The Trucial Coast Diaries (1948-1957):
On the Way from Pearls to Oil
in the Trucial States of the Gulf

Gulf Studies at Gerlach Press

The Gulf Region: Economic Development & Diversification.
Luciani, G.; Hertog, S.; Woertz, E.; Youngs, R. (eds.), (4 vols set),
ISBN 9783940924001, 2012

The GCC in the Global Economy.
Youngs, Richard (ed.), ISBN 9783940924018, 2013

Resources Blessed: Diversification and the Gulf Development Model.
Luciani, Giacomo (ed.), ISBN 9783940924025, 2013

GCC Financial Markets: The World's New Money Centers.
Woertz, Eckart (ed.), ISBN 9783940924032, 2013

National Employment, Migration and Education in the GCC.
Hertog, Steffen (ed.), ISBN 9783940924049, 2013

Asia-Gulf Economic Relations in the 21st Century: The Local to Global Transformation.
Niblock, Tim (ed.), ISBN 9783940924100, 2013

Gulf Charities and Islamic Philanthropy in the Age of Terror and Beyond.
Lacey, Robert; Benthall, Jonathan (eds.), ISBN 9783940924322, 2014

A New Gulf Security Architecture: Prospects and Challenges for an Asian Role.
Gupta, Ranjit; Bagader, Abubaker; Ahmad, Talmiz; Janardhan, N. (eds.),
ISBN 9783940924360, 2014

Political Economy of Energy Reform: The Clean Energy-Fossil Fuel Balance in the Gulf States.
Luciani, Giacomo; Ferroukhi, Rabia (eds.), ISBN 9783940924407, 2014

The Silent Revolution: The Arab Spring and the Gulf States.
Seikaly, May; Mattar, Khawla (eds.), ISBN 9783940924346, 2014

State-Society Relations in the Arab Gulf States.
Al-Zoby, Mazhar A.; Baskan, Birol (eds.), ISBN 9783940924384, 2014

Security Dynamics of East Asia in the Gulf Region.
Niblock, Tim; with Guang, Yang (eds.), ISBN 9783940924483, 2014

Sustainable Development Challenges in the Arab States of the Gulf.
Bryde, David; Mouzughi, Yusra; Al Rasheed, Turki (eds.),
ISBN 9783940924629, 2015

Employment and Career Motivation in the Arab Gulf States: The Rentier Mentality Revisited.
Kropf, Annika; Ramady, Mohamed (eds), ISBN 9783940924605, 2015

The Changing Energy Landscape in the Gulf: Strategic Implications.
Bahgat, Gawdat (ed.), ISBN 9783940924643, 2015

The United States and the Gulf: Shifting Pressures, Strategies and Alignments.
Hook, Steven W.; Niblock, Tim (eds.), ISBN 9783940924667, 2015

Africa and the Gulf Region: Blurred Boundaries and Shifting Ties.
Abusharaf, Rogaia Mustafa; Eickelman, Dale F. (eds.),
ISBN 9783940924704, 2015

Kropf, Annika
Oil Export Economies: New Comparative Perspectives on the Arab Gulf States. With a Foreword by Giacomo Luciani.
ISBN 9783940924582, 2016

Wahhabism – Doctrine and Development. (2 Vols) (Critical Surveys in Islamic Denominations)
Peskes, Esther (ed.), ISBN 9783940924506, 2016

Iran's Relations with the Arab States of the Gulf: Common Interests over Historic Rivalry.
Warnaar, Maaike; Zaccara, Luciano; Aarts, Paul (eds.),
ISBN 9783959940047, 2016

The Arab States of the Gulf and BRICS: New Strategic Partnerships in Politics and Economics.
Niblock, Tim with Sun, Degang; Galindo, Alejandra (eds.),
ISBN 9783959940085, 2016

The Arms Trade, Military Services and the Security Market in the Gulf States: Trends and Implications.
Des Roches, David B.; Thafer, Dania (eds.), ISBN 9783959940160, 2016

Heard-Bey, Frauke
Abu Dhabi, the United Arab Emirates and the Gulf Region: Fifty Years of Transformation.
ISBN 9783959940009, 2016

Science and Technology Development in the Gulf States: Economic Diversification through Regional Collaboration.
Siddiqi, Afreen; Diaz Anadon, Laura (eds.), ISBN 9783959940023, 2017

Higher Education Investment in the Arab States of the Gulf: Strategies for Excellence and Diversity.
Eickelman, Dale F.; Abusharaf, Rogaia Mustafa (eds.),
ISBN 9783959940122, 2017

Egypt and the Gulf: A Renewed Regional Policy Alliance.
Mason, Robert (ed.), ISBN 9783959940061, 2017

Intellectual Property Rights: Development and Enforcement in the Arab States of the Gulf.
Price, David; AlDebasi, Alhanoof (eds.), ISBN 9783959940108, 2017

Strategies of Knowledge Transfer for Economic Diversification in the Arab States of the Gulf.
Bertelsen, Rasmus Gjedssø; Noori, Neema; Rickli, Jean-Marc (eds.),
ISBN 9783959940146, 2017

Yemen and the Gulf States: The Making of a Crisis.
Lackner, Helen; Varisco, Daniel Martin (eds.),
ISBN 9783959940306, 2017

Conflict Resolution and Creation of a Security Community in the Gulf Region.
Niblock, Tim; with Ahmad, Talmiz; Sun, Degang (eds.),
ISBN 9783959940368, 2017

The Future of Labour Market Reform in the Gulf Region: Towards a Multi-Disciplinary, Evidence-Based and Practical Understanding.
Jones, David B.; Sahraoui, Sofiane (eds.), ISBN 9783959940344, 2017

Battaloglu, Cihat
Political Reforms in Qatar: From Authoritarianism to Political Grey Zone
ISBN 9783959940429, 2018

Gulfization of the Arab World
Jones, Marc Owen; Porter, Ross; Valeri, Marc (eds.),
ISBN 9783959940320, 2018

El-Radhi, Yesenn
Economic Diversification in the Gulf States: Public Expenditure and Non-Oil Economic Growth in Bahrain, Oman and Qatar
ISBN 9783959940528, 2018

The Gulf States, Asia and the Indian Ocean: Ensuring the Security of the Sea Lanes.
Niblock, Tim; with Ahmad, Talmiz; Sun, Degang (eds.),
ISBN 9783959940580, 2018

Heard, David
Oil Men, Territorial Ambitions and Political Agents. From Pearls to Oil in the Trucial States of the Gulf (2 Volumes)
ISBN 9783959940641, 2019

Alebrahim, Abdulrahman
Kuwait's Politics Before Independence: The Role of the Balancing Powers
(Exeter Critical Gulf Series), ISBN 9783959940726, 2019

Kelly, J. B., edited by S. B. Kelly
Desert Dispute: The Diplomacy of Boundary-Making in South-Eastern Arabia (3 Volume Set)
ISBN 9783959940788, 2020

The Trucial Coast Diaries (1948-1957)

On the Way from Pearls to Oil in the Trucial States of the Gulf

Edited and commented by David Heard

Gerlach Press

First published 2020
by Gerlach Press
Berlin, Germany
www.gerlach-press.de

Cover Design: Frauke Schön, Hamburg
Set by Anne Jeschke, Gerlach Press
Printed and bound in Germany

British Library Cataloguing in Publication Data.
A catalogue record for this book is available from the British Library.

Bibliographic data available from Deutsche Nationalbibliothek
http://d-nb.info/1202283942

ISBN: 978-3-95994-080-1 (Hardcover)
ISBN: 978-3-95994-081-8 (eBook)

Contents

Common Acronyms

ADMA	Abu Dhabi Marine Areas
APOC	Anglo Persian Oil Company
AIOC	Anglo Iranian Oil Company
ARAMCO	Arabian American Company
BAPCO	Bahrain Petroleum Company
BISNC	British Indian Steamship Navigation Company
BP	British Petroleum
CFP	Total
FO	Foreign Office
HMG	His (Her) Majesty's Government
IAL	International Aeradio Ltd.
IPC	Iraq Petroleum Company
PA	Political Agent
PCL	Petroleum Concessions Limited (IPC associated company)
PD(TC)	Petroleum Development (Trucial Coast) (IPC associated company)
PO	Political Officer
PR	Political Resident
RA	Residency Agent
RAF	Royal Air Force
Rs.	Rupees
TC	Trucial Coast
TOL	Trucial Oman Levies
TOS	Trucial Oman Scouts
UAE	United Arab Emirates

Names and Transliterations

The transliteration of Arabic words and names is fraught with difficulties. I apologise for adopting the easy opt out which may not please many of my friends. In my own writing I have employed commonly used English equivalents attempting to be at least consistent in my spelling. I have naturally not changed the spelling of names which appear in texts of 'The Trucial Coast Diaries'. I hope that this does not lead to confusion, but as the reader will see the various authors of the letters and reports have not themselves adopted a common spelling. Indeed one writer may employ more than one spelling for the same name. In the reports and diaries the name Zayed is invariably spelt as Zaid. I do not change this but I have used in my text the current spelling, Zayed. Similarly Rashid bin Saeed is frequently written Rashid bin Said.

I am tempted to follow the example of T.E. Laurence who in the 1935 preface to his book[1] 'The Seven Pillars of Wisdom' found a simple solution. He wrote 'only three vowels are recognised in Arabic, and some of the consonants have no equivalent in English ... the sound of many Arabic words can legitimately be represented in English in a variety of ways, but also because the natives of a district often differ as to the pronunciation of any place-name which has not already become famous or fixed by literary usage.' When challenged by his editor saying that he had written Sherif el Mayin, which later became el Main, el Mayein, el Muein, el Mayn, and el Muyein, he responded 'Good egg. I call this really ingenious.'

However I would not like to follow Laurence's example too closely any more than I care for his style of writing!

1 First published privately in 1926 with most of the pictures in colour. The first edition for general circulation was published in 1935 with 54 full page pictures in black and white and with four maps.

Acknowledgements

Without the example and encouragement of my wife Frauke, and the support of our children Nicolas, Miriam and Theresa, I would probably never have started on what has been a journey of nearly two decades. It has been a journey that I sometimes have had my doubts about – there are so many other activities that I could have enjoyed in these years after retiring from the Abu Dhabi Petroleum Company that I was with for my whole working life. This was the company whose forerunner was PD(TC) which operated in all the Trucial States and is the subject of this account.

I am very grateful for the friendship of so many nationals of Abu Dhabi and the UAE. I have lost contact with some, such as the geological assistant who, sitting on a sand dune near oil well Murban 29 in 1963 (the third Bu Hasa well) tried to teach me my first words of Arabic.

There are so many nationals of the UAE whose friendship we enjoyed forty or fifty years ago, and we are very fortunate and grateful to still enjoy their comradeship to this day. They have so enriched my, and Frauke's, experience of life in Abu Dhabi over these memorable and unique decades. I mention here only a few of these people. The first must be Ahmed Khalifa Al-Suwaidi who, with his keen interest in recording events for posterity, encouraged me to access the reports, written by the Company employees more than half a century ago, some of which I reproduce in this volume.

I also include Sheikh Mohamed bin Zayed, whose father appears in this account as the active 'Sheikh in waiting'. Sheikh Nahyan bin Mubarak whose grandfather, Sheikh Shakhbut bin Sultan bore very great responsibility as Ruler (1928-1966). There are also Sheikh Soroor bin Mohamed, Khalaf bin Ahmed al-Otaiba, Mohamed Habroush al-Suwaidi and Dr. Mana Saeed al-Otaiba who themselves and their forefathers would have been familiar with the events recounted here in the following pages.

There have also been so many expatriates, Arab, British, German, Dutch, French, Indian and from the USA, as well as from many more nationalities, who have signed and filled the pages of our guest books and have retained a place in our hearts to this day. Among them are Adnan Pachachi, Bill Clark, Paul Bergne, Jessie Brom, Ian MacPherson and Marie-Hélène Colin de Verdière.

Many of these have run their course on this world and have passed away. It is for all these friends, their children, their grandchildren and their families that this work is completed, and to whom it is dedicated.

I am not a historian, but being employed in the oil industry in Abu Dhabi all my working life, I having watched the development of the State of Abu Dhabi and the federation of the United Arab Emirates from extreme poverty to great wealth. We have observed, Frauke and I, the effect of this transformation on society; I hope that I may be able to employ my insights and experience, for the benefit of you, the reader.

Foreword

The events recounted below belong to another age, a time of poverty and deprivation on the Trucial Coast. Yet the people lived in a well ordered society, where Islam provided guidance and discipline and the Sheikhs were responsible for leadership and order. The people knew their position in their world.

It was a world dependent on the date palms in the oases for the staple food and on camels for travelling across expanses of rolling sand dunes.

These people knew the hundreds of names, largely forgotten today, that were associated with dates and camels, a sophistication unknown to the present generation, it was very real and it has vanished. It has been replaced by a language of computers and megabytes, of barrels of oil and scf[1] of natural gas, of the stock market and shares.

The explorer Wilfred Thesiger (locally known as Mubarak bin London) feared that exposure to the modern world would lead to the end of the values he so admired in the 'Noble Bedouin'. Thesiger spent many months in the desert with the bedouin and never lost, even decades later, his respect and admiration for his companions. He admired their loyalty and companionship, generous even in poverty. Thesiger relates that in hunger they offered unexpected guests the morsel of fresh meat, a hare, which they had looked forward to sharing amongst themselves.[2]

It was a world where the benefits from the fruits of the sea, fish and pearls, depended on the skills of the boat builders, the navigators, the divers as well as the boat owners and merchants.

Then there were the fruits of the desert for other people, consisting of dates, herbs and in season truffles, the occasional hare, a dhub (large lizard), a bird and its eggs, which were the subject of everyday conversation and essential for life in a harsh environment.

Before the days of computer games, or inter-city football matches and Aston Martins, young men on their camels and with a rifle slung under their arm, looked for excitement not just in racing their camels but also sometimes in less legal activities encouraged by inter-tribal rivalries and jealousies.

Sheikh Shakhbut bin Sultan in Abu Dhabi and the other rulers were well aware of the abilities and the limitations of their people. They knew that the people had to be

1 Standard cubic feet.

2 THESIGER, Sir W., *Arabian Sands*, (1959).

ruled with a firm hand which in days of great poverty and hardship had little to give in return for their loyalty.

Sheikh Shakhbut, and many others too, were apprehensive of the effect on the people of the arrival of the oil company, the locust survey or the Political Officers who to the people seemed to be all one and the same. They were foreigners who were willing to pay a reasonable wage, and perhaps thereby steal the loyalty of his people. Some people suggested that the intruders would steal the land. Sheikh Shakhbut demonstrated his respect for these foreigners and for their ways including their religion, but he still had to protect his people, their religion, their values and their way of life.

This intrusion of foreigners into this society also brought corrupting and undesirable habits, some of which were new to many of the people of the Trucial Coast. This unfamiliar behaviour produced a desire among some of the Arabs to imitate – often with unfortunate consequences. An example of this was the 'leakage' of alcoholic beverages from the Naafi in the RAF camp in Sharjah.

I think we should regard with tolerance and understanding the misdeeds of long ago by some individuals, perhaps a grandfather or an uncle of you, the reader, as indeed both Sheikh Shakhbut and Sheikh Zayed did at that time.

Society today in the UAE is increasingly 'in tune' with the wide world and better able to confront such matters and avoid excesses.

I have tried to gauge the feeling of people as to whether I should, or should not, reproduce the reports of certain events as recorded in these diaries. I realise that some readers may be critical of my decision, but I did find that most people favoured receiving the total and not a shortened account. However all archives do have to hold back some information, for a period of time. I have therefore deleted some words and sentences, and this is indicated in the text, but I have reduced my deletions to a minimum and I ask for the readers' tolerance.

Introduction

I have included these diaries under my subtitle "From Pearls to Oil" so as to keep the oil company records together and maintain the distinction between them and the British Government archives or any other sources of information about the early days on the Trucial Coast.

One cannot stress too much that the Trucial Coast in those days bears very little resemblance to the United Arab Emirates of these days. These reports illustrate how very much it is to the credit of the several Rulers and their people, who in 1971 decided to put the past differences behind them and move rapidly from the individual Sheikhdoms, jealously guarding their own interests, to the modern President-led state of the United Arab Emirates.

The Trucial Coast Diaries are secret reports written in Dubai, between the years 1948 and 1957 by representatives of the oil company PD(TC), (Petroleum Development (Trucial Coast)) which was exploring for oil in the United Arab Emirates (formerly Trucial Coast). Many years ago I was entrusted with the safe-keeping of these documents and I believe that it is now time to make them available for researchers and anyone who is interested in the history of the Emirates. Sadly all the main players in these reports, and even some of their sons have passed away.

Unfortunately some reports are missing, some were never written, and although some were written after 1957 I do not have them. Some reports are short and of little interest to most readers but I have included them as even they have some significance.

In this volume the oil company, in keeping with the custom on the Trucial Coast at that time, is referred to as PD(TC) or just the 'Company'. Sir Easa Saleh Al-Gurg in conversation with me referred to the company as Lermitte's company. This is a reference to a representative of the company from 1937 to 1953, Basil Lermitte, who was based in Bahrain but who travelled throughout the Trucial Coast and south into the Sultanate of Oman.

The Iraq Petroleum Company (IPC) and its bunch of associated companies, PD(TC) was one of those companies, ceased to exist when the last concession expired in Abu Dhabi in January 2014. In its heyday, roughly the years 1930 to 1960, the IPC engineers and particularly the exploration geologists and geophysicists were pre-eminent in the whole of Arabia. The records of their work are copious and still preserved to this day in the BP archives at the university of Warwick in England.

PD(TC) was one of the IPC (Iraq Petroleum Company) associated companies based in London. It was a consortium which since 1928 included BP, Exxon-Mobil, Shell, Total and Gulbenkian, collectively named 'The Groups'. In my first book 'From Pearls to Oil',[1] this same company is referred to as PCL (Petroleum Concessions Limited). The name PCL was used to cover all IPC operations beyond the main oil producing area in Iraq, at Kirkuk. The employees, who generally were not employees of the Groups, were mostly British or natives of the land in which the company operated.

The IPC, in its day, operated in most countries of the Middle East. Before the emergence of ARAMCO in Saudi Arabia, it was the second largest oil consortium in the Middle East, after Anglo Iranian (later BP). Some of the great pioneers and geologists of the Middle Eastern oil industry worked for this company, their enormous contribution to finding the oil and developing the oilfields to feed an ever more energy-hungry world should not be forgotten.

Unfortunately the files containing political or social reports, in particular relating to Iraq and Syria, have largely been destroyed. The fear in London was that after political turmoil in much of the Middle East in the 1950's and 1960's, these files could contain information that might compromise, or offend employees and Government officials in these host countries. I remember that there was often a reluctance to share sensitive information with the Groups, particularly when it was clear that the recipients of the reports in their American or European offices would not appreciate the significance of such information, and could easily subsequently innocently cause embarrassment.

Further to this, as the Company reduced in size and scope the cost of storage in central London of vast amounts of files was seen as an unnecessary burden. Both the authors and the recipients of the reports written in Dubai, retired from the Company and new executives arrived, particularly from among the Groups.[2] These newcomers frequently had little knowledge of, or interest in the history and way of life on the Trucial Coast. Files were discarded, or 'weeded' by these people. Although I was occasionally aware that this was going on there was little that I could do about it at the time.

For this volume I have carefully copied each diary report and have left very little out. I have deleted a few incidents which anyone would regard as being too personal and not for public display. I have indicated where there are such deletions. However I cannot stress too often that these reports should be read bearing in mind the situation on the Trucial Coast and the world at that time. The writers recorded events that they witnessed or were reported to them. They may have misunderstood certain events, believed rumours, or listened to people who deliberately set out to mislead them. However their accounts, often in the absence of any other, stand as a record of activities in those days 70 years ago.

---

1 Published by Motivate, Dubai 2011.

2 IPC owners. See below.

The footnotes are all mine, and in these I have provided explanations which I hope will help readers who are not familiar with the land. Since readers may wish to delve into this volume and not read it systematically, I have often repeated information contained in the footnotes to help such users.

The reader will obtain the greatest benefit from these diaries if they are read in conjunction with or after reading my second work 'Oil Men, Territorial Ambitions and Political Agents.'[3] I could, in my comments, have included with these diaries many references again and again to this work, but I leave it to the reader to decide when you would wish to refer to those two volumes which cover the period from the Second World War (1939-1945) to the end of 1955.

The diaries reproduced here were sent from Dubai to the company office, initially in Bahrain and later in Dukhan in Qatar, and we know that some of them, at least in part, were also copied to the company headquarters in London. However, there are no copies among the company files saved in London, and the offices in Bahrain, Dukhan in Qatar and in Dubai have long ceased to exist. I have not searched widely for more copies which possibly may exist in the archives of one or another of the Group companies. We have here enough to fill one volume, and perhaps someone else can continue the search.

For many years these diaries were considered to be too sensitive to risk exposure to the public. Time has passed and the decades have rolled by and since they provide a useful, and modest, supplement to the British India Office archives, which are available to the general public, it is perhaps time to lift the veil of secrecy and provide this information for those who are interested in the history of the United Arab Emirates.

There is one word of caution which I cannot repeat too often, and that is that events taking place 60 or 70 years ago must be understood and if need be, judged, bearing in mind the conditions which prevailed at that time.

My wife, Dr. Frauke, and I have welcomed into our house for the past 50 years many citizens of this country, the United Arab Emirates. We have shared with them accounts of their past but we observe that, even today, many UAE nationals are sadly lacking in knowledge about their own history.

Whereas, not so long ago, very few foreigners, including students, were aware of and understood the way of life in the UAE, now the Emirates are better known and even experienced at first hand by ever more people. In recent years we have observed that there is an ever increasing thirst for information about the past among more and more nationals. Foreigners too, from all walks of life across the world, are researching the history of the Emirates, and I hope that they will all benefit from this publication.

I have reproduced here the diaries which were typed on papers, nearly always flimsy and fragile with age, and sometimes difficult to read. The original writers,

3 Published by Gerlach, Berlin 2019.

Codrai, Henderson, Jackson, Kirkbride, Morgan, Thomson and Watt reported on what they observed. They admit that their observations may be incorrect as it was often very difficult for them to distinguish between rumour, propaganda and reality. On occasion they have corrected themselves in a following report when they found that they had been misinformed.

They were, at times, 'closer to the action' than the British Political Officers and Agents, in that they, such as Codrai, remained on or near the Trucial Coast for longer periods of time. Codrai and Henderson in particular were very familiar with the area and spoke good Arabic. Some, such as Thomson arrived with no local experience, and yet often adapted well. We see in the reports that Henderson, who had years of local intimate experience on the Trucial Coast and the Sultanate of Oman, was not pleased[4] when the total newcomer Thomson was promoted above him. However Thomson produced some good reports.

The company men also travelled more extensively into the interior, across high dunes and through rugged mountain passes, than almost any British Government official. Codrai, for example, walked from Dibba on the Indian Ocean across the mountains and through the wadis to Ra's al-Khaimah on the coast of the Gulf. Codrai too was the first to take a vehicle, a Landrover, over the – previously considered impassable – dunes to the Liwa oases. The two exceptions to this were the intrepid Viscount Buckmaster, the first Political Officer to reside in Abu Dhabi, and Walker.[5] Buckmaster enjoyed passing through the sandy desert to the Liwa oases, while Walker was trying to determine the boundaries between the sheikhdoms in the sand dunes and the rocky mountains of the Northern Emirates.

It is characteristic of almost all the reports that, unfortunately, the writers give little, or no, credit to the Arab and other companions without whose assistance they would have been very much less well informed, and without whom they would not have achieved very much. Every expedition would have first needed to collect cars, drivers, interpreters, cooks as well as petrol, water and sufficient livestock, such as

4 See INNES, N.,(1987), p. 106. "He was in a furious and aggrieved mood because he had heard that the post of Senior Political Officer of the Company in the area had been given to a man named Thompson who, according to Edward (who had hoped for the job himself), knew no Arabic, and nothing about the tribes or the area, and was utterly unsuitable." The Company management in London and the Group representatives did not look favourably on their employees who became (in their minds) too familiar with the people of the area.

5 I have been told, by people who were with him, that Buckmaster was popular among the Bedu because he would arrive at a settlement, buy a goat from the people and then invite them all to a feast to eat the goat. It was assumed that he used his own money for this pleasure. Buckmaster first came to Abu Dhabi in March 1952 when he, accompanied by Sheikh Zayed, conducted a survey of the Liwa settlements. They travelled by camel. He returned in 1955 when he was appointed as the first Political Officer in Abu Dhabi. (1955-1958).

chickens and goats to last several days away from base. That base in early days would have been Dubai or Sharjah and later included the temporary drilling camps at Jebel Ali, Tarif or Al Hamra.

Probably chief among these Arabs was Ali Tajir whose time with the company dates from the 1930's until the 1950's. Ali contributed to a large part of the 'Henderson papers' which were used to support the Abu Dhabi territorial case in the face of Saudi Arabian territorial claims.

The Bahraini Ibrahim Arayadh should also be mentioned who was with the company from 1937 until 1967. He was described as 'long distinguished in the Arab world as a man of letters and in particular as a poet and critic, having published a total of 22 books.'[6] After retiring from the company he went on to chair the Bahrain Constitutional Council. Before he passed away in 2002 at the age of 94 he had been honoured by the King of Bahrain as a leading poet and for 'appreciation of his efforts to serve the nation and his immense contribution to the country's cultural life.'[7] He is on record, in the diaries, as having started to visit the Trucial Coast more frequently after Ali Tajir retired in 1956. I remember that he attended the official inauguration of the start of oil exports from the desert at Jebel Dhanna in March 1964. The event took place in the presence of the Ruler Shaikh Shakhbut and his brother Sheikh Zayed. By this time the company in Abu Dhabi was no longer named PD(TC). It was the Abu Dhabi Petroleum Company. (ADPC).

6 The Crescent January/February 1973. The Crescent was the IPC monthly magazine for company employees.

7 Gulf News 2002. Gulf News is a prominent Dubai based English language daily newspaper.

Preliminary Notes

You, the reader, may wish to refer to these notes from time to time as you read the main text. They will be helpful for you, if you are not familiar with the Trucial Coast, or with the situation in the land at that time. I refer you to the map to see the positions of the major regions, oases and towns. These include the seven emirates Ra's al-Khaimah, Umm al Quwain, Ajman, Sharjah, Dubai, Abu Dhabi and Fujairah as well as the oases of Dhaid, Hatta, Al Ain/Buraimi, and the Liwa oases.

Some of the following notes will also appear as footnotes at the bottom of the diary pages as a reminder for the reader.

Today visitors arrive in the Emirates and find themselves immediately in a land of plenty. They travel along broad tree lined avenues, to their hotel, which could, in appearance, be in any wealthy country. They see shopping malls which host shops that frequent the high streets of Europe. There are buildings, roads and parks which could be the envy of long established cities elsewhere. These diaries take us back to another land, a land inhabited by the ancestors of today's Emirati. To him the names of towns, villages and oases, and the names of his forbears will be familiar. But in these reports they represent a time past, a time of great hardship and yet a history to be proud of.

Hopefully you, the reader, will have taken note of my introduction above and you are ready to cast aside, while you read this book, the familiar images that we have now all around us.

1. The Land. The Trucial Coast

The Trucial Coast was also known as 'The Trucial States' or 'The Coast of Oman' or 'Trucial Oman' or even on occasion 'The Pirate Coast'. The land occupies the southern and eastern end of the Gulf. The border with Saudi Arabia starts in the west near Qatar, running south before turning east continuing south of the Liwa oases until it reaches the territory of the Sultanate of Oman. Thereafter the border continues northwards, in due course running along the foot of the mountains up to north of Ra's al-Khaimah near the entrance to the Gulf. The Emirates also stretch across the Hajar mountain range to the Indian Ocean in the east separating the Musandem peninsula from the rest of the Sultanate of Oman.

The Trucial States were seven in number, Kalba[1] having earlier separated from Sharjah it rejoined Sharjah in 1951, and Fujairah first acquired the status of a Trucial State in 1952. These vary in size, in geography and in population.

The Treaties between the rulers of the individual sheikhdoms and the British Government date back to 1820, and primarily concerned the maintenance of peace at sea. All the rulers who signed these treaties were based on the coast.

We see in the narrative of the diaries how the sheikhs of large tribes in the interior tried to assert their independence in spite of The British Government (H.M.G.) declaring that the inland territory all came under either one or another of the coastal sheikhs or the Sultan of Oman in Muscat.

The British Government unilaterally abrogated the treaties with the rulers of the seven sheikhdoms in 1971 who then combined to form the United Arab Emirates.

Before oil there was no necessity to clearly define borders in the sands, the mountain foreland or the wadis. In those days the most important geographical and economic features for the inhabitants were the coastal towns and harbours, the inland oases and the water wells in the desert. Although people were aware of their traditional grazing areas these were not clearly defined with distinct borders. At the time of the first of the diaries there were still no mapped borders between the various sheikhdoms, and also none with the Sultanate of Oman or Saudi Arabia. These only became necessary after the Company arrived and needed to know in whose territory they were conducting surveys.

We also find that in every case the name of the capital, the coastal town, is also applied to the Sheikhdom, the Emirate as a whole.

During the time of this narrative the group of oases in the mountain foreland in the east of Abu Dhabi and on the border with the Sultanate of Oman were commonly collectively known as the Buraimi oasis to the foreigners. Only some of the oases in this group are named in these dairies. These are Buraimi and Hamasa in the present day Sultanate of Oman and the Abu Dhabi oases are Muwaiji and Jahili. According to a May 1937 report compiled by Packer of PCL the local people referred to the oases as a whole as Oman.

I remember in the 1960's that some Abu Dhabi people still used to say 'I am going to Oman' when they were going to Al 'Ain or to any of the oases in the whole group. Similarly it was only Europeans who would refer to Buraimi when they meant the entire group of oases.

1 Kalba is situated on the east (Indian Ocean) coast. Sheikh Khaled bin Ahmed was the regent for many years as the sheikh was a youth at the time of the death of his father in 1937. Sheikh Khaled's influence, when he signed an oil concession agreement with Longrigg in 1938, probably extended over an area further at that time than might later have been attributed to Kalba.

However since the early 1970's the Abu Dhabi oases, chief of which is now Al 'Ain, have grown to cover a vast area with many new townships extending into what was previously desert. People in Abu Dhabi now speak of going to Al 'Ain and no longer talk of Buraimi, or Oman, unless they are going to the Sultanate of Oman. The three Oman oases, chief of which is Buraimi, have also expanded into the desert but not to the same extent as those on the Abu Dhabi side of the border.

We see in the accounts that there was considerable traffic between Dubai and Sharjah in the Gulf and the Batinah[2] coast on the Indian Ocean leading on to Muscat in the Sultanate of Oman. The main route, which was motorable, to the Batinah was through the wadi Qor which lies to the east of Dubai. The route east from Al 'Ain/Buraimi through the Wadi Jizzi was still not open to wheeled transport in the 1950's. Security, in particular in the mountain foreland was a problem and probably inhibited travel. But we see that, for example, the Ruler of Ajman would leave his coastal capital to visit his family properties in Ibri more than 100 kilometres south of Buraimi, stopping on the way to see his relatives at Hamasa next to Buraimi. He would have taken a large entourage including his guards and so would have not been an easy prey such as the lonely taxi loaded with men, women and children. Bandits provided as much, if not more of a hindrance or inconvenience to travellers than the difficult terrain, and we see that nervous villagers might shoot at passing strangers before asking any questions.

By the end of the 1940's cars were slowly taking over from camels as the preferred mode of transport, but they were still banned from the oases and towns in the interior of Oman where the Imam ruled and the Sultan had little influence.

Sheikh Zayed bin Sultan, the Abu Dhabi Ruler's brother, was very familiar with the terrain to the east and west of the Hajar mountains and frequently spent time in the Sultanate, often to help in settling disputes. He visited Suneinah[3] and Ibri many times as well as going as far as Muscat to call on the Sultan or to seek treatment at the hospital nearby at Muttrah.

At the time of the diaries men were leaving the Trucial Coast to seek work in the Gulf countries further north. Kuwait, Saudi Arabia and Qatar were already all benefiting from their increasing oil based wealth. The remittances back home to families on the Trucial Coast meant that the population[4] started to increase and

2 Indian ocean coast extending the full length from near the entrance to the Gulf to as far as Muscat.

3 Sheikh Zayed's first wife, 'Alia, the daughter of Mohamed bin Salameen bin Rahma al Shamsi, was from Suneinah. Suneinah is about 90 kilometres south of Buraimi and Ibri a further 80 kilometres south.

4 A population census was conducted in 1968 when numbers had already risen considerably. The figures below are taken from FENELON, KEVIN, (1973), *United Arab Emirates, An Economic and Social Survey,* Longman.

poverty was becoming less acute. We also read of the complaint that men found work with contractors where remuneration and conditions were not as well regulated as in the oil industry. We find too that although some whole families left the Trucial Coast, in many cases men went alone and returned, for example, to attend to the date harvest. The increase in population on the Coast was inevitable as money was available to pay immigrant servants. This is illustrated in the well-known story of the poor man who bought a fish for a rupee and paid another a couple of fils to carry it home for him.

Ports anywhere in the world attract immigrants, many of whom stay if they find the conditions better that those at home. As the Trucial Coast slowly became more wealthy Dubai was becoming a good destination for such people.

a) Abu Dhabi

The Ruler was Sheikh Shakhbut bin Sultan (1928-1966). His family, now Al Nahyan,[5] was from the Al bu Falah section of the Bani Yas. Sheikh Shakhbut was assisted by his brothers Sheikhs Khalid, Haza and Zayed. Their mother Sheikha Salamah bint Buti al-Qubaisi was a very real 'power behind the throne'. The most notable other person was the merchant Ahmed bin Khalaf al Otaiba. Sheikh Shakhbut ruled over the land which was geographically by far the largest, but at the time of these diaries not the largest in population.

At that time the loyalty of Bedouin tribes such as some sections of the Manasir and the Murra was a problem for the Ruler in the face of Saudi Arabian subversion.

Sheikh Shakhbut signed an oil concession agreement in 1939 with Longrigg working for the IPC associated company. The company was known as Petroleum Development (Trucial Coast) or PD(TC). The company announced in October 1960 that oil had been discovered in commercial quantities. The name was changed to Abu Dhabi Petroleum Company (ADPC) in 1962 and oil exports commenced from Jebel Dhanna in December 1963.

Abu Dhabi is the capital today of the United Arab Emirates. The land of Abu Dhabi held within its territory original oil reserves which amounted to about 95% of the total for all the Emirates. The Abu Dhabi land area, 26,000 square miles, represents some 85% of the Emirates.

The population at the time of the 1968 census was 46,375. It would have been probably less than 10,000 at the time of the diaries, due to emigration to find work in Qatar, Kuwait or Saudi Arabia. The depopulation in the area was at its starkest in Abu Dhabi.

Abu Dhabi town is on an island beside the Gulf coast about 160 kilometres south west from Dubai. Apart from Abu Dhabi town, and Batin a village on Abu Dhabi island, the main centres of population were in the Abu Dhabi villages bordering the

5 Sheikh Shakhbut introduced the name Al Nahyan in the last years of his rule.

Sultanate of Oman, the chief being Muwaiji, next to Buraimi. The third important area was the one hundred kilometre long crescent of settlements in the high dunes in the south, the Liwa. Here the population was scattered among oases as well as, in earlier days, being seasonally absent in the surrounding desert or on the sea fishing for pearls.

b) Dubai

The Ruler was Sheikh Saeed bin Maktoum (1912-1958). The Al Maktoum family is from the al Bu Falasa section of the Bani Yas. In 1833 the chief leader, Maktoum bin Buti led the al Bu Falasa to join a small fishing community on the western shore of the natural creek of Dubai. Sheikh Saeed's first wife, Sheikhah Huzza[6] came from the Omani coastal town of Bakha further north in the Gulf.

Sheikh Saeed's difficulties stemmed chiefly from differences within the ruling family. He also had to consider the interests of the prominent merchant community.

Dubai lies on the coast of the Gulf centrally placed between Abu Dhabi and Ra's Al-Khaimah. The land area is approximately 1,500 square miles. Population at the time of the 1968 census was 58,971. It was possibly about 30,000 at the time of the diaries.

The coastal town of Dubai was famous for the Creek, a stretch of water reaching inland to the extent that early cartographers showed it as a river mouth. However the Creek was affected by variations in the currents in the Gulf. As Sharjah's and Umm al Quwain's creeks became limited by growing sand banks so Dubai's creek became freer from the sand although the sand bar at the entrance was still a serious hazard.

Sheikh Saeed signed an oil concession agreement in 1937 with Holmes on behalf of PD(TC). Dubai, although its oil reserves initially amounted to only 5% of the total for the seven states, has leapt ahead as a trader, and then a major world renowned destination for tourists and industries.

The Ruler owned a substantial oasis at the foot of the mountains at Hatta. In the latter part of his rule Sheikh Saeed depended increasingly on his son Sheikh Rashid, while he was often reported to be tending his gardens in Ra's al-Khaimah.

The move of the British Political Agency from Sharjah to Dubai was completed in February 1954. There were reports that people in Dubai were not particularly pleased with this move, as they thought that it would lead to unwelcome greater British scrutiny of their trading activities.

c) Sharjah

The Ruler was Sheikh Sultan bin Saqr Al Qasimi (1924-1951) until he was succeeded upon his death in London by his son Sheikh Saqr bin Sultan (1951-

6 Her mother was from Dubai.

1965). Sheikh Saqr's uncle Sheikh Mohamed bin Saqr was regarded as being a better organizer, but his early attempts to become ruler were not successful, a situation which he accepted.

The land area of Sharjah is about 1,000 square miles. The population at the time of the 1968 census was 31,668. It was possibly about 20,000 at the time of the diaries.

The Rulers had difficulty in asserting their authority over tribes of the interior, in particular the Bani Kitab near Jebel Faiyah.

Sharjah lies on the Gulf coast directly north of Dubai.

Sharjah was the seat of the representative of the British Government until 1954. The first British national to take up residence there as Political Agent was P.D. Stobart (1948). Previously British interests were in the hands of the Residency Agent (1829-1949), an Arab.

Sharjah benefitted from having a sheltered creek for local shipping, and since the early 1930's an airport for international flights. The original airport buildings have been expanded to house a very informative museum, the Mahatta museum.

The Ruler signed an oil concession agreement with Lermitte on behalf of PD(TC) in 1937.

Sharjah is today the cultural leader with its many museums, an annual Book Fair and many other events.

d) Ra's al-Khaimah

Shaikh Sultan bin Salem Al Qassimi was Ruler (1921-1948). In February 1948 he was replaced in a bloodless coup by Shaikh Saqr bin Mohamed (1948-2004). Sheikh Sultan lived for many years after his deposition in the mountain village of Huwailat in the southernmost part of Ra's al-Khaimah territory.

Ra's al-Khaimah has a land area of 650 square miles. The population at the time of the 1968 census was 24,387. Ra's al-Khaimah town lies on the coast of the Gulf about 100 kilometers north of Dubai. The long established gardens benefit from the good fresh ground water aquifers due to the proximity of the Hajar mountain range.

The Rulers of Ra's al-Khaimah held within their territory tribes who were difficult to control. The Khawatir (a branch of the Naím) were on the Jiri plain. The Tunaiji in the coastal village of Rams held out against Sheikh Saqr for several years after his accession. The Zaab of Jazirat al Hamra were a special case, while the Shihu and Hubus were often unruly when they descended from their mountain villages (in the Sultanate of Oman) in the summer.

The Ruler signed an oil agreement with Longrigg of PD(TC) in 1939.

Ra's al-Khaimah, lying in red sand dunes between the sea and the mountains, now has a number of substantial industries, such as cement factories and quarries, and more recently developed tourism.

e) Fujairah

The Ruler was Sheikh Mohamed bin Hamad Al Sharqi (1952-1974)

Fujairah on the Indian Ocean has a narrow coastal strip, between the sea and the mountains, with ample supplies of fresh water. The territory stretches inland and through the mountains to touch the mountain foreland on the west.

The land area is approximately 450 square miles. The population at the time of the 1968 census was 9,735.

Fujairah was accorded by the British the status of a Trucial State in 1952.

The Ruler signed a three year oil exploration agreement in 1953 with PD(TC), which was extended for one further three year period.

Fujairah taking advantage of its position outside the Gulf on the Indian Ocean, today serves innumerable oil tankers preparing to enter the Gulf.

f) Ajman

Sheikh Rashid bin Humaid Al Naimi was the Ruler of Ajman (1928-1981. His family is from the Khuraiban section of the Na'im.

The area of Ajman is approximately100 square miles. The population at the time of the 1968 census was 4246.

Sheikh Rashid, based on the coast about 25 kilometres north of Dubai and Sharjah, included in his territory the mountain foreland oases of Manama and Masfut. Manama is north east of Dhaid while Masfut is next to the oases of Hatta (Dubai) and Hadhf (Sultanate of Oman).

The Ruler was noted in those days for his ability to settle disputes, particularly among the sheikhs and tribal leaders. He maintained contact with his Khuraiban relations in Buraimi and Ibri.

The Ruler signed an oil agreement with PD(TC) in 1939.

Today Ajman has its own industries and benefits from the close proximity of Dubai and Sharjah.

g) Umm al Quwain

The Ruler was Sheikh Ahmad bin Rashid Al Mu'alla (1929-1981). Sheikh Ahmed was from the Al Ali tribe.

The land area is approximately 300 square miles. The population at the time of the 1968 census was 3744. Umm al Quwain lies on the Gulf coast north of Ajman.

The Ruler signed an oil concession agreement in 1945.

Today Umm al Quwain engages in fish research and has a couple of fine museums.

h) Kalba

The Regent was Sheikh Khalid bin Ahmed Al Qasimi (1937 -1950). He had been the Ruler of Sharjah from 1914 to 1924.

When the Ruler, Sheikh Said bin Hamid died in 1937 the elders of Kalba appointed his son who was still a minor. They also appointed Barut, a trusted slave, as his advisor. The British did not agree and Sheikh Khalid was appointed Regent and was initially very active[7] expanding his territories as far as Dhaid. In later years his influence seems to have declined and he spent much of his time at Hira on the coast next to Sharjah delegating authority to Humaid bin Abdulla. Sheikh Khalid signed an oil concession agreement with PD(TC)'s Longrigg in 1938.

The young Sheikh Hamid bin Said succeeded in 1950. (1950-1951). After Sheikh Hamid was murdered Kalba reverted to Sharjah in 1952.

Kalba town is on the coast of the Indian Ocean and lies about 15 Kilometres south of Fujairah.

The total Kalba area was possibly about 50 square miles (difficult to determine) and the population perhaps a couple of thousand.

2. The British Interest

The initials H.M.G. are short for His, or Her, Majesty's Government, the British Government. R.A.F. are the initials for the British Royal Air Force. Similarly H.M.S. stands for His (Her) Majesty's Ship.

The Political Resident (P.R.) was the title of the senior officer representing the British Government in the Gulf. He was based in Bushire until 1946 when his office moved to Bahrain. He was appointed from among the officers in the civil service of the British Government in India. The last to hold this post, appointed from Bombay was Sir Rupert Hay (1946-1953). Thereafter the P.R. and his staff were appointed from the Colonial and Commonwealth Office in London.

The Political Resident (P.R.) was supported by Political Agents (P.A.), Political Officers (P.O.) and the Residency Agent (R.A.) in Sharjah.

The Residency Agent in Sharjah, first appointed in 1829, was an Arab national reporting direct to the Political Resident. The post was abolished in 1949. The first British Political Officer to stay in Sharjah through the year was P.D. Stobart, appointed in 1948. The post was raised to the rank of Political Agent in 1953 and moved to Dubai in 1954. The first Political Officer in Abu Dhabi Buckmaster arrived in 1955. The post was raised to Political Agent in 1961 when Colonel Sir Hugh Boustead was appointed.

7 HEARD-BEY (1982), p.89ff and ABDULLAH (1994), p. 312ff.

The British interest in the area was chiefly concerned with security of the route between London and India where it passed through the waters of the Gulf. The first treaties, mainly about peace at sea, date from 1820. These safeguarded both vessels passing through the Gulf and the many pearling boats venturing out from the towns and settlements along the length of the Arabian coast.

The British attention was only drawn towards the interior of the land after the discovery of commercial oil in the lands at the northern end of the Gulf, Iran, Iraq and Bahrain. The oil industry inevitably expanded its efforts towards the south of the Gulf, while ears in the suqs of the coastal towns heard stories and rumours of unimaginable wealth, which the tongues gladly passed on suitably embellished and dramatized.

The British Government, at times reluctantly, found the need to exercise some authority over the Rulers and their people and to be assertive in the interior of the land. We see in these diaries examples of the, often uneasy, relationship between the British Government and the Rulers and their people, and at times the Company.

H.M.G., familiar with events further north in the Gulf, feared that the Rulers would be faced with strangers offering 'concession agreements' which were not in the best interests of the Rulers. Perhaps they had in mind the situation in Iran (Persia) where many entrepreneurs, without adequate financial or technical backing had come and gone, leaving the rubbish, environmental damage and disappointment of their failed ventures. There were also many, such as Holmes, who hoped to obtain oil concessions which they would sell on to large companies.

3. The Oil Company

The London based consortium, the Iraq Petroleum Company (IPC) originated in the years before the First World War (1914-1918). The Company took its final form in 1928 when the owners were the companies known today as BP, Mobil-Exxon, Partex, Shell and Total. They agreed in that year to operate together and not in competition with one another in most of the countries of the Middle East within the 'Red line'. The IPC established 'associated companies' to operate in areas other than their major discovery at Kirkuk in Iraq. One of these associated companies was P.C.L., Petroleum Concessions Limited, which operated throughout the Middle East. When operations were preparing to start on the Trucial Coast the company Petroleum Development (Trucial Coast), PD(TC) was established.

For many years the Company, PD(TC) was known on the Trucial Coast as 'The Company', 'As Sharikat'. The Company was the first on the Trucial Coast to provide employment for hundreds of men since the decline of the pearling industry. All the Skeikhdoms of the Trucial States benefited from the arrival of the Company, whether it was from the payments made to each Ruler or employment provided for the people.

Geological, geophysical and geographical survey parties sent out by the Company covered all the emirates, employing men from each sheikhdom as guides, guards and helpers.

In the days before the Second World War (1939-1945) the activity on the Trucial Coast was confined to negotiating agreements with the Rulers and then sending geological survey parties. Information about the work undertaken in this period is described in my book 'From Pearls to Oil'.

During the war years the payments to the Rulers continued to be made and, where necessary, agreements were extended to enable payments to continue and to allow the Company to return when the war was over.

After the war geological and geophysical survey parties returned. But their activities were at the start limited due to the shortage in the UK of suitable men, material and equipment in the immediate post war years. The Rulers were well aware of the difficulties that the Company faced, but they frequently expressed their displeasure at the slow progress in making surveys and then starting to drill wells in their lands.

The Company had other competing interests such as in Iraq where it was important to maintain oil exports through the pipelines to the Mediterranean. Drilling soon got underway in Palestine, but this was stopped by war in that land.

The Company had concession agreements with the Sultan of Oman and with the authorities in Hadramaut and Aden protectorate and geological parties were active there. Several successful wells had been drilled in Qatar and oil production from there was the next priority.

In spite of these other pressing requirements the Company did send the first survey parties to the Trucial Coast at the end of 1946. They came to a land with no infrastructure of roads, harbours, drinking water, electricity and modern communications. They had to bring all their requirements of fuel, food and fresh water. They had to offload from ships (landing-craft) heavy equipment onto the soft sand and establish themselves in a strange distant land which had little to offer in assistance and presented uncertain difficulties and dangers.

The first survey parties employed helpers and guards provided by the Ruler of the territory that they were operating in. The wages were one Rupee[8] a day before the War and two Rupees after the War. When the party moved from one sheikhdom to another the men were discharged and men from the next sheikhdom were engaged.

In 1949 at the start of preparations for drilling at Ra's Sadr in Abu Dhabi territory the people experienced for the first time on the Trucial Coast, the possibility of regular employment for longer periods than the few months each year on a pearling boat. Many of the pearl workers, divers and haulers, were constantly in debt as they had to finance in advance their living costs for the time spent on the pearl banks, before they left the harbour. In contrast the Company provided the men with food

8 In those days there were Rs. 13.33 to the £1 sterling.

rations and a steady income. The word 'rations' entered the local vocabulary. Many years later a friend of mine told me that his father, living in Liwa, was visiting Abu Dhabi suq to collect his Russians. I felt slightly confused until I realized that he was talking about his weekly shopping trip to buy his 'rations'.

During the days of the Trucial Coast Diaries, and for many years until the middle of the 1960's the employees in the geological and geophysical parties or on the drilling rig floor were all nationals of the sheikhdom where the operations were taking place.

The Company announced in October 1960 that they had found oil in commercial quantities at Murban (now Habshan) and would be preparing to start exports. When I arrived at Tarif, on the coast west of Abu Dhabi town, in August 1963 there was little more than a pile of pipes at Habshan, the pipeline to the oil export terminal at Jebel Dhanna was still under construction when I climbed onto the roof of a recently completed oil storage tank. The first oil was exported from Jebel Dhanna before the end of the year.

Perhaps as a memorial to earlier difficult times the Company Petrol store, established in the 1940's, stood for about 40 years beside the road into Al 'Ain. It was in later years empty. I used to pass it on the left side of the road from Al Muwiaji to Al Jimi until it was demolished in the early 1980's to make way for modern shops.

I hope that you, the reader, will enjoy reading these diaries which are a valuable record of events long ago on the Trucial Coast.

1948

Petroleum Development (Trucial Coast) Limited

From: Dubai
To: Bahrain 26th October 1948

CONFIDENTIAL

TRUCIAL COAST DIARY FOR PERIOD ENDING 26th October 1948

RAS AL KHAIMAH:

The new Ruler Shaikh Saqr bin Moh[1] continues to strengthen his relations with tribes in his area. In particular he has taken considerable pains to bring under his influence the tribes who inhabit the mountains east of Ras al Khaimah. It is understood that he is now on good terms with everyone in his area save the Shaikh of Rams,[2] who although he manifests no hostility has not yet come in to greet Saqr since the latter took over the government of Ras al Khaimah.

Shaikh Sultan bin Salim,[3] whose activities, culminating in his becoming an outlaw, have previously been described, is living quietly at Huwailat in Wadi al Gor.[4] No further intrigues on his part have so far come to light.

---

1 Sheikh Saqr deposed his uncle Sheikh Sultan bin Salim (Ruler 1921-1948) in February 1948 in a bloodless coup.

2 Rams is on the coast about 15 kilometres north of Ra's al-Khaimah town. The main tribe there are Tunaij.

3 Previous Ruler.

4 Huwailat is a Ra's al-Khaimah mountain village in the Wadi al Qor (Gor) commanding the then main route between Dubai/Sharjah and the Batinah (Indian Ocean) coast of the Sultanate of Oman. The route from Dubai passes eastwards through Sharjah, Ra's al-Khaimah and Sultanate of Oman territory.

UMM AL QAIWAIN:

Shaikh Ahmed bin Rashid[5] is still busy trying to settle the Shakhbut[6] camel dispute, for which he was appointed arbitrator in May of this year. Briefly this concerns certain camels of Shakhbut, put out to graze by him with the Manasir[7] and taken by Dubai, when the latter raided the Manasir. Shakhbut's claim has been substantiated but the Shaikhs of Dubai are now demanding that he give details of the ages and condition of the camels so that they may return camels of the same type.

It is reported that some of the buoys, planted by the Company's hydrographers in Umm al Qaiwain earlier this year have broken loose and are lost. Khan Sahib Hussain bin Hasan Amad[8] is at present engaged in replacing them.[9]

AJMAN:

The Ruler of Ajman[10] paid a visit to the Company's Representative on 24th October 1948. Previously on very bad terms with his kinsman, Shaikh Saqr bin Sultan of Biraimi,[11] he now claims to have settled all outstanding differences including the disputed village of Masfut.[12]

SHARJAH:

The Ruler of Sharjah[13] is still under H.M.G's displeasure for his part in the escape of Shaikh Sultan bin Salim.[14] It is interesting to note that the naval sloop,

5 The Umm al Quwain Ruler, Sheikh Ahmed bin Rashid was noted in those days for settling disputes, particular among the Sheikhs and tribal leaders.

6 Sheikh Shakhbut bin Sultan, Ruler of Abu Dhabi (1928-1966).

7 The Manasir are a large Bedouin tribe. They were to be found chiefly in the western and southern part of Abu Dhabi territory. They were also present across the border in Saudi Arabia.

8 Khan Sahib Hussain Ahmed was Residency Agent in Sharjah in 1935. He reported to the British Political Resident in Bushire. He formed a contracting company which provided services to the oil industry from the very earliest times of the industry on the Trucial Coast and is still prominent to this day.

9 The creek at Umm al Qaiwain provided the best possibility for the Company to bring heavy equipment ashore. The creeks at Dubai and Sharjah had sand banks at the entry while the creek at Umm al Quwain was judged to be safer for the barges bringing material from the ocean going ships which had to lie some kilometres out at sea.

10 Sheikh Rashid bin Humaid.

11 Both of the Al bu Kharaiban section of the Na'im tribe.

12 Ajman territory next to Dubai's Hatta Oasis on the edge of the Hajar mountain range 100 kilometres south east of Dubai.

13 Sheikh Sultan bin Saqr.

14 Previous Ruler of Ra's al-Khaimah.

which recently visited the Trucial Coast called at Dubai and not Sharjah, its usual port of call, as being the seat of H.M.G's representatives and the R.A.F. Station.[15]

The Beni Kitab tribe,[16] under Mohd bin Ali bin Huwaidin, are at present on bad terms with Shaikh Mohd bin Hamad ash Sharqi[17] of Fujaira.[18]

DUBAI:

Shaikh Said bin Maktum[19] left for Bahrain by air on 21st October for eye treatment.

H.M.S. Loch Quoich[20] visited Dubai on 19th October 1948; the Ruler of Dubai and his son Shaikh Rashid went on board to pay a courtesy visit. Their visit was returned the following day.

ABU DHABI:

Shaikhs Shakhbut and Hiza' are at present in Abu Dhabi. Shaikhs Zaid and Khalid[21] are still in the Biraimi Oasis.[22]

No further information regarding Shaikh Shakhbut's relations with the Manasir has come to hand.

The Company proposes to start building an explosive[23] store at Mandar Farida[24] in the very near future.

---

15 There had been a Residency Agent (Arab) living in Sharjah since 1829. The post was abolished in 1949. He reported direct to the Political Resident, the senior British Officer in the Gulf based in Bahrain (since 1946). The first Political Officer (British national) living full time in Sharjah arrived in 1948. The post was raised when a Political Agent was appointed in 1953. The office was moved to Dubai in 1954.

16 This refers to one section of the tribe inhabiting the area around Jebel Faiyah in Sharjah territory. The tribe also was found in the territory of Abu Dhabi and the Sultanate of Oman (Wadi Bani Kitab).

17 Sheikh Hamad was not yet recognised as 'Trucial Ruler'. He was finally admitted in 1952 after the re-absorption of Kalba into Sharjah.

18 On the Indian Ocean coast.

19 Dubai Ruler.

20 His Majesty's Ship Loch Quoich, a small British naval ship.

21 The Ruler Sheikh Shakhbut bin Sultan (1928-1966). The four sons of a previous Ruler Shaikh Sultan bin Zayed. Their mother was the formidable Sheikhah Salamah bint Buti al Qubaisi.

22 In those days the oasis villages of Abu Dhabi and the Sultanate of Oman were referred to as the Buraimi oasis. The Abu Dhabi villages now are towns including Al Ain. Buraimi is one of the three Oman villages, present day towns. They are found about 160 kilometres east of Abu Dhabi.

23 Explosives for seismic surveys.

24 On the Abu Dhabi coast.

700 tins[25] of petrol were recently sent by the Company to Abu Dhabi en route for their Petrol Stores at al Mawaiqi[26] in the Biraimi oasis.

KALBA:

Shaikh Khalid bin Ahmed, Regent of Kalba,[27] is still in residence at al Haira.[28] Shaikh Hamad bin Abdullah represents him in Kalba.

VISIT:

Mr. W. Thesiger,[29] explorer, arrived in Sharjah by air on 20th October 1948, and came to stay with the Company's Representative in Dubai. He left for Abu Dhabi on 26th October 1948, by launch. He proposes to stay a few days with Shaikh Shakhbut and then to proceed by camel to Biraimi. His ultimate intention is to cross the sands once again and emerge in the Hadhramaut.[30]

ARRIVAL:

Mr. E.F. Henderson,[31] a Company employee, arrived by air on 19th October 1948 at Sharjah.

GENERAL:

Very heavy rain[32] fell all over the Trucial Coast on the 25th October 1948.

H. Jackson
Representative in Dubai.

---

25 Petrol came from the Anglo-Persian refinery at Abadan in Iran in four gallon cans. The cans were not returned empty and were so numerous and useful that they performed many functions varying from building blocks (when filled with sand or cement) to seats at the cinema (outdoors) They were not very robust and there were many complaints that much petrol was lost due to leaks and spillage, such as when an over-loaded camel rolled on its side.

26 The main Abu Dhabi village in those days.

27 Kalba, situated on the Indian Ocean coast was one of the seven Trucial Sheikhdoms from 1936 to 1952. Longrigg (PCL) signed a concession agreement with Sheikh Khalid bin Ahmed the Regent of Kalba in 1937.

28 Haira is on the coast a few kilometres north of Sharjah, now absorbed into Sharjah town.

29 THESIGER, WILFRED, *Arabian Sands*, Longman, London, 1959, ISBN 0 00217005 1.

30 South Yemen.

31 Recently recruited to work for the Company (1948-1956). Henderson was seconded to the Foreign Office for three years from 1956. Thereafter he remained with the Foreign Office until he retired in 1974.

32 In many countries people complain when rain falls. Not so in lands such as the United Arab Emirates (Trucial Coast) where rain is regarded as blessing from God, coming to relieve the parched desert.

TRUCIAL COAST DIARY FOR WEEK ENDING 2 NOVEMBER 1948

RAS AL KHAIMAH:

Nothing to report.

UMM AL QAIWAIN:

The Company's representative accompanied by Mr. Read, Camp Boss of Party No.3[33] and Khan Sahib Hussain visited Umm al Qaiwain on 30th October 1948, to inspect the suitability of the roads for the heavy seismic equipment likely to be landed in the near future at Umm al Qaiwain from the Company's vessel Jasura. It was decided that very little if any road repair work would be necessary. After the inspection a visit was paid to the Ruler of Umm al Qaiwain.

AJMAN:

Nothing to report.

SHARJAH:

The Residency Agent,[34] Sharjah left for Bahrain by plane on 28th October 1948.

The dispute between the Bani Kitab[35] and the Sharqiyin[36] is not yet settled.

DUBAI:

The Company began to erect a camp for their Seismic Party No.3 at a site 6 miles south west of Dubai in an area disputed by both Dubai and Abu Dhabi. Guards from both Shaikhdoms have been asked for by the Company.

Said bin Suwaid, chief of the Al bu Rahma section of the Manasir[37] is at present in Dubai on a visit.

---

33 Geophysical party.

34 Jasim bin Mohamed al Kadmari. The Residency Agent was a Gulf local reporting to the Political Resident in Bahrain. Prior to 1946 the Political Resident was based at Bushire. The post of Residency Agent was abolished in 1949. Political Officers (British nationals) were first appointed to Sharjah in 1937, but they did not remain there during the summer months before 1948 when P.D. Stobart arrived.

35 The Bani Kitab tribe were spread between the desert and mountain foreland in Sharjah territory (east of Dubai) including Jebel Faiyah and south as far as Wadi Bani Kitab in the Sultanate of Oman.

36 The Sharqiyin are a tribe largely in Fujairah territory, an area which includes much of the Hajar mountain range between the desert and the Indian Ocean.

37 The Manasir are divided into four main groups. Al Bu Rahmah, Al Bu Mundir, Al Bu Sha'ar, Al Bu Hamir with a fifth group the Al Bu Khail who are usually regarded as being separate.

ABU DHABI:

The Ruler of Abu Dhabi[38] has replied to the Residency Agent, Sharjah on the subject of the Manasir. He claims that the writer of the letter mentioned in our DO/DB/TC/9 dated 19th October 1948 has been instigated by evil people and that he will take steps to punish those of the Manasir concerned.

KELBA:

Nothing to report.

ARRIVAL:

Mr. E.G. Read, Camp Boss Party No.3 arrived in Sharjah by air on 28th October 1948.

PUBLIC BAZAAR PRICES:

One maund equals nine lbs. (9 Pounds)
16 Annas equal one Rupee.

Rice	per maund	Rs. 8	
Flour		Rs. 3	
Sugar		Rs. 4	
Ghee		Rs. 20	
Mutton		Rs. 8	
Beef		Rs. 6	
Tea		Rs. 3	
Coffee		Rs. 4	
Dates (Basri)[39]	basket	Rs. 12	
Eggs	dozen	Rs. 1	As. 4

GENERAL

The heavy rains reported last week would appear to have passed and the weather is now fair and mild. The effects of the rain are already apparent in the desert.

Two Vampire jet aircraft[40] landed at Sharjah on 2nd November 1948. These are the first jet aircraft to land here.

Jackson
Representative
HMJ /KAZ.

---

38 Sheikh Shakhbut bin Sultan.

39 From Basra.

40 Small Royal Air Force fighter aircraft. They were based at Habbaniyeh in Iraq.

TRUCIAL COAST DIARY FOR WEEK ENDING 9 NOVEMBER 1948

GENERAL:

The recent heavy rains, the effect of which is already apparent in the desert, would seem to have had a most salutary effect on the political atmosphere as well. The usual reports of lawlessness in the desert and intrigue in the towns are conspicuous by their absence. The inhabitants of the desert are apparently too busy talking about the rains and the revived pasturage, while the townsmen are still busy repairing leaking roofs.

RAS AL KHAIMAH:

Nothing to report.

UMM AL QAIWAIN:

Mr. Read, Camp Boss Party No.3, visited Umm al Qaiwain in the company of Khan Sahib Hussain on 9th November 1948 for the purpose of siting a stores compound, into which he intends to discharge the equipment arriving in the near future by the Company's vessel Jasura.

AJMAN:

Nothing to report.

SHARJAH:

The Company hopes to erect a permanent building alongside its garage compound outside Sharjah for the purpose of a Seismic Equipment Stores and Workshops.

DUBAI:

Shaikh Said bin Maktum[41] returned from Bahrain by launch on 5th November 1948.

Shaikh Rashid bin Said[42] since the rains is devoting himself entirely to hawking.[43]

The Seismic Camp near Jebel Ali[44] is nearly completed. A shortage of tent pegs however is likely to hold up further work on it. Two guards each from Abu Dhabi and Dubai are now in camp.

---

41 Dubai Ruler Sheikh Said bin Maktum (1912-1958) and his son Sheikh Rashid bin Said. (Ruler 1958-1990)

42 Sheikh Rashid bin Said. Son of Ruler. Later Dubai Ruler (1958- 1990).

43 A favourite past time for many of the Sheikhs, until this day.

44 The prominent dome shaped hill south of Dubai.

ABU DHABI:

Until recently the Abu Dhabi sabkha[45] has been very treacherous even for camels owing to unusually heavy rains.

KELBA:

Nothing to report.

ARRIVALS:

M/S Bird[46] and Clark[47] arrived in Sharjah by air on 3rd November 1948.

DEPARTURES:

M/S Bird and Henderson left[48] for Muscat by launch on 5th November 1948. A Company car was dispatched the following day to meet them at Sohar.[49]

DUBAI BAZAAR:

As for last week.

H. Jackson
Representative.

---

45 The sabkhah is a coastal strip of low-lying land consisting of a gypsum saline sandy mud. It extends from south of Dubai in the north-east to the border with Saudi Arabia in the west. It reaches approximately 10 kilometres inland in the north and centre and 50 kilometres in the far west. The sabkhah can also be flooded by the sea when there is a very high tide at the same time as a strong northerly wind.

46 Bird was based in Jahili (Buraimi) to negotiate with the various Omani sheikhs to obtain permission for the Company to send in geologists.

47 There is no indication of who he was.

48 They left from Sharjah.

49 On the coast of the Sultanate of Oman and due east of Al Ain/Buraimi.

TRUCIAL COAST DIARY FOR PERIOD ENDING 23 NOVEMBER 1948

RAS AL KHAIMAH:

Mr. R.E.R. Bird and Mr. E.F. Henderson arrived at Ras al Khaimah on 17th November 1948 by launch on their way back from Muscat. While there, they took the opportunity of calling upon Shaikh Saqr bin Mohamed, the Ruler. They continued their journey to Dubai the same day by Company car.

UMM AL QAIWAIN:

All preparations for the arrival of the much delayed Jasura[50]are now ready.

AJMAN:

Nothing to report.

SHARJAH:

Peace has now been made between the Beni Kitab (Mohamed bin Ali bin Huwaidin) and the Shargiyin (Mohamed bin Hamad ash Shargi).[51] It is also reported that the dispute between the Bani Kitab on the one hand and the Awamir and Rawashid[52] on the other has also been settled. The Dubai Shaikhs were intermediaries in both cases.

DUBAI:

An unconfirmed report states that Said bin Suwaid, chief of the Al Bu Rahmah section of the Manasir while in Dubai recently, sent a messenger (a Dubai subject) to the Baraimi Oasis,[53] instructing all Manasir there to leave Baraimi and return to their area.

---

50 Company landing craft.

51 Fujairah Sheikh.

52 Large desert tribes found not only in the UAE (Trucial Coast) but also in the Sultanate of Oman and Saudi Arabia.

53 In those days the term 'Baraimi or Buraimi Oasis' referred to all the villages both in the territory of Abu Dhabi and in that of the Sultanate of Oman. The name was used commonly by the British, among others. I remember, years ago, many national people saying that they were going to Oman for the weekend, they were referring to one of the Abu Dhabi villages. In recent times Abu Dhabi's Al 'Ain has grown into the largest town and most Abu Dhabi people would no longer refer to Baraimi or Oman as their holiday destination, unless they were crossing the border.

ABU DHABI:

A report from the Baraimi Oasis states that Shaikh Zaid bin Sultan[54] (Al Bu Falah)[55] is very worried over the present attitude adopted by the Manasir and is seriously concerned over possible repercussions from neighbouring states should hostilities break out between the Manasir and the Al Bu Falah. The same report states that the attitude of the Manasir towards the Al Bu Falah has hardened and that they have sworn to pursue the matter to the end.

Mr. W. Thesiger,[56] who recently left Dubai for the Baraimi Oasis, has now set out for Liwa,[57] from where he will return to Baraimi.[58]

KALBA:

Nothing to report.

ARRIVALS:

The new Political Officer, Trucial Coast Mr. P.D. Stobart, arrived in Dubai by steamer from Bahrain on 11th November 1948. The Residency Agent, Jasim bin Mohd al Kadhmawi, returned to Sharjah by air on 10th November 1948 from sick leave in Bahrein.

Messrs. R.E.R. Bird and E.F. Henderson returned to Dubai from Muscat on 17th November 1948.

GENERAL:

The considerable delay in the commencement of the Company's operation this season is the subject of much adverse criticism locally.

---

54 The brother of Shaikh Shakhbut, Shaikh Zayed bin Sultan, features prominently in these diaries. He was his brother's representative in Al 'Ain. His name is spelt throughout the diaries 'Zaid' and I have not changed the spelling. He ruled Abu Dhabi (1966-2004) and was President of the UAE (1971-2004).

55 At the time of writing this diary the use of the name 'Al Nahyan' had not yet been introduced. The Abu Dhabi ruling family came from the Bani Yas tribal group Al bu Falah. The Dubai ruling family came from the Bani Yas tribal group Al bu Falasi.

56 The explorer. Known by his Rashidi companions as 'Mubarak bin London'. He was the first European to reach the Liwa oases in the south of Abu Dhabi territory. He arrived by camel from the south, crossing the Empty Quarter from Salala in the Dhofar province of the Sultanate of Oman.

57 The crescent shaped string of oases extending over more than 100 kilometres in the high dunes in the far south of Abu Dhabi territory.

58 See THESIGER, WILFRED, (1983), *Arabian Sands*. Longman, London, 1959, Collins, London, 1990, ISBN 0 00 217005 1.

Rice	per maund	Rs. 7	As. 10
Flour	" "	3	2
Sugar	" "	4	
Ghee	" "	19	
Mutton	" "	8	
Beef	" "	6	
Tea	" "	3	
Coffee	" "	8	
Dates	" basket	12	
Eggs	" dozen	1	14
Onions	per maund	1	12

Jackson
Representative
HMJ/KAZ.

TRUCIAL COAST DIARY FOR PERIOD ENDING 7 DECEMBER 1948

RAS AL KHAMAH:

Nothing to report.

UMM AL QUWAIN:

The Company's landing craft M.S.Jasura arrived Umm al Quwain on the morning of 29th November 1948 crossing the bar of the creek at low tide and anchoring finally off Bury Bakhut. At the turn of the tide the vessel was brought to the landing site on the shore and all cargo was very successfully landed. Unloading was completed by 1430 hours. M.S. Jasura left again for Basra on the following morning at 0700 hours.

The Ruler of Umm al Quwain[59] came on invitation to witness the unloading operations. Capt. Retti, the master of the Jesoura, Capt. Pilditch and Mr. Gore, both of the Marine Dept. London were introduced to the Ruler. Capt. Ritti apologised to the Ruler for remaining such a short time at Umm al Quwain and for not calling upon him, but promised to do so on his next visit, on which occasion he hoped the Ruler would honour him by coming aboard the vessel.

AJMAN:

Nothing to report.

59 Sheikh Ahmad bin Rashid (1929-1981).

SHARJAH:

The ban on the issue of travel permits to Sharjah subjects imposed by the Political authorities as a result of the Ruler's connivance at the escape of Shaikh Sultan bin Salim,[60] has still not been lifted.

Shaikh Sultan bin Salim is still living at Hawailat in the Wadi al Gor.

DUBAI:

Shaikh Juma' bin Maktum[61] left by car for Muscat on 26:11:48 and returned on 3.12.48. There would appear to be greater liaison than usual at present between the Sultan of Muscat and the Dubai Shaikhs.

Shaikh Said bin Maktum, Ruler of Dubai visited the Company's camp near Jebel Ali on 4.12.48.

ABU DHABI:

It is understood that Shaikh Shakhbut bin Sultan, Ruler of Abu Dhabi has admitted that the Manasir are being incited by evilly disposed persons against him but that he does not consider the situation serious. The Manasir, he claims, are still as firm allies of his as ever.

KALBA:

Nothing to report.

CAMP:

Seismic Party No.3 whose members arrived at Umm al Quwain by Jasura on 29.11.48 started operations from their Jebel Ali[62] Camp on 1st December 1948. The area being worked at present lies between the camp and Jebel Ali. All members of the party are at present living in camp.

4 additional guards from Dubai and 4 from Abu Dhabi arrived in camp on 1st December 1948 making a total of 6 guards from each Shaikhdom.

It is not expected that the party will change their camp site this season.

VISITORS:

Mr. Banta of the Company's geophysical department arrived with Seismic Party No.3 by Jasura on 29.11.48 to assist in the opening of the party's operations. He left by R.A.F. plane on 1st December 1948.

60 The previous Ruler of Ra's al-Khaimah. The British authorities were considering deporting him to Bahrain.

61 Brother of the Dubai Ruler.

62 Jebel Ali is a low hill near the coast in Dubai territory and close to the border with Abu Dhabi.

Mr. C.J. Pelly, Political Agent, Bahrein arrived by air in Sharjah on 1st December 1948. After visiting the Rulers of Sharjah, Ajman, Kelba, Umm a1 Quwain, Dubai and Ras al Khaimah he left on 4.12.48 by road accompanied by the P.O.T.C. and R.A.[63] on a visit to Abu Dhabi and the Baraimi Oasis. He expects to return to Sharjah from Baraimi by the Ramlat al Anaij[64] route on 8th December 1948.

DEPARTURES:

Mr. R.E.R. Bird left for Abu Dhabi by road on 3.12.48 and from there proceeded to the Baraimi Oasis. He expects to return to Dubai on 8th December 1948.[65]

Mr. E.F. Henderson left for Bahrain by air on 1st Dec. 1948 to undergo further medical examination at the Bahrain hospital.

DUBAI BAZAAR PRICES:

One maund equals 9 lbs.

16 Annas equals one Rupee.[66]

Rice	per maund	Rs. 7	As. 10
Flour		Rs. 3	As. 2
Sugar		Rs. 4	
Ghee		Rs. 19	
Mutton		Rs. 8	
Beef		Rs. 6	
Tea		Rs. 27	
Coffee		Rs. 8	
Dates	basket	Rs. 12	
Eggs	doz.	Rs. 1	As. 14
Onion	maund	Rs. 1	As. 12

Jackson
Representative.

63 Political Officer Trucial Coast and Residency Agent.

64 The Ramlat Anaij (Anaij sands) are a particularly high group of sand dunes which block the direct route between Dubai and Buraimi/Al 'Ain. The sand extends right up to the mountains.

65 Bird spent several months living at Jahili in the Al Ain area. He was negotiating with the Omani sheikhs to try to obtain their permission for Company geologists to work in their territory and to pass through to central Oman. See HEARD, DAVID, (2018), *Oil Men, Territorial Ambitions and Political Agents.* Gerlach Press, Berlin, 2019, ISBN 978 3 95994 064 1.

66 There were Rs. 13.33 to the £1 sterling.

VISIT OF SUPERIOR OIL COMPANY TO ABU DHABI:

Please refer to my letter PO.A/257 of 17th December 1949.[67]

The Superior Oil Company party consisted of Mr. Smith a geologist an interpreter (Weightman's)[68] and two others. Galloway[69] was not, as at first thought, in the party. They went down by road and returned by air to Bahrein, the KLM Dakota landing without any trouble at Abu Dhabi. According to Hiza they spared no effort to pour contempt on us -one well in 14 years. Hiza explained our difficulties to them, and the war in which Britain was engaged totally. It is not thought that their discussion reached any conclusion.

I passed the party on my way down and took one member of it to be Galloway, but did not have a very good view of him through the windscreen of their truck. Opinion in Sharjah had it that Galloway was there, but Hiza assures me this was not the case.

Henderson
Representative
ERH/KAZ.

TRUCIAL COAST DIARY FOR PERIOD ENDING 21 DECEMBER 1948

GENERAL:

Heavy rain fell in the Ajman, Umm al Qaiwain and Ras al Khaimah area during the night of 18/19 December 1949.

RAS AL KHAIMAH:

Shaikh Saqr bin Mohamed, the Ruler of Ras al Khaimah, accompanied by his brother Shaikh Humaid bin Mohd, arrived in Dubai on 16.12.48 on an official visit to the Dubai Shaikhs. They left for Sharjah the following day and have now returned to Ras al Khaimah.

UMM AL QAIWAIN:

One of the Company's buoys marking the entrance to the Umm al Qaiwain creek was recently reported to have been damaged by rough seas. It has now been repaired by Khan Sahib Hussain bin Hasan Amad.

---

67 This letter is not included.

68 Victor Hashim.

69 Both Weightman and Galloway had retired from the Diplomatic Service and were both former Political Agents.

AJMAN:

Shaikh Rashid bin Humaid, Ruler of Ajman is at present busy trying to settle the dispute, which has recently broken out between Shaikh Saqr bin Sultan[70] of Biraimi and the Bani Kitab under Mohamed bin Ali bin Huwaidin. It is understood that camels have been stolen on both sides.

It is also reported that Shaikh Rashid is among those who are trying to dissuade Saqr bin Sultan from going in to Muscat to make his peace with the Sultan. It will be recalled that as a result of Seyyed Ahmed Ibrahim's[71] visit to the Biraimi Oasis in the summer of this year it was considered possible that Saqr would visit Muscat.[72]

SHARJAH:

Two incidents involving Company personnel and vehicles took place in Bani Kitab territory during the period under review. These have been reported fully under our DB/PL/57 dated 19.12.48.[73]

It appears that a Shaikh of Dubai is as usual mixed up in the matter, with the motive apparently of causing trouble for the Shaikh of Sharjah. Mohamed bin Ali bin Huwaidin, Shaikh of the Bani Kitab and large numbers of his tribesmen, are frequently visiting Dubai these days.

DUBAI:

A large number of Manasir Shaikhs and tribesmen are at present in Dubai. It seems that Rashid bin Said[74] is still busy trying to widen the rift between the Manasir and al Bu Falah,[75] a rift which he was to a very great extent responsible for creating in the first place.

ABU DHABI:

Reports from the Dhahirah, Bainuna and Liwa[76] areas indicate that the Manasir continue to adopt a hostile attitude towards the Al Bu Falah and insist that no 'Christian' will be allowed to enter their area. One of the excuses they apparently give

70 Sheikh Saqr bin Sultan al Naimi, Al Bu Khuraiban section, was the Representative of the Sultan of Oman in Buraimi. Sheikh Rashid bin Humaid, Ruler of Ajman is also Al Bu Khuraiban.

71 The Sultan of Oman's Minister.

72 See HEARD, D. (2019) chapter 3.11. Ahmed Ibrahim came to reassert the Sultan's authority after Bird had signed agreements with several tribal leaders to permit PD(TC) geologist to work in and pass through their territories going towards central Oman.

73 This is recorded in HEARD, D. (2019).

74 Son of Dubai Ruler. Later Ruler of Dubai.

75 Al Bu Falah of Abu Dhabi.

76 East, central and southern areas respectively of Abu Dhabi.

for their present behaviour is that the Al Bu Falah gave them no help when the Dubai Shaikhs raided them in the early part of this year.

Mr. W. Thesiger has now returned to Biraimi after visiting the Dhahara, Bainuna and Liwa areas. His Rashidi followers are once again at feud with the Bani Kitab and it is understood that the Ghafiri tribes in the south have intimated that they do not wish Thesiger and his Rashidi followers to come to their area. The Rawashid are of course Hinawi.[77] Mr. Thesiger will be leaving for the central sands probably after Christmas.

KALBA:

Nothing to report.

SEISMIC CAMP:

The Party's operations are making good progress in spite of transport difficulties. The survey is now being carried south of the camp.

Shaikh Said bin Maktum Ruler of Dubai again paid a visit to the camp on the afternoon of 19th December 1948.

The Party hope to spend the 24th and 25th December 1948 in Sharjah in order to celebrate the Xmas season. It is hoped that M/L Jasura will bring the party's Xmas fare in time.

VISITORS:

Mr. Bertram Thomas[78] formerly director of the School of Arab Studies[79] and now working for the Shell group in some liaison capacity, arrived in Sharjah unexpectedly from Bahrein on 15th Dec. 1948. He told the Company's Representative that he is merely renewing old acquaintances, though it is understood from the Political Officer Trucial Coast that Mr. Thomas has come here in accordance with his intention to visit all areas where his Company has interests. He is at present engaged in visiting the Trucial Shaikhs and has so far called upon the Rulers of Dubai, Abu Dhabi, Sharjah and Ras al Khaimah. He hopes to return to Bahrein by the steamer arriving Dubai on 22nd Dec 1948. Mr. Thomas is being escorted on all his visits to the Trucial Shaikhs by either the Political Officer Trucial Coast or the Residency Agent Sharjah.

---

77 Ghafiri and Hinawi. Two sects of Islam. The Bani Yas are also Hinawi. The distinction is not so relevant today.

78 Finance Minister to Sultan Taimur bin Faisal 1925-1932. Crossed the Rub' al Khali (Empty Quarter) 1930-1931. His account of the journey is in his book THOMAS, B. (1932), Arabia Felix.

79 In Jerusalem.

The following arrived Sharjah on 12th Dec. 1948 by Company Dove.[80] Messrs. De Metz, Benezit, Dalmont, Heseldin, Wellings and Gibson. The party left immediately for the Jebel Ali camp of Party No.3 where they had lunch. They returned in the afternoon via Dubai to Sharjah where they spent the night. The following day the party went on a survey flight into the interior, returning to Sharjah for lunch, after which they left again for Bahrein. Mr. P.D. Stobart Political Officer Trucial Coast accompanied them on the survey flight.

DEPARTURES:

Mr. E.I. Grizzell, Party chief of Seismic Party No.3 left for Basra by R.A.F. plane on 16th Dec. 1948. He hopes to return to the Trucial Coast after Xmas.

Mr. L.C. Williamson, employed as recorder with Seismic Party No.3 left Sharjah for Bahrein on 16th Dec. 48 on his way to U.S.A. Mr. Williamson has gone on leave.

Dr. Abdul Latif Inayatullah, Company Medical Officer on the Trucial Coast, left for Karachi on 9th December 1948 by S.S. Barjora. He has been granted 61 days leave. A replacement is expected to arrive soon.

Jackson
Representative.

80 Aircraft used by the Company. The reader can see one in the Mahatta museum in Sharjah.

1949

TRUCIAL COAST DIARY FOR PERIOD ENDING 5 JANUARY 1949

RAS AL KHAIMAH:

The Company's Representative visited Ras al Khaimah on 21st Dec. 1948. In addition to conducting some Company business with the Ruler,[1] he took this opportunity to present on behalf of the Company a Ford Pilot Station Wagon, which was very much admired and appreciated by the Ruler.

UMM AL QAIWAIN:

All arrangements were made for the arrival of the Jasura[2] at Umm al Qaiwain before Christmas. Owing however to bad weather the Jasura has so far not been able to sail from Zekrit.[3]

AJMAN:

The Ruler of Ajman[4] recently accompanied Shaikh Mohamed bin Ali bin Huwaidin[5] to Biraimi with a view to making peace between the latter and Shaikh Saqr bin Sultan of the Na'im.[6] The latter however insisted that the Bani Kitab should return all the Na'im camels, after which he would agree to discuss a settlement. It is

---

1 Sheikh Saqr bin Mohamed.

2 The PD(TC) landing craft.

3 On the coast a short distance north of Dukhan on the west coast of Qatar.

4 Sheikh Rashid bin Humaid.

5 Al Kitbi from the Jebel Faiyah area south of Dhaid.

6 Sheikh Saqr bin Sultan, the representative of the Sultan in Buraimi. Sheikh Saqr bin Sultan and the Ajman Ruler Sheikh Rashid bin Humaid were both from the Al Khuraiban section of the Na'im and were related.

understood that Mohamed bin Ali did not agree to this and left Biraimi with Rashid bin Humaid. On their way out of the oasis the Bani Kitab took the opportunity of looting 45 camels. It is not considered likely in view of this that Saqr will fulfil his intention of going to Muscat.[7]

SHARJAH:

As was reported recently, Sharjah subjects are not at present being issued with travel permits by the Political Authorities. The Ruler of Sharjah therefore with remarkable ingenuity has started to issue his own, but it is understood that he has been warned that such permits will not be recognised by any of the States in the Gulf, who require permits from travellers.

DUBAI:

Large numbers of Awamir,[8] including Salim bin Musallem bin Ham[9] have recently been visiting Dubai. It is understood that they came in connection with their dispute with the Beni Kitab.

ABU DHABI:

Nothing to report.

KALBA:

Nothing to report.

SEISMIC CAMP:

Speed of operations is being seriously held up by transport difficulties.

The Party[10] spent 24th and 25th Dec. 1948 in Sharjah.

DEPARTURES:

Mr. P.D. Stobart, Political Officer, Trucial Coast left for Bahrein by plane on 22nd December 1948.

---

7 This report of the incident proved to be an exaggeration. It illustrates the difficulty that the writer had in differentiating between truth, gossip and malicious gossip.

8 The large desert tribe found in the southern desert of Abu Dhabi as well as The Sultanate of Oman and Saudi Arabia.

9 Shaikh of the Awamir and a strong supporter of Sheikh Zayed.

10 The geophysical party.

Mr. R.E.R. Bird[11] left for Bahrein by air on 22nd Dec. 1948 for further medical treatment.

Mr. Martin, Seismic Party No.3, left for Bahrein by air on 30th Dec. 1948 for medical treatment at the Bahrein hospital.

ARRIVAL:

Mr. E.I. Grizzell, Seismic Party No.3 returned from local leave in the Lebanon on 29th December 1948.

DUBAI BAZZAR PRICES:

One maund equals 9 1bs. (9 pounds or about 4 kilograms)

There are 16 Annas to the Rupee.

Rice	per maund	Rs. 7	As. 10
Flour		Rs. 3	2
Sugar		Rs. 4	
Ghee		Rs. 19	
Mutton		Rs. 8	
Beef		Rs. 6	
Tea		Rs. 27	
Coffee		Rs. 8	
Dates per basket		Rs. 12	
Eggs per doz.		Rs. 1	14
Onions	maund	Rs. 1	12

Jackson
Representative.

11 Bird had been seeking agreements with the tribal leaders in the Buriami area to allow PD(TC) geologists to enter the Sultanate of Oman across their territory. See HEARD, D. 2019.

TRUCIAL COAST DIARY FOR PERIOD ENDING 18 JANUARY 1949

RAS AL KHAIMAH:

Nothing to report.

UMM AL QAIWAIN:

M/V Jasura[12] Voy.2 arrived Umm al Qaiwain on 6th January 1949 with a miscellaneous cargo including Xmas rations for the Trucial Coast. No difficulties occurred in off-loading and every facility was offered to the Company by the Ruler, Shaikh Ahmed bin Rashid and by the A.I.O.C.[13] Agent, Khan Sahib Husain bin Hasan Amad.

Capt. Ritty[14] called upon the Ruler on 8th January 1949. The Shaikh returned his visit the following day and while aboard was taken on a conducted tour of the vessel. Rockets were fired as the Shaikh went ashore and there is no doubt that the visit was a very great success. Capt. Ritty and the Company's representative were then entertained to lunch ashore at the Ruler's fort, when Capt. Ritty took the opportunity of saying goodbye. M/V Jasura sailed for Bahrein on 10th January 1949.

AJMAN:

Relations between Shaikh Rashid bin Humaid and Shaikh Saqr bin Sultan[15] have considerably deteriorated as a result of the Bani Kitab raid mentioned in our last report. Shaikh Saqr believes that Rashid bin Humaid at least connived at the Bani Kitab action if he did not actually take part in it.

SHARJAH:

Nothing to report.

DUBAI:

Nothing to report.

ABU DHABI:

The Company's representative visited Abu Dhabi on 10th and 11th January 1949. He was accompanied by O.C. R.A.F. Station,[16] Sharjah who examined the Abu

12 The Company landing craft.

13 Anglo Iranian Oil Company, later BP.

14 The captain of the Jasura.

15 The Ruler of Ajman and his cousin the sheikh in Buraimi.

16 Officer Commanding Royal Air Force Station Sharjah.

Dhabi airstrip with a view to its use by company aircraft. It was decided that the strip was fit for use by Rapides[17] and Doves[18]. Two runways were roughly marked out for subsequent final marking with crude oil.[19]

The Political Officer, Trucial Coast[20] arrived Abu Dhabi by launch on 10th January 1949 on a visit to the Ruler. He left for Sharjah the following morning.

Tribesmen of the Murra, who normally live in Saudi Arabia, are at present pasturing their camels at Al Muqatara near the Abu Dhabi sabkha.[21] The pasturage in the Abu Dhabi shaikhdom as a result of the recent rains, is everywhere good.

W. Thesiger[22] is still in the Biraimi Oasis and spends much time hunting with Shaikhs Zaid and Khalid, the brothers of the Ruler of Abu Dhabi. He expects to go off south very soon and to return to the Trucial Coast about April.

Shaikh Shakhbut asserts that the machinations of the Dubai Shaikhs to provoke enmity between him and the Manasir[23] have been to no effect and that he is still assured of the latters' loyalty.

KELBA:

It is reported that eight tribesmen of the Awamir[24] are at present in prison at Kelba. They were attempting to abduct individuals with a view to selling them into slavery but were captured by the Regent of Kelba's deputy Shaikh Humaid bin Abdullah.

ARRIVALS:

Mr. P.D. Stobart, Political Officer, Trucial Coast returned to Sharjah by launch from Bahrein on 11th January 1949.

Messrs. Bird, Henderson and Martin returned from hospital treatment in Bahrein on 6th January 1949. Mr. N.R. Fallon[25] also arrived the same day. The following

---

17 Small bi-plane, several of these aircraft were used by IPC group of companies across the Middle East.

18 The De Havilland Dove was still in service when I arrived 14 years later. One may be seen in the Sharjah Mahatta museum, hanging from the ceiling.

19 The first runway was prepared by the RAF during the Second World War for emergency use. This is the first mention of a runway at Abu Dhabi in the Company records. It was used by Longrigg who landed there with Lermitte on 19 January 1949. Longrigg was the Company Manager in London and Lermitte the Representative in Bahrain.

20 P.D. Stobart.

21 He refers to the first sands that one reaches after crossing the sabkhah east of Abu Dhabi island.

22 The explorer, known by the Arabs as Mubarak bin London.

23 Large desert tribe found chiefly in Abu Dhabi territory, also in Saudi Arabia.

24 A large desert tribe who range through Oman, the Emirates and Saudi Arabia. They were not responsible for this kidnapping.

25 PD(TC) surveyor.

personnel arrived by Company Dove on 7th January 1949:- Messrs. Wellings, Browne, Ion, Wetzel and Dr. Lehner.[26] On the same day they visited the seismic camp at Jebel Ali and returned to Sharjah for the night. The following day a survey flight was carried out over the Oman mountains. Mr. Henderson and Mr. Fallon accompanied them on the trip, which took them also to Masirah.[27] The Dove left on 8th January 1949 for Bahrein with Mr. Wellings as the only passenger.

DEPARTURES:

Mr. Read, camp boss Party No.3 left for Bahrein by air on 7th January 1949. He returned on 13th January 1949.

Mr. Charles of seismic Party No.3 left for Bahrein by air for sick treatment on 7th January 1949.

Mr. R.E.R. Bird left for Muscat by road on 9th January 1949.

Messrs. Henderson, Fallon, Browne, Wetzel, Ion and Dr. Lehner left for Muscat by road on 10th January 1949 to spend 3 weeks to a month doing geological work at Seh Hatat.[28]

SEISMIC CAMP:

Operations have now been carried approximately 25 kilometers south west of Jebel Ali.[29] Transport difficulties are still slowing up operations.

Jackson
Representative.

26 All geophysical or geological people. IPC and PD(TC).

27 The large island off the coast of Oman. The BBC operated a radio relay station on the island from 1969 to 2002.

28 Near Muscat.

29 Dubai territory south of Dubai town.

TRUCIAL COAST DIARY FOR PERIOD ENDING 2 FEBRUARY 1949

RAS AL KHAIMA:

Nothing to report.

UMM AL QAIWAIN:

Nothing to report.

AJMAN:

It now appears that Shaikh Rashid bin Humaid[30] did not accompany the Beni Kitab Shaikh Mohd bin Ali Huwaidin to Biraimi recently with a view to making peace between the Na'im and the Beni Kitab, but because he hoped with the aid of the latter to assassinate or at least depose Shaikh Saqr bin Sultan of Biraimi. It is likely however that the latter was forewarned of this intention by Shaikh Rashid of Dubai or others and the coup d'etat was therefore unsuccessful. The subsequent theft of the Na'im camels, already reported, rather supports this view that the motive of the visit was war and not peace.

The number of camels stolen was 42 and not 45 as previously reported and one Na'im was wounded not two killed. Since then truce has been effected between the Na'im and the Bani Kitab and the latter have returned 40 camels. Peace still remains to be made.

As a result however of these events the situation in the Biraimi Oasis is somewhat disturbed and the Company's Representative has requested the Political Officer Trucial Coast to take steps to warn Shaikh Rashid bin Humaid that he must cease from his interference in the affairs of his relation Shaikh Saqr since our operations in the Oasis would inevitably be affected by any deterioration in the peace and security of this area.

SHARJAH:

Shaikh Sultan bin Saqr[31] occupied the fort of Al Haira[32] by force on 21st January 1949. Shaikh Rahma bin Abdulrahman[33] has taken refuge with Rashid bin Humaid of Ajman.

---

30 The Ruler of Ajman.

31 The Ruler of Sharjah.

32 The settlement on the coast about halfway between Sharjah and Ajman towns, since absorbed into Sharjah.

33 The Haira sheikh.

Shaikh Sultan was compelled to take this action by the uncompromising attitude adopted by Rahma, who refused to cooperate in the arresting of certain individuals living in his village and concerned in carrying out recently a particularly brutal ... three girls and one boy with the object of selling them into slavery. It is almost certain that Shaikh Rahma was himself closely concerned in the ... .The Political Officer Trucial Coast first of all tried to persuade Rahma to hand over those responsible but was met with an insolent and indifferent attitude in the matter, Rahma claiming that one of the people concerned was missing and the other sick and could not be moved! The Political Officer Trucial Coast then asked the Ruler of Sharjah to co-operate. The latter first tried to use persuasion but received the same insolent replies, including a demand for an increase in his annual payment from the Shaikh of Sharjah, or otherwise he (Rahma) would stop Company cars on the road north of Sharjah. Shaikh Sultan then decided to use force with the results already described.

Shaikh Rahma appears to be meeting with little sympathy from the other Shaikhs of the Trucial Coast but it is possible that Shaikhs Rashid bin Humaid and Rashid bin Said[34] will use him as a means of threatening Shaikh Sultan in the future.[35] It is known that Rahma is very friendly with Dubai.

DUBAI:

On 28th January 1949 the Political Officer Trucial Coast left by car with Shaikh Rashid bin Said to be shown what Dubai claim to be their southern frontier with Abu Dhabi. It is to be expected that the Ruler of Abu Dhabi will supply a representative in the near future to show his northern frontier.[36] In the course of his frontier visit the Political Officer Trucial Coast spent one night at the Company Jebel Ali camp.

ABU DHABI:

Brigadier S.H. Longrigg and Mr. B.H. Lermitte[37] arrived at Abu Dhabi by air on 19th January 1949. After a few hours spent on a visit to the Ruler, they proceeded by air to Sharjah to spend the night.

The airstrip at Abu Dhabi though originally prepared by the R.A.F. as an E.L.G.[38] has long been out of action and it was necessary to do considerable clearing

34 Son of the Ruler of Dubai.

35 This sort of behaviour was not rare before the establishment of an overall security authority, initially the Trucial Oman Levies in 1951.

36 Both Rulers had previously agreed that they would accept the adjudication of the Political Resident.

37 Longrigg was the London based IPC manager and Lermitte was the Company Representative based at Bahrain.

38 Emergency landing ground. This airstrip was very close to the fort.

and levelling work in advance. Markings were also made with crude oil.[39] Wind direction was given by smoke.

Mr. W. Thesiger left on 29th January from the Biraimi Oasis on a camel trek into the southern sands. He hopes to be back on the Trucial Coast in May 1949. Mr. Thesiger advises us that in his opinion the relations between the Manasir and the Al bu Falah[40] are definitely strained.

The general attitude in the oasis towards Shaikh Rashid bin Humaid of Ajman is hostile. They consider his interference in the affairs of his relation Shaikh Saqr bin Sultan as quite uncalled for.

KELBA:

The eight tribesman reported previously as in prison in Kelba are now known to be of the Afar and not Awamir, though the former are generally but wrongly said to be a subsection of the Awamir by the Arabs of the Trucial Coast.

It is now reported that under their leader Tuwairish al Afari they made their escape from Kelba with the assistance of Shaikh Mohammed bin Hamed ash Sharqi of Fujaira. After some days under the protection of the latter and after intervention on their behalf by Shaikh Zaid bin Sultan, Shaikh Shakhbut's representative in the Biraimi oasis, they were allowed to go and at once looted a taxi belonging to Dubai, in the vicinity of Jebel Faiyah. Shaikh Rashid bin Said of Dubai at once sent a party in pursuit. Tuwairish al Afari, who is in tribal alliance with Dubai, was located in Dhank[41] and explained that of course he did not realise that it was a Dubai taxi. He had supposed it was from the Batinah and therefore legitimate prey! All the loot was returned including one pregnant woman, who had also been seized from the taxi.

Individuals such as Tuwairish al Afari, Hilal Harsusi etc. represent a permanent menace, by their brigandage, to the law and order of the Trucial Coast. It appears that not one of the Shaikhs, coastal or interior, is strong enough to deal once and for all with such people. Each is compelled to ally himself with one or all of these brigands in order to protect himself against their depredations, though at the same time by means of such alliances the Shaikhs can use these brigands to their advantage against enemies.[42]

39 Brought from Dukhan in Qatar.

40 The Abu Dhabi ruling family.

41 An oasis and town, about 100 kilometres south of Buraimi.

42 In 'Arabian Sands' Thesiger wrote, 'Zayed had many of these outlaws in his entourage, since it suited him better to have them with him than in some rival sheikh's fort'. THESIGER, W. (1959), p.270 ff.

ARRIVAL:

Brigadier S.H. Longrigg and Mr. B.H. Lermitte arrived Sharjah by air on 19th January 1949. They left the following morning for Muscat by air and returned to Sharjah in the evening. They returned to Bahrain by air on 21st January 1949.

Mr. R.E.R. Bird returned from Muscat by road on 22nd January 1949.

Messrs Henderson, Ion, Wetzel, Browne, and Dr. Lehner returned from Seh Hattat[43] by road on 31st January 1949.

Messrs. Wellings and Quinlan arrived Sharjah by Company Dove on 1st February 1949. They went immediately to the Seismic Party's camp at Jebel Ali where they had lunch before returning to Sharjah for night stop. On 2nd February 1949 accompanied by Messrs. Lehner, Ion, Browne, Wetzel, Bird and Fallon they carried out two survey flights into the interior of Oman.[44]

Messrs. Swafford and Charles, both of Independent Prospecting Company arrived Sharjah by Dove on 20th January 1949.

DEPARTURES:

Mr. R.E.R. Bird accompanied by Mr. H.M. Jackson left for Biraimi by car on 21st January 1949 via Ramlat al Anaij.[45] The latter returned via the Haza' al Bosh[46] route on 28th January 1949. Mr. Bird returned to Dubai via Abu Dhabi on 1st February 1949.

SEISMIC CAMP:

It is understood that the present operations will not be carried any further south this season than the distance reported in our last summary. The rest of the season will be spent filling in detail of the area already covered.

Shaikh Said bin Shakhbut[47] visited the camp on 24th January 1949.

43 Near Muscat.

44 The company (IPC associate) also had a concession signed with the Sultan Saeed bin Taimur. But access to the interior of the Sultanate was barred by tribes who did not always acknowledge the Sultan's authority.

45 The Ramlat al Anaij (The Anaij sands) form a belt of relatively high dunes rising from the desert and extending right up to the Hajar mountains. They represent a formidable barrier to vehicles on the direct route between Dubai/Sharjah and Buraimi. They could only be bypassed if one took a considerable detour towards the coast. Later in the 1950's a route was cleared through the mountain wadis.

46 This is the most direct 160 kilometre long route between Buraimi/Al 'Ain and Abu Dhabi. The big sand dunes at Hazza al Bosh about 30 kilometres before Buraimi were quite an obstacle, even for camels.

47 Eldest son of Sheikh Shakhbut bin Sultan, Ruler of Abu Dhabi.

GENERAL:

Dr. Willem Drees, Prime Minister of Holland accompanied by his staff arrived Sharjah by air on 21st January 1949 on his way back to Holland from Indonesia. At the request of Messrs. B.O.A.C.[48] whose transport was all out of action, the Company's Representative took Dr. Drees on a sight-seeing tour in Sharjah. Dr. Drees expressed his thanks for this kindness extended to him and his party.

Dr. Lehner and Messrs. Ion and Wetzel spent 1st February 1949 doing geological work in Wadi Mileh in Ras al Khaimah area. They were accompanied by the Ruler of Ras al Khaimah, Shaikh Saqr bin Mohd.

Jackson
Representative.

TRUCIAL COAST DIARY FOR PERIOD ENDING 15 FEBRUARY 1949

RAS AL KHAIMAH:

Nothing to report.

UMM AL QAIWAIN:

Nothing to report.

AJMAN:

Shaikh Rahma bin Abdurrahman formerly of Haira, is still residing in Ajman.

Shaikh Rashid bin Humaid of Ajman visited Dubai a few days ago accompanied by Mohamed bin Ali bin Huwaidin of the Bani Kitab. It is understood that their visit was in connection with their dispute with Shaikh Saqr bin Sultan of Buraimi.

SHARJAH:

The ban on the issue of travel permits to Sharjah subjects has now been lifted by the Political Authorities.

A Dubai taxi was fired upon by brigands in the area of Jebel Faiyah.[49] This same vehicle was attacked and looted in the same area only a short time ago. Vide our DB/TD-49/79 dated 2nd February 1949 under Kelba.

---

48 British Overseas Airways Corporation.

49 A ridge of hills in the mountain foreland south of Dhaid. This is Bani Kitab territory. The sheikh Mohamed Ali Huwaidin prevented the Company from sending geologists in to look at what appeared, from a distance, to be a very interesting geological structure.

Two women were stolen from the vicinity of Khan (near Sharjah) by beduins thought to have been Bani Kitab. Shaikh Mohamed bin Saqr[50] has now gone off to Biraimi to attempt to recover them.

DUBAI:

Nothing to report.

ABU DHABI:

Shaikhs Hiza' and Zaid, brothers of the Ruler of Abu Dhabi arrived at the Company's Jebel Ali Camp on 14th February 1949. The purpose of their visit is to take the Political Officer Trucial Coast over what they claim to be their boundary with Dubai.

KELBA:

Nothing to report.

SEISMIC CAMP:

Party No.5 is at present working near Khor Ghanadha.[51] Operations are going ahead well. Transport difficulties have now been reduced to a minimum.

VISITORS:

Sir Rupert Hay, Political Resident in the Persian Gulf[52] accompanied by his wife and daughter, arrived in Abu Dhabi on s. s. NEARCHUS on 6th February 1949 and in Sharjah on 7th February 1949. Owing to bad weather the NEARCHUS was unable to return to Bahrain until 12th February 1949. During his stay on the Trucial Coast he paid calls upon all the Trucial Shaikhs and also made a flight over Biraimi and the Batinah in a R.A.F. plane. Sir Rupert returned to Bahrain on 12th Feb. 1949 by plane.

Mr. N. Jackson,[53] formerly Political Officer Trucial Coast Sharjah arrived by air in Sharjah on 2nd Feb. 1949. His visit was in connection with the Resident's tour of the Trucial Coast. He left for Bahrain by air on 10th February 1949.

Mohamed maintained that the Company should pay him for the permission while the Company insisted that they had already paid the Sharjah Ruler and they should settle the matter between themselves.

50 Brother of the Sharjah Ruler and father of present Ruler, 2020.

51 On the coast between Abu Dhabi and Dubai. Later the first well to be drilled on the Trucial Coast is nearby at Ra's Sadr.

52 The senior British Officer in the Gulf based in Bahrain since 1946. Sir Rupert was the last Political Resident to be appointed by the India Office.

53 Not to be confused with H.M. Jackson, the Company representative.

Khan Bahadur Seyyed Abdurrazzaq ar Razzuqi,[54] formerly Residency Agent Sharjah[55] arrived in Sharjah on 2nd February 1949 and left on 10th February 1949. The purpose of his visit was apparently to visit his family and attend to various business interests.

ARRIVAL:

Mr. E.F. Henderson returned from Bahrein by air on 10th February 1949.

Messrs. Browne, Morton[56] arrived Sharjah by company Rapide[57] on 14th Feb. 1949.

DEPARTURES:

Mr. R.E.R. Bird left for Muscat by road on 8th February 1949.

Jackson
Representative.

TRUCIAL COAST DIARY FOR PERIOD ENDING 1 MARCH 1949

RAS AL KHAIMAH:

Shaikh Sultan bin Salim,[58] who recently left Wadi al Gor on a visit to Muscat, is now back in his village in the Wadi. While in Muscat, it is reported, he approached the Political Authorities and terms were communicated to him from the Resident.[59] Since his return from Muscat, he has sent an emissary to the Political Officer Trucial Coast apparently to discuss these terms which he considers at present unacceptable.

UMM AL QAIWAIN:

The Ruler of Umm a1 Qaiwain paid a visit to Sharjah on 26th February 1949. As already reported he is acting as arbitrator at the request of the Political Officer Trucial Coast in the dispute between Dubai and Abu Dhabi over the latter's camels.

---

54 1936-1945.

55 The representative of the Political Resident. Traditionally an Arab occupied this post. The post was abolished in 1949. The first Political Officer (British) in Sharjah was appointed in 1945.

56 Two geologists.

57 The Rapide was a small two-engined bi-plane. Seated 6 passengers. The Company used these throughout the Middle East as they were light, rugged and could land on simple air-strips.

58 Former Ruler of Ra's al-Khaimah.

59 The Political Resident, who was the chief British representative in the Gulf. Based in Bahrain after 1946.

AJMAN:

It is understood that Shaikh Sulaiman bin Himyar of Tanuf, Jebel Akhdhar,[60] who is at present on a visit to the Trucial Coast, is attempting to reconcile Shaikh Rashid bin Humaid[61] and his relation Shaikh Saqr bin Sultan of Buraimi.

SHARJAH:

Nothing to report.

DUBAI:

Shaikh Mohd bin Ahmed of Bakha,[62] father-in-law of Shaikh Said bin Maktum, is at present on a visit to Dubai.

It is reported that the Dubai Shaikhs are considerably perturbed by what they consider the outrageous claim of the Abu Dhabi Shaikhs in connection with their boundary with Dubai. It has already been reported that both parties have now demonstrated on the ground to the Political Officer: Trucial Coast their territorial claims.

ABU DHABI:

Shaikhs Hiza' and Zaid bin Sultan of Abu Dhabi are at present on a hunting trip in the desert south of our Jebel Ali camp, which they left on 18th February 1949 after having been the Company's guests for 3 days. Shaikh Khalid bin Sultan is at present representing his brother, the Ruler, in the Buraimi Oasis.

KELBA:

Nothing to report.

SEISMIC CAMP:

An area stretching roughly from several miles north of Jebel Ali[63] southwards to the vicinity of Khor Ghanadha[64] has now been surveyed in general outline. The rest of the season, we understand, will be spent filling in detail.

---

60 Sultanate of Oman. Sheikh Sulaiman was largely independent of both the Sultan in Muscat and the Imam in the interior of the land. Tanuf is a well-watered oasis and town at the western foot of the 3,000 metre high Jebel Akhdhar, Green Mountain. At that time and for many years to come communication and therefore commerce was easier through Dubai for these people than through Muscat.

61 Ajman Ruler.

62 Bakha (Bukha) is on the Gulf coast of the Musandam peninsula (Sultanate of Oman territory). A short distance north of the border with Ra's al-Khaimah territory.

63 Dubai territory.

64 Abu Dhabi territory.

GEOLOGICAL PARTY BURAIMI:

This party, consisting of 2 geologists, one surveyor and 2 liaison officers, set out from Sohar on 19th February 1949 and reached Biraimi on the same day by the Wadi Jizzi[65] route which was discovered to be unsuitable except in emergency for wheeled transport. It is understood that their passage through the Wadi Jizzi was not without incident politically.[66] On arrival in the Biraimi Oasis camp was pitched at Sidairi[67] near Biraimi village in Na'im territory. It is understood that difficulties are being experienced not unexpectedly by the party in respect of their relations with the Na'im.

Shaikh Sulaiman bin Himyar of Tanuf, Jebel Akhdar, arrived recently at Ajman from Buraimi. After a few days there, he came to Dubai and has since gone to Abu Dhabi. He is expected to return to Dubai in the near future. It is understood that the purpose of his visit was to sort out relations between Rashid bin Humaid and Saqr bin Sultan. It is also reported that he offered to intervene in the Dubai-Abu Dhabi frontier dispute. The offer was not accepted.

H.M.S. 'Wild Goose'[68] is expected at Sharjah on 2nd March 1949. It is expected to be bring cargo for the Royal Air Force, Sharjah.

Jackson
Representative
HMJ/KAZ.

65 Due east from Buraimi/Al Ain.

66 They were fired on.

67 In the 1960's-1980's there was the almost completely vanished Sudairi fort to the south of the reasonably maintained Qazar al Khandaq. The latter fort is outside and on the south side of the Buraimi oasis. The main Buraimi fort is inside the gardens and next to the suq. It appears that the geologists camped on or near the site of the Sudairi fort, in territory of the Sultanate of Oman.

68 Her Majesty's Ship. A British Royal Navy, small vessel.

TRUCIAL COAST DIARY FOR PERIOD ENDING 15 MARCH 1949

RAS AL KHAIMAH:

H.M.S. WILD GOOSE[69] visited the Ruler of Ras al Khaimah[70] on 3rd March 1949. The Political Officer, Trucial Coast was in Ras al Khaimah for the occasion.

UMM AL QAIWAIN:

The Ruler of Umm al Qaiwain[71] has again visited the Political Officer, Trucial Coast[72] in connection with the Dubai Abu Dhabi camel dispute, in which he is arbitrator.

AJMAN:

Shaikh Rashid bin Humaid accompanied Shaikh Sulaiman bin Himyar of Jebel Akhdhar[73] to Abu Dhabi and from there went with him to the Biraimi Oasis. The purpose of their journey was to try to make peace with Shaikh Saqr bin Sultan of Biraimi. It is understood that Shaikh Sulaiman has now left for the south. He has taken back with him a 3 ton lorry recently purchased in Dubai.[74]

SHARJAH:

Shaikh Sultan bin Saqr, who is a diabetic, has recently been suffering from a variety of diseases including malaria, bronchitis and a poisoned arm. On the advice of the Government and Company doctors he left for Bahrein by air on 10th March 1949. News has now reached Sharjah that his condition is greatly improved.

Two women were stolen by beduin on 13th March from the Falaj near Sharjah. A pursuit party has gone out after them. Such thefts are becoming frequent in the Sharjah Shaikhdom and demonstrate clearly the weakness of the Ruler's control.

H.M.S. WILD GOOSE visited Sharjah on 2nd March 1949 but owing to bad weather was unable to land its R.A.F. cargo. No visits to or from the vessel were possible and she left for Ras al Khaimah on the following morning.

DUBAI:

Nothing to report.

---

69 This Royal Navy vessel was well known in the Gulf.

70 Sheikh Saqr bin Mohamed.

71 Sheikh Ahmed bin Rashid.

72 P.D. Stobart.

73 The Green Mountain. The 3000 meter high mountain in the Sultanate of Oman.

74 Vehicles had already reached Tanuf and Nizwa a year earlier.

ABU DHABI:

Shaikh Zaid bin Sultan has apparently now returned to Biraimi though Shaikh Haza' is still in the desert hunting.

Sir Hugh Weightman[75] visited Abu Dhabi in an amphibious aircraft on 10th March 1949. He stayed until the following day. The aircraft, a Mallard, landed successfully in Khor Baghal.[76]

The Ruler of Abu Dhabi was taken for a trip in this plane, which also returned to Abu Dhabi on the 12th carrying fresh water from Sharjah for Shaikh Shakhbut. The arrival of the plane caused a very considerable sensation. On its second visit the pilot brought it down successfully in the open sea off Abu Dhabi town.

Mr. E.F. Henderson[77] visited Abu Dhabi on 10th March 1949 for purpose of measuring the airfield and looking for an alternative site.

KALBA:

Nothing to report.

GEOLOGICAL PARTY:

This party left Biraimi on 2nd March 1949 and returned through the Wadi Jizzi to Sohar accompanied by Seyyed Ahmed Ibrahim.[78] They arrived back in Sharjah on 5th March 1949.[79]

---

75 Sir Hugh Weighman was Political Agent in Bahrain in 1938/'39 when Longrigg (IPC) was negotiating the Abu Dhabi 1939 concession with Sheikh Shakhbut. Weightman retired and at the time of this report was working for Superior Oil Company who were seeking concessions to search for oil offshore in the Gulf. Weightman died in an accident at London Heathrow airport.

76 Khor Baghal is the water between Abu Dhabi and Sadiyat islands. It those days there was a larger expanse of water than today, but much of it was shallow with many sandbanks exposed at low tide. The main channel, however, would have been adequate for landing the Mallard.

77 Company employee recently arrived in Dubai. He remained with the Company until 1955, mostly in Bahrain, but also in Dubai, Abu Dhabi and the Sultanate of Oman.

78 The Sultan's representative in Sohar on the Batinah coast (Indian Ocean). 'Wali Mudhafir who was a slave and son of a slave, yet governor of a large district in the Oman Sultanate. This man was an example of the power to which a born slave could attain and had on occasions opposed the Sultan's own brother.' STANTON-HOPE, W.E, *Arabian Adventurer, The Story of Haji Williamson*, Robert Hale Ltd., London, 1951. p.307.

79 They had spent 9 fruitless days camped beside Buraimi.

Mr. R.E.R. Bird[80] returned from Biraimi to Dubai via Hiza' al Bosh[81] on 3rd March 1949.

Messrs. Browne and Morton[82] spent two days working in the Jebel Ali area, before returning to Bahrein[83] on 11th March 1949 accompanied by Messrs. Fallon[84] and Bird. The outstanding features of this expedition were politics and track rods.[85] The latter suffered particularly in the Wadi Jizzi which was found unsuitable for wheeled transport except in an emergency.

VISITORS:

Mr. N. Pelly, Political Agent Bahrein, arrived in Sharjah by air on 3rd March 1949 and returned the following day to Bahrein.

Three representatives of the civil engineering firm Holloways arrived at Dubai by launch on 4th March 1949 and after a few days in Sharjah left for Muscat by road.[86] It is understood that they have gone to Muscat in connection with water work on behalf of the Muscat Government.

Sir Hugh Weightman accompanied by an American, Mr. Wood and one Lebanese interpreter[87] arrived in Sharjah on 9th March 1949 by an amphibious aircraft. They visited Abu Dhabi on 10th and 11th March 1949 and returned to Bahrein on 12th March. It is understood that they also paid a brief visit to Sharjah by the same craft on 5th March to make the necessary arrangements for their second trip.

A Company Rapide[88] with Messrs Tomkins and Monks of the Company's Aviation Department and one photographer arrived in Sharjah on 4th March 1949.

80 Company representative who was part time resident in Jahili Fort (Al Ain) while he negotiated with the tribal leaders in the area to obtain their permission for geologists to pass through their territory. His modest success with the tribal leaders was repudiated by the Sultan in Muscat.

81 The high dunes on the route between Abu Dhabi and Buraimi/Al Ain. The last, and most difficult to cross, they were just before reaching the oases.

82 Company geologists.

83 The Bahrain office was opened in 1936 and was closed in 1966. The First Manager was E.V. Packer who was joined by B. Lermitte and they both remained in Bahrain during the war years (1939-1945) occasionally visiting the Trucial Coast and maintaining the regular payments to all the Rulers.

84 Company surveyor.

85 Track rods were often referred to as the part most liable to break in the vehicles. A repair or replacement, was frequently undertaken in the desert.

86 They travelled through the Wadi Qaur. (Gor or Qor)

87 Victor Hashim from the Lebanon became a regular visitor before entering into business in Abu Dhabi in the early 1960's.

88 Small biplane that the company used throughout the Middle East.

It had been hoped that this plane might go on to Biraimi and Muscat but owing to various difficulties it was unable to proceed and returned to Bahrein on 5th March.

Messrs. Parry and Brown of the Company's Commissariat Department arrived in Sharjah by Dove on 11th March 1949 and returned to Qatar by same day. Mr. R.E.R. Bird also arrived by this plane and left the same day for the U.K. by Norwegian Skymaster[89] via Cairo, Rome and Amsterdam.

Dr. Lees and Mr. Ion of A.I.O.C. and Messrs. Wetzel and Damesin of I.P.C. arrived at Sharjah by Dove on 2nd March 1949, carried out a flight to Masirah[90] and back on 3rd March and returned to Bahrein on 4th March 1949.

ARRIVALS:

Messrs. Brownfield, Coull and Kirkland of Independent Exploration Ltd., arrived Sharjah by Dove[91] on 4th March to join Seismic Party No.3 at Jebel Ali.

Dr. Abdullatif Inayatullah returned to duty on the Trucial Coast on 13th March after 2 month's home leave in Pakistan.

Jackson
Representative
HMJ/KAZ.

89 4 engined Douglas DC4 aircraft. World War 2 vintage.

90 The large island in the Indian Ocean and near the coast of the Sultanate of Oman.

91 De Havilland Dove aircraft. There is one suspended from the ceiling in the Mahatta Museum in Sharjah.

TRUCIAL COAST DIARY FOR PERIOD ENDING 30 MARCH 1949

RAS AL KHAIMAH:

Nothing of importance to report.

UMM AL QAIWAIN:

One of the Company's buoys in the Umm al Qaiwain creek has been reported broken loose. This present system of temporary buoys is proving very expensive and inconvenient. It is considered essential that these buoys be replaced by permanent ones at an early date.

Seismic Party No.3 is now moving equipment, not at present in use, to our stores yard at Umm al Qaiwain with a view to its being ready for loading on M/V Jasura[92] when the party closes down its operations on the Trucial Coast at the end of April.

AJMAN:

Rashid bin Humaid[93] has returned from Biraimi and along with Rashid bin Said of Dubai has been busy trying to make trouble between the Bani Kitab and the Jawasim Shaikhs of Sharjah. Fortunately their efforts would appear to have been unrewarded.

SHARJAH:

The Ruler of Sharjah is now undergoing treatment for his various illnesses in Bombay, where he proceeded by sea from Bahrain.

Shaikh Mohd bin Saqr[94] has been very active recently arranging for the Seismic party to work in Sharjah territory. He has been successful in his efforts and it is understood that the Bani Kitab are satisfied with the settlement made between them and Sharjah. Details of this settlement will be given when known.[95]

The two women reported in our last issue stolen from the Falaj near Sharjah, were recovered by the energy and prompt action of Shaikh Mohamed bin Saqr, who appears to be able to cope with the affairs of Government much more efficiently than his brother.

---

92 Company landing craft.

93 Ajman Ruler.

94 Brother of the Ruler, and father of the present Ruler.

95 The Company geologists had been long denied access to Jebel Faiyah by Sheikh Mohamed Ali Huwaidin. From a distance the Jebel held many attractions for the geologists, however when they finally obtained access they were disappointed.

DUBAI:

Seismic Party No.3 has moved from Jebel Ali and is now working in Dubai territory along the Oud al Matinah track to distance of about 20 kilometres.

ABU DHABI:

Messrs. H.M. Jackson and E.F. Henderson visited Abu Dhabi on 19th and 20th March 1949.

A Dubai sailing vessel belonging to Murshid al Usaimi was recently wrecked off Dalmah.[96] It is understood that the Ruler of Abu Dhabi gave the Dubai party who went to inspect it very considerable assistance and hospitality.

KALBA:

Nothing to report.

VISITORS:

Messrs. Baker, Wellings and Gibson of I.P.C. Ltd. accompanied by Dr. Dozy of Shell and Dr. Skeels of Standard Oil of New Jersey arrived by Company Dove GAICY on 15th March 1949. The following day they made a survey flight to Masirah and left on 17th March for Bahrein via Dukhan.[97]

Messrs. Lermitte[98] and Banta of I.P.C. Ltd. accompanied by Dr. De Cizancourt of Compagnie Francaise des Petroles[99] and Sir Rupert Hay, Political Resident in the Persian Gulf arrived by Company Dove on 25th March 1949. They made a survey flight to Masirah the following day and returned to Bahrein via Dukhan on 27th March 1949. The Political Resident remained behind in Masirah to travel by R.A.F. plane on 27th from Masirah to Aden.

A Dakota of Arabian-American Oil Company arrived in Sharjah from Dhahran on 15th March 1949, and the following day made a survey flight into the interior returning the same day direct to Dhahran.

ARRIVAL:

Mr. R.A.T. Codrai arrived Sharjah by R.A.F. plane on 16th March 1949 to join the staff of the Company on the Trucial Coast.

Jackson
Representative
HMJ/KAZ.

---

96 A large island in the west of Abu Dhabi waters.

97 The base for the company operations in Qatar.

98 Company manager based in Bahrain from 1937 to 1951.

99 Now Total.

TRUCIAL COAST DIARY FOR PERIOD ENDING 13 APRIL 1949

RAS AL KHAIMAH:

The Ruler Shaikh Saqr bin Mohamed, visited the Company's Representative in Dubai on 2nd April 1949.

Mr. R.A.T. Codrai visited Ras al Khaimah on Company business on 3rd and 10th April 1949.

UMM AL QAIWAIN:

Seismic Party No.3 is about to commence operations in Umm al Qaiwain territory. The Company's Representative visited the Ruler in connection with this on 13th April 1949.

AJMAN:

The Ruler, Shaikh Rashid bin Humaid has recently been raising the question of his frontiers with Sharjah on the grounds that the Company has been using Sharjah guards in Ajman territory. The matter for the time being has been satisfactorily settled.

SHARJAH:

Nothing to report.

DUBAI:

Nothing to report.

ABU DHABI:

Very considerable activity has been reported from this Shaikhdom during the period under review.

A party of 6 Americans with 4 vehicles and accompanied by 4 beduin guards were reported between Abu Dhabi and Dubai on 2nd April 1949. The beduins were believed to have consisted of three Murra tribesmen and one Amiri. The party is thought to have travelled from Saudi Arabia along the coast via Sabkha Matti and Al Mirfa. It is understood that they returned the following day by the same route. The purpose of their visit is not known but their coming has created considerable consternation and anxiety in Abu Dhabi. A full report on the activities of the party has already been sent.[100]

Sir Hugh Weightman accompanied by Mr. Woods of Superior Oil Company once again visited Abu Dhabi on 5th April 1949 arriving by amphibian plane. They

---

100 This incident and subsequent events are recorded in HEARD, D. (2019).

returned on the following day to Sharjah and left for Rome via Bahrain and Cairo on 7th April 1949.

Mr. P.D. Stobart Political Officer, Trucial Coast visited Abu Dhabi on 5th April 1949 and returned to Sharjah on 6th April 1949. Mr. C.J. Pelly, Political Agent, Bahrain arrived Sharjah by air on 6th April 1949 and visited Abu Dhabi accompanied by the Political Officer, Trucial Coast on 7th April 1949. They returned to Sharjah the following day.

Mr. B.H. Lermitte, Manager Bahrein, visited Abu Dhabi by air on 31st March 1949, 2nd April, 4th April and 9th April 1949.[101]

Captain Holden the Company's Marine surveyor, with M/V Jamila M/L Nasr and one L.C.T. arrived Abu Dhabi on 5th April 1949. They left the following day to carry out a marine survey on Abu Dhabi waters after taking on board a party of 20 coolies and 6 Abu Dhabi representatives. Mr. E.F. Henderson arrived Abu Dhabi on 5th April 1949 to join Captain Holden's party.

Mr. R.E.R. Bird left for Baraimi on 10th April 1949. He has since reported that Mr. W. Thesiger, the explorer, has returned to Baraimi from the south after a very successful expedition.

The Company's Representative visited Abu Dhabi on 11th April 1949 in connection with the abovementioned marine survey. While there, he arranged for the Ruler and his brother to speak on R/T[102] to M.V. Jamila. He returned the same day accompanied by Shaikh Hiza', the Ruler's brother, who proceeded to Sharjah to visit the Political Officer, Trucial Coast.

KALBA:

Nothing to report.

SEISMIC PARTY:

Work is proceeding well in Sharjah territory. The Party is accompanied by Bani Kitab guards.

VISITORS:

Mr. B.H. Lermitte, Manager, Bahrein, visited Sharjah on 6th April 1949 and returned the same day to Bahrein. He again arrived by air on 9th April 1949 and paid visits to the Rulers of Dubai, Ras al Khaimah, Umm al Qaiwain, Ajman and Kalba. It is expected that he will return to Bahrein on 14th April 1949.

---

101 The frequent visits were in connection with PD(TC's) claim that the waters beyond the territorial waters should be included in the concession area.

102 Radio telephone.

As already mentioned Mr. C.J. Pelly Political Agent, Bahrein arrived in Sharjah on 6th April 1949 by air and returned by Company Rapide on 10th April 1949.

ARRIVAL:

Mr. R.E.R. Bird arrived back in Sharjah by air from U.K. via Bahrein on 6th April 1949.

Jackson
Representative
HMJ/KAZ.

TRUCIAL COAST DIARY FOR PERIOD ENDING 26 APRIL 1949

RAS AL KHAIMAH:

Shaikh Humaid bin Mohd, elder brother of the Ruler, visited the Company's Representative in Dubai on 19th April 1949.

Shaikh Rashid al Badi of Shamal[103] (where Shaikh Said bin Maktum[104] has date gardens) has written to the Ruler of Ras al Khaimah to the effect that the Company may not operate in his area. Though this is of little importance, it illustrates yet again evil intriguing activities of Dubai shaikhs.[105]

UMM AL QAIWAIN:

Nothing to report.

AJMAN:

Nothing to report.

SHARJAH:

In spite of reports that the health of the Ruler is improving, we understand that the opposite is the truth.

DUBAI:

A rumour that a cousin, and confirmed enemy, of the Ruler, was attacking the latter's desert camp, caused a party of men to be sent off to investigate on 24th April

103 Close to and northeast of Ra's al-Khaimah town.

104 Dubai Ruler.

105 The writer, expressing his opinion of some of the Dubai Sheikhs.

1949. The party found no evidence of an affray, and the only ammunition expended was to announce its happy return to Dubai, the same night.

Messrs. R.E.R. Bird, W. Thesiger and R.A. Codrai attended a dinner given by the Ruler, Shaikh Said, at his desert camp, on the night of 20th April 1949.

ABU DHABI:

The fixing of boundaries, by H.M. Government, on the Trucial Coast, will greatly lessen the possibilities of internal dispute, when the result of the Company's activities becomes apparent. As yet, these activities have not furnished grounds for serious dispute within the Shaikhdoms. Recently, however, the unsettled boundary to the West of Abu Dhabi territory has given rise to an immediate problem, the settlement of which will no doubt rest between H.M. Government and the Saudi Arabian Government.

Following several reports of Aramco activities within the "understood" boundary to Abu Dhabi territory, Mr. H.M. Jackson, in company with P.D. Stobart, Political Officer, Trucial Coast, set off on 19th April 1949 to make contact with the party. They were joined at Abu Dhabi by Shaikh Haza with seven retainers. The results of this journey have been the subject of a separate report by the Representative,[106] who returned to Dubai on 24th April 1949: the Political Officer and Shaikh Haza left Abu Dhabi on the Company's M/V Nasr for Bahrein, the same day.

The Marine Survey of Abu Dhabi waters has now been completed and M/V Jamila M/L Nasr and one L.C.T., left Abu Dhabi during the night of 21st April 1949 for Bahrein. Next day the Nasr returned to Abu Dhabi to pick-up the Political Officer, Trucial Coast, and Shaikh Haza.

Mr. R.E.R. Bird and Mr. W. Thesiger returned from Biraimi by road to Dubai on 14th April 1949.

A Messenger from Shaikh Saqr bin Sultan of Biraimi has recently visited the Company's Representative. Shaikh Saqr now expresses himself ready to deal direct with the Company. The same messenger advises that Shaikh Saqr's Wali in Dhank,[107] Samsoum, has recently been murdered by Shaikh bin Salim also of Dhank. There is now fighting between the sons of Samsoum and Sheikh Mater bin Salim. It is also reported that the Sultan of Muscat has recently written to Saqr inviting him to visit Muscat.[108]

---

106 See HEARD, D. (2019).

107 Dhank in the Sultanate of Oman about one hundred kilometres south of Buraimi.

108 Bird wrote on 22nd March 1949. 'Dhank is occupied by Naim and Al bu Shamis (Ghafiri). Dhank al Ulya (upper portion). Naim under Shaikh Saqr bin Sultan of Baraimi who has a wali there called Salim bin Samsoon. Dhank al Sufla (lower portion) Al bu Shamis. (i)Shaikh Mohd bin Hamad al Hiyayi (Eastern portion). (ii) Shaikh Matar bin Salim al Azizi. (central portion). (iii) Shaikh Hamad bin Salim al Wahahi (western section)'.

SEISMIC PARTY:

The Party finishing its work in Umm al Qaiwain territory on 24th April 1949 and is now back in Dubai territory, where it will operate for two or three days. It will then, most probably, return for experimental work to Umm al Qaiwain until its departure, at the end of April.

DEPARTURE:

Mr. R.E.R. Bird and Mr. W. Thesiger, left Dubai on the Agency launch for Bahrein on 21st April 1949. They sighted the M/V Jamila[109] at Abu Dhabi, and transferred to that vessel for the remainder of the journey.

Mr. B.H. Lermitte, Manager, Bahrein, returned to Bahrein on 14th April 1949.

ARRIVALS:

Dr. Joseph Adler of Independent Prospecting Co. Houston Texas arrived in Sharjah by Dove on 21st April 1949 on a visit to Party No.3. To date he is still in Sharjah.

Messrs. Parry, Brown and Banta arrived in Sharjah by the same plane and left the following day.

Jackson
Representative.

109 IPC/PD(TC) vessel.

TRUCIAL COAST DIARY FOR PERIOD ENDING 10 MAY 1949

RAS AL KHAIMAH:

It now appears that in addition to the instance of truculence already reported, Shaikh Said bin Badi (incorrectly mentioned previously as Shaikh Rashid al Badi of Shamal) has continued to cause trouble for the Ruler of Ras al Khaimah.

Dictated by a strong determination to show his subjects that disobedience would be dealt with by a strong hand. The Ruler, Shaikh Saqr, arrested Shaikh Said on 1st May and subsequently burnt .... Relations of the victim retaliated by seizing and damaging date plantations belonging to the Shaikh of Ras al Khaimah. Shaikhs Said and Juma' of Dubai are at present in Shamal attempting unsuccessfully to effect a settlement.

SHARJAH:

A recent strike of the employees of the Golden Valley Ochre & Oxide (Colours) Ltd[110] in Abu Musa, reached such proportions that Shaikh Rashid bin Saqr, one of the Ruler's brothers, had to go over and intervene. Two of the ringleaders, who escaped from Abu Musa with the intention of proceeding via Sharjah to Sir Bu Nair,[111] where the company also operates, were arrested in Sharjah and sent back to Abu Musa. There, at the orders of Shaikh Rashid bin Saqr, they were beaten in public.

DUBAI:

The recent infiltration of Aramco[112] under Saudi Arabian auspices into Abu Dhabi territory produced a crop of fantastic rumours in Dubai. A Dubai sheikh was unable to conceal his pleasure, and among other things spread abroad the rumour that the Saudis had already taken over Abu Dhabi territory as far as Khor Ghanadha[113] and that very soon a Saudi force would arrive to take over the Biraimi oasis. It will be recalled that earlier this year Dubai Shaikhs made great efforts to cultivate the

110 This British company held a concession for producing and exporting red oxide.

111 A large Sharjah island nearly100 kilometres north of Abu Dhabi in Abu Dhabi waters, and about 100 kilometres south west of the island of Abu Musa.

112 Arabian American Oil Company.

113 On the coast about 15 kilometres from the present border with Dubai. This would have included in the "Saudi Invasion" almost all the territory of Abu Dhabi! It is illustrative of the nature of rumours at that time, and also, perhaps, ignorance of the geography of their own land.

friendship of bin Mansur the Saudi tax collector, who entered Abu Dhabi territory, ostensibly to collect Zikkat[114] from the Murra.[115]

Since, however, they were advised by the Political Officer, Trucial Coast, that the Aramco and the Saudis had left Abu Dhabi territory the Dubai Shaikhs have had to turn their attention to other intrigues. The part they are playing in the present Ras al Khaimah dispute has already been mentioned: they have always shown a preference for the previous Ruler, Shaikh Sultan bin Salim, and are therefore, under the guise of peacemakers, doing their utmost to aggravate the difficulties of Shaikh Saqr.[116]

Light has now been thrown on the reported attack into Dubai territory by Manasir tribesmen, reported in our last issue. It now appears that in addition to trying to embarrass Shaikh Shakhbut of Abu Dhabi, whose subjects the Manasir are, the Dubai Shaikhs are trying to make out that Shaikh Suhail bin Mana'[117] who last year unsuccessfully tried to murder Rashid bin Said and then fled to Biraimi, is now collecting together Manasir with the intention of attacking Dubai. It seems that Suhail bin Mana' is due to come to Sharjah in the near future on business, and Shaikh Rashid bin Said by means of all these rumours and alarms is trying to make out that the real motive of the visit is an attack on Dubai. He hopes by this means to justify any attack on Suhail when the latter leaves Biraimi for Sharjah.

Shaikh Rashid bin Said is reported to have been disappointed that Sir Hugh Weightman[118] did not visit him during the latter's recent visit to the Trucial Coast. He has, moreover, spread abroad a rumour that the Dubai possessions in Wadi Hatta are not included in the Petroleum Concessions Limited[119] concession and that he intends to offer them to Sir Hugh Weightman.

ABU DHABI:

The following paid visits to the Ruler of Abu Dhabi on the dates mentioned:

Mr. H.M. Jackson – 29.4.1949 by road

Mr. B.H. Lermitte – 3.5.1949 by air

---

114 A tax which it is the duty of every Moslem to pay. The proceeds should then be distributed among the poor.

115 A desert tribe found in Abu Dhabi territory and Saudi Arabia.

116 Perhaps the writer, Jackson, is given to exaggeration. But in a society where the first question after formal greeting is 'what is the news?' people may well exaggerate for effect. Then there is the way the message is passed through many mouths changing on the way.

117 Sheikh Suhail bin Mana' bin Rashid bin Maktoum distant cousin of Dubai Ruler Sheikh Saeed bin Maktoum bin Hasher bin Maktoum.

118 Sir Hugh Weightman was a former Political Agent in Bahrain. After he retired he helped the USA company, Superior Oil Company in their pursuit of oil concessions.

119 PCL, the Company.

Sir Hugh Weightman and Mr. Wood of Superior Oil Company – 4.5.1949 by air.

The latter during their visit showed the Shaikh a film on oil exploration and production.

It is understood that Aramco have almost completed their evacuation of the western area of Abu Dhabi territory, where they were previously reported to be working.

The Ruler of Abu Dhabi is anxiously awaiting the return of his brother, Shaikh Hiza', from Bahrein. The latter is expected to return to Abu Dhabi on Wednesday 11th May 1949 by Company Rapide.[120] Mr. B.H. Lermitte will take this opportunity to visit Abu Dhabi again.

SEISMIC PARTY:

Having completed its original programme, the Party was preparing for its departure from the Trucial Coast, when on 28th April it learned of the location of a new camp, in Abu Dhabi territory, from where it is to operate until sometime in June. Work was immediately started in erecting the camp, and the main body of the Party moved out to it on 8th May.[121]

ARRIVALS:

Mr. R.E.R. Bird and E.F. Henderson returned to Dubai on 27.4.49 from Bahrein, and left for Muscat the following day. Mr. P.D. Stobart, Political Officer, Trucial Coast, returned to Sharjah on 6.5.49, following his recent visit to the western area of Abu Dhabi territory, and his subsequent journey to Bahrein.

VISITORS:

The Political Resident, Sir Rupert Hay, arrived by a Company Rapide on 8th May accompanied by Mr. Burrows of the Foreign Office. They visited the Company's Representative in Dubai, and travelled on to Muscat the following day.

Mr. B.P. Warburton arrived from Basra on 4.5.49 and stayed with Party No.3 until his return on 10th May.

Jackson
Representative
RAC/KAZ.

---

120 Small aircraft which could land on rudimentary airstrips. The Company used these aircraft in many countries of the Middle East.

121 The Party were expecting to leave before the summer heat, but interpretations of their work showed the possibility of an attractive rock structure deep underground. The geologists, who were under pressure to approve a location to drill for oil required one last confirmation from the geophysicists that they had indeed found a good prospect.

TRUCIAL COAST DIARY FOR PERIOD ENDING 24 MAY 1949

RAS AL KHAIMAH:

The dispute, mentioned in our last report, between the Ruler and the family of Said al Badi of Shimal, has apparently been settled through the intervention of Said bin Maktum of Dubai. It is understood that the Ruler will pay Rs. 800 compensation for the injury done to Said al Badi.

In the meantime however the Tenaiji Shaikh of Rams, Salim bin Saleh, who had declined all contact with the Ruler since the latter's accession to the throne last year, has begun to organise active opposition to be Ruler, (In the recent Badi affair he actively encouraged the relations of Said al Badi, to whom he is related in marriage, to avenge the injury done to one of their family.) It is understood that he has obtained a considerable tribal following, including many of the Shihuh.[122] The Shaikhs of Ras al Khaimah are considerably alarmed and have requested the Political Officer, Trucial Coast to assist them in crushing the revolt.

UMM AL QAIWAIN:

The Representative visited Umm al Qaiwain on 16th May and on the following day accompanied by Messrs. O.S. Dickson and T.F. Williamson visited Falaj al Ali,[123] Dhaid and Umm al Qaiwain.[124]

AJMAN:

The Ruler[125] is still absent and is understood to be in Dhank where he hopes to benefit from the confusion and lawlessness prevailing as a result of the recent murder of Samsoom, Wali of Shaikh Saqr bin Sultan of Biraimi. He no doubt hopes to acquire some or all of Saqr's possessions in Dhank.[126]

---

122 The tribe from the mountains of the Musandam peninsula in the Sultanate of Oman. They would descend in the summer months to the plain in Ra's al-Khaimah territory, and the wadis leading into the mountains. They have, in recent years largely abandoned their mountain retreats and gardens for more steady employment in the Emirates.

123 An Umm al Quwain oasis near Dhaid.

124 Dickson (IPC Iraq) and Williamson (Geologist) had come to find out more about the Trucial Coast such as the availability of water, nature of transport difficulties, and materials that might be locally available and could be employed when the planned drilling operations commenced.

125 Sheikh Rashid bin Humaid.

126 The Ruler of Ajman Sheikh Rashid bin Humaid and the Buraimi Sheikh Saqr bin Sultan were cousins. Both Al bu Khuraiban section of the Na'im tribe.

SHARJAH:

The Residency Agent, Sharjah,[127] left by boat on 16th May for Bahrein. He is proceeding on leave. Wishful thinking in Sharjah and Dubai has created the rumour that he will not return to the Trucial Coast. As the Political Officer, Trucial Coast,[128] himself is also due to leave for Bahrein in the very near future, the next few months on the Trucial Coast may produce some very interesting events.

No recent news has come from Bombay of the progress of the Ruler's illness. It is understood that he has undergone six operations.

DUBAI:

The Shaikhs of Dubai have been busy in Ras al Khaimah 'settling' the dispute between the Ruler and the Badi family.

Rashid bin Said is still there, probably giving encouragement to Salim bin Saleh, Shaikh of Rams.

ABU DHABI:

Shaikh Hiza' bin Sultan, the Ruler's brother, returned from Bahrein to Abu Dhabi by Company plane on 12th May. He was accompanied by Mr. B.H. Lermitte[129] who after visiting the Ruler, Shaikh Shakhbut, night-stopped in Sharjah and left the following day for Bahrein.

The P.O.T.C. Mr. P.D. Stobart visited Abu Dhabi on 14th May in a Miles-Gemimi plane owned and piloted by an independent traveller Mr. Winch, who is on his way back to the U.K. after a tour of India.

Shaikh Hiza' bin Sultan[130] arrived in Sharjah by road on 16th May on a visit to the Political Officer, Trucial Coast. He left again for Abu Dhabi on 18th May.

KELBA:

Reports of misrule in Kalba and Khor Fakkan[131] on the part of the Regent's representatives there keep arriving here. It is understood that they are giving the P.O.T.C. considerable concern. The Regent, Shaikh Khalid bin Ahmed[132] and his

127 Jasim ibn Mohamed Kadmari. The post was abolished soon afterwards.

128 P.D. Stobart.

129 Manager PD(TC) Bahrain office. A post he held through the war years (1939-1945).

130 Brother of Abu Dhabi Ruler, Sheikh Shakhbut bin Sultan.

131 North of Kalba and Fujairah on the east coast (Indian Ocean). Now part of Sharjah.

132 The Regent, Sheikh Khalid bin Ahmed was very active ten years earlier when he was expanding his influence. He negotiated the oil concession agreement with Longrigg of PD(TC) in 1938. By the time of this diary he was suffering from bad health and the 'fire

nephew and representative, Humaid bin Abdullah are at present in Hira.[133] The Regent however is contemplating not before time, a visit to Kelba.

SEISMIC PARTY:

Work is proceeding from the new camp in Abu Dhabi territory, though drilling[134] is more difficult than in the area previously worked, and has slowed up the party considerably. A second drill is soon to be brought into operation. The Party Chief, Mr. I.E. Grizzell, rejoined the party on 19th May, after his recent visit to Tripoli.

ARRIVALS:

Mr. R.E.R. Bird and Mr. E.F. Henderson returned to Dubai from Muscat on 16th May, and left again for Biraimi on 22nd May1949.

Mr. O.S. Dickson and Mr. T.F. Williamson arrived by air from Tripoli on 15th May and remained on the Trucial Coast until 19th May. During their stay, they visited the Seismic camp, Khor Ghanadha, Ras Sadr, Bandar Farida and the Abu Dhabi Maqta. They also inspected Jebel Ali, Falaj al Ali, Dhaid and Umm a1 Quwain.[135]

Doctor McCaully,[136] the new Government doctor, arrived on 18th May and is at present living in the R.A.F. Station, Sharjah.

Jackson
Representative.

---

seems to have gone out in him'. He was spending most of the time in Hira on the Gulf coast near Sharjah town.

133 Hira, now part of Sharjah town.

134 Drilling shallow hole to hold the explosive charge.

135 This was a reconnaissance visit in anticipation of bring in a drilling rig.

136 Dr. McCaully came to Dubai after serving with the British army in India. He moved to Abu Dhabi in the early 1960's where he remained for a decade. He was eccentric, with a kind heart.

TRUCIAL COAST DAIRY FOR PERIOD ENDING 8 JUNE 1949

RAS AL KHAIMAH:

It is understood that the Ruler of Umm al-Qaiwain[137] has been asked by the Political Officer, Trucial Coast to try to settle the differences between the Ras al Khaimah Shaikhs and the Shaikh of Rams. Up to now there are no developments to report.

UMM AL QAIWAIN:

Nothing to report.

AJMAN:

Shaikh Rashid bin Humaid has now returned to Ajman after a fruitless trip to Dhank into which he was not permitted to enter by any of the Dhank parties. He was accompanied in his expedition by tribesmen of the Beni Kitab including Mohd bin Ali Huwaidin. Though unsuccessful in acquiring any pickings from Saqr's[138] properties in Dhank it appears he was successful in estranging the Beni Kaab Shaikh Ubaid bin Juma' from Saqr.[139] Messrs R.E.R. Bird and E.F. Henderson met Rashid and his retinue returning northwards over the Ramlat Anaij. One of them made a half-hearted attempt to prevent their onward passage to Biraimi. Rashid is at present somewhat of a laughing stock on the Trucial Coast for imagining that the Biraimi Na'im must prefer him to Saqr, but there is general admiration for his 'nerve' which makes him ready to try again after repeated failures.

SHARJAH:

Nothing to report.

DUBAI:

The Dubai Shaikhs would appear to be very pleased with the boundary award recently announced by the Political Agent, Bahrein. Had they been otherwise the bazaar would have been full of it. As it is no one seems to know anything about it. Now that summer has come Rashid bin Said[140] is spending more and more time in his gardens in Ras al Khaimah. We can therefore expect things to happen there rather than in Dubai. A rumour in the Dubai bazaar says that the Superior Oil Company

---

137 Sheikh Ahmed bin Rashid. He had a reputation for being a good mediator.

138 Sheikh Saqr bin Sultan of Buraimi.

139 Sheikh Saqr bin Sultan in Buraimi and the Kaabi Sheikh Obaid bin Juma were frequently reported to be 'on bad terms'.

140 The Ruler.

is now busy drilling in Abu Dhabi. This rumour has been occasioned by the fact that Superior's amphibian plane arrived in Sharjah on 4th June and has been making daily trips to Abu Dhabi since then.

ABU DHABI:

Mr. H.M. Jackson and Mr. R.A. Codrai visited Abu Dhabi, on 24th May 1949.

Mr. P.D. Stobart, the P.O.T.C., Sharjah visited the Ruler of Abu Dhabi on 2nd June 1949 and among other things announced the Political Agent's decision in the Abu Dhabi/Dubai boundary dispute. He reports that all the brothers were very considerably disturbed and regarded the decision as most unjust. It is possible that Shaikh Haza' will visit Bahrein in the near future to put their objections before the Political Resident.

Sir Hugh Weightman accompanied by Mr. Adams of Superior Oil Company visited Abu Dhabi by air on 8th June 1949 and up to the present are still there. Their arrival on the Trucial Coast coincided with the announcement on the part of the Political Officer Trucial Coast that the Trucial Shaikhs were free after 4th June 1949 to make arrangements with Oil Companies to cover the mineral rights of the continental shelf adjoining the territorial waters. Draft copies of any such agreements made by the Trucial Coast Shaikhs must however be submitted to H.M. Government for approval before signature by the Shaikhs.

Mr. R.E.R. Bird and Mr. E.F. Henderson proceeded to Biraimi on 23rd May 1949 and returned[141] on 31st May 1949 accompanied by Shaikh Zaid bin Sultan who left them en route to go to Abu Dhabi. Mr. Bird's negotiations with the Na'im and Al bu Shamis Shaikhs of Biraimi oasis were once again unsuccessful. It appears that the Sultan of Muscat's name there means even less than before.

KELBA:

Nothing to report.

SEISMIC PARTY NO.3:

The party had planned to conclude this season's operations on 15th June, but it is now thought that its programme will continue beyond this date. Its camp at Khor Ghanadha will not however be dismantled during the period of its absence but will be left in charge of guards.

The seismic survey has now been carried southwards to the vicinity of Bandar Farida.

141 To Dubai.

DEPARTURES:

Mr. R.E.R. Bird left the Trucial Coast for Tripoli on 2nd June 1949, upon completion of his work there.[142] Mr. E.F. Henderson left on a visit to Bahrein on a Company Rapide, on 6th June, in company with the Political Officer, Trucial Coast who was returning to Bahrein.

Jackson
Representative.

TRUCIAL COAST DIARY FOR PERIOD ENDING 22 JUNE 1949

RAS AL KHAIMAH:

The good offices of the Ruler of Umm al Qaiwain[143] and Rashid bin Said[144] assisted by the Shaikh of the Beni Qitab have restored peace between the Shaikh of Ras al Khaimah[145] and the Shaikh of Rams.[146]

UMM AL QAIWAIN:

Nothing to report.

AJMAN:

Nothing to report.

SHARJAH:

Reports from Bombay suggest that the health of the Ruler[147] improves. He has sent for two of his wives.

---

142 The Company, IPC, held a concession agreement with the Sultan of Oman. He was more often referred to as the Sultan of Muscat reflecting the extent of his authority. Access to the interior of the Sultanate, where the geologists wished to examine interesting rock structures, was impeded by the tribes over which the Sultan had little control. Bird had hoped to negotiate agreements with the tribes in the Buraimi area to permit the geologists to pass through their territory. Access through the Wadi Jizzi from the Batinah Coast to Buraimi proved to be difficult because of the terrain and the tribal problems. After failing to gain access from this direction the Company turned to an alternative route from Duqm.

143 Sheikh Ahmed bin Rashid.

144 Ruler of Dubai.

145 Sheikh Saqr bin Mohamed.

146 Sheikh Salim bin Saleh al Tunaiji.

147 Sheikh Sultan bin Saqr.

Toweirish, who was recently well received by Mohammed the Ruler's brother, and given a present, has held up yet another taxi in the Jebel Faiyah -Wadi al Ghor area, killing a lady passenger and wounding the driver, By way of explanation he said he thought it was a car of the Imam's.[148] In fact it was a Sharjah taxi. He is now week-ending in Biraimi.

On the 14th and 15th two R.A.F. light bombers paid flying visits to all coastal towns from Abu Dhabi to Rams. To the West they visited Liwa and Khor al Odaid. They flew low several times over each town. Inland they visited Dhaid, Hamasah and Hafit.

The population on the coast does not appear to be greatly impressed by this demonstration of armed might. The people of Sharjah and Dubai, at least, are well accustomed to low flying aircraft. Opinion in the suq is divided as to whether the aircraft belong to P.C.L. or to the Americans. At any rate two aircraft do not equal one sloop in local estimation. The Shaikhs of Sharjah and Rashid of Dubai were shown over the aircraft on the ground.

On the 18th the Flamingo[149] paid a welcome visit to Sharjah.

DUBAI:

On the 18th S.S. LUTTERKERK 11,000 tons ran ashore opposite the Shaikh's winter palace but floated off 24 hours later. The attempt of the Dutch to get a hold on the dried fish trade in the Gulf appears to be unprofitable to them, since the quantity taken back to Europe on each trip is not adequate to fill their large ships. They may well give up the struggle before long.

Shaikh Mohamed bin Salimeen bu Rahmah[150] is in Dubai and frequently visits the Company's Representative but finds him very busy. His purpose in visiting Dubai apart from cadging money is not yet clear.

The Ruler[151] is on a visit for health reasons to Ain Khamir,[152] to bathe in sulphur waters, but is expected back soon.

Shaikh Rashid pays daily visits to his date gardens near Ras al Khaimah.

148 Imam Mohamed bin Abdullah al Khalili from Oman interior. He controlled the tribes in the interior where the authority of the Sultan was very weak.

149 Royal Navy Ship.

150 Shamsi from Sunainah and Qabil in the Sultanate of Oman.

151 Sheikh Saeed bin Maktoum.

152 On the Iranian coast opposite Qesham island.

ABU DHABI:

Strongest rumours from Abu Dhabi are to the effect that the Ruler[153] has signed with Weightman. The latter's aircraft was observed in the area on the 19th, so that rumour is as usual a little ahead of fact.

Ahmed bin Fadhil[154] is visiting Dubai and Sharjah over the camel question. The camels are already collected. There only remains the oath of the Ruler of Abu Dhabi which is said to be unlikely to be forthcoming, since the latter has a conscience in the matter.

Mr. Lermitte visited most of the Trucial Coast Shaikhdoms between the 9th and 12th including Ras al Khaimah and Abu Dhabi.

SEISMIC PARTY NO.3:

The Party has now nearly all dispersed. Mr. Maude who arrived on the 16th is in process of taking over from Mr. Read.[155] The camp will remain at Ras al Ghanadha, with nine guards in occupation, ready for the move down to the area in the autumn.[156]

DEPARTURES:

The bulk of the Seismic Party left on the 16th and Mr. Jackson left for Bahrain on 17th.

Henderson
Representative.

153 Sheikh Shakhbut bin Sultan.

154 Ahmed bin Fadhil al Mazroui. Acting on behalf of Sheikh Shakhbut.

155 Camp boss. The administrative overseer of the camp.

156 The Geophysicists believed they had found an interesting geological structure deep underground which it was considered promising enough to explore by drilling a well. The well was drilled at Ra's Sadr and may still be visited today.

TRUCIAL COAST DIARY FOR PERIOD ENDING 7 JULY 1949

RAS AL KHAIMAH:

It is reported that Shaikh Sultan bin Salim[157] is now charging 10 Rupees per vehicle for the right to travel through Wadi al Ghor.

UMM AL QAIWAIN:

Nothing to report.

AJMAN:

Nothing to report.

SHARJAH:

The Ruler's health is said to be still improving.

Shaikh Khalid bin Ahmed[158] has gone to Kelba for the summer.

DUBAI:

On the 6th of July Shaikh Rashid bin Said with 4 or 5 companions, including Ahmed bin Sultan bin Saleim, as secretary interpreter, left by air for Bombay. His official reason for the visit is medical; he is supposed to have some stomach trouble.

Ahmed bin Fadhil (mentioned in the last diary) returned to Abu Dhabi without the camels. No oath is yet forthcoming from the Ruler of Abu Dhabi. Ahmed claims that any way the camels were not worth taking.

Shaikh Mohd bin Salimeen[159] has returned to the interior without divulging his reason for wishing to see the Representative.

ABU DHABI:

Weightman did not after all visit Abu Dhabi, as was reported probable a fortnight ago. His aircraft returned to Bahrain without alighting at Abu Dhabi.

Shaikh Zaid with all the younger generation has returned to Baraimi after an unusually prolonged stay in Abu Dhabi of one month. In his absence Said bin Shakhbut[160] was in charge at El Muaiji.

The pearl fleet returned at the beginning of the month: the pearlers and their families returned to Baraimi to spend Ramadhan in the drier climate.

---

157 Former Ruler of Ra's al-Khaimah.

158 The Kalba regent.

159 Sheikh Mohd bin Salimeen bu Rahma Shamsi.

160 Elder son of Ruler Sheikh Shakhbut.

The Ruler has been spending a lot of money in Dubai, where his new car is frequently seen.

The Representative visited Abu Dhabi.

VISITORS:

Messrs. Dickson[161] and Jackson visited the Coast, and made a reconnaissance accompanied by the Representative in the Khor Ghanadha area, and to the South West.

Mr. Dickson returned by Rapide[162] to Bahrein on July 6th.

Henderson
Representative
EFH/KAZ.

TRUCIAL COAST DIARY FOR PERIOD ENDING 19 JULY 1949

RAS Al KHAIMAH:

The Wadi al Ghor tax has been confirmed in some quarters, but it is said that the sum of ten rupees reported in the last diary is seldom achieved. It is claimed that some services, water etc., are supplied in exchange. It will be interesting to observe the reaction to company vehicles.

UMM AL QAIWAIN:

Nothing to report.

AJMAN:

The fasting of Ramadhan seems to be confining the Ruler to his narrow domains as nothing else can.

SHARJAH:

Nothing to report.

DUBAI:

The ailment afflicting Rashid bin Said has turned out to be hernia. It is said that he is frightened to have an operation. If however the doctors in Karachi insist,

161 Dickson was the IPC Fields Superintendent in Iraq. They came to learn about the situation on the Trucial Coast before sending the drillers. They first visited in May 1948.

162 Small bi-plane used by PD(TC) and IPC.

he is likely to go to Bombay for it. That town is becoming an old crocks home for the Trucial Coast.

Weightman is reported to have written to the Ruler suggesting that he should shortly pay him a visit. The Ruler is believed to have replied to the effect that he would rather postpone talks with Weightman until the return of his son. However a prolonged absence on the part of Rashid is unlikely to prevent the arrival of Weightman.

ABU DHABI:

Weightman is expected on the 28th or 29th of this month.

GENERAL:

Ramadhan has put a stop to most activities. The chief subject of conversation in the suq is the whereabouts of the Company's proposed wild cats.[163] Details of the amounts received in royalties by the Shaikhs of Kuwait and Bahrain have been spread by Weightman to the Shaikhs, and thence have reached the man in the street in exaggerated form.

COMPANY ACTIVITIES:

Captain Pilditch and Captain Ritty[164] in the Jasoura visited the Ras al Ghanadha and Ras Sadr areas[165] with a view to examining the possibilities of landing vehicles and equipment on this difficult coast. The Representative joined them in the Sea Urchin, and several reconnaissance trips were made in the latter craft into the creeks and inlets.

At the same time Mr. N.R. Fallon[166] made a brief land survey in the same area. He naturally experienced much difficulty with the bad visibility, and was forced to do much of the work at night by means of lights.

The mariners returned by sea, after three days on the coast, and Mr. Fallon returned by Dove[167] to Bahrein on the 12th.

Mr. Clarke left for Bahrein on the 7th July 1949 for a medical check-up returning on the 13th

STOP PRESS:

A party of Awamir raiding into Abu Dhabi territory North West of Baraimi made off with eight camels. It is not known whether the camels were Manasir property

163 Oil exploration wells.

164 IPC marine department.

165 About half way between Abu Dhabi and Dubai towns, in Abu Dhabi territory.

166 IPC surveyor.

167 De Havilland Dove aircraft.

or not. The thieves made off and a large party gave chase without effect. The leader of the raiders is said to have been Bu Sabai.

Henderson
Representative
EFH/KA.

TRUCIAL COAST DIARY FOR PERIOD ENDING 16 AUGUST 1949

RAS AL KHAIMAH:

Saqr bin Mohamed[168] is actively engaged in trying to get news from the other Shaikhs regarding any agreement they might have made with Weightman. His father, Mohamed bin Salim, paid a two-day visit to Rams in an attempt to improve relations with the Shaikh there, after the recent peace-making, and seems to have had some success.

UMM AL QAIWAIN:

Ahmed bin Rashid has spent most of the time since Ramadhan at Fali al Ali,[169] from where he is keenly watching for reactions in other Shaikhdoms to any proposals that Weightman may have made. From all accounts, he is anxious for the return of the Political Officer, Trucial Coast.

AJMAN:

Nothing to report.

SHARJAH:

The Ruler is now expected back from India within the next two months.

DUBAI:

Rashid bin Saeed arrived back suddenly from India on 4th August. It became known later that he had been called back by his father, who had already received a visit from Weightman. However, he seems to be in good enough health, but denies having had hernia and states that he was suffering from chronic dysentery which has been cured by injections. He was visited by Weightman on 9th August 1949.

---

168 Ra's al-Khaimah Ruler.

169 His oasis in the sands before the mountain foreland.

The trade slump which has been gradually closing in on Dubai for the past year is becoming more apparent in the suq, and has been talked about more during the past few weeks than at any other time.

ABU DHABI:

Weightman visited Abu Dhabi on 9th August but only his interpreter saw the Ruler. The fact most noted about the visit, is that the interpreter, a Lebanese,[170] travelled from the Beit ash Shammal[171] to the fort on a camel.

GENERAL:

Ramadhan and the Eid, followed by a very hot spell, seems to have temporarily put an end to political activities, and the period under review has been a very quiet one. In fact, the more usual situation seems to have given way to a period of waiting and watchfulness, brought about by the activities of Weightman. Tempted by the latter's offers, or reputed offers, the Trucial Shaikhs are restrained only by the feeling that something must be wrong for them to be able to get extra concession money so easily, and they are now watching carefully the moves of the others whilst reaching a decision. Their attention, of course, remains focused on Abu Dhabi. It is worth noting that interest in Weightman seemed to develop considerably during the recent long period that he was away from the Trucial Coast, and one reliable source has it that people from Abu Dhabi have been used to spread his gospel.[172]

R.A. Codrai visited all the Shaikhdoms except Ras al Khaimah during the Eid, and also Abu Dhabi on three other occasions on Company business.

COMPANY ACTIVITIES:

Although politically quiet, the period has certainly been a very active one for the Company, due to the early start of Phase One Operations.[173] Messrs Ball and Upton arrived on 27th July, and. moved out to Khor Ghanadha to start the new camp there on 7th August. K.M. Maude i/c Services, arrived on 9th August and moved on to camp the following day. Messrs. Dickson, Hamilton and Robinson visited the camp on 16th August accompanied by Mr. Haddad of the CAT Company.[174]

---

170 Victor Hashim.

171 The northern house, located on the sea shore.

172 Weightman's message of 'good news'.

173 Preparing to drill the first well on the Trucial Coast at Ra's Sadr in Abu Dhabi territory.

174 Contracting and Trading Company from the Lebanon.

LABOUR:

25 Coolies, 6 watchmen and one head-coolie from Abu Dhabi were engaged for the Khor Ghanadha Camp on 8th August.[175] On 15th August it was found necessary to introduce the Company's ration scale, as a result of which the coolies refused to work, and were sent off back to Abu Dhabi. The matter was taken up with the Ruler, and the 25 coolies were returned to camp on 16th August, accompanied by Shaikh Haza. The latter was shown one man's ration of food for one day, and seemed quite satisfied with it, though, of course, he asked that they be given more. The ration of rice has now been temporarily increased a little, and the men are all back at work.[176]

Codrai
Representative
RAC/KAZ.

TRUCIAL COAST DIARY FOR PERIOD ENDING 30 AUGUST 1949

RAS AL KHAIMAH:

Sultan bin Salim[177] is now living at Bu Bagara in the Wadi al Qor,[178] and it is reported that he is asking the Ruler of Ras al Khaimah for a share of the Company's Concession payment, on the grounds that when he was Ruler, he himself paid the present Ruler a share of the payments.

Shaikh Mohd bin Salim[179] recently stayed a few days in Sharjah for medical attention.

AJMAN:

Nothing to report.

175 All Abu Dhabi nationals. Although men had been engaged to work for the seismic party, this new recruitment marks the start of a process which led to the employment of hundreds of Abu Dhabi nationals. Money spent by the company, PD(TC), was starting to reach the people in large numbers.

176 Over the years the food or rations provided by the Company, or later the Company's contractors, were too often the cause of complaints, often quite justifiable.

177 Previous Ruler and uncle of current Ruler Sheikh Saqr.

178 There are various spellings of this name.

179 Father of Ruler.

SHARJAH:

Baluchis from Sharjah living in a camp near Falaj al Ali recently rescued a small party of Baluchis travelling from Sharjah to Batinah who were being attacked by the Bani Kitab. There were no casualties.

Mohamed bin Saqr[180] has been noticed to have greatly increased his guards during his frequent visits to Ras al Khaimah, an indication of the troubled atmosphere that is attributed to that part.

DUBAI:

Dubai people gave chase and rescued camels stolen from them during a raid near Buraimi by Shaikh Aumair Muttawa, Shaikh of Falaj.[181] This was Shaikh Aumair's second raid; the first time he captured six camels from the sons of Ubaid bin Nasir of Qattara,[182] after which he immediately went to the Shaikh of Mahdhar[183] and asked for protection.

Dubai merchants, suffering from the gradual trade slump, seem to be getting a little impatient in waiting for benefits from the Company's operations, and recently tried unsuccessfully to persuade the Ruler to prevent other than Dubai launches and dhows from being used by the Company for bringing goods from Bahrain or Qatar, or for shipping them elsewhere.

H.M. Jackson and R.A. Codrai visited Shaikh Rashid on 18th August.

ABU DHABI:

As will be seen under 'Labour', the Abu Dhabi Shaikhs are taking a very keen interest in the Company's operations at Khor Ghanadha. Shaikh Haza has been appointed by Shaikh Shakhbut as his representative on all matters relating to labour and problems arising at the new camp.

H.M. Jackson visited Abu Dhabi on 17th August and R.A. Codrai on 26th August.

---

180 Sheikh Mohamed bin Saqr was the brother of the then Sharjah Ruler Sultan bin Saqr and father of Dr. Shaikh Sultan bin Mohamed, Ruler since 1972.

181 It is not clear what the writer means. Falaj is an underground water course common in Buraimi/Al Ain and the Sultanate of Oman. The name is also attributed to a particular place in Oman. Perhaps the place about 20 kilometres south west of, and inland from Saham on the Batinah Coast of Oman. This would be about 80 kilometres from Buraimi.

182 Qattara is one of the Abu Dhabi oases in the Buraimi/Al Ain group.

183 Mahdhar or Mahdhah is a large oasis in the mountain foreland north of Buraimi/Al Ain. The Sheikh was Obaid bin Juma al Kaabi.

COMPANY ACTIVITIES:

Work at the construction camp is keeping fairly close to the programme. The Jasura[184] arrived on 22nd August and spent two days just outside Khor Ghanadha off-loading her cargo. An attempt is being made to find and mark a channel outside the Khor, and it is hoped that the Jasura will be able to use it on her next trip, early in September.

Messrs. Rennie and Burges spent about 2 weeks based at Sharjah, from where they did an aerial photographic survey of certain parts of the coast at high tide, from a Company Rapide.

LABOUR:

Abu Dhabi coolie labour is not good,[185] and it was found necessary to bring in ten Dubai coolies to assist in the unloading of the Jasura. This was afterwards strongly objected to by Shaikh Haza, who refused to allow them to remain in his territory. He was persuaded to permit them to assist in off-loading the Jasura, but only on condition that they did not work ashore between trips. In the meantime old and unsuitable Abu Dhabi coolies are being weeded out and returned to Abu Dhabi, and are being replaced by others a little better. Thirty coolies are at present being employed from there, ten of whom were recently replaced.

Representative
Codrai
RAC/KAZ.

184 Company landing craft.

185 'When the prospecting operations were restarted, it was quickly apparent that their daily diet of fish and rice gave locally recruited workmen little stamina. When they were first engaged, many of them could barely lift a basket of dates. After one year of Company feeding, the same men could easily lift a 200lb. sack of rice. The most difficult employees were former slaves, who, after years of pampering by their masters, were inclined to be intolerant of the Company's hours and conditions of work.' LONGHURST, H. (1959), *Adventure in Oil. The story of British Petroleum*, Sidgwick and Jackson, London, 1959, p. 210.

TRUCIAL COAST DIARY FOR PERIOD ENDING 12 SEPTEMBER 1949

RAS AL KHAIMAH:

Nothing to report.

AJMAN:

Nothing to report.

SHARJAH:

Nothing to report.

DUBAI:

Nothing to report.

ABU DHABI:

Shaikh Shakhbut has paid a long overdue visit to El Muaiji.[186] Hiza[187] is shortly to visit Bahrein at the request of the Resident, having failed to catch the routine aircraft last week.

Zaid has come to an agreement with Saqr[188] on all outstanding points - he has finished building the new fort at El Ain.[189] Relations between the two shaikhs are said to be unusually cordial.

The Representative visited Abu Dhabi and ascertained that there are no launches[190] of the size shape and speed the Company require. This is not surprising.

BIRAIMI:

Saqr is in correspondence with the Sultan. The latter is said to be raising a coalition to chastise him, even smuggling a few rifles to the confederates, among whom is Rashid bin Hamden of Dhank.[191] Saqr has made tentative approaches

186 One of the Abu Dhabi oases in the 'Al Ain/Buraimi group. In those days it was the most prominent. Earlier PD(TC) reports wrote 'Lumwaiji'.

187 Brother of Shaikhs Shakhbut, Khaled and Zayed.

188 Shaikh Saqr bin Sultan of Buraimi.

189 Al Muraba' Zayed.

190 Today many people would call them dhows.

191 One of the Dhank shaikhs? Has Henderson made a mistake? There is neither Rashid nor Hamden in Codrai's list of Dhank sheikhs. There is on the list a sheikh Rashid bin Ali in Wadi Dhank.

to the Company via Khan Sahib Hussain,[192] but as yet they do not amount to anything concrete.

COMPANY ACTIVITIES:

The Jasura, a "Z" lighter and five booms landed their cargoes without undue trouble at Khor Ghanadha[193] between the 8th and 12th. The Jasura tried without success to enter the creek herself. Reconnaissance in the Jassairah Fahad area[194] has shown the possibility of a better harbour and landing place for heavy equipment, but a survey is needed to confirm this.

Work on the new camp on Sadr itself is proceeding.

Dubai coolies have assisted in unloading craft with the permission of the Ruler of Abu Dhabi. Labour troubles at present centre round the problem of feeding in the newly constructed camps, but whatever the food it still requires 8 men to do one man's work.

Henderson
Representative.

TRUCIAL COAST DIARY FOR PERIOD ENDING 26 SEPTEMBER 1949

RAS AL KHAIMAH:

It is reported that Jasim bin Dalam uncle of the Shaikh of Jazirat Zaab[195] was assassinated when he was at evening prayers. The assassins had previously asked the Shaikh of Ras al Khaimah for a share from concession payment, but the Shaikh rejected them, and they believed that Jasim was responsible for the refusal.

AJMAN:

Nothing to report.

---

192 One time Residency Agent in Sharjah, 1935-1936. The first contractor for the Company and agent for Anglo-Iranian Oil Company.

193 On the Abu Dhabi coast between Abu Dhabi and Dubai towns and near the first drilling location at Ra's Sadr.

194 Near Ra's Sadr but much nearer to Abu Dhabi town.

195 Jazirat a' Za'ab or Jazirat al Hamra is in Ra's al-Khaimah territory and a short distance south from the town of Ra's al-Khaimah. The headquarters of the Za'ab tribe.

SHARJAH:

Nothing to report.

DUBAI:

Nothing to report.

ABU DHABI:

On Sept. 22nd Shaikh Haz'a left Sharjah by R.A.F. plane for Bahrein. The story was put about that he was going on the Haj, but others thought that it was to a conference at Jeddah.[196]

Shaikh Khalid visited construction camp.

Shaikh Shakhbut is now back in Abu Dhabi and has become his own representative to the company once more. He claims to have made an important agreement with Shaikh Saqr.[197] He says that all the Naim and the Bani Kaab[198] are now in friendly relations with the Al bu Falah.[199] Zaid he says is now the major power in Biraimi. Saqr appears to have burnt his boats with the Sultan. Whether Saqr has been driven into this agreement through fear of the Sultan or through fear of Zaid's new fort in al 'Ain, is not clear.

BIRAIMI:

It is reported that Na'im arriving from Biraimi were met by people of the Bait Kathir,[200] there was a fight. Two men were killed, and their camels and dates were taken. A party on camels from Dubai set-off in pursuit, carefully too late.

COMPANY ACTIVITIES:

Jasura entered the creek at Khor Ghanadha and began unloading.

Jamila arrived off Abu Dhabi on the 20th and explored the Khor es Sadiyat South West of Ras el Gharab and later came up to Khor Ghanadha to meet Jasura.

196 Shaikh Haza attended the conference in Jeddah called to discuss the Saudi Arabian claim to much of the territory of Abu Dhabi.

197 Shaikh Saqr bin Sultan at Buraimi.

198 The Bani Ka'ab occupied Mahadha in the mountain foreland to the north of Buraimi as well as many neighbouring settlements, often in the valley (wadi) before it opens onto the plain. The Ka'ab are associated, not only by name, with people in Qatar and as far as Basra and Arabistan.

199 The Abu Dhabi ruling family tribe.

200 A Hadramaut tribe from South Yemen.

VISITORS:

Mr. Hoogwerf visited location No.1[201] and Dubai, Mr. Tussler location No.1 and Sharjah. Mr. Brown visited camp.

Henderson
Representative.

TRUCIAL COAST DIARY FOR PERIOD ENDING 11 OCTOBER 1949

RAS AL KHAIMAH:

Nothing to report.

UMM AL QAIWAIN:

Nothing to report.

AJMAN:

Mr. Codrai presented the Ruler[202] on behalf of the Company with a Ford Pilot car, for which the Ruler appeared grateful.

KALBA:

There has recently been considerable trouble between the people of Khor Fakkan[203] and the Shaikh, owing to the greed and licentious life of the latter. The people of Khor Fakkan are said to wish for Hamad bin Said[204] to take over as Ruler in fact. Khalid[205] is in Ajman unable or unwilling to curb his unpleasant relatives. At Khor Fakkan there is a truce after a period of open revolt. As usual no casualties are reported, though the incident is described as a minor war.

---

201 Location No.1 was the site for the first oil exploration well to be drilled on the Trucial Coast at Ra's Sadr, near Ghanadha.

202 Sheikh Rashid bin Humaid.

203 A Kalba port on the east coast, now part of Sharjah. The main tribe in Khor Fakkan was the Naqbiyin.

204 Sheikh Hamad bin Saeed, Ruler 1950-1951. In 1937 after the Ruler of Kalba, Said bin Hamad, died, he was succeeded by his son Hamad who was a 12 year old minor. Sheikh Khalid bin Ahmed who had been Ruler of Sharjah (1914-1924) was chosen to be the Kalba Regent. He was ambitious and extended the territory under his control. He signed an Oil Concession Agreement with Longrigg of PCL in 1938.

205 Sheikh Khalid bin Ahmed the Regent of Kalba.

SHARJAH:

The Ruler[206] sufficiently forgot himself during an Eid visit to ask us why we were not drilling in his territory. Otherwise the Eid passed pleasantly.

DUBAI:

Eid visits were exchanged without any gauche remarks on either side. A representative of Holloways[207] has appeared, and says that he intends to build a house near the new hospital site for himself and his wife. He also intends to build and maintain a power station.

ABU DHABI:

The Ruler[208] appears to have entered upon a mood of Celtic gloom leavened occasionally by hysteria.

COMPANY ACTIVITIES:

Jamila has completed her work[209] in Khor Ghanadha and is now working near Ras al Gharab.[210] Construction is continuing at the Ras Sadr camp to which a move is shortly to be made.

VISITORS:

Mr. Heseldin[211] visited camp on the 28th September 1949. Mr. Lermitte visited camp on the 5th. Mr. Fielding is staying in Dubai and hopes that before he leaves to be able to move the signal station to Ras Sadr. There have been several other visitors to camp, and two new arrivals.

Henderson
Representative.

---

206 Sheikh Sultan bin Saqr.

207 A British construction company who did not achieve much on the Trucial Coast.

208 Sheikh Shakhbut bin Sultan.

209 Conducting marine surveys along the coast.

210 Ra's Gharab is a headland on the island of Gharab, looking south west over the wide channel which separates that island from Sadiyat Island.

211 IPC later PD(TC).

TRUCIAL COAST DIARY FOR PERIOD ENDING 24 OCTOBER 1949

RAS AL KHAIMAH:

Nothing to report.

UMM AL QAIWAIN:

Nothing to report.

AJMAN:

The Ruler has sold the car which the Company gave him and bought a Chevrolet with the proceeds.

KALBA:

Nothing to report.

SHARJAH:

Nothing to report.

DUBAI:

The pearl fleet has returned.[212]

ABU DHABI:

Nothing to report.

COMPANY ACTIVITIES:

The work of transporting stores to Ras Sadr is proceeding slowly owing to transport difficulties. A one day strike took place.

VISITORS:

Dr. Colenso Jones[213] visited camp.

212 The safe return of the pearl fleet, often several months away on the pearl banks, was an occasion for celebration. The main pearling season was between April and September. However they may have stayed out for longer of gone again for a short period.

213 Chief Medical Officer based in London, still in that position when he passed me fit, in July 1963, to go to Abu Dhabi.

ARRIVALS

Dr. Ayoub came to take over as Resident Medical Officer. Mr. P.D. Stobart P.O.T.C.[214] returned to Sharjah.

Henderson
Representative.

STRIKE – CONSTRUCTION CAMP

On 22nd October 1949 a day's strike took place on account of food. The strike virtually ended at mid-day when Mr. Codrai, who happened to be present, insisted on the labour returning to work before the food could be discussed, and the Shaikh's representative agreed to their resuming work. Mr. Dickson however would not allow them to return as he said they must forfeit the whole day's pay. It is thought this weakened the Company's position. In the evening Dickson, Henderson and Codrai met Shaikh Khalid and discussed the matter. The following was decided.

1. No strike would be tolerated.
2. Complaints to be passed through the normal channels and time to be allowed to solve such questions as food.
3. One or two changes in food agreed to in respect of dal[215] and rice.
4. As far as possible Abu Dhabi (Biraimi) or Batinah dates to be issued in preference to the stale Basra dates on sale at present.
5. If possible better quality flour to be obtained.

There is no doubt that the dal and flour issued by Qatar is scarcely eatable, likewise the ghee,[216] (this is now being bought locally).

We are doing what we can to improve the rations locally, but we would like Qatar to send much better quality coolie rations and also it is suggested someone from commissariat to go into this question on the spot. In other words to concentrate for the moment on the coolie food alone, and its preparation. I am quite certain that the full scale as laid down in a recent commissariat instructions is not being issued. Is the coolie ration the same as the normal daily paid scale?

Henderson
Representative.

214 Political Officer Trucial Coast.

215 Dal or Dhal is split pulse (a vegetable like pea or bean) that is common in India.

216 Indian butter from buffalo milk, clarified to appear like oil.

LETTER HENDERSON TO LERMITTE

Dubai
2nd Nov. 1949

Dear Mr. Lermitte,

I took the P.A. round both camps for a brief visit before going to Abu Dhabi. He has retained the impression that while conditions are better than normal conditions in Abu Dhabi they are not quite what is expected from a high-powered oil company. I think it will be difficult to dissuade him until improvements can be made.

They do not appear to have sent any kitchen equipment for the coolie cook-houses. We rely on local purchases entirely. Some of the cooking is still being done in petrol tins. We hope to remedy this to a certain extent from local sources. Wood fires are used in the absence of any alternative, at a great expense. There are no tables, cupboards, fly-proof safes for fish, meat etc and as a result the food is covered in flies.

The rice is a kind that does not swell. The 12 ozs.[217] allowed on the scale that is followed at present appears to be small when cooked. The fish available varies with the amount caught locally by the representative of the Shaikh, of course there is nothing to take its place if the supply fails. There are no vegetables except onions; and the coolies refused to eat the dhal provided, as they are not used to it, and it was anyway of very poor quality. In view of this it was agreed by the representative of the Shaikh and Mr. Dickson and myself to issue 6 ozs.[218] dates in place of 4 ozs. Meat is issued once a week, and the flour, ghee and odds and ends, such as curry, seems to be adequate, except that some of the Qatar ghee is rancid.

In view of the fact that there are virtually no vegetables except onions, it is thought that 6ozs. of dates are not enough. The Abu Dhabi people are accustomed to live almost entirely on dates.

The food complaints seem to come from two sources. The Shaikh's representative, family and guards deliberately stir up discontent, but at the same time the coolies are of the opinion that there is not enough bulk in the ration.

Since I am not myself convinced that there is no ground for complaint it is the more difficult for me to persuade the P.A. and the Shaikh's representative, that there is nothing in fact wrong. Up to date I have protested, contrary to my own belief that all is well and good, but I cannot continue to do so.

I do not know what the correct coolie scale of rations are or the scale of utensils for coolie kitchens. How commissariat personnel can visit camp time and again

217 12 ounces or ¾ pound. About ⅓ Kilogramme. 16 ounces to the pound.

218 6 ounces.

without apparently noticing that the food was being cooked virtually without any recognised form of utensils I do not understand.

It appears that the company intends to learn hygiene and cooking from the Abu Dhabi example. I should have thought the reverse should be the correct policy.

As I have repeatedly said, a British camp boss could do more at present to solve labour troubles than we can do ourselves.

Yours sincerely
Edward Henderson.

TRUCIAL COAST DIARY FOR PERIOD ENDING 9 NOVEMBER 1949

RAS Al KHAIMAH:

Recent minor troubles seem to have settled themselves.

UMM AL QAIWAIN:

Nothing to report.

AJMAN:

Nothing to report.

SHARJAH:

Advance guard of anti-locust mission has arrived.[219]

DUBAI:

Shaikh Saqr bin Sultan[220] and Ahmed al Salf[221] are visiting the Shaikhs. Shaikh Khalid has returned from pilgrimage. Shaikhs Saqr and Ahmad al Salf paid a social visit to the Representative and threatened to come again.

---

219 The Desert Locust Survey, initially based in London in 1940's, searched for breeding grounds of locusts in Arabia and the Horn of Africa. The team was at times welcome and other times treated with suspicion that they were spies for the British. Sometimes they laid poison bait for the locusts. People protested fearing that they would poison camels and goats. However if locusts appeared the Survey people were more welcome. Henderson was very critical of them. They also sponsored the trips that Thesiger, the explorer, undertook crossing the Empty Quarter.

220 Sheikh of Buraimi. (Na'im).

221 Sheikh Ahmed as Salf (Na'im) from Hafit village near Baraimi.

ABU DHABI:

Shaikh Khalid[222] has returned to the fort[223] after protracted stay in camp.[224] Mohammed bin Khalifa[225] and Mubarak[226] with two others have left Sharjah by air for Bahrein. Hamdan[227] was to have been of the party, but was sent for by Shakhbut at the moment the aircraft was due to leave. It is hoped that the summons was in connection with Hamdan's last visit to Construction Camp when he made himself a nuisance. Shakhbut appears to disapprove of Hamdan's activities.

COMPANY ACTIVITIES:

Work on the new living quarters at Ras Sadr proceeds apace. Shakhbut has produced another launch, which will probably be hired in place of a Dubai launch. Jasura made another successful trip. Some trouble with the labour centred again on food. In the absence of any representative from Abu Dhabi it is hoped that the workers will regain their lost content. This appears to be happening.

Henderson
Representative
EFH/KAZ.

TRUCIAL COAST DIARY FOR PERIOD ENDING 23 NOVEMBER 1949

RAS AL KHAIMAH:

Nothing to report.

UMM AL QAIWAIN:

The Wild Goose[228] naval party headed by S.N.O.P.G.[229] arrived at the fort riding camels, which they commandeered on the beach.

---

222 Brother of the Ruler.

223 In Abu Dhabi.

224 At Ra's Sadr.

225 First cousin of Sheikh Shakhbut.

226 Sheikh Mubarak bin Mohamed bin Khalifa.

227 Sheikh Hamdan bin Mohamed bin Khalifa.

228 A British naval vessel.

229 Senior Naval Officer Persian Gulf.

AJMAN:

Nothing to report.

KALBA:

Nothing to report.

SHARJAH:

A Company truck was in collision with a truck driven by the Ruler's son. It is hoped to settle the matter peacefully.

DUBAI:

Shaikhs Saqr bin Sultan of Biraimi and Ahmed al Salf[230] stayed with the Ruler. They visited Ras al Khaimah before returning to Biraimi.

Wild Goose visited Dubai the 16th.

ABU DHABI:

From a description of Colonel Miles of his travels in the 19th century "At a distance of twelve miles from Abu Thubi[231] is said to be the best creek on the Pirate Coast called Khor Girab." Presumably he refers to what we are calling Sadiyat.[232]

Wild Goose visited Abu Dhabi on the 15th and S.N.O.P.G. called on the Shaikh.

The Company M.O.[233] treated the Queen mother[234] as a patient, apparently with success.

VISITORS:

The General Manager[235] Mr. H.S. Gibson, with Mr. Heseldin[236] and party visited the construction camps on November 12th and stayed the night at Sharjah.

---

230 Naim Khawatir Sheikh from Hafit village.

231 Abu Dhabi.

232 Ra's al Gharab is a headland at sea end of the wide channel between Sadiyat island and Gharab the next large island to the north. However there is some confusion and some people place the Ra's at the northern end of the narrow and shallow channel which opens out at the northern end of Sadiyat island.

233 Medical Officer. The Company had a small medical centre which although it was strictly for employees, no one was turned away and sometimes people would come long distances for treatment.

234 Sheikh Shakhbut's mother Sheikha Salama bint Buti.

235 General Manager Qatar and Trucial Coast.

236 IPC later with PD(TC).

ARRIVALS:

At Ras Sadr, a camp boss Mr. J. Harrison arrived.

COMPANY ACTIVITIES:

No.3 Party are working, with the knowledge and consent of the Ruler on the island of Es Sadiyat.

The last of the very heavy lifts to be carried from Khor Ghanadha to Ras Sadr beat the advent of the first rain by a short head. The Shaikh says he is relieved, so I understand are we.

Henderson
Representative
EFH/KAZ.

TRUCIAL COAST DIARY FOR PERIOD ENDING 17 DECEMBER 1949

There is little of interest to report regarding internal politics during the period under review, and activity has been centred mainly around visitors to the Coast. The Political Resident[237] accompanied by his wife and daughter, arrived at Abu Dhabi on 7th Shortly afterwards, the new Representative of the Superior Oil Company, Colonel Galloway,[238] an ex-Political Agent from Bahrein, arrived on the coast to start his negotiations with the Rulers. Local feeling is very much confused by the manner in which ex-Political Agents reappear on the scene representing an American Company, and it remains to the seen whether this will weaken the position of the local Political Officer in dealing with any Company problems that may fall into his lap.

RAS AL KHAIMAH:

Nothing to report.

UMM AL QAIWAIN:

Nothing to report.

237 Sir Rupert Hay.

238 He replaced Sir Hugh Weightman who also had previously been a Political Agent. Weightman died in an accident at London Heathrow airport.

SHARJAH:

With the recommencement of work of the Red Oxide company on Abu Musa, the Shaikh of Sharjah has imposed a 'Foreign Labour Tax' of Rs. 10 for European and Rs. 3 for every other non-Sharjah subject. Only the Red Oxide Company seems to be effected by this.

All the members of the Anti-Locust Mission, at present based with the R.A.F. at Sharjah, have now arrived, together with most of their transport. As yet, the mission has confined itself to training trips, and has not yet settled down to any programme. It is reported from Biraimi that opposition there to the work of the Mission is mainly because of its use of poisoned bait.

Col. Galloway of the S.O.C.[239] arrived at Sharjah in a K.L.M.[240] Chartered Dakota on 7th December. He did not visit any of the Shaikhs on this trip, though he flew over Abu Dhabi. The crew of the Dakota, were unable to contact Abu Dhabi control tower, however, and returned to Sharjah. They reported a circle of barasti huts across the runway, so it is unlikely that they saw the actual landing ground.

The Shaikh of Sharjah is reported to be planning the building of a new harbour, and intends raising a loan from the Company. The plan was introduced to the Shaikh by Mr. Lindsay, representative of Holloway Bros., who has other schemes which include the building of a power station for Dubai, a pontoon bridge across the Dubai creek, and a bridge across the Ford at Abu Dhabi.

A tender from the H.M.S. Flamingo overturned at the entrance to Sharjah creek on 8th December during darkness, but there were no casualties.

DUBAI:

In December a party of Superior Oil Company representatives visited the Ruler of Dubai and are said to have offered one lac[241] cash, and a 20% royalty on all oil. They left for Abu Dhabi the following day by road.

ABU DHABI:

Shaikh Haza' arrived back in Abu Dhabi on 2nd Dec from his visit to Saudi Arabia and Bahrein.

Mr. Pocock, representative of the Red Oxide Company working on Abu Musa, recently spent two days in Abu Dhabi, negotiating with the Ruler for a lease of certain Abu Dhabi islands, but met with no success, and is to try again sometime in the future. The Ruler demanded a first payment of one lac rupees, on the grounds that he had been cheated by the oil company and had to make it up in other ways.

---

239 Superior Oil Company.

240 Royal Dutch Airline.

241 One hundred thousand (Rupees).

COMPANY ACTIVITIES:

Work has now been begun on the derrick structure[242] at Ras Sadr.

VISITORS:

The Political Resident,[243] accompanied by his wife and daughter, the Political Agent from Sharjah[244] and Lt. Comd. Godden of the H.M.S. Flamingo[245] visited Khor Ghanadha and Ras Sadr camps on 8th December.

W. Thesiger arrived on 23rd November and left for Biraimi on 30th Nov. He was expected to leave Biraimi to commence his travels on 16th Dec. but he has so far been unsuccessful in obtaining either M.T. Dollars[246] or silver rupees, and is reported to have arrived at Abu Dhabi on 17th December.

Codrai
Representative
RAC/KAZ.

<u>Subject VISIT OF SUPERIOR OIL COMPANY TO ABU DHABI</u>

Please refer to my letter PO.A/257 of 17th December 1949.

The Superior Oil Company party consisted of Mr. Smith a geologist an interpreter (Weightman's)[247] and two others. Galloway was not, as at first thought, in the party. They went down by road and returned by air to Bahrein, the KLM Dakota landing without any trouble at Abu Dhabi. According to Hiza they spared no effort to pour contempt on us -one well in 14 years. Hiza explained our difficulties to them, and the war in which Britain was engaged totally. It is not thought that their discussion reached any conclusion.

I passed the party on my way down and took one member of it to be Galloway, but did not have a very good view of him through the windscreen of their truck.

---

242 The tower of the drilling rig in those days was erected, piece by piece. It was to be another 10 years before the masts were raised, lowered and transported in one piece.

243 Sir Rupert Hay.

244 P.D. Stobart.

245 His (or Her) Majesty's Ship Flamingo. A Sloop such as used for escorting (protecting) cargo ships. The Flamingo was sold to the German (West) navy in 1959, where it was used for training.

246 Maria Theresa Dollars were silver coins in common use in the area and as far afield as the Horn of Africa.

247 Victor Hashim.

Opinion in Sharjah had it that Galloway was there, but Hiza assures me this was not the case.

Henderson
Representative
ERH/KAZ.

1950

TRUCIAL COAST DIARY FOR PERIOD ENDING 4 JANUARY 1950

RAS AL KHAIMAH:

A section of the Khawatir[1] are being troublesome, and notice would be required of any Party intending to work in the Ras al Khaimah, Falaj al Ali[2] area.

UMM AL QAIWAIN:

Nothing to report.

SHARJAH:

Shaikh Mohd bin Saqr[3] of Sharjah was entertained to lunch at the Company rest house at Sharjah on 2nd January 1950.

---

1 The Khawatir are a section of the Na'im and were found on the Jiri plain south of Ra's al-Khaimah and also in Hafit village near Buraimi. They knew that the Company had paid the Ruler of Ra's al-Khaimah for the right to survey an area which included the Jiri Plain. The Khawatir believed they had the right to receive payment from the Ruler or the Company and so they obstructed the operations of the Company hoping thereby to receive satisfaction. This was a problem that the Company faced with several tribes of the interior. Each time that the Company faced a confrontation with a tribe the others were watching closely to see how the dispute was resolved. The Company had agreements with the coastal sheikhs and the Sultan of Oman and HMG declared that all the tribes of the interior came under either the coastal sheikhs or the Sultan.

2 Falaj al Ali is an Umm al Quwain oasis north of Dhaid and south of the Jiri plain.

3 Brother of Ruler and father of present Ruler, Dr. Sheikh Sultan bin Mohamed.

DUBAI:

Khalifa bin Abdulrehman al Qusaibi[4] intends drilling water wells to a depth of 2500 feet (sounds incredible) in Dubai. Ed Richardson informs me that this may have serious effects if gas or even oil were struck, and might damage any oil deposits that are present. It might be as well if he were warned of the damage he may run into. Khalifa Qusaibi intends to contact P.C.L.[5] with the intention of offering drilling samples to the Company.

ABU DHABI:

The launch trouble goes on.[6] Abdullah Sani of Kuwait is at Abu Dhabi whispering in the Shaikh's ear about contracts and other unpleasant things. Trouble may brew up in this quarter.

GENERAL:

Henderson and Codrai visited Hairah, Ajman, Umm al Qaiwain, Ras al Khaimah, Dhaid, Kelba, Fujeira and Khor Fakkan, over the Christmas period and paid visits to all the Shaikhs. The general impression is, as usual, one of extreme impatience with the Company for not drilling, and of envy of Abu Dhabi.

Shaikh Mohd bin Ahmed es Sharqi[7] seems to own more of Kelba than ever. While camping near Marbat[8] he provided guards and not Shaikh Humaid.[9] He claims all the coast from exclusive Kelba to exclusive Khor Fakkan and exclusive Khor Fakkan to Dibba. Local opinion seems to uphold Mohamed's claim rather than Kelba's. The situation is however muddled, and it appears to be anybody's game so far.[10]

Saqr and Khalid sons of Sultan bin Salim[11] greeted us with an unfriendly shot in Wadi al Qor, which should by rights have made a hole in somebody (about 50 yards range).

---

4 The Qusaibi or Gusaibi are a large Saudi Arabian family.

5 The IPC (Iraq Petroleum Company) used the name P.C.L. (Petroleum Concessions Limited) for operations throughout the Middle East except at Kirkuk in Iraq. PD(TC) was the same company, an IPC associated company operating only on the Trucial Coast.

6 This refers to the problems the Company had with hiring suitable boats. (Dhows often referred to as launches).

7 The – yet to be recognised by HMG – Ruler of Fujairah.

8 On the coast between Fujairah and Khor Fakkan.

9 Sheikh Humaid bin Abdulla, deputy to Sheikh Khalid, the Kalba Regent.

10 This paragraph refers to places along the coast of the Indian Ocean. The main access route to the Indian Ocean from the Gulf towns such as Dubai was across the Hajar mountains and through the Wadi al Qaur. This necessitated passing through territory of the Sultanate of Oman to go from Dubai to Kalba.

11 Previous Ruler of Ra's al-Khaimah.

Apologies and coffee followed, but we were not clear as to how one should negotiate the pass without incurring target practice on oneself (presumably by pretending to be a taxi). We did not pay the customary 10 rupees for the privilege of using the Wadi.

Codrai
Representative.

TRUCIAL COAST DIARY FOR PERIOD ENDING 22 JANUARY 1950

RAS AL KHAIMAH:

Shaikh Mohamed[12] visited Sharjah as a result of the last letter he received from us, in order to consult the Political Officer. Detachment of Anti-locust Mission[13] complete with Hareem visited Ras al Khaimah. There have been no developments so far.

AJMAN:

The Ruler[14] has been chasing a stolen female subject and has just returned to base.

UMM AL QAIWAIN:

Nothing to report.

SHARJAH:

It is reported that after March the B.I. steamers[15] will call only at Dubai.[16] The Shaikh is thinking of building a jetty and is looking for funds.

DUBAI:

Kanoo[17] and Zayani[18] are opening Agencies. A new store, called the London Store opened recently and gave a tea party to the leaders of Dubai commerce.

---

12 Father of the Ra's al-Khaimah Ruler.

13 The Desert Locust Survey.

14 Sheikh Rashid bin Humaid.

15 The British India Steamship Navigation Company provided a regular service between India and the Gulf.

16 The ships called at Sharjah.

17 Yusuf bin Ahmed Kanoo was a frequent visitor to the Trucial Coast in the 1930's.

18 Bahraini merchants.

ABU DHABI:

The Ruler has visited Seismic[19] and is now hunting in the vicinity of Bu Merikha.[20] He has bought a jeep. Messrs. Jackson and Henderson visited Abu Dhabi in a G.M.C.[21] and returned over the Maqta[22] on camels owing to an unusally bracing shimal.[23]

COMPANY ACTIVITIES:

The main structure of the Derrick is complete and the draw works are being moved into place.[24] Work on convenanted[25] staff buildings is temporarily held up by lack of material for ceilings which is expected shortly. The Political Officer and the Shaikh have promised to attend the spudding in ceremony.[26]

Henderson
Representative
EFH/KAZ.

---

19 The Company Geophysical Party conducting seismic surveys. The early geophysical surveys measured changes in the magnetic field, or in the pull of gravity. Seismic surveys involving small explosions and the measurement of the shock waves passing through the earth, are much more complicated providing information about rock formations deep down in the ground. The rock reservoirs in Abu Dhabi are mostly more than 8,000 feet below the surface.

20 Near the coast about 20 miles north of Maqta.

21 G.M.C. General Motors Corporation car. Generally known as 'Gimcy'.

22 The wind raised the water level at the ford crossing to Abu Dhabi island. When this happened the water was too deep for cars, but camels could still cross.

23 North wind.

24 The drilling rig. Preparing to drill the first well on the Trucial Coast at Ra's Sadr.

25 A word borrowed from the Indian Civil Service. Staff under contract.

26 The start of drilling.

TRUCIAL COAST DIARY FOR PERIOD ENDING 14 FEBRUARY 1950

RAS AL KHAIMAH:

The anti-locusts have been operating in the area.

KELBA:

The regent[27] has been very ill, but is recovering. Shaikh Humaid[28] has also been ill. The young Ruler[29] has been attempting to get himself recognised.

SHARJAH:

The wall protecting the aerodrome from the sea broke and the aerodrome was flooded.

DUBAI:

A Bahreini launch was wrecked at Jamaira[30] with the loss of eleven lives. A boom[31] is reported to be lost at sea with 60 passengers.

ABU DHABI:

Several jolly boats[32] lost at sea. One wrecked at Khor Ghanada, but no lives lost. Later report suggests large casualty list.

OMAN:

Mohamed bin Ahmed al Hiyayi from Dhank[33] visited us in Dubai. He states that he has recently been to Muscat to have a tribal affair settled by the Sultan, of whom he claims to be the devoted subject. He states that the Dhahira[34] tribes are annoyed with the Shaikhs of the Naim because of their attitude to the Company.

27 Sheikh Khalid bin Ahmed.

28 This is Sheikh Humaid bin Abdulla, the deputy to Sheikh Khalid bin Ahmed.

29 Sheikh Hamid bin Said.

30 A short distance south of Dubai. Now part of Dubai.

31 Ocean going dhow.

32 Small boat.

33 Dhank is in the Sultanate of Oman about 100 kilometres south of Buraimi. Bird's March 1949 list names Mohamed bin Hamad al Hiyayi al bu Shamis, sheikh of the eastern portion of Dhank. HEARD, D. (2019), Chapter 3 Appendix 36.

34 The Dhahira is a large area extending from Buraimi south beyond Ibri and towards Nizwa. It encompasses the plain area nearer to the Hajar mountains rather than the desert areas to the west.

Mr. Thesiger is reported to be past Ibri[35] and going South.

The locust Mission have set an ugly precedent by paying Rs. 5 per car to Obeid bin Juma'.[36]

THE COMPANY:

Spudding in at Ras Sadr is predicted for the 15th February. The Political Officer visited Abu Dhabi with the Representative.

Mr. Dickson states that Seismic have reported some time ago the presence of shale in Abu Dhabi territory, near Abu Dhabi. Mr. Dickson hopes one day to go down and see if it is suitable.

Henderson
Representative.

TRUCIAL COAST DIARY FOR PERIOD ENDING 8 MARCH 1950

RAS AL KHAIMAH:

Two European members of the anti-locust mission were met by a more business like party of Shahu'[37] in the foothills near Qalila, east of Ras al Khaimah. The Shahu' relieved them of some of their clothing and other effects (according to one account their trousers), and took the rifles of the Sharjah guards. Shaikh Mohd bin Sultan[38] of Sharjah has since recovered some of the stolen property, and the Ruler of Ras al Khaimah[39] has been trying to recover the remainder.

Shaikh Humaid bin Mohamed[40] was entertained to lunch at the Company house at Dubai on 19th February 1950.

---

35 Ibri is in the Sultanate of Oman about 140 kilometres south of Buraimi.

36 Bani Ka'ab sheikh. He erected a tower beside the large dune obstacle, the Ramlat Anaij, on the main route between Dubai and Buraimi and demanded a toll be paid by travellers.

37 The mountain tribe of the Musandem Peninsula, Sultanate of Oman. Many of them descend, in the summer, from their terraced gardens high in the mountains. They come down onto the coastal plain, habitually entering Ra's al-Khaimah territory. Their strange language is, by some people incorrectly, attributed to Portugese influence of several centuries earlier.

38 The father of Dr. Sheikh Sultan, Ruler of Sharjah from 1972.

39 Sheikh Saqr bin Mohamed.

40 An elder brother of the Ra's al-Khaimah Ruler.

KELBA:

Shaikh Humaid bin Abdullah of Kalba[41] died on 20th February 1950. Shaikh Khalid[42] has recovered from his illness. He accompanied the P.O. on a visit to Kelba. The people of Kelba have asked for the recognition of Hamad bin Said[43] as Ruler and have stated that they do not wish Khalid to play any part in the government, and requested him to return to Haira,[44] which he has done.

AJMAN:

Two persons were killed in Ajman when a party of Harasis[45] raided the outskirts of the town as a reprisal for a raid made on them (itself a reprisal) by the Ruler during his visit to Dhank last year. The raiders were chased to Biraimi, but were not caught.

DUBAI:

Khalifa Qasaibi's water-drilling operations have begun outside the Ruler's summer palace. However, after a few days of drilling at a depth of less than 100 feet the bit stuck, until rescued by a local Nakhoda, Ra'ay al Boom.[46] The new drilling location is now but a few feet away from the old one.

THE COMPANY:

Location No.1 T.C. officially spudded in on 16th February 1950 at a depth of about 80 feet.[47] The Ruler, his brothers Hiza and Khalid and the P.O.T.C. were all present at the ceremony, but Shaikh Zaid was unable to throw off a very large following, and very considerately stayed away.[48]

On the following day, Shaikh Shakhbut was taken up for a flight in a Company Dove,[49] to see the location from the air. He also caught a fleeting glimpse of Brigadier

41 The deputy of the Regent, Sheikh Khalid.

42 Sheikh Khalid bin Ahmad, the Regent.

43 The son of the previous Ruler. He was a youth when his father died and Shaikh Khalid was appointed Regent.

44 Haira is on the coast a very short distance north of Sharjah. Shaikh Khalid had recently been spending most of the time in Haira and not Kalba.

45 A large tribe from an area of the same name, central in the Sultanate of Oman.

46 Ship's captain. This man seems to have been a 'Jack of all trades' in a society where mechanical skills would have been confined to few such people.

47 Well Ra's Sadr. The first well to be drilled on the Trucial Coast (UAE). The site is marked today. It is beside an asphalted road a few kilometres south of Tawilah. The well was a 'dry hole' and abandoned in 1951. Today it is surrounded by a high wire fence.

48 Sheikh Zayed was a frequent visitor to the drilling rig and the camp.

49 De Havilland Dove aircraft. There is one hanging from the roof in the Mahatta museum in Sharjah. This was the Sharjah airport building dating from 1932/33 and owned by the

S.H. Longrigg,[50] Mr. B.H. Lermitte[51] and Mr. H.M. Jackson[52] who refueled at Sadr[53] before paying a short visit to Sharjah.[54]

NEW ARRIVAL:
Mr. T.L. Hedgcock arrived on 21.2.50 to take charge of the Sharjah Rest House.[55]

Henderson
Representative.

TRUCIAL COAST DIARY FOR PERIOD ENDING 21 MARCH 1950

RAS AL KHAIMAH:
The American sea-plane tender Duxbury Bay visited the town.[56] The news of the robbery of the anti-locust mission has spread throughout Oman[57] to the detriment of our prestige. If they are to continue their activities, travelling in this part of the world will become hazardous.

Ruler. The construction was supervised by an officer from the British Royal Engineers based in Bagdad. The design was based on the fort at Rutbah Wells in Iraq where Imperial Airways already had a refuelling and stop over rest house. The Sharjah Fort was still used as a guest house after airlines moved to new airports in the 1970's. My wife, Frauke, and I attended a dinner hosted there by the late Ruler Shaikh Khalid bin Mohamed in 1969. For more information see STANLEY-PRICE, NICHOLAS, *Imperial Outpost in the Gulf*, The Book Guild Ltd., Brighton, 2012, ISBN 978 1 84624 684 5.

50 IPC Manager from London. He negotiated the 1939 concession agreement with Sheikh Shakhbut.

51 Manager PD(TC) Bahrain.

52 Qatar Petroleum Company (QPC) and PD(TC).

53 Ra's Sadr. PD(TC) had a landing ground and fuel storage for aircraft near Ra's Sadr.

54 Surprisingly they failed to show usual courtesy and call on Sheikh Shakhbut, in part due to a misunderstanding.

55 Then the BOAC later (BA) night stop station. Now the Mahatta Museum.

56 The passengers were from the USA from the Superior Oil Company and Victor Hashem (Lebanese) was among them. They came to negotiate with the sheikhs for oil concessions in the waters of the Gulf. Years later Victor Hashem became a prominent businessman in Abu Dhabi.

57 In those days one might apply the name 'Oman' to the Sultanate and the Trucial Coast, Trucial Oman.

SHINAS:

It is reported that the Wali of Shinas[58] beat off an attack of tribesmen from the Hawasina in reprisal for a raid made some time ago by the Wali. Four of the attackers were killed.

SHARJAH:

Shaikh Mohammed bin Hamad al Sharqi[59] (on a visit to Ajman) was a guest to lunch with the P.O.T.C. in Sharjah. The Rulers of Ajman and Sharjah were present. It is understood that Shaikh Mohammed asked[60] for his independent status to be recognised. This request is a hardy annual.

DUBAI:

The water drilling has again come to a stop. Mohd al Sharqi visited us with view to getting a concession – he even began discussing marine rights. The issue was laughed off.[61]

ABU DHABI:

A strike of coolies – excluding those on the rig – put a stop to the construction work, and work in the stores etc. for 24 hours. The workers returned to work without any concessions being granted. A load of commissariat laundry and the head guard left camp on the same day; only the latter, unfortunately has returned since.

Hiza' and Khalid[62] have spent most of the last month hunting.

A limited liability company consisting of Said bin Shakhbut, Rais Abdul Rahim and Abdullah al Sania'[63] has been formed. All the directors met in Abu Dhabi. Its primary objective is said to be the collection of bird lime from Abu Dhabi islands. This seems a limited objective for so international a concern. Our Company has not been worried by them to date.

Sir Geoffrey Prior[64] accompanied the Representative on a trip to Abu Dhabi. They were entertained to a dinner of cold boiled eggs and coffee.

---

58 On the Batinah coast of the Sultanate of Oman.

59 Ruler of Fujairah, not yet recognised by HMG as a Trucial Coast Ruler.

60 The Political Officer, P.D. Stobart.

61 The geologists only interest in Fujairah was to look at the rocks in the mountains to obtain a greater understanding of regional geology. In those days the oil prospects in the mountains and coastal plain were ranked as negligible, and off-shore not even worth considering.

62 Brothers of Sheikh Shakhbut.

63 From Kuwait.

64 British Member of Parliament.

VISITORS:

Messrs. Thesiger, Salim bin Qabina and bin Ghabaish[65] have returned from Oman and are staying in Dubai.

Henderson
Representative.

LETTER 13 APRIL 1950

Subject: Biraimi

The following brief notes are the result of my last visit to Biraimi.

Mohamed Salimineen[66] is on his way back from the Batina[67] where he has been living on the land and begging money. It is not certain whether he has got any money out of Said Saiyid.[68] He is said to owe from 9,000 to 12,000 rupees in Biraimi Suq. He is said to be on good terms with Zaid,[69] bad terms with Saqr[70] and moderately bad terms with his cousin Mana.[71]

Saqr is at present at feud with Rashid bin Hamid[72] over a question of a date plantation of which the ownership is disputed. The latter is in Abu Dhabi seeking the support of the Ruler. Saqr is alone and on bad terms with Zaid.

Obaid bin Juma'[73] is levying a tax of 10 rupees each way on cars crossing Ramlat el Anaaj.[74] This he claims is his method of proving ownership of the country. He is still on bad terms with Saqr, but the camel dispute is solved.

Mohamed bin Awad in Hafit is perpetually expressing his desire to come to terms with the Company; and Mohamed Salimeen is said to be. Saqr says he will not discuss things with the Company unless the other shaikhs have come to an agreement.

---

65 Two of Thesiger's Rashidi companions from the Sultanate of Oman.

66 Mohamed Salimeen Al bu Rahma al Shamsi from Hafit, Qabil and Sunainah, south of Buraimi in the Sultanate of Oman. Sheikh Zayed's father-in-law for a few years.

67 Coast of Oman.

68 Sultan Said bin Taimur, The Sultan of Oman. In those days sometimes referred to as the Sultan of Muscat and Oman, or just the Sultan of Muscat.

69 Sheikh Zayed bin Sultan.

70 Sheikh Saqr bin Sultan in Buraimi.

71 Mana' bin Mohamed.

72 Al Shamsi, of Hamasa, the village next to Buraimi in the Sultanate.

73 Ka'abi sheikh from Mahadhah, Sultanate of Oman.

74 The sands blocking the way to the north of Buraimi, the route to Dubai.

He still however claims to be paramount Shaikh of the Na'im. Apart from Wahshi[75] at Dhank and possibly Ahmed Salf, all the Naim and Al Bu Shamis claim complete independence of Muscat and will not discuss oil on any other basis.

The slavery flourishes more than ever in Biraimi. Abdullah bin ...[76] and his brother are among the major Najdi operators. Abdullah is still away in Riadh. Prices seem high, nice looking girls apparently fetching Rs. 4,000. The lowest prices are doubled or trebled on selling in Saudi Arabia.

Rashid bin Hamid of Hamasa seals and witnesses documents relating to slavery sales but does not take further part. Members of his retinue however do so.

Zaid still has political ambitions. He still however wants the government[77] to put a P.O.[78] in Biraimi to keep order and stop slaving. He says he would also be agreeable to Said Sayid[79] taking over proper control. He may not mean this. He thinks that if we conclude an agreement with Mohamed Salimeen the remainder will sign. This looks extremely doubtful.

Henderson
Representative.

75 Sheikh Hamad bin Salim al Wahshi of Dhank, western section.

76 My wife, Frauke, recorded a conversation with Abdullah. Unfortunately the tape recording has faded with time.

77 HMG.

78 Political Officer.

79 The Sultan of Oman.

TRUCIAL COAST DIARY FOR PERIOD ENDING 20 APRIL 1950

KALBA:

The Resident,[80] visiting Kalba, is expected to recognise the Ruler as having gained his majority.[81]

SHARJAH:

Superior Oil Company[82] arrived by special K.L.M.[83] and embarked in the launch JENNINGS returning after a four day visit to Abu Dhabi. The Representative also visited the Ruler of Dubai. The K.L.M. charter and the JENNINGS have come back again to Sharjah.

DUBAI:

Qasaib's water well has begun again in a third place. Having come to grief in the second hole. The third hole is about 10 feet away. The Ruler has been spending considerable money on improvement to the water front at various points.[84]

ABU DHABI:

Haza' and Khalid, and the younger generation have returned from a two month hunting trip in Biraimi,[85] and Mr. Lermitte, paid two visits by air. Mr. Stobart[86] paid five visits by air and sea. The Representative paid six visits.

COMPANY ACTIVITIES:

The Seismic Party have moved from Mirfa to Ruwais.[87] Two strikes occurred in Ras Sadr. The second was begun by Hamdan.[88] The guards ran amok and as a result

---

80 The Political Resident, Sir Rupert Hay, based in Bahrain.

81 Sheikh Hamad bin Said, who was only a youth when his father died, hence the appointment of Sheikh Khalid bin Ahmed as Regent.

82 The U.S. company seeking concessions to search for oil in the land under the waters of the Gulf.

83 Royal Dutch Airlines.

84 Henderson was probably referring to the Creek and not the open sea?

85 The desert around Buraimi.

86 Political Agent, Sharjah.

87 Ruwais is 80 kilometres west of Mirfa which is 150 kilometers along the coast west of Abu Dhabi town.

88 Hamdan bin Mohamed. Son of cousin of the Abu Dhabi Ruler.

S.N.O.P.G.[89] called on the Shaikh, later landing with an armed party at Ras Sadr on the 11th April. The situation returned to normal in camp by that date.

GENERAL:

Locusts have been seen in the Mahdha[90] area. Anti-locusts have been seen in the Hadbat Shakhbut[91] area. Swarms are not reported to be as yet large.

Henderson
Representative.

TRUCIAL COAST DIARY FOR PERIOD ENDING 11 MAY 1950

RAS AL KHAIMAH:

The Ruler is having more trouble than ever with the badu. The Zaab are still agitating about the injustice done to them after the murder of one of their number in Ras al Khaimah some months ago, which the Ruler chose to ignore. In fact they are probably only after cash, but went so far as to claim the right to choose a new Ruler. They appear to have been appeased for the time being, but the security in this area is likely to be shakier than before.

Sultan bin Salim[92] is again a free man, and is naturally the centre of a vortex of rumour. He called on the P.O.[93] in Sharjah. The meeting was without incident. The younger generation of his family still maintain the toll on the Muscat road at Huwailat, in the Wadi al Ghor.[94]

SHARJAH:

Superior Oil Company, by aircraft and by their ship, the Jannings, have been frequent visitors on their way to Abu Dhabi and Dubai.

89 Senior Naval Officer Persian Gulf.

90 The large oasis 30 kilometres northeast of Buraimi in the Sultanate of Oman. The Ka'abi headquarters.

91 This is where the land rises to the first sand dunes after the sabkhah a few kilometres due east of Abu Dhabi island. The locusts and the anti-locusts are separated by 130 kilometres of sand dunes.

92 Former Ruler, deposed in 1948.

93 Political Officer.

94 The main, and only motorable route through the mountains when one travelled from Dubai or Abu Dhabi to Muscat.

The Ruler[95] is reported to be undergoing yet another operation in Bombay. He is an unconscionable long time spending his people's heritage.

The Ruler of Umm al Quwain[96] was entertained to lunch in the Company house by Messrs. Lermitte, Codrai, and Henderson.

DUBAI:

Shaikh Mohamed bin Ali al Huwaidin of the Bani Kitab is staying with the Ruler. It is said that he gets more cash out of Dubai than he does out of Sharjah. Possibly this is true. The Ruler[97] and his family were entertained by the Company to a lunch in the new house.[98] The Shaikh of the Bani Kitab was also present.

Gray Macs[99] have a British agent here for the first time.[100]

ABU DHABI:

A snooping party sent by Rashid bin Said[101] arrived in camp but was not permitted by the head guard to see anything. The P.O. has been requested to inform the Shaikhs that the Company cannot give permission to people to enter Abu Dhabi territory, and that we will only consider showing people the camp after they have obtained the permission of Shakhbut.

All four brothers have been in Abu Dhabi for some time, although Zaid is always about to come to camp. It appears he has so far been prevented by the Ruler, who is posing as an injured innocent, and has sent the Company to Coventry.[102] This has not caused the Company any particular discomfort.

OMAN:

Mohammed Salimeen bin Rahmah recently killed two of his own men out of hand, at a wedding, when one of them had accidentally shot a fellow guest from the Bani Kitab. This shooting was contrary to accepted custom in such a case, and the matter may well end with Mohamed Salimeen's own demise if he is not careful.

---

95 Sheikh Sultan bin Saqr.

96 Sheikh Ahmed bin Rashid.

97 Sheikh Saeed bin Maktoum.

98 Company house on the creek.

99 British shipping agent. Gray Mackenzie.

100 George Chapman, still living in Dubai in 2020, was one of first.

101 Son of Ruler of Dubai.

102 In other words not talking to the Company.

Shaikh Rashid bin Hamad al Shamsi[103] came to lunch with us in Dubai (at the same time as Rashid bin Humaid of Ajman). He is spending a fortnight between Dubai and Sharjah.

COMPANY ACTIVITIES:

Mr. Lermitte visited all the rulers with the exception, this time of Abu Dhabi. He called on the ex (?) Regent Khalid at Haira.[104]

Drilling continues without interruption, and the second string of casing has been set.

GENERAL:

The Government doctor[105] is much exercised at the inactivity on the part of Messrs. Holloway and sons, who have been supposed to have been building a hospital in Dubai for some six months. They appear to have achieved nothing, and their local representative has suddenly left the firm with no more to his credit than one barasti[106] hut. Perhaps a local building now would be better than a reinforced concrete one in 1952.[107] The Politicals think otherwise.

The anti-locusts are still with us, as are the locusts. Neither are in strong force. They now have no one here with any even professed, knowledge of the locust or of Arabic. This goes for their Somali interpreter, who does not speak English either. The fact that they get into trouble when they go out does not cause surprise. Fortunately they usually stay at home.

Henderson
Representative.

103 The sheikh of Hamasa – Buraimi.

104 Henderson did not know whether the Regent, his host, was still in charge in Kalba.

105 Dr. D. McCaully.

106 Palm frond or Basra board (reeds) construction.

107 In two years.

TRUCIAL COAST DIARY FOR PERIOD ENDING 24 MAY 1950

RAS AL KHAIMAH:

Ruler still in trouble with his badu. Part of the Bin Qidib gang who murdered Jasim bin Dalim of the Zaab are more or less refugees in Ras al Khaimah and Khat.[108] When Abdullah bin Hassan[109] moves to Khat for his estivage[110] trouble is expected. The Khawatir are agitating for money as usual.

H.M.S. Wren[111] visited the town on 22nd May.

SHARJAH:

Khalid bin Mohamed[112] and Ibrahim Midfa[113] visited Abu Dhabi to settle with Zaid the old question of the date palms in the Biraimi area belonging to the Bani Kitab. The latter have been denied access to them since the Dubai – Abu Dhabi war.[114] A solution is not expected.[115]

The Ruler is thinking of issuing regulations in regard to motor traffic.

DUBAI:

The water well is supposed to be 800 feet deep. No water has been found.

ABU DHABI:

Shaikh Zaid paid a three day visit to camp and saw two film shows. The second was also attended by his mother.

I visited Abu Dhabi, and ate four goats, in the company of Khan Sahib Hussain, who has been accepted by the Shaikhs as a contractor to the Company.

The site of a house at Ras al Bur[116] was tentatively fixed.

The Ruler seems to have made his peace with the Company.

---

108 The warm springs in Ra's al-Khaimah territory about 20 kilometres south of the town.

109 The Sheikh of the Za'ab.

110 To aestivate is to spend the summer and/or to be in a state of torpor (sluggishness).

111 British Royal Navy sloop. (Small warship).

112 Sheikh. Sharjah Ruler 1965-1972. Elder brother of present Ruler Dr. Sheikh Sultan bin Mohamed.

113 A leading Sharjah family and confident of the Ruler.

114 Often referred to as a war 1945-1948. It was in reality more like occasional small skirmishes and Bedouin raids. There were few casualties, with the exception of the Ruwaihah tragedy in January 1948 when more than fifty men died.

115 A solution may not have been expected then, but it did come later.

116 Northeast end of Abu Dhabi island, later in the port area.

OMAN:[117]

Shaikh Zaid, by enlarging wells near Al Ain claims to have doubled the flow of water in the falaj.[118]

Five Rawishid, two of whom were ex-Thesiger's party attacked two Bani Ali and stole their camels. One Bani Ali killed and one wounded; one Rashidi wounded and seeking treatment in Dubai.

Henderson
Representative.

TRUCIAL COAST DIARY FOR PERIOD ENDING 5 JUNE 1950

RAS AL KHAIMAH:

There appears to have been no new development on the bedu situation, which remains tense however.

KELBA:

Towairish the Afari has stolen three women. The Ruler[119] has been lunched by the politicals. He later came to lunch with us in Dubai, and was 2 ½ hours late. When he has had more experience perhaps he will be a day late, like the Al bu Falah.

AJMAN:

Rashid bin Hamid al Shamsi[120] has been paying a prolonged visit to his relatives. The Ruler is building some sort of a house in Dhaid.[121] Perhaps this is part of his policy of aggrandizement.

---

117 In those days, and until recently people in Abu Dhabi who were going to Al 'Ain/Buraimi would say 'I am going to Oman'.

118 The Buraimi/ Al 'Ain oases are fed with water, from aquifers in higher ground nearby, through an extensive network of underground channels. Recent archaeological work indicates that such 'falaj' have existed in the area for 5,000 years.

119 Sheikh Hamad bin Saeed.

120 Sheikh at Hamasa, Buraimi.

121 The writer may mean Manama which is the Ajman oasis about 10 kilometres north of Dhaid.

SHARJAH:

Mr. Pelly[122] is on tour with Mrs. Pelly, and visiting all Shaikhdoms by launch, with the exception of Abu Dhabi.

DUBAI:

Abdullah bin Madhad, has been touring the Shaikhdoms looking for 5 camels stolen by a Mansuri from Hiza'.[123] He ran them to ground in Dubai where the Ruler relinquished the camels readily enough, but declined to punish the miscreant.

Dr. Henry Field paid an anthropological visit to the neighbourhood.

ABU DHABI:

Enemy[124] activity reported near Sir Beni Yas.[125] The Ruler on being informed appeared interested, but not sufficiently to take any action. He scarcely deserves to keep his realms.[126]

Work at the drilling camp was somewhat held up by porous rock, and hence much cementing.

The labour appears contented and the men are working well despite the onset of warm weather.

Henderson
Representative
EFH/KAZ.

122 Political Agent Bahrain.

123 Sheikh, the brother of Sheikh Shakhbut bin Sultan of Abu Dhabi.

124 An ARAMCO party.

125 The large island near Jebel Dhanna and Ruwais in the mid-west of Abu Dhabi territory.

126 Perhaps Sheikh Shakhbut had other ideas? There is evidence that he wanted the Company PD(TC) and HMG (the British Government) to confront Saudi Arabia on his behalf. The King Ibn Saud was held in awe by people on the Trucial Coast.

TRUCIAL COAST DIARY FOR PERIOD ENDING 26 JUNE 1950

As it is Ramadhan there are no reports of anything happening North of Sharjah.

SHARJAH:

The American ship Greenwich Bay[127] paid a visit on the 23rd. The Consul General at Dhahran was on board.

DUBAI:

The old Mana[128] trouble has begun again and heavy guards are mounted at night in all the Daira towers. They make a real effort to stop motor cars at night, but casualties have not been heavy up to date.

The trouble is complicated by the fact that Hamad bin Juma'[129] whose followers murdered two people recently, at his orders, is taking umbrage since the Ruler had occasion to chide him concerning his conduct. He is said to have asked the Al bu Falah[130] to send Manasir to his help, and he is allied to Rashid bin Batti limited and the remains of the old Mana group.[131] A battle is expected nightly, even though it is Ramadhan.

ABU DHABI:

Greenwich Bay and the Consul General Dhahran[132] visited Abu Dhabi. The Political Officer Sharjah accompanied him. It is doubted whether a daylight visit in Ramadhan occasioned much joy.

Hiza'[133] returned from Oman.

Henderson
Representative.

---

127 USA ship and Consul General from Dhahran in Saudi Arabia.

128 The Dubai ruling family may be traced, (for this note) back to Maktoum who died in 1852. He had three sons Hasher, Rashid and Suhail. **Son 1, Hasher** had a son Maktoum. Maktoum had sons Saeed (the father of Rashid and grandfather of present Dubai Ruler Sheikh Mohamed) and Juma, who had a son Hamad. **Son 2, Rashid** has son Mana the father of Suhail and Rashid. **Son 3 Suhail** has a son Buti (Batti here below) and his son was Rashid. HAWLEY, DONALD, *The Trucial States*, George Allen and Unwin Ltd., London, 1970, ISBN 0 04 953005 4.

129 Juma' was a brother of the Ruler Saeed bin Maktoum.

130 Abu Dhabi.

131 Rashid bin Batti (Buti) is a cousin of Mana bin Rashid and Maktoum bin Hashar.

132 The USA Consul General.

133 Sheikh Hazza bin Sultan, brother of Sheikh Shakhbut.

TRUCIAL COAST DIARY FOR PERIOD ENDING 15 JULY 1950

RAS AL KHAIMAH:

The badu who are at present annoying the Shaikh for money appear to be remaining quiet until the end of Ramadhan.

SHARJAH:

Mr. Coulson, solicitor for Fox Andrews K.C.[134] paid a visit with Kanaan al Khatib.[135]

DUBAI:

The likelihood of trouble seems about evens; but it is not thought that anything will occur till after the Eid.

The water drilling continues beyond 1,000 feet, though the quest is now hopeless.

ABU DHABI:

A messenger from Said bin Maktum of Dubai has gone to Biraimi to ask Zaid why he appears to be assisting the Rashid bin Batti – Rashid bin Mana – Hamad bin Juma' faction with many of the Manasir.

Saqr bin Sultan[136] has proclaimed that he will not permit Zaid's men to cross his territory. He does not explain how he will prevent them. Zaid's boasted control over Saqr appears to have evaporated once more.

COMPANY ACTIVITIES:

Drilling continues at Ras Sadr.[137] New pumps are being fitted to increase the sea water supply for the well. Work will begin at the end of Ramadhan on the airstrip, which has a soft patch at the end of the runway, making it unsuitable for Vikings.[138]

Mr. Hamilton[139] paid a visit to Ras Sadr and stayed one night in Dubai with G.W. Henderson.[140]

Henderson

---

134 London based lawyers.

135 Lawyer from prominent Lebanese family.

136 Sheikh at Buraimi.

137 The first oil exploration well drilled on the Trucial Coast. It is in Abu Dhabi territory on the coast and near to the border with Dubai.

138 Aircraft made in UK by Vickers. Carried about 30 passengers.

139 From the London office of IPC.

140 G. Henderson in charge of operations at Ra's Sadr.

Chief Local Representative
EFH/ KAZ.

TRUCIAL COAST DIARY FOR PERIOD ENDING 29 JULY 1950

RAS AL KHAIMAH:

Ramadhan ended with a bang which might well have resulted in dislodging the present Ruler, had it not been for intervention by H.M.G.

On 17th July the Shaikh of Zaab[141] attacked Sha'am[142] killing two people and wounding another four. Realizing that this shooting affair would probably bring all the unrest in his territory to a head the Ruler called for assistance from H.M.G., and H.M.S. "Flamingo"[143] was sent to the scene. In the absence of the P.O.T.C., the Commander of the sloop acted as mediator.

The trouble has been patched-up for the time being, but has, once again, proved the need for a Political Officer on the Trucial Coast at all times.

UMM AL QAIWAIN:

Nothing to report.

KALBA:

Shaikh Khalid bin Ahmed,[144] who is at present living at Hira; is due to go to Bahrein for medical treatment within the next few days.

SHARJAH:

The aerodrome is being extended in preparation for jet-aircraft.[145]

Shaikh Mohd bin Saqr tells a story about propaganda which is being made against the Company. His brother, Shaikh Sultan bin Saqr[146] was visited in hospital in Bombay by an American, who showed him several bottles of oil. "This bottle", he said, "comes from Bahrain, this bottle from Kuwait, and this bottle from Sharjah. The

141 The Zaab tribe were based on the Hamra (Zaab) headland about 10 kilometres south of Ra's al-Khaimah town.

142 Sha'am is about forty kilometres north of Ra's al-Khaimah, near the border with the Omani Musandam peninsula.

143 Royal Navy sloop, (ship).

144 The Regent of Kalba.

145 Small fighter aircraft.

146 The Sharjah Ruler.

R.A.F.[147] found it when they were digging for water[148] - but has the British Company found any?"

DUBAI:

There is still much uneasiness in the air regarding expectation of war with Zaid, and the Ruler's reason (customs!) for doubling the guards in the watch-towers does not carry much weight. Zaid refused to admit two messengers who were sent to Biraimi by Rashid. The possibility that Shaikh Zaid is using Dubai as a cover to mass forces for use against another neighbour cannot be ruled out.

Rumours that the Company is to start drilling operations at Jebel Ali ceased to be rumours, to the practical mind, when Messrs. Browne and Beydoun[149] visited Jebel Ali to plot a geographical position and mark it with a cairn. The rumours, in the first instance, were started when the Company began to run into drilling trouble at Ras Sadr; for the rest, it seems to be public knowledge that Jebel Ali is the best structure on the coast.

Water well drilling near the creek in Dubai has been abandoned, and the rig taken a short distance inland.

ABU DHABI:

Despite the heat, Shakhbut is more than usually friendly and seems to be taking greater pains over his guests these days.

The 'Jamila'[150] arrived at Abu Dhabi on 25th July, and picked up two representatives of the Ruler before starting its operations (looking for signs of unauthorised activity)[151] around the islands of Abu Dhabi.[152]

Ali bin Saif, an ex-Company driver, and one of the first of the Dubai employees to become an Abu Dhabi subject, is in gaol at Abu Dhabi on a charge of murder. It will be of interest to see whether the Ruler exercises any leniency towards him, so as not to discourage others from becoming Abu Dhabi subjects.

COMPANY ACTIVITIES:

Very little progress has been made with the drilling at Ras Sadr. The Company Representative visited Umm al Qaiwain, Ajman, Sharjah, Dubai and Abu Dhabi during the Eid.

---

147 Royal Air Force.

148 No chance of finding oil at the depths that the R.A.F. were drilling to.

149 PD(TC) geologists.

150 PD(TC) landing craft.

151 ARAMCO.

152 Island survey.

Codrai
Chief Local Representative
RAC/KAZ.

TRUCIAL COAST DIARY FOR PERIOD ENDING 15 AUGUST 1950

RAS AL KHAIMAH:

The Ruler, Shaikh Saqr bin Mohamed, visited the Company Representative in Dubai on 2nd August, the same day having been summoned to Sharjah by the P.O.T.C.[153] in connection with the recent trouble in his territory. There have been no further outbreaks of unrest in Ras al Khaimah, but the Ruler seems to be having his usual financial difficulties, trying to raise sufficient cash with which to keep quiet some of his dissident subjects.

UMM AL QAIWAIN:

The Ruler has been living at Falaj al Ali[154] for several weeks past; and little is heard of him except that he is suffering the summer rather badly.

SHARJAH:

The Political Agency in Bahrein made the usual attempt to abandon its responsibilities on the T.C. this summer, but was unsuccessful. The P.O.T.C. was sent to Doha on permanent transfer at the end of June, the post there having been up-graded due to the seniority of the Ruler's Adviser, but events on the T.C. soon necessitated his return, and he arrived back in Sharjah on 24th July.

DUBAI:

There has been noticeable activity among the merchants in Dubai, opening commercial agencies that many of them have held for years without troubling about. A large party of Indian merchants arranged an excursion to Ras Sadr, but were referred to the P.O.T.C. when they asked the Company Representative for permission for their visit. The power-station project is still in the air, and the engines have actually been ordered, but the Ruler will not say whether it is to be a private or a state-financed Company until he sees the engines!

---

153 Political Officer Trucial Coast.

154 His inland oasis and gardens. North of Dhaid. During the hot and, on the coast, humid summer months people would retreat to their inland oases where the climate was much more bearable. It is hotter inland, but drier.

ABU DHABI:

The Jamila finished her operation in Abu Dhabi waters on 4th August.[155] During the operation, she was compelled to go to Umm Said[156] for three days, owing to an outbreak of sickness aboard. Shaikh Shakhbut left Abu Dhabi for a few days to go hunting – a rare excursion for him.

COMPANY ACTIVITIES:

Drilling operations have continued very slowly[157] and a depth of about 6,600 feet has been reached.

On 31st July two Abu Dhabi subjects (non-Company employees) were electrocuted at Ras Sadr whilst playing with an electrical drill in the M.T.[158] workshop, which they entered without permission. They were brothers, and their father,[159] a Company guard, was on duty outside the workshop when this sad and unfortunate incident occurred.

The water distillation units at Ras Sadr ceased to function properly for a short spell and Ras Sadr was kept supplied from the wells at Dubai for about a week.

Codrai
Chief Local Representative.

TRUCIAL COAST DIARY FOR PERIOD ENDING 30 AUGUST 1950

AJMAN:

On about 23rd August, Shaikh Rashid bin Humaid[160] was reported missing, presumably killed, from an operation against a section of the Awamir tribe that had been troubling his people. However, a few days later the P.O.T.C. received a verbal message from him saying that he was very much alive, and unhurt.

155 The IPC marine surveyor was on board conducting a survey of Abu Dhabi islands.

156 Oil export terminal in Qatar. IPC associated company QPC.

157 At Ra's Sadr.

158 Motor transport.

159 Ali bin Shaiban from a prominent Abu Dhabi family.

160 The Ajman ruler.

SHARJAH:

On 24th August a Sharjah taxi, which was stuck in the sand between Tawi Rashid[161] and Falaj al Ali[162] was attacked by Tuwairish, who made off with about Rs. 25,000[163] and a female slave. It is significant that two Dubai subjects including one woman who were passengers in the taxi, were not robbed. Perhaps the Ruler of Sharjah now regrets the present of a rifle and money which he made to Tuwairish recently.

Shaikh Saqr bin Sultan,[164] followed later by Shaikh Mohd bin Saqr[165] gave chase to Tuwairish, but all their vehicles broke down, and three days later they returned to Sharjah in a taxi.

DUBAI:

Great excitement was created, early during the period under review, when a messenger dashed into Dubai one night with the news that water was gushing out of the ground at Ruwaiya,[166] the site of the water-well drilling operations. A night of celebrations followed this news, but next day visitors to Ruwaiya saw only a trickle of sea water. Casing has been put down the hole and drilling continues.

Shaikh Rashid, accompanied by a party of about sixty, (including thirty women) is due to leave Dubai on 31st August to go on pilgrimage. He is taking seven cars and going by the overland route and, with the permission of Shaikh Shakhbut is going through Abu Dhabi territory and stopping the night at Ras Sadr. Shaikh Rashid told the Company Representative that he thinks that the differences between Abu Dhabi and Dubai will soon be settled, and that he hopes to arrange a meeting with Shakhbut when he returns from Mecca. Apparently, the ball was started rolling in this direction by a visiting Qadi from Al Hasa, who approached both Rashid and Shakhbut in turn and told them they should end their unholy quarrel.

A local type of launch, loaded with a thousand tins of Company petrol, which had been hired for a single trip from Dubai to Ghanadha,[167] caught fire near the A.I.O.C. [168] Agents Depot in Dubai creek and was a total loss.

The Ruler has been informed verbally, by the Representative that the Company plans to drill in his territory next year.

161 About ten miles west of Dhaid.

162 About ten miles north east of Dhaid.

163 Rupees 25,000.

164 Son of Sharjah Ruler.

165 Brother of Sharjah Ruler.

166 About fifteen miles south of the inland extremity of the Dubai Creek.

167 The petrol was for operations at Ra's Sadr.

168 Anglo Iranian Oil Company at Abadan. Later BP.

ABU DHABI:

Shaikh Shakhbut has informed the P.O.T.C. that he intends to visit Bahrain, in the near future, and make his peace with the Political Agent.

Shaikh Shakhbut was summoned to Bahrain by the Political Agent four months ago, following the Hamdan incident[169] and visit of the H.M.S. FLAMINGO to Ras Sadr.

COMPANY ACTIVITIES:

Drilling operations at Ras Sadr have reached a depth of about 7,500 feet.

Shaikh Haza and Shaikh Hamid bin Buti[170] visited Ras Sadr in August and were entertained there for two days. Although the main purpose of the trip was to discuss Company business with the Representative, both Shaikhs, and practically the whole of their party, received medical attention from the A.M.O.[171] Doctor Semmenkian.

Codrai
Chief Local Representative.

TRUCIAL COAST DIARY FOR PERIOD ENDING 13 SEPTEMBER 1950

SHARJAH:

Bin Gatim, and not Tuwairish (as previously reported) was responsible for the raid on the Sharjah taxi on 24th August. However, not to be outdone, Tuwairish and his party raided another Sharjah taxi on about 8th September and killed one Sharjah guard and wounded another two. Shaikh Saqr bin Sultan[172] gave chase to the raiders, and succeeded in recapturing two slaves and some ammunition. Tuwairish is reported to still be in the Wadi al Qor- Falaj al Ali area, and all traffic to the Batinah[173] has stopped.

The Ruler of Ajman has been asked by the Rulers of Sharjah and Umm al Qaiwain to lead a combined force from the three Shaikhdoms against the Awamiri[174] bands in their territories. He has agreed to this provided that the P.O.T.C.[175] gives

---

169 At Ra's Sadr.

170 Shaikh Hamid bin Buti was the maternal uncle of Sheikh Shakhbut and all his brothers.

171 Acting Medical Officer.

172 Sharjah Ruler.

173 The Indian Ocean coast, Sultanate of Oman.

174 It seems that this large desert tribe, who were found in inland areas of the Trucial Coast, the Sultanate of Oman and Saudi Arabia, had some unruly and criminal elements who enjoyed the Bedouin sport of raiding.

175 Political Officer, Trucial Coast.

permission, and the others consent to the killing of the principal culprits as soon as they are caught.

On 8th September the P.O.T.C. publicly announced that the Trucial Coast Levy Force would be formed next winter. Apparently, about twenty Arab Legionnaires[176] are to be sent here for the initial recruiting and training, and the force is to be based with the R.A.F.at Sharjah.

DUBAI:

Shaikh Rashid[177] and his party stopped the night at Ras Sadr on 31st August, when he left by the overland route for Mecca. Shaikh Saeed,[178] and very nearly all the other Dubai Shaikhs, surprised everyone by arriving at Ras Sadr shortly after Rashid. It seems that they only intended to see Rashid as far as Jebal Ali, but after Saeed had hunted a rabbit or two he found himself so near to Ras Sadr that he just had to have a look at the camp. The Abu Dhabi guards at Sadr were not overjoyed to see the party, although one of their members was later reported missing, gone on a pilgrimage with Rashid.

News has been received that Rashid arrived at Mecca on 13th September.

Work has begun on the foundations of the hospital in Derra.[179]

A Dubai launch carrying about 80 passengers sank off Doha[180] on 1st September and 36 people are reported to have been drowned.

There has been a fresh outbreak of stories about a Manasir attack on Dubai, and most of the Dubai Badu have moved in near to the town.

The drilling of the well at Ruwaiya was stopped at 700 feet, and no further attempts at finding water are to be made until Rashid returns.

ABU DHABI:

The ex-Company employee, Ali bin Saif, who is imprisoned in the fort at Abu Dhabi, has had more shackles put on him following an unsuccessful attempt to escape.

---

176 Recruited from Jordan. From the British point of view these men were very suitable. However did the British take into consideration that at this time when relations between Britain, acting for Abu Dhabi, and Saudi Arabia were strained it would be unwise to bring Hashemite soldiers to the Trucial Coast? 'Ibn Saud's increasingly agitated complaints about the TOL ... and what was obviously a conspiracy to encircle him with his Hashemite enemies'. KELLY, J.B. Edited by S.B. Kelly, *Desert dispute*, Gerlach Press, Berlin, 2018, p. 317. ISBN 978 3 95994 024 5.

177 Son of Dubai Ruler.

178 Dubai Ruler and father of Sheikh Rashid.

179 Deira, (Derra) is on the north side of the creek, while Dubai is on the south side.

180 Qatar.

COMPANY ACTIVITIES:

Drilling operations at Ras Sadr have continued to a depth of about 8,000 feet. Casing[181] has been laid to about 7,500 feet.

The camp ran dangerously short of water on 9th September, and was supplied from the wells in Dubai.

Shaikhs Saeed and Rashid, and about a hundred relations and followers were entertained to dinner by i/c Operations and the Representative, when Rashid's party stopped the night at Sadr.

Shaikhs Khalid bin Sultan[182] and Mohamed bin Khalifa[183] visited the camp on 12th September.

Codrai
Chief Local Representative.

TRUCIAL COAST DIARY FOR PERIOD ENDING 8 OCTOBER 1950

RAS AL KHAIMAH:

Shaikh Mohamed al Sharji[184] recently visited Ras al Khaimah to settle a minor dispute within the territory.

SHARJAH:

The Awamiree have caused Shaikh Mohamed bin Saqr[185] much concern of late, not so much because of their taxi raiding activities (although they recently made another attack on a Sharjah taxi), but because of the flagrant manner in which they are able to threaten and insult him. The Awamiree bands boast that they are strong enough to attack Sharjah town itself, and many of the people in Sharjah are quite ready to believe them. They have also threatened to fire at the P.O.T.C.'s car if they see it. It is estimated that bin Gatami and Tuwarish[186] have about thirty-five and forty followers respectively.

---

181 A 7,500 foot long pipe run in the well which is cemented in to prevent the sides of the hole from falling in. Drilling is then resumed through the pipe.

182 Brother of Sheikh Shakhbut.

183 Cousin of Sheikh Shakhbut.

184 From Fujairah.

185 Brother of Sharjah Ruler and father of the present Ruler Dr. Sheikh Sultan bin Mohamed.

186 Tawarish was from the small tribe, Ifar.

Shaikh Mohamed[187] has had a bad time listening to the criticism directed at him by the northern Shaikhs, each of whom has in turn reminded Mohamed of the present he made Tuwarish[188] last year. They accuse him of being too mean, and of not looking after his followers well enough. The Awamiree bands have now been reported as having withdrawn to the 'Ibri[189] area, and Mohamed has escaped to Ras al Khaimah for a few days rest.[190]

Towards the end of September, the P.O.T.C. called the northern Shaikhs together to discuss the plan to send a combined force against the Awamiree, but it fell through when Ahmed bin Rashid[191] of Umm al Qaiwain suggested that it would be neither proper nor effective unless Dubai and Abu Dhabi joined forces with them.

KALBA:

Shaikh Khalid bin Ahmed, the ex-Regent of Kalba, who has been admitted to the Government Hospital, Bahrein, is reported to be very ill.

DUBAI:

The Superior Oil Company Representative visited the Ruler of Dubai[192] on 8th October. He arrived by Boswerth's[193] 'plane, landed on the road at Derra, and took-off again about five hours later. The purpose of the visit was to present a Chevrolet saloon car (which arrived by B.I. Boat the previous day) to Shaikh Saeed, and to measure the house of Shaikhs Saeed, Juma, Hasher etc. for wiring, and the fitting of a generator which Superior are going to present to the Shaikhs.

---

187 Ruler's brother.

188 Kelly wrote 'Tuwarish who Thesiger describes as a 'notorious outlaw' performed several services for the Saudis in 1954 and 1955. In January 1955, for example, he successfully guided an arms caravan to Buraimi by a route south of Liwa.' KELLY, J.B. *Eastern Arabian Frontiers*, Faber & Faber London, 1964.

189 In the Sultanate of Oman south of Buraimi.

190 Dr. Sheikh Sultan bin Mohamed, Ruler of Sharjah wrote of a meeting between his father Shaikh Mohamed bin Saqr and Stobart, the Political Officer 'My father said angrily, 'the bandit attacks will not cease as long as the British Government restricts its interests to the coast, and gaining full control of that area alone. They have failed to take control of the interior regions". AL-QASIMI Sheikh Dr. SULTAN MOHAMMAD, *The Myth of Arab Piracy*, Routledge, USA, 1988, ISBN 0 415 02973 2, p. 54. The British Government did take note and had already set in motion the establishment of a military force; the Trucial Oman Levies, later called the Trucial Oman Scouts. The Primary function of the force was to maintain law and order.

191 Ruler of Umm al Quwain.

192 Sheikh Saeed bin Maktoum.

193 Founder of Gulf Aviation, now Gulf Air.

ABU DHABI:

The Ruler, accompanied by his son Saeed, and Hamdan[194] left Abu Dhabi for Bahrein by launch on 18th September. He is expected to arrive back in Abu Dhabi about 12th October. Shaikh Mohd bin Khalifa,[195] who accompanied Shaikh Shakhbut to Bahrein, has gone to the Lebanon for medical treatment.

COMPANY ACTIVITIES:

Drilling Operations at Ras Sadr have continued to a depth of about 8,700 feet. At 8,300 feet the bit twisted-off,[196] but was recovered the next day.

Shaikhs Zaid and Khalid visited Ra Sadr on 4th October 1950.

Codrai
Chief Local Representative.

TRUCIAL COAST DIARY FOR PERIOD ENDING 27 OCTOBER 1950

RAS AL KHAIMAH:

Shaikh Saqr bin Mohamed, the Ruler, visited the Representative in Dubai on 12th October, 1950.

SHARJAH:

The Anti-Locust Party is preparing for its winter activities, and most of its European members are due to return to the T.C. at the beginning of November. Arrangements are being made for the Party to work in the Biraimi area.

The third Trucial Memsahib[197] is expected to arrive shortly. The British community on the T.C. is gradually getting larger, as can be seen from the following figures:

194 Hamdan bin Mohamed bin Khalifa, The eldest son of Sheikh Shakhbut's cousin.

195 Sheikh Shakhbut's cousin.

196 When a very deep well is drilled the vertical hole is not exactly straight as the drilling bit 'wanders'. The drill pipe may stick against the side of the well and torque may build up in the pipe which, when released, may unscrew part of the pipe. There follows a 'fishing job' which may, or may not, be successful. In the case described here the drill bit became unscrewed. The driller then tries to screw back into or grab the drill bit 'the fish' with a 'fishing tool'. The drill bit is the cutting tool at the bottom end of the drill pipe.

197 European lady.

	Autumn 1948	Autumn 1949	Autumn 1950
Dubai	1	2	3
Derra	1	1	6
Sharjah (excluding R.A.F. and Main Locust Party)	6	7	8
Total	8	10	17

DUBAI:

Shaikh Rashid bin Saeed returned from Pilgrimage by the overland route arriving in Dubai on 20th October, 1950. Shaikhs Saeed and Juma, and many others, were entertained by the Company for three days at Hassian,[198] where they awaited Rashid's return.

It is remarkable that all seven of Rashid's overloaded vehicles should have returned to base. The journey on return from al Hasa to Dubai took 5 days.

To everyone's surprise, Rashid returned empty-handed from Riyadh,[199] although since his return Dubai has been disturbed by a siren, said to have been removed from the King's escort car.

This year's pearling season has been good and very profitable, although at the moment the market in Bombay is said to be poor. One of the many merchants who have come to Dubai to buy pearls is Jassim Derwish of Qatar.

P. Stobart, the P.O.T.C., is leaving the T.C. shortly, on transfer to the Foreign Office. Before he departs, he hopes to effect a reconciliation between the Rulers of Dubai and Abu Dhabi. Shaikh Saeed has already expressed his willingness to meet Shakhbut.

ABU DHABI:

The Ruler returned to Abu Dhabi from Bahrein on 19th October, having visited Umm Saeed,[200] Dalmah,[201] and many other places in his territory en route. On his return, he was entertained to lunch by the Representative aboard the hired-launch Simen, anchored outside Bait ash Shammal.[202]

---

198 On the coast in Dubai territory near the border with Abu Dhabi.

199 This is surprising and unusual. Kelly's view is also contrary to normal custom. 'Ibn Saud was more likely to bully the shaikh than treat him generously' KELLY, J. (2018), p.321.

200 In Qatar territory, but Sheikh Shakhbut never gave up his claim to Umm Said.

201 Large island in western Abu Dhabi waters.

202 Abu Dhabi sea front.

Since his return, the Ruler has also been visited by the Superior Oil Company Representative, who landed at Abu Dhabi by 'plane.

Shaikh Mohamed bin Khalifa and his party, is leaving Baghdad for Bahrain by air on 30th October.

KALBA:

The Ruler, Hamad bin Saeed, came to Dubai to visit the Representative on 17th October, during the latter's absence.

COMPANY ACTIVITIES:

Gravity meter Party No.4 started work in Abu Dhabi territory on 13th October. Drilling operations at Ras Sadr have continued to a depth of about 9,200 feet.

Shaikh Haza visited Party No.4 on 15th October and Ras Sadr on 16th October.

BIRAIMI:

A ... member of W. Thesiger's parties, killed a man and a woman in Saqr bin Sultan's[203] territory recently, and escaped into the southern sands, taking a captured slave-girl with him.

Codrai
Chief Local Representative.

TRUCIAL COAST DIARY FOR PERIOD ENDING 20 NOVEMBER 1950

RAS AL KHAIMAH:

There have been two further attacks on Sham,[204] and trouble in the Rams[205] area caused by Mohammed bin Hamid al Malik the Shaikh of Bakha.[206] The P.O.T.C. intervened with the Flamingo.[207] The Muscat Wali of Khasab[208] "persuaded" the Shaikh of Bakha to accompany him to Muscat.

---

203 Sheikh Saqr bin Sultan was the representative in Buraimi of the Sultan, Saeed bin Taimur of the Sultanate of Oman.

204 Sha'am on the Gulf coast about 40 kilometres north of Ra's al-Khaimah town.

205 Rams, Tunaiji tribe, on the Gulf coast about 15 kilometres north of Ra's al-Khaimah town.

206 In Sultanate of Oman territory. On the Gulf coast a few kilometres north of the border with Ra's al-Khaimah.

207 Naval vessel, a sloop.

208 The main town on the Musandem peninsula.

There have been other minor troubles in the Ras al Khaimah area. Two of Abdullah bin Hasan's men from Jez. Zaab[209] were killed near Ras al Khaimah apparently at the orders of … . This is thought to be a reprisal for previous killings.

UMM AL QAIWAIN:

The Resident visited Umm al Qaiwain on seventh November and formally presented the Ruler with the M.B.E.[210] A guard of 24 sailors and approximately 30 sailor spectators were present. The ceremony went off very well, except that the townsfolk feared their Shaikh was about to lose his head when the officer of the guard drew his sword to salute him.

Bin Qitami the robber has "made peace" with Sheikh Mohammad in exchange for a fat bribe, thus ensuring a further period of insecurity in the area.

DUBAI:

The proceeds from the customs have been reckoned by a reliable source to be over a lac[211] a month. These are net proceeds and exclude the slice taken by the customs chief.

ABU DHABI:

Shaikh Shakhbut came within 20 miles of Sadr while hunting and i/c operations paid him a visit. Shaikh Mohammed bin Khalifa is still in Abu Dhabi after his return by air from the Lebanon. The Company arranged (and paid for) his direct arrival by air to the capital.

BIRAIMI:

A queer customer is visiting Biraimi, and all stations south, under the name Abdulla Farij and Abdulla al Zamil al Sulaim. He appears to use the first name for the general public and the second when talking to shaikhs. He carries a letter purported to be signed by one Abdullah Karim an alleged Saudi official, introducing himself to the shaikhs of Oman. The letter is believed to be written and signed by the bearer, as his handwriting is well known. This Ruritanian character states that he is an emissary of Bin Saud and an American oil company and holds forth on the subject of the lavishness of American concession payments.

Mohd bin Salmeen Bin Rahama and Shaikh Yasir[212] of the Janiba called on the P.O.T.C. and P.D. (T.C.) Dubai.

---

209 Jezirat al Hamra.

210 Member of the Order of the British Empire.

211 A Lac Rupees. One hundred thousand Rupees.

212 Yasir bin Hamud al Haja'li was the Sheikh of the Janiba at the time of writing, A large tribe scattered along the eastern and southern parts of the Omani coast as well as in the desert.

Negotiations to get the locust party past Biraimi and on to Sunaina[213] (reported as completed in my DO to you) appear to be creaking to a probable impasse.

Saqr of Biraimi has sent an emissary with the news that he wants to come to an agreement with the British Government on the subject of oil and is following shortly in person. It is too early to place much significance on this message, but it is thought that it may not be unconnected with the visit of the self-styled representative of an American company. The temptation to try to play A off against B would be too much for Saqr to resist.

COMPANY ACTIVITIES:

The Gravity Party are in the last stage of the campaign in the far west.

Jamila[214] with Captain Holden and a survey party have arrived at Khor Ghanadha, and two representatives from Abu Dhabi have been sent to meet them.

Mr. Fortescue has arrived to take over from G.W. Henderson[215] as I/C operations while the latter is on home leave.

P.S. According to the P.O.T.C. Abdullah al Zamil is a discredited Saudi official who has probably being bought up by A.R.A.M.C.O. He is believed to have taken photographs, spent Rs. 10,000 in tips and visited Dhank, Ibri, and possibly even the Batina.

Henderson
Representative.

Bird wrote that 'he does not exert much control over the scattered portions of his flock'.

213 In the plain about 70 kilometres south of Buraimi.

214 PD(TC) survey vessel.

215 Not to be confused with E.F. Henderson, who wrote this report.

TRUCIAL COAST DIARY FOR PERIOD ENDING 29 DECEMBER 1950

RAS AL KHAIMAH:

The shaikh of Bakha has returned via Dubai (where he was saluted and welcomed), from Muscat. It is not known what exactly Said Ahmed bin Ibrahim[216] has said to him, but there is peace at present in the Rams – Sham area.

The Ruler of Ras al Khaimah visited Dubai and called on the Representative PD(TC).

KALBA:

The locust mission are establishing a post at Kalba. A large swarm of locusts came and went while the locust officers were enjoying Christmas and New Year's entertainment. Otherwise this area has been free of the pests and little or no damage has been done.

An American ship visited Khor Fakan, about a month ago, but no one came ashore.

Recent rain has made the emergency landing ground unsuitable for use, unless in grave emergency, owing to new growth of plant life.

SHARJAH:

A raiding party of eight bedu seeking to attack cars and caravans on the Faiya[217] route ran into a larger band of Bani Kitab ... One Rashidi and the remaining Amiris talked their way out of it and arrived at Dubai and Sharjah respectively, less all their weapons, camels, money etc. Codrai and Henderson missed this little foray by an hour or so.

DUBAI:

The customs jetty is now equipped with a crane. Trade appears to be increasing daily. Jamila and Nasr[218] visited Dubai, and Captain Holden[219] declared the creek navigable to all Company craft.

---

216 Minister of the Sultan of Oman.

217 Jebel Faiyah is on the route from Dubai and Sharjah to the Wadi al Quor and on to the Batinah coast. Faiyah is south of Dhaid and the sands reach as far as the Jebel, there is then a wide mountain foreland plain before entering the valleys (wadis) in the mountains.

218 PD(TC) vessels.

219 The IPC/PD(TC) marine surveyor.

ABU DHABI:

It is fairly reliably reported that Shaikh Zaid has left for Muscat, at short notice, and Hiza and Khalid have gone to Biraimi in his place. This is remarkable in view of Zaid's statement after his last visit that he would not go there again.

Trouble was caused by the coolies at Ras Sadr when the leave routine was altered. Order was restored without any coolie actually downing tools.

BIRAIMI:

There is no further news from Biraimi, nor any sequel to the activities of Saqr mentioned in the last diary. It is thought possible that as Abdullah al Zamil was so well equipped with money he must in fact have represented an oil company or Bin Saud, in spite of the repudiation by the Saudi Government.

One locust officer is proposing to establish himself in Biraimi.

OTHER ITEMS:

The Arab legion officers and men who were expected have been delayed as their transport cannot be sent here as early as had been planned.

The Bani Kitab will remain in charge of police activities.

P.S. Since this diary was written information has been received that Shaikh Zaid has arrived at Muscat.

Henderson
Chief Local Representative
EFH/KAZ.

LETTER 29 DECEMBER 1950

Henderson wrote to Lermitte:

The new Ruler[220] appears to have the situation in Kalba and Khor Fakan under reasonable control. However he was hampered at the outset by three difficulties. His accession was preceded by considerable disorders. At the same time the Sheikhly family's popularity was at a low ebb. Thirdly the financial position left by Khalid[221] was

220 Sheikh Hamad bin Said, Ruler of Kalba. When his father Sheikh Said bin Hamad died in 1937 Sheikh Hamad was a minor and a regent, Sheikh Khalid bin Ahmed the former ruler of Sharjah (1914-1924) was appointed. Sheikh Hamad bin Said became ruler in April 1950.

221 Sheikh Khalid bin Ahmed, the Regent.

bad; taxation was most irregular, and, because it was resented, was effectively resisted by the bigger merchants. In addition Khalid retained the car given by the Company and has now sold it. As there is no car in Kalba or Khor Fakan, the new ruler was obliged to buy one, and to the purchase of this his reduced concession payment will be devoted for many months.

The ruler has made several requests for assistance. I informed him that the Company was not prepared to assist him at present, but that of course I would mention his comments to you, without however any hope that anything could be done for him.

Although the situation is quiet and orderly, there is no doubt that the ruler is in a weak position. There is no relation to help him rule his scattered domains, except the ineffective Saqr who has gone to Dibba. The ruler is anxious to learn, but lacks any good advisors. His chief companion at present is a certain Mubarak bin Esa who is quite intelligent, but is a Baluch and does not appear to command much respect. Mohd bin Hamid al Shirqy[222] seems to be pressing him on all sides, though officially the ruler and Mohd. are on good terms.

In general it appears that unless the ruler receives some financial aid and advice his land is likely to continue to dwindle to the gain of Mohd. On the other hand he is obviously taking interest in the local crops and growing of vegetables, which are sent to Sharjah for sale. He is however debarred from making any notable improvement by lack of funds. For example the petrol engine of the water pump in Kalba has broken down and it seems doubtful he can get it going again. It looks like a return to cow and rope tactics.[223]

The ruler was most hospitable and friendly during our recent visit and spent two days with us. He appears to appreciate his difficulties and is indeed somewhat bitter about them. No doubt there is no way in which we can help him, but I thought you might be interested to hear something of the present situation.

222 Fujairah sheikh.

223 To old traditional way to raise water from the well.

1951

TRUCIAL COAST DIARY FOR PERIOD ENDING 16 JANUARY 1951

RAS AL KHAIMAH:

At the end of December the Locust Mission set up a camp North of Jazirat al Hamra[1] at the beginning of the sand dunes. They were surrounded by the Zaab and forced to move out. The Zaab stated that they were at war with the Shaikh of Ras al Khaimah, and that the locust camp was in the way. This was of course an exaggeration. The Ruler and the shaikh of Jazirat al Hamra are not on good terms as a result of inter-tribal murders over the past twelve months. The Ruler of Ras al Khaimah states emphatically that the Locust Mission did not ask for his permission to camp, and he has not yet heard officially of the incident. If this is true it is yet another instance of the locust party provoking trouble.

The Bakha – Sham trouble seems to have died down altogether.

The Ruler appears to be a little nervous of Sultan bin Salim's[2] activities in Dubai and Sharjah. As the latter is however without any cash, it is not apparent what damage he can do.

SHARJAH:

The new P.O. Mr. Michell returned from Bahrein after his marriage; his wife is accompanying him. This is some-thing new in Sharjah history. They both left on the 5th for Khor Fakkan by launch.

---

1 On the coast a few kilometres south of Ra's al-Khaimah town. The Jazirat al Hamra was the home of the Za'ab tribe.

2 Previous ruler of Ra's al-Khaimah.

The acting ruler of Sharjah[3] is doing his best to invite himself to Ras Sadr. The Company, aided by the P.O., are doing their best not to invite him. The acting ruler of Sharjah was seen recently on the road to Umm al Qaiwain with 15 guards in his truck. He recommended that the Company should carry many guards owing to the danger of robbers. He was informed that the Company is not accustomed to fear robbery in his lands, but the shaikh was unable to endorse this sentiment.

Bin Gabaish was released on the request, apparently, of Shaikh Hiza.[4] The acting ruler has evidently decided not to take a strong line with robbers. Probably Bin Qataimi will be week-ending with him again before the winter is over.

DUBAI:

The first guard arrived at Location No.1[5] on the 9th of December, but work did not begin until after Christmas. There are now 4 covenanted staff in residence at Jabal Ali; the sea line is laid,[6] and many of the roads are cut. The site is exceptionally difficult owing to loose sand. There are 70 coolies at work on the site. Shaikh Rashid[7] keeps visiting the camp, and a very careful eye is kept on our recruitment in Dubai in order to exclude "foreigners".[8] All the minor shaikhs have been making futile attempts to get us to employ their useless hangers on.

The ruler has a very much improved lighting plant installed, apparently, by courtesy of American oil.[9]

ABU DHABI:

Shaikh Zaid is reported to have returned to Biraimi,[10] having visited Matrah[11] in order to see Dr. Tomes.[12] Zaid has been suffering from malaria. Members of his family also saw the doctor.

Khalid and Hiza'[13] are still away hunting in the Biraimi area. Shakhbut is still petulently claiming Jabal Ali as his territory.

---

3 Sheikh Mohamed bin Saqr. Father of present ruler of Sharjah, Dr. Sheikh Sultan bin Mohamed.

4 Sheikh Hazza bin Sultan brother of Abu Dhabi Ruler, Sheikh Shakhbut bin Sultan.

5 The second drilling location on the Trucial Coast at Jebel Ali (Dubai location No.1).

6 To bring sea water to Jebel Ali.

7 Son of Ruler Sheikh Said bin Maktoum.

8 That is, that only Dubai subjects could be employed by the Company.

9 Superior Oil Company. They were trying for offshore concessions.

10 Not Buraimi in The Sultanate of Oman. Probably Muwaiji, an Abu Dhabi oasis in the Buraimi group of oases.

11 The town next to Muscat.

12 At the Mission Hospital.

13 Sheikhs Khalid, Hazza and Zayed. All brothers of the Ruler Sheikh Shakhbut bin Sultan.

Drilling continues at Ras Sadr, at a depth of over 11,000 feet. The dismissal of 10 coolies caused a slight stir. Perhaps it was regarded as a red light.

The Al bu Falah[14] are reduced to one car again; that presented to them by the Shaikh of Bahrein.

BIRAIMI:

Saqr[15] has sent a message asking after our health. We replied that it was good, and asked after his. He appears to be quite isolated. Mohamed bin Salimeen[16] is reported to have left Bahrein for the Mamlakah.[17]

It is now said that the tower which Obaid bin Juma[18] constructed on the Ramlat al Anaij by the motor track, was built on Zaid's advice. All cars pay Rs. 10 to pass it. It is said that Zaid – early last year – sent his own car to pay the tax first. The idea was to provoke Saqr[19] to fight for his territory or else to force his public acknowledgement that he did not own Ramalat al Anaij. Saqr's car was the second to pay the Rs. 10.

This is part of Zaid's policy, which he has been fairly consistently carrying on over the past year, of hemming Saqr in, and isolating him. Saqr's brief hegemony seems to have been completely dissolved in the space of a year, but Zaid's boasts that he would do away with him altogether have not come to anything.

Zaid is probably perfectly happy to see the Naim and Al bu Shamis disunited and weak, and probably has no intention of abolishing so useful a thorn in the flesh of all his neighbours.

It is now reliably reported that the reason for the Locust Mission's failure to penetrate South of Biraimi is chiefly that the shaikhs are convinced that they are really looking for oil. They apparently cannot decide whether it is P.D.T.C. – or Oman and Dhofar[20] – in disguise, or competitors of ours. The Locusts[21] do not know of this, and there are other reasons for their failure to date, such as fear of the poison which they use.

Henderson
Chief Local Representative.

---

14 Sheikh Shakhbut and his family.

15 Sheikh Saqr bin Sultan, Sheikh of Buraimi and representative of the Sultan of Oman.

16 Shamsi sheikh from Sunainah and Qabil in the Sultanate of Oman and close to the Abu Dhabi border. Father of Sheikh Zayed's first wife, 'Alia, since divorced without issue.

17 The Kingdom (Saudi Arabia).

18 Ka'abi sheikh from Mahadhah, in the mountain foreland in the Sultanate of Oman, north of Buraimi.

19 Sheikh Saqr bin Sultan of Buraimi, Sultanate of Oman.

20 The same IPC associated company Petroleum Development Oman and Dhofar.

21 Meaning the survey team.

TRUCIAL COAST DAIRY FOR PERIOD ENDING 4 FEBRUARY 1951

RAS AL KHAIMAH:

The ruler by subterfuge and force, in equal proportions, gained control of Jaz. Al Hamra.[22] The key was the tower on the mainland near the well - one of the two guards was suborned, the other persuaded to go away to collect firewood. At this moment 15 of Saqr's men, who happened to be about the place, walked into the tower. Saqr was sent for and arrived with the army. The son of the Zaab shaikh Hasan bin Abdullah sallied forth to the mainland to war and was captured. A nice little note was sent over to his father: "Dear sir unless." Abdullah bin Hassan[23] came across, gave up the island to Saqr and himself to durance, pretty vile, in Saqr's fort.[24]

Saqr's brother has been put in charge of the Jazira, taxes on the export of charcoal and firewood have been reduced from 20% to 5% ad valorem. The inhabitants express their loyalty and love of the Qawasim. They have not much alternative.

The shaikh of Bakha is said to be continuing his policy of encouraging the Habus[25] to rebel. However Saqr's victory in the south[26] may give people seriously to think in the north. It is said that he is intending to chastise Rams. We may be in time to join in with geological hammers.

KALBA:

The Locust party seem to be firmly established on the aerodrome.

The Falaj at Dhaid[27] dried up for 20 days. It is now running again, but with less water owing to the collapse of the sides.

Khalid bin Ahmad is reported to be setting up house in Daira.[28] He is in better health this year.

---

22 The Za'ab island (peninsula or island) Jazira al Hamra or Jajira al Zaab..

23 Sheikh of the Za'ab.

24 Perhaps I need to remind the reader that Hassan bin Abdullah means Hassan the son of Abdullah, and Abdullah bin Hassan means Abdullah the son of Hassan. It happens sometimes that we have Hassan bin Abdullah bin Hassan bin Abdullah, representing 4 generations.

25 The Hubus and Shihuh are the mountain tribes on the Musandam peninsula, (Sultanate of Oman).

26 Jazira al Hamra and Rams on the coast to the south and north of Ra's al-Khaimah town respectively.

27 The Kalba ex-Regent, Sheikh Khalid bin Ahmed was still claiming Dhaid as part of Kalba territory. The falaj at Dhaid was famous for the volume and strength of the water flow. But a falaj does need regular maintenance.

28 Dubai territory across the creek from Dubai town.

SHARJAH:

It has now got abroad that the ruler is intending to go to London.

DUBAI:

Shaikhs Mohamed bin Salimeen and Obaid bin Juma[29] called on the Representative.

Cable & Wireless Ltd. have concluded an agreement with the ruler and intend installing telephones in the town and possibly some form of communication with Sharjah.

It is reported that a box containing 5 lacs[30] of currency, being smuggled out of Bombay on behalf of high Dubai personages, has been seized and confiscated by the Indian authorities.

The first Company aircraft landed on Jabal Ali airstrip.

ABU DHABI:

Two cars were landed at Khor Ghanadha.[31] The Ruler has recruited several drivers. More are expected to be landed at Dubai and taken down by road. Some or all these cars are presents from Superior Oil Company. The Ruler returned the launch he bought recently from Murshid because he did not like it. He had not paid for it anyway.

Henderson
Chief Local Representative.

29 Shamsi and Ka'abi sheikhs. Sultanate of Oman.

30 500,000.

31 The temporary wharf created by PD(TC) before drilling the well at Ra's Sadr.

TRUCIAL COAST DIARY FOR PERIOD ENDING 22 FEBRUARY 1951

RAS AL KHAIMAH:

The shaikh of Bakha[32] has renewed his attacks on Sham.[33] Reports of the fighting give casualties as 7 Shihu and 5 from the ruler's people. Nearly half the casualties appear to be women. A five day Truce was agreed on the 20th. The P.O.[34] was to go up to establish terms at Sham on the 22nd, but was summoned precipitately by news that the ruler had been captured, and that Sultan bin Salim[35] was in occupation. This proved to be false. The P.O. returned to Sharjah. He is now proposing to go up by launch on the 23rd. The P.O. asked the P.A. for a sloop, in response to Shaikh Saqr's appeal for assistance against a foreign enemy from outside his lands. The P.A. refused to send one, saying that the shaikh must fight his own battles. The shaikh wanted to know, rather pertinently, what in that case is the point of having a treaty with H.M.G., which imposes restrictions and bestows no tangible benefit?

In the midst of all these alarums and excursions a geological party with Dr. Hudson, and Messrs. Browne and Beydoun was moving, under the direction of Codrai, in the area, without radio communication, and with rather shaky transport. They reached the watershed of the Wadi Milaha, on foot, on the 21st. The Ruler was most co-operative, but a great variety of guards was needed to ensure their safety among the Habus; and even then they were restricted in their movements in any direction but along the Wadi itself.

The situation in Jazirat Zaab (Hamrah) is quiet. Abdullah and son are still imprisoned, but have been given a carpet to sit on.

AJMAN:

A Sharjah boat with a very valuable Bahrain cargo was taken by its Ajmany Nakhoda to Ajman without the owner's permission. The shaikh of Sharjah sent a launch in pursuit and a fight ensued. The boat ran aground and the cargo was "salvaged" by the people of Ajman. This promises to outdo Mis'ilat al Baush[36] in Trucial litigation.

---

32 On the coast north of Ra's al-Khaimah and in the Sultanate of Oman, Musandum peninsula.

33 It was reported in the December 1950 diary that the Sheikh Mohamed bin Hamid al Malik of Bakha had been to Muscat and met the Sultan's Minister Said Ahmed bin Ibrahim and although it was not known what was said it was reported that there was peace in the north. Was this renewal of serious fighting provoked by the people of Sha'am? Whether or not, the Ruler of Ra's al-Khaimah, Sheikh Saqr bin Mohamed, supported his Sha'am people.

34 Political Officer.

35 Previous Ruler of Ra's al-Khaimah, deposed in 1948.

36 Camel court cases.

SHARJAH:

The P.R. and the Ambassador[37] for Jeddah visited Sharjah and Dubai. Their aircraft unfortunately killed a Sharjah guard.[38] They did not have time to call at Bait Lermitte,[39] having asked us, in writing, to be ready for them (as usual): last time they had the grace to wave, this time they did not.

The ruler has gone to London by air.

DUBAI:

The hospital may be ready in June. It is to be opened by Lady Hay in November. It is to be hoped they will use it in the meantime. Rashid has gone to Persia, and came to lunch with us, before leaving. The ruler is shortly leaving for Karachi for eye treatment. Rashid will return first. Most of the shaikhs have made several visits to Jabal Ali, but have caused no trouble at all, and only want to be left alone to look. Entertaining them frequently in Dubai has provided a way of bypassing the need to do anything for them at Jebel Ali.

The levy officer[40] brought his soldiers to tea, and afterwards presented them to the ruler.

ABU DHABI:

More cars have arrived from Superior.[41] The Ruler has engaged a fitter.

Zaid is hunting near Biraimi and is recovered from an operation for hernia. He is shortly visiting Abu Dhabi.

It is very nearly certain that an American Sloop and a British Political Officer managed to arrive simultaneously in Abu Dhabi with a Superior[42] representative in an aircraft.

It is hoped shortly to confirm or not this information. If it is confirmed by signal it will be referred to as "paragraph X" of our letter of the above reference.

BIRIAMI:

Shaikhs Mohd. Salmeen Biraham[43] and Obaid bin Juma[44] called here several times in the past days. There have also been other visitors from Biraimi.

---

37 British ambassador.

38 Not so. The man was killed by a saluting gun.

39 The PD(TC) house. Lermitte was the Bahrain manager through the war years (1939-1945) and until 1952.

40 The recently established 'Trucial Oman Levies'.

41 The American company seeking concessions to search for oil off-shore.

42 Superior Oil Company.

43 Shamsi sheikh in Qabil and Suneinah. Sultanate of Oman.

44 Ka'abi sheikh in Mahadha. Sultanate of Oman.

Shaikh Saqr bin Sultan appears to be isolated for the time being, as a result of the activities of Zaid bin Sultan, and Obaid bin Juma. He has been territorially constricted as previous reported, by Obaid's tower in the Ramlat al Anaij. Zaid has, for the time being, suborned the allegiance of Mohd. bin Salimeen from Saqr.

Mohd. appears to have picked up some money and clothes on his travels. He visited Dhahran and Riyadh, but makes no veiled threats about any conversations or understandings with American interests.

Mohd. states that in an interview with the P.R.[45] in Bahrain he agreed to meet Saiyid Said[46] in Muscat, in the presence of the P.R. and admit his allegiance to him. He acknowledges that he can only come to any understanding with us through Saiyid Said. He stated that, while the Muscat meeting was not what Zaid wanted, he hoped to remain on good terms with him. He said, that what he wanted was for Zaid to arrange an agreement between the Al bu Shams and the company, and that he proposed this to the Resident, who pointed out that the matter was nothing to do with Zaid, but was the affair of Muscat. Mohd. then stated that he would do whatever the Resident asked, and would happily agree to be a subject of Bahrein if that would please him.

Mohd. said no more about requesting a treaty with the Dawlah,[47] but stated that he wanted an oil agreement with us in which, as long as "his rights" were recognised, any other ruler whom the Resident named could participate. He states that he refused entry to the Locust Mission because he wanted to prove his good faith with us first and not allow anyone in before us.

What percentage of the reported conversation with the Resident is true there is no means of telling from here. However it shows something of his present state of mind. The reason given for refusing the Locusts is probably the opposite of the truth, as I understand that he really believes that Locust Mission is a cunning move on our part to gain access under new colours.

I gained the impression that Mohd. has been improved by his travels, and his interview with the Resident. He appeared much more responsible and reasonable than before.

Other sources state that if all the Al bu Shams shaikhs go to Muscat, Saqr will go, for fear of being left out. The difficulty of getting Saiyid Said and his shaikhs in the same place at the same moment is well known. One can believe in this meeting when one has seen it happen in fact.

Henderson
Representative.

---

45 Political Resident, the senior British official in the Gulf, based in Bahrain since 1946.

46 The Sultan of Oman, Saeed (Said) bin Taimur.

47 The British Government.

TRUCIAL COAST DIARY FOR PERIOD ENDING 21 MARCH 1951

RAS AL KHAIMAH:

A geological party consisting of Dr. Hudson, Browne, Beydoun and Codrai spent nearly a month in the Wadi Milaha area, and also to the South around Adthan.[48] Their visit coincided with the war between the Ruler and the Shaikh of Bakha.[49] There is no doubt that the Shaikh of Bakha is being supported by the Muscat Government. After several people had been killed in the Rams area the P.O. arranged a truce. Juma bin Maktum of Dubai also attempted to mediate. The Habus[50] did not support the invaders as expected, but remained loyal to their ruler. This may have been due to the fact that owing to the shortage of water in the hills they are relying this year on the wells in the plain, and these are controlled by the Ruler.

The Ruler attached too great an importance on the expedition,[51] and he expects a rig[52] to follow at once. He spent thousands of rupees paying each little tribe in each wadi for the right of enter the Wadi. The Habus and Masari'a,[53] who had not received what they expected from the concession money, were able to extract sums from the Ruler, but no settlement was reached between Saqr and the Khawatir.[54] Much additional trouble was caused by the fact that the geologists originally asked only to see the Wadi Milaha itself. The Ruler had to enlarge his plans at very short notice. If no further work follows, any subsequent geological expedition will probably experience much more trouble getting into the area.

The telegram stating that the geologists wished to visit Jabal Shuam was of no use whatever. A special visit was paid to Ras al Khaimah to inform the Ruler of proposed visit to this mountain. No one had heard of it. This is not surprising as we subsequently discovered that the name was invented by Glyn-Jones. The inventing of names, that sound like Arab names can cause considerable confusion and trouble. If no names exist, perhaps the Himilayan practice of using letter and figure symbols could be employed.

---

48 In the hills about 20 kilometres northeast of Dhaid, Ra's al-Khaimah territory.

49 In the Sultanate of Oman, on the coast a few kilometres north of Ra's al-Khaimah territory.

50 A tribe who divided their time between the mountains of the Musandam peninsula and the plain.

51 The geologist's expedition.

52 Oil drilling rig.

53 Ra's al-Khaimah branch of this tribe, Mazroui.

54 The Khawatir are a large Na'im tribe occupying the Jiri plain south of Ra's al-Khaimah town and north of Dhaid. Bird wrote that a small number of the tribe (Saloof section) were also in Hafit village. Hafit is in Abu Dhabi territory south of Buraimi.

The Ruler has again requested an advance.

UMM AL QAIWAIN:

The Ruler is suffering from serious diabetes. It is thought that he will seek treatment shortly in India or Bahrein.

SHARJAH:

The levies[55] are installed at Sharjah now number 35 men of the Arab legion[56] under Major Hanken Turvin.

Mr. Wilton has taken over as P.O. from Mr. Michell.

The Ruler's family returned from Pakistan on the 20th. The steamer made a special call for them.[57]

DUBAI:

The Ruler left for Pakistan on the 1st of March. A strike in Jabal Ali camp on March 1st was settled under the direction of the I/C operations. The strikers demand for higher pay for 6 rig coolies was granted. This is the first strike the company has lost on the Trucial Coast. The Representative has not yet been informed that it took place.

A further car has been landed for Abu Dhabi, a present from Superior.

Shaikh Khalid[58] has been prevented by the Qawasim from selling Dhaid to Dubai.

ABU DHABI:

Hiza' is alone in Abu Dhabi. Zaid has returned and paid a visit to Abu Dhabi. His operation for hernia by Dr. Tomes in Matrah[59] was successful. Shakhbut is in the South West, and said to be moving towards Liwa. He has sent a load of water to Mirfa.

55 Trucial Oman Levies. Later Trucial Oman Scouts.

56 Jordanians.

57 The British Indian Steamship Navigation Company was no longer calling at Sharjah, having transferred to Dubai. This was a special stop for the Sharjah Ruler who was very displeased at the change.

58 Sheikh Khalid bin Ahmed, Regent of Kalba.

59 At the Mission hospital.

Seismic have camped at Tarif,[60] near Radaim.[61] They experienced great trouble in landing, as Mirfa[62] was denied to them by the Politicals.[63]

Ras Sadr has reached 13000 ft. and work has stopped, awaiting fresh orders from London.

Henderson
Representative.

TRUCIAL COAST DIARY FOR PERIOD ENDING 15 APRIL 1951

RAS AL KHAIMAH:

The ruler is seeking a large subsidy from politicals. Sultan bin Salim[64] is trying to get a larger cut from the ruler's subsidy. The ruler therefore called on us; and asked, for the hundredth time, for a fat loan. He was referred to previous conversations he has had with the Manager P.C.L.

Sultan bin Salim has, of course, been mixed up with the intrigues surrounding the office of ruler in Sharjah. He is supporting Mohamed.[65]

Mohammed bin Salim[66] of Ras al Khaimah was called in to Sharjah to solve the succession problem.[67] After a week he admitted himself defeated.

No further news on the Bakha front.

---

60 Tarif is on a hill beside the sea about 100 kilometres west of Abu Dhabi town. The centre for oil operations in the desert for about 30 years.

61 Radaim (Rudaim) is on the coast about 10 kilometres west of Tarif.

62 Mirfa is on the coast about 30 kilometres west of Tarif. The Levies (Trucial Oman Scouts) later had a post here for many years but at the time of writing the Saudi Arabian territorial claim had not been resolved. HMG, to avoid a confrontation or provocation, prevented the Company PD(TC) from operating in areas claimed by Saudi Arabia.

63 The Saudi Arabian border claim extended to Mirfa. The tide goes out a very long way for most of the coast commencing from about 50 kilometres west of Abu Dhabi town and extending towards the west as far as beyond Sila in the far west.

64 Previous Ruler and uncle of Ruler Sheikh Saqr bin Mohamed.

65 Mohamed bin Saqr, brother of deceased Sharjah Ruler, Sheikh Sultan bin Saqr. Father of present ruler, Dr. Sheikh Sultan bin Mohamed.

66 The Ra's al-Khaimah Ruler's father.

67 After the death of the Sharjah Ruler, Sheikh Sultan bin Saqr.

UMM AL QAIWAIN:

The Ruler has left for Matrah,[68] presumably for hospital treatment, in view of his diabetic condition.

SHARJAH:

The Ruler died in London on the 23rd of March. His body was brought in an Airworks Dakota, chartered specially by the I.P.C. to Sharjah. The aircraft arrived on the 2nd of April. The funeral was something of a fiasco. The P.O. was away meeting the P.R. in Dubai. (on his way to Muscat by the B.I.).[69] The levy commander had been away, and in his absence a levy officer had arranged with Shaikh Mohamed,[70] against the latter's wish, that the levies should participate. The outcome was a proof that such ceremonies were better left to the local people to arrange. There rose an argument as to whether the body should be carried, or put on a truck, and if so whose. The levies occupied the centre of the scene. Eventually a levy jeep was produced, closely followed by an R.A.F. ambulance. The jeep was decided upon. The coffin was put on board and four levies climbed in with it. As a result the crowds who hoped to have the honour of carrying the coffin, were unable to do so, and were kept at a distance by files of levies who marched behind.

Meanwhile various members of the British community climbed on the roof of taxis to take photographs.

However the Shaikhs were most grateful to the Company for their assistance in supplying a special plane. – whatever the shortcomings of the funeral the Company was in no way to blame – very much the contrary.

When the news of Sultan's death first came, Saqr[71] gave up his claim, in front of his uncles, to Mohammed.[72] He subsequently retracted this, and, after prolonged discussions in which other Qawasim[73] shaikhs were called in, it was decided that the Shaikhs should meet in the Agency in the presence of the P.O. The issue is still undecided. Hiza'[74] visited Sharjah, probably concerning the affair.

---

68 Next to Muscat in the Sultanate of Oman. A medical clinic was opened in Matrah in 1904 by an American nurse. The story of the work of the American Mission that followed can be found in the book DR. DONALD AND LOUISE BOSCH, (2000) *The Doctor and the Teacher.*

69 British Indian Steamship Navigation Company.

70 Sheikh Mohamed bin Saqr. Brother of the deceased.

71 Saqr bin Sultan son of the deceased.

72 Mohamed bin Saqr, brother of deceased and father of Dr. Sheikh Sultan bin Mohamed.

73 The Ra's al-Khaimah and Sharjah Qasimi sheikhs are closely related.

74 Haza bin Sultan, brother of Sheikh Shakhbut, Ruler of Abu Dhabi.

The Bani Kitab, or a large part of them,[75] are partly in revolt against Shaikh Ali bin Mohamed bin Hawaidin.[76] They claim that they are not receiving enough of the concession payment. Shaikh Ali in turn says that he hardly gets anything at all. The malcontents robbed a Sharjah truck near Dhaid. They say that they are going to go on robbing until they get some money from Ali.

Shaikh Ali asked Rashid bin Said[77] to meet him and the tribal leaders to settle the matter. No one however was at the rendezvous when Rashid arrived owing to a rumour that some Rashidis,[78] and Amiris[79] were about to attack the Bani Kitab.

DUBAI:

Rashid has refused the generator Superior[80] offered him, as it is too old. He has asked for a new one.

The Ruler of Ras al Khaimah was taken round Jebal Ali camp by the Representative.

A man, accidentally shot near the company house, was flown in special charter at the Ruler's expense, to Bahrain.

Superior representatives visited the ruler.

Shaikh Juma and Hashir[81] are having a serious row about a land settlement. The latter appears to have fixed the matter in his favour, in his own court, and his brother is somewhat vexed.

The ruler began a transport service on April 12th for coolies from Jabal Ali, going on leave. Two vehicles carried the 106 men quite comfortably and only broke down once.

ABU DHABI:

Superior have paid more visits to Abu Dhabi, on one occasion bringing counsel with them to discuss the arbitration.[82]

Shakhbut has returned from his hunting trip.

---

75 Living near Jebel Faiyah south of Dhaid.

76 The writer means Mohamed Ali al Huwaidin. Mohamed features prominently in the Company reports. His nephew Ali is Ali bin Abdulla.

77 Dubai Ruler.

78 From the Sultanate of Oman.

79 Awamir.

80 Superior Oil Company.

81 Younger brothers of the Ruler Sheikh Saeed bin Maktoum.

82 The arbitration to take place in Paris where Sheikh Shakhbut claimed that the whole sea area was not included in the PD(TC) concession. PD(TC) claimed that the entire sea area was included, both territorial waters and continental shelf. Superior were seeking concessions to search for oil in the sea waters of several sheikhdoms.

Zaid is trying to improve the Hiza al Baush[83] road, and has cut a new route.

A Pontiac has arrived for the ruler, a present from Superior. It is fitted with air-conditioning. The ruler has, for the time being, quite a fleet of vehicles, and a mechanic to maintain them.

Hiza' refused the offer of a lighting plant, which Superior made.

Superior's apparent generosity to the Al bu Falah is creating an impression up and down the coast.

An unconfirmed report states that Shakhbut is to visit some of the northern shaikhs at the instance of Superior to do their business. This seems improbable, and the validity of the report will be further checked.

A further unconfirmed report has it that Shakhbut has given the ruler of Umm al Qaiwain a launch.

Seismic party are experimenting, fairly successfully, with a Tourneau Dozen[84] in the heavy sand south of Tarif.

Shaikh Hiza' paid a visit to the Jassoura[85] at Khor Ghanadha.

Henderson
Representative.

83 The high dunes about 20 kilometres west of Al Ain/Buraimi and on the main route to Abu Dhabi.

84 Large truck made by Chevrolet.

85 The PD(TC) landing craft.

TRUCIAL COAST DIARY FOR PERIOD ENDING 9 MAY 1951

AJMAN:

On 1st May, Ali bin Rashid[86] gave chase to a troublesome band of Harassis,[87] and killed two. Another two escaped, and were given sanctuary by Ahmed bin Rashid[88] of Umm al Qaiwain.

SHARJAH:

An impressive and well-arranged ceremony took place in Sharjah on 8th May, at which the Political Resident made a short speech in Arabic, bestowing official recognition on Shaikh Saqr as Ruler. Within the family, the question of inheritance had been settled nearly two weeks before the ceremony, when the Political Officer and other members of the British Community attended a dinner given by Saqr, although the reason for the party was not made known at the time. The delay in H.M.G.'s recognition of Saqr was caused by the Foreign Office.

Shaikh Khalid bin Sultan[89] and the Midfa family seem to have been the organisers of the ceremony, which was held outside the fort, where the principal guests were seated in a covered enclosure at the end of an open rectangle, which was thickly lined by the people of Sharjah, one side having been reserved for the womenfolk. A well-arranged group of some two hundred schoolboys sang during the ceremony, and the T.C. Levies provided a guard of honour. However, the coffee servers and Fuwala[90] carriers seemed to be operating without orders, and took pity on the guard of honour, which was standing to attention in the sun. The persuasive powers of the slaves won over the Army Handbook, and one by one the levies stood at ease to swallow a peach and drink a cup of coffee.

The announcement that Saqr was to be Ruler was well received in Sharjah, and, in particular, among the other Trucial Shaikhs. Shaikhs Rashid and Juma of Dubai, Rashid bin Humaid and Ali of Ajman and Hamid of Kalba, were among the many shaikhs present.

The day following the ceremony the Political Resident, escorted by the T.C. Levies, left by the Wadi al Qor route for Kalba.[91]

---

86 Eldest son of Ruler of Ajman.

87 From Sultanate of Oman.

88 Ruler.

89 Younger brother of new Ruler of Sharjah.

90 Small sweet snacks.

91 News only came later that this visit was cancelled.

DUBAI:

At the beginning of the month there was another scare that Sohail bin Mani,[92] Manaseer[93] and Bin Hiraz[94] were about to attack Dubai, and Shaikh Rashid took all the usual precautions and doubled the number of guards in the watch-towers, etc.

There is a gradual expansion around the fringes of Dubai, and every day the Ruler's Court has to deal with disputes about land or property.

Shaikh Saeed[95] returned by boat from Pakistan on 18th April where he underwent treatment for his eye and knee troubles. He claims that his condition is much improved by the treatment he received.

ABU DHABI

R.A. Codrai visited the Ruler in Abu Dhabi on 17th April, and afterwards met E.F. Henderson who took him on a visit to Zaid and initiated him into the Biraimi scene.

The Anti-Locust Party has abandoned its watching activities in Biraimi for the time being, and has retired to Sharjah where it will tick-over for the summer.

COMPANY ACTIVITIES:

The General Manager Persian Gulf, and I/C Operations Trucial Coast spent the night in Dubai on 5th May, where they met the whole British Community from Dubai and Sharjah.

The 1st June has been announced as the provisional spudding-in date for Jebal Ali.

The Seismic Party has had several labour troubles, during the period under review, which are the fruits of the poor basis which the party started-off on this season. This is the subject of a separate report.

R.A. Codrai visited the Ruler of Abu Dhabi on 9th May, following an incident in the Seismic camp in which an Abu Dhabi guard struck the M.P. Camp Supervisor. Credit goes to the Ruler for removing the guard without further ado, but he was well informed of events in the camp, and had several criticisms to make concerning them.

Codrai
Representative.

---

92 From the disaffected branch of the Ruling family. Suhail bin Mana' bin Rashid bin Maktoum. The Dubai Ruler was Said bin Maktoum bin Hasher bin Maktoum. Hasher and Rashid were brothers.

93 Presumably allied to Abu Dhabi.

94 There is no indication of who this was.

95 Dubai Ruler.

TRUCIAL COAST DIARY FOR PERIOD ENDING 17 JUNE 1951

UMM AL QAIWAIN:

The Ruler is not enjoying good health and spends much of his time at the Falaj.[96]

SHARJAH:

The Levy mutiny of last month, which took place on day of the coronation,[97] and at the last moment prevented the P.R. from visiting Kalba by land, seems to have been a very serious affair.[98] A Lt. Col. from Amman has been down, and one of the officers has been sent away. The incident will not raise the levies, by now not very high, prestige. None of the dozen or so new recruits are said to have been implicated. The policy of bringing so many obviously non-badu, and probably non-Arab, officers and men with the newcomers, is seen to be part of the trouble.

Bin Qitami held up one of the Sharjah Shaikhs – Humaid bin Saqr and robbed his vehicle.

The Bani Kitab appear to be at peace again internally, after several months of trouble.

DUBAI:

Jabal Ali No.1 was officially spudded in on June 2nd at about 700 feet. The G.M.[99] was present, and the ruler was entertained to dinner after the ceremony. Mr. Lermitte came, as did some people from Qatar. Mr. Jackson[100] not being invited did not come.

On the 4th a strike, affecting one shift on the rig and for half an hour all the camp coolies, was ended by the arrival of the Ruler. Complaints were raised about water shortage, and the food, especially the frequent Dhall and rice meals.

An ice factory belonging to Mustafa Abdul Latif began to function in June.

The Ruler is suffering from Jaundice.

ABU DHABI:

For a month or more 11 armed men have been encamped on the Abu Dhabi side of the Muqta, guarding the island against unknown enemy.

The Company house is said to be completed.[101]

---

96 His inland oasis.

97 Queen Elizabeth in London.

98 Two officers and a sergeant were returned to the Arab League.

99 Company General manager.

100 Presumably a Political Officer. A.J. Wilton was the Political Officer at the time. Did Henderson have a problem with him?

101 The house was at the far north eastern end of Abu Dhabi island.

A strike took place as a result of Friday working on the 8th June. This is the first strike in Abu Dhabi and Khor Ghanadha since April 1950. As a result the Jassoura, picking up Seismic party No.3, was delayed a day in her departure.

Hiza' and Khalid have just returned from Biraimi. Shakhbut has just left for Muscat, where he is taking some of his women folk to visit the American Mission Hospital. Salama[102] was with the party which so far has made a snail-like progress, reaching a point near the Dubai-Abu Dhabi frontier in two days. The transport seems plentiful for once, but the M.T.[103] available in A.D. is reduced to the normal level i.e. one Chevrolet, less wheels, outside the entrance to the fort.[104]

The majlis in the fort is now graced by a cheap table, said to be for the Americans to eat on, as they have been complaining of cramp in the legs.

BIRAIMI:

There appears to be a fresh declaration of everlasting friendship between Zaid and Saqr bin Sultan.[105] Recently Said bin Rashid al Baluchi,[106] Mohd. bin Salimeen Birahma,[107] Ahmed al Salf,[108] Obaid bin Juma[109] and others all gathered at al Muaiqi[110] to have a palaver with Zaid. It is said that oil was discussed, and that one or other of these Shaikhs is likely to call on us shortly. Mohamed. bin Salimeen is said to have left for Muscat.

The levies chasing Bin Qitami reached Dhank. They found their quarry sheltering with Mattar bin Salim[111] and could not touch him. They have nothing particular to report. Zaid helped them, Saqr did not. Several new recruits were collected from the Al bu Shaams and others. It is said that the people of Dhank thought some of the levies were Nasranies[112] and were annoyed about it. Some of the soldiers have red hair.

Henderson
Representative.

102 Sheikh Shakhbut's mother. Salama bint Buti.

103 Motor transport.

104 The party going to Muscat would have been on camels.

105 The Buraimi sheikh.

106 From Mazam near Ibri, west of Dhank and 100 kilometres south of Buraimi in the Sultanate of Oman.

107 Al bu Shamis from Qabil and Sunaineh in the Sultanate of Oman.

108 From Hafit in Abu Dhabi territory. Khawaitir section of Na'im.

109 From Mahadha. Ka'abi. All four sheikhs from the Sultanate of Oman meeting in Sheikh Zayed's majlis in Muwaiji.

110 In those days the main Abu Dhabi village in Buraimi oasis.

111 Mattar bin Salim Al Azizi Al bu Shamis sheikh.

112 Christians.

TRUCIAL COAST DIARY FOR PERIOD ENDING 13 JULY 1951

KALBA:

On the last day of Ramadhan the ruler, Hamid bin Said[113] while sleeping in his room in the castle was awakened by the appearance of Saqr bin Sultan bin Salim,[114] Ali bin Amir and three others. The Ruler was with Ali bin Hazim and four of his men. None had arms within reach. They were murdered ... who were armed with rifles. It is not known whether Saqr's brother Khalid was party to the affair.

Khor Fakkan[115] and Kalba are now in the hands of Saqr and his men. Khalid is said to be in control of Khor Fakkan.

Saqr bin Abdulla[116] is said to be still in the Kalba part of Dibba.[117]

It will be remembered that Ali bin Amir was at one time chief adviser and secretary, in the regency period, to the acting ruler Hamad.[118] He was however driven out by Ali bin Hazim, who supplanted him when Hamid bin Said became Ruler.

This event has caused a considerable stir on the coast. It is said that if the murderers are not brought to justice by His Majesty's Government, the new ruler of Sharjah will be in a difficult position. He is on bad terms with his brothers, and he constantly fears a coup d'etat on the part of Mohammed bin Saqr, his uncle.

This example in Kalba will give all other Qawsim rulers seriously to think, unless the usurpers can be punished.

Sultan bin Salim[119] is said to have written to Saqr bin Sultan of Sharjah to disown his son's acts. Opinion in general holds that this action would not have been taken by the son without the advice of the father. Opinion as to whether Mohamed al Sharqy[120] is implicated or not, is divided. Since he profits by a weak ruler in Kalba, the likely answer is in the negative.

It seems incredible that the deceased ruler of Kelba was fool enough to leave the palace unguarded. Stories of his misrule, and the connivance of the towns-men of Kalba in the crime, are now current as a matter of course. Imprisonment and ill-

---

113 Ruler of Kalba.

114 Son of former Ruler of Ra's al-Khaimah.

115 Now Sharjah territory on east coast.

116 Qasimi Shaikh. His grandfather and great grandfather were Qasimi Walis in the Qasimi part of Dibba. Today Dibba is divided between Sharjah Qasimi Dibba, Fujairah Dibba and Sultanate of Oman Dibba, (Baiyah).

117 Dibba lies across the border between the Emirates and the Sultanate of Oman (Musandam).

118 Does he mean the Regent Sheikh Khalid bin Ahmed?

119 Previous Ruler Ra's al-Khaimah.

120 Of Fujairah, awaiting British recognition as a 'Trucial State'.

treatment of the Shaikh of the Naqbyin,[121] who appealed to Saqr bin Sultan bin Salim, is said to have been the excuse for the attack.

RAS AL KHAIMAH:

There has been further raiding by the Amaris and other tribes, this time in the Ras al Khaimah area. Bin al Gabaisha and others have got away with six camels.

Bin Rakadh of the Awamir declared war on all Qawism Shaikhs and Ajman and Umm al Qaiwain as well. Later bin Hamm[122] arrived and patched up a general peace all round.

UMM AL QAIWAIN:

Shaikh Ahmed who has been suffering from diabetes is said to be a little better, and proposes going on the next haj. He has patched up a little family squabble with Ajman, The rulers are again on good terms.

SHARJAH:

Saqr's rule appears to be satisfactory within the town, but he is having trouble with his relatives, as reported above.

His brother Khalid, having seen the world and learned to speak English, is now too big for his boots and may be calculated to cause some sort of trouble sooner or later. He appears to be on good terms with one of the locust officers. They evidently have not learned the danger of being on intimate terms with young and ambitious relatives of rulers, in Arab countries.

The non-arrival of the Gulf aviation Anson[123] on the 20th June caused considerable alarm. It was found to have force-landed outside the fort in Abu Dhabi.[124] Having filled up with M.T. spirit it took off again the following day. Local opinion is not favourably impressed by this performance.

The American Air Sea Rescue amphibian flew over this aircraft at approximately 800 feet, in daylight, without seeing it.

It is reliably reported that the ruler of Sharjah has purchased the oasis of Dhaid from Khalid bin Ahmed[125] for the sum of Rs. 6,000. His guards are said to be in occupation. It will be remembered that Shaikh Khalid attempted to sell Dhaid some time ago to the ruler of Dubai, but the Qawasim prevented him.

---

121 A large East Coast and valleys tribe.

122 Of the two Awamir sheikhs Salem Bin Ham was closer to, and a strong supporter of Sheikh Zayed.

123 Small passenger aircraft. The reader can see one in the Sharjah Mahatta museum.

124 The first Abu Dhabi airstrip was outside the Fort (Husn).

125 The ex-Regent of Kalba.

DUBAI:

The hospital being complete, the contractors have left, but Dr. McCaully[126] refused to take over the hospital on some feeble excuse. The local ward is being completed by a local contractor.

The ruler's son is meddling with the Bani Kitab to such an extent that he has now more control over the tribe than has the Shaikh of Sharjah. He claims to have settled the outstanding trouble between two sections of the tribe, and to be on the way to settling Bin al Gabaisha's[127] difference, in favour of the latter.

The ruler has recovered from jaundice.

With Rashid's approval a known agitator was discharged from Jabal Ali[128] without any trouble resulting. Fish has been very short[129] locally and there have been complaints from the coolies. However two fishermen are now employed at Jabal Ali and it is hoped that the situation will improve.

The attitude of an American driller to his coolies caused a serious situation in camp, and very nearly a general strike, The American was taken off duty and the trouble subsided of its own accord, leaving a few problems in its wake. The coolies are undoubtedly touchy, and liable to cause trouble. However with the exception of this incident relations in general have been good with the labour in the camp, in the last three weeks.

The ruler and Shaikh Rashid continue to be very helpful towards us.

ABU DHABI:

The Company house is complete,[130] apart from a few very small points, the wind tower works well.

The ruler having reached Awhai near Sohar where Mohamed bin Khalifa[131] has a garden, had news that the mission doctor was not in Matrah.

Shortly afterwards an Abu Dhabi truck, said to have driven by Said bin Shakhbut overturned, killing one slave and injuring another.

After a stay of some days, Shakhbut made his way to Biraimi, via Wadi al Gor[132] and Ramlat al Anaij. At the time of writing he is still there. He may still go to Muscat before returning to Abu Dhabi.

---

126 Arrived in Dubai May 1949 from service in India.

127 One of Thesiger's Rashidi companions. His adventures are reported in earlier diaries.

128 The second drilling location on the Trucial Coast, in Dubai territory.

129 In short supply.

130 At the far north east of Abu Dhabi island, now in the port area.

131 Sheikh Shakhbut's paternal uncle.

132 Various spellings of Gor.

Rashid bin Hamid of Hamasa and his brother Mohammed were in the Anson that landed at Abu Dhabi. They refused to take off with the aircraft (wisely perhaps), and later made their way to Biraimi via Dubai, by car.

Having been refused travel papers by the Political Officer, Trucial Coast, who insisted on conferring with Bahrain before granting facilities, they left Sharjah originally without papers. They have now returned proudly bearing Saudi documents. It is not, however, thought that these documents are valid for more than one journey. It is generally believed locally that they have sold Hamasa to the Saudis. The Al bu Falah[133] deny this.

It is felt that the visits of Mohammad Salimeen, Said bin Rashid Al Baluchi, and Rashid bin Hamid al Shamsi to bin Saud cannot altogether be without significance. Their one object is money, but what queer documents or promises do they give in return?

Zaid claims to have the confidence of all these shaikhs, and states that none of them will give away anything to the Saudis. It is difficult to share his confident opinion without reserve.

Zaid went by launch to Sharjah, and from there to Sohar to see the Ruler,[134] returning a few days later by the same route.

The Anti-Locusts are intending to go to Bireimi to rescue three vehicles they left there at the end of last season.

Henderson
Representative.

133 Abu Dhabi ruling family.

134 Sheikh Shakhbut.

TRUCIAL COAST DIARY FOR PERIOD ENDING 13 AUGUST 1951

KALBA:

There has been little change in the situation since ... murdered the ruler. Sultan[135] himself loudly protests that he had no prior knowledge of the crime and that as a result of his deeds his son is in disgrace. The father may protest too much.

The P.O.T.C with the Levy Commander and several car loads of troops made the pilgrimage to the new shrine.[136] They were held up for a short time at Huwailat, and again at the entrance to the Batina plain. At the latter point only one car with the P.O. and the major was allowed to proceed, the remainder being held up while awaiting word from the de facto ruler, granting permission to proceed.

The party camped on the airfield. The P.O. expressed his displeasure at the murder and usurpation. He was shown members of the dead man's family, who appeared to be free and in good health. Saqr is a great showman and brought a very large number of armed men to the P.O.'s. camp. Sultan refused to see his son.

It is not thought H.M.G. will take any action in this matter. Oman[137] in general disapproves of the murder, but regards the succession of the ... to the position of ruler as inevitable. Saqr is not repentant and asked to be officially recognised.

The P O. later visited the Shaikh of Fujaira.

The other Saqr (brother of the dead Hamaid[138]) is said to be still in residence in Dibba.

RAS AL KHAIMAH:

Continued pressure is reported to have been put on the people of Sham[139] by the Shaikh of Bakha.

The P.O. in H.M.S. Wren visited Rams and Sham. The levies also went up by road and were fired at by the people of Rams. The shaikh of Rams appears to have taken sides finally with the shaikh of Bakha and Sham is therefore cut off effectively

---

135 Sultan bin Salim, former Ruler Ra's al-Khaimah.

136 There is no explanation. Looks like the writer meant Kalba. The route from Dubai/ Sharjah to Kalba would be as described.

137 Trucial Oman, ie the Trucial States.

138 Hamad.

139 Sha'am, loyal to Sheikh Saqr of Ra's al-Khaimah. The sequence of towns north from Ra's al-Khaimah is:-Ra's al-Khaimah – Rams – Sha'am – Bukhah – Khasab. (The latter two in the Sultanate of Oman).

from Ras al Khaimah. The Ruler can only visit these areas in company with the levies or a man of war.[140]

The P.O. read him a lecture, and told him to get on with ruling his country. His father and brothers do nothing to help him. One of the latter took his pick-up to Dubai and sold it. Security in the area is as bad as ever.

UMM AL QAIWAIN:

The Ruler is still far from well, and spends most of his time at Falaj al Ali. His proposed Haj is now not likely to come off.

AJMAN:

The Ruler[141] finally paid up a fine of Rs. 5,000 for the part played by his subjects and members of his family in seizing a cargo and sailing craft in February. (TCD/3/51 refers). The cargo was mostly damaged by sea water, but some of it found its way into the ruler's household.

The Ruler has spent some time in his oasis in the Wadi Hatta. He is disputing Rashid bin Said's[142] right to cross his land on the latter's way to Masfut.[143] In return, Ali bin Rashid was not permitted to enter Dubai bearing arms. As both Rashid bin Hamaid[144] and Rashid bin Said[145] are in Wadi Hatta at one and the same time, at the present moment, amusing consequences may result. Rashid bin Said professes great friendship for Rashid bin Hamaid, which is not altogether reciprocated.

The G.M.[146] and Mr. Phelps visited Rashid bin Hamaid, but found only Ali bin Rashid at home. It happened to be the hottest day this month, and owing to the late arrival of the aircraft, the time of this audience was 1430. Even the shaikh showed signs of the heat.

SHARJAH:

The ruler appears quite unperturbed by the activities of Rashid bin Said among his Bani Kitab. It is publicly admitted in Sharjah that he has lost their allegiance. Whether Rashid[147] has gained it is another matter. Cupboard love was never very sure.

---

140 A 'man of war' was the term used to describe a ship from the navy.

141 Rashid bin Humaid (Hamaid).

142 Son of Dubai Ruler.

143 There is some confusion here. Masfut is Ajman and Hatta is Dubai territory.

144 Ajman Ruler.

145 Son of Dubai Ruler.

146 PD(TC) General Manager.

147 Rashid bin Said (bin Saeed) of Dubai.

The arrival of a big locust officer occasioned a pilgrimage from Sharjah to Biraimi, reported elsewhere in this diary.

DUBAI:

After leaving Ajman the G.M. and Mr. Phelps of SOCONY[148] visited Dubai. The ruler was impressed by having his photograph taken and developed immediately. The G.M. has promised him a camera[149] that does this.

Trade has been, temporarily at least, affected by the trouble at Abadan.[150] Merchants are unwilling to risk large quantities of goods in smuggling ventures while cash is in short supply in Persia.

On the news of the production stoppage at Abadan all launches immediately reported to Bahrain to pick up gas oil. There is already a black market in fuel, but the A.I.O.C.[151] agent is taking some steps to ration petrol to taxis. He will not sell more than one tin at a time, and is insisting on filling the tanks himself. To what extent he is also helping behind the scenes in the creation of the black market can be guessed, but not estimated exactly.

The Company is obtaining gas oil from Bahrain, and in two months' time all fuel for P.D. (T.C.) Ltd., will come from B.A.P.C.O.[152] A sea line will be laid for Jabal Ali camp for unloading in bulk.

The cost of living is going up. Tinned food is scarce and has increased in price. This is partly due to an increase in two years of nearly 50% in freight charges. A further increase of 15% is expected. The chief increases in prices in the last two years are house rents – about 100%, coffee, ghee, tinned food, cloth, and nearly all manufactured articles. Fresh meat is expensive and hard to obtain owing to the lack of rain last winter.

The following list gives only an approximate comparison of prices today (Rupees and Annas) and the equivalent, in summer, two years ago. Several items have not followed the general upward trend in price, but increases in many cases are now expected.

148 One of the American group of companies in IPC group.

149 Poleroid camera.

150 Events leading to the nationalization of Anglo-Iranian Oil Company.

151 Anglo Iranian Oil Company.

152 Bahrain Petroleum Company.

			1949		1951
Rice	Per maund[153]		Rs. 3/8 to 4/-		Rs. 3/8 to 4/
Flour	"		Rs. 3/-		Rs. 3/-
Sugar	"		Rs. 5/-		Rs. 5/-
Omani Ghee	"		Rs. 19/-		Rs. 23/-
Mutton	"		Rs. 8/-		Rs. 10/- to 12/-
Beef	"		Rs. 6/-		Rs. 8/- to 10/-
Fat Sheep		Upto	Rs. 40/-		Rs. 50/- to 55/-
Goat for killing		Upto	Rs. 25/-	upto	Rs. 35/-
Dates Per basket			Rs. 5/-		Rs. 5/-
Eggs Per dozen			Rs. 1/-		Rs. 1/12
Coffee beans			Rs. 9/-		Rs. 24/-

Rice while it is at the same price as in the summer of two years ago is cheaper than the winter price of 1948-49 when an average price of Rs. 7/- per maund (9 pounds) obtained. It is thought likely to return to this price and exceed it.

Dates are at present at their normal summer price, but may exceed the normal winter price of Rs. 12/- later in the year.

Fish is scarce at present at 12 annas per pound, but will of course go down again in the winter.

Fewer people have gone pearling. Gray Mackenzie pay a coolie Rs. 2/4 annas with food, for work in Dubai or on ships, which represent a small increase.

A larger number than usual of illegal immigrant (there are virtually no legal ones outside the European firms and their staff) has swelled the population of Dubai, and there is more obvious unemployment than before. A very large number of Somalis have recently arrived. A few of the ex Qatar Dhofaris have remained here. There is the usual stream of discharged people from Kuwait.

Wages in general have gone up. The increase in the Company rate of Rs. 1/- per diem[154] for coolies will be partly, if not wholly offset by price increases, and if the present price trend continues it will not be long before the new rate will amount to much the same thing for the wage-earner as the old.

It is clear that the increase in cost of living is not so steep as in some parts of the Gulf. However general seasonal fluctuations, and expected rapid fluctuation in the price of rice, may make living very difficult at times for the working classes.

Work in Jabal Ali has progressed, though there have been difficulties on the well. The spirit of the coolies has improved as the result of Rashid's efforts. We are

153 A Maund is about nine pounds. Rs. Rupees. 16 Annas to the Rupee. Rs. 3/8 means three Rupees and eight Annas.

154 Day.

experiencing the same trouble as in Qatar with national feeling (only in a very mild way). Three of the ruler's men were recently discharged as redundant. The ruler asked us to discharge some "foreigners" instead, despite the fact that these "foreigners" were sent by the ruler with a request that we should employ them. We are not accepting any employee without a certificate from the ruler or his son. The company is still regarded as a Philanthropic institution for destitute relatives of shaikhs.

ABU DHABI:

The Ruler returned from his trip in Oman, and a few days later set off with Zaid and Hamdan for Europe as the guest of Superior Oil Company.[155] An extraordinary scene took place when Dr. McCaully and the P.O. flew to A.D. to have him vaccinated. The ruler refused on the grounds that Zaid was not with him. He will probably have to be done in Bahrain. Meanwhile Hiza' is in Buraimi, and Khalid alone in Abu Dhabi.

Fortescue and Henderson visited Khalid in order to look at the ford. Khalid expressed neither surprise nor pleasure when we said we were intending to improve the crossing for them. He said nothing must be done until the ruler returned. He even sent a guard with us to the ford to see that we did not do anything.

The shaikhs are very perturbed about a building said to have been erected on HALLUL island.[156] They are not perturbed sufficiently, however, to go and see what it is.

BURAIMI:

Mohammed Salimeen appears to have made a written treaty with Zaid putting all oil matters in Zaid's hands as far as his part of the tribe is concerned. It will be interesting to see whether Zaid attempts to take up this matter with anyone while in Europe.

The Locusts and the Levies with the P.O. went in a monster convoy to Biraimi. They ran into floods in the wadi approaches to Ramlat al Anaij. There has been continuous rain for two days in the mountains.

Shaikh Sulaiman bin Hamyar[157] called at Dubai. He was cheerful and friendly and suggested as this month's bright idea that we should land an aircraft on the flat plain on top of Jabal Akhdhar.[158]

Henderson

---

155 The arbitration concerning the dispute over exploration for oil under the waters of the sea.

156 An island in Qatar waters 100 kilometres north east of Doha. Sheikh Shakhbut's claim to the island was refuted by the British.

157 From Oman, His base was at Tanuf at the western foot of the Jebel Akhdhar.

158 The Green mountain. The mountain is 3000 metres high. It would probably have been quite feasible to land an aircraft on the Sayq plateau at 2000 metres, once a level surface was cleared of stones and vegetation.

Representative
EFH/ARK.

TRUCIAL COAST DIARY FOR PERIOD ENDING 17 SEPTEMBER 1951

RAS AL KHAIMAH:

The ruler appears to have had no successes against his revolting subjects. He looks to the Dawla[159] for help. The latter tells him to look to his own business himself. It is not thought likely that security in the area will improve in the near future.

A very large number of fish died in the sea. There is said to have been a big patch of yellow water which poisons the fish off the Oman peninsular. Dead fish floating on the sea reached Sharjah.

UMM AL QAIWAIN:

The ruler claims to be better. He is on a very strict diet and is becoming thin. He does not now, apparently, take insulin.

AJMAN:

The unreformed Dutch church continues to suggest that the setting up of a mission hospital with a woman doctor is imminent. Dr. McCaully strongly disapproves.

The damaged and quite useless cargo mentioned in TCD/3/51 was picked up in a Gray Mackenzie barge (which entered the creek), and shipped by the agent of the owner to Bombay at a cost of Rs. 1,000.

It is not thought that the owner will appreciate this further waste of his money. Apparently a barge had to be sent, as no local boat owner would trust his craft inside Ajman harbour, after the last incident.

SHARJAH:

The young "Prince" shaikh Khalid[160] is marrying this month.

The negotiations for signing the new airfield agreement, which began in 1949 are still going on. Apparently the F.O.[161] at home have quietly re-drafted the agreement which the present ruler's father approved. It took them 18 months. Apparently the

---

159 H.M.G.

160 Brother of the Ruler.

161 Foreign Office in London.

object was to bring it in line with the Kuwait agreement. Shaikh Mohamed[162] spends much of his time at Ras al Khaimah.

The ruler is disputing with Mohamed bin Ali Hawaidin the payment of Rs. 15,000 which his father used to make to the Bani Kitab.[163]

He complains he cannot guard the newly acquired property at Dhaid effectively, as the P.O. will not let him have enough rifles.

DUBAI:

The trouble between the Bani Kitab and the badu group of Awamir (including the Rashidi, Bin al Gabaisha) was settled in the wadi Hatta by Rashid bin Said,[164] after Ahmed bin Rashid[165] had put his finger in it. The final settlement agreed to by all parties was that the Bani Kitab should pay Rs. 5,000 to the Awamir (who, though raiders, had been their "guests" at the time). The payment was held up, as the Bani Kitab had no money. An easy solution was found by Rashid bin Said who made the payment himself.

The manumitting by the Political Officer of a Company employee caused a slight stir.[166] When the freed man (a Dubai subject) returned to work at Jabal Ali, he was thrown out of camp by the head guard, and threatened with worse should he return. He retired to Sharjah. The P.O.[167] is attempting to reinstate him, and shaikh Rashid bin Said has reluctantly agreed. The Company has remained aloof from the struggle, being unwilling to become involved in so delicate an affair. The P.O. appears to believe that he can stamp out slavery by following the careers of individuals he has manumitted. He is likely to be kept busy. The Company's relations with the ruler have not been, as yet, adversely affected by these antics; and the P.O. has been informed that the Company does not wish to sacrifice good relations on the altar of missionary work. However we are not in any way obstructing these good works.[168]

162 Mohamed bin Saqr, uncle of the Ruler and father of the present Ruler Dr. Sheikh Sultan.

163 The problems that Mohamed bin Ali Hawaidin made for the Company PD(TC), and the Sharjah Ruler, are documented at length in previous volumes. The surprising result is recorded there too.

164 Dubai son of Ruler.

165 Ruler Umm al Quwain.

166 Slaves who held onto the flagpole at the British Political Agency were granted their freedom.

167 A.J. Wilton.

168 Slavery presented a real problem. Generally slaves were well treated and cared for even into old age. Some rose to prominent positions in business or administration. In society on the Trucial Coast in those days there was often no material advantage to be obtained for a man who achieved freedom.

The ruler and two of his sons have received treatment for dysentery and other ills at the hands of the company doctor. The results have been good, and the shaikhs are very grateful. Dr. McCaully has so far raised no objection. He has been kept in the picture. It is not too late for adverse reactions from this quarter, but he may remain tolerant.

Shaikh Rashid bin Hamaid of Ajman is on bad terms with Rashid bin Said as a result of the latter's use of the wadi Hatta for negotiations with the Awamir. Rashid bin Hamaid claims most of the wadi and is on bad terms with the Awamir.

Mr. Parker, the first representative here of Africa and Eastern[169] has set up his office in Dubai near the abra[170] station. His arrival coincides with a trade slump. His competition may not be welcomed by the merchants, who are already finding business slow.

ABU DHABI:

In the absence of the two leading personalities, quiet reigns. Khalid chews the cud[171] in Abu Dhabi and Hizza in Biraimi. The brothers are expected home from Paris this week.

Rumours that Herbert Morrison[172] has given away all the islands to Ibn Saud are rife.

Henderson
Representative.

TRUCIAL COAST DIARY FOR PERIOD ENDING 20 OCTOBER 1951

RAS AL KHAIMAH:

The Ruler remains perpetually hardup. He has called again on us asking for money. It is understood he has received Rs. 15,000 from Damalmal Iserdas[173] on security of his next quarterly concession payment.[174] He appears to have made little or no headway in the north of his kingdom.

---

169 British international trading company.

170 Literally 'across'. The abras are the small boats carrying people across the creek between Dubai and Deira. In those days men rowed the abras across the Creek while today they are powered by the 'chug' of diesel engines.

171 One might write 'relaxes peacefully'.

172 British Foreign Secretary (Minister) Labour Party. February to October 1951.

173 Indian Merchant.

174 The PD(TC) oil exploration concession agreement with the ruler.

UMM AL QAIWAIN:

The health of the Ruler is said to continue to improve. He played some part in the bringing together of the Awamir and Bani Kitab in the recent arbitration settled by Rashid bin Said.

SHARJAH:

The Political Officer, Trucial Coast, has begun his attempt to define and settle the Trucial Coast boundaries. His activities are unpopular with the Shaikhs; he is taking them one at a time to establish their claims. In this way he is hearing extravagant claims which rulers would not dare make if they were not on their own. The other rulers are annoyed that he has begun with the ruler of Sharjah by himself, and fear that the Ruler has claimed much territory belonging to others.

The Political Officer requested the presence of Company Representative, with the party, but when it was seen, on the first day how unpopular his methods are likely to be, we withdrew on an excuse concerning non-availability of transport (no idle excuse, as it turns out). The withdrawal of the Company was generally commended by the other shaikhs, and was not criticized by the Shaikh of Sharjah. The Company will not therefore be implicated in any of the claims put forward. The Seismic Surveyor has been asked to establish the position of certain points on the map, which are not marked. Precautions are being taken to ensure that this will have no political significance.

The shaikhs all fully realise that the boundary question does not concern the Company politically, since all land must belong to one shaikh or another and all shaikhdoms will be covered by concessions wherever their boundaries lie. We did not even point this out to some of the shaikhs who saw the point for themselves.

Salim bin Sultan bin Salim[175] was arrested in Dubai by the levies when visiting the bank. The full details are not available at present. It appears however that the Political Officer has ordered a sort of blockade of Kalba and intends cutting off the usurping ruler – Khalid[176] – from his supplies and money. The attempt to discomfort the ruler is belated and childish. The moment to take action was at the time of the first incident. Since then both the Political Officer and the navy have visited Kelba without achieving anything. Salim bin Sultan bin Salim is admittedly the brother of the present "Ruler". He has for a large number of years contended himself with driving a taxi in Sharjah and had not interfered in Politics. His arrest in Dubai appears to be unwise for the following reasons. He is the wrong man. Had the Political Officer sent a note to the Ruler of Sharjah any day this year, Salim would have been produced on demand without the need of any dramatic arrest. His arrest in Dubai is an insult to the Ruler of Dubai, which the latter feels very keenly. His arrest by levies is likewise an

175 Son of the previous Ruler of Ra's al-Khaimah.

176 The writer is wrong, he meant Saqr bin Sultan bin Salem.

affront to the ruler of Sharjah. The levies were already becoming most unpopular. This arrest brings to light the problem up till now obscure, as to what legal rights have they to interfere in political matters and arrest people inside the Coastal Towns.

The whole incident and the general behaviour of the Political Officer is causing considerable and justifiable criticism from the sheikhs and from the people. Shaikh Said[177] is incensed that such a thing should have happened. Conversation with the rulers is becoming most embarrassing as a result of their open criticism of the Political Officer.

DUBAI:

On the 17th the Ruler of Dubai was presented with the C.B.E.[178] by the Political Resident on behalf of His Majesty.[179]

On the 18th the hospital was opened by the Political Resident.[180] It was made very plain that the credit was due to the British entirely and not to the Shaikh and his people who contributed so much money. The contributions of the merchants were not mentioned, though they amount to lacs.[181] The help given by the "Ladies of Sharjah" in making the sheets was mentioned. The Ruler was tactfully told that this was "the first sign of progress" in his country.

The usual chaos ensued from all arrangements that had been entrusted to the Political Officer.

Shaikh Said has recently visited Muscat to have his leg inspected in hospital. The results have not been encouraging.

Shaikh Suleiman bin Hamyar[182] visited Jabal Ali.[183]

All Trucial rulers except Abu Dhabi and Kalba came to Dubai for the C.B.E. ceremony.

ABU DHABI:

The ruler has returned from Paris.[184] He is to be entertained in the Company's house in two days' time.

---

177 Dubai Ruler.

178 Commander of the Order of the British Empire.

179 King George VI.

180 Sir Rupert Hay.

181 Hundreds of thousands of Rupees.

182 From Tanuf and the Jebel Akhdhar in the Sultanate of Oman. Sheikh Suleiman was a frequent visitor to Dubai. He was powerful in his area, an area much larger than that of many other sheikhs who also often denied or defied the authority of the Sultan.

183 The Company camp near the drilling rig.

184 The reason for going to Paris was to attend the arbitration of the dispute between himself, the Ruler, and the Company, PD(TC) over rights to explore for oil in the waters of the

COMPANY'S AFFAIRS:

Seismic party No.5 are operating from Sharjah house in Sharjah, Ajman and Umm al Qaiwain territories.

When setting casing at Jabal Ali two pumps broke down leaving 4,000 ft. of cement in the hole solid. The ruler took this news with a smile.

POSTSCRIPT:

It now appears that Khan Sahib Hussain was also arrested for a time. The details of this extraordinary case will be made the subject of separate correspondence.

Henderson
Representative.

LETTER HENDERSON TO WILTON

21st October 1951

Dear John,[185]

The recent trouble the levies have caused in Dubai has made it a matter of some embarrassment for any member of the Company to associate with the levies until the matter is satisfactorily cleared up. I wonder if it would be possible to postpone the expedition with the surveyor until this matter can be properly settled, and public opinion became a little less bitter?

As you probably are aware Khan Sahib Hussein and Salim bin Sultan bin Salim were enticed into the bank, when the building was empty, by a trick. There they were insulted by the levies, and held prisoner, and threatened with a pistol by one (who was in civilian clothes) called Da'ud. Da'ud appears to have offered Salim his hand with a greeting and then struck him with the other. The two suffered various indignities and insults and were driven publicly in arrest through the main suq, with rifles levelled at their backs (there are about 3,000 witnesses to this part of the episode).

Khan Sahib is our contractor and Salim is his driver. They were employed on Company business at the time of this arrest. On the previous day they appear to have been obstructed in their lawful business by some subterfuge. Khan Sahib has stated

Gulf. PD(TC) claimed that the original concession agreement included all the area under the waters. The Judge found in favour for the Company concerning the territorial waters and in favour for the Ruler in respect of the water beyond the territorial waters and up to the median line in the Gulf. The judgement made international legal history.

185 Political Officer A.J. Wilton.

that under no circumstances can he now visit the bank to cash our cheques and claim documents for goods for us. This will hold up our affairs.

General opinion here was at first that Khan Sahib had been caught doing something illegal with a Company cheque and was only forgiven because of his known lengthy service with British Companies (and indeed at one time with H.M.G.). His more intimate friends have now heard his own story, and bizarre and nearly incredible as it is, believe him. The general populace have no means of hearing his story; and unless some public restitution is made in the way of an apology on the part of Da'ud – and one would like to think his punishment – backed by some gesture on the part of the authority concerned to confirm his innocence of any crime, the public may continue to think ill of him.

However whatever the public have heard about Khan Sahib and Salim, there is no doubt, of the universal condemnation of the action of the (already unpopular) levies. In the last three years nothing that has happened in Dubai has caused such a stir as this has done. The ruler was very angry saying that he had never experienced any such incident in his territory before, and that he had understood that he himself was supposed to be responsible for law and order. Nor could he understand why such a dramatic arrest should be needed in the case of Salim, when an application to Shaikh Saqr any day of any week would have produced his person, whenever required, and without recourse to any levy force. It has become most embarrassing to speak to the ruler of Dubai since he constantly returns to this topic, and it is difficult to see what rejoinder one can give.

The relations of this Company with the local ruler, it seems, must inevitably suffer with those of every British concern on account of this incident; and we are most anxious to know whether there is any argument we can put forward when confronted with accusations concerning it, and whether any action to rectify the damage is contemplated.

As you know I do not meddle in politics and my only concern is the relations of the Company to the local people and their rulers. However this business touches us nearly, and the locals see little difference between oil companies, levies, locust officers and government officials. When H.M.G. or the levies or anyone else is criticised we come in for our share, and have to stick up for our side. It has been heavy going recently.

I hope you will excuse my putting my views on paper; you may disagree with them, but you will find that my description of local feeling as a result of this incident is accurate enough, and I feel that it is vital that you should know what is being said in Dubai.

Yours sincerely
Signed
Edward Henderson.

P.S. K.S. states that while under arrest he had to put up with the jeers of the people, who thought he had robbed the bank. It is ironical that the one man who has consistently stuck up for the British in public and private, and worked mainly for our firms, should be the first to be arrested - without cause under this new, unexpected and extraordinary system.

To
A J. Wilton, Esq.,
Political Officer,
Trucial Coast,
Sharjah.

LETTER HENDERSON TO LERMITTE

26th October,

Dear Mr. Lermitte

The facts of the recent arrest appear to be as follows. On Wednesday 17th October Salim bin Sultan bin Salim, brother of Saqr (the present ruler of Kalba) was; sent by Khan Sahib, whose driver he is, to Dubai. He brought a cheque from P.D.T.C. to pay into Khan Sahib's account, and a note asking for some bills of lading for some goods which were lying in the customs, and had been ordered by us. The bank officials decided Salim was really Saqr (no one knows why on earth they did), and asked him to return on the 18th (when the bank would be closed for the hospital opening ceremony).

On the eighteenth, Khan Sahib called at the hospital[186] himself leaving his driver outside. In the meantime the Political Officer, acting on the wrong information from the bank, had posted levies inside and outside the bank. Khan Sahib entered and found no one in the bank except the clerk, and two levies. The levies detained him. The clerk went away and brought back a corporal, Da'ud in mufti, and another soldier, and then left the bank to the levies. Khan Sahib was then asked to produce Shaikh Saqr, and asked why he was supplying Kalba. Khan Sahib was unable to give a reply satisfactory to them, and was insulted by Da'ud and put in another room. Salim was brought in, insulted and hit in the face for denying he was Saqr. Khan Sahib was brought back and received further insults, but eventually convinced them that perhaps they had the wrong man. The two were then taken in close arrest in Landrovers to the outskirts of the town, with rifles pointed at their backs. Khan Sahib then insisted on being taken to the hospital where the Resident was. On the way the bank manager diverted them

186 He must mean 'the bank'?

to the watch tower. He apologised to Khan Sahib for any trouble he had caused, and had Khan Sahib taken back to the bank by the levies.

When Codrai and I returned from the hospital to go over to lunch with the Resident and others at the palace someone gave Codrai a brief description of how Salim had been arrested. Codrai therefore took the Political Officer aside, and warned him of his extraordinary mistake. The Political Officer seemed to think the matter a joke. He told Codrai that he was after Saqr, and that Kelba is now "Blockaded" (The locusts[187] have however been given permission to go there!).

Salim remained in close arrest for 24 hours in the levy camp in Sharjah, the Political Officer having apparently disregarded Codrai's warning.

Next day Salim was released and Khan Sahib made a complaint to the Political Officer which was received with indifference, and a casual "Sorry to have troubled you".

The feeling in Dubai was so high that I later wrote a note to the Political Officer to warn him of how the people and the ruler were reacting.

As a result of this note (in addition Gray Mackenzie and Dr. McCaully wrote and spoke in similar terms) the Political Officer went round to Khan Sahib's house to apologise as publicly as may be, and likewise sent Ali Bustani to pacify the ruler of Dubai. The latter having just received the C.B.E. made no official complaint, but remained very angry, and several times raised the point when speaking to me.

He claims that it is illegal for the levies to arrest anyone within Dubai.

Khan Sahib refuses to visit the bank again.

Public opinion has not been altogether appeased by the apology. It is difficult however to see what else the Political Officer could do.

The Political Officer appears somewhat shaken by the unanimity of the advice he received from three independent sources. He replied politely enough to my note, explaining the action he would take, but he implies that the only mistake made was in arresting the wrong man. He also denies that the levies are unpopular.

I feel, as I said in my note, that Company interests are endangered in the ways I described. However the levy commander has been asked to take disciplinary action against Corporal Da'ud, who has been made to apologise to Khan Sahib. The levies, by the arrogant behaviour of the Transjordians are likely to become more unpopular, and we shall have as little to do with them as possible while this unpopularity lasts.

I do not know what you feel about the matter, but it seems to me that if any further major errors of this nature are made we might mention it to the P.A.[188] In the mean-time, since the Political Officer has taken the advice given to him, could we not wait and see what happens next?

---

187 He probably means the locust survey team!

188 The next senior man, the Political Agent, then resident in Bahrain.

If any such incident occurs again, one which really affects us closely, I will let you know. I do not intend writing again to the Political Officer on any such similar occasion, and would not in fact have done so this time, had not Khan Sahib been so deeply involved. The letter seems to have had the required effect, however.

Yours sincerely,

E. Henderson.

There are no diaries for November and December 1951.

1952

TRUCIAL COAST DIARY FOR PERIOD ENDING 26 JANUARY 1952

GENERAL:

The most notable event during the period under review has been the heaviest fall of rain on the Trucial Coast for several years. The Sharjah, Jabal Ali and Ras Sadr airstrips were unusable for sometime after the rain, and the Jabal Ali airstrip is still flooded, as are all the car tracks which run across the sabkas.[1] Some of the Shaikhdoms have been cut-off by road for several days. The coast is already looking much greener, and the badu is a very happy man; it is only the Europeans with tight programmes or two wheel drive vehicles who have lifted their eyes hoping to see a blue sky.

KALBA AND THE JAWASIM:

Although seven months have passed since the Ruler of Kalba[2] was murdered, it is still the intention of the Politicals to punish ... [3] to prove that accession to power

---

1 The sabkhah is the salt/gypsum/sand mud flat that lies between the sea and the sand dunes. It is largely found from Dubai south and westwards. It extends inland only a few kilometres in the north and over 100 kilometres in the far west. It is dangerous to drive vehicles on sabkhah as they will sink in, particularly after rain. The worst situation is when a vehicle had sunk to resting on the chassis. A very long cable was left beside the track to the south of Jebel Dhanna for many years to await the arrival of, and to pull out, another careless driver. However a good track can be built across the sabkhah by vehicles, one after another, running across at a good speed and under the right conditions. This track is depressed below the surrounding sabkhah and after rain may hold water and be very slippery.

2 Kalba is on the Indian Ocean coast and was still one of the 7 sheikhdoms in treaty arrangement with the British government.

3 The usurper and temporary Ruler of Kalba.

by assassination is now out-dated in Oman.[4] With nothing in particular in mind, the Political Officer Trucial States called together the Jawasim Shaikhs[5] to discuss the situation. Several proposals were put forward at the meeting, but the Shaikhs were unable to reach any agreement.

One of the proposals was that Kalba should be brought under the direct control of Sharjah: another that Humaid bin Mohd[6] of Ras al Khaima should be installed as Ruler - a proposal by Mohd bin Sallim which only received the support of his hard-up relations. The third, and by far the most popular proposal with all but the Political Officer Trucial States was that Sultan bin Salim, the father of the present Ruler[7] should be made Ruler of Kalba.[8]

The reason for the popularity of the latter proposal (although there is no possibility of it being agreed to by HMG[9]) is two-fold: firstly, Sultan bin Sallim is a thorn in the side of the Ruler of Ras al Khaima, and his instatement in Kalba would not only remove one of the Ruler's many troubles, but it would no longer be necessary for him to make him any grant from the concession payments. Secondly, during the period he spent there in exile, Sultan bin Sallim got on good terms with Muscat, and it is thought that if he became Ruler of Kalba he might use his influence to regain the small pieces of Kalba territories that in the past years have been lost to Muscat, via Fujaira.

More than one observer has commented that if only the Shaikh of Fujaira would seize Kalba two problems would be solved, that of Kalba and of the unrecognised Fujaira Shaikhdom - Fujaira becoming absorbed into Kalba territory, and sliding into the position of being in treaty terms with HMG. However, it is hardly likely that the Jawasim Shaikhs would stand-by and allow this to happen.

Meanwhile, in spite of the 'one man' boycott of Kalba by the Political Officer Trucial States, Saqr bin Sultan continues to reign, and according to most accounts is quite a popular and successful Ruler.

SHARJAH:

On 1st December 1951, the designation of the Political Officer Trucial Coast was changed to Political Officer Trucial States, and similarly the Agency is now known as

---

4 Trucial Oman.

5 The sheikhs of Sharjah and Ra's al-Khaimah.

6 Humaid bin Mohamed bin Salem, an elder brother of Sheikh Saqr, the Ruler of Ra's al-Khaimah. Proposed by his father, Sheikh Mohamed bin Salem.

7 Sheikh Saqr bin Sultan bin Salem, the usurper.

8 Sheikh Sultan bin Salim was former Ruler of Ra's al-Khaimah. He was the father of the Ruler/usurper, Shaikh Saqr bin Sultan. (Neither the same Sheikh Saqr bin Sultan, Ruler of Sharjah, nor the Sheikh Saqr bin Sultan of Buraimi).

9 The British Government.

the Political Agency Trucial States. Whether or not this is intended to bring about a change of name for the Trucial Coast is not known, and as yet there has been no attempt to substitute States for Coast or Shaikhdoms. Visas are still issued for "The Trucial Shaikhdoms".

An attempt is being made by Shaikh Khalid, the brother of the Ruler,[10] to start a "Sports and Cultural Club" in Sharjah. Membership is to be confined to those who "Speaka der Ingleez language". It is difficult to judge whether this is a genuine attempt by Khalid to bring about something worthwhile, or whether he is merely interested in providing himself with reasonable quarters outside of the fort. He seems to have succeeded in having the Ruler's majlis renamed the Library.

Shaikh Mohd,[11] the former acting-Ruler, is said to be causing the Ruler some embarrassment, and to be continuously asking for more money. Also, it is said that he collects some of the taxes and keeps the proceeds himself.

An Assistant Political Officer, the Hon. Martin Buchmaster, a Class B Officer, arrived during the middle of December, and his main function will be to run the consular affairs of the Agency.

A new detachment of Levies[12] arrived by a special Charter just before Christmas, and would appear to be better chosen than the detachment which they replace. However, the Levies will have to do much to make a good name for themselves, and at present their stock is not very high.

Shortly after Christmas the anti-Locust Party left for Baraimi, from where they started out on a month's camel excursion to Liwa.[13] The Politicals arranged this trip with both the Ruler of Abu Dhabi and the Saudi Arabian Government,[14] both of whom readily agreed to this excursion into 'each others' territory, in view of the forthcoming boundary settlement. The trouble the Politicals take with any organization not having the stamp of commerce is very noticeable, even though it is very doubtful indeed whether any good will arise from such activities. One also wonders how much harm is done when an organization places itself almost entirely in the hands of one interpreter.

The anti-Locust Party has not returned at the time of going to press and, according to plan, a relief expedition organized by the Levies has set out to meet it.

A new agreement for the Sharjah aerodrome has been concluded with the Ruler, one of the new clauses of which is that he is allowed to signal, via Cable and Wireless,[15] several thousand words free, every year. He took advantage of this at Christmas and

10 Sheikh Saqr bin Sultan.

11 The uncle of the Ruler.

12 The Trucial Oman Levies. These men came from the Arab Legion in Jordan.

13 See HEARD, D. (2019) for their report on the trip.

14 An illustration of just how far the British Government was going to avoid irritating Saudi Arabia.

15 Cable and Wireless was the company providing international communication.

sent a large bundle of greeting telegrams. A fairly heavy bill was then presented to him, no one in I.A.L.[16] having been told of this new clause.

RAS AL KHAIMAH:

The Ruler is treading deeper into financial difficulties, and has mortgaged his concession payments[17] for the next two periods. Pocock of the Golden Valley Oxide Company reached agreement with him, after a hard battle, for the oxide concession on Tunb Island.[18] The agreement was for Rs. 10,000/- cash, plus a royalty of Rs. 4/- per ton exported, with a guaranteed royalty of Rs. 2,000/- annually. However, the Golden Valley Company has gone back on its instructions to Pocock, and now states that the cash payment is too high.

Shaikh Saqr is not, as might be expected (because of his financial plight), an easy man to bargain with. He holds the view that his present troubles are partly due to his predecessor having signed agreements that give him little benefit, and he intends to get his 16 oz. 's[19] worth in the future.

A Geological Party camp, was established near Shammal[20] on 12th January, and the party has since been operating in the hills in this area. The Party has also been on a short reconnaissance as far as Sha'am.[21] Shortly after this visit, the O/C Levies, accompanied by the APO,[22] visited the Shaikh of Rams,[23] and did him honours. They also listened to his complaints against the Company, with whom he requires a concession. This is yet another example of the damage which can be done when people are allowed to wander forth, without knowing how to conduct themselves; when they do not realise that it is improper to call on a dissident subject before the Ruler of the territory.

Shaikh Saqr claims that Shaikh Mohammad[24] of Bakha has used his influence with the Shihu[25] to try and prevent the Company from operating in Ras al Khaima territory. It was fairly certain that the Habus (a sub-section of the Shihu) were acting

16 International Aeradio Limited. The company providing airport communication services.

17 Due to him from the Company PD(TC).

18 They were already working on Abu Musa island under an agreement with the Sharjah Ruler.

19 A reference to Shakespeare's Jew and his demand for a pound of flesh, according to the agreement. 16 ozs is sixteen ounces, or one pound.

20 A short distance north of Ra's al-Khaimah town.

21 On the coast about 40 kilometres north of Ra's al-Khaimah.

22 Acting Political Officer.

23 The Ruler's problems with the Sheikh of Rams (10 kilometers north of Ra's al-Khaimah) have been reported in previous diaries.

24 The father-in-law of Sheikh Said, Ruler of Dubai.

25 The Musandam mountains tribe who are subjects of the Sultan of Oman, but they also come down onto the coastal plain during the summer months, where they come under the

under orders other than those of Ras al Khaima, and it took a show of force to arrange for the entry of the geologists into their territory, where some were quite frank in stating that they did not want the Company to operate there.[26] A full report on this area will follow later.

AJMAN:

On about 20th January Shaikh Rashid bin Humaid of Ajman shot at two baduin whom he thought to be of the Awamir tribe, and killed one of them. Unfortunately, his victim turned out to be Khalifah bin Sallim, the nephew of Mohd bin Ali bin Huwaidin of the Bani Kitab. For a time the situation looked critical, but Mohd bin Hamad Ash Sharji,[27] who was in Ajman at the time, mediated between the two parties and arranged a forty-five days truce. It is not now thought that the consequences of this incident will be very serious, as the victim was the sister of one of Rashid bin Humaid's wives who is the mother of Nasir bin Rashid.

An unconfirmed report says that a missionary hospital is shortly to be built in Ajman, and is to be run by Dr. (Miss) Houseman, from Saham,[28] on the Batinah.

ABU DHABI:

The Ruler has been kept active by visitors laden with questionnaires regarding his territory, in preparation for the coming talks as to the settlement of the Abu Dhabi/ Saudi Arabian frontier problem. On 24th January he left for Bahrain, to attend the first meeting, which is to be held[29] towards the end of this month.

The Company camp at Ras Sadr is slowly getting smaller, as more and more stores are gradually moved to Jabal Ali.[30]

Ruler of Ra's al-Khaimah. Today, in the 21st century, many of the mountain settlements have been abandoned and the terraces which earlier provided grain are falling into decay.

26 This is the same problem as the Company faced elsewhere on the Trucial Coast. The Company had agreements with the coastal Rulers, for which the Company paid. HMG decreed that all the land either came under the authority of one or another coastal ruler who was in treaty arrangement with HMG, or under the Sultan of Oman. Several tribal leaders in the interior sought agreements with the Company or at least payment to be able to work in their area, from either the Company or the Ruler. When this was not forthcoming they prevented the Company from working in their areas.

27 The Fujairah Ruler.

28 Saham on the coast of the Batina was famous for the export of limes to Basra. This was important enough for the British Bank of the Middle East to establish a branch there. (Information provided by the late Sir Geoffrey Arthur, the last Political Resident in Bahrain).

29 In Riyadh.

30 The well at Ra's Sadr was abandoned in March 1951, but there was still activity at the site and work for Abu Dhabi men.

DUBAI:

A trade slump is slowly making itself felt on the Dubai market. African and Eastern Company[31] have opened a branch in Dubai with an English Manager, and a state of cut-throat competition with Gray Mackenzie & Co[32] is now raging for all to see. African and Eastern seem to have the support of both the bank and the Political Officer Trucial States. The competition has now reached an undesirable and unhealthy peak, regarding the supply of liquor. With the approval of Political Officer Trucial States, African and Eastern have imported supplies, but Gray Mackenzie have succeeded in getting the Ruler to see the undesirability of having liquor distributed from another source, and the Ruler has refused to allow African and Eastern to take delivery of these supplies.

Apparently with the approval of P.O.T.S. African and Eastern are now offering to pay the Ruler a considerable customs duty on liquor. Even consumers who are interested in cheaper liquor (which African and Eastern are offering) are critical of the Politicals allowing a third supplier of liquor to be established here, particularly when they have so little control over the NAAFI supplies in Sharjah – unquestionably the source of leakage for the whole of the Trucial Coast.

The Ruler of Kuwait visited Dubai on 15th December and stayed for four days. There has been much speculation as to the reason for his visit, but no one explanation seems to be very plausible, and the mystery remains. It is quite certain, however, that he did not come here to improve his relations with Dubai, for according to local standards he behaved very badly during his stay here.

During December, Suhail bin Mana'a bin Rashid[33] tried to enter Dubai in a taxi from Baraimi, dressed as a woman. It is thought that he was trying to get here to organise a force to overthrow the Ruler, particularly as many notorious Manasir baduin had already lodged themselves in various parts of the town. One of them, Said bin Sidairi was carried here on a Company vehicle. However, Suhail bin Mana'a was detected by the driver of the taxi who, once he saw the manner in which 'this woman' performed her ablutions (and subsequently her beard) refused to bring her further.

COMPANY ACTIVITIES:

The well at Jabal Ali[34] has now reached a depth of over 7000 feet, but it has just been reported that the hole has caved in at one point, threatening the loss of the well.

Seismic Party No.5 have continued to operate in Sharjah territory, but are withdrawing from the Trucial Coast at the end of January.

31 A British trading company.

32 The British company, shipping agent and trader.

33 A dissident Dubai sheikh.

34 The second well drilled by the Company on the Trucial Coast.

Khan Sahib Hussein's canteen at Ras Sadr was destroyed by fire during November. Also, during November a Viking aircraft ran off the airstrip at Jabal Ali, and sank into the sabka up to its belly, after having tipped up on its nose and damaged one of its propellers. It was dragged out of the sabka the same day, but did not take off until nine days after schedule. This is the first accident which Airwork[35] have had, and that only due to very bad luck.

BARAIMI:

Baduin Shaikhs near Baraimi who have, until recently, been claiming independence, are now reconsidering their position in the light of the Saudi claims to the whole area.

On 20th January Obaid bin Juma' of Mahadha left Dubai for Saudi Arabia with some thirty attendants.[36]

Cordai
Representative.

35 The company providing aircraft for PD(TC) operations.

36 Ka'abi from Mahadha north of Buraimi in the Sultanate of Oman.

TRUCIAL COAST DIARY FOR PERIOD ENDING 10 MARCH 1952

RAS AL KHAIMAH:

The Shaikh[37] of Rams[38] has been captured by the Ruler of Ras al Khaimah and is a prisoner in the fort. The Shaikh's cousin Mohammad bin Ismail was killed in the scuffle, as was his sister (accidentally).

His brother has taken to the hills and is raising part of the Shihuh[39] against the Ruler. An attack by part of the Shihuh is expected. The Ruler with his brothers and all his armed retainers are in the Rams area prepared to defend the place. The forts on the Sha'am track are in his hands.

The Shaikh of the Zaab, Abdullah, is understood to have petitioned the Ruler to be allowed to return, as a humble citizen, to the island.[40]

The father of the Ruler has asked for assistance from H.M.G. yet again, in the Rams affair. It is not thought that it will be forthcoming.

KALBA:

The levies[41] are still in the entrance to the Wadi al Ghor. It is understood that they are not stopping anyone. It is not clear what is the object of the maintenance of this standing patrol.

In a skirmish between the levies and the Bani Ka'ab the former claim to have had 30 shots fired at them. They allege that they replied with 70 rounds. No one on either side in this battle was scratched.

AJMAN:

The Ruler is still at war with the Bani Kitab and likely to remain so for a month or more.

SHARJAH:

The Ruler's brother is still away on his begging trip in Saudi Arabia, or Kuwait.

The Ruler has grandiose ideas as to planting Dhaid, and is understood to have brought a large number of fruit trees.

---

37 Sheikh Salim bin Saleh. Tunaiji.

38 On the coast about 15 kilometres north of Ra's al-Khaimah town.

39 The mountain tribe.

40 Jazirat al Hamra, the traditional home of the Za'ab tribe.

41 Trucial Oman Levies, Later Trucial Oman Scouts. Founded in 1951 by the British Government. The officers were British and the men were initially from the Arab legion in Jordan and later from Aden while local men were being trained to take over.

Pocock's new assistant has explained to the Ruler how he should dredge his creek and has offered to help him to do so. No outcome is expected.

Shaikh Shakhbut stopped an hour or two at Sharjah on his way back from Boundary Conference in Saudi Arabia. He seemed very anxious to move on home.

The American Mission Hospital are establishing themselves in a house in Sharjah which they have been given free by the Ruler.

DUBAI:

A stolen Abu Dhabi camel was caught near Jabal Ali. The claimant and an alleged culprit were sent on by the head guard[42] to Rashid.

Sir Roger Makins[43] landed at Jabal Ali, briefly saw the camp and went on to lunch with the Ruler of Dubai, and dinner with the Ruler of Sharjah. He came in a Company aircraft and stayed in the Company House at Sharjah. A party was apparently given in his honour by the P.O.

Four days later (the 8th) the P.R. paid a routine visit to Dubai and Sharjah.

The depth of the still dry[44] well (9,500 feet) is causing gloom.

The hospital funds appear to be lower than usual. The Shaikh of Umm al Qaiwain has however contributed Rs. 2,500/- and more than one merchant has given as much as Rs. 2,000/-. The Ruler of Dubai is expected to produce Rs. 75,000/-.

Shaikh Rashid has had a week's hunting in Persia. He took his own cars, as usual.

Shaikh Said is in good health as far as his leg is concerned, but has been treated by the M.O.T.C.[45] for stomach troubles.

ABU DHABI:

The Ruler and Zaid returned from Bahrain. Zaid went straight on to Oman.[46] Bird visited the Ruler by air. Hiza and Khalid are still in Oman.[47] Hiza seems to have had a long and successful trip to Sohar and Muscat, and to be on good terms with Saiyid Said.[48]

The inhabitants of Batin[49] are still threatening to go over to Dubai with their families. Individuals may already have done so. Abu Dhabi is suffering from a slump

42 Head guard at the Company camp.

43 British Ambassador to USA 1952-1956.

44 Dry meaning no oil.

45 The Medical Officer, Trucial Coast.

46 People on the coast going to Buraimi/Al Ain/Muwaiji would frequently say 'I am going to Oman'.

47 Probably in Muwaiji, one of the Abu Dhabi oases in the Buraimi group of oases.

48 The Sultan of Oman.

49 Village on Abu Dhabi island inhabited by Muhairi and Sudan (Suwadi).

that tends to outdo its normal chronic slump. This is thought to have depressed the Ruler somewhat.

Bin Mansur[50] is reported to be at Agaila[51] in the Bainuna,[52] returning the Zakat[53] last collected, with interest.

Buckmaster[54] is leaving on the 10th of March for a trip to Liwa,[55] probably in the company of Zaid. Ali Bustani[56] will be going with him.

Henderson
Representative
efh/ i.

TRUCIAL COAST DIARY FOR THE PERIOD ENDING 28 MARCH 1952

RAS Al KHAIMAH:

It is reported confidentially from a reliable source, which should not be quoted outside the Company, that the P.R.,[57] met the Shaikh of Bakha[58] in Muscat. He granted him an interview, and listened patiently, and did not refute his complaint that

---

50 The Saudi tax collector who was well known in the Bainunah and Liwa areas. He did not always receive a warm welcome.

51 About 40 kilometres south of Ruweis between Markhia and Bida Matawa.

52 Extensive desert area central to Abu Dhabi territory.

53 Tax which every Moslem should pay. The money should be given to the poor in the same area or near to where it was collected.

54 Political Officer in Sharjah, later Political Officer in Abu Dhabi. Buckmaster was sent by HMG to survey the Liwa settlements, which form a 150 kilometre crescent in the high dunes in the far south of Abu Dhabi territory. The purpose was to ascertain the loyalty of the people in the light of the Saudi claim to the whole territory. His survey was made after the less detailed locust party survey earlier in the year. Sheikh Zayed did go with the party. They visited many villages and recorded the names of inhabitants. It was not until September 1955 that Viscount Buckmaster was appointed the first Political Officer in Abu Dhabi.

55 The Liwa oases were the original homeland of the Abu Dhabi Bani Yas and Manasir tribal groups.

56 The Arab employee at the Political Agency.

57 P.R. Political Resident. (Bahrain) Sir Rupert Hay. P.A. Political Agent (Bahrain and Muscat). P.O. Political Officer (Sharjah). In that order of seniority.

58 Mohamed bin Sulaiman was the Sheikh of Bakha which lies on the Gulf coast in Sultanate of Oman territory on the Musandam peninsula. A few kilometres north of Ra's al-Khaimah territory. About 10 kilometres north of Sha'am in Ra's al-Khaimah. Rams is

the Levies[59] accompanied by the Ruler of Ras al Khaimah invaded his territories. The Levies have admittedly caused embarrassment in this area (see previous diaries), but the evils of which they were accused were not those which they committed.

In fact the Shaikh of Bakha is himself the cause of the trouble. He had been sent a year ago to Muscat to be reprimanded - and was, we believe, complimented by the Muscat Government, and encouraged to go back and cause more trouble. Now he[60] has been worsted by the Ruler of Ras al Khaimah. In this the Levies played no part - rather the contrary - for they had tacitly supported the Shaikh of Rams by calling on him.[61] Now that Rams is lost to the rebels,[62] the Shaikh of Bakha (with the cheek of a Russian) is blaming the Levies. The P.R., in giving audience to the Shaikh and in not refuting his complaints has demonstrated once more our habit of failing to assist the Shaikh of Ras al Khaimah despite our treaty. We believe that this is because the P.A. Muscat fitfully supports the Shaikh of Bakha, while the P.O. Sharjah, even more fitfully and unsuccessfully, supports his protégé - Ras al Khaimah. It seems that the P. R. does not appreciate this curious conflict inside his own organisation, or see the damage he is doing to the Ruler of Ras al Khaimah by condoning the actions of the Shaikh of Bakha. In the meantime, the Ruler of Ras al Khaimah is doing remarkably well on his own.

KALBA:

The Levies are still at their camp near the Wadi Ghor.[63] No one professes to understand why, and their maintenance of a patrol in that area is an open joke among the rulers. Their presence in the Wadi appears to cause no embarrassment so far to the Ruler of Kalba. It may of course be cleverer than we think it is.

FUJAIRA:

The Ruler has been granted a treaty as an independent shaikh. He does not realise that in so doing he has defeated one of his two cherished but hopeless aims.

---

south along the coast and about 15 kilometres north of Ra's al-Khaimah town. The wife of Sheikh Saeed bin Maktoum, Ruler of Dubai came from this family.

59 The Trucial Oman Levies, later the Trucial Oman Scouts were first formed in 1951. The officers, British, and men, Arab Legion from Jordan, had a lot to learn about the Trucial Coast and its political complications.

60 He, the Sheikh of Bakha, was supporting the Sheikh of Rams in his rebellion against Sheikh Saqr the Ruler of Ra's al-Khaimah.

61 It was only a courtesy call. Probably the levies did not realise the great significance attached, on the Trucial Coast, to such calls.

62 He means that the rebels have lost Rams.

63 The main route from Dubai/Sharjah to the Batina coast and on to Muscat runs through the Wadi Ghor.

The first is to produce his own postage stamps and sell them to collectors. His other aim is to sign up with an Oil Company. It is indeed understood that his pertinacity in persuading H.M.G. to give him a treaty is solely with this latter object in view.

AJMAN:

The Ruler is not yet reconciled with the Bani Kitab and except for visits to Sharjah is confined to barracks.

SHARJAH:

The Rulers of Fujaira, Ras al Khaimah, Ajman, Umm al Qaiwain and Sharjah, and representatives of Dubai (Rashid) and Abu Dhabi (Said and Hamdan)[64] met at the Agency. They were summoned by the P.O. to discuss various problems including the matter of locust bait.

Hamdan[65] came to see the Representative in the Company house in Sharjah. This is the first time really friendly relations have been re-established between him and the Representative since the riot caused by the former in April 1950. The hatchet is now well buried[66] and relations are excellent once more. Perhaps it was about time.

Pocock has completed a successful season[67] on Bu Musa[68] and Sir Bu Na'ir.[69]

DUBAI:

The Rulers of Sharjah and Ajman called on the Ruler to discuss the pearl problem. They have made an arrangement to inspect pearls that are sold or bought in Dubai, and to test for cultured ones. A recent sale by Mohammed Balai of Dubai in Bombay of cultured pearls has caused the Rulers trouble. These he claimed were Dubai pearls. It is said that he obtained Rs. 400,000 from the sale before the fraud was discovered. The Rulers fear that this will dishonour all T.C. Merchants, and ruin the pearl trade. They have agreed to outlaw Mohd. It is understood that he did this same thing some years ago in Bahrain, but on a smaller scale.

It is said that three camels in Dubai territory died by Locust bait. It is said that as a result the Ruler of Sharjah may retreat the permission he has given to spread bait

64 Sheikhs Said bin Shakhbut and Hamdan bin Mohamed bin Khalifa (Sheikh Shakhbut's son and son of his cousin).

65 Sheikh Hamdan bin Mohamd bin Khalifa from Abu Dhabi.

66 Friendship restored.

67 His company was mining red oxide.

68 Out in the Gulf, about 70 kilometres north west of Sharjah.

69 About 110 kilometres west of Dubai and about 80 kilometres north of Abu Dhabi.

in his territory. The attitude of Dubai is not known, but the mission have established a camp at Tawi Ashush[70] and are apparently happily installed there.

Admiral Cunningham[71] called at Jabal Ali, but did not have time to see the Shaikh.

On the same day Admiral Rose of the U.S.N.[72] was taken by Shaikh Rashid hunting gazelle. It is understood that the P.O. arranged this trip but was not present himself.

Several thefts have recently been reported in Jabal Ali. A driver is in Dubai jail in consequence. A truck was recently taken from the camp during the night and returned without its spare wheel. The guards did not notice this.

ABU DHABI:

On the 18th Zaid and the A.P.O.[73] set off with 50 camels from Dahan for Liwa. They may be away five weeks.

Pocock is intending to have another attempt to make an agreement with Shakhbut for the Red Oxide concessions on the various islands.

Bin Mansur[74] is said to have departed, having taxed and bribed many Bani Yas and other tribesmen in the Bainuna.[75]

As has been previously reported, representatives of 70 families from Batin village[76] went to Rashid of Dubai asking him to accept them as immigrants. Rashid agreed to have them, and Hiza to let them go. Their main complaints were lack of work and the extortions of a Persian usurer. Shakhbut, on his return, gave them some money and forbade their departure.

Henderson
Representative.

70 A well at the eastern end of the border between Dubai and Abu Dhabi.

71 IPC / PD(TC) Chairman.

72 United States Navy.

73 Acting Political Officer Buckmaster.

74 The Saudi tax gatherer.

75 The area between the Liwa oases in the south and the coast of Abu Dhabi.

76 On Abu Dhabi island.

TRUCIAL COAST DIARY FOR THE PERIOD ENDING 26 APRIL 1952

KALBA:

The situation is unresolved. The levies are still stationed in the Wadi Qor[77] and at Jabal Faiyah.[78] The P.R. visited the area. Some activity is expected in the near future. Sultan bin Salim[79] passed through again on his way to Manama,[80] and although he was halted, was not prevented from passing. The politicals are still keeping up the pretence that he has nothing whatever to do with the Kalba affair. These activities have thrown the Wadi somewhat into the limelight. It is understood that when it comes to settling the boundaries the Bani Kaab will claim half the Wadi.

Shaikh Saqr – brother of the dead Humaid[81] is still in residence in the Kalba part of Dibba, and no one questions his right to be there. He recently underwent a successful minor operation in Dubai Hospital.

RAS AL KHAIMAH:

The ruler's father is still very ill. It is thought to be malaria again.

UMM AL QAIWAIN:

The ruler is now in very much better health. A theft of paint from the Jassoura which took place at Umm al Qaiwain is now attributed to Sharjah subjects.

AJMAN:

The ruler has made a truce with the Bani Kitab lasting up to the month Dhu al Haj.[82] The ruler however was shot up by the Bani Kitab who claimed they thought he was Shaikh Rahmah bin Abdul Rehman of Sharjah (ex Haira), as their cars are similar. No one was injured, but Rashid was very angry. On the whole he has little right to be, considering ..., and the incident is regarded by everyone else as being rather comic.

---

77 Ghor or Qor.

78 Jebel Faiyah is south of Dhaid and in land occupied by the Bani Kitab under Sheikh Mohamed Ali Huwaidin. He denied the Company geologists access to the Jebel maintaining that it was his territory and that he should be rewarded financially. The Company insisted that the concession agreement was with, and the payment was made to, the Sharjah Ruler and so they should resolve the matter between them.

79 Previous Ruler of Ra's al-Khaimah. 1921-1948. Father of the Kalba 'ruler'.

80 The Ajman oasis in the foothills about 10 kilometres north east of Dhaid.

81 Former Ruler of Kalba. 1937-1951. Hamad bin Said (not Humaid, Henderson's mistake) was a boy in 1937 so the ex-Ruler of Sharjah, Sheikh Ahmed bin Khalid was appointed as Regent.

82 In that year August 22.

SHARJAH:

Some of the Bani Kitab, who appear to be on worse terms than usual with the ruler of Sharjah stole one of Saqr bin Sultan's[83] camels. He sent Rahmah bin Abdul Rehman[84] after them. Having shot up the ruler of Ajman on the Dhaid track (see above) the Bani Kitab came up with the levies. Apparently a Jordanian levy officer intervened, and the ruler of Sharjah got his camel back. The Bani Kitab appear to be very much out of control, and Rashid of Dubai may be partly responsible.[85]

However the presence of the levies in the Faiyah area seems to be having a good effect.

The levies are shedding Jordanians in exchange for locals. Some of the Jordanians are seeking to stay on down here with the locust mission or with anyone who will give them a job. Apparently their pay in Jordan is inadequate.

Mohammad bin Sultan[86] brother of the shaikh of Sharjah has joined the levies as a sort of ensign, or junior officer. He appears to be taking it seriously. Affairs seem to have taken a turn for the better as far as the levies are concerned.

Pocock[87] had to return before he intended to South Africa, because his wife was suffering from acute appendicitis. He left a Major Lippet in charge. He appears to have reversed all Pocock's policy, and seriously upset relations between his company and the ruler and people of Bu Musa.[88] He dismissed many of the skilled labour – the miners themselves – on the grounds that their pay (Rs. 4/-) was too high. He employed unskilled labour instead. This has caused serious unrest.

He has also had trouble with the boat crews, whom he sent out in bad weather, at risk to their lives. Subsequently he appears to have broken a promise to the ruler in regard to pay of labour.

He has offered to dredge Sharjah creek, build a jetty – a floating harbour and goodness knows what. The shaikh took it all seriously for a time, but his eyes are opened at last.

Among other futile activities he sent a letter to us recommending a consulting engineer to help us in Jabal Ali.

The second meeting of the Trucial Council[89] is appointed for the first of May to discuss, among other things, the Kalba succession question.

83 The Ruler's camels.

84 Sheikh of Hira.

85 The writer, Henderson's opinion!

86 Cousin of present Sharjah ruler.

87 Manager of the Golden Valley Red Oxide Company mining red oxide.

88 Large Sharjah island in Sharjah territory where the Red Oxide Company was operating a mine.

89 Trucial States Council 2nd meeting. Attended by all the Rulers and chaired by the Political Agent until 1965. Thereafter it was chaired by the Rulers in turn until its dissolution in

Dr. Hausmann[90] and a nurse are now established in a house in Sharjah and are at work. It is said that they are to be joined by more Americans later. The ruler of Ajman is much put out that they preferred Sharjah to Ajman. It is said that the ruler of Sharjah has permitted them to practise as religious missionaries, whereas the ruler of Ajman would not permit any conversions.

The ruler has ordered a lot of fruit trees to plant in Dhaid, and is said to have made many improvements there already.

DUBAI:

The first appendix was removed in Dubai Hospital, the Company doctor assisting. The patient is a levy corporal, and is doing well.[91]

A Lebanese water-divining company have been active in the area. They say that water is to be found at 400 feet under the site of the old aerodrome on the Sharjah road (Qarhud). Shaikh Rashid does not think much of them, and has not allowed them to continue.

Shaikh Rashid is thinking once more of having his hernia operated on. He wants to go to Muscat, but may end up in Bahrain.

Ganshyam of Damanmal Issardas is reported to be the new chief pearl inspector (the establishment of a system of inspection was reported last month).

There will be no main pearling season this year till after Ramadhan.

Four hundred people are reported to have left Dubai in the last 10 days for Saudi Arabia. Some are Dubai subjects, others from the interior, or from other coastal towns.

Lord Inchcape[92] called on the Shaikhs of Dubai and Sharjah.

The Ruler of Dubai had hoped to agree his frontier with the ruler of Sharjah direct. To this end they have had several meetings. He is now forced to admit that they cannot agree on a single point anywhere on their frontier, and he has referred the matter, with regret, to the P.O.T.S.

The P.O.T.S. sited two cairns (one on the track and one on the coast) on the Abu Dhabi/Dubai frontier. The Company under his guidance dug the holes and made the cairns. The P.O.T.S. promised to make it clear to the rulers concerned that the Company are in no way concerned with the siting, but merely assisted, as a matter of convenience, with the materials etc. This short frontier still remains the only one that has yet been defined on the whole coast.

1971. HEARD-BEY, F.U. (1982, 1996), p. 311.

90 One of the The American medical missionaries.

91 See TCDs October 1951 for more information about hospital. Also HEARD-BEY, F. U. (1982, 1966), p. 266.

92 The Chairman of Gray Mackenzie who provided marine services.

The locust mission still have their post at Ashush.[93] There have been other cases of animals alleged to have been poisoned by bait. However the shaikhs appear to be more on the side of the mission, who are not unduly worried by the attitude of a few individual badu.

A company consisting of Shaikh Khalifa[94] and Badri have been given monopoly rights to start a cinema (15 years monopoly) in Daira. They have purchased equipment from Persia.

ABU DHABI:

The Lebanese water diviners have had more success with the ruler than with Shaikh Rashid. It is said that they have already been paid between 12,000 and 16,000 rupees. It is not known if they have declared a find yet. They do not have with them any drilling apparatus, so far, but appear to have an instrument of some sort, which they claim gives them knowledge of the presence, the depth, and the purity of water.

They say that water should be available on the island itself but that it will not come up under its own pressure. It would be interesting to know whether it would be technically possible for any known instrument to give this information from the surface.

Buckmaster, having crossed by camel from Dahan to Liwa and back to Markhiya,[95] is now doing the Bainuna by car, and is said to be about to leave for Dalma.[96] Ali Bustani is with him, and Shaikh Zaid has personally conducted them everywhere. The anti-locust mission have lent them a car.

Shakhbut seems to have no transport at all and hires cars from Sharjah.

He appears to be transforming the camp at Maqta end of the island into a permanent building or fort. The garrison is still quite considerable.

There is no further news of any Saudi activity. The Ras Sadr camp and rig[97] is largely dismantled.

Henderson
Representative
efh/i.

---

93 A well at the border with Abu Dhabi in the far southeast of Dubai territory.

94 Sheikh Khalifa bin Saeed. Second son of the Ruler.

95 The Government post about 30 kilometres south of Ruwais.

96 Large island in the west of Abu Dhabi waters.

97 In those days a drilling rig tower was built piece by piece and later dismantled. This report is from more than a year after the well was abandoned. It was to be another decade before drilling rigs were introduced to Abu Dhabi where the tower was raised, lowered and transported in one piece.

ADDENDA TO TRUCIAL COAST DIARY 26 APRIL

DUBAI:

Locusts in swarms of hoppers have reached Jumaira.[98] The ruler has changed his mind about bait on the strength of the alleged deaths of animals. The results to his palm trees and camel grazing may be serious.

The ruler of Abu Dhabi has agreed to the use of bait.

A locust contingent from the Hajaz in three cars has arrived direct from Al Hasa. A representative of Bin Jaluwi[99] is said to be with the party.

The head legal adviser of the Foreign Office is paying a three day visit to the T.C. He is staying at the Company house, but having his meals at the Agency, at the request of the P.O. The arrangement seems to work satisfactorily.

Henderson
Representative.

TRUCIAL COAST DIARY FOR THE PERIOD ENDING 31 MAY 1952

GENERAL:

The Fast of Ramadan began on 25th May, but it is a comparatively cool month, and compared to previous years its coming has not made the usual impact on town life, although it has necessarily resulted in a quietening of the political scene. A few pearling boats from each of the Shaikhdoms went out to the banks before Ramadan, but they have returned to harbour and will remain there until after the Eid.

The steady, but noticeable, exodus of people from each of the Shaikhdoms to Bahrain, Qatar, Kuwait and Saudi Arabia continues. Many are finding employment whilst others have been disappointed and are returning to the Trucial Coast. Those of them who have returned and have succeeded in getting employment, are disgruntled with the local working conditions and rates of pay, and the various British organisations in Sharjah have experienced a new wave of labour troubles, due no doubt to this reason.

KALBA:

On 15th May HMG recognised the reincorporation of Kalba territory into the Shaikhdom of Sharjah. This annexation was brought about by peaceful means, ostensibly by Shaikh Saqr of Sharjah, but in fact by HMG, after nearly a year of

98 On the coast a few kilometres south of Dubai, now part of Dubai city.

99 The Saudi Al Hasa Governor.

unsuccessful and badly handled attempts to demonstrate that "succession by force" is out-dated, and no longer recognised on the Trucial Coast.

The POTS left for Wadi al Qaur (where the TC Levies had been stationed for sometime past) on 11th May, from where he despatched a letter to Saqr bin Sultan bin Sallim informing him that if he did not allow the entry into Kalba of the Ruler of Sharjah on the following day, HMG would have no alternative but to excercise force against him. This threat was not intended to be accompanied by a show of force, but due to extremely bad timing the P.R. was out visiting, and was landed from a Sloop near Fujaira the same day as the POTS's letter was received in Kalba!

Saqr bin Sultan bin Sallim left Kalba (for Muscat territory where he is still living) and Saqr bin Sultan of Sharjah marched in, accompanied by the POTS, a small force of Sharjah soldiers and the Levies. They were then called on by the P.R., after his visit to Fujaira, although this visit had not been previously planned.

Saqr bin Sultan bin Salim was evidently quite popular as Ruler of Kalba, for the POTS was confronted by a small demonstration of people who wanted Saqr to return, but these dissidents were taken in hand by Saqr of Sharjah.

Apart from the jubilations of Sharjah and the POTS, the only other reaction has been one of disappointment on the part of the Shaikhs of Ras al Khaima, who themselves hoped to benefit from HMG's removal of Saqr from Kalba.

Shaikh Saif Abdul Rehman, an uncle of the Ruler of Sharjah has been appointed as Wali of Kalba.

RAS AL KHAIMA:

All remains quiet in the territory and at Rams.

The P.R., on a recent visit to Muscat, again listened to the Sultan's complaint about intrusions into his territory by the Jawasim of Ras al Khaima. His complaint refers to the area of the Habus (in the hills immediately facing Ras al Khaima) and is presumably because of the recent Geological Party reconnaissances in this area. Although the Habus claim allegiance to the Shaikh of the Bani Hadiyah at Bakha,[100] there is little doubt that they are living in Ras al Khaima territory. During the summer they are forced to evacuate their hills and wadis[101] and migrate onto the Sir plain,[102] which is undisputably under the control of Ras al Khaima. It is interesting to note that the Sultan has not complained against the Company for operating in his territory without permission, which strictly speaking he should do to reinforce any claim he may make to the area.

100 On the Gulf coast in Sultanate of Oman territory a few kilometres north of the border with Ra's al-Khaimah.

101 Sultanate of Oman territory.

102 South of Ra's al-Khaimah town and north of Dhaid.

FUJAIRA:

Since his recognition as an independent Shaikh, the Ruler is reported to be very concerned because the Company has not yet sought a concession from him. He is at present in Ajman, still trying to reconcile the Ruler with the Bani Kitab.

SHARJAH:

The POTS,[103] A.J. Wilton, and his family, left Sharjah on his posting to Cairo on 19th May. His successor will probably be Pirie-Gordon, from Aden, but in the meantime The Hon. Martin Buckmaster, who arrived back from his Liwa trip just before the departure of Wilton, is the Acting P.O.

DUBAI:

The trade slump in Dubai is slowly making itself more felt, probably due to the dismal news from Jabal Ali, and there is a shortage of money.

Shaikh Rashid, accompanied by his father, sister, a large hareem, and fifteen specially chosen followers (all suffering from hernia) left for Muscat on 12th May. He was successfully operated on 24th May.[104] This was only after his fellow sufferers had been successfully dealt with, but even then he had to be tricked into having the operation. Shaikh Saeed returned to Dubai on 25th May, but Shaikh Rashid is not expected back until about 8th June.

Doctor D. G. McCaully left on home leave at the end of the month, and Dr. Mohd. Yasin remains in charge of the hospital, which seems to have become little more than a clinic. People wanting treatment still travel forth to Bahrain and Muscat.

The Ruler's approval to the building of a Cinema in Dubai has not yet been given and, in view of the present trade slump, is not expected.

ABU DHABI:

With the exception of his son, Saeed, Shaikh Shakhbut is still in Abu Dhabi on his own, and is already suffering the heat rather badly. Haza is with Zaid, in Baraimi, whilst Khalid is elsewhere in the desert. Both Haza and Khalid are said to have quarreled with Shakhbut regarding their share of the revenue, and since Shakhbut's return from Saudi Arabia they have each spent only a few days with him in Abu Dhabi.

Shakhbut has now built a stone bungalow for his new guard post, a short distance on the Abu Dhabi side of the Maqta ford.

The concrete blocks for the causeway are being made in Abu Dhabi, and work is expected to begin on the Maqta towards the end of Ramadan.[105] Having himself

---

103 Political Officer Trucial States.

104 At the American mission hospital in Mutrah.

105 The contractor was Khan Saheb Hussain, paid by PD(TC).

spent several months obstructing us in building the causeway, Shakhbut is now critical of the speed of the operation.

On the 26th May Shaikh Shakhbut was informed of the Company's intention to drill near MANDAFANA (Murban), south of Radaim. He was far from being overjoyed, and wanted to know why the Company was not going to operate in the area between Ras Sadr and the new location.[106]

Buckmaster (P.O.T.S.) returned from his Liwa trip about the middle of May, and claims that the information gathered by him is in favour of Abu Dhabi. Apparently Zaid spent a lot of money on the trip, and was as popular as ever among the baduin, but one wonders, for this reason, whether the party attracted a bias in the information which it gained on its travels.[107] It is interesting to note that Zaid is finding Shakhbut more intolerable than ever, and many of the baduin met with en-route were themselves very critical of Shakhbut.

COMPANY ACTIVITIES:

Drilling operations at Jabal Ali have reached a depth of slightly more than 12000 feet, and due to a crack in the casing, it is expected that drilling will finish earlier than was previously anticipated, possibly after a further 200 feet has been drilled.

A reconnaissance and visits to the site of new location in Abu Dhabi territory have already been made.

Codrai
Representative.

106 In other words, nearer to Abu Dhabi town.

107 See also TCD 10 March 1952.

TRUCIAL COAST DIARY FOR PERIOD ENDING 30 JUNE 1952

GENERAL:

The ill-famed Persian Gulf summer arrived on the Trucial Coast during the Eid al Fatr, after an unusually cool month. The Eid fell on Tuesday 24th June in all the Shaikhdoms except Ras al Khaima which, acting on radio news from Iraq and Egypt, declared Monday to be the Eid.

Owing to a heavy mist the Hallal[108] was not sighted from anywhere except Umm al Qaiwain, and the Eid began according to the law of Kamil (the end of thirty days of fasting). All the Shaikhdoms, with the exception of Fujaira, were visited by the representative[109] during the Eid.

Hundreds of people who went to Saudi Arabia in search of work have now returned to the Trucial Coast, having been refused permission to enter Saudi Arabia. A quarantine restriction is said to be the reason for this. Until recently people possessing letters from Shaikh Saeed bin Maktum were refused entry, but others bearing letters from Obaid bin Juma (of the Bani Kaab) were allowed to enter the country. Consequently Obaid bin Juma made a good thing of his favoured relations with the Saudis, and sold his letters for sixty Rupees each.

Henceforward, and since the re-incorporation of Kalba territory into the Shaikhdom of Sharjah (as reported in the Diary for May) events in Kalba will be reported on under the heading of "Sharjah."

RAS Al KHAIMA:

Saif bin Abdul Rehman, the former Shaikh of Rams; is still in shackles in the fort at Ras al Khaima.[110] The undersigned was introduced to him by the Ruler, and from appearances the prisoner seemed to be fairly well looked after. At any rate, he had been presented with a new shirt for the Eid, and had recently been under a torrential fall of rose-water. It is thought that he will be released as soon as he agrees to certain terms which are to be imposed on his freedom to prevent him creating any further trouble for the Ruler. It is now becoming more apparent that Saif was urged on in his policy of trouble-making by Said bin Badi (the victim of the ... episode of May, 1949) who is said to be dying in his house in Shammal,[111] and with his last energy is

108 New moon heralding the arrival of the fasting month Ramadan.

109 Codrai.

110 The treatment of prisoners varied. It was not uncommon for a prisoner, in his shackles, to seat inside the entrance to the fort where he could converse with any visitors. However the wretched conditions that some prisoners endured was rather severe.

111 A short distance north of Ra's al-Khaimah town. Now absorbed into the town.

still spreading hate against Saqr bin Mohammad. Saqr, on the other hand, is slowly endeavouring to strengthen his position among the Tanaij,[112] the Bani Shamaili and the Habus, and he took a great deal of trouble over visitors from these tribes during the Eid. He seems to be forever floundering between the weak advice of his father and his brother Humaid, and his own impulsive desires to fly into action and to put an end to all the trouble-makers. As always, he still feels that given the money he could bring all his dissident subjects under control. However, he is at present restraining himself from any act which might have harmful effects for him in the event of the Politicals trying to reach a settlement regarding the boundary between Ras al Khaima and Muscat territories.

Shaikh Mohammad bin Sallim is still suffering from a fever.

The Golden Valley Red Oxide Company[113] are to begin operations on Tunb Island[114] next winter.

UMM AL QAIWAIN:

Shaikh Ahmed bin Rashid seems to have fully recovered from his illness and is back to his former corpulent state, much to his own liking.

AJMAN:

Shaikh Mohd. bin Hamid of Fujaira has successfully mediated between Shaikh Rashid bin Humaid and the Bani Kitab. The settlement was for Rs. 1400/-, to which Rashid agreed and added a present of Rs. 1,000/. However, he is still very indignant that he should have been shot at by the Bani Kitab (The Diary of April) and refuses to see that it is a parallel case to that of his own misdemeanours.

Ajman has been infected with a little of Sharjah's enthusiasm for improving their Majlis, and now boasts what closely resembles a pre-fabricated kitchen, but which is many times hotter.

---

112 Tanaij people at Rams.

113 A British company mining for red oxide. A company which over the years caused problems for the British Political Agent, and indeed almost anyone who came into contact with them.

114 One of the two Ra's al-Khaimah islands, both on the north side of the median line between the Trucial Coast and Iran.

SHARJAH:

Shaikh Saqr bin Sultan has become very ambitious territorially, since his gain in Kalba, and has asked the Politicals to draw the Kalba/Shihu (Muscat)[115] boundary, and he has made claim to Dibba.[116]

Shaikh Mohd bin Hamid of Fujaira is the most apprehensive of all regarding the growth of Sharjah territory and is reported to have asked Saqr bin Sultan[117] for a written assurance guaranteeing his safety, if he goes to Sharjah. The reason for this remains very obscure, but one authority says that although Fujaira has been recognised as an independent Shaikhdom by HMG, Saqr of Sharjah is still claiming Fujaira as Jawassim[118] territory. Another more doubtfu1 source reports that Saqr has refused Mohd's request, and that the latter has openly declared a hostile attitude to Sharjah as the result.

Shaikh Saqr is fortifying his position in Kalba by marrying the sister of the former Ruler, Shaikh Hamid, and he leaves for the wedding in Kalba at the beginning of July. Shaikh Mohammad, the former acting Ruler of Sharjah, seems to be on good terms with Saqr, but outsiders distrust him, for he seems to be furthering his own interests rather than those of Sharjah.

DUBAI:

Shaikh Rashid bin Saeed and his party returned from Muscat by the overland route on the 8th June, and everyone including Rashid seems to be recovered; Rashid began fasting as soon as he arrived.[119] He is very impressed with the American Missionary Hospital at Matrah, but has brought back a very unfavourable impression of Muscat and the Sultan.

The trade slump in Dubai continues to make itself felt, and has been somewhat worsened by a tightening of control on the Persian coast round about Lingeh. The carriage of gold to Pakistan seems to be a flourishing trade at the moment, but this is of little benefit to trade in Dubai.[120]

---

115 In those days the Sultan, based in Muscat or Salalah in Dhofar province, exercised little control over the interior and parts of his land distant from Muscat; he was often referred to as the 'Sultan of Muscat'.

116 The large coastal oasis on the Indian Ocean shared between Sharjah, Fujairah and Muscat.

117 Sharjah ruler.

118 Qassimi.

119 He would have been excused fasting while he was on a journey and when he had been ill.

120 Gold smuggling through Dubai to the sub-continent of India was, for decades, a very profitable business for a number of merchants based in Dubai. There were times when the amount of gold passing through Dubai made Dubai one of the largest gold markets of the world. Gold arrived by air from Switzerland. Then fast launches based in Dubai Creek,

ABU DHABI:

The Ruler continues to remain alone in Abu Dhabi, and has still not yet been visited by any of his brothers. It has been confirmed that Shaikh Khalid and Haza have quarelled with Shakhbut on a question of finance.

COMPANY ACTIVITIES:

Drilling operations at Jabal Ali came to a sudden end (by order from London) on 26th June at a depth of approximately 12,300 feet. About 8000 feet of casing is to be recovered. A Seismic Party was here for the final week of drilling, making tests near the rig.[121] In the meantime, work has been progressing on the road to Tarif, and a C.A.T. Company[122] Representative has arrived to dismantle the buildings at Ras Sadr, which are to be re-erected at Tarif.[123]

Codrai
Representative.

TRUCIAL COAST DIARY FOR THE PERIOD ENDING 31 JULY 1952

GENERAL:

More interest than has been shown in the past is now being taken in the Saudi Arabian scene, and this may be partly attributed to the large number of people from the Trucial Coast who have recently been to Saudi Arabia. Most of them went in

and vests with pockets to each hold a gold thaler made by Dubai tailors, were all part of the system to evade Indian and Pakistani customs officials.

121 Seismic surveys are normally carried out by drilling a shallow hole to take an explosive charge, and laying strings of microphones to detect the resulting shock waves. The geophysicists could obtain more valuable information by placing the explosive charge deep in the earth and near to the rock formations that they were particularly interested in. In this case deep down in this well.

122 CAT Company was a prominent Lebanese company founded by Emile Bustani. "Emile had started out in a small way as a civil engineering contractor to the IPC in Haifa but moved to the Lebanon in 1948 and built his company until as CAT it had become one of the biggest contracting companies in the Middle East, working for all the oil companies and for several Governments" Mike Gardiner in the IPC Society Newsletter Issue 132 October 2006.

123 This was all in preparation for drilling the first well on, what was then and for many years named, the Murban geological structure. Tarif jebel was to be the base for the oil industry operating in the desert for the next thirty years. When I joined the company in 1963 I lived in Tarif – for three years.

search of work, but only a few were allowed to land there, and the remainder have come back to the Trucial Coast. This excursion has made many of them disgruntled with their lots here, now that they have seen other more developed parts, and those of them who have found employment since their return are now critical of the local rates of pay and working conditions.

The refusal of the Saudis to accept some (but not all) of the passes issued by the T.C. Shaikhs and the Sultan of Muscat raises a point of interest. Whatever the Saudi regulations and policy, they are not consistent: quarantine regulations may well be the reason for not allowing some of the immigrants to land, but the fact that Rs. 70/ is said to suffice to gain admittance points to a rather more oriental reason. It is possible, though not very likely, that there may be political reasons behind the Saudi policy of accepting a pass bearing, say, the Ruler of Sharjah's seal and not another from the Ruler of Dubai, but if this is intended to annoy any of the Shaikhs it has failed, although perhaps some success can be reported from Muscat.

Saudi activity in Oman has, of course, been another reason for this focus of interest.

RAS AL KHAIMAH:

On about 8th July a party of Tanaij, assisted by members of the Bani Hadiyah section of the Shihu,[124] raided and occupied Thayih and Ghara, two small settlements adjoining Rams. Fighting broke out when Saqr bin Mohd's[125] soldiers arrived on the scene, and this continued for several days, during which time a small number of casualties was inflicted on either side.

Shihu reinforcements were daily expected to arrive from Dibba to assist the raiders, but never appeared (it is about a three days walk over the hills from Dibba to Rams, in the frightful heat of summer of these barren hills).[126] The raiders then captured three of Saqr's followers, and held them as hostages, threatening to deal with them in the same manner that Saqr dealt with Saif bin Abdul Rehman, the imprisoned Shaikh of Rams.

There is little doubt that this trouble was instigated by Saif bin Abdul Rehman's relations in Rams, although as with most of the troubles in these parts, it was by no means disconnected from the politics of Bakha.[127]

124 The Omani tribe high up in the mountains of the Musandem peninsula who would, in the summer months, descend to the coastal plain in Ra's al-Khaimah territory.

125 Ruler of Ra's al-Khaimah.

126 The writer, Codrai, had himself walked this route.

127 Bakha is the coastal oasis north of Ra's al-Khaimah in the Musandam peminsula, (Sultanate of Oman).

The moment that fighting broke out, Saqr placed the matter in the hands of the P.O.T.S, and shortly after the outbreak a sloop[128] arrived at Rams, together with a detachment of T.C. Levies, and the trouble was squashed, although not until automatic weapons had been brought into use. Three of the Shihu are said to have been killed by this force, but this is denied by the P.O.T.S., but without any particular reason. Ten of the trouble-makers have been removed to Sharjah, where they have been joined by Saif bin Abdul Rehman, who was brought there by Saqr at the request of the P.O.T.S.

For reasons which are by no means clear, the Politicals now wish to reinstate many of the trouble-makers in Rams, where they have property. Saqr has protested against this move, but is bound to adhere to the wishes of the Politicals, knowing that it will not be long before he again needs assistance in this troublesome area. He has offered to give the people concerned property in Ras al Khaima town, equal to their possessions in Rams, rather than to have them returned to the scene of their misdeeds, and the matter has been submitted to the Political Resident for settlement. The Levy detachment, which has for some time past been stationed at Wadi al Qor, is to be moved to Rams.

Saqr has arranged a small loan with B.B.I.M.E.[129] Dubai, at a lower rate of interest than he has been paying to Dubai merchants, for advances on his concession monies.[130] H.M.G's support of Saqr, and the swift manner in which it was suppressed, has had a quietening effect on the Habus, the behaviour of whom has considerably improved recently. Nearly all the Habus migrate from the hills to the Sir Plain during the summer, where they frequently cause petty troubles and are always stealing dates, even from the gardens of the Ruler of Dubai. However, there is little hope of a permanent peace settling in this neighbourhood until the Muscat/ Ras al Khaima Boundary has been demarcated.

UMM AL QAIWAIN:

There is nothing to report from Umm al Qaiwain except the deep sighs of Shaikh Ahmed, which can be heard above the din of the troubles elsewhere.

AJMAN:

Since his unhappy experience in the desert, Rashid and his sons have remained in the town where they are striving to compete with Sharjah in modernising their fort.

128 Also known as a frigate. Small naval war-ship. The Swan class sloop, The Wild Goose, used in the Gulf carried 14 guns. It was 299 Feet (about 91 metres long) and displaced 1250 tons.

129 British Bank of Iran and the Middle East, now HSBC.

130 The money paid to the ruler by PD(TC) according to the agreement to allow geologists study the rocks in the hills.

SHARJAH:

Serious trouble broke out among the Bani Kitab during the month, but seems to have been silenced without a settlement having been made. The tribesmen have for some time past been demanding that their share of the Sharjah Concession payments be paid to them direct, and not to Ali bin Huwaidan,[131] their Shaikh. The latter flatly refused to give them anything (he receives but very little from Shaikh Saqr[132]), and the tribesmen then threatened a campaign of raiding and trouble-making, to show their independence. Ali[133] told them to do as they wished, and various incidents then took place near Dhaid, but these quickly came to an end when the Levies and soldiers from Sharjah began touring the area. All is quiet at present, but the Bani Kitab are still nursing their grievance.

Saqr went to Kalba at the beginning of the month and married a cousin of the murdered Ruler, who is said, by those who can see through Saqr's politics, to be a toothless old Hag. Saqr stayed but a short time to enjoy his nuptials, returning to Sharjah a few days later, leaving his new wife in Kalba.

Saqr is still not popular in Kalba, and the Wali who he has appointed seems to be as bad as Shaikh Humaid[134] (a former Ruler) for his drinking and drug-taking.

The Sharjah fort is undergoing extensive alterations, and has already taken on the appearance of a wedding cake, and the Shaikhs are making one or two minor efforts to improve their lot (and their view). They are growing increasingly jealous of Dubai's trade, and whenever they are able to, they insist that goods destined for Sharjah should not be off-loaded in Dubai. B.I. Steamers still have to drop anchor off Sharjah, even though it may only be for a few minutes, and they have neither goods nor passengers for Sharjah.

An attempt is being made to join together by a canal the Sharjah and Khan creeks, in the hope that a greater flow of water would open up the badly silted entrance to the Sharjah Creek. Labourers employed by the R.A.F., Anti Locust Party and other organisations are forced to work on this project, without pay, on their days off, and the unpopularity of this measure may easily be imagined.

Shaikh Saqr appears to be on bad terms with all his relatives, and has no strong ally among them.

A tense situation exists between Fujaira and Sharjah, which seems to have been brought about by a demand from the Ruler of Fujaira that if Saqr did not repay certain debts incurred by the former Ruler of Kalba (Saqr bin Sultan bin Sallim) he would declare war on Kalba. The debts seem to relate to transfers of property which have for

131 Does he mean Mohamed Ali Huwaidin?

132 Sharjah Ruler.

133 Mohamed Ali Huwaidin or his nephew Ali Abdullah?

134 Shaikh Hamad bin Saeed. HAWLEY, D. (1970), p. 356.

some time past been made between Fujaira and Kalba, but the issue is not a clear one, and has not yet been brought to a head.

Shaikh Saeed bin Maktum, accompanied by his son Khalifah and about one hundred and thirty followers, including women and children, is going on pilgrimage this year. Obaid bin Juma[135] is the only other notable Shaikh in the party. Saeed planned to travel with his party by launch to Dammam, but early in the month he received a cable from Coulson (at present acting as the Ruler's legal adviser on the question of his sea rights) requesting him to remain in Dubai until 7th August, when he is due to arrive there from London. The launch party is to depart about 3rd August, and Saeed is to join it at Dammam, having chartered an aircraft to take him there immediately after Coulson's visit. Three launches are being sent, with six vehicles which will be used for the overland journey to Mecca loaded on them. The party is to return by the same route.

Dubai has been a very active port during the month, and has averaged the arrival of one steamer a day. Large quantities of goods ordered before the present trade slump have overflowed from the custom's wharf, and are piled high at every suitable landing point. However, the illicit trade with Persia now seems to have re-started and the stacks of rice and sugar are slowly losing their former height.

It is interesting to note that the trade with Persia has taken on a new form: instead of the Dubai merchants smuggling their goods into Persia, near Lingah, as in the past, Persian merchants are themselves coming and buying direct from Dubai. Goods sold in this way still fetch the old smuggling prices (a sack of sugar costs a Dubai merchant about Rs. 100/- is resold for Rs. 150/ -) but the freight charges have been reduced to about Rs. 2/- per sack instead of the old charges of Rs. 5/-, due to the Persians using their own launches. This may well mean that the Persian market has become very competitive and merchants are being driven further afield, or it may merely mean that the reduced freight charge is the attraction.

Towards the end of the month Dubai saw the beginning of a new trade, the export of camels (Yazur, for eating) to Saudi Arabia, where they are in great demand. Some 50 to 100 have already been dispatched on launches. A camel costing Rs. 200/- to Rs. 500/- on the Trucial Coast fetches from Rs. 1000/- to Rs. 1500/- in Saudi Arabia. (The Dubai Subject, however, never allows high profits and good trade to stifle his flow of criticism, and he deplores the Saudi's choice of flesh.)

Work on the new Political Agency is to be started about the end of September, and it is thought that it will take about eighteen months to complete. The building is to comprise offices and living quarters for the P.A. and A.P.A. The site chosen for it is on the Dubai side of the creek, near the old AIOC[136] depot, and although this site has been criticized by everyone who has seen it the P.R. firmly adheres to his choice, claiming it

135 Obaid bin Juma al Ka'abi from Mahdha.

136 Anglo Iranian Oil Company.

would take two years to get Treasury permission to select a new site. The Ruler of Dubai is far from being pleased at the prospect of having the Agency in Dubai.[137]

A site for the new BBIME[138] building has been cleared (in the old fish market, next to Gray Mackenzie & Co.), and work is also to begin on it during September. Married accommodation for two families is to be built over the bank.

Everyone in Dubai has been greatly disappointed by the Company's unsuccessful attempt to find oil at Jabal Ali, but the Ruler and Shaikh Rashid (though none of the other Shaikhs) have led the people onto a path of philosophical acceptance of this sad news, despite much criticism of the Company by a handful of aggrieved merchants, and people who have visited some of the luckier Gulf States. Enquiries as to the Company's plans for the future became very earnest when the move to Tarif began, and particularly when the discharge of Dubai labour was begun. Until then it was never fully realised, not even by the Ruler, that operations at Jabal Ali were to be completely abandoned.

Shaikh Rashid and a large party were entertained to an Arabic film at Jabal Ali on 28th July, and the Ruler and all his relatives were entertained to lunch in the Representative's house in Dubai on 30th July, before the departure of the pilgrims.

A leading personality in Dubai, Shaikh Mubarak (a Senior Qadi) has been offered a teaching post in Doha, and is wavering on the edge of acceptance.

ABU DHABI:

The quarrel between Shajkh Shakhbut and his brothers seems to have taken on a serious aspect. Zaid, Haza and Khalid have become firmly united in their grudges against Shakhbut, and have been joined in Baraimi by their Mother, who is said to be as peeved as they are (she is also said to be very ill). The main issue is one of finance, regarding Shakhbut's division of the revenue, but other matters seem to be coming out in the boil. The brothers are voicing their distaste of the behaviour of Shakhbut's sons, Saeed and Sultan, rightly objecting that these boys are being given all the money they ask for to spend on … , cars and their other pleasures, whilst Zaid is deprived of money which he needs to strengthen Abu Dhabi's influence among the baduin. Saeed's behavior certainly deserves censure … .He[139] strongly objects to Saeed being made acting Ruler, on occasions when Shakhbut is away from the town.

Shakhbut has further aggravated the situation by proclaiming Saeed to be his lawful heir. With Zaid and Haza still alive, this is nothing short of an insult, and no one is more sensitive to this than the Abu Dhabi badu.

137 The Ruler and his people were not happy about having the British Political Agent so close, they feared that he might try to influence matters where his interference was not welcome.

138 British Bank in the Middle East. Now part of HSBC.

139 Sheikh Zayed strongly objects.

Shakhbut seems to be well aware of the difficult position he has placed himself in, and with side glances to the family tree he has set about fortifying his position. He has greatly increased the numbers of his followers, and has kept back and armed many people who would otherwise have gone pearl-diving.

Shaikh Mohammad bin Sultan,[140] who has always made known his friendship for the Abu Dhabi Shaikhs, spent several days in Baraimi and Abu Dhabi, with a view to mediating between the brothers, but failed to even elicit an admission that all was not well in the House of Bani Sultan bin Zaid,[141] and has returned to Sharjah without achieving anything. Mohd bin Khalifah[142] is said by outsiders to be mediating, but he has so far failed to put in an appearance at Abu Dhabi.

Shaikh Zaid arrived in Abu Dhabi shortly after the middle of the month, and remained there for a week, during which time he went off for several days on a hunting trip by launch. The shaikhs are being so reticent regarding their troubles that it is not known as to whether Zaid has yet done anything towards lessening their difficulties, but his return to Oman[143] and non-arrival of his brothers indicates little change. A party of 25 of Shakhbut's followers, led by Ahmed bin Fadhal, were recently sent off on a trip to Liwa to endeavour to strengthen Abu Dhabi's position there. Ahmed bin Fadhal, has, however, returned to Abu Dhabi and the party is now being led by Rashid bin Jabir, a former Head Guard at Ras Sadr.

It is not to be wondered why the Company has experienced difficulties in its dealings with Shakhbut, when one sees the troubles that his own brothers are having with him.

OMAN:[144]

The number of Saudi visitors to Oman[145] seems to be on the increase. Most of them appear, in some way or other, to have some connection with bin Jaluwi of Al Hasa.

Shaikh Rashid bin Hamid[146] is away on another visit to Riyadh.

The Imam[147] recently summoned the Shaikhs of the Bani Baluch to his presence, no doubt to rebuke them for making agreements with the Saudis. A messenger was instantly dispatched to inform the Saudis of this, and to seek guidance, and he was

140 Uncle of Sharjah Ruler.

141 Meaning the four brothers, all sons of Sultan bin Zayed bin Khalifa.

142 Sheikh Shakhbut's cousin, Sheikh Mohamed bin Khalifah bin Zayed bin Khalifa.

143 Muwaiji/Buraimi.

144 Buraimi.

145 Meaning Buraimi, Hamasa.

146 Shamsi from Hamasa (Buraimi).

147 The Imam of Oman, Mohamed Abdulla Khalili (1920-1954) exercised authority over much of the interior of Oman.

very well received by bin Jaluwi and sent by air to Riyadh. He was then given letters for the Bani Baluch Shaikhs, Obaid bin Juma and others, and given a verbal assurance that the Saudis would give all the support necessary to the Bani Baluch, and would shortly be sending a party in that direction.

COMPANY ACTIVITIES:

The new operations have been getting well under way, and a track to Tarif from Ras Sadr has already been graded. Abu Dhabi labour is slowly being recruited, whilst Dubai labour is being discharged from Jabal Ali. Towards the end of the month three Cov. Staff moved into temporary, air-conditioned quarters at Tarif, and work is in full swing there. The C.A.T. Company have nearly completed taking down the buildings at Ras Sadr, which are to be re-erected at Tarif.

A Saudi vehicle carrying five passengers visited Tarif at a point near Ras Kahaf[148] about the middle of the month, and then turned back to go westwards. This party was said to be looking for runaway slaves. A report that a larger party was camped at Al Agaila,[149] holding discussions with the Manasir Shaikhs, has not been confirmed. Towards the end of the month a Dakota aircraft bearing green markings seemed to be making fairly close observations of our activities in Western Abu Dhabi.

Codrai
Representative.

TRUCIAL COAST DIARY FOR THE PERIOD ENDING 31 AUGUST 1952

GENERAL:

The outstanding event of importance has been the recent meeting between Shaikh Shakhbut and Shaikh Rashid bin Saeed. (whose relations since the Dubai/Abu Dhabi war in 1946/47 have been strained). This is reported on below, under the heading of Abu Dhabi.

All the Trucial States are suffering an unhealthy period of economic depression. Trade is bad, the cost of living is rising and despite the present immigration difficulty into neighbouring countries, a considerable proportion of the T.C. population is slowly drifting away.

---

148 A headland on Dabiiyah about 30 kilometres due west of Abu Dhabi town.

149 About 20 kilometers south of Jebel Dhanna and a few kilometres west of Markhia, the Abu Dhabi Government post and a few kilometres northeast of Bida Mutawa, the Manasir settlement.

The Persians are now carrying out what would appear to be their first full-scale operation to prevent smuggling by local boats, and the effect of this has been felt in Bahrain and Kuwait, although the effect on trade is not as important to the trading communities in these countries as it is serious on the Trucial States. The rise in cost of living during the past four years is shown by the following figures:

Dubai Market Prices.[150]

		Nov. 1948.	Aug. 1952.
Ghee, Omani.	per maund	Rs. 19- 0-0	28- 0-0
Mutton,	per maund	8- 0-0	12- 0-0
Beef.	per maund	6- 0-0	10- 0-0
Coffee.	per maund	8- 0-0	24- 0-0
Onions.	per maund	1-12-0	2- 0-0
Tea.	per pound	5- 0-0	5- 0-0
Sugar.	per maund	4- 0-0	4- 4-0
Flour.	per maund	5- 2-0	4- 8-0
Rice.	per maund	7-10-0	8- 0-0

The Eid al Haj was celebrated on 27th August in Dubai, Sharjah and Ajman, and on the following day at Umm a1 Qaiwain, Ras al Khaima and Abu Dhabi.

RAS AL KHAIMAH:

Shaikh Mohammad bin Sulaiman of Bakha left on pilgrimage at the beginning of the month, travelling by air to Dammam from Sharjah.

The Levy post referred to in the diary for July has now been installed at Rams, and although it is manned by only a small detachment, about ten in number, the effect of its establishment has been very favourable, and this troublesome area has known a whole month of peace. Petty pilfering of the date harvest on the Sir Plain, which has been the blight of the lives of the owners of the date gardens for many years past, has now practically ceased.

On 26th August Saqr made peace with the Shihu of Dibba for a period of six months. These are the Shihu who were expected to rally to the support of the Rams trouble-makers, but who failed to arrive at the scene of battle. This conciliation was

150 Rupees, Annas and Pais. 4 Pais to the Anna and 16 Annas to the Rupee. Maund is about 9 pounds or 4½ kilogrammes.

effected by Shaikh Rashid, the Sharqiyeen[151] Wali of Hab Hab,[152] and both parties were brought together near Khatt, the Shihu after a two day walk from Dibba and Shaikh Saqr after a thirty minute drive from Ras al Khaima. The Shihu had no leaders, and Saqr touched hands with three or four of the elders, the meeting lasting less than a minute.

Two minor, but interesting facts have manifested themselves as a result of this meeting. Firstly the Shihu have no recognition for anything except their complete independence, and the name of Muscat is quite foreign to their politics. The Sultan of Muscat will have difficulty in establishing his claim to their territory on any but vague historical facts. Secondly, the Wali, so-called, of Hab Hab, by no means regards himself as being a subordinate of the Ruler of Fujaira, and although the comparatively large area which he controls is inhabited by Sharqiyeen he has little contact with Fujaira, and a greater friendship with Ras al Khaima. Shaikh Saqr is well aware of the value of this friendship, and when the boundaries are drawn in this area the Ruler of Fujaira may well find that he has lost territory to Ras al Khaima.

Having excelled themselves at dealing with the Rams trouble, the Politicals have embarked on a policy which lesser brains find difficult to understand. The Political Resident has decreed that the trouble-makers, Shaikh Saif bin Abdul Rehman and his relatives, should be reinstated in Rams, despite the indignant protests of the Ruler.

Camping in the grounds of the Political Agency, these dissidents have seized every opportunity that this policy has placed in their path, and their demands on the Political Officer (even had they been the winners, in this affair, instead of the losers) have become so ridiculous, not even stopping at HMG's recognition of them as being completely independent, that the P.O. has been once again forced to submit the matter to the P.R.

Shaikh Khalid bin Ahmed, the former Regent of Kalba, died at Shammal, near Ras al Khaima, on 14th August. He had been ill and very weak for some time past.

The Ruler signed a Sea-Rights Declaration in favour of the Company[153] on 26th August.

Shaikh Saqr of Ras al Khaima and Shaikh Saqr of Sharjah have made an agreement which should be of considerable help to them in keeping control of their territories. They have arranged that trouble-makers from Khawatir[154] will no longer be able to escape to Sharjah territory, and similarly the Bani Kitab will find no sanctuary in Ras al Khaima. Letters to each of these tribes have been despatched by each of the Saqrs.

151 Fujairah tribe.

152 A Fujairah settlement in the mountain foreland 20 kilometres south of Ra's al-Khaimah town and a few kilometres south of Ra's al-Khaimah's Khatt. The latter is known for its hot springs.

153 The Company, PD(TC).

154 The large Naim tribe on the Jiri Plain south of Ra's al-Khaimah and north of Dhaid.

SHARJAH:

The Ruler has complained to the P.O.T.S. about the encroachment by the Sultan of Muscat beyond Aswad, at the end of Wadi al Qor.

A new Political Officer, M.S. Weir, arrived Sharjah during the month, and is to remain until the arrival of the new P.A., about the end of the year. Weir was previously P.O. at Doha, prior to which he was secretary to the P.R. assisting on the Abu Dhabi/ Saudi Arabian Frontier talks, in Saudi Arabia.

Gray Mackenzie & Co.,[155] are meeting with increased difficulties in the course of their business in Sharjah. B.I. Steamers with very small cargoes for Sharjah have been delayed, waiting for local lighters, and on some occasions the Ruler has tried to insist that the Steamer waits off Sharjah a whole day or more, until it has been possible to send out a lighter.[156] The Ruler's jealousy of Dubai is such that he now makes strong complaints to Gray-Mackenzie & Co., whenever the smallest cargoes for Sharjah is, by necessity, off-loaded in Dubai.

In an attempt to revive trade, and steal a little of Dubai's business, Sharjah merchants are importing a large quantity of rice: by a chartered steamer, but it is expected that they will lose on the deal, mainly due to the state of Sharjah creek which does not permit speedy discharge of a large cargo, and it will cost the merchants £350 a day whilst the ship is standing-to. Gray Mackenzie & Co., are not prepared to risk more than one barge on the operation for, much to the Ruler's annoyance, the steamer is afterwards to discharge a cargo at Dubai.

This is a trifling detail of news, but it serves to illustrate the situation created by the Ruler's efforts to build up his seaport and to make Sharjah completely independent of Dubai. It is the warning light of the situation as it will develop everywhere along the Trucial Coast in the future, as the Rulers slowly become more and more conscious of their boundaries, and the Company will no doubt be faced with the same difficulties as it experienced in Abu Dhabi, in keeping its operations in one territory independent of facilities in the next.

DUBAI:

Shaikh Saeed left on Pilgrimage on 8th August, having chartered an aircraft to take him to Dammam, where he caught up with his party who had travelled on ahead

155 Shipping agents based in Dubai.

156 In those days, in the shallow waters of the Gulf, the ships had to discharge their cargoes a mile or two offshore onto barges. The barges had then to negotiate the way into the creeks, Dubai, Sharjah or Umm al Quwain. The entrance to the creeks were often obstructed by sand banks as tides carried sand back and forward, sometimes laying new sandbanks or scouring out a different channel.

by sea. Shaikh Rashid, espying a vacant seat in the aircraft, made a last minute decision to accompany his father to Dammam, from where he returned two days later.

During his short stay he had a long meeting with bin Jaluwi,[157] and the latter presented him with a gold sword. One source reports that Rashid was very outspoken in his talk with bin Jaluwi, and told him that the Omanis did not want the Wahabis in their country. The Saudis evidently think a lot of Shaikh Saeed, and made a great fuss of him, placing many cars at his disposal.

The day before he departed, the Ruler signed a Sea Rights Agreement with the Company.[158]

Dubai's relations with Abu Dhabi are reported on under the heading Abu Dhabi.

Three Foreign Office Works people have rented a house in Derra,[159] where they are to live for the next year or more to supervise the building of the new Agency.

The BBIME[160] has asked the C.A.T. Company[161] to give them an estimate for the building of the new Bank.

ABU DHABI:

Shakhbut, accompanied by his son Sultan and Hamdan bin Mohammad, and four other followers, arrived unexpectedly in Sharjah during the night of 29th August, and asked for an aircraft to be chartered to take him to Bombay, where he is going for medical treatment. He shortly afterwards changed his mind, and the aircraft was diverted in flight, and Shakhbut is now going to India on the B.I. Steamer on 6th September.

As soon as Rashid bin Saeed of Dubai heard this news he sent a letter to the P.O.T.S. asking him if there would be any objection to his visiting Shakhbut. The reply from the P.O. was favourable, and Shaikh Rashid and Juma, accompanied by the undersigned, met Shakhbut in the B.O.A.C. Fort[162] on the evening of 30th August. The meeting was very friendly, and great credit goes to Rashid for having made this gesture. It was most interesting seeing these Shaikhs together, and the contrast in their personalities. Rashid was very nervous, which made him even more talkative and vivacious than usual, in contrast to which Shakhbut sat in silent dignity, but not unsmiling, although rather uncertain of the boisterousness which was going on

157 Al Hasa Governor.

158 The agreement was negotiated with the ruler by PD(TC)'s Heseldin and then transferred to AIOC (BP).

159 Part of Dubai territory and north across the creek from Dubai proper.

160 British Bank of Iran and the Middle East. Later British Bank of the Middle East. Now HSBC.

161 Contracting and Trading Company. Still very big in the Middle East.

162 The British Overseas Airways guest house, now the Mahatta museum in Sharjah. Well worth a visit.

around him. Juma,[163] as the Senior Dubai Shaikh, sat with Shakhbut with apparent disconcern for the occasion. He was in one of his winking and pipe-filling moods, and seemed to spend much of the time appealing to the large and distinguished majlis for a cut-out for his car.

It was an occasion which anyone who had any feelings for these Shaikhs could not be unaffected by, though on sober reflection after the flabbergasting suddenness with which this event was brought about, the value of it appears less certain. It was an outward show of friendliness between the Shaikhs, and thanks to Rashid, a big step in the right direction towards an ultimate reconciliation, which one can hardly claim has already been effected by this meeting. It is unlikely that Zaid[164] will approve of this happening, and Saeed bin Maktum[165] has yet to give it his blessing.

After a truly magnificent lunch given for Shakhbut by Rashid in Dubai, all the Dubai Shaikhs made repeated attempts to persuade Shakhbut to stay with them in Dubai, until the arrival of the B.I. Steamer, but Shakhbut said that he preferred to live quietly in the B.O.A.C. Fort[166] so that he could enjoy the air-conditioning. He was also invited by Shaikh Saqr of Sharjah to stay with him, and the Company Representative offered to accommodate him in the Company House. After he had refused all these invitations, Shakhbut was then told by the Manager of the Fort that he will have to move out, as there is no longer any room for him, and it is not yet known where he is going to stay. The P.O.T.S. seems to see nothing amiss in the ejection of Shakhbut from the Fort.

Shakhbut is to be entertained to a meal in the Company House in either Dubai or Sharjah, before he departs on 6th September.

Mohammad bin Khalifah,[167] mediating between Shakhbut and his brothers, visited Abu Dhabi on about 21st August, and returned to Oman a few days later to fetch Haza and Khalid back with him to Abu Dhabi. However, Haza and Khalid feel that it is now up to Shakhbut to visit them in Baraimi, and no settlement has yet been effected. Zaid is said to be desperately in need of money. Saeed bin Shakhbut is the acting Ruler in Abu Dhabi, during Shakhbut's absence.

COMPANY ACTIVITIES:

Work on the move to the new location at Tarif is actively under way, though the usual water supply and transport difficulties have manifested themselves. Slight labour trouble during the month, caused by the fact that Abu Dhabi labourers were having to

163 Brother of the Ruler, Sheikh Saeed bin Maktoum.

164 Sheikh Zayed bin Sultan of Abu Dhabi.

165 Dubai Ruler.

166 The B.O.A.C. rest house.

167 Sheikh Shakhbut's cousin.

spend most of their off days journeying to and from Abu Dhabi, was quickly settled, and it is hoped that the causeway across the Abu Dhabi ford will soon be completed, and will make the leave arrangement much simpler.

OMAN:

The much talked about Party which was to be sent from Saudi Arabia to Oman (see TCD July) arrived in Hamasa[168] on 31st August. The Party, which is led by the former Amir of Ras Tanura, Turki bin Ataishan, consists of some sixty to eighty soldiers, and includes some Manasir who they picked up en route. The Party arrived in four large vehicles, and two jeeps, and was accompanied by Rashid bin Hamid[169] and his brother Mohammad, who were travelling in a car presented to them by the Saudis. The Party is equipped with a W/T set.[170]

The moment the Party arrived, Shaikhs Zaid, Haza, Khalid, Mohd bin Khalifah and Hamid bin Bati[171] visited Saqr bin Sultan (Naim)[172] and had a long discussion with him, as a result of which a letter was immediately dispatched to the P.O.T.S. requesting him to send a Levy detachment to sit in Baraimi, to show that it was under British protection. The P.O.T.S.'s reply has not yet been received.

Codrai
Representative.

168 Oasis next to Buraimi oasis in the Sultanate of Oman.

169 Hamasa sheikh, Shamsi.

170 Wireless transmitter for communication.

171 Maternal uncle of Sheikh Shakhbut.

172 Buraimi sheikh.

TRUCIAL COAST DIARY FOR PERIOD ENDING 29 SEPTEMBER 1952

GENERAL:

The Saudi "invasion" of Baraimi has taken prominence over all other events on the Trucial Coast.[173] No Shaikhdom which claims authority over any badu tribe, and hence the area in which they live, has been unaffected by this event. At the same time the rulers look to Ibn Saud as the Great Arab King. The shaikhs as a whole therefore attempt to remain aloof from these events leaving any action to H.M.G.[174]

RAS AL KHAIMAH:

Shaikh Saif[175] remains in Sharjah with his party. Mr. Weir[176] is shortly to visit Ras al Khaimah. It is believed that he will try to make an arrangement that the Ruler shall pay Saif and his people annually Rs. 5, 000/-, provided they remain outside the sheikhdom and leave their property in Rams in the hands of an agent.

Sultan bin Salim, the former ruler of Ras al Khaimah is pressing for an allowance from the present ruler, Shaikh Saqr. It is understood that Saqr is prepared to pay Rs. 10,000/- a year provided Sultan moves out of the Wadi Ghor and resides in the Batinah.[177] It is believed that the P.O. will support Sultan's claim for Rs. 12,000/ and permission to remain in the Wadi. The Politicals seem willing to be liberal with Saqr's money.

A traveller from Dibbah says there is no longer any Muscat Wali there. The Qasimi half of the town is run by Saqr bin Abdullah the brother of Humaid,[178] who died in Kalba in 1951. He appears to be completely independent.

AJMAN:

The Ruler is contemplating a visit to Kuwait. His son 'Ali did well, financially, out of a visit to that place. The ruler does not appear so far to have meddled in Baraimi, but has watched the situation keenly. He is amused at his cousin Saqr's predicament.

---

173 For a fuller account of this event see HEARD, (2019), Chapter 9.6.

174 H.M.G., His Majesty's Government, The British Government. The writer, Henderson was only partly correct. Sheikh Shakhbut left for India. Sheikh Zayed, however, was active, calling on the Political Resident, who happened to be in Sharjah. He forcefully stated his concerns and a detachment of the Trucial Oman Levies did come to Buraimi.

175 The Tunaiji sheikh. The last we read of him in the diary was that he was camping in the grounds of the Political Agency in Sharjah having been released from his chains in the Ra's al-Khaimah fort.

176 The Political Officer.

177 The Indian Ocean coast of the Sultanate of Oman.

178 Deputy to the Regent Sheikh Khalid bin Ahmed. Hamad not Humaid.

He is worried however at the number of his own people who have gone to Saudi Arabia and elsewhere. He claims that his town is fast losing its population. He has spent some of his recently acquired money on a lighting plant, which doesn't work, and on beautifying the palace.

The Ruler has left by air for Kuwait leaving his uncle Rahmah bin Abdulrehman[179] in charge.

SHARJAH:

Damanmal Issardas[180] has imported 1600 tons of rice in a Danish vessel, paying only 1½% import tax. The cargo took many days to land, but it was done at last. Most of the rice will be exported by sea and a little by land. The landing was costly and there is likely to be loss. This consignment was landed at Sharjah because D.I.'s agent Gunshyam filed a suit against Rashid bin Said for blocking his view from his house by heightening a building. Rashid was so incensed that he forbade the import of rice by D.I. The ruler of Sharjah agreed to have it landed there at a much lower import tax. Much of it however is still in the open. Gunshyam it is believed will have to leave Dubai.

The Resident came ashore for a few hours conference with the P.O. about Baraimi. He met Zaid, the mother of the ruler of Abu Dhabi, Ahmed bin Rashid of Umm al Qaiwain, Rashid bin Said of Dubai and others.

Shaikh Khalid has returned from Kuwait richer than he went. However he says that his brother the ruler with whom he is on bad terms, has stopped his allowance. His brother Mohd.[181] is said to be doing well in the Levies and may shortly go to O.C.T.U. in Amman. Projects for draining the creek are being discussed.

Pocock has left the Golden Valley Company of Bu Musa and Major Lippet, who caused the labour trouble and who is said to have supplanted Pocock, is to arrive shortly to begin work on Bu Musa.

DUBAI:

Shakhbut sailed to India from Dubai on September 6th by B. I. Zaid stayed for several days with the ruler's son.[182] They were both entertained to lunch at Company house. The rapprochement should have very good results as far as the Company is concerned. Zaid thinks he has persuaded Rashid bin Said to dabble no more in Baraimi. Possibly this may be so as dabbling may no longer be necessary.

179 Formerly Sheikh of Hira.

180 Indian merchant.

181 Sheikh Mohamed bin Sultan.

182 Sheikh Rashid bin Saeed.

The trade slump has grown if anything-worse. The bank are forging ahead with plans to build their new establishment on the South side[183] of the creek. It is said that CAT Co. have been offered the contract.

The ruler returned from pilgrimage on the 21st. He appears to be very well after all his travels. Rashid had flown to meet him in Saudi Arabia, but the launch sailed with Said four hours before Rashid arrived. Rashid returned by air in time to meet him in Dubai. Jum'a met the party in Riyadh, with an eye to his own benefit, and was not disappointed. Shaikh Said travelled back by car to Riyadh from Mecca. At the capital the King entertained them and gave them a big dinner. The ruler then continued by train to Dammam where he stayed with Bin Jaluwi. The latter entertained them well, but with his usual grim, taciturn, demeanour. The ruler seemed much better pleased by the Saudis than the Al Bu Falah[184] have been.

Four British Ministry of Works officials have come to begin the construction of the new Agency.

ABU DHABI:

Said bin Shakhbut has been left in charge in Abu Dhabi, though it is believed that Zaid is in general charge, from Baraimi. Rashid bin Jabir al Khaili has been appointed representative in Shakhbut's Western territory. He is encamped at Markhia in Bainuna, with about 20 men. This is a belated attempt to administrate the area. It is significant however that this man is a Mansuri of the Al bu Khail section (the closest to Bani Yas of all of them.) [185]

BARAIMI:

The Baraimi debacle has been reported week by week in letters.[186] However a summary may be useful.

(i) The Amir Turki established himself at once in Hamasa and set up a passport office. He gave presents and passports to all comers: 9,000 have been issued in September.

(ii) Zaid came to Sharjah to ask help from the P.O. The P.O. referred to Bahrain and the P.R. to London. The P.R. in the meantime came himself to Sharjah, and stayed a few hours. Zaid put his case clearly and forcefully, but received no promise of support. He finally on his own returned to Baraimi and announced there that the levies would follow. As he said he had nothing to

183 The Dubai side.

184 Abu Dhabi ruling family.

185 Usually said not to be Manasir.

186 These letters are missing from these files.

lose. If the Levies had not come within a few days all his people with the exception of 50 or so would have gone over to the Saudis.

(iii) Luckily 2 days later the word came from London to send the Levies. P.O.T.S., Brigadier Baird and the Levies went to Baraimi via the Ramlat al 'Anaij. The Levies stopped near Suara[187] and the P.O. went on to Al 'Ain. The party stayed a few days. Apparently their arrival frightened the Saudis as did the R.A.F. Vampires[188] which flew low over Hamasa. However P.O. and Levies withdrew to Sharjah.

(iv) The Levies were sent back again and the same party accompanied them. By this time the Saudis were getting used to the aircraft.

(v) Nearly all the shaikhs of the Dhahira went over to the Saudis almost at once. Saqr bin Sultan al Naimi of Baraimi alone held out. Considerable pressure was put on him and he was asked to fly the Saudi flag. He refused and said he would only negotiate with the King himself.

(vi) The P.O. left the Levies in Al 'Ain and returned to Sharjah.

(vii) A lorry with 9 Saudis on board was held (after it had broken down) on the Baraimi track near Awad al Matinah, by the Levies. The Saudis were taken to the P.O. One was sentenced to deportation, the remainder who, it was found had not, owing to a technicality, broken the visa regulations, were released. They were warned however that in future Saudis without visas would be arrested.

(viii) 3 Shamsi Levy soldiers in Al 'Ain deserted to Turki with their rifles. Turki returned them and their rifles. They were discharged from the Levies.

(ix) A day or two ago a group of shaikhs left for Saudi Arabia in two Saudi cars. Each Shaikh has one retainer. Their objective is thought to be Riyadh and the King himself. They are:- Ahmed Salf of Hafit, Said bin Huwaidan (cousin of Ali bin Huwaidan), Mohd bin Salamin bin Rahmah al Shamsi, Obaid bin Jum'a al Kaabi, Abdullah bin Salim al Kaabi (of the formerly dissident faction), (not yet confirmed Matar bin Salim of Dhank), and Bin Rakadh al Amiri. 150 followers were to go by sea. However at Jabal Faiyah they were met by the Saudi party -who had been held by the P.O. and were warned that if they reached the coast they might be arrested.

GENERAL:

It is clear that much of the Dhahira is now firmly in Saudi hands. Saqr alone holds out, but he must by now be almost without influence outside his village. Many

187 The third Buraimi village in the Sultanate of Oman. Buraimi, Hamasa, Suara. Suara is on the east side of Buraimi while Hamasa is on the west side.

188 Small jet fighter aircraft.

of the Dur'u and individuals from the tribes have become Saudis. Otherwise 'Oman from Ibri and beyond is not much affected as yet. The Baluch shaikhs have all become Saudi and so we believe have the tribes represented by the shaikhs in the above list of those who are visiting Riyadh. It is not known what proportion of the Bani Kitab are now considered Saudis, but it is reported by the P.O. himself to be 200 adult males, i.e.; a very large part of the tribe.[189]

It is still believed that the Imam[190] and Saiyid Said[191] have made contact (as reported before).

The arrival of the Levies alone saved the Al bu Falah[192] in Baraimi and possibly in the whole of Abu Dhabi shaikhdom. To their disastrous delay however many defections (perhaps the Bani Kitab) may be attributed.

It is not thought that the Saudis are likely to leave Liwa alone and if H.M.G. cannot provide counter-action to whatever they may do there, this may seriously damage the Al Bu Falah.

The Saudis may have reached a temporary high-water mark in their success in Baraimi, but there would seem to be no limit to the possibilities if they set to work systematically in the Dhafara.[193]

Henderson
Representative.

---

189 Henderson appears to assume that ever one who has taken Saudi money had become a Saudi citizen. In hindsight, this would not be a reasonable assumption.

190 The Imam of Oman who ruled the interior of the country. Mohamed Abdullah al Khalili.

191 The Sultan whose influence was weak away from the coast.

192 The Bani Yas tribe to which the Abu Dhabi ruling family belong.

193 The area south of Buraimi as far as Ibri and beyond in the Sultanate of Oman. Although the situation appeared to be very alarming, I think Henderson was unduly pessimistic. The reports from that time, such as written by Bird indicate that the people would give their allegiance to all, or any, of the competing interests, the Sultan in Muscat, the King in Saudi Arabia and a Trucial Coast sheikh, while asserting their own independence and dignity.

TRUCIAL COAST DIARY FOR THE PERIOD ENDING 31 OCTOBER 1952

GENERAL:

Summer has been lingering, and the weather has remained rather warm, although first signs of winter have appeared over the mountains. There have been slight, isolated showers of rain at Dhaid, Ras al Khaima and in 'Oman. The last of the pearling boats have now arrived back in harbour.[194]

Despite the troubled state of affairs in 'Oman,[195] which to some extent or other has cast a general gloom over every Shaikhdom on the coast, the shaikhs have greeted the hunting season with their usual gay abandon. The Jawasim shaikhs have contented themselves with a little gazelle shooting, but the Dubai and Abu Dhabi shaikhs have given themselves over to catching and training and hunting with their hawks with their usual enthusiasm, and inconvenience to those who have business with them.

Trade remains very bad in all the coastal towns, and the inhabitants continue to slowly drift away to other parts.

RAS AL KHAIMAH:

The Politicals have not yet succeeded in arranging a settlement between the Ruler of Ras al Khaima and Shaikh Saif and his relatives from Rams, but it is expected that the Resident himself will intervene and try and settle the matter when he arrives on his annual tour, at the beginning of November.

Shaikh Mohammad bin Sallim, the Ruler's father, has been taken to Derra,[196] where he lies seriously ill. He has, for some years past, been suffering frequent attacks of malaria and his present illness seems to be a bad attack of the same ailment.

The Seismic Party No.5 Camp is at present established near Labana, south of Khatt on the Jiri Plain.

The Company vessels Jessoura and Afri have both been inside the Ras al Khaima creek, discharging seismic equipment at Maria. The Party is at present operating in Khawatir territory only, and is using the Kuran/Umm al Qaiwain track for communications with Sharjah and Jabal Ali. Later, when the Party moves further

194 Perhaps a bit late for the main pearling season. Boats often went out again for a short period after the main season. 'The pearling season starts in May and lasts until the middle of September. This is known as the *Ghaus al Kabir* – the Big Diving. There are, however, two other seasons of no real importance. One falls in April, and the other extends from mid-September to the second or third week in October. This late diving is known as *al Raddah* meaning the Return.' STANTON HOPE, W.E., *Arabian Adventurer, The Story of Haji Williamson*, Robert Hale Ltd., London, (1951), p.261ff.

195 Buraimi.

196 Dubai north side of the Creek. Where the Maktoum hospital was due to open.

south, it is proposed to begin using the Manama/Dhaid track to Sharjah which will, of course, mean employing Bani Kitab guards to accompany the vehicles.

Said bin Maktum of Dubai, and several of his relatives, continue to develop the gardens at Shammal,[197] and are at present having new wells dug, and are installing new water-pumping equipment.

The Ruler, Shaikh Saqr, is reported to have made a temporary peace with Mohammad bin Hamad of Fujaira, though it is not yet clear as to what events have made this hand-shaking ceremony necessary.

AJMAN:

The Ruler, Shaikh Rashid bin Humaid, is due back in Ajman sometime during the beginning of November. He is said to have been to Kuwait, and to have travelled as far afield as Baghdad.

SHARJAH:

Towards the end of the period under review, the Ruler, Shaikh Saqr, was stopped by the Levies – between Dhaid and Wadi al Qor. This was merely a routine check on vehicles, but the Ruler was most annoyed: Ibrahim Midfa,[198] who was accompanying him, felt it his duty to be even more verbose in his objections than the Ruler, but words soon failed him and he was accidentally hit on the brow with his own rifle, during a slight scuffle. Ibrahim was sent back to Sharjah with a letter of complaint to the Political Officer, signed by Saqr. The Levies who stopped the vehicle were of the Bani Kitab.

The system of recruitment by the Levies, and sub-sequent placing of its members, is not always easy to understand. Shaikh Khalid bin Sultan bin Salim, who was involved in the last round of Kalba trouble ... is in the Levies and rapidly rising to the top. At the moment he is stationed at Tarif, engaged on a responsible and confidential matter.

The Ruler is still being troubled by domestic matters with members of his family, particularly with his brother Khalid and his uncle Mohammad.

Major Lippet arrived in Sharjah towards the end of the month as the Manager of the Golden Valley Oxide Company. He was accompanied by an assistant. It is the intention of the Company to work Tunb, as well as Bu Musa island, this season.

Early in the month two members of the anti-Locust party set out for Kalba and the Batinah, where the arrival of locusts was reported. During their absence very large swarms arrived everywhere on the Trucial Coast, and particularly large swarms were reported from the Baraimi direction.

---

197 North and east of the nearby town of Ra's al-Khaimah.

198 Confidant of the ruler. Prominent Sharjah family.

DUBAI:

A fact which for some months past has not been generally known is now apparent to all:

Shaikh Rashid is forever having a difficult time in his Majlis standing between the Company and a powerful group of merchants who are demanding that the Ruler adopt various means to force the Company to operate in Dubai territory. These merchants are all powerful, as far as Dubai politics go. Moreover, their interests being in Dubai they are far from appreciative that the Company is operating in neighbouring territories, and any benefits which their neighbours may gain from the Company's operations elsewhere, particularly in Sharjah, merely serve to irritate them.

News that the Company is to establish a base at Sharjah has already become public, and merchants and shaikhs alike are asking what it is that Sharjah has to attract the Company, that doesn't already exist at Jabal Ali. And, in this respect, they are as puzzled as many of the Company employees themselves. Any suggestion that Sharjah is geographically central for the Company's operations on the Trucial Coast does not ring true, and in Dubai, as well as in Sharjah, this move to establish a base is said to be a cunning plan to take the Jabal Ali rig out of Dubai territory to Sharjah. There have been suggestions that a group of merchants have been endeavoring to bludgeon Rashid into not allowing the Company to move the Jabal Ali installations away from Dubai territory, but Rashid has remained firmly opposed to quarrelling with the Company. Despite this reasonable attitude on the part of Rashid, there is no knowing what tricks the merchants may be driven to, if the present trade slump lasts.

ABU DHABI:

Said bin Shakhbut remains in Abu Dhabi; whilst Zaid, Haza and Khalid are in Baraimi.

It is only during Shaikh Shakhbut's absence that the full weight of his unpopularity among his people is making itself felt, and there is much speculation as to whether he will ever return to Abu Dhabi. If Shakhbut himself is fully aware of his precarious position at this present time, he cannot fail to be very conscious of the history of his family tree.

BARAIMI:

The Saudi party under the leadership of Emir Turki remains encamped at Hamasa. Compared with the damage to the Al bu Falah cause which is being done by the mere presence of this Saudi gift-giving-force, the details of its actual size, and movements of vehicles connected with the supplying of it, are insignificant. The maintenance of a status quo under the present circumstances is a very doubtful thing: to the local observer there is no apparent change in the position since the Saudis first arrived. They remain, and are continuing with their tactics of burrowing into 'Oman through the greed of the baduin.[199] On the other hand, neither the Al Bu Falah nor HMG have yet found a means of manifesting their intention to oppose the Saudis.

Rumours of Saudi victories are frequently being spread along the Coast, and it is difficult to ever get confirmation of the events reported, or to trace the origin of the news. One such rumor in current circulation has it that the Imam has tired of wearisome 'Omani politics, and has told Turki to "come". Other reports state that a very large party of Janaba[200] recently visited Turki in Hamasa, that the Saudis are about to dispatch cars to Dhank and Ibri, and that King Ibn Saud has sent a message to Turki that Zaid is to visit him in Riyadh and, if necessary, he is to be taken there by force. The latter seems most impolitic and unlikely, but it is difficult to sift such reports, which sound very convincing when first voiced.

The following have left the Trucial Cast via Sharjah on a visit to Riyadh during the month, and are reported to have included PCL Office, Bahrain, in their itinerary:

(a) Ya'aya bin Abdullah bin Sulaiman al Kindi, brother in-law of Sulaiman bin Himiyar of Jabal Al Akhdhar,
(b) Talib bin Ali bin Hilal, a Hinawi Minister of the Imam, and
(c) Mohammad bin Abdullah al Khalifah of Nezwa.

During the month, several Saudi vehicles were reported to have arrived in Baraimi from Al Hasa, following a route which skirted the Company camp at Tarif.

Turki now signs himself "The Emir Turki of Baraimi."

The Saudi system of making payment to the badwin is that when a visitor presents Turki with a present (Hadiyah) he is asked whether he is a follower of the Al bu Falah or of the Saudis. If he says "of the Saudis" he is then paid approximately Sixty Rupees if it is a goat, and three hundred Rupees if it is a small camel. If, however, he replies "of the Al bu Falah", his present is returned, but sometimes he is given an ex-gratia payment. Visitors who do not bring a Hadiyah are given smaller sums.

COMPANY ACTIVITIES:

Mr. G. Heseldin, the General Manager, visited Jabal Ali, Tarif, Sharjah and Dubai on 30th October accompanied by the Representative, he also flew over the Seismic Camp at Ras al Khaima, and over Baraimi.

Large swarms of locust were everywhere sighted en route, and the Dove aircraft ran into one swarm at 2000 feet, having to climb to 3500 feet to get above it.

---

199 The writer, Henderson, was well aware of the poverty of these people. Thesiger also described the generosity of the Bedouin even when they had very little, while Walker refers to their independence of any authority.

200 Large Oman tribe.

The move from Jabal Ali to Tarif continues, and work is shortly expected to begin on establishing a base in Sharjah.

Codrai
Representative
c.c. E.F.Henderson Esq., PCL. Bahrain.

TRUCIAL COAST DIARY FOR PERIOD ENDING 30 NOVEMBER 1952

GENERAL:

The month has been one of great activity, but the day to day events which keep alive the feeling that the Trucial Coast is undergoing a critical period of its history, have done little to change the situation as it existed at the beginning of the period under review. Few issues that arise today are seen other than through a pall of uncertainty and unrest which hangs low over Oman, and by people who suffer the sensitiveness of those living in lands without frontiers.

The most notable event of the month has been the unexpected return of Shaikh Shakhbut, reported on below.

RAS AL KHAIMA:

The Political Resident,[201] his wife, and daughter Mary, paid a one day visit to Ras al Khaima on 4th November, as part of the Resident's annual tour (made earlier this year to avoid the shammals,[202] which on previous tours have proved so disastrous). This year's tour included the usual half day's shooting on the Jiri Plain, and did little towards helping to reach a settlement over the Rams affair, which remains unsettled. The party visited the Seismic Camp during its shooting trip, without notice, and having declined an invitation to include this visit in its itinerary.

As already stated, the solution with regard to Rams remains as before. The dissident Shaikh Saif, and some of his relatives, are still in Sharjah, living at the expense of HMG whilst the Politicals, who originally brought them to Sharjah, are endeavoring to arrange their return to their homes and property at Rams. Shaikh Saqr has remained adamant in refusing to allow them to return to the scene of his last round of trouble (See T.C. Diary for July, and onwards), and as a third alternative

201 Sir Rupert Hay.

202 Strong northerly winds.

(Arabia, and Ras al Khaima town itself, having been mentioned in the past) now offers to rehabilitate these people at Khor Khawair.[203]

The initial mistake made in dealing with the Rams trouble lies with the Politicals for removing the trouble-makers without having fixed intentions as to their banishment. The Politicals now find themselves under obligation to look after the welfare of these people, and wish to reinstate them in Rams. Shaikh Saqr, on the other hand, is determined to keep them away from their kinsfolk (the Tanaij). From the humane point of view the Politicals are right: from the viewpoint of his political interests, so is Saqr.

The Ruler and most of the principal Ras al Khaima shaikhs were very successfully entertained at a dinner given for then at the Seismic Camp on 21st November. The highlight of the evening was provided by a tape recording machine, which played back for the party some of the unique noises made by the hillmen,[204] recently recorded by a member of the Party. On his departure the Ruler left in two new Landrovers, which were due to him according to the arrangements made for his Sea Rights Agreement.

Two Geologists arrived at the Seismic Camp the same day, to begin a five-day reconnaissance in the Jebel Qamar area. Last minute arrangements had to be made for an additional trip to Wadi Hagil and Khatt, but apart from a four-hour visit to the latter the geologists confined themselves to the Qamar area.

Ali bin Saif, Shaikh of the Khawatir (who inhabit the area in which the Seismic Party is at present operating) left on a visit to Turki, in Baraimi, at the beginning of the month, as also bin Hamid, the Shaikh of the Mazaria tribe, which inhabits the Jebel Qamar area where the Geologists carried out their reconnaissance. The Khawatir are Na'im, and the Mazaria Bani Yas.

Shaikh Mohammad, the Ruler's father, virtually leapt from his sick-bed in Derra when he learned of the P.R.'s visit to Ras al Khaima, and rallied to his son's support over the Rams affair. He is now at Ras al Khaima, and still very weak.

The remains of a boy who had been devoured by a wolf were discovered on the main track between Khatt and the Seismic Camp. The wolf's lair was later said to have been discovered a short distance into the hills, in Fujaira territory, and the Camp guards did their best to try and persuade members of the Party to go and dynamite it. A more original excuse for doing Seismic work in Fujaira territory would be difficult to think of.

A drum erected by the Seismic Party as a surveyor's marker on the Labana outcrop was several times hauled down by the Sharqiyeen,[205] as soon as it was replaced. Shaikh Mohd bin Hamid ash Sharqi, the Ruler of Fujaira, protested to the P.O.T.S.

---

203 On the coast about 15 kilometres north of Rams.

204 The Shihu.

205 Fujairah tribe.

against this unauthorised intrusion into his territory, but by the time the matter came to a head, the use of the Labana marker had been discontinued.

The boundary settlement in this area is going to be a most difficult matter for the P.O.T.S., but fortunately for him the matter seems to get a low priority on his list of functions.

Five Political Officers have dabbled with the problem, but have heaved a sigh of relief and retired from it at the ends of their tours, leaving the matter unsettled. Despite the fact of there now being an assistant P.O. in Sharjah, the P.O. is as harassed as ever with other affairs, and there seems to be little likelihood of an early settlement of the boundary questions, and it is felt that an officer should be posted here to deal exclusively with this matter until it is satisfactorily settled, not only in Ras al Khaima, but everywhere along the Trucial Coast.

AJMAN:

The Ruler, Shaikh Rashid bin Humaid, returned to Dubai by B. I. Steamer on 11th November, having travelled as far as Baghdad. He was ill with fever for nearly two weeks after his return.

There is little doubt but that the high-spirited Ajman Shaikhs are among the most dissident along the whole coast and, perhaps, with less territory to lose than any of the others, would like to feel the immediate warmth of the Saudi gold.

The Ruler has quickly orientated himself to his old ways of tongue-in-cheek trouble-making, since his return, and is said to be having a round of trouble with his father-in-law, Shaikh Ali bin Saif of the Khawatir.

SHARJAH:

Shaikh Saqr bin Sultan has risen above any apprehensions which were felt when he first became Ruler, and is now quite a popular and a successful leader. Shaikh Mohammad bin Saqr the one time acting Ruler, who himself hoped to succeed his brother, has now quietly faded from the political scene, and lives in his date gardens at Ras al Khaima. Minor differences between Saqr and his younger relatives, which have enlivened the Majlis since Saqr's coming to power, are no longer major issues, but it is felt that they will always exist, until such times as the younger shaikhs are able to play the part of Princes of the Kingdom of Gold.

Shaikh Saqr was greeted on his return from a trip to Kalba by the sight of his new car, which had been carefully storing for ceremonial occasions, which had been involved in a crash in the R.A.F. Camp, whilst being driven by his brother Khalid, who had broken the garage lock to take it out.

The Political Resident arrived in Sharjah on 1st November with his wife and daughter, and after a visit to Dubai travelled on to Ras al Khaima in the Wren.[206]

206 Yacht.

Sharjah and Dubai have been inundated with official and other visitors during the month, the most notable of whom have been General Packard, Judge Haines, Mr. Poisson of Sharq al Adna Radio Station, The Crown Prince of Siam and his wife, the A.O.C., R.A.F., and the Bishop of Jerusalem. Whereas, in the past, the arrival of the mail bearing plane in Sharjah has always been a welcome sight, the three times weekly Gulf Aviation service is now of doubtful benefit to the representatives of most of the British organisations, each of them being visited by his own visitors, and practically everyone else's besides. The P.O.T.S. is the worst hit in this respect, and many matters of importance, as far as local affairs are concerned, have had to be left undone for this reason, in particular, any attempt to finish the boundary work.

Doctor Hosnan, and her assistant, of the Dutch Reform Mission, are back in Sharjah, where they are installed in the house given them by the Ruler, much to the disgruntlement of the Ajman Shaikhs, who originally attracted the Mission to the Trucial Coast. Another two doctors (man and wife) are expected to come to join them in the near future.

Major Lippet, of the Golden Valley Red Oxide Company, continues to get himself into disrepute in handling his Company's affairs. He is apparently suffering a neurosis regarding his predecessor, and seems to make changes merely to spite him. Khan Saheb Hussein, for many years the Golden Valley Co's Agent has been dismissed, but hurriedly, recalled within a few days to load a ship at Sir bu Nair. Lippet has taken Shaikh Khalid to live with him in Bu Musa, as the Sharjah Representative.

Many of the new generation of shaikhs on the Trucial Coast are getting themselves frowned upon for their drinking and other questionable habits. Sharjah continues to be the best centre for procuring British liquor, and some of them have no difficulty in procuring invitations from members of the British Community for their drinking bouts. The Politicals are, at long last, becoming concerned about the large quantity of liquor which is finding its way onto the local markets, particularly in Sharjah.

Sulaiman bin Hamyar[207] arrived back from Riyadh at the beginning of the month, and shortly afterwards arrived in Sharjah, ostensibly to await the arrival of some new cars coming for him from Bahrain. Obaid bin Juma was reported to have arrived with him, but it later turned out, as it frequently does, that it was one of Sulaiman's followers who looked like Obaid.

Sulaiman arrived back from Riyadh in three cars which he had been given as presents and, it is said, with a radio transmitter.

To the relief of the R.A.F. labourers, who have been working on the project on their days off, without pay, the Ruler has finally abandoned work on the canal which was to join the Sharjah and Khan creeks, This was an attempt to increase the flow of water through the Sharjah creek and thereby improve the entrance to it.

207 From Tanuf and the Jebel Akhdhar in the Sultanate of Oman.

An attempt by Gulf Aviation[208] to start a weekly service from Muscat to Sharjah has, as with most other things, been torpedoed by the Sultan, who seems to be adhering to his policy of keeping away foreigners from Muscat. Aircraft are now only allowed to land at Muscat if they are carrying passengers who have business with the Sultan, or officials who have urgent work with the Consul.

DUBAI:

Shaikh Rashid had made an order that no one is to travel on vehicles leaving Dubai for Baraimi without a barwa from him. This is a good move on his part to keep check of the opportunists who have been going on visits to Turki for their slices of the Saudi gold. Earlier in the month, before this order came into effect, one of Rashid's soldiers, a slave, went on a visit to Turki. As soon as it became known who his master was, a special feast was given in his honour, and the slave was given five hundred Rupees on his return to Dubai.

On 11th November Shaikh Shakhbut arrived in Dubai by B. I. Steamer from Bombay. The only news of his coming was received by Ali Awazi (who seems to have become the Abu Dhabi agent in Dubai) despite a promise given by Shakhbut to Rashid bin Saeed that he would send him a signal notifying him of his return. On the eve of Shakhbut's arrival the greater part of Dubai was split into two camps, hotly debating as to whether Rashid should go out to the ship to welcome Shakhbut, in the absence of a 'tel' having been received. Rashid himself was keen to go, but was dissuaded from the idea, and instead sent a representative to invite Shakhbut ashore. Representatives of many other shaikhs and organisations arrived out at the ship, thronging the decks looking for Shakhbut, who had chosen to slip quietly over the windward side of the ship, where three Abu Dhabi launches were waiting for him, together with Hamdan bin Mohd[209] and his son, Sultan. The undersigned succeeded in being the only representative to visit Shakhbut, and found him in very good spirits. Before the other visitors arrived, the Abu Dhabi launches set off for Abu Dhabi. These launches returned the same evening due to bad weather, and anchored off Sharjah. Shakhbut and his party disembarked and after dining with Ali Awazi set out for Abu Dhabi by road.

Whatever the reasons for Shakhbut's behaviour, and they probably amount to very little, the effect has been the same, and the Rulers of both Sharjah and Dubai consider that they have been slighted. As far as Dubai is concerned the manner of Shakhbut's return has thrown their relations with Abu Dhabi back to what they were before Shakhbut's visit to Dubai, prior to his departure for India.

---

208 Later became Gulf Air.

209 Codrai wrote bin Hamdan bin Mohd. A typing error.

Mohd bin Hamid ash Sharqi[210] stayed in Dubai on 23rd November and left for Bahrain by B.I. Steamer on 25th November. Ostensibly, the reason for his visit is to seek medical attention but, as in the case of anyone who travels forth from the Trucial Coast these days, there is the possibility that he will go to Riyadh, particularly if he fails to get any satisfaction from the Company regarding his request for a concession.

An interesting visitor to Dubai during the month, who made no bones as to his destination, was Shaikh Salih bin Kalut of the Ar Rashid tribe, who accompanied Bertram Thomas[211] on his crossing of the Rub al Khali. He left for Bahrain by local launch.

ABU DHABI:

The Ruler seems to be very much better after his treatment in Bombay, and he claims to be cured, though some of his followers say that this is not the case. He was recalled from Bombay by the Politicals regarding some matter relating to the means of settlement of the boundary dispute.

Shakhbut's quarrel with his brothers seems to have been temporarily shelved, and to have advanced beyond a state of bickering, although Shaikhs Haza and Khalid remain in Baraimi, together with their mother Salama.

BARAIMI:

The various events and items of news in connection with the situation in Baraimi, which have already been reported by letter and signal, serve to make two facts clear.

Firstly the 'Standstill Agreement',[212] one-sided though it is, has not been honoured by the Saudis. Furthermore, H.M.G. has realised the futility of raising complaints about the isolated incidents which infringe it, and despite the businesslike, though badly planned, activity of the Levies in establishing bases to report on vehicle movements, the Saudis have come and gone to Baraimi and Dubai without hindrance. Secondly, it is absolutely clear that even if the Saudis did adhere to the terms of the Standstill Agreement, these in themselves would be quite inadequate as far as preventing them from carrying out their activities, so long as Turki and his party are allowed to remain in Oman.

---

210 Fujairah Ruler.

211 Bertram Thomas was engaged in 1925 by the Sultan Taimur bin Faisal of Oman to sort out the poor state of the government finances. During the next five years, after a good start, he succeeded in leaving the finances in an even sorrier state. TOWNSEND, J., *Oman, The Making of the Modern State*, 1977, Croom Helm, London, 1977, ISBN 0 85664 446 3, p.193. Thomas did travel extensively in Oman including crossing the Empty Quarter from Salala in Dhofar (Sultanate of Oman) to Doha (Qatar) in the years 1930-1931. THOMAS, BERTRAM, *Arabia Felix: Across the Empty Quarter of Arabia*, Jonathon Cape, 1938.

212 Agreement dated 26 October 1952 between HMG and the Government of Saudi Arabia. See HEARD, D. (2019). p.323.

Judging the problem locally, without knowledge of other issues which may be influencing the case, H.M.G. has allowed the tail of the Lion to be twigged unceasingly, and this, of course, as far as can be judged by a foreigner, is the reaction of the T.C. Shaikhs.

However, one or two, at least, realise that the most powerful animal is frequently the slowest moving, and it is hoped that before long they will hear the roar of the Lion.

The main anti-climax of the month, which for a short time looked as though it would bring about a major change in the Baraimi situation, centred around Saqr bin Sultan al Na'im. On 12th November he set out for Muscat, accompanied by the P.O.T.S. and two lorries carrying Muscat troops lead by Feisal. Before reaching Aswad[213] the P.O.T.S. decided to return to Sharjah, and to signal Muscat and ask the Sultan to despatch a car to meet Saqr. On arriving at Aswad, Saqr become the victim of his own apprehensions, and when he met the T.C. Levy Officer, on his way back from Muscat, and learned that the P.R. was no longer there (the P.R.'s visit being quite incidental, and in no way connected with the arrival of Saqr) he hired camels and set out to return to Baraimi. In the meantime, the P.O.T.S., fearing that this might happen, dispatched the Levies to look for Saqr, but he was not found until he arrived back home. Until the actual facts of this event became known, it was followed by a period of several days during which time practically everyone with pro-Saudi feelings gave birth to a stream of rumours, Dubai more than anywhere, being active in this respect.

As a result of this episode, the P.O.T.S. was rebuked by the Sultan for interfering in the affairs of 'Oman, and the situation reverted to its former state.

Codrai
Representative.

---

213 Near the border.

TRUCIAL COAST DIARY FOR PERIOD ENDING 31 DECEMBER 1952

GENERAL:

The Rulers of all the Trucial States are gravely concerned about the loss of a considerable number of their people who have gone to work in the oil-producing Gulf States, during the past two or three years. Not all the emigrants have been get-rich-quick adventurers, but mainly those who are genuinely finding it difficult to make ends meet. Everyone readily makes use of the Company as the only possible scapegoat in this matter. It is fairly certain that the discovery of oil in any of the Trucial States would very quickly bring about the economic death of the neighbouring and less fortunate Shaikhdoms, but until oil is discovered it seems to be only a matter of time before the whole of the Trucial Coast meets the same fate, due to the increasing wealth of the other Gulf States.

The Sultanate of Muscat must be as hard hit as anywhere as regards loss of its people, mainly from the Batinah Coast, Muscat, Matrah and Dhofar.

On the whole, it is fairly certain that given employment and reasonable wages, most of the local people would prefer to work near their homes on the Trucial Coast than to go elsewhere, to States where the attraction of high wages is usually offset by inflated costs of living, and that the majority of people who have already migrated would return to the Trucial Coast as soon as there is plenty of work for them.

In the towns of the Trucial Coast, as in other Gulf States, the increased cost of living is to a small extent due to an increased standard of living. Apart from improvements in diet, an example of this is that in Dubai and Sharjah, in particular, the moment anyone can afford an extra ten to twenty Rupees a month he invests in a radio on the hire-purchase basis. Following up this one example, the possession of a radio then gives the owner a new social status, and he finds himself spending more of his income on coffee, etc., with which to entertain his guests.

Also, the charging of his battery adds a few Rupees to his expenditure, and even the most humble father of a radio engages a coolie to carry his battery for him, in line astern, through the market-place.

The following list is not very comprehensive, but serves to show the increase in price of a few foodstuffs during the past four years.

Dubai Market Prices[214]		Nov. 1948.	Aug. 1952.	Dec. 1952.
Ghee, Oman,	per maund	19-0-0	28-0-0	28-0-0
Mutton	per maund	8-0-0	12-0-0	16-0-0
Beef.	per maund	6-0-0	10-0-0	14-0-0
Coffee.	per maund	8-0-0	24-0-0	28-0-0
Tea.	per pound	3-0-0	5-0-0	5-0-0
Onions.	per maund	1-12-0	2-0-0	2-8-0
Sugar.	per maund	4- 0-0	4-4-0	3-8-0
Rice.	per maund	7-10-0	8-0-0	9-0-0

International Aeradio,[215] Sharjah, is about to increase the minimum rate for a labourer to four Rupees a day, which will probably mean every other organisation which does not provide food for its staff making the same increase. Several members of the Dubai Office staff, who are not fed or accommodated by the Company, have been asking for transfers to the Company locations where they are given the same pay and have all found.

The following list, showing the increase in the size of the British community in Dubai, Derra, and Sharjah, may be of some interest:

	Autumn 1948	Autumn 1950	Dec. 1951.
Dubai.	1	3	4
Derra.	1	6	9
Sharjah. (including RAF)	6	8	12 (includes 2 American missionaries.)
Total	8	17	25

Other arrivals are expected during the next few months. There has also been an increased flow of visitors to the Trucial Coast, corresponding to the increased size of the community.

RAS AL KHAIMAH:

The Ruler is to follow up a suggestion made to him by the P.O.T.S., and intends to establish a post at the southernmost point of the Jiri Plain, in the near future. The

214 Rupees – Annas. 16 Annas to the Rupee. And 4 Pais to the Anna.

215 Airport and communications company, a subsidiary of BOAC (British Overseas Airways Corporation).

place he has chosen is on the border of Khawatir/Mazaria territories (near Umm Hamad), and is on the motor track to Ras al Khaima from Wadi al Qor.

The problem of the displaced Shaikh and his relations from Rams has not yet been settled, and is causing everyone concerned to get more and more angry. The Politicals are no doubt influenced by a desire not to drive anyone into the Saudi Camp in a fit of anger and, if this is so, then the problem will be interminable.

Sultan bin Sallim, the former Ruler of Ras al Khaima, who has retained considerable influence among the people of Ras al Khaima territory and who still makes claim to a controlling interest in Wadi al Qor, has gone off on a trip to Turki, the Saudi representative in Baraimi.[216]

The people living in Khatt have complained that the Seismic Party encamped at Labana has taken so much water from their spring as to endanger their gardens. The watering of the gardens at Khatt is worked on a rota basis, and in the past every garden has been given its turn every eight days, but there is now only a sufficient flow from the spring for a turn every twenty days. The complaint is justified, and the Party will have to haul its water from Hail, a few miles further north. Drilling on the Camp site has found water, but so far it has not been found possible to pump this to the surface.

Sometime during January the Party is due to move into the sands, nearer to the coast, a short time after its return from Christmas leave.

AJMAN:

The Ruler has broken off relations with Ali bin Saif (Shaikh of the Khawatir), his father-in-law, which leaves them on much the same terms as they have been on for the past few years.

SHARJAH:

A most tragic and unfortunate accident over-shadowed a successful sports meeting, which was arranged by Buckmaster, of the Political Agency, Sharjah on Boxing Day. A Desert Locust Control lorry, which was loaded with singing children on their way back to Derra, over-turned after a real-wheel blow-out. Three children were killed, another still unconscious, was taken to Bahrain on 29th December, and several others are still in the Maktum Hospital, apart from which there are many in their own homes suffering from minor injuries. Another Locust Control vehicle knocked down an onlooker at the sports meeting.

Anti-British and Anti-Christian comments were heard from many quarters after this accident, but fortunately any such feeling quickly subsided. Sharjah, Derra and Dubai have been in partial mourning for several days.

216 Turki was in the Buraimi oasis village of Hamasa. Buraimi village itself was still under Sheikh Saqr bin Sultan.

The Rulers, or representatives, of all the Trucial States except Abu Dhabi were called together at Sharjah by the P.O.T.S., during the month, and asked to raise a further Rs. 20,000 towards the upkeep of the Maktum Hospital. No contributions were forthcoming, and one representative considered it pertinent to ask how much H.M.G. was giving.

The hospital finances are in a very precarious state, and neither McCaully[217] nor the P.O.T.S. has yet found a means of raising the necessary funds to keep it going.

Claims to the territory at either end of Wadi al Qor, and the Wadi itself, are being pushed forward by everyone with any interest in this area, and relations between Sharjah and Muscat are very strained as a result of the Sultan's setting up of various posts on the motor tracks at the Batinah[218] end of the Wadi. The Ruler of Sharjah endeavours to visit Kalba once a month, and is quite successfully strengthening his position in that quarter.[219]

DUBAI:

Shaikh Rashid bin Said and many followers left to go on a hunting trip to Persia on 24th December. They travelled in two launches, which also carried two of their vehicles. They were not allowed to land when they arrived at Lingeh, and are said to be at present hunting on Farur Island, on their way back to Dubai. On past occasions the Dubai shaikhs have always succeeded in bribing the Persian officials to allow than to land with their arms. The reason why they failed on this occasion is not yet known in Dubai, but presumably it is some matter connected with the latter.

Shaikh Said returned to Dubai after a prolonged hunting trip in the Ras al Khaima area, and has remained in town during the absence of his son Rashid. He has approached the Company with a request that arrangements be made for him to visit England for medical treatment at the beginning of summer.

Major Lippett, the Representative of the Golden Valley Red Oxide Company, has broken the two contracts to supply stone for the new Bank and the new Agency in Dubai, which he snatched from Khan Sahib Hussein. He is said to be paying the Ruler of Sharjah in royalties nearly as much as he himself is receiving for the stone.

Ali Awazi, the Bapco Distributor for the Trucial Coast, is one of the most up and coming merchants in Dubai at the moment, an advancement made partly at the expense of his former partner of the AIOC Agency, Khan Saheb Hussein. He is the principal contractor for the building of the new Bank, and is engaged on several smaller projects besides it would seem that he has been successful in persuading Bapco

217 The doctor. Ex Indian army.

218 Oman end of the Wadi.

219 The Ruler would have to travel through Sultanate of Oman territory to reach his possessions on the East coast, (Indian Ocean).

to make the Company purchase its drummed supplies from him possibly hoping to deliver it to the Company locations on his lighters.

Sultan bin Shakhbut, younger son of the Ruler of Abu Dhabi, came to Dubai on Christmas day, and had a gramophone needle extracted from his ear. He claims that it was pushed in whilst he was asleep.

ABU DHABI:

Following many rumours that the Manasir in Liwa[220] were creating trouble for the Al bu Falah, the Ruler received a letter from Rashid bin Jabir, his representative at Maria,[221] saying that the lives of himself and his eight followers had been threatened by Nasir bin Said bin Suwaid of the Al bu Rahma,[222] if they remained at Maria. Shortly before this the Ruler's other representative at Markhia,[223] Jabir bin Rashid, resigned, having come under Saudi influence at the hands of one called Bandar.

These events, coupled with the one sided trend of the general situation, stirred the Ruler into a state of activity which was quite surprising. He armed as many retainers as he was able, and dispatched them as fast he could on his two serviceable vehicles, to establish a base at Markhia. However, a shortage of rifles, ammunitions and money, coupled with transport difficulties in keeping this post supplied, soon made themselves felt, and the Ruler approached the Company and the P.O.T.S. for immediate assistance. The Ruler seems to be very satisfied with the prompt, and considerable aid which he received from the Company within only a few days of his request.

The Markhia base, which is considered to be of considerable strategic importance in this area, is garrisoned by approximately sixty armed soldiers led by Ahmed bin Fadhil. Said bin Shakhbut took an active part in establishing the post. The small Maria detachment has been increased only to twenty, but the establishment of a base at Markhia has provided the necessary support for the Maria representative.

There has been no news from the area since the establishment of the Markhia base, but there is no saying how bad the tidings might have been had this strategic move not been carried out.

---

220 The crescent shaped string of oases in the high dunes in the far south of Abu Dhabi territory.

221 Central oasis in Liwa, as yet only accessible by camel or by air.

222 Manasir.

223 The post in the west a short distance south of Ruwais and Jebel Dhanna, in the west of the Bainuna area. It is situated near the edge of the sands and easily accessed.

The Ruler was due to leave on a hunting trip to Bainuna[224] towards the end of the month, but it is not known whether he has yet left. Shaikhs Zaid and Mohd bin Khalifah were in Abu Dhabi during the preparations for establishing the Markhia base.

The Levy post at Muqatara[225] has been withdrawn, having proved to be of no strategic value.

MUSCAT AND BARAIMI:

The P.O.T.S. has now been instructed by the P. R. to visit Baraimi only if he considers such a visit necessary, having been given orders forbidding him to go there earlier in the month.

However, he finds himself fully occupied in Sharjah, and has recently summoned Shaikh Zaid to Sharjah for consultations.

The refusal of the Sultan of Muscat to take part in a visa agreement with the Gulf States has just bounced back on him. Followers of Saqr bin Sultan of Baraimi, who recently travelled to Kuwait via Sharjah, were turned back because of the P.O.T.S.' s endorsement that they were Subjects of the Sultan of Muscat.

Sayid Kamil returned from Muscat on 29th December with letters for his master, Saqr bin Sultan,[226] and for Zaid. During his stay in Muscat he was twice seen by the Sultan, the first time he has ever met him, despite other visits to Muscat. The Sultan is sending Saqr a car and two rifles, which are to be collected from Sohar within a few days. He has not given Saqr a definite answer regarding his request that Ahmed Ibrahim[227] be sent to Baraimi and it is most unlikely that he does, in fact, intend to send him.

Abdul Wahid, who together with Abdullah Salim[228] claims to control the Bani Kaab, is still in Muscat on a visit to the Sultan. In the meantime, Abdullah Salim has gone over to Turki.

A vehicle sent out by Turki to collect firewood in Bani Kaab territory, and accompanied by followers of Obaid bin Jum'a,[229] was stopped by members of the Bani Kaab and the wood was unloaded from it and burnt.

---

224 Markhia is in the west of the Bainuna area and on the edge of the, more difficult to traverse, sand dunes.

225 On the approach to Abu Dhabi island.

226 Buraimi sheikh.

227 Sultan's Minister in Sohar.

228 Prominent Kaabi sheikh.

229 Mahadhah sheikh supplanted by Abdullah bin Salim.

These events go to prove the troublesome state of affairs existing within the Bani Kaab, and to show the nonsense of any claim put forward by any one of its shaikhs to control the whole tribe.[230]

COMPANY ACTIVITIES:

Members of the Seismic Party left for the Lebanon on Christmas leave on 15th December, and are due back on 5th January. Preparations at Tarif are well under way, and it is hoped to spud-in early in the new year.

Work has begun on reconditioning the RAF Hospital in Sharjah, ready for establishing the Company base there.

On 4th December Mr. G. Heseldin,[231] accompanied by a director of C.F.P.[232] visited Tarif, Dubai and Sharjah, and flew over the Seismic Camp.

On 16th December the General Manager and Mr. H.M. Jackson[233] came on a two day visit to the Trucial Coast and visited the Rulers of Abu Dhabi, Dubai, Sharjah, and Ajman, and also met the Ruler of Ras al Khaima. The members of the British community were entertained at a cocktail party given for them by the General Manager in Dubai, during his visit.

Codrai
Representative.
rc/ i.
c.c.E.F. Henderson Esq.,Bahrain.

---

230 This was copied to a political report where the word 'tribe' was changed to 'territory'.

231 General Manager.

232 Compagnie Française des Pétroles. Today known as Total who have a 23 ¾ share in IPC/ PD(TC).

233 IPC London.

1953

TRUCIAL COAST DIARY FOR THE PERIOD ENDING 31 JANUARY 1953

GENERAL:

Security Force:

The month under review has been full of activity, and the sudden arrival on the Trucial Coast of new detachments of the British Forces, to be used in connection with the Saudi/Trucial States boundary dispute will no doubt become a noteworthy event in the history of these parts.

The various happenings in connection with the arrival of these forces took place under a veil of secrecy, but this was seen through with greater ease than was contemplated, and there are few people who could not read the intentions written on the countenances of H.M.G. Now that the situation has unravelled itself, the need for secrecy in the first place seems rather doubtfully justified, and failure to keep it has kept those with grandstand privileges entertained with comic opera activities. The whole operation should be regarded as a lesson in Security and, what is most important, in co-ordinating the assistance which was to be sought from nearly every member of the small British community on the spot.

The decision to bring forces to the Trucial Coast was made by the Foreign Office whilst it was engaged in fresh talks with the Saudi Government as to the means of having the boundary dispute arbitrated. The talks broke down, but it is understood that the Foreign Office is having a last try to reach an acceptable solution. In the meantime, the forces are being used for flag-waving, and are familiarising themselves with the area in preparation for any calls that may be made on them. One such call has already been made, to deal with some Bani Kaab trouble-makers, as reported on below. The P.O.T.S has been given a free hand in using this Security Force to restrain the Saudis from any further infiltration into Trucial Oman and to uphold the terms of the Standstill Agreement.[1] Gratifying that it may be, that the F.O. should have decided to adopt a strong-handed approach to the problem, this is rather offset by the fact that at present, at any-rate, our show of strength amounts to upholding the Restriction line.[2] However, it is likely that sometime in the near future action may be taken against Saudi convoys passing through the Restricted Zone.

At present the Security Force consists of a complete R.A.F. Regiment Armoured Car Squadron, and a Squadron of thirteen Vampires and two Meteor Jet Fighters.[3] Also, the T.C. Levies are being expanded, many supernumeraries are being recruited and instructors from the Aden Levies are due to arrive shortly, and a new British Officer is on his way here.

The arrival of these forces was preceded by a flow of official visitors, who were so pointed in their questioning as to leave little doubt as to the type of operation they were contemplating. The A.O.C.,[4] R.A.F. arrived unexpectedly by air (even as far as the P.O.T.S. was concerned) with a self-contained party, including road transport, and carried out a survey of all the T.C. landing strips. At the same time, the H.M.S. Dalrymple carried out a survey of beaching points along the coast. Shortly afterwards, H.M.S. Wild Goose and a tank landing craft arrived off Jabal Ali, and with a light sea running, following a shammal, began to bring vehicles and supplies ashore. The S.N.O.P.G. was present, and acknowledged that the materials actually landed were only done so with the aid of Company personnel, winches P.S.P. etc. The remainder of the supplies were offloaded in Dubai by Gray Mackenzie barges. Ten thousand tins if kerosene were afterwards written off as being unsuitable for jet purposes, for which they were intended.

The P.O.T S. has been concerned at the leakage of information during the operations, and was ill-advisedly about to rebuke the Dubai Shaikhs from their knowledge of events, when he became aware that the shortcomings on the question of

1 The standstill agreement. The main provisions of the standstill agreement were 1. The Parties (to the agreement, Saudi Arabia and Abu Dhabi) in Buraimi were to remain in their present positions. Replacements and supplies were allowed but not reinforcements. 2. Neither side was to make any threatening move. 3. Life in the oasis was to return to normal without restrictions. 4. Visits were allowed but not to spread propaganda among, or try to influence the tribes. KELLY, J. B., (1964), p. 163.

2 The Restricted Zone where the oil companies of both parties were not to operate. PD(TC) operations were limited to north of 23°15". Placing Liwa in the south of Abu Dhabi 'out of bounds' to both parties. This delineation was formalised in the agreement which was still to come, dated 30 July 1954. However at the time of this diary entry HMG was preventing the Company from operating in the western half of Abu Dhabi territory, land which was claimed by Saudi Arabia.

3 15 modern jet fighter aircraft.

4 Area Officer Commanding.

security were mainly on our side. In any case, it seemed unreasonable to expect Shaikhs with pro-Saudi feelings to close their ears to news of our activities, no matter what the source of their information. Astute observers were even endeavouring to estimate the strength of the 'surprise' force by counting the cases in a large consignment of beer, which an efficient Naafi Manager had ordered for the visitors. Judged by this means, the force would seem to be a good deal larger than it actually is, unless, as one person put it, people were actually bathing in the stuff.

Since its arrival, the jet squadron has been carrying out daily sorties over the disputed area, but the sight and noise of low flying aircraft no longer seems to have the desired effect on the onlookers, and unless one is the father of a click-shutter Polaroid camera[5] (which two of the Rulers are), the speed of the jets goes comparatively unnoticed compared with the speed which rumours of Saudi victories reach Dubai. The introduction of armoured cars to the Coast is a far better strategical move, and armoured plating and automatic weapons are to the baduin as the jet-noise is to the British Community.

At the end of the period under review a small detachment of the Armoured Car Squadron remains encamped about two miles from the Company location at Tarif, whilst another small detachment is about to go out on tour in the Ras al Khaimah area. Company Dodges have played a prominent part in extracting the armoured cars from various sabkhas, and this is one of many happenings which might well have been avoided had the strangers to this difficult terrain been more carefully briefed. Criticism of the various activities connected with the grand entrée of these forces comes easily to an observer, no matter what his prejudices, and it is a great pity that this fact has not been taken into account before allowing these otherwise experienced performers to act independently over this difficult terrain. The P.O.T.S. is, during these active times, far too busy to assume active command of the forces (although he is, of course, nominally in charge of them), and this responsibility has been vested in Group Captain Price who is resident in Bahrain. The main part which has so far been enacted by the latter[6] was in flying a drug down from Bahrain in record time, to save the life of a British sailor. The drug was also available in the Maktum Hospital, Dubai. In the meantime, the sailor's tummy-ache has worn away, and he was found to be standing waist deep in the sea, as part of a human chain which was man-handling kerosene ashore.

The reaction among the more enlightened of the local populace in Dubai and Sharjah to the arrival of these forces was based on what was a very good line of propaganda for the Saudis. That is, it was generally put about that we had brought tanks and aeroplanes, but this was through fear of, rather than superiority over the

5 Polaroid Camera. The film in this camera was such that on pulling it out, one exposure at a time, that exposure was already developed.

6 Group Captain Price.

Saudis, and that no shots would be fired. However, H.M.G.'s business-like and rapid treatment of the Bani Kaab trouble[7] has done much to prove that we are not as timid as the Saudis have said us to be, after their round of temporary victories.

The British Cruiser, H.M.S. Ceylon, accompanied by three frigates, is coming to the Trucial Coast on 7th February and will be remaining in the Sharjah/Dubai area for four days. All the Rulers of the Trucial States are to be summoned aboard the Cruiser to meet the Admiral, and to be entertained to a barrage from the ships and a display by the jet squadron.

RAS AL KHAIMAH:

The Ruler's reluctance to reach a compromise over the Rams affair, and his unwillingness to establish a security post in Khawatir territory, for fear of further antagonising his relations with the Khawatir, have caused him to be frowned upon by the P.O.T.S., who regards him as a difficult fellow. (very obstinate).

Shaikh Ali bin Saif, of the Khawatir, is said to be thinking of imposing a tax on every foreigner (possibly meaning Ras al Khaimah and Sharjah subjects only) employed by the Seismic Party in his territory. If this is the case, then his potential source of income is about to move out of his grasp, to Falaj al Ali, in Umm al Qaiwain territory.

On 10th January Admiral Towner of the U.S. Navy accompanied by eight of his officers were entertained at the Seismic Party Camp, and were taken on a tour of the Ras al Khaimah area. Nearly all the members of the Seismic party were entertained on board the Duxbury Bay the same evening concluding a very successful day. Prior to the visit, the Admiral had been on tour of some of the Trucial Shaikhdoms. He plans to visit Fujaira on 15th February.

Shaikh Humaid bin Mohd, brother of the Ruler, has brought himself into disrepute with the Bani Kitab, having tricked one of their girls into believing that he had married her (Humaid himself acted as the Qadi at a brief ceremony), but abandoning her after the first night of their supposed wedding.

AJMAN:

The Ruler has allowed a large party of his followers to go to Hamasa on a visit to Turki, the Saudi Representative in the Baraimi area.

SHARJAH:

A second Assistant Political Officer (Class A) is due to arrive in Sharjah shortly. He is to be the Political Liaison Officer with the British forces.

---

7 The Bani Kaab trouble. See below under Muscat, Baraimi and Oman.

An attempt is being made to exercise greater control over the flow of legitimately imported liquor on the Trucial Coast, and Major Lippett, of the Red Oxide Company, has been refused a liquor permit by the P.O.T.S. who considers his purchases excessive.

The B.B.M.E.[8] is to open a small branch in Sharjah, which for the time being will function on two half days a week.

The (American) Dutch Reform Mission[9] in Sharjah is now staffed by five Americans, including a new Doctor and a Padre who arrived at the end of January.

On 12th January Mohd bin Ali Huwaidan of the Bani Kitab arrived in Hamasa from Riyadh. It is said that the Ruler of Sharjah, whose subject he is in theory, is to stop his share of the Company concession money.

The Ruler is establishing a new post in the Sharjah section of the Wadi al Qor.

DUBAI:

Shaikh Rashid and his followers arrived back in Dubai from Persia on 3rd January, having been refused permission to land in Lingeh. On his way back to Dubai he visited Farar and Bu Musa islands. The former has a Persian Wali, living on it, but Rashid found it as easy to bribe him as he had expected it to be to bribe the officials at Lingeh. Orders to prevent Rashid from landing at Lingeh apparently came direct from Teheran, and the Persian officials on the spot were in no position to bend before Rashid's bribes, apart from allowing one of the party ashore to purchase supplies.

Rashid was quick to avoid creating the impression that the refusal to allow him to land was because of any past misdemeanours on his part, and he put it about that he was being punished for his association with the British, and it was all part of the "Abadan Smell".[10]

Persian merchants in Dubai felt rather uneasy for some time after this happening, but Rashid's goodwill towards them soon relieved their anxiety. They naturally made the most of any suggestion that the Abadan trouble was the cause of all the trouble.

Messrs Gray, Mackenzie & Co.,[11] in common with most other merchants and commercial organisations in Dubai, are undergoing difficult times, and are having to reconsider their decision to have a European here as a Branch Manager. An increase in labour costs has hit them rather hard, as a result of which their landing and other charges have had to be increased, and some shipping lines are no longer finding it worth their while to call at Dubai.

8 British Bank of the Middle East, now HSBC.

9 This is the same organisation which also ran a hospital in Mattrah (Sultanate of Oman) and Bahrain.

10 This is a reference to the problems Anglo-Iranian was facing in Abadan and with the Government of Iran.

11 Shipping agents and merchants.

ABU DHABI:

The situation with regard to Shaikh Shakhbut's quarrel with his brothers has, unfortunately, not improved. Despite various reports during the past few months that a reconciliation between them was about to be effected, there has been no progress made in this respect, and the only question that arises is, to whether the relationship between them has worsened, or remained as it was when the split first occurred, sometime last March, 1952.

The pro-Saudi propagandists are making the most of these domestic troubles of the Al bu Falah,[12] and several times during the month rumours have been spread abroad that Haza and Khalid[13] had gone over to the Saudis. Shakhbut is a man without friends, and the Dubai Shaikhs, making the most of his unpopularity, let it be understood that it is with him and not the Al bu Falah as a whole, with whom they are on bad terms. In this respect, it is difficult to sum up whether the Dubai Shaikhs are, at the present time, pro-Saudi because they like the Saudis, or because they revel in the harm the Saudis are doing to Shakhbut. There are many people outside of Dubai who have taken a malicious pleasure in watching the Saudi triumphs over Shakhbut, and if popular stories possess any degree of truth, Shakhbut's own mother is now among them.[14]

On 5th January Shaikh Zaid travelled to Sharjah to see the P.O.T.S. about Shakhbut's handling of the Markhia post affairs. Said bin Shakhbut had gone to Markhia and behaved in a most disreputable manner and had dismissed Ahmed bin Fadhil from his command of the post. Troubles had arisen as a result of this, but Shakhbut would not reinstate Ahmed bin Fadhil. Instead he had sent Hamdan bin Mohd bin Khalifa to Markhia to settle matters, but according to Zaid, Hamdan behaved as disreputably as Said and merely made things worse. Ahmed bin Juma, (the head guard whom the Company had so much difficulty in removing from Ras Sadr) has now been placed in charge of the post.

Zaid also reported to the P.O.T.S. that various leading personalities of the Al bu Mundhir and the Al bu Rahma had come to him in Baraimi and expressed their loyalty to the Al bu Falah. He quickly went to report this to Shakhbut to arrange a payment for them, but Shakhbut had not only refused Zaid any money for this purpose, but had been very rude to him into the bargain. Apparently Shakhbut is conscious of his own unpopularity, for he accused Zaid of bettering his own position at his expense.[15]

12 The Al bu Falah are the section of the Bani Yas tribe to which the Abu Dhabi ruling family belong.

13 Brothers of the Ruler Sheikh Shakhbut.

14 Very unlikely. Any such ideas could be malicious rumour.

15 Sheikh Shakhbut would have been well aware of his brother's popularity.

The P.O.T.S. has summoned the brothers to Sharjah to meet Admiral Slayter on 9th February, and is hoping that their coming together may help them to settle their differences. Shakhbut has not met either Haza or Khalid since they left Abu Dhabi during March 1952. According to Zaid it seems unlikely that anything less than the most severe curbing of the activities of Said and Hamdan is likely to satisfy Haza.

With unblushing calm Shakhbut has asked the Company for a loan of two million Rupees, as an advance against future Royalties. His argument is that he wishes to enjoy the Royalties during his lifetime.

Major Lippett of the Golden Valley Red Oxide Company has been trying to secure a concession from Shaikh Shakhbut to mine red oxide on one of Abu Dhabi's islands. Shakhbut agreed to the royalty rate, and Lippett was within majlis-distance of success when Shakhbut mentioned a minimum payment which was quite out of the question. Lippett has come away from Abu Dhabi and is referring the matter to his superiors.

The causeway at Abu Dhabi ford, built by the Company, was opened to traffic on 5th January when the first vehicle crossed. This belonged to Hamdan bin Mohd bin Khalifah who was on his way to Markhia, carrying with him a 33½ gallon drum ....

Rain fell in many parts of the Trucial Coast during the early part of the month, making the Abu Dhabi sabkha difficult, though not impassable, as also parts of the road from Jabal Ali to Tarif.

MUSCAT, BARAIMI AND OMAN:

During the early part of the month an Iraqi doctor with two assistants arrived by the overland route from Al Hasa, and are now working with Turki in Hamasa.

The Sultan of Muscat is to be treated to a display by the Jet fighter Squadron from Sharjah, when he leaves Muscat by ship for the U.K. during the beginning of February.

Abdullah bin Salem, one of the Shaikhs of the Bani Kaab, has now definitely thrown in his lot with the Saudis. Together with Abdul Wahid, Abdullah bin Salem has been Obaid bin Juma's chief competitor in claiming control of the Bani Kaab. Sometime ago Abdullah bin Salem made an approach to the Sultan of Muscat for an agreement, through Abdul Wahid, who met with indifferent success and is still reported to be in Muscat. On his own, Abdul Wahid's position among the Bani Kaab amounts to very little. It has, for sometime past, been the hope of the Politicals that the Ruler of Sharjah would reach an agreement with Abdullah bin Salem and in this way put himself in a position to extend his territorial claim to include Bani Kaab territory, and the Ruler was on the point of despatching an emissary to Abdullah when news was received of his going over to the Saudi side.

Shortly after this news became known, and towards the latter end of January Abdullah bin Salem and a large band of followers surrounded the Levy Post in the Sharjah part of Wadi al Qor and gave orders for the Levies to leave. A message was quickly sent back to Sharjah and an armoured car detachment was rushed to the trouble spot, and in turn surrounded the trouble-makers. The jet fighters arrived on the scene and eased the tension, after which the party broke up and Abdullah bin Salem crept off with his followers back to Hamasa.

The Ahl Mazam[16] (Bani Baluch), in the Dhahira, are said to be suffering internal dissentions caused by the recent visit of some of their leaders to Riyadh.

Sayid Kamil, Shaikh Saqr bin Sultan (Na'im)'s representative has been to Sohar and collected a vehicle and two rifles which the Sultan has sent as a gift to Saqr.[17]

COMPANY ACTIVITIES:

Drilling operations began at Tarif on 18th January,[18] but it has not, so far, been possible to hold an inauguration ceremony there, owing to the uncertainty of the Ruler's plans. Shaikh Shakhbut has been wavering on his decision to tour the Bainuna area (and possibly visit Baraimi) since the beginning of the month, much to the annoyance of the P.O.T.S. who understood that the tour was coming to an end, when in fact Shaikh Shakhbut had not even left Abu Dhabi. Together with the other Trucial States Rulers Shakhbut has been summoned to Sharjah to meet the P.R. and Admiral Slayter on 9th January, and his plans after that date are undecided.

The Seismic Party operations on the Jiri Plain are coming to an end, and the party will shortly be basing itself on the Falaj al Ali area for operations along the Umm al Qaiwain and Sharjah/ Dhaid tracks.

R Codrai
Representative
cc. E F Henderson Esq.
Representative Bahrain.

---

16 The people of Mazam, which is an important Baluch settlement half way between Ibri and Dhank in the Sultanate of Oman.

17 Sheikh Saqr bin Sultan, Buraimi sheikh.

18 Well Murban 1.

TRUCIAL COAST DIARY FOR THE PERIOD ENDING 28 FEBRUARY 1953

GENERAL:

On 7th February all the Rulers of the Trucial States, with the one exception of the Ruler of Fujaira, were summoned to the agency in Sharjah, where they were entertained to lunch by the P.O.T.S.[19] and presented to the C. in C. [20] East Indies, Admiral Slayter. The Political Resident was unable to attend the gathering owing to the unserviceability of Sharjah airfield, which was flooded after the recent rains. Apart from the frequent meetings of the Trucial Rulers in Sharjah, to listen to the P.O.T.S. appeals for contributions to the Maktum hospital, noted for their absenteeism, this is thought to be the first time that the Rulers have been summoned together since the visit of Lord Curzon.[21]

After lunch the Rulers were taken aboard the Cruiser "Ceylon" which, in company with three frigates gave a demonstration lasting two to three hours, including an impressive gunnery display. Shaikh Shakhbut was reported as having a curious smile on his lips, as he sat in a 6 inch gun turret with Dubai in the sights.

For the same reason which prevented the Political Resident arriving, The R.A.F.[22] jet fighter squadron was unable to take part in the demonstration.

RAS AL KHAIMAH:

H.M.G. has made small grants, to assist the Rulers of Ras al Khaimah, Sharjah and Abu Dhabi. The latter two have already been paid, but the P.O.T.S. has delayed the payment to the Ruler of Ras al Khaima, as he wishes to make it conditional on something (which he considers to be worthwhile) being done with it, such as constructing a post in Khawatir territory or, alternatively, improving relations with Ali bin Saif of that tribe.

The Ruler is, as always, hard up and has again started borrowing from merchants, against the security of his concession monies.[23]

---

19 P.O.T.S., Political Officer Trucial States.

20 C in C., Commander in Chief.

21 Lord Curzon was Viceroy (King's representative) in India. He visited the Gulf in 1902/3 and held a Durbar in Sharjah where he addressed the Rulers. The visit was said to be in response to the visit to the Gulf of a Russian four funnelled ship. The Royal Navy did not have a ship to match this number of funnels, but British prestige was at stake!

22 R.A.F., Royal Air Force.

23 Concession agreement with the Company PD(TC).

Shortly before the seismic party moved to Falaj al Ali,[24] a Company Dove[25] carrying Messrs Wellings, N.V. Brown, Jackson and Codrai, landed on the Jiri plain near the camp. This is probably the first time that an aircraft has landed on the hinterland of Trucial Oman.

UMM AL QAIWAIN:

On 14th February Seismic Party No.5 moved camp from the Jiri plain to Falaj al Ali, in Umm al Qaiwain territory. It is to operate along the motor track to Umm al Qaiwain, after which it will do a traverse along the Dhaid/Sharjah track, moving camp to Dhaid if the Falaj al Ali water supply becomes impoverished. Much of the Dhaid/Sharjah track runs through territory claimed by the Ruler of Ajman.

SHARJAH:

The Ruler of Sharjah is reported to be in very impecunious straights. He has requested an advance of his annual payment from the R.A.F. agreement, and has been given an advance of his concession monies by the Company. He is reported to be anxiously enquiring as to why the Company has not shown any interest in taking his Sea Rights,[26] although he has made no official approach to the Company Representative in this respect.

The Sharjah airfield has been out of action for several days during the month, after the rains.

The R.A.F. Jet Squadron left Sharjah during the middle of February, to return to Habaniyah.[27] Earlier in the month the Squadron was due to give a demonstration over the ship in which the Sultan of Muscat was leaving Muscat but, as in the case of the naval demonstration off Dubai, was grounded in Sharjah at the time.

---

24 Umm al Quwain territory north of Dhaid. The oasis is the where the Ruler and his people retreat in the summer to escape the high humidity on the coast.

25 De Havilland Dove Aircraft on contract to the Company. The reader may see one in the Mahatta museum in Sharjah, suspended from the ceiling over a Dakota DC3.

26 The mineral/oil rights for territory under the sea bed and beyond the territorial waters had become an issue of international interest after the Second World War (1939-1945). Sheikh Shakhbut made international legal history in November 1951 when he successfully challenged PD(TC)'s right to include the waters beyond the territorial waters up to the mid-Gulf median line in the territory covered by the 1939 concession agreement. See HEARD, D. (2019) chapter 6. Sheikh Shakhbut had awarded the Superior Oil Company a concession to search for oil in the offshore areas beyond the territorial waters. The other rulers were considering following suite.

27 The British R.A.F. base in Iraq.

Mr. Buckmaster,[28] one of the two Assistant Political Officers, was sent to Abu Musa island during the month to investigate unsavoury reports which have been circulating, regarding the misdemeanours of Major Lippett of the Red Oxide Company. The disposal of liquor was the main question of interest to the Politicals, but many other matters came out in the wash, and a strike of the Sharjah labourers on the island provided a lively background for the A.P.O.'s visit. One of many things bearing down on Lippett is that an ex-foreman, recently discharged by him, is putting about a story that Lippett has been adding a low grade of oxide and sand to piles of high grade oxide which Pocock, Lippett's predecessor, had mined, and is trying to substantiate his story by obtaining written statements to the same effect from labourers who are supposed to have been employed on this task.

The R.A.F. Armoured Car Squadron still remains based in Sharjah and during the middle of the month the Trucial States Levies were reinforced by a detachment of from 200 to 250 Aden Levies, the primary purpose of which is to relieve the Trucial States Levy force whilst it is undergoing training and expansion.

There have been many visitors to Sharjah during the month, and Company Doves on special flights have made 11 landings there during this period.

DUBAI:

During the visit of H.M.S. Ceylon Shaikh Rashid excelled himself entertaining Admiral Slayter, the P.O.T.S., and many officers, and members of the British Community, to an Arab meal – believed to be the first of its kind on the Trucial Coast, served in European style with knives and forks, table and chairs. Those who were eating with their hands found the table to be rather too high and, in preparation for the next feast (given in the same style to the visiting representative of Cable and Wireless) a slave was ordered to cut several inches off the legs of the tables. Unfortunately, he also sawed off the legs of several chairs, before he was stopped.

The Cable and Wireless visitors had come to negotiate an agreement with Shaikh Rashid, to allow them to install a telephone system in Dubai, but have met with no success. Had they succeeded, they were planning to extend the system to Sharjah, as soon as they had finished the installation in Dubai (estimated to be about one year's work).

One of the Ruler's camels, which was with calf, was found shot dead on the motor track near Hassian.[29] An R.A.F. armoured car squadron vehicle had passed along the track, a short while before this discovery was made by the driver of a Company vehicle. Shaikh Rashid has protested to the P.O.T.S. about this, on behalf of his father, who has been away from Dubai for most of the month, on a hunting trip.

28 The Hon. Viscount Buckmaster.

29 Towards the border with Abu Dhabi.

Shaikh Said bin Shakhbut came on one of his periodic visits to Dubai for medical treatment, having turned-tail from Jebel Ali[30] rather than see the Company doctor in the presence of an interpreter. After his treatment at the Maktum hospital he lost no time in celebrating the return of his health, and news reached Shaikh Rashid that Said's car was stuck in the sabkha at the end of the creek, and that Said had 'gone mad'. Rashid immediately dispatched a car to rescue him, and took pains to try and cover up Said's misdemeanours.

Trade is still very bad on the Trucial Coast, and several hundred cases of piece goods, mostly Japanese, lie in the Dubai Customs Jetty, uncollected.

A dense swarm of locusts arrived over Dubai during the month, and stayed for half a day – the thickest swarm to come over the town for many years.

A British deserter from the "Wild Goose"[31] was brought to the Representative by Shaikh Rashid, who found him wandering along the track at the end of the Dubai Creek. The deserter said that he had tried to explain to the Shaikh that he was merely out for a stroll, looking for a boom[32] to take him to Bombay. But he misinterpreted the 'tafadiling'[33] from the Shaikh's followers, and decided that he had no alternative but to get in the car. He had been missing for two days, during which time he travelled to Jebel Ali, and spent the day there in custody before making his escape and spending the night at Jumaira.[34] He was handed over to the R.A.F., who made him comfortable in the O.C.'s bedroom, whilst the patrols were out looking for him.

It is said that Shaikh Rashid has received permission, direct from Teheran, to visit Lingeh[35] and to go on a hunting trip in the hinterland, but he seems to have no intention of taking advantage of this permission, just yet awhile.

ABU DHABI:

Shaikhs Zaid and Haza came to Sharjah to meet Admiral Slayter, as well as Shaikh Shakhbut, with whom they afterwards spent several days encamped a short distance from Sharjah. Ziad was taken ill, and spent two days in hospital during his visit.

Everyone with any interests in Abu Dhabi was closely watching events, wondering whether a reconciliation between Shaikh Shakhbut and Haza would be brought about by this visit. Shaikh Mohammed bin Sultan of Sharjah again made efforts to get himself accepted as mediator (having once travelled to Abu Dhabi and Baraimi with this intent) but he was again told by Shakhbut that there were no

30 The Company camp at Jebel Ali.

31 A British naval vessel.

32 Ship.

33 "Welcoming".

34 South of Dubai town on the coast, now absorbed into Dubai town.

35 On the Iranian coast.

differences with his brothers to settle. Shaikh Rashid claims that Shakhbut asked him why he did not [want him to] mediate - he did not mind someone from his own tribe knowing of his troubles, but he did not want any of the Jawasim to know that there was anything wrong in his house. Haza and Zaid both accompanied Shakhbut back to Abu Dhabi, but left for Baraimi shortly afterwards, leaving Shakhbut to deal with Messrs. Macpherson and Stockwell of the D'Arcy Exploration Company,[36] who had come to negotiate for the Abu Dhabi Sea Rights. As on their previous visit, the representatives found Shakhbut a difficult person to deal with.[37]

The R.A.F. Armoured Car Squadron detachment near Tarif has been reinforced by 17 of the newly arrived Aden Levies.

Shakhbut is complaining that the security of his island has been weakened by the building of the causeway, and he is now asking that the Company should either make a junction of the causeway to join it to his old watch-tower, or that a new guard post should be built at the side of the causeway. Khan Saheb Hussein, the Company's Contractor for the building of this causeway, has also been having a difficult time with Shakhbut, who seems to have very fixed ideas as to the style of the gate he requires across the causeway. He is also doing his best to relieve Hussain of a goodly percentage of "his own idea" of Hussein's profits – both from the causeway and from the camp canteen.

BARAIMI AND OMAN:

The tide in the affairs of 'Oman appears, at last, to have turned in favour of the Sultan and Abu Dhabi. This, at the moment, amounts to little more than that the Saudis are observing the terms of the Standstill Agreement, but the reason for their succumbing in this respect are not altogether clear. It may be that the recent show of force on the part of H.M.G. has had the desired effect or, of course, it may be that the present cessation of Saudi activities has been decided upon to place the Saudis in a stronger position to complain against H.M.G., should the new forces be used to their detriment. One thing which is quite clear is that the Saudis are suffering burnt fingers over the recent Abdullah bin Salim affair,[38] and that they are anxious not to risk a similar rebuff in any other area.

There have been many, but rather flimsy, rumours of late suggesting that some of the newly won Saudi followers (Sulaiman bin Hamyiar[39] being particularly mentioned)

36 Anglo-Iranian or BP.

37 The negotiations with Sheikh Shakhbut ended in the agreement on 9th March 1953 leading to the establishment of the company ADMA. Abu Dhabi Marine Areas. ADMA (⅔ BP. ⅓ Total) started exporting oil from the offshore Umm Shaif oilfield in 1962.

38 At the Wadi Qor. Mentioned in the previous month's diary.

39 The Bani Riyam sheikh from the Jebel Akhdar and Tanuf in the Sultanate of Oman.

are turning their attention to the wicket being batted[40] by H.M.G., but a lapse of time is necessary to confirm these stories. In the meantime, it is apparent that Turki has closed the door of the Hamasa stronghold, and has stopped his entertaining of anyone who wishes to visit him. It is even reported that gift bringing baduin are actually being turned away with their presents, unless, of course, they are philanthropically minded enough to leave them without promise of reward, but it is understood that Turki's doorstep has so far not been littered in this fashion.

Codrai
Representative

TRUCIAL COAST DIARY FOR PERIOD ENDING 31 MARCH 1953

GENERAL:

Early in the month the Foreign Office made a general release to the press of the facts of the Trucial Oman/Oman boundary dispute with Saudi Arabia, and on 8th March newspapers began publishing the British case, quickly followed by Saudi charges and British counter-charges.[41] Both British and Saudi Arabian radio stations have broadcast several items of news on the subject, in Arabic.

The Foreign Office campaign of publishing was well timed to forestall a similar campaign which the Saudis had threatened, to attract international sympathy for their case against Britain.

The mustering of British Forces in Sharjah has been in full swing during the month, and a total of five hundred Aden Levies are now based on the Coast. These Levies, together with the R.A.F. Armoured Car Squadron, have been shouldering most of the duties since they arrived, leaving the T.S. Levies[42] free to continue with their recruiting and training programme, ready for their gendarmerie duties once the boundary troubles have been settled. There has also been a considerable amount of aerial and naval activity, carrying out of reconnaissances over the "Restricted Zone", and landing of vehicles and supplies for the ground forces. A jet fighter squadron, consisting of four Meteors, is based in Sharjah for reconnaissance purposes.

---

40 As in cricket. Meaning 'the actions of H.M.G.'

41 The reader will recall that the Saudi Arabian Turki bin Ataishan arrived in Buraimi (Hamasa) on 31st August 1962 with a substantial military force.

42 Trucial States Levies.

The arrival of Adenese seems to have caused no unfavourable criticism and, on the whole, they are more popular than the rather more arrogant Syrians and Jordanians who were sent here to form the T.S. Levies.

It appears that the Adeni N.C.O.[43] instructors who have long been awaited by the Muscati Levy Commander at Sohar, spent some time in Sharjah, where they arrived by mistake and were claimed by the Commander of the T.S. Levies.

Towards the end of the month a new Group Captain took over from Group Captain Brice,[44] the Senior Air Staff Officer in the Persian Gulf, who is in charge of the forces on the Trucial Coast.

March has been a month of variable weather, of dusty, hot, south winds, and of cool north-westerlies which brought a few light rain showers with them. As appears to happen at least once a year, a particularly strong wind (a westerly rather than a shammal)[45] caught many of the mariners napping, with the usual disastrous results. Ali Awazi of Dubai was the hardest hit of all. One of his launches (an ex-R.A.F. seaplane tender) sank off the entrance to the Dubai Creek and four people were drowned (two of them having been washed overboard, a short while before the launch sank). At the time of the strong wind two ships were discharging off Dubai, and several lighters had to weather the storm. One of Ali Awazi's booms, loaded with Bapco[46] petrol ran aground at the entrance to the creek as it was trying to get in, and was broken up by the sea. No lives were lost and the cargo was saved. A Graymacks[47] barge loaded with forty tons of dried fish was washed ashore at Shandaga,[48] and the dried fish was ruined. African and Eastern were acting as agents to a local merchant for the shipping of this cargo (valued at approximately two thousand pounds) but neither they nor Graymacks stand to lose by this mishap.

RAS AL KHAIMA:

During the early part of the month Shaikh Saqr filled in the water well at Sahaila. It is difficult to imagine what exactly he hoped to achieve by this. It was an angry action, presumably wrought about through boundary jealousies, though there is no doubt that the withdrawal of the Company Seismic Party from his territory has increased his wrath.

Shaikh Saqr is getting himself into bad odour with the P.O.T.S. for frequently failing to appear at the Agency, when he is summoned there.

---

43 Non Commissioned Officers.

44 Earlier in diaries named Price.

45 North wind.

46 BAPCO (Bahrain Petroleum Company) had, and still have, a refinery at Bahrain.

47 Grey Mackenzie.

48 At the entrance to the Dubai Creek.

UMM AL QAIWAIN:

A Seismic Party Dodge crashed into the Ruler's car in town recently, and apparently the drivers of both vehicles share the blame for this accident, out of which the Ruler's car emerged the most badly damaged.

The Ruler has been caught up in the "brighter-majlis" movement, and has reconditioned a stable in his fort, which he now uses as the principle guest room.

The Wadi Batha track from Umm al Quwain to Falaj al Ali is practically unserviceable except for the Landrover style of vehicle, and the Ruler and the Seismic Party have to use the Sharjah/Falaj al Ali track. The Seismic Party plan to operate along this track, but not until it has first been tackled by a grader.

AJMAN:

Now that the situation has turned against the Saudis, public opinion is quick in trying to fend off criticism from each particular Shaikhdom and, not a little, to excuse the misdeeds of the Saudis. The basic facts of the present review are that the Saudis had no intention of extending their interests beyond the frontiers they claimed from Abu Dhabi, but the door was open, H.M.G. appeared disinterested, and the Saudis were beckoned into these parts by such people as Rashid bin Humaid, and his son Ali.[49]

SHARJAH:

On 10th March the Political Resident[50] journeyed overland from Sharjah to Kalba, Fujaira and Khor Fakhan, escorted by a detachment of the Armoured Car Squadron. Apart from the Resident, who made claim to the only tent and whatever bedding was available, the parties seemed to be badly lacking in camping experience, and the P.O.T.S. and R.A.F. Officers were the worse for wear on their return to Sharjah.

On 23rd March the Resident visited Abu Dhabi in the frigate Lock Glendhu, after which he called at Abu Musa Island[51] to see for himself the state of affairs there, which have been reported on recently. It is thought that Major Lippett will not be returning to the Persian Gulf, after he leaves at the end of the oxide working season, sometime next month. Some embarrassment was caused when the Resident returned the visit of Shaikh Khaled,[52] the Sharjah Representative on the island, who was found to be living in the pantry of Lippett's bungalow. Amidst pin-up girls and

---

49 Sheikh Rashid bin Humaid was the Ruler of Ajman, and his eldest son was Ali. The writer seems to have confused him with Rashid bin Hamad of Hamasa, Buraimi, who accompanied the Saudi Turki bin Ataishan when they arrived at Hamasa from Saudi Arabia on 31st August 1952.

50 Sir Rupert Hay.

51 The Sharjah island due north of Abu Dhabi and in the middle of the Gulf.

52 Khalid bin Ahmed.

empty Brylcream[53] bottles the Resident, P.O.T.S. and the Commander of the frigate solemnly seated themselves to eat a fuwala[54] consisting of a plate of broken biscuits. Investigations of the various reported happenings on the island seem to have left Shaikh Khalid's character comparatively unblemished.

The P.R. went fishing off Abu Musa, and the launch he was on broke down, delaying the frigate for a few hours, and by the time it reached Sharjah a strong shamal was blowing and the party was unable to land, although this was not fully realised until the Trenchard-Fowle[55] had broken a few timbers getting alongside the frigate. Both the P.R. and the P.O.T.S. were over-carried to Bahrain.[56]

The Ruler is still toying with the idea of dredging Sharjah Creek, and has been offered a German dredger. He is badly lacking advice on the subject, and has asked for the assistance of the Company's Marine Department, in this respect. Whatever the physical chances of this project, it is most unlikely that the opening up of Sharjah Creek would bring the trade which the Ruler supposes it would, particularly if trade on the T.C. fails to rise above the present slump level, despite the attraction of a lower Sharjah Customs tariff (2 ½%) compared with Dubai's (4 ½%).

A water diviner (Colonel, ex-sappers) has been brought to the Trucial States by the Politicals, to carry out a preliminary survey of the coast and to report on the possibilities of benefiting the Rulers by finding fresh supplies of water. He is an independent operator (sponsored by the Foreign Office), who has already had some success at Kuwait, and seems to be much sought after. He is remaining on the coast until about 10th April, after which he is going to carry out a survey at Jeddah, travelling there via Bahrain. He is both a natural and a scientific diviner, and is using a new radionic[57] aid which he claims to have designed and to have had specially made. He is one of the few visitors to the coast who is unreservedly wished the greatest of success by everyone.

The P.O.T.S., the Mr. M.S. Weir, is still in the throes of departing and being relieved by C. Pirie-Gordon.[58] The rooms of the Sharjah Agency have been divided and dubbed under the terms House of Commons and House of Lords, affairs of state being discussed in the principal majlis presided over by M.S. Weir, whilst applications for liquor permits and visas are carried through the portals to the Hon. M. Buckmaster,[59]

53 A common hair cream in those days.

54 Small meal, usually more generous than on this occasion.

55 The Residency Yacht named after a previous Political Resident.

56 Instead of landing at Sharjah.

57 His name for his instrument.

58 I have corrected Codrai's spelling of his name. Incorrectly spelt Perrie.

59 Martin Buckmaaster, 3rd Viscount Buckmaster.

and the Hon. I. Lucas,[60] in the House of Lords, noted at the present time for its shortage of chairs which [would] enable both members to be seated at the same time.[61]

A Liquor Regulation has been introduced into the Trucial States Order in Council.[62]

Early in the month a Kuwaiti boom carrying six hundred sacks of rice ran aground at Zubaira, to the north of Khor Fakhan. The Sharqiyin[63] of the nearby village of Badiyah, and surrounding hills, raided the boom and looted its cargo. Zubaira it's claimed by the Ruler of Sharjah, who has lodged a complaint against the Sharqiyin with the P.O.T.S.[64]

DUBAI:

Early in the month the Politicals placed an embargo on the carriage of goods to Hamasa from Dubai. Shortly afterwards a Dubai taxi bound for Hamasa with a Banyan[65] and his wares was turned back by the Levies and followers of Zaid, acting together, after the goods had been seized. It is said that the Banyan has been compensated by Turki. A further incident relating to the turning back of a Dubai vehicle occurred at the latter end of the month, but the details of it are not known.

This embargo is a good move, for supplies in Hamasa are already reported to be none to plentiful, but this restriction needs to be continuously imposed so as not to offend the Ruler of Dubai. The actual destination of Dubai taxis going Baraimi-wise is always open to doubt until they actually arrive, and it would be easy to commit a mistake in turning back vehicles, as the Ruler claims has already happened. Shaikh Rashid was himself asked by the P.O.T.S. to bring an end to trade between Dubai and Hamasa, and he has agreed to do whatever he is able in this respect, although he claims that his own people will not find it easy to investigate the intentions of every passenger leaving Dubai by car. Also, it is not easy to control the flow of goods leaving Dubai by camel.

A Dubai prostitute has complained to the Ruler against an attempt which was made to abduct her, and to carry her off to Hamasa, from where she would be sent to Saudi Arabia and sold as a slave. Several others of the ladies of little leisure have been reported missing from their establishments recently, and this complaint has given rise to the belief that they have been carried off by the slavers. Applicants from among the Rulers' followers to investigate these charges were frustrated by the appointment

---

60 Second son of George Lucas 1st Baron Lucas of Chilworth.

61 Sir Ivor Lucas describes this as 'The Hons' cupboard'. The Honourable's cupboard.

62 Order in Council is an order issued by the Monarch in London on the advice of ministers.

63 The chief tribe of the emirate of Fujairah on the Indian Ocean coast.

64 Khor Fakkan, on the east coast, is Sharjah territory.

65 Indian merchant.

of Mausa,[66] Shaikh Rashid's mother, for this task. The outcome of the investigations is not quite certain. The Suq stories implicate a number of Dubai people, including one Khalifah bin Majid who [is], distantly related to Shaikh Said, and several others including taxi drivers. The Saudi who buys the slaves in Hamasa, and dispatches them to Saudi Arabia, is said to be bin Gharab, who has a house there. A Bahraini taxi driver and one of the Ruler's M.T. mechanics have been arrested in connection with this incident, and are now in Dubai gaol.

The mother of a girl stolen from Derra several months ago has just heard that her daughter is now in service in Kuwait.

In the past, the Foreign Office has been rather reluctant to expose such slaving activities, in its case against the Saudis, but the P.O.T.S. now seems to consider that opportunities may be taken to publicise various happenings in this respect. However, H.M.G.'s position as far as the state of slaving goes may not be unimpeachable, judged on an international level, and one wonders whether it would be wise to turn back the blanket and expose the Saudis at this stage, particularly as very few of the Rulers with whom H.M.G. has treaties have clean sheets as a result of this black slaving traffic.

Trade with Persia seems to have fallen off even more recently, and in Dubai there is now a shortage of fresh foodstuffs which usually come from Persia. The African and Eastern Company is feeling the pinch, and is about to withdraw its Representative for the summer, leaving behind an Indian in charge. If this arrangement is successful, and unless trade picks up considerably, it is unlikely that a European will be sent to Dubai after the summer.

There has been another accident between two vehicles on the Derra/Sharjah track, and three people have been killed.

ABU DHABI:

Shaikh Shakhbut still continues to suffer bad health, and seems more conscious of this since his return from Bombay, than previously. Three times during the month Dr. McCaully was summoned to Abu Dhabi to treat the Ruler, but on each occasion he found him to be suffering only a mild ailment. The Ruler will not acknowledge that he is unwell until the doctor is on the scene, and he then clings to him and will not let him go until he claims to feel better.

Apart from these trips to Abu Dhabi, Dr. McCaully has spent a few days in Baraimi. This was at the request of Shaikh Zaid, the recommendation of the P.O.T.S. and the order of the Political Resident.

66 Codrai is mistaken. Sheikh Rashid's mother was Sheikha Hussa bint Al Murr. She came from Bukha, a coastal town in the Sultanate of Oman north of Ra's al-Khaimah. Sheikha Hussa was reputed to have been a forceful lady with a strong personality.

Messrs. MacPherson[67] and Stockwell of the D'Arcy Exploration Company have recently made two visits to the Coast, and spent several days in Abu Dhabi, negotiating with the Ruler for his off-shore rights. They have been successful, but not on their own terms.[68]

After leaving the Company location at Tarif the Ruler visited his base at Markhia.

BARAIMI AND HAMASA:

Bin Mansur, the Saudi tax collector, arrived in Hamasa during the month and spent several days there, during which time he travelled a short distance to the south, but without reaching Dhank. Apparently he had been encamped near Baraimi when a Saudi vehicle arrived from the west, bringing him instructions to extend his tour to Hamasa. The purpose of his visit, to establish the Saudi right to collect taxes in this area (which on this occasion the taxpayers could immediately get refunded, with a possible bonus, from Turki) does not seem to have been successfully fulfilled, and bin Mansur left the area sooner than was generally expected.

Abdullah bin Salim of the Bani Kaab has accepted in writing, through the P.O.T.S., the sovereignty of the Sultan of Muscat over himself and the Bani Kaab under his control. At the first time of being asked for his acceptance of this in writing he submitted a letter which, after compliments, read "Na'am".[69] Shortly afterwards, and with the assistance of the Levies and Shaikh Zaid (who takes full credit for his handling of Abdullah) he installed himself at Sharm,[70] after a brief skirmish which the Saudi press and radio was quick to make the most of. Abdul Wahid has been acting as Abdullah Salim's go-between. Slight troubles have been experienced at Sharm, since Abdulla installed himself there, but these have been quickly dealt with.

Establishing a footing among the Bani Kaab cannot be regarded as a major victory, but it is one of many happenings which have considerably brightened the general situation.

Rumours from the Baraimi direction have been rife, and seem to contain fewer truths than ever before. For this reason suq news has to be discounted, and it is difficult to keep in touch with anything but the major events. Even reports from the Levy Post at Baraimi frequently turn out to be inaccurate these days.

67 D. MacPherson of BP, not I.G. MacPherson of IPC.

68 They were negotiating a concession on behalf of BP ⅔ and Total ⅓. In due course the company ADMA was established, Abu Dhabi Marine Areas. Sheikh Shakhbut demanded that they should accept the same terms as the Superior Oil Company had agreed to. These terms included payments far in excess of Stockwell's instructions from London.

69 "Yes."

70 Between Mahadha and Buraimi in the Wadi Sharm.

COMPANY ACTIVITIES:

There has been a further cessation of drilling at Tarif, due to loss of circulation at approximately 4800 feet.[71] The Seismic Party operations from the Falaj al Ali camp are continuing, and the Party is due to cease work on 5th April for one week's local leave. The Area Superintendent and his staff moved to the Sharjah base from Jebel Ali at the end of the month.

On 24th and 25th March the Ruler of Abu Dhabi was successfully entertained by the General Manager to a rather belated inauguration party at Tarif. The Ruler was accompanied by his brother Haza and Mohamed bin Khalifa.[72]

As was expected, the Seismic Party has been experiencing one or two difficulties, due to the undemarcated state of the area in which it is operating. Early in the month a party of Tanaij (claiming allegiance to Sharjah) was unexpectedly encountered along the Umm al Quwain track, and the Party was only allowed to proceed with its operations after arrangements had been made for it to use Sharjah, as well as Umm al Quwain guards, in the disputed area. Later in the month the Party was again threatened with stoppage, this time by the Ruler of Sharjah, when its operations had to temporarily be transferred to the Sharjah track. The Ruler objected to the camp being based in Umm al Qaiwain territory, but he climbed down from this when he was told the temporary nature of the work in his territory. Slight friction was occurring between the Umm al Qaiwain and Sharjah guards in the camp, and arrangements were made to establish the latter at Tawi Rashid.[73]

On 3rd March the General Manager, companied by Mrs. Heselden, Captain Holden, Codrai and Glencross, boarded the M/V Jamila off Dubai, for a marine reconnaissance to other parts.

Codrai
Representative.

STOP PRESS – 3rd April '53

On the morning of 2nd April a detachment of the R.A.F. Armoured Car Squadron and the Adeni Levies, which had been forming up at Tarif, set off for Jebel Dhanna, where an R.N.[74] Supply Ship was offloading water and supplies for them. All the vehicles are reported (by a reconnaissance aircraft) to be stuck in the sabkha,

---

71 The drilling mud is circulated down the drill pipe and back up the hole through the annulus between the drill pipe and the wall of the hole. Sometimes the drilling mud escapes into the rock formation (lost circulation).

72 The Ruler's cousin.

73 Near Dhaid.

74 Royal Navy.

a few miles to the east of Dhanna, and they have not yet made contact with the naval off-loading party.

This operation is a result of a decision of H.M.G. to uphold the right to unrestricted movement within the limits of the boundary claimed by H.M.G. on behalf of Abu Dhabi, and wave aside the Standstill Agreement. It is also the intention of the British Forces to turn back any Saudi vehicles which they may make contact with. To assist them in this task the ground forces are aided by the R.A.F. which (with four Meteors, two Ansons and two Lancasters)[75] does daily reconnaissances over the area, giving the ground force details of any vehicles which they spot.

The Forces are to go as far west as Sila, and in a southerly direction wherever they have cause to, and wherever the terrain makes this possible.

The B.B.C. news bulletin in Arabic announced this move westwards on the night of 2nd April.

Two of the women reported missing above (under Dubai) have been recovered by the Ruler and returned to their 'homes'.

Codrai.

TRUCIAL COAST DIARY FOR PERIOD ENDING 30 APRIL 1953

GENERAL:

There has been no great change in the political situation in Abu Dhabi, since the move into the restricted zone by the British Forces.[76] Ground and air forces have spent the month in carrying out patrols and systematic reconnaissances in the western part of the territory, and around Baraimi and have successfully effected the blockade of Hamasa. No reliable news of the Saudi reaction to this sudden reversal has been received locally, although the propaganda machine has been pouring forth rumours of a Saudi offensive to relieve Hamasa, and indeed, to take the whole of Oman. However, the enthusiasm with which these rumours are put about by local sympathisers seems to be waning with the passing of time.

The principal happenings during the month has been a meeting of the Trucial States Council, and the departure of Shaikh Shakhbut for London.

Apart from many Foreign Office News releases to the Press, the Baraimi problem has been brought into the public eye during the month after the visit to these parts by Daily Express and Daily Mail correspondents. The latter arrived in Sharjah and

75 Lancaster bomber. Sometimes used to drop hay for the sheikhs' camels.

76 HEARD, D. (2019), p. 331ff. 'Turki (Bin Ataishan) does not honour the Agreement'.

was conducted on a tour of Baraimi by the Political Officer Trucial States. The Daily Express's correspondent was flown direct to Baraimi, via Tarif from Bahrain by the Group Captain in charge of operations, without the knowledge of the Political Officer Trucial States.

The British elements of H.M.G.'s forces out on patrol have been having an uncomfortable tour, and are shortly to be withdrawn. The plan which is about to be put into effect is that the R.A.F. armoured car squadron is to be withdrawn forthwith from the Trucial Coast, and the Aden Levies sometime later, when the local Levy Force has been expanded to about five hundred strong. Many Adenese will, however, be integrated in the local Levy Force.

The R.A.F. Lancasters which have been daily carrying out long and arduous reconnaissances are showing signs of wear, and arrangements will have to be made to replace them with other aircraft, very shortly.

From the Company's point of view the most important event of the month has been the lifting of the restriction West of 53° 30' which has been in force since February 1951. This has led to preparations being made for a speedy re-entry into this area, and by the end of the month the move of Seismic Party No.5 from the Sharjah/ Umm al Quwain camp to its new site in the Jebel Dhanna area had already begun. It is expected that Seismic operations will begin about the middle of May.

Admiral Towner of the U.S.N., in the Duxbury Bay, is about to begin another tour of the Trucial States, including calls at Rams and Fujairah. Whenever possible he is met by one of the Political Officers, who acts as his interpreter with the Shaikhs.

RAS AL KHAIMA:

Two of the Ruler's younger brothers, Hamad and Abdallah and several others, including the former Head Guard with the Seismic Party and the eldest son of Shaikh Humaid have returned from a scrounging tour to Bahrain and Kuwait.

Boundary troubles have occurred between Ras al Khaima and Fujairah, and the Rulers of these two Shaikhdoms recently met at Habhab[77] to declare a temporary truce between the people living near the frontier of that place. These are Sharqiyeen, who pay date taxes[78] to Ras al Khaima. Shaikh Humaid, brother of the Ruler of Ras al Khaima is about to go on a trip to Dibba, and this may well be connected with these disputes.

The ill feeling between the Ruling family of Ras al Khaima and Shaikh Ali bin Saif of the Khawatir, and his followers seems to have increased and no hope of an improvement in their relationship can be hoped for whilst Saqr continues his efforts to keep them down with a strong hand.

77 In Fujairah territory close to Qat in the mountain foreland. The west side of the Hajar mountains.

78 Their date crop was largely for their own consumption.

AJMAN:

Shaikh Ali, the Ruler's eldest son, recently caused a little consternation, in Ajman and Sharjah, by marrying in Sharjah. His bride was the daughter of a distant relative of Saqr bin Sultan,[79] and the sister of a former Company houseboy. Earlier in the month he arrived back from a visit to Bahrain and Kuwait.

The Ajman/Sharjah frontier problem came near to stopping the Seismic Party, within a few days of its withdrawal from this area, and it was about to link up with earlier traverses. This is reported on below.

SHARJAH:

On 23rd April a meeting of the Trucial States Council was called, so that Sir Rupert Hay could say goodbye to the Rulers. He is due back on the coast sometime during Ramadan, to make his farewell to the British community. The Rulers seem genuinely concerned that Sir Rupert was leaving, and there is little doubt but that they have formed a personal attachment to this diplomat of the Old School.[80]

The remainder of the Council Meeting took to a dismal trend, as far as the Rulers were concerned. They were asked to make contributions towards the upkeep of the Maktum hospital, but this appeal was offset by Rashid bin Said, who then held-forth on the failures of the hospital, and his expectations of it, making particular reference to the fact that his people had to travel far afield to get medical attention, which should be obtainable in Dubai. In principle, he was no doubt right, but his arguments were weakened by demands for equipment, doctors, specialists and staff, without his being able to suggest the means of maintaining the hospital financially.

Rather prematurely perhaps after the recent round of political troubles, the slavery question seems to have leapt to the head of the political agenda and the suppression of slavery was discussed and the Rulers were asked to free their slaves. This appeal must have been made without [even a] little hope of it leading to anything like a settlement of this difficult problem, and it would better have been left unmade until it could be backed up by a practical proposition or determination to see it through to the end. However, allowances have to be made for the fact that this move may have been forced on the Politicals themselves, due to the focus of outside interest on this area, and the necessity for putting into effect one of the prime reasons for the British being here – the suppression of slavery.

As far as could be judged, reactions to the Political Resident's appeal to end slavery were very mixed, although no doubt the Arab argument of "who would make our coffee or work in our harims if we didn't have slaves" appeals to them all. Shaikh

79 Sharjah Ruler.

80 Sir Rupert Hay was the last Political Resident to be appointed from the Indian Civil Service.

Zaid afterwards reported Mohamed bin Salim (of Sharjah), and one of two others, as saying that the Christians should live their way, and leave the Muslims to live as they wished. On the other hand, Saqr of Sharjah and Juma of Dubai were rather too verbose in their insistence that slavery had ended years ago. The Rulers of Fujairah, and others adopted a more practical attitude and after the meeting told his slaves to go inside the Agency and obtain their freedom, knowing full well that he would depart with the same size retinue as had accompanied him on his arrival.

It appears that the Company is not to go untroubled by the anti-slavery question, and the Politicals still have it in mind to persuade the Company not to employ slaves. The Company cannot afford to offend the Rulers in this way, and the only practical way to proceed would be for the Politicals to inform the Rulers not to send slaves for employment with the Company. But even then it seems hardly worth the trouble for the little good it could possibly do to further their cause.

As far as Company employees are concerned there seems to be little difference between a slave who takes his pay to his master, and a free man who parts with most of his pay in the perpetual struggle to free himself of a pearling debt[81]. Such people are probably as numerous as slaves, among the Company's employees.

Shortly after this meeting of the Council the Political Officer received information of a plan to embark slaves on a launch at Khan near Sharjah, and carry them off to Kuwait.

The Levies lay in wait for the slavers, but a thick mist prevented them from making contact with them until it was too late, and the launch had sailed off into the mist with the slaves aboard. The Levies blindly fired their automatic weapons after it. The car, with its driver and mate, which brought the slaves to the rendezvous, was captured, but the mate made his escape by diving into the sea, crying out that he would fetch the launch back. He reappeared in the Dubai Suq the following morning. The Trenchard-Fowle, the Agency launch,[82] was at the time, high and dry in Sharjah creek, and unable to give chase until the following day, when it embarked on a tour of some of the islands where it was thought that the slave-carrying launch might have sheltered.

The Political Officer made a brief, unenthusiastic, attempt to begin work on the internal boundaries question, but has made no headway beyond getting Rashid bin Said's refusal to accept H.M.G.'s judgement as binding.[83]

---

81 Men working on the pearling boats had to borrow to pay for food etc while they were on the water. This was in anticipation that they would return home at the end of the season with cash from the sale of the pearls. However frequently they failed to earn enough to pay off the debt. Debts accumulated and were even passed from father to son.

82 Named after a previous Political Resident.

83 All the Rulers were required to give their agreement to accepting the boundaries between the individual sheikhdoms as determined by the 'politicals'.

There has been much coming and going between Baraimi and Sharjah during the month by the R.A.F. Anson, and Shaikh Zaid was flown in to attend the meeting of the Trucial States Council. But only after he had signed an R.A.F. 'blood chit'[84] which had to be sent back to Sharjah by car.

Rashid bin Humaid of Ajman failed to arrive for the meeting of the Council, and was represented by his son Ali who was cold shouldered by the Political Resident, having rather prematurely explained that his father was unable to attend the meeting, owing to car trouble near Masfoot.

There is still a small Levy post in Wadi al Qor, but it is of little use, having neither a radio nor a vehicle at its disposal.

Major Hankin-Turvin, who has been the Officer Commanding the Trucial States Levies since they were first formed, is shortly leaving the Service and is to be replaced by another officer, not yet named. His relief is expected shortly.

The present Political Officer Trucial States, M.S. Weir, is now due to leave Sharjah about the middle of May on home leave but there is still no news of the arrival of his replacement C. Perrie-Gordon.[85] Buckmaster is due to go on leave this summer, leaving Lucas behind.

The Ruler has made his first formal approach to the Company as regards his Sea Rights.

DUBAI:

Shaikhs Juma bin Maktum and Khalifa bin Said now wish to accompany Said on his visit to London, and to fall in with their wishes Said is now considering going by sea. The number of followers who are to accompany the Ruler seems to be growing, and it is not unlikely that the Ruler may be persuaded to visit Bombay, rather than England.

Following the departure of Shakhbut for London, and the meeting of the Trucial States Council, Shaikh Rashid entertained Shaikhs Haza, Zaid and Hamid bin Bati in Dubai for a day and a night. They now get on very well together, but Shaikh Said seldom appears when the Abu Dhabi Shaikhs are present. The general opinion is now that Shaikh Shakhbut is the only n... in the woodpile as far as improving relations between the two Shaikhdoms is concerned. The Abu Dhabi Shaikhs seemed in the best of spirits, at being left to deal with the situation themselves, since the departure of Shakhbut.

A mobile clinic, together with a European attendant, is to be attached to the Maktum hospital for one year, at the expense of the International Red Cross. As soon as it arrives, it is to be sent to the Baraimi area, where an R.A.F. doctor is already functioning.

84 To relieve the RAF of demands for restitution, should an accident occur.

85 Pirie-Gordon.

ABU DHABI:

On 5th April Shakhbut arrived unexpectedly in Sharjah on the Company Charter,[86] and was admitted to the Maktum hospital the same day, where he remained until he left for London on 22nd April. Prior to this, he had been treated by Dr McCaully in Abu Dhabi. The latter rather over publicised the fact that he did not consider that Shakhbut was ill, and had everyone from the Political Officer to the Dubai Shaikhs guessing at political motives for the visit. While he was in hospital he was visited by Haza, Zaid, Hamad bin Bati, Mohammed bin Khalifa and his mother. This, coupled with the visit of Suheil al Mana,[87] created an uneasy state of tension in Dubai, and the usual precautions of imposing a curfew and of doubling the guards in watchtowers etc, were taken. To the time of Shakhbut's departure, McCaully was unable to find anything wrong with him, and readily gave his confirmation to the popular belief that Shakhbut was a neurotic. Despite this, Shakhbut appeared very ill and weak.

Shakhbut is making his own arrangements for his visit to London, and has engaged Victor Hashim, formerly of Superior Oil Company, as his interpreter. He is also accompanied by Shaikh Khalifah bin Muhammad, and his secretary Khalifa bin Yusuf, and one other follower. During his absence, his brother Haza is to act for him in Abu Dhabi and on the coast, and Shaikh Zaid in the interior.

Shaikh Haza is planning to go on tour in Bainuna, and to try and find a motor route to Western Liwa. He is fairly confident of reaching Suaitiya by car, and hopes to get to Arada,[88] where it is said that a Saudi vehicle once penetrated. If the track is suitable, the Levies hope to establish a post[89] to the South West of Suaitiya. Haza may be accompanied by Zaid on this tour.[90]

The Levy post at the Naval off-loading point at Jebel Dhanna is to be withdrawn.

FUJAIRAH:

The Ruler was visited in Fujairah by the Company Representative, during the month, and a first approach was made to him for the Exploration Rights of his Shaikhdom. After going on a tour of his territory, to find out what the reaction of his people would be if he accepted the Company's offer, and if he did not insist on getting the same as the other Rulers, he arrived in Dairah where he rented a small house, apparently in preparation for protracted negotiations. Shortly after this he had to hurry back to Fujairah, in time for a visit from Admiral Towner, but he remained

86 Aircraft.

87 One of the Dubai dissidents, cousin of the ruler.

88 Arada is a small oasis on the western side of the Liwa crescent.

89 This did not happen as even getting as far south as Suaitiya was not easy.

90 It was to be another couple of months before Codrai and Chatton took the first car to Liwa, via Suaitiya arriving at Arada in June 1953.

in Dubai long enough to express his disapproval of the Company's offer, and it seems unlikely that he will accept it, when he returns.

BARAIMI AND OMAN:

There have been many reports that the Imam's Wali at Ibri formerly Qadhi in Muscat has been expelled by Sulaiman bin Hamyar.

One of Turki's cars, on its way back from Ibri to Hamasa was caught by the Levies, who escorted it over the border, into Saudi territory. Turki is now left with about four vehicles. The blockade of Hamasa is being very effectively maintained.

The new Levy force at Sohar has only succeeded in recruiting a few people during the past few months, and is now between 30 and 40 strong.

COMPANY ACTIVITIES:

About 80 Abu Dhabi labourers went on strike at Tarif on 26th April, and had to be discharged and replaced by new recruits. The reason given for the strike was their objection to riding in open lorries between camp and the rig, and a demand to be transported in buses. This followed an accident, in which one of their number was injured when he fell from the lorry, but an offer by the company to install benches and guardrails in the lorries was rejected. No other complaint against the company was voiced by the strikers, but it seemed reasonable to suppose that they are reflecting a little of the unhappy spirit and discontent which exists, to a very noticeable degree, among the covenanted[91] staff.

A few days before the Seismic Party was due to finish its operations along the Dhaid/Ajman track, and near the Sharjah/Ajman disputed territory, the Ruler of Ajman stopped the Party from working with a demand that they should take Ajman guards. The Ruler of Sharjah naturally refused to permit this, and was adamant about the ownership of this particular area to the point of not allowing the Party to proceed with guards from both Shaikhdoms. This difficulty was, eventually, overcome and the Party finished its operations ready for its move to Dhanna, a few days later. Both Rulers manifested a greater determination than ever to uphold their claims to this particular area, and the Politicals are going to meet with considerable difficulties when they eventually tackle this boundary problem again.

Codrai
Representative

91 The Covenanted staff. The men under contract.

EXTRACT LETTER: 26th April 1953

A meeting of the Trucial States Council was called yesterday, and the Resident said goodbye to all the Rulers. Shaikh Zaid was brought in from Baraimi by R.A.F. Anson, to attend this meeting.

Last night I dined with Shaikhs Rashid, Zaid, Haza, and Hamid bin Bati.[92] They were all in the best of spirits, and seemed to be getting on very well together. Shaikh Said and Shaikh Juma[93] were not present, although they were both in town.

Codrai

TRUCIAL COAST DIARY FOR PERIOD ENDING 31 MAY 1953

GENERAL:

Ramadan began on 13th May on the Trucial Coast, although a few people began fasting the previous day, acting on the radio news from Cairo and Mecca. The principal pearling season will not get in full swing until after the Eid al Fitr.

Mr. M.S. Weir left Sharjah on posting on the 18th May, going home to England to attend the Coronation.[94] Mr. C. Pirie-Gordon, O.B.E.[95] arrived on 20th May, and assumed his duties as Political Agent, this post superseding that of Political Officer.[96]

Ground and air forces have kept up their patrol duties in the western part of Abu Dhabi territory, during the month, but there have been no reports of Saudi activities from this area. The merger of Adenese into the T.S. Levy Force is nearly completed and, as soon as the latter have been brought up to strength, the balance of the Adeni Levies will be withdrawn. There are now six British Officers in the Local Levies, with Lieutenant Colonel Martin (formerly of the Military Mission to Saudi Arabia) in command. The former Commander, Major Hankin-Turvin, is shortly to go on leave, after which he is to be posted on other duties.

RAS AL KHAIMAH:

Mid-way during the month it appeared very much as though the Ruler, Shaikh Saqr bin Mohd, was about to reach a reconciliatory agreement with the former Ruler, Sultan bin Salim. The terms of the proposed agreement were that Saqr was to pay

92 Sheikh Rashid, son of Dubai ruler. Two brothers of Sheikh Shakhbut and their maternal uncle.

93 Dubai ruler and cousin.

94 The coronation of Queen Elizabeth.

95 O.B.E. Officer of the Order of the British Empire.

96 Representing an up-grade of the political presence in Sharjah.

Sultan Rs. 14,000/-annually, in return for which Sultan would renounce any rights which he claimed to territory in the Wadi Al Qor and, in particular, he would cease to exercise the influence he had retained among the Ras Al Khaimah subjects, notably the Khawatir tribe, to the detriment of the present Ruler. However, they are now no nearer to reaching agreement than they were before the present negotiations began, the Ruler of Sharjah having intervened and interrupted the negotiations, interpreting this settlement to mean that Sultan bin Salim was selling the whole of the Wadi Al Qor.

The Ruler, his father and brother Humaid were entertained to lunch by the Representative before Ramadan.

SHARJAH:

The American Mission clinic in Sharjah is about to re-open, having been closed for two or three months, for reasons unknown to the public. However, it will only be functioning for two or three weeks, as Dr. Hosman and her four colleagues are due to go on summer leave to India, early next month.

As usual, the Red Oxide Company on Abu Musa has ceased operating for the summer, but this year it has been asked by the Royal Navy to remove its stock of dynamite from the island, for fear of a visit there by the Persians.

DUBAI:

The Ruler and his eldest son, Shaikh Rashid, narrowly escaped with their lives, when the driver of the car, in which they were travelling to Sharjah at night, missed the main track, and drove straight into the creek at high speed. The car came to rest in about 12 feet of water, and was completely submerged but fortunately all the occupants managed to escape. The car was a Plymouth Saloon, which was presented to the Ruler by the Company, last year.

Shaikh Juma, the Ruler's brother, has been on a tour to Bahrain and Kuwait, and received a gift of a car from the latter and money from Bahrain.

ABU DHABI:

Khalifah Bin Yusif, Shaikh Shakhbut's Secretary, returned from London for a few days towards the end of the month, to conduct some business in Dubai and Abu Dhabi, but he has since re-joined Shakhbut in London.

Shaikh Haza has temporarily established himself in the Bainuna, near Al Agaila,[97] at a spot which is now known as Bada Haza, since the recent discovery of a good supply of sweet water from a well, which Haza ordered too be dug. The Abu Dhabi post at Markhia is still being maintained, and the Levy Force is still centred at Al Agaila.

97 South of Jebel Dhanna and Ruweis.

In company with Major Hankin-Turvin, Shaikh Haza is conducting a reconnaissance south of Bainuna, with a view to establishing other posts in Manasir territory, particularly on the western approaches to Liwa. The Levies also intend to establish posts in this area. Haza seems to be very happy, and to be enjoying his tour. He is accompanied by Hamid bin Bati.[98]

Towards the end of the month Zaid occupied Falaj Maziad,[99] which was taken from Ahmad as Salf,[100] and his followers. The only casualties were on Zaid's side, being two killed and two wounded. Falah Maziad is now garrisoned by about sixty of Zaid's followers. Rumour has it that Obaid bin Juma, of the Bani Kaab, has joined forces with Ahmed as Salf, and other Na'im supporters, and that both sides are mustering forces, but this rumour has not been taken seriously, and it is not thought that the situation will develop.

Zaid is said to have expressed his concern to the P.O.T.S. about the amount of money which the Al Bu Falah are spending on matters which are really in the interest of the Sultan of Muscat, whereas, as far as they are concerned, the Sultan still seems to view the situation with indifference.[101]

COMPANY ACTIVITIES:

Ramadan was heralded by a round of labour troubles in the Company camps although prevailing discontent, rather than Ramadan itself, seemed to be the root of these troubles. Most of the Sharjah employees working with the Seismic Party went on strike for the most flimsy reasons connected with complaints about their rations and leave arrangements, and the majority of them were dismissed and sent back to Sharjah. At the same time, troubles were being experienced at Tarif in connection with the opening of the local staff kitchens, for Northern Area personnel,[102] by a tool-pusher.[103] Also, the insistence on the part of the drillers for the return of their old rig crews, who had recently been dismissed (at the demand of the tool-pusher himself - see TCD April) when they had gone on strike. However, these matters were smoothed over without any further dismissals being made, and without suffering any stoppage of work. Shortly afterwards the remainder of the Dubai labourers and guards at Jebel

98 The maternal uncle of Sheikh Shakhbut.

99 Falaj Maziad. The spoken 'j' is very soft like 'y'. Maziad is south of Buraimi and under the shadow of Jebel Hafit, near the border with the Sultanate of Oman. Jebel Hafit is the prominent 1000 metre high mountain between the sand and the Hajar mountain foreland. It is divided between Abu Dhabi and the Sultanate of Oman.

100 Khawatir section of the Na'im.

101 The Saudi force was in Hamasa, Sultanate of Oman territory.

102 Arabs from Iraq or Jordan.

103 Drilling foreman. Company man.

Ali went on strike in protest at the poor quality of dates which they were being given. Their complaint was found to be justified, and this matter was quickly put right.

Preparatory to the arrival of a Gravity Meter party in the area south of Bainuna, Messrs. F.A. Gibson, Codrai and Hedgcock made a brief reconnaissance to a point a few miles north of Ghatail[104] towards the end of the month. A short time prior to this, F. Brooks, who is making a similar reconnaissance in this area, encountered Said bin Suwaid and Gharan Mana, two Manasir leaders who had pledged their allegiance to the Saudis, near Bada Mattawa, and was not allowed to proceed further. This was just prior to the arrival of Shaikh Haza, on his tour in the Bainuna.

Codrai
Representative.

TRUCIAL COAST DIARY FOR PERIOD ENDING 30 JUNE 1953

GENERAL:

Ramadan ended on 12th June in all the Shaikhdoms, after the new moon had been sighted.

As is the custom, the Eid al Fitr was announced in Dubai by a burst of cannon fire but, due you to a poor quality chappati,[105] there were fewer casualties than usual. Two people were slightly injured when one of the Eid canons exploded in a rather spectacular fashion, outside the Ruler's Palace, sending fragments as far as the Creek, one piece landing in the Majlis in which the Ruler was seated. It is thought that this is the best bang Dubai has had, since a slave was transported over to Derra[106] on the end of a ram-rod.[107]

Some of a group of children, including Khalifa bin Said's son, were injured, one seriously, when they tried to react the same incident, by igniting some gun-powder which they had been stuffed in a piece of water-pipe.

Fewer boats than ever before have gone out to the pearling banks this year, due to the drift of a considerable proportion of the working class population to the Northern oil states.

The T.S. Levies now have seven British Officers and a British Sergeant-Major. They are not now expected to take over completely, from the remaining Aden Levies,

104 Western Abu Dhabi, south west of Jebel Dhanna, north of the continuous dune country.

105 Flat bread.

106 Across the creek from Dubai to Deira.

107 An unlikly event which nevertheless entered local folklore.

until about October. The former Gray Mackenzie building in Sharjah, is to be taken over by the Levies as an Officers Mess.

Apart from feasts which were given for some of the Rulers at the Agency and the Representative's house, the Coronation Celebrations[108] were confined to the British community.

Only a few people are going on Pilgrimage next month, from the Trucial Coast. The most notable of them are Shaikh Khaled, the brother of the Ruler of Sharjah, and Khan Sahib Hussein, the Company Contractor.

FUJAIRAH:

The Ruler is still undecided as to whether to accept the Company's offer for the Exploration Rights of his territory.

SHARJAH:

The Foreign Office has made a grant of £4,000 to £5,000 for the building of a school in Sharjah. The Political Agent is to be responsible for the spending of this money, and for approving the plans.

Jassim al Midfa, a former employee of the Company, is preparing for a visit to Ibn Saud by having a "Tree of Life" made for the King, from silver and gold. The cost of it is ten thousand Rupees, which is generally regarded as being a safe sum to invest, as the giver of it can reckon on at least receiving an American car (worth Rs. 12,000 to 15,000) in return.

DUBAI:

Shaikh Said bin Maktoum left Dubai by B I steamer on 27th June, with 15 followers. He is first of all going to Bombay, to see an eye specialist, after which he is to go to Miraj, to have his knee treated. Shaikh Juma and Shaikh Khalifah, who were to have accompanied the Ruler, both change their minds at the last moment, the latter when he was actually aboard the steamer.

The Ruler had previously declined the Company's offer to pay his expenses to go to England for treatment, on the grounds that there were too many people wanting to accompany him.

It is planned to have the new Political Agency in Dubai ready by next February.

A Dubai launch carrying about 90 passengers sank on the way to Bahrain, towards the end of June. Six survivors reached Jebel Baraka,[109] floating on drums. The remainder of the passengers are presumed to have been lost.

108 The coronation in London of Queen Elizabeth on 2 June 1953.

109 On the Abu Dhabi coast west of Jebel Dhanna.

ABU DHABI:

The Ruler has arrived in Egypt, whence he came from London, via Paris, but it is not yet known when he will be returning to Abu Dhabi. Stories of how he left England in a huff, shortly before the coronation, have quickly circulated on the coast. The reason which is given for his hurried departure is that he had a disagreement with his doctors, rather than that he was dissatisfied with the arrangements made for him to attend the coronation.

The D'Arcy Exploration Company is awaiting the Ruler's return, with a view to establishing a base in Abu Dhabi.

Together with Shaikh Haza, the Levies have been active in carrying out reconnaissances to the south of Bainunah, as a result of which a few new posts were established in that area making the disposition of forces as follows:

Markhia.	Shaikh's post	
Bida Haza.	Shaikh's post	
Suaitiya.	Shaikh's post.	(Camel post)
Al Agaila.	Levy post.	(Camel post)
Bada As Suwaila.	Levy post.	(Camel post)
Arada.	Levy post.	(Camel post)

Following a Company reconnaissance by Chatton and Codrai, as far as Arada[110] and Suaitiya, the post at Suaitiya was withdrawn. The difficulty of keeping this post supplied had already been realised, as Lancasters[111] have been dropping grass for the Shaikh's camels, at this place.

BANI KAAB:

Towards the end of June, Obaid bin Juma of the Bani Kaab sent out about eighty of his followers, led by a slave called Marzug from Mahadha, to attack Sharm. The latter was being held by Abdullah bin Salim and about forty followers. When the attacking forces reached Nuwei, the defending force at Sharm[112] took to defensive positions in the hills, at the same time sending news of the attack to Zaid. The latter immediately arranged the dispatch of about sixty Levies, who arrived at Sharm without encountering the attacking force. Fighting did not break out until Obaid's force at Nuwei fired on six Levy vehicles carrying reinforcements, which had been

110 Chatton and Codrai drove from Jebel Dhanna to Arada in Liwa in June 1953. This was the first record of a vehicle reaching Liwa.

111 RAF transport aircraft.

112 Mahadha, Nuwei and Sharm are all within a short distance, less than 20 kilometres, of one another.

sent from Sharjah, whereupon the force of Sharm joined in the fray and surrounded Obaid's force, which surrendered after five of its members including Marzug, had been killed, and five injured.

The Levies then turned their attention to Mahadha, and sent Obaid bin Juma a warning that they would attack him the following morning. Obaid fled during the night, with a handful of followers, and apart from a brief visit to an old friend living near Wadi Jizzi, nothing has been heard of him since. His two sons, Nasser and Ahmed, have also gone into hiding, although they made their escape sometime after their father. Obaid's womenfolk have gone to Abdul Wahid[113] for sanctuary.

Mahadha was taken without trouble, the only opposition coming from one soldier in a watchtower, who fought on until he was killed by machine-gun fire. Accounts of this incident vary considerably in stating the number of bullets which it took to kill this warrior, some claiming as many as eighty. Whatever the number the unfortunate defender of Mahadha was buried without a post-mortem.

Some of the goods which had been stolen from Dubai and Sharjah vehicles, after they had been raided by the Bani Kaab, were found at Mahadha.

Abdullah bin Salim has now been recognised as the Shaikh of Bani Kaab.

BARAIMI AREA:

All is quiet on the Hafit side of Baraimi. Zaid's followers are still occupying Falaj Masiad, and Ahmed as Salf is sucking his gums in Hafit village.

Turki and about twenty five Saudi followers remain cut-off in Hamasa, together with about fifteen of the Al Bu Shams, including the brothers Rashid and Mohamed Bin Hamad, and their cousin Abdul Aziz. The only other inhabitants of Hamasa are slaves. The Saudis still have three cars with them but, it is said, no petrol.

A few days before the beginning of Ramadan a small party of Bani Kitab, with about a dozen camels laden with food, entered Hamasa at night by breaking through the walls of the date gardens on the Baraimi side. They were arrested by the Levies on leaving Hamasa, but were released at the request of Shaikh Zaid.

During the above mentioned trouble at Sharm and Mahadha, a large party of about fifty men with two hundred camels was reported to be en route for Hamasa, carrying foodstuffs from Dubai. They were of mixed origin, and are said to have included Awamir and Bani Kitab tribesman. Zaid got news of this party, and sent word that it was either to return to Dubai, or deliver the foodstuffs to him. The party returned to Dubai – some say at the orders of Rashid bin Said, while others say that it was Turki who ordered them to go back.

A member of the Bani Baluch is said to have been killed recently, in a skirmish between the people of Ibri and the Bani Baluch, over the usual Falaj trouble.

---

113 Ka'abi associate of Sheikh Abdullah bin Salem.

TAIL PIECE:

A four engined Aigle Azur charter aircraft, which was in trouble over the Ruus al Jabal area,[114] having lost two of its engines, jettisoned most of the baggage of the crew and nine passengers, in order to retain its height and clear the hills. The aircraft landed safely in Sharjah, followed shortly afterwards by a Dakota of the same Company, which was carrying two spare engines for another craft which had broken down elsewhere. The bad advertisement this may have created for this Air France sponsored company in Sharjah, could not undo the good which this inadvertent publicity campaign had done among the Shihu. Not all of the raiments from heaven were appreciated to the full, however, and the effect of a "wild hatchet man" wearing a beach suit, carrying his axe in a golf club bag, went almost unnoticed when his goat was seen to have its milk protected by a black nylon garment with "Bon Soir, Mon Ami" embroidered on it.

Codrai
Representative.

TRUCIAL COAST DIARY FOR PERIOD ENDING 31 JULY 1953

GENERAL:

All the Rulers of the Trucial States are away from the coast, at the moment, with the exception of Ras al Khaima and Fujairah. The Ruler of Sharjah has gone to India, where the Ruler of Dubai is still having medical treatment. Shaikh Shakhbut has not yet returned to Abu Dhabi from Bahrain, on his way back from London. The Rulers of Ajman and Umm al Qaiwain have gone on the pilgrimage.

UMM AL QAIWAIN:

The Ruler left by B.I. steamer, on 21st July, and is going on pilgrimage.

AJMAN:

The Ruler left on pilgrimage on 21st July, travelling by B. I. steamer to Bahrain.

SHARJAH:

The school which is to be built in Sharjah with the Foreign Office grant is to be run by Lebanese or Iraqi teachers. The running costs of the school are to be paid for by the Ruler of Kuwait.

114 Musandam peninsula.

The Ruler, Shaikh Saqr bin Sultan, accompanied by several members of his family, left for Bombay by B.I. steamer on 26th July. He intends to remain about one month in India, for medical treatment and a holiday.

The Ruler is still endeavouring to get Gray Mackenzie and the Sharjah merchants to use Sharjah as a port, and to encourage steamer traffic, but he is unlikely to meet with any success.

Shaikh Saqr has, for sometime past, been actively engaged in trying to prevent drinking, or trading in Liquor, in Sharjah, and has been dealing very harshly with any culprits who have been detected. Himself a member of the rather large drinking community in Sharjah, before becoming Ruler, he is well informed in the activities of those who indulge in this illicit past time, and conducts most of the raids himself, and it is said that he sometimes goes out alone at night in order to gain admittance to houses where he believes people to be drinking.

Towards the end of June Shaikh Saqr cut off the hand of a local fisherman, who had been found guilty of theft.

The T.S. Levies have, at long last, received a F.O. grant with which to buy a local launch, to use for supplying their forces in western Abu Dhabi territory.

DUBAI:

Three people died from alcoholic poisoning in Dubai during the month. They are believed to have all drunk methylated spirits.

Shaikh Rashid had several bottles of whisky and beer confiscated from Arab and Pakistani visitors to one of the B.I. steamers. Some of the culprits were put in goal, for a short time.

A local Persian went mad, and shouted down the Mullah, during a Friday service in one of the mosques, at which Shaikh Rashid was present. He was removed and put in goal.

Shaikh Said has written to his son, Rashid, to say that he has derived benefit from the treatment which he has been having for his knee, at Miraj, and that he will be leaving for Bombay, where he is to have treatment for his eye, at the beginning of August.

Sulaiman bin Hamyar[115] and his son Sultan arrived in Dubai during the month, and stayed about a week as the guest of Shaikh Rashid before travelling to Bahrain on 4th August. They also spent two days in Sharjah. Sultan is suffering from a disease of the eye, and bin Hamyar says that he is going to take him to London, if necessary, to have him cured.

Shaikh Rashid considers that the local drivers are too reckless, and has forbidden them to use the Company graded track, from Jebel Ali to Sharjah. There have been several more minor accidents involving local taxis, during the month.

---

115 From Tanuf and the Jebel Akhdhar in the Sultanate of Oman.

ABU DHABI:

Hillyard, who is to be the Representative of the D'Arcy Exploration Company[116] in Abu Dhabi, arrived on a visit to Abu Dhabi on 23rd July, to make arrangements for the building of a house there. Having got permission for this from Shaikh Shakhbut in Bahrain. Hillyard is married, and hopes to bring his wife with him when he arrives to take up his appointment after the summer.

Hillyard would have liked to have lived on a suitable launch in Abu Dhabi, but his Company is bound to a clause of the Agreement, which it took over from the Superior Oil Company, which makes it necessary for its Representative to be based onshore.

The D'Arcy Exploration Company plans on beginning its Geophysical programme, next winter. It is also going to establish an office in Dubai.

Shaikh Shakhbut arrived in Bahrain on 17th July, where he had come from London, via Egypt. He is expected to return to Abu Dhabi, early in August. His eldest son, Said, travelled up to meet him in Bahrain, at the end of the month.

MUSCAT AND OMAN:

After approximately nine months of recruiting, the Levy Force at Sohar[117] has raised only thirty eight recruits, apart from which it consists of two British Officers and four Arab instructors. The Living conditions for the Officers at Sohar are said to be very bad, and Maxwell, the Commander of the Force, has suffered a lot of illness during his stay there. Small though it is, the Force has been on the brink of three mutinies, during its brief history.

The Sultan attributes the difficulty in raising recruits to a restriction which he felt obliged to impose on the force, limiting the area of recruitment to the coastal stretch, in the immediate vicinity of Sohar. This restriction has, however, been lifted for about three months, without any noticeable improvement in the recruiting programme of the force.

The Advisor to the Sultan, Woods-Ballard, is about to have his contract terminated, the Sultan having arranged for a replacement during his recent visit to England. Subsequent to Woods-Ballard learning of this, he has discovered that his Chief Accountant has defrauded the State of about Rs. 20,000/-.

Sultan is still in Dhofar, and it is thought that he may remain there next winter.

Midway during the month the Levies fired on, and severely wounded, one of the followers of Turki,[118] who had wandered out of the gardens at Hamasa. The report of this incident which reached Dubai, said that a Mullah had been shot at by the

116 Also known as Anglo Iranian Oil Company, or BP.

117 The town on the Batinah coast. The Wadi Jizzi route across the mountains from Buraimi led to Sohar. At that time it was not suitable for motor vehicles.

118 The Saudi Arabian Turki bin Ataishan in charge of the occupying force in Hamasa.

Levies, whilst he was praying, and this is a typical example of the effectiveness of the distortions produced by pro-Saudi news-carriers.

The blockade of Hamasa continues, but there is a mystifying number of people who appear to come and go to Hamasa, with comparative ease. Recently arrived in Dubai from Hamasa, via Baraimi, is the son of Shaikh Mubarak (Formerly Qadi of Dubai, now with Turki). Although only 12 years old, he has been a radio operator with Turki, and claims that he is on his way to Saudi Arabia for further training.

COMPANY ACTIVITIES:

The death occurred during the month of Rihan bin Sultan, a fitter who was one of the first employees to be recruited for the Trucial Coast. He was greatly respected for his unusual skill, and aptitude for anything mechanical, and will be missed by all who knew him.

Codrai
Representative.

TRUCIAL COAST DIARY FOR PERIOD ENDING 31 AUGUST 1953

GENERAL:

The Eid al Adha was celebrated in all the Trucial Shaikdoms except Abu Dhabi, where it was a day later, on 20th August.

As usual, August has been the hottest month of the summer, and this year's claim made by the "Grey Beards" as to it being the hottest period within their memories, has, to some extent, been borne out by various manifestations of intense heat, notably, a large number of cases of heat exhaustion, and the death of many camels in the hinterland. The arrival of slightly cooler weather at the end of the month has resulted in a widespread epidemic of fever and colds.

The new Political Resident, Persian Gulf, Mr. B.A.B. Burroughs, C.M.G.[119] made his first visit to the Trucial Coast during the month, and remained for a week, during which time he made a two-day visit to the Sultan of Muscat, in Dhofar, flying to Salala by Lancaster.[120] Local conditions, low tides and the "Trenchard-Fowle" (The Sharjah Agency launch) quickly had their effect on the Resident's tightly packed programme, as they have done so many times in the past for his predecessor, but

119 The first Political Resident to be appointed by the Foreign Office in London. All previous appointments were made by the India Office in Bombay.

120 A World War 2 bomber aircraft, still in use at that time by the RAF.

the Resident won high regard from those with him for facing the difficulties with a smile, despite the fact that he himself was affected by heat exhaustion. Apart from a visit to the Ruler of Ras al Khaima, the tour was mainly concerned with the Official Organisations, particularly the rapidly expanding Trucial Oman Levies. It is expected that he will visit the Coast again later, when all the Rulers are present.

The air search of Western Abu Dhabi territory continues with praiseworthy regularity, but it is only just being realised how formidable the task of scanning this area is, and the value of the present system is open to doubt. The task of maintaining the Levy Post in this area is proving to be a heavy burden on the Trucial Oman Levies and, again, the effectiveness of the degree of control which these posts extend over the area is not as great as was first thought. However, the value of all these operations in showing the intentions of H.M.G. to remain firm on its boundary claim is considerable, and this alone justifies operations which are otherwise open to criticisms and which are frequently demoralising, particularly in the heat of summer, to the Services concerned.

A further example of this situation has existed in the Baraimi area for sometime past, and is now quite clear. Hamasa remains surrounded by Levy Forces, and followers of Zaid, who, from the positions they occupy, are correct in their claim to be blockading Hamasa. But the back door to Turki, through the Baraimi settlements is wide open, and has been for some time. Saqr bin Sultan[121] refuses to allow the Levies to carry out patrols in his settlement,[122] and seemingly for a very good reason, as he taxes all supplies which are taken to Turki (Anna's eight per maund).[123] Apart from which his followers collect considerable baksheesh for allowing this trade. This makes little difference to the status quo of the present situation, but the effect which it has on the Forces carrying out day-to-day patrol duties on the other side of Hamasa can be well imagined.

FUJAIRAH:

The Ruler of Fujairah, Shaikh Mohammed bin Hamid ash Sharqi, signed a three-year Exploration Agreement with the Company on 18th August.

Ruler has a confused conception of the Passport and Visa Regulations which are in force, but with some justification he complains that although he himself is not allowed to issue travel documents, many of his people are taking passes from the Rulers of Ras al Khaima, Sharjah and Dubai, and selling his rifles before travelling on to their destinations. More than seventy members of the Sharqiyeen tribe recently

121 Buraimi sheikh.

122 The three Omani settlements are Baraimi, Hamasa and Sa'ara.

123 A Maund is about 9 pounds and 8 annas were half a Rupee.

arrived in Sharjah with the Ruler and after he had arranged passes for them they travelled on to the Oil States, in search of employment.

The Ruler is very critical of the failure on the part of H.M.G. to delineate the boundaries of his territory, as he is being perpetually troubled these days by the Rulers of the adjoining Shaikdoms, namely Sharjah and Ras al Khaimah, who are busy reinforcing their territorial claims. One of the factors which prompted him to sign the Exploration Agreement with the Company was, no doubt, the fear that he would get less than his fair share of territory if the Company had no interests in Fujairah. Dibba and Habhab (adjoining Khatt) are two of the places where the Ruler and his neighbours have most noticeably being jockeying for position.

One of the worst Locust attacks for many years occurred in Fujairah territory just as the dates were ripening, and the dates had to be harvested before they were ripe, causing a considerable loss to the people.

RAS AL KHAIMA:

A fight broke out among members of the Habus[124] near Khatt, on 16th August, and one person was killed and several injured. Ali bin Saif, (Khatiri), was called in to act as mediator, and succeeded in postponing the issue until after the Eid. The cause of the trouble was that a goat which had been sold by one Habsi[125] to another as being with milk, ceased to deliver the goods as soon as it has changed hands.

The standard of living of the Habus in the hills is very much lower than that of the average Bedu in the hinterland, and it frequently happens that fights occur for such trivial reasons as the one mentioned. The beginning of quite big fights, with high casualties, in the past, has often been a Habsi gesticulating with his little axe,[126] as he bargains over an article of pathetic value. A large number of Habus visitors to Ras al Khaima usually results in a hurried closing of the market place, in the old style of the American West.

SHARJAH:

The Political Agent is endeavouring to introduce a measure of protocol into the Agency's business, and has himself retired out of range of Arab callers. He is also trying to reduce the number of calls made to the Trucial Coast by Naval Frigates. In the past, these have averaged one every three weeks, and apart from the Political Agent most of the burden of receiving the Commander of the Frigate and returning his call has fallen on the Ruler of Sharjah.

---

124 A mountain tribe who descend onto the plain in the summer.

125 Member of the Habus tribe.

126 Every man would carry the small axe about 2 inches long, on a wooden handle about 30 inches long.

On the night of 3rd August an Orient Airlines (Pakistani) Dakota crashed in Sharjah, shortly after taking off. It had come from Karachi, and was carrying Pilgrims. Of the twenty five passengers and crew, six were injured, and one died, after being flown to hospital in Bahrain.

A lorry overturned on the Sharjah/Batinah track, near the entrance to the Wadi al Qor, during the month, and seven of the Omani passengers were killed, and many others injured.

DUBAI:

The recent news from Persia brought about a sudden revival of trade between Dubai and the southern Persian ports, but it was only short-lived and trade remains bad in Dubai.

Khalifa bin Majid, one of the persons concerned in the slaving incident reported in March has been arrested by the Trucial Oman Levies and sent by air to Bahrain. It is understood that his arrest was made with the approval of Rashid bin Said.

ABU DHABI:

Shaikh Shakhbut returned to Abu Dhabi on 8th August. He travelled back from Bahrain by a Gulf Aviation Aircraft, but the pilot was unwilling to land at Abu Dhabi, and put the Ruler down at Tarif. Most of the Ruler's close relatives, including all his brothers (Khalid among them, with whom he had not spoken for nearly a year), and the Representative were awaiting his arrival at Abu Dhabi, and had to repair to Tarif where they were entertained by the Company. The following day the Ruler and his whole party travelled back by road to Abu Dhabi, where they narrowly missed disaster. Swiftly turning the corner of the Fort, to get through the sand, the leading car, carrying the Ruler and the Representative were fired on at point blank range by one of the line of cannons which had been loaded to fire a welcome. Fortunately the canon had been packed with nothing harder than palm fronds, which were sprayed all over the car. The following cars braked to a standstill alongside the other cannons, when suddenly the advancing committee of welcome, which had been waiting outside the Fort, took to its heels, and disappeared back into the Fort. At the same time the Ruler's party saw that one of the cannons was furiously belching smoke out of its rear end, and everyone quickly dismounted and disappeared from sight round the corner of the fort, until the cannon, which had looked very much as though it would explode, had exhausted self.

Shaikh Shakhbut claims to be feeling much better, although he still appears to be very weak.

Travellers to Abu Dhabi who have spent long hours at the ford waiting for the tide to recede, would now find the scene much changed. A causeway now connects the island to the mainland, and there is a stone-built guards' post a short distance from it, on the Abu Dhabi side.[127] A two storeyed post, with a majlis for the Shaikhs, has now been completed at the end of the causeway, on the mainland.

MUSCAT, OMAN AND BARAIMI:

Sulaiman bin Hamyiar has joined the ranks of the illicit drinkers. During his recent visit to the Coast he was seen inebriated in company with Said bin Shakhbut. He also pestered Zaid for some of the "Christian's Special" which he insisted that Zaid had brought back with him from Paris. "I know you are a drinker, Zaid," he said, "I can see it in your eyes".[128]

Bin Ham,[129] one of the Shaikhs of the Awamir tribe, and the constant companion of Zaid bin Sultan, visited Turki recently with the permission of Zaid, and collected a present of Rs. 600/-.

It is said by Zaid that a Najdi[130] brought Turki a large sum of cash (paper Rupees) at the end of July.

At the beginning of August about sixty members of the Wahiba[131] tribe accompanied by their Tamima, Shaikh Mohd bin Sultan bin Mansur, arrived in Dubai, where they remained for two days before travelling on to Saudi Arabia. They had come from Ibri in a Dubai lorry calling on Zaid en route. Zaid would not allow them to visit Turki, but gave them a present of a thousand Rupees and supplies. Rashid bin Said of Dubai paid for the launch which took them to Dammam, and also gave them liberal supplies. Mohammed bin Sultan made no secret of the fact that his party had mixed intentions, some of them desiring to go on Pilgrimage, whilst all of them were hoping for substantial presents from the King. The Wahiba have in the past, frequently visited Saudi Arabia, journeying by camel on a southern route, but this is the first time that a large party of them has travelled by the Trucial Coast.

Mr. B. Woods-Ballard the Minister of Foreign Affairs in Muscat, is retiring at the end of September, Mr. Innis[132] his replacement, is due to arrive about the same time.

Codrai
Representative.

---

127 The causeway was constructed by Khan Sahib Hussain and paid for by the Company (PD(TC)).

128 Could not be further from the truth.

129 Sheikh Salem bin Ham was a constant loyal supporter of Sheikh Zayed. At the time the chief Sheikh of the Awamir in the Buraimi region. Sheikh Salem needed cash to enable him to maintain the loyalty of his tribe.

130 From Saudi Arabia.

131 From the Sultanate of Oman.

132 Innes wrote a very interesting book about his experiences in The Sultanate. INNES, N. M., *Minister in Oman, A Personal Narrative*, The Oleander Press, 1987, ISBN 0 900891 89 0.

TRUCIAL COAST DIARY FOR PERIOD ENDING 30 SEPTEMBER 1953

GENERAL:

During the month there has been little news of importance, other than from the Baraimi area, which continues to occupy the limelight of local affairs, normally shed upon lesser boundary problems or tribal troubles.

There seems to be but little doubt that the new Political Resident is hastening a decision to change the existing, unsatisfactory, state of affairs relating to the presence of Turki bin Ataishan in Hamasa, and it likewise seems to be fairly certain that the eve of some decisive action on the part of H.M.G. has been reached. Recent happenings in Baraimi area are reported on below, under that heading, and they amount to a general tightening up of the blockade of Hamasa by the T.O.L. and local forces. Furthermore, the situation has reached the Churchill/Eisenhower level of international affairs, and the fact that the Political Resident has been called home for consultations adds weight to the belief that an important decision is about to be made.

A bad epidemic of sand-fly fever and malaria has grown out of the post-summer period of ills, reported on last month, and nearly half the people of Dubai have already been affected by it. This epidemic has become popularly known as "A'ker bagr" – cow's stiffness, apparently because of the effect of mild paralysis of the legs, which is brought on by the fever.

RAS AL KHAIMA:

All is quiet, for the time being, among the Habus, and the trouble reported upon last month has been settled, and the goat which was the cause of all the fighting was devoured at the peace talks.

UMM AL QUWAIN:

The Ruler of Umm al Quwain returned from the Pilgrimage on 5th September 1953.

AJMAN:

The Ruler of Ajman returned from the Pilgrimage on 19th September, 1953. He is reported as being displeased with the reception he got when he visited bin Saud. This may be due to his Na'imi relationship to Saqr bin Sultan of Baraimi (despite Rashid's reputation as a Saudi sympathiser), although any disinterest shown by the King is more likely to be due to the size of Ajman territory, which could hardly be expected to ensure a Regal welcome for its landlord.

SHARJAH:

As a result of a sympathetic hearing given to the T.O.L. Commander by the Political Resident, during his recent visits, thirty five badly needed one ton vehicles are on their way to Sharjah from the U.K.

A "Times" correspondent recently visited Sharjah and Baraimi, en route to another assignment.

Doctor Hosman, and her colleagues of the American Mission, returned to Sharjah at the end of September, and has reopened her clinic.

Khan Sahib Hussein, the Company Contractor, returned from the Pilgrimage on 2nd September 1953.

A T.O.L. 3 ton lorry overturned when travelling between Derra and Sharjah early in the month, killing one Levy and seriously injuring seven others.

An Airman was accidentally electrocuted in the R.A.F. station, during the month.

The Golden Valley Red Oxide Company has hit the headlines sooner than even the closest observer of its activities would have forecast. Major Lippett unexpectedly returned to conduct this season's operations, and with him came a new, handpicked assistant, who announced his arrival by blackening eyes in the B.O.A.C. Fort to the extent of £10 sterling, which sum he handed over after the hammer had fallen in the Political Agent's Court. En route to the promised island, he later fell off the launch before it had cleared the creek, and then followed a scuffle in which a greater part of the Sharjah population seemed to find itself searching for him in the water, several rescuers themselves getting into difficulties. The new assistant is now back in the U.K., perhaps in the same bar from which he was recruited, vaguely wondering who it was that had promised him a job on some island or other.

DUBAI:

The Ruler of Dubai returned from Bombay on 1st September. He claims to be feeling very much better after the treatment he received for his knee, and is certainly as lithesome as ever. The day after his return he escaped from the well-wishers and made off to his date gardens in Ras al Khaima.

ABU DHABI:

The Ruler seems to be very weak, and has again called in Dr. McCaully.

Earlier in the month Shaikh Said bin Shakhbut, accompanied by a party of about six womenfolk of the Ruling family, all of whom are seeking medical treatment, left Sharjah by air to Bahrain, thence to Bombay, in a very happy state, after a three day sojourns in the B.O.A.C. Fort. He was first told by his father to go to the Lebanon, but in typical Al Bu Falah fashion he received a two inch letter on the eve of his departure from Sharjah, telling him to go to Bombay instead, making no mention, of course, of the reasons for the revised instructions.

The Ruler has bought another three launches, so that the Company will have no reason to engage Dubai and other local launches, for its operations in Abu Dhabi territory.

Shortly after the Ruler of Qatar had complained to the Company that the Gravity Meter Party IA had crossed into Qatar without his consent, Shaikh Shakhbut quickly took up the cudgels and complained to the P.A. that the Qataris (presumably the Qatari beduin who had reported the movements of the Party to the Ruler) had entered his territory. Although he has since dropped the matter, without further ado, this incident has added fuel to Shakhbut's dislike of Darwish, and the Qatari Shaikhs, which seems to have become inflamed shortly after his return from Europe.

The Representative[133] transported two R.A.F. Officers to Arada,[134] in Western Liwa, during the month, to enable them to establish an airstrip there. The party had a hazardous journey, and took eight days for the round-trip from Tarif. The site for an airstrip was chosen, and one of the R.A.F. Officers remained behind to supervise the clearing of it. His Levy helpers, who had arrived by camel, needed much convincing that this was their job, but were eventually persuaded to clear a short strip, on which a fully loaded Anson[135] subsequently landed. The Anson only just managed to take off again, and the strip is at present regarded as being unsatisfactory, and the question of lengthening it has resulted in an argument between the R.A.F. and T.O.L., as to who is to pay for the work. Meanwhile, their enthusiasm aroused by the thought of getting more food supplies, the handful of Levies manning the Arada post have got busy with the shovels which were flown in by the Anson, and have cleared a further stretch of ground, though unfortunately not in line with the rest of the strip. The "Round the Bend" phrase, now has a slightly varied meaning for the R.A.F. on the Trucial Coast.

It is worth recording that the average midday temperature reading in the Dhafara sands, whilst on this trip, was 122°F.

The R.A.F. took the opportunity of this trip to Arada to organise an air search exercise and in the eight days that the Party was out failed to locate it once. This has given rise to doubts, which have already been expressed, as to the value of the aerial search of Western Abu Dhabi territory, which has so arduously been carried out since it was first instituted. This is by no means a criticism of the work of the R.A.F., but it does show just how formidable their task is. The discomfort of long, low, daily flights in the hot weather could well be imagined, and is a noteworthy achievement for all

133 Codrai. He probably took the same route as he had driven in June via Ruweis, Bida Mutawa, Markhia, Suaitiya and on to Arada.

134 The settlement in the west of Liwa, where Codrai took the first vehicle, a Land Rover, to reach Liwa in June 1953. See HEARD, (2019), Appendix 106.

135 There is an Anson in the Mahatta museum in Sharjah.

those who have carried them out, as well as for those who have managed to keep the R.A.F.'s last squadron of Lancasters airborne.[136]

BARAIMI AND OMAN:

Two incidents occurred in the Baraimi area on 15th September. A party of about twelve Bedouin, said to be Awamir, tried to enter Hamasa from Abu Dhabi territory, and fired upon the Trucial Oman Levies, when called to halt. The T.O.L. returned their fire, killing and injuring several people. The Levies claim that shots were also fired on them from Hamasa. Later the same day the T.O.L. fired on another beduin attempting to enter Hamasa, as a result of which are about eighty armed soldiers advanced out of Hamasa on the Levy post in Jimi Fort, but withdrew when the T.O.L. open fire. These incidents occurred on the day that both the P.R. and the P.A. were visiting Baraimi.

Saudi sources of propaganda made the most of these incidents, and slight twist of the facts (which travel so quickly that it is not possible to suppress them completely), and the announcement that several of the casualties were women, dressed up this incident to make it appear as a rampant case of British aggression.

It is reported that three members of the Al Murra recently travelled by camel to Hamasa, through Abu Dhabi territory, with further supplies of cash for Turki.

The R.A.F. still has a medical officer stationed with the T.O.L. in Baraimi.

Obaid bin Juma, formerly the Shaikh of the Bani Kaab, is still living at Khatwa,[137] in the Wadi Jizzi. His successor, an unimpressive bedu, Abdullah bin Sallim, seems to have the support of the whole tribe, and takes his orders from H.M.G., without whom he would never have been able to usurp Obaid. There now seems to be no likelihood of the Beni Kaab forming an allegiance with the Ruler of Sharjah. The Ruler of Sharjah lost his opportunity of gaining control of this tribe several months ago, when he turned down Abdullah's offer of allegiance; the latter then went off in a huff to the Saudis.

It is reliably reported that the Political Resident has had some success in persuading the Sultan of Muscat to take a more active interest in the Baraimi situation. It was a sorry day when H.M.G. stopped the Sultan sending his forces to Baraimi through the Wadi Jizzi, and this act has been regretted ever since.[138]

Codrai
Representative.

---

136 Codrai had served with the R.A.F.

137 Khatwa is actually a few kilometres north of the east-west Wadi Jizzi.

138 Soon after Turki bin Ataishan arrived at Hamasa (Sultanate of Oman territory) on 31st August 1952 the Sultan of Oman assembled a large force at Sohar and was preparing to go through the Wadi Jizzi to expel the Saudis. HMG intervened and ordered the Sultan not to attack.

TRUCIAL COAST DIARY FOR PERIOD ENDING 31 OCTOBER 1953

GENERAL:

The epidemic of "Agr al Bagr" has not yet abated, and a large number of people continue to be affected by it, particularly in Dubai. Dr McCaully has diagnosed this illness as being dengue fever.

Light showers of rain fell through the month in several places, notably in Baraimi, the Bainuna and Falaj al Ali.

The hawking season has already begun, and the Dubai and Abu Dhabi Shaikhs are busy training their birds. Large numbers of Hibara[139] have already appeared in the hinterland. Prices for the hawks, particularly those from Persia, are very high this year, no doubt due to the attractive prices being offered for them in the Oil States, and Shaikh Rashid of Dubai has paid as much as fifteen hundred Rupees for a single bird.

There has been no change in the political situation with regard to Baraimi, and it is hoped that the problem will soon be settled by arbitration, once the question of the presence of the Saudis in Hamasa has been settled between H.M.G. and the Saudi Government.

The pearl divers returned earlier this year, than in the past, and although the pearl trade still continues to suffer a considerable decline, profits this season have been good for those who took part. A diver from Ajman was badly injured near the Jabal Ali banks when he was attacked by a barracuda.

RAS AL KHAIMA:

The Trucial Oman Levies are considering re-establishing a post at Rams, to assist their recruiting in that area.

SHARJAH:

The Ruler signed an offshore rights declaration for the Company on 10th October.

The Assistant Political Agent, the Hon. Ivor Lucas, has gone on a temporary posting to Bahrain, and has been relieved by Michael Weir, who is later to take over from the Political Agent, C. Pirie- Gordon, when he goes on leave in December. Weir is going to be joined by his bride, sometime towards the end of November.

During the month a Class B Officer arrived at the Agency to take over his duties as Administrative Officer.

F.N. Lee-Oldfield[140] of the Desert Locust Control has arrived back in Sharjah with his wife and child, for another tour of duty on the Trucial Coast. Lee-Oldfield

139 A Bustard. The bird that the people of the Emirates hunt.

140 Lee-Oldfield led the camel party from Al 'Ain to Liwa in January 1952. He was accompanied by Sheikh Mubarak bin Mohamed.

has been warned by the Anti-Locust Organisation not to become involved in any political activities, which he is reported to have done in the past, presumably by giving help to the P.O.T.S.[141] H. Platt, who Lee-Oldfield relieves, has been posted to Kuwait.

The Ruler is endeavouring to persuade Gray MacKenzie & Company to arrange a scheduled call with the B.I. steamers to Khor Fakkan, every fortnight. He has promised a large cargo and nearly a hundred passengers for every ship.

Dissensions within the Ruler's family are occurring again, after a period of quiet during which Shaikh Saqr gained considerable popularity. The principal antagonists this time are Rashid bin Saqr, one of the Ruler's uncles, and the sons of Humaid bin Saqr, another uncle who died last year. The Ruler recently lost face when he climbed down to a state of meekness, having threatened strong action against members of his family, notably the aforesaid, who have been engaging in drunken revelry in public.

Now that the Red Oxide Company has finished its work in Sharjah territory, the Ruler and many others have become openly vitriolic regarding the activities of Major Lippett, particularly Khaled, the Ruler's younger brother, who was for some time the Ruler's representative on Abu Musa.

DUBAI:

Shaikh Rashid of Dubai is seeking permission from the Governor of Bandar Abbas to go hunting in Persia this winter.

The British Bank of the Middle East, Dubai, has invited a British dredging expert from Kuwait to visit the coast and to give an opinion on the possibilities of improving the Dubai and Sharjah Creeks.

Winant, an American pearl merchant, has come back on another pearl buying trip to Dubai, and is considering staying longer this year to organise a work room for making the pearls up into articles of jewellery. By doing this he hopes to take advantage of cheaper labour, and to avoid revenue difficulties such as he is experiencing with another branch of his business in Bombay.

ABU DHABI:

An Officer of the Trucial Oman Levies has been on a reconnaissance through the Liwa settlements, but having no knowledge of Arabic he has not been able to add to the political knowledge of this area. He was landed by an Ansom at Arada, from where he travelled Eastwards to Baraimi by camel.

141 Political Officer Trucial States.

Shaikh Haza to is about to go on a tour of central Liwa, but has been delayed by an attack of dengue fever. He plans to travel as far as Hawaiya[142] by car, from where he will journey onwards by camel.

Early in the month Shaikh Shakhbut was reported to be very ill, and he sent for Dr McCaully, one of his many troubles was a carbuncle on his chest. He quickly recovered after treatment by McCaully and was afterwards looking fitter and more cheerful than he had been for some time. McCaully was presented with a Land Rover apart from a generous cash payment.

Later in the month Shaikh Shakhbut went to Dubai for further treatment, during which he declined all offers of hospitality from the Shaikhs of Dubai and Sharjah, and lived in a tent which was, very significantly, pitched on the Abu Dhabi side of the Dubai/Abu Dhabi frontier, at Hassian.[143]

Shaikh Said bin Shakhbut returned to Abu Dhabi from Bombay, via Bahrain, on 22nd October. He is said to have spent a fantastic amount of money on his trip, and to have taken cash advances in his father's name from many people.

Major Lippett of the Golden Valley Oxide Company is about to establish his new base on Dalma Island, from where he will be prospecting on several of the Abu Dhabi islands. Apparently he concluded an agreement with Shaikh Shakhbut at the end of last season.

Said bin Suwaid, one of the Shaikhs of the Manasir tribe, is very ill.

Now that they are no longer receiving presents from the Saudis, and Shaikh Shakhbut has shown no signs of loosening his purse strings, the Manasir are growing very discontented, and many of them have approached the Company Representative for financial aid, as well as for the full right to use Company vehicles and launches in their territory whenever they wish.

T. Hillyard, the D'Arcy Representative is due to arrive in Abu Dhabi early in November. It is said that Shakhbut is going to insist on his Company using an Abu Dhabi contractor for it supplies, and the D'Arcy Concession Agreement which was originally signed by the Superior Oil Company, contains certain clauses which place the company in a weak position in this respect. Nevertheless, the Ruler is allowing Khan Sahib Hussain to build Hilliard's house in Abu Dhabi.

OMAN:

Salih bin Isa[144] arrived in Sharjah by air during the month, on his way south after his visit to Bahrain, Kuwait, Egypt and Saudi Arabia. He was met by the Ruler

142 There is a place named Heyaymah about 30 kilometres north of Liwa. Map Centre for Documentation and Research. Abu Dhabi 1972. Probably the same place.

143 Near the Coast.

144 Sheikh Saleh bin Isa of the Harth tribe, Sultanate of Oman.

of Sharjah, with whom he stayed for three days, after which he moved to Dubai as the guest of Shaikh Rashid. He was then sent as far as the Baraimi in one of Rashid's cars.

Sulaiman bin Hamyiar[145] also arrived back from his travels, by steamer, and stayed in Dubai for nearly a week as Rashid's guest, during which time he shared the guest room for 1 or 2 days with Salih bin Isa. The disease of his son's eyes has not been cured, and his father has expressed the intention of taking him to India for further treatment.

During his stay in Bahrain, Sulaiman went to the cinema every night. During his tour, bin Saud sent him a special aircraft to take him from Kuwait to the Hijaz. He left Dubai by his own car, for Baraimi.

COMPANY ACTIVITIES:

The Company has been prohibited from exporting water from Umm Said[146] for its operations on the Trucial Coast, and the two geophysical parties operating in Abu Dhabi territory are now having to be supplied with water from Sharjah, which is being loaded onto Abu Dhabi launches in Dubai. This prohibition does not affect the drilling location at Tarif, which has its own distillation unit, neither does it affect the foodstuffs and materials which are supplied from Umm Said to the Trucial Coast.

The Company contractor, Khan Sahib Hussain, is having difficulty in his dealings with Shaikh Shakhbut. Shakhbut allows him to operate in Abu Dhabi territory in return for a quarter share of his profits. It is generally believed that Khan Sahib makes considerably more out of the Company then is in fact the case, and Shakhbut is demanding from Khan Sahib considerably more than the latter claims as being his total profits.

Codrai
Representative.

145 Sheikh from Tanuf and Jebel Akhdhar, Sultanate of Oman.

146 The Company oil export terminal, Qatar.

TRUCIAL COAST DIARY FOR PERIOD ENDING 30 NOVEMBER 1953

GENERAL:

At the beginning of the month the General Manager,[147] Mr G. Heseldin, accompanied by the Chief Local Representative and the Representative Trucial States, visited all the Trucial Shaikhdoms, on the Company vessel "Jamila". The tour[148] was very successful, and all the Rulers with the exception of Fujairah, who was visited by road from Khor Fakhan, and Dubai, who was entertained to lunch in the Company House, were feasted aboard the "Jamila". The Ruler of Sharjah was visited in Khor Fakhan. At the beginning of the tour the British community in Dubai and Sharjah was entertained by the General Manager to supper in the Company House, Sharjah.

The Naval C.-in-C. Far East Forces visited the Trucial Coast during the month, aboard the Cruiser "Newfoundland". His visit coincided with the new Political Resident's tour of the Shaikhdoms, and of the holding of a meeting of the "Trucial States' Council", and a minor state of chaos, worsened by the inevitable M.T. troubles and the absence of a tide-clock on the hard, reigned in Dubai and Sharjah until the "Newfoundland" left on its visit to Muscat ahead of schedule to investigate the pirating of a boom somewhere on the east coast of Oman.

All the Rulers attended the meeting of the Trucial States' Council, at which the long-standing dispute between the Ruler of Ras al Khaima and Sultan bin Salim (the former Ruler) was finally settled, following agreement by the two parties before the meeting. Sultan bin Salim has surrendered all his rights to Hawailat and the territory in the Wadi al Qor area over which he had previously retained control, in return for which he is to receive an annual grant of Rs. 16,000 from the Ruler of Ras al Khaima. Also, the Ruler has been given the option to buy Sultan's property in Ras al Kaima town, but if he fails to exercise it then Sultan is free to dispose of it to others, but in either case the sale is to be conducted under the supervision of representatives of the Rulers of Dubai and Sharjah. Sultan bin Salim is still not permitted to live in Ras al Khaima, and is at present living in Mina'i[149] village in the Wadi al Qor.

The usual appeals for support for the Maktum hospital were made to the Rulers, but from the opinions expressed by two of them after the meeting it would seem that these appeals would be more successful if made to the Rulers privately.

A tragic incident occurred on 11th November which resulted in the deaths of three Britishers and a Palestinian, and brought to a head a period of trouble and unrest

---

147 General Manager Qatar and Trucial States.

148 The tour commenced on 30th October and I attach to the end of this Diary note the report of the tour.

149 A few kilometres north of Huwailat.

in the Trucial Oman Levy Force. Many of the Adeni members of the force have for some time past been known to be troublemakers, and four of the most dissident ones were stationed with the garrison at Al Ain. Several unsuccessful attempts to have these troublemakers posted were made by the I/C Garrison, but it was not until the situation grew ugly, and threats had been made on the lives of some of the Levy Officers, that orders were given from Sharjah to have them arrested. An unarmed party led by Major O. Thwaites then encountered these four Adenis on the outskirts of Hamasa. Whether it was intended to carry out the arrest of them at that particular time is not clear, but the Adenis opened fire on the party killing Major Thwaites, the RAF Medical Officer, and the Levy Sergeant Major, a Palestinian called Da'ud, and wounding a British Sergeant and a Corporal. The Sergeant later died of wounds, after he had been taken to Bahrain. Major Thwaites was for a short time, a camp boss with B.P.C.[150]

Two of the Adenis were captured shortly after the incident, but the other two escaped to the south after (it is believed) they have been refused sanction by the Saudis in Hamasa. They were eventually caught near Dhank by a mixed party of Levies and followers of Zaid.[151]

There have been many accounts of an unpleasant incident which occurred about the time when the Adenis were being most troublesome, and before the above affair. It is not easy to say exactly what bearing this incident had on the subsequent happenings, but it appears that the four troublesome Adenis were on Guard duty one night, and they shot dead a Rashidi lad who had just spoken to them, after leaving Hamasa. The Rashidi had been a member of the Levy Party that had recently been on tour through Liwa, and he had been granted permission to enter Hamasa and collect his rifle, which he had left there some time ago. One account suggests that the Rashidi was shot by mistake, as the guard had not been properly briefed regarding his movements, while another story claims that the Adenis shot the Rashidi in cold blood after they had sold him some ammunition, and when they thought that he was about to report them. Whatever the truth, it seems fairly certain that the Adenis mutilated the face of the victim, so that it would be thought that he was one of Turki's followers who had been shot.

Practically all the Adenis in the Levies have been flown back to Aden, and for the time being their place has been taken by a detachment of the R.A.F. Regiment.

All the Shaikdoms were alive with stories and rumours as soon as the news of the flow of oil at Murban got about. Celebrations immediately started in Abu Dhabi, and a sample of the oil was immediately sent by Shaikh Shakhbut to his mother and brothers in Baraimi, and he was naturally very disappointed when he eventually learned of the nature of the find. The Ruler is being kept fully informed

150 B.P.C. Basra Petroleum Company, an associated Company in the Iraq Petroleum Company Group of Companies.

151 Sheikh Zayed bin Sultan.

of developments but he tends to find the information he has been given so far rather baffling, and he is naturally awaiting a definite indication as to whether or not the Company has discovered an oilfield.[152]

All the Shaikdoms went into mourning for King Ibn Saud, the day following his death, and the market places were closed four days in Dubai, seven days in Sharjah and three days in the other Shaikhdoms.

The epidemic of dengue fever seems to have practically come to an end, but has given way to a lesser number of cases of sandfly fever and influenza.

Large numbers of Pakistani pilgrims have been landed on the coast during the month, and have been walking westwards. Many of the Shaikhs are indignant that the Pakistani Government should be doing nothing to stop them. One old man was found ill on the road and brought back to Dubai by a Company vehicle, where he died shortly afterwards. The plight of these pilgrims is, to some extent, eased by the presence of the Company camps along the coast, but many of them still die by the wayside.

SHARJAH:

The usual flow of R.A.F. visitors has this month been headed by several high-ranking Officers, including the Inspector General of the R.A.F. Also, the C.-in-C. M.E.L.F.[153] visited the R.A.F. and T.O.L. bases in Sharjah, Baraimi and Tarif. It is a noteworthy sign of the changing times that one service visitor, travelling by Anson, went to Sharjah, Baraimi, Liwa (Hamar)[154] and Tarif in one day.

The Ruler of Sharjah, accompanied by his brothers Khaled and Mohamed, and his secretary Ibrahim Midfa, left for Saudi Arabia on 23rd November, to pay his respects to King Saud. It had been the intention of the Dubai Shaikhs to arrange a party to visit the new King, but they changed their minds when they learned of Saqr's visit.

B.P. Aviation is anxious to overhaul it supply system to the Sharjah aerodrome, and an engineer is expected to come shortly to investigate the possibility of constructing

152 The oil was retrieved from the first Murban well. The Company experienced several unexpected problems with this well. The rock formation that interested them was much deeper that the limestone rocks where oil was later found. They drilled through the oil bearing rock without realising it contained oil as they had masses of shale entering the hole from above which, in volume, swamped the cuttings from the limestone below. They set casing which held back the shale but which also concealed the limestone. The oil probably came from a leak in the cement or in the casing. They drilled on to the target zone where they encountered, very dangerous high pressure, sour gas. There was an accident when a petroleum engineer and his helper died of gas poisoning. In those days the industry did not yet have the equipment to handle high pressure sour gas.

153 C.-in-C. M.E.L.F. Commander in Chief, Middle East Land Forces.

154 West of Arada. They used the airstrip constructed by the levies.

a supply line from the shore to the aerodrome. At present the aviation fuel is brought ashore in drums at Dubai and is then taken to Sharjah by road.

DUBAI:

T. Hillyard, the D'Arcy Representative,[155] arrived on the Coast early in the month, and is at present based in Derra, having taken a short lease there on the African and Eastern Company's house (African and Eastern having withdrawn their representative until trade improves). Hillyard is still awaiting news from his Company regarding the Dubai Sea Bed Concession, which was signed in the name of Mr Heseldin, so that he can inform the Ruler of the formation of the Company which is to take it over. In the meantime, one of the difficulties facing him is that of importing his supplies through Dubai where his Company has, as yet no customs exemption.

Shortly before leaving on a visit to Bahrain at the end of the month, Hillyard was informed by Shaikh Shakhbut that he had changed his mind, and could not now let him have Bait ash Shamal (the Ruler's Guest House) which Hillyard had arranged to take on lease for his Company, for use as an office and stores base.

Shaikh Rashid has received permission from the Governor of Bandar Abbas to go hunting on the mainland, but the Governor does not wish the Shaikh to go direct to Bandar Abbas, but to go first to Qishm, where he himself will meet the Shaikh and arrange for him to go to the mainland. Shaikh Rashid is, however, trying instead to get permission to land at Lingeh. These matters are handled for him by Dubai merchants who originate from these places.

A cinema in Derra which is being built by Murshid al Asaimi in partnership with Latifa, the wife of Shaikh Rashid, is nearing completion, and the generators and projectors have all been ordered. This cinema has been the cause of a quarrel between Rashid and his brother Khalifah, the latter having failed to obtain his father's permission to build a cinema nearly a year ago, and finding himself out in the cold, now that Saeed[156] has agreed to the proposal.

ABU DHABI:

The R.A.F. is continuing its searches over Western Abu Dhabi territory, and to enable it to do this with Ansons has established a refuelling and servicing base at Tarif. The establishment of this base coincided with the first burst of rumours regarding the discovery of oil at Tarif, and without the foes actually being named, it quickly got about that there was a likelihood of Tarif being attacked, and the R.A.F. was going to defend it.

155 B.P.

156 The Ruler, Saeed or Said.

Shaikh Haza left Abu Dhabi on his tour of Liwa at the beginning of the month, and has visited the T.O.L. post at Hamar,[157] where there is an airstrip. He is said now to be in the area of Al Khis.[158]

Immediately Shaikh Shakhbut heard of the Levy incident in Baraimi he sent his son Said, with thirty men and five vehicles, to report to Zaid, and assist in the search for the runaway Adenis.

When Shaikh Shakhbut travelled to Sharjah, to attend the recent meeting of the Trucial States' Council, he camped near his boundary at Hasian, rather than accept the hospitality of the other Rulers. Shakhbut is growing very peeved at being called to attend meetings with the other Rulers in Sharjah, and the Politicals may well be over-exercising their prerogative in summoning him to the Council meetings.

Bu Hailaiba, the Shaikh of the Manasir, and a close follower of Zaid, has gone to Bahrain to be operated on for a hernia.

Salih bin Kabut, a Shaikh of the Al Rashidi, who is best known for his crossing of the Empty Quarter with Bertram Thomas, is very ill and probably dying, and has been sent to Dubai by Shaikh Zaid.

OMAN:

Early in the month the Levies fired on a party of the Duru entering Hamasa, and are said to have killed one and injured another.

BARAIMI:

The R.A.F. has, for the fourth or fifth time, changed the site of it airstrip near Al Ain. The usual difficulty of ruts and soft patches on the strip is partly the reason for this, but also the fact that the Anson propeller blades are easily damaged by small stones of which there are plenty on the plain at Al Ain.

COMPANY ACTIVITIES:

The Dar as Salaam, an Abu Dhabi launch on hire to the Company, sank near Abu Dhabi at the beginning of the month, but without loss of life. It was loaded with drums of water for the Gravity Meter Party, too many of which were on deck when the launch was hit by a shamal.

P.D. (T.C.) is again permitted to draw water from Umm Said, for its geophysical parties in Abu Dhabi territory.

The rig and buildings at Jebel Ali were taken down during the month, and are now ready to be taken elsewhere.

---

157 North east of Arada. About half way between Arada and the centre of the Liwa crescent.

158 A settlement on the east side of Liwa.

Codrai
Representative.

<u>REPORT OF THE GENERAL MANAGER'S TOUR OF THE TRUCIAL SHAIKHDOMS</u>.

30th October to 8th November, 1953.

The M.V. "Jamila" sailed from Umm Said on the morning of 30th October and arrived in Dubai earlier in the morning of the following day.

The General Manager, Mr. G. Heseldin, was accompanied on his tour by the Chief Local Representative, Mr. H. M. Jackson, and the Medical Officer Trucial Coast, Dr. J. F. Doherty, as well as the Representative, PD(TC), Mr. R. A. C. Codrai, who joined the party in Dubai. Mr. K. M. Maud, Area Superintendent, Trucial Coast, joined the party ashore in Sharjah and again in Abu Dhabi.

31st October.

During the morning the G.M. Called on the acting ruler of Dubai, Shaikh Rashid Bin Saeed, the acting ruler apologized for the absence of the ruler, his father, who was away on the Batina Coast. Shaikh Rashid was later entertained to an Arab feast in the company house, to which he brought several of his relations and retainers, including the following:

Shaikh Juma bin Maktoum	brother of the Ruler
Shaikh Khalifa Bin Said	son of the Ruler
Shaikh Obaid bin Juma	nephew of the Ruler
Shaikh Thani bin Juma	nephew of the Ruler
Shaikh Mohd bin Hasher	nephew of the Ruler

Whilst in Dubai the G.M. called on the Manager of the B.B.M.E., K. Bradford, and also met P. Townsend, the B.B.M.E. accountant, Mr. Winant an American pearl buyer, and Colonel Gerald De Caucey, a guest of the Political Agent. After lunch the "Jamila" sailed for Sharjah, anchoring about 1 hour before sunset.

During the evening the G.M. called on the Political Agent, C. Pirie-Gordon, in Sharjah, after which he entertained the British community from Dubai and Sharjah to a buffet supper party at the Company house, Sharjah. The P.A. was unable to attend this party, as he himself was that evening retaining a visiting party of doctors, including Sir Eric Pridie, the medical adviser to the Colonial Office. The non-Company guests who attended the G. M.'s party were:

Lt. Col. B. Martin	o/c T.O.L.
Captain Rowecliffe	T.O.L.
Wing commander R. Watts	R.A.F.
Flight Lt. Whitsun-Jones	R.A.F.
Flying Officer D. Maguire	R.A.F.
Mr. and Mrs. F.N. Lea-Oldfield	Anti locust mission
Mr. and Mrs. G. Baker	Gray MacKenzie & Co.
Messrs. D. Phillips	Gray MacKenzie & Co.
K. Bradford	B.B.M.E.
P. Townsend	B.B.M.E.
T. Winant	American pearl buyer
R. Coleman	Administrative officer, Agency
S. Hidge	I.A.L Sharjah
R. Parrott	I.A.L. Sharjah

1st November.

The Ruler of Sharjah, Shaikh Saqr bin Sultan, had left earlier for Khor Fakhan, and it was arranged that the G.M. should visit him there, instead of in Sharjah.

The G.M. went ashore to inspect the Company's installations at Sharjah, and then the "Jamila" sailed for Ajman where the G.M. went ashore and visited the Ruler, Rashid bin Humaid. Ruler was then invited to an Arab lunch aboard the "Jamila", and was accompanied by his sons Ali, Humaid and Nasr, and many retainers.

The "Jamila" left for Umm al Qaiwain, and entered the creek at sunset. This was the first occasion that the G.M. had visited Umm al Qaiwain.

2nd November.

The G.M. visited the Ruler Shaikh Ahmed bin Rashid, during the morning, and invited him to an Arab lunch aboard the "Jamila". The Ruler was accompanied by his sons Ali, Abdullah and Sultan, and several followers. After the Ruler's visit the "Jamila" left Umm al Quwain for Ras al-Khaimah, and entered the creek there shortly before sunset.

3rd November.

The G.M. called on the Ruler, Shaikh Saqr Bin Mohd, during the morning, after which he invited him aboard the "Jamila" to an Arab lunch. Whilst the party was having lunch the "Jamila" sailed out of the creek on the high tide, and anchored at sea off the town, landing the ruler's party later by L.C.P. The Ruler was accompanied by his elder brother, Humaid Bin Mohd, his son Khalid, and two of Humaid's sons, Abdullah and Ahmed, as well as many of his retainers. During discussion, the Ruler asked the G.M. when the Company would be operating again this area. In reply the

G.M. told him that unfortunately the Ras Al Khaimah area was only of secondary interest from the point of view of finding oil owing to the proximity of the mountains. He stressed however that although we were not operating actually in his area, the work we were doing elsewhere had a direct bearing on it. The G.M. in conclusion stated that there was a possibility that the Company might operate in future in Ras al Khaimah territory. The Ruler appeared to be satisfied by this answer.

After the Ruler's party had been landed, the "Jamila" sailed for Khor Khasab[159] where she anchored for the night.

4th November.

The "Jamila" left Khor Khasab early in the morning and arrived in Khor Fakhan[160] a short time before sunset. Mr. Jackson then called upon the Wali, Shaikh Hassan Bin Abdullah, and ascertained that the Ruler of Sharjah Shaikh Saqr bin Sultan, was due to arrive in Khor Fakhan from Kalba the following morning after breakfast. This was the first occasion that Mr. Jackson had visited this part of the coast.

5th November.

The G.M. visited the Ruler of Sharjah in Khor Fakhan and was later shown around some local gardens by the Ruler. Afterwards the G.M. invited him aboard the "Jamila" for an Arab lunch. The Ruler was accompanied by her younger brother, Shaikh Mohd bin Sultan, and his Secretary/Adviser, Ibrahim Midfa, as well as several of his retainers.

During the afternoon the G.M. drove by car from Khor Fakhan to Fujairah, where he called on the Ruler, Sheikh Mohd bin Hamad ash Shargi, who entertained the visitors to a late lunch, after which he showed them his seaport village of Ghurfa, the port of Fujairah. The G.M. then drove back to Khor Fakhan and rejoined the "Jamila", which then sailed for Abu Dhabi shortly after sunset.

This was the first occasion that Messrs Heseldin and Jackson had met the Ruler of Fujairah.

6th November.

The "Jamila" spent the day at sea, but anchored off Abu Musa island from 1430 hours to sunset in order to arrive at Abu Dhabi the following morning at first light. The party went ashore and inspected the recently abandoned workings of the Golden Valley (Colours and Oxide) Company Limited. This company has now transferred its activities to the islands of Dalma and Das in Abu Dhabi Territory.

---

159 Large harbour/bay on the northern part, accessed from the west, of the Musandam peninsula. Khasab itself is a substantial town with a fort.

160 On the Indian Ocean coast north of Fujairah. Khor Fakhan is in Sharjah territory.

The G.M. called upon the Ruler, Sheikh Shakhbut bin Sultan. After much general conversation the subject of the Company's operations in the Abu Dhabi area was discussed. The G.M. took the opportunity to tell the Ruler that the favourable indications which had appeared some time ago in Murban number one had unfortunately receded. Another 500 feet or so of drilling would determine whether this well had any oil or not. The depth to date was then 10,015 feet. The G.M also stressed that there was every indication that the prospects would improve as operations proceeded westwards. The geophysical parties had turned up promising indications in the area west of Jebel Dhanna. In order to help in assessing the value of a feature near Shuwaihat island the G.M. said that it had been decided to do some seismic work in the sea between that island and the mainland. A special marine seismic party was due soon for that purpose. In the meantime the rig at Jebel Ali will be taken down and removed to the Dhanna area until such time as a suitable drilling location was found. He also mentioned that in view of the difficulty of some of the terrain in which the geophysical parties were now working, the Company was exploring the possibility of using helicopters. The Ruler was also told that the gravity party next year would be increased from a single to a double crew.

After inviting the Ruler to lunch, the G.M. before returning aboard visited the new causeway at the Maqta' and also the site of the D'Arcy company's new house, where building operations were already in progress.

The Ruler then had lunch aboard. His two sons, Saeed and Sultan and Khan Saheb Hussain Ahmed, the Company is contractor, were also of the party.

"Jamila" sailed for Umm Said about 1500 hours.

7th November.

The "Jamila" arrived at Umm Said[161] about 1230 hours.

TRUCIAL COAST DIARY FOR PERIOD ENDING 31 DECEMBER 1953

GENERAL:

The Trucial Oman Levy Force is still having its troubles, and it seems as though the R.A.F. Regiment Armoured Car Squadron will be remaining on the Trucial Coast for some time to come. There are still many Adenis in the Force as Officers, Radio Operators and instructors, and the facts of the recent Baraimi incident, and that they have no career to look forward to (they are not A.P.L. seconded) do not make them the most loyal soldiers. A fault on the part of the administration is that these Adenis

161 The Qatar Petroleum Company oil export terminal on the southern coast of Qatar.

are frequently given command at key positions, such as in Liwa. At the end of the month it was reported that a local man in the Levies at Al Khis had been shot dead by an unknown attacker, but investigations are beginning to show that he was killed by a member of the Force. The P.A. has had to ask for the withdrawal of an Adeni Officer stationed in Baraimi, who is putting about anti-British talk.

The case of the three Adenis imprisoned in Sharjah on a charge of murder is becoming very involved, and the statements by witnesses are so conflicting that the case is far from being clear-cut. In particular, it seems that no charge will be made against the Adeni ringleader, of whom it is said that he was undoubtedly selling ammunition, owing to lack of evidence.

It is inevitable that a Force which has expanded so quickly, and which covers such a large area, should be having its troubles, but they cannot all be pinned on the presence of the Adenis. Presumably the Force has only been expanded to its present size to enable it to deal effectively with the troubles arising out of the frontier problems, and it will be reduced to a much smaller gendarmerie force when these are over, yet most of its efforts are centred upon building up the H.Q. base in Sharjah to an extent which is not justified by its training programme. It is thought that more attention should be paid to the outposts. Of the nine British officers in the Force (and there will shortly be another two) only two are out on fieldwork. It is sad to note that there was more liaison with the Shaikhs and tribes when the Levies were "a one man show", than there is at the present time.

During the C. in C. M.E.L.F.'s[162] visit to the Trucial Coast, he was critical of the small number of Arabic speaking Officers in the Force, and arrangements have been made for more students of M.E.C.A.S.[163] to be posted here in the future.

Colonel Martin, the o/c Levies, has arranged to rent the D'Arcy bungalow in Abu Dhabi for the summer months, and he is going to live there with his wife and children.

RAS AL KHAIMA:

The Ruler of Ras al Khaima has complained to the Political Agent that a Ras al Khaima car was shot at by the Sharqiyeen tribe when it entered one of the wadis of Jebel Khadra. On being called to account for the incident by the P.A., the Ruler of Fujairah simply replied that vehicles are forbidden in this particular wadi. He rightly adds that it is necessary to make advance arrangements for visitors to these hills, whether in Fujairah or Ras al Khaima territory.

---

162 C. in C. M.E.L.F. Commander in Chief Middle East Land Forces.

163 M.E.C.A.S. Middle East Centre for Arabic Studies, in Lebanon.

FUJAIRAH:

The Ruler plans to keep his two Land Rovers (which he is expecting to receive shortly, under the terms of the Company's Exploration Agreement) at Manama. He will then travel by camel or donkey between Fujairah and Manama, to avoid using the Wadi al Qor.[164] He is trying to interest the Company in making a motor track in the Wadi Ham, which runs from Adhan[165] to Fujairah. The Ruler is hoping to visit the P.R. In Bahrain, sometime next month.

DUBAI:

It has been announced that a Company has been formed to take over the Sea Bed Concession for Dubai, which was signed in the name of Mr. G. Hesledin in 1952. As in the case of the Company formed to take over the Abu Dhabi Sea Bed Concession (first taken out by Superior Oil Company and later transferred to a A.I.O.C.), A.I.O.C.[166] will hold two thirds of the capital and C.F.P.[167] one third. The name of the new Company has yet to be decided and, in the meantime preliminary operations are being conducted in the name of the D'Arcy Exploration Company.

Shaikh Salih bin Kalut of the Ar Rashid tribe, who has been ill in Dubai died on 15th December. Two of his sons who were with him at the time have returned to Baraimi, on their way south.

The Ruler is building a small causeway to join Dubai and Shandaga, two sections of the town which are separated by about 18 inches of water at high tide.

Shaikh Rashid left for Qishm on 16th December, where he was met by the Governor of Bandar Abbas. Apparently a difference of opinion between the Governor and the Military Commander prevented his landing at Bandar Abbas, but later he was, rather surprisingly, allowed to land at Lingeh. The Shaikh has sighted large numbers of bustard, and has sent back to Dubai for two of his cars.

A few of the new type of Landrover pick-ups have been bought by the Shaikhs, and they have won immediate popularity. One of them, carrying about 12 people, including Hamdan bin Rashid, turned over on a steep sand-dune when out on a hunting trip, but only one of the passengers suffered injury.

SHARJAH:

The month has been a black one for the Anti-Locust Party. Lee-Oldfield, the head of the local party, resigned, after he had been called to attend an enquiry at his

164 Qassimi territory, Ra's al-Khaimah and Sharjah, and territory of the Sultanate of Oman.

165 Adhan is a settlement, now a town, on the west side of the Hajar mountains north of Dhaid. The west end of the Wadi Ham is further south.

166 Anglo Iranian Oil Company, later BP.

167 C.F.P. Companie Française des Pétroles, now Total.

H.Q., and he left Sharjah with his wife and child shortly before Christmas. An auditor of the name of Henderson temporarily took over for him, and on Christmas Eve his Office strong-box was broken open and over Rs. 5000/- was stolen. On New Year's Eve Henderson was found dead in his bed. Owing to the foregoing circumstances, and the fact that he had been locking himself in his room at night out of some fear arising from his investigations connected with the theft, it was decided to send his body to Bahrain for an autopsy. It is thought that a prima facie case exists for further investigation, and Judge Mawdsly and Hewitt (from the Anti-Locust H.Q.) are now handling the matter.

The Political Agent, C. Pirie-Gordon, left Sharjah on home leave on 12th December, and has been replaced by M.S. Weir. J. Walker, who has just finished the M.E.C.A.S. course, has arrived in Sharjah as the new Assistant Political Agent.

The move to the new Agency building in Dubai is expected to take place sometime during February. One room of the old Agency in Sharjah is to be retained as a Passport Office, while the remainder is to be taken over by the T.O.L. as an Officers' Mess.

Gulf Aviation[168] now runs a direct flight between Bahrain and Sharjah on Mondays. The other flights, on Wednesdays and Saturdays, call at Doha, as before. A new move to establish a service to Muscat seems to be doomed from the outset.

Mr. Crawford, the agricultural advisor to B.E.O. (Development Branch, now in Beirut) has spent a week or so touring the Trucial Coast, investigating the possibilities of following up the recommendations made by Colonel Merilly,[169] a water diviner.

Work has started on the new school, which is to be situated on the sands just outside Sharjah, near the Cultural Club. The school is being built with a grant of five thousand pounds, which has been given for the purpose by H.M.G. The cost of the teachers, books and accessories is being borne by the Ruler of Kuwait. The first two teachers, (Palestinians), have already arrived in Sharjah.

It is understood that the R.A.F. is considering the possibility of having to establish a larger base on the Trucial Coast, such as might be necessary if the Habbaniya Command[170] has to be resolved into larger units. A survey of the coast is expected to be carried out in the near future, to find the most suitable site. Also, the need for longer runways than are available in Sharjah is beginning to be felt, as the Sharjah strips are not suitable for being extended any further.

The Ruler returned from his visit to Saudi Arabia at the middle of the month. He returned laden with cameras, electronic flash units and many photographic accessories which he had bought in Bahrain, as well as a 16 mm sound projector. Local opinion

168 Gulf Aviation, now Gulf Air, based in Bahrain was founded in 1949.

169 Previous accounts give his name as Meriless.

170 The R.A.F. base in Iraq.

has it that he was not very well received by King Saud, due to the aid which is given to the British forces in Sharjah.

The Ruler still divides his time between Sharjah, where he has his generators, Kalba, where he has his new wife, and Dhaid, where he has planted many orange trees, and several other types of imported fruits.

Dr. Hosman, of the American Mission in Sharjah, and her assistants, are doing good work in the town, and in Dubai, particularly among the local women. One of her assistants, a male nurse, the Rev. G.A. Fearnow, now holds Sunday services in the R.A.F. church.

Mr. Kinnersley, the Managing Director of the Golden Valley Red Oxide Company, has come on a visit to the Trucial Coast to work out a program of operations for his Company, and arrange various matters with the Rulers. He finds the place much changed since he was first here, in the early 1930's.

A representative of B.P. Aviation has been in Sharjah, investigating the possibilities of constructing a pipeline to deliver aviation spirit from Layah Point to the aerodrome. At present the supply is lightered ashore in drums at Dubai, and transported by road to Sharjah.

ABU DHABI:

The Ruler was informed that the Company had encountered a flow of light gravity oil[171] at Murban, on 3rd December. Drilling there was then discontinued on 5th December due to a very high gas pressure, and special equipment is now awaited from America, before operations are restarted.

Shaikh Haza returned to Abu Dhabi from his tour of Liwa during the month, but shortly afterwards he left for Baraimi where he intends to remain for some time.

The Ruler has again changed his mind, and is allowing Hillyard to take the Bait Ash Shamal as an office, as was originally agreed between them.

The Calepso,[172] the D'Arcy Exploration ship, has been delayed by fire, and will not now be arriving until the end of January. The season's program, which will consist of gravity meter work and bottom sampling, will last only up to the end of May.

The D'Arcy, (originally Superior) Concession contains several difficult clauses regarding labour matters. All their recruitment has to be done through the Shaikhs, consequently the Ruler is now engaging artisans who are not available in Abu Dhabi, through Murshid al Asaimi, a Dubai merchant. Also, the Company is not allowed to dismiss any employee without prior reference to the Majlis of Shaikhs.

171 This light oil would not have been the same as the oil found in the previous month. This light oil would have been associated with the gas.

172 Codrai's spelling.

It is now known on the whole of the Trucial Coast that oil has been found at Murban and, of course, no attention is given to the fact that it may not be in commercial quantities, and the many other reservations that have to be made at this juncture. Many merchants from Dubai and Sharjah have been calling on Shaikh Shakhbut, and the Manager of the British Bank of Middle East[173] has been to see him several times, although apparently he has not yet been able to reach any agreement with the Ruler as to the future.

Shaikh Shakhbut seems to be re-organising his Civil Service. Khalifa bin Yusif has now resigned from all posts under the Shaikh in favour of branching out more as a merchant. Khalifa seems to have his eye on one or two contracts which D'Arcy will be giving to local merchants.

The 4 gallon petrol tin is about to make its reappearance on the Coast.[174] Seven thousand tins have arrived in Dubai, and Hillyard is about to present them to the Ruler of Abu Dhabi (less one hundred which he has given to the Ruler of Dubai to ease the customs problem).

Early in the month Hillyard presented two new Landrovers to the Ruler, but one of them, which was taken out on a hunting trip by Sultan, is already u/s.[175]

OMAN:

A slave-trading incident occurred during the month which brings into the open the value of Saqr bin Sultan Na'im's[176] friendship with H.M.G. Earlier in the month Abdallah bin Gharab, (who is said to be a Qatari, but who seems to have changed his nationality several times in the past) left Hamasa, via Baraimi, with the permission of Saqr, taking with him several slaves. It is said that he shipped them off to Kuwait with the help of Ali bin Saif of the Khawatir tribe (also Nai'mi) via the Khor al Batha, in Umm al Quwain territory. The Levies, and later the "Trenchard-Fowle" gave chase but without success. Abdullah bin Gharab is a man with an adventurous past, who was at one time imprisoned by bin Jaluwi for his misdeeds in Saudi Arabia. Some say that he originates from the Al Murra tribe.

Codrai
Representative.

173 B.B.M.E. British Bank of the Middle East.

174 This was the familiar can coming from the Abadan refinery. Supplies were interrupted during the troubles in Iran. The can was not returned for refilling. It was highly valued on the Trucial Coast and used for many purposes from filling with cement for building, to seats for the cinema. It was not very robust and so when it was transported on camels, spillage or breakage was common.

175 u/s. unserviceable.

176 At Buraimi.

1954

TRUCIAL COAST DIARY FOR THE PERIOD ENDING 31 JANUARY 1954

GENERAL:

As from 1st March travel documents issued by the Rulers will only be valid for travel to Bahrain, Kuwait and Qatar when bearing a Visa issued by the British Agency. Local subjects travelling on documents issued by the Agency will not require visas for Bahrain or Qatar, but will continue to require visas for Kuwait.

A Baghdadi author, Dr Haji Abdullah El Askari, who describes themselves as a delegate of the World Muslim Conference, visited these parts during the month, and was a guest of several of the Rulers. He has a good knowledge of local affairs and is engaged in writing a book on Oman.

The three Adenis who are held on a charge of murder are still imprisoned in Sharjah, awaiting trial. Earlier in the month it had been decided that the trial was to take place in Muscat, HMG, and the Sultan have mutually agreed that the crime had taken place on Muscat territory, but the Politicals have now had to withdraw their agreement to this, as the Sultan will not permit a defending officer to be present at the trial.

A very strong shammal hit the coast at the beginning of the month. One launch travelling from Bahrain to Dubai is said to have been sunk, whilst another ran aground at Zirko,[1] but without loss of life. Two Gray MacKenzie barges were caught outside the creek when the shammal started, and were washed ashore where they filled with water. Five sacks of mail, and general cargo, mainly Japanese piece goods to the value of about 12 lacks[2] of Rupees was ruined. The "Dwarka"[3] broke her moorings during

1 An island about half way between Abu Dhabi and Doha.

2 12 hundred thousand Rupees.

3 BISNC passenger ship.

the night and left for Bahrain, taking with her all the Gray MacKenzie clerks and visitors from Dubai.

The Rulers of Ras al Khaima, Sharjah and Fujairah appear to have started claim-jumping, and the Political Agent is again being forced to consider the internal boundary question. There is every reason to believe that Sharjah and Fujairah are uniting in their attempts to push their claims against Ras al Khaima. There are now four claimants for Manama[4] – Ajman, Sharjah, Ras al Khaima and Fujairah.

Twelve thousand young orange trees were brought from Basra to Dubai in a Boom, and have been sold at two Rupees each and taken to many parts of the Coast for transplanting.

The Golden Valley Red Oxide Company is having its ups and downs, and Major Lippett has, at last, been dismissed. The company has given up its interests in Abu Dhabi, and hopes to make a new arrangement to continue working in Sharjah territory. This seems rather mystifying, but it appears that when Mr Kinnersley recently visited Dalmah, and other Abu Dhabi islands he found only a poor grade of burnt oxide, which was most unlike the samples that had been sent to the U.K. office. Moreover, it seems that the Abu Musa supply of oxide is far from being exhausted, although the mining of it has now become more difficult. It will be remembered that the Red Oxide Concession for Abu Dhabi contains a minimum production clause, which the Company has failed to observe. The Ruler of Abu Dhabi has not yet been informed that the concession is to be abandoned.

RAS AL KHAIMA:

A party of T.O.L. has been sent out to arrest Saif bin Ali, the son of the Shaikh of the Khawatir tribe, who was concerned in the recent slaving incident.

The Ruler's father is claiming compensation from the company for a 50% loss of the date harvest at Khatt, which he says is due to the Seismic Party having overdrawn water from the spring from October to December, 1952.

SHARJAH:

Ninety five bivouac tents were stolen from the R.A.F. Station during the month, but most of them were recovered when trackers caught the thieves, who were labourers employed on the Station garbage truck. The culprits were severely flogged, under the personal supervision of the Ruler.

The anti-Locust party is beginning to settle down again, after its round of ill fortune, and two new field officers have gone out on reconnaissance on the Batinah.

4 North east of Dhaid towards the mountains.

FUJAIRAH:

The Political Agent, Sharjah, has fined the Ruler of Fujairah Rs. 300 for the incident reported on in the TCD for December.

DUBAI:

The Ruler of Qatar[5] called at Dubai on 17th January, en route to India by B.I. steamer. He was unable to accept the invitation of Rashid bin Saeed to lunch ashore in Dubai, owing to the leg trouble from which he is suffering, and the fact that there was a rough sea at the time. He was, however, visited aboard the ship by Shaikh Rashid of Dubai, the Ruler of Sharjah and the Company Representative, all of whom were entertained to an Arab lunch on deck. Shaikh Ali has promised both the Sharjah and Dubai Shaikhs to try and visit them on his way back from India, towards the end of February.

A gold sword was presented to Shaikh Ali by the Ruler of Sharjah.

Shaikh Rashid returned to Dubai on 14th January, after an enjoyable hunting trip in Persia. The Shaikh was able to achieve most of his aims by bribing officials, but he tells one amusing story of an escapade with the Customs at Lingeh. All his followers and their arms and belongings were allowed through Customs, but Khalifa bin Mohamed, one of the Shaikhs followers, who was carrying a portable wire-recording-machine, was stopped. To satisfy the Customs Officials that the machine was only the thing he declared it to be, he pulled out one of many spools and proceeded to play it. The spool turned out to be a recording of the B.B.C. Arabic news from London made early in 1953, which included a resume of a speech by Mussadeq[6]. The machine was impounded until the Shaikh's return to Dubai.

The loss or damage of the valuable cargoes (reported on above) is causing much ill feeling among the merchants concerned, and most of the criticism is being levelled against Gray Macks. A Lloyds surveyor from Bahrain is having to spend about three months in Dubai, settling the insurance claims and disposing of the damaged goods.

The extent to which Dubai is used as a centre for re-shipping goods to other ports (mainly Persia) may be judged from this particular shipment. It is estimated that less than five percent of the consignment which was lost or damaged was for internal consumption.

It has been a gay month for Dubai. At night, the many bright lights of the new cinema in Derrah have shone out over the town, whilst during the daytime long lengths of brightly coloured cloth, which were being dried after having been awash in the Gray Mack's barges have been fluttering all over the town.

---

5 Sheikh Ali bin Abdullah.

6 Prime Minister of Iran 1951-1953. Overthrown in a coup, organised by the CIA in August 1953.

A petrol driven launch belonging to Ali al Awazi caught fire when full of passengers, who were being carried out to a ship to Kuwait there were no casualties, although most of the baggage was lost and the launch destroyed.

ABU DHABI:

An A.R.A.M.C.O. aircraft from Dhahran flew on a reconnaissance over Tarif and Baraka areas of operations on the 25th January.

The Representative of D'Arcy Exploration Company Mr. Hillyard, went to Baraimi during the month to visit Shaikh Zaid.

Khan Saheb Hussein is building himself a house and shop in Abu Dhabi, on the foreshore near the Bait Ash Shamal.

The Abu Dhabi causeway was covered with fish which were left behind by a very high tide, after a strong Shamal.

The Ruler has again quarrelled with his brothers over financial questions, and apart from occasional visits from his sons and Hamdan bin Mohd bin Khalifah he has been left on his own in Abu Dhabi for over a month. He has infuriated Zaid by telling him that he is squandering money on his attempts to improve the Baraimi falaj system.

Buti and Ahmed, two sons of Hamad bin Buti, left Abu Dhabi for Dubai, a short time ago, but have now been persuaded by Zaid to return to Abu Dhabi. It seems that they were discontent with the treatment they are receiving from Shakhbut.

Shaikh Sultan bin Shakhbut is suffering from some ailment which cannot be cured at the Maktum hospital, and he is being taken to Muscat for treatment.

The Ruler has invoked the clause of the Company's Concession calling upon it to pay duties on the personal effects of its employees. The matter is still under discussion.

The authorities have realised the absurdity of the o/c T.O.L. summering in Abu Dhabi, and have prevented his continuing with his plans. The o/c has yet to visit Abu Dhabi which is reason enough for his optimism in even considering the idea.

Codrai
Representative.

TRUCIAL COAST DIARY FOR THE PERIOD ENDING 28 FEBRUARY 1954

GENERAL:

There is a steady increase in the amount of outside interest being taken in Trucial Oman and not all of the limelight falling on these parts comes from the boundary dispute with the Saudis, although it is true to say that the situation as it exists in Baraimi is a "pièce de résistance" for any journalist who is able to penetrate the cordon of the Foreign Office caution, which unsuccessfully tries to guard the situation from critical eyes. Commercial organisations with their appetites whetted by the other Gulf States, send representatives to explore the possibility of driving in a stake, so as to be ready to reap the benefits of any oil developments. Many commercial travellers find themselves in the ridiculous position of kicking their heels in Sharjah, awaiting the next aircraft to take them away, having booked themselves to the end of the line without knowing what lies there. Some degree of aesthetic interest is also shown in these parts by those who find them more congenial than other countries of the Arab World. The net result, however, is that much more interest is being taken in Trucial Oman then is justified by its present state, which has undergone very little change since the time when Trucial Oman was regarded as being on the edge of the unknown.

The flood of visitors continued during February and, apart from high ranking Service Officers, included Hammond-Innes, the novelist, Waterfield, the Director of the Eastern Department of the B.B.C., twenty five Kuwaiti students (who are spending some time here), a student from Oxford, who is to remain here until August, to write a thesis on the Persian Gulf, many salesmen, several journalists, and the usual flow of fine weather V.I.P.s.

Most places in the Trucial Oman enjoyed a good fall of rain, during the month. The airfield in Sharjah was made serviceable after the rains much more quickly than in past years, due to a new pumping system which has proved to be fairly successful. The large part of the local Staff House in Dubai collapsed during the rains, and is now being made serviceable by the Ruler.

The move of the Political Agency from Sharjah to Dubai was completed at the end of the month.

RAS AL KHAIMA:

Several attempts have been made to arrest Saif bin Ali bin Saif of the Khawatir tribe but without success. He is wanted by H.M.G. for his part in the recent slaving incident. The report of how he is being harboured by his father, and how he hides over the sand dunes when the T.O.L. or Ruler's vehicles appear, has caused some amusement in the other Shaikdoms. A member of the Sharqiyeen tribe, known as

Tuwairish,[7] has been named as an accomplice in this slaving incident, but he has sought sanctuary with Turki in Hamasa.

FUJAIRAH:

The General Manager, Mr. G. Heseldin visited the Ruler of Fujairah on 7th February, and entertained him to an Arab lunch aboard the M.V. «Jamila».[8] The "Jamila" was anchored off Ghurfat, which is a small village belonging to Fujairah on the coast near Kelba.

SHARJAH:

The inquest on Henderson, the Anti-Locust Party Officer who died suddenly in Sharjah at the end of the year (T.C.D. December) has again had to be postponed, due to a difference of medical opinion as to the cause of his death.

No progress has yet been made in arranging the trial of the Adenese who are being held in Sharjah on murder charges. Judge Mawdsley, of the British Residency, is kept busy with the Trucial Coast part of his circuit, mainly with cases between merchants.

The U.S. Navy supply ship "Duxbury Bay" visited Sharjah and Khor Fakhan during the month, to introduce the new American Admiral.

DUBAI:

Fighting broke out between Arab and Indian deck passengers aboard the B.I. steamer "Dara", while it was anchored off Dubai on 16th February, and the Captain signalled ashore asking for the help of the police. The Political Agent, who was in Dubai at the time, sent for a detachment of T.O.L. and although these Levies were not actually used to quell the trouble, their arrival in Dubai without the knowledge of the Ruler caused much indignation and ill feeling amongst the Shaikhs which has not yet worn off. Several casualties occurred aboard the ship as a result of the trouble. The Ruler now sends several armed soldiers aboard each passenger ship that comes to Dubai.

ABU DHABI:

The situation in Abu Dhabi seems to be worse than it has ever been before, due almost entirely to the universal unpopularity of Sheikh Shakhbut. The summing up of the events of the month does not, alone, portray the gravity of the situation but, on the other hand, it is difficult to give a balanced view of the situation without attaching too much importance to the various happenings, and without being swayed by the general

7 The reader will remember that we have come across this rogue a few years earlier.

8 PD(TC) boat.

interpretation of events through the eyes of those who are already deeply prejudiced on the subject.

It would seem that the only members of Shakhbut's family with whom he is still on good terms are his sons Saeed and Sultan. His relationship with his brothers has, for sometime past, been most uncertain, but it would appear that it has now deteriorated more than ever before, particularly with Zaid. The latter, who has been doing a magnificent job in the Cold War against the Saudis, is now practically out of funds, and has been refused any further cash by Shakhbut. This is a tremendous embarrassment to him, as he now has to refer his followers and visiting Baduin to Shakhbut for payment, but very few of them will go to Abu Dhabi. Zaid has said that he would not commit any drastic act to change the present situation but, apparently, he has once or twice, in moments of despair, said that he would have to leave the territory and go elsewhere.

Shakhbut's unpopularity among the Manasir is now legend, but it seems to have spread to many of his former followers among the Bani Yas. There is no doubt that he must feel that much of Zaid's popularity has been won at his expense, and with his money, and the realisation of this has probably caused him to be less liberal in his dealings with Zaid.

It is now reported that Shaikh Hamid bin Bati, (Shakhbut's maternal uncle) and his sons and followers have left Abu Dhabi after a quarrel with Shakhbut, and have gone either to Qatar or Saudi Arabia. Shortly afterwards Shakhbut's mother, Salama, also left Abu Dhabi without Shakhbut's knowledge, and returned to Baraimi. The number of Abu Dhabi's subjects going away to Dubai, Qatar and Saudi Arabia, seems to have increased of late.

This picture of the state of affairs which exists in Abu Dhabi must be viewed against the background of past events, when, from the point of view of the baduin, money flowed more freely, when the Saudis were on the scene. Also, about this time, the Ruling house was able to enjoy the large payments which were being made to it by Superior Oil Company and, later D'Arcy Exploration Company. The present situation must be regarded as an anti-climax to those more prosperous times.

The Political Agent visited Shaikh Shakhbut during the month for the purpose of asking him to give more assistance to Zaid.

Shaikhs Zaid, Khaled, Hazza and Mohamed bin Khalifa spent most of the month out hunting in the Khatam[9] area. Zaid claims that the purpose of the trip was to establish contact with the baduin in that area and to find out more about them, but he also had some good sport, and everyone acknowledges that he has had a well-earned holiday.

9 Between Al 'Ain and Abu Dhabi.

No progress has yet been made in settling the Abu Dhabi customs problem, which arose last month when the Ruler invoked the clause of the Company's concession calling on it to pay duty on the personal effects of its employees. The Ruler interprets the clause to mean any goods which are for the use of the Company's employees, such as passenger cars, staff quarters, foodstuffs, etc.

Another A.R.A.M.C.O.[10] aircraft was sighted on reconnaissance over Tarif area during the month.

D'ARCY EXPLORATION COMPANY:

The chartered survey ship "Calypso" arrived in Abu Dhabi waters during the month, just in time to enable D'Arcy to fulfil its obligations to begin exploration within one year of signature of its agreement. This Company has also undertaken to drill within five years if a suitable location can be found.

The Commander of the "Calypso", the famous underwater explorer, Cousteau, has contracted with D'Arcy to make an underwater film of the operations.

The D'Arcy representative's offices in Dubai and Abu Dhabi are nearly ready, and his home in Abu Dhabi is nearing completion. A special launch has been built for him by Khan Sahib Hussain.

Under the terms of its concession, D'Arcy has to pay each of the Ruler's three brothers the sum of Rs. 60,000/- every year, apart from the main annual payments to the Ruler. Shaikh Shakhbut has asked for these payments to be made through him (as they were last year), but in view of the financial difficulties confronting the brothers, the Political Agent has asked for these payments to be made direct. There is no doubt that Shakhbut wishes to use these payments to try and appease his brothers without expense to himself.

The Ruler has signed an agreement giving the British Bank of the Middle East[11] the option to open in Abu Dhabi when the trade there justifies a branch. He also has opened an account with the Dubai branch, into which D'Arcy has made its annual payment.

BARAIMI AND OMAN:

Obaid Bin Juma has made an attempt to regain his control of the Bani Ka'ab. Sometime towards the end of the month, the present Shaikh, Abdulla bin Salim discovered that Obaid and a handful of followers had returned to Mahadha where they were trying to influence the people with gifts of money, which, presumably they had received from the Saudis. A shooting incident followed this discovery, and one of Abdulla's followers, and one of Obaid's, were killed. Order was restored by the T.O.L.

---

10 Arabian American Oil Company. Saudi Arabia.

11 BBME, Now part of HSBC.

and Abdulla bin Salim has moved his headquarters from Sham[12] to Mahadha. Abdul Wahid, One of the Shaikhs of the Bani Ka'ab, who supported Abdulla bin Salim in overthrowing Obaid bin Juma, died of heart failure on the night of the incident.

Dr Haji Abdulla bin Askari, a Baghdadi author has recently travelled a great deal in Oman and during his stay he has been on a visit to Nezwa. He states that he was in Majlis with the Imam[13] when news was received of the D.E.F. landing.[14] The Imam's first reaction was to send troops to the area, but he later decided to call a Majlis of the principal Shaikhs, and no course of action had been decided upon up to the time of the informant's departure. It is also reported that several Saudi emissaries have been on visits to Nezwa, and have distributed money there.

Dr Askari is now thought to be a confidence trickster, who has quite a long criminal record. At one time he was travelling in the Far East, posing as the Imam's Representative. However, no ulterior motive has yet to come to light as being the reason for his visit.

The RAF Medical Officer in Baraimi was withdrawn sometime ago, and Dr McCaully, of the Maktum hospital in Dubai, visited during the month and treated over two hundred patients.

Codrai
Representative.

---

12 Sharm in the Wadi Sharm north of Buraimi and in the western foothills of the Hajar mountain range.

13 Following the 1920 Treaty of Sib the Imam Mohamed Abdullah al-Khaili, to quote Innes, 'had established and maintained an ascendancy through the virtue of his own integrity and moral character and the respect in which all men held him. The Sultan shared this respect for the man, as a man, and corresponded with him on friendly terms.' The Sultan was unable to assert himself in much of the interior of Oman where the Imam was dominant. INNES, N. M. (1987), p. 73.

14 Was this a reference to the IPC (Petroleum Development, Oman) preparations at Duqm, to penetrate into central Oman with a military escort? Clark wrote '400 mercenaries were recruited to serve in the Muscat and Oman Field Force (MOFF). It had been agreed eventually that the Sultan would be responsible for it, the Company would foot the bill, and the British Government would arm and train it.' In mid-March the Sultan inspected the troops at Duqm accompanied by a number of Company personnel. Initially the Company was only permitted to go as far as 50 miles inland. CLARK, Sir T., *Underground to Overseas, The Story of Petroleum Development Oman,* Stacey International, 2007, p.19f. And HENDERSON, E. (1988).

TRUCIAL COAST DIARY FOR THE PERIOD ENDING 31 MARCH 1954

POLITICAL AGENCY:

The Acting Political Agent, Mr. M.S. Weir, accompanied by his wife, left on posting to the Foreign Office on 27th March. Mr. C.M. Pirie-Gordon, C.B.E., returned from leave on 20th March, and is expected to resume his duties sometime in the future.

A Foreign Office Inspector, a former Ambassador to Siam, spent a fortnight at the Agency during the month, and has made some slight changes in the administration.

The Political Agent is still being pressed by the Residency in Bahrain to settle the internal boundaries, and has chosen the least disputed Ras al Khaimah/Umm al Quwain boundary for his first attempt. However, the respective claims of the Rulers of these territories have enlarged since they were last heard: roughly speaking, the Ruler of Ras al Khaimah now claims as far along the coast as the Wadi Batha, and the Ruler of Umm al Quwain as far as Jezirat al Zaab.[15]

Col. Merilees, a water diviner whose visits to these parts is sponsored by the Foreign Office, (see TCD April, 1953) spent a further two weeks touring Baraimi and the Trucial Shaikhdoms during the month. He is returning here in September to begin drilling operations, and the Foreign Office is making arrangements to hire a percussion drilling rig. He is most confident that he has 'found' an abundant supply of water in each Shaikhdom, but it would, perhaps, have been preferable[16] had the Rulers not been imbibed with so much optimism until he has had some success. It is, indeed, to be wondered what his record of past success is, that gives the Foreign Office the confidence to spend so much money on this project.

RAS AL KHAIMAH:

Saif bin Ali bin Saif of the Khawatir tribe continues to elude arrest by the T.O.L.

FUJAIRAH:

The Ruler fell off his camel when travelling from Fujairah to Dibba at the end of the month, and injured his back. He is being treated at the Maktum hospital, Dubai. He is planning to go on pilgrimage this year, and to visit Bahrain, Saudi Arabia, Kuwait and the Lebanon. The Ruler is well known for his travels during Ramadan, and he makes no attempt to conceal his inability to fast.

Large swarms of locusts have descended on the Fujairah/ Batinah coast, and are ravaging the plantations there.

---

15 Overlapping claims by a long way!

16 Codrai wrote 'preferably'.

SHARJAH:

T.O.L. vehicles have been involved in two more road accidents during the month. On 7th March a British Officer was injured when the Land Rover he was driving struck a local taxi near Jebel Faiyah, and on 12th March an Adeni driver was killed when his lorry turned over outside the Maktum hospital, Derrah.

The Ruler has issued an order stating that all drivers of motor vehicles in Sharjah territory are to apply and be tested for driving licenses, and have to pass a test.

The Ruler has imprisoned two of his cousins, the sons of the late Shaikh Humaid. Since their father's death about two years ago, they have been squandering the family fortune and drinking heavily.

Saqr bin Abdullah, the Sharjah Wali of Dibba, and the brother of Shaikh Humaid,[17] a former Ruler of Kelba, is trying to assert his independence, but has been rebuffed in his claim by the Political Agent.

The old Agency building in Sharjah has been taken over by the T.O.L. as an officers' mess. It is said that the R.A.F. is trying to have the T.O.L. camp moved outside the perimeter of the R.A.F. camp.

The Manager (formerly Asst. Manager) of the Golden Valley Red Oxide Company is now planning to work on Abu Musa Island the whole year round, and to have his family there.

DUBAI:

On 2nd March, the Ruler of Qatar visited Dubai, on his return to Qatar from Bombay by B.I. Steamer. A lunch was given for him ashore by the Ruler of Dubai, at which the Ruler of Sharjah, Shaikh Rashid, Abdullah Darwish, The Political Agent, the Company Representative, and many others were present. The occasion was not regarded as a great success, due to an apparent aloofness on the part of Shaikh Ali of Qatar, who was also rather agitated in case he should miss the tide and be unable to return to the steamer. He seemed to have received but little benefit from his treatment in Bombay.

The largest circumcision ceremony on the Trucial Coast for many years was held in Dubai during the month. Dances, camel races, and numerous feasts were held during the nine days of celebrations, after which several hundred youths, ranging in age from about five to twenty five, were circumcised. The expenses of the whole ceremony were paid for by Shaikh Rashid, whose eldest son, Maktum, was circumcised at the ceremony.

A new B.B.M.E. Manager, and a new Manager for Messrs Gray Mackenzie & Co., arrived during the month to take over from the present managers who are shortly going on leave and will be posted elsewhere.

A British Red Cross orderly arrived in Dubai at the end of the month, in full regalia.

17 The dead brother. Codrai insists on calling him Humaid while elsewhere he is called Hamad.

He is being accommodated in the R.A.F. Officers mess, Sharjah. His ambulance (a converted Land Rover), which is to be attached to the Maktum Hospital, is due to arrive shortly.

ABU DHABI:

The dissentions within the Ruling house reached a new climax during the month, and rumours that Shaikh Shakhbut had abdicated became widespread in the Persian Gulf States as well as on the Trucial Coast. However, after a visit of Haza and Zaid to Abu Dhabi the chief differences, mainly financial, between the brothers seem to have been settled, until- as the local commentators put it, 'the next Shammal blows'.

Naturally enough everyone is still awaiting more definite news of the Company's operations at Tarif, and the extent of their success.

Following the departure of Hamid bin Bati from Abu Dhabi (reported upon last month), Shaikh Haza has been given the task of establishing a post in the Khor Odaid area. As the leader of the Qubaisat, Hamid bin Bati has historical claims to the Odaid area, and it is feared that he may encourage the Saudis to establish a post there.

Fahad bin Rashid, a merchant who is the leading personality on Dalma island, has been thinking of leaving Abu Dhabi for good, to go to Saudi Arabia. Apparently the only thing which has discouraged him from this move has been the prospect of a contract to supply water to D'Arcy, next winter.

Shaikh Khalid's wife has been admitted as a patient to the Maktum hospital, and Khalid has been encamped outside the hospital, where he has been visited by Zaid (whose wife was also admitted to the hospital for a few days) and Haza. Zaid was feasted by Shaikh Rashid during the Circumcision ceremony in Dubai.

Another A.R.A.M.C.O. aircraft was sighted on reconnaissance over the Tarif area during the month.

D'ARCY EXPLORATION COMPANY:

The 'Calypso' has developed many troubles which have delayed its operations and she has spent much time in Doha and Bahrain while undergoing repairs to her radar apparatus. In the meantime, her commander and his wife have been on a trip to Europe. D'Arcy is far from pleased with the Commander for the manner which he has set about the operations, and the many delays which have occurred, and there seems to be a likelihood that the Company may end his contract. The 'Calypso's' operations are, in any case due to end early May.

The D'Arcy Company is being pressed by Shaikh Haza to work more to the westwards, particularly around Halul Island.[18] It is understood that H.M.G. has forbidden much of this area, without apparently informing the Ruler.

18 Halul island is in Qatar waters. Sheikh Shakhbut maintained his claim to the island in spite of HMG informing him otherwise.

BURAIMI AND OMAN:

The Representative made a visit to Buraimi during the month, and this has been the subject of a separate report (20th March).[19]

The T.O.L. post on the Ramlat Anaij track near Mahadha (the so called 'toll-post') is being enlarged, ready for use in case of a joint withdrawal by Saudis and the British forces from Buraimi, should any such agreement be made with the Saudis.

An officer of the anti-Locust party has been on a motor reconnaissance of the approaches to Liwa from Buraimi, and succeeded in reaching Al Khis by Landrover, after much difficulty.[20]

Codrai
Representative.

TRUCIAL COAST DIARY FOR THE PERIOD ENDING 30 APRIL 1954

POLITICAL AGENCY:

It is understood that instead of seeking the means of arbitration, H.M.G. and the Saudi Government have now agreed to negotiate settlement of the Abu Dhabi / Saudi frontier problem.

The Ras al Khaima/Umm al Quwain boundary settlement having proved more difficult than the Political Agent had anticipated, he is now tinkering with the idea of settling the Trucial Oman/Muscat Boundary, in the Rus al Jibal area, first.[21] It is understood that he asked for an Officer to be attached to the Agency who can deal fulltime with the boundary problems until they are settled.

The Agency is endeavoring to procure the use of a water well drill from the Company, to follow up the recommendations of Colonel Merilless.

H.M.S. "Wild Goose" visited Dubai on 11th April, this being the first visit of a frigate since the opening of the new Agency.[22] The "Wild Goose" afterwards toured the other Shaikhdoms.

---

19 This report is missing from this file.

20 Codrai and Chatton PD(TC) were the first to reach Liwa in a vehicle, also in a Land Rover, in June 1953. Al Khis is on the eastern side of the Liwa crescent, while Codrai and Chatton went to Arada on the western side.

21 Ra's al -Khaimah and Sultanate of Oman border.

22 The Political Agency moved from Sharjah to Dubai.

The Ruler of Fujairah has been fortifying his position in the Jebel Khadra area, where he recently clashed with the Ruler of Ras al Khaima, for which he was fined Rs. 300/-, and the Agency has fined him a further three thousand Rupees.

RAS AL KHAIMA:

The Company has now settled the claim for compensation for the loss of the date harvest at Khatt arising out of Seismic Party 5 operations in that area last year, and the sum of three thousand Rupees has been paid to the Ruler.

Shaikh Skhar of Muscat travelled through Ras al Khaima territory en route to Khasab.[23] via Bakha and Sha'am on 12th April. It is said that he was seeking information regarding the Muscat/ Ras al Khaima boundary, although it also seems likely that the reason for his visit was the annual collection of taxes from the Muscati Wali of Khasab.

FUJAIRAH:

The Ruler of Fujairah is suffering acute financial embarrassment, and his only relief from his troubles seems to be based on the hope that he will be given substantial presents of money, when he shortly goes on tour of Bahrain, Kuwait and Saudi Arabia. Apparently some of the Shargiyeen tribe on the Ras al Khaima side of his territory are squeezing him for gifts, threatening to take their allegiance elsewhere if they are not given them.

UMM AL QUWAIN:

Abdulla al Masawi, the Company's Head Guard at Umm al Quwain, who was also the pilot for Company craft entering the creek, died on 12th April.

SHARJAH:

The Ruler's uncle, Shaikh Mohd, left Sharjah to visit the Ruler of Qatar in Doha on 7th April.

Arrangements have been made by the Agency to make the T.O.L. the testing authorities to deal with applications for Sharjah driving licences, but there the matter seems to rest, and the actual system has not yet been brought into effect. It is considered that the Agency has fallen short in not making provisions for the interchangeability of licenses between the Shaikdoms, before giving its support to this administrative move in Sharjah, and it now finds Rashid bin Sa'id unwilling to agree to any arrangements in this respect, due to the apparent unpopularity of the T.O.L. in Dubai.

The Ruler has released two of his cousins whom he arrested last month, and one of them has left Sharjah to live in Dubai.

---

23 Khasab. The main town and good harbour on the Musandam peninsula. Bakha (Bukha) is also in the Sultanate of Oman near the Ra's al-Khaimah border. Shaam is in Ra's al-Khaimah.

Gray Mackenzie & Co., Ltd. has had to inform the Ruler that it is unable at the present time, to arrange for the B.I. steamers to call at Khor Fakhan.

The new school in Sharjah, which was built with a grant by the F. O.,[24] and is staffed with Kuwaiti teachers and financed by the Ruler of Kuwait, is now open, and a very successful sports day was held on 28th April, which was attended by most of the British community.

DUBAI:

Shaikh Rashid's wife gave birth to a son, Ahmed, on 10th April. In typical happy-go-lucky style, Rashid was away in Ras al Kaima, supervising the building of a new house at Koran, in which his wife was to have her baby, when he received news of the birth. The house is expected to be completed in a few weeks' time.

Shaikh Rashid is expected to go to India after Ramadhan, for a further operation on his hernia. His brother, Khalifa, is expected to return shortly from Miraj where he has spent about a month, without having been cured of the dysentery with which he has suffered for a number of years.

The new cinema in Dairah, probably the first publicly owned one on the Trucial Coast, opened during the month, but has not yet proved to be very successful, due to the difficulty of obtaining reasonably up-to-date films.

The cost of living has been steadily creeping up during the past few months, most noticeably with meat and livestock. The inflated prices of the latter are mainly due to the lack of control on the export of livestock to the profitable markets in Kuwait and Saudi Arabia. The Ruler has temporarily forbidden this export during Ramadhan, and has issued an order controlling the prices of the following foodstuffs, to approximately what they were a few months ago.

		Controlled price During Ramadan	old price
Mutton	per Maund	Rs,.12/-	Rs. 20/- to 24/-
Beef		Rs. 10/-	Rs. 20/- to 24/-
Coffee		Rs. 22/-	Rs. 48/-
Tea		Rs. 3/-	Rs. 4/-
Eggs per dozen		Rs. 1/8	Rs. 2/4
Chickens each		Rs. 3/-	Rs. 5/- to 6/-

24 Foreign Office London.

The B.B.M.E. is suffering from a round of staff troubles. Offered a 5% increase in salaries (the staff received a substantial increase not long ago) the employees[25] held a meeting at which they drew up a list of demands which included a 30% increase and longer leave, and each member took an oath on the Koran to support any employee who might have action taken against him by the Bank. The demands were presented to the Manager who called in his Bahrain Manager to assist him in dealing with the trouble. Shaikh Rashid is said to have intervened and asked the employees to wait a reasonable time for a reply to their demands, before taking any drastic action.

Chinese crackers, which have been on sale in Dubai for several years, have suddenly become the craze, and vast quantities are being bought, one merchant having ordered a further Rs. 25,000/- worth. Shaikh Rashid made a round trip from Ras al Khaima – where he amuses himself making bombs out of Ras al Khaima mud, and rolling the crackers in his home-grown tobacco – to replenish his supply. Shaikh Said has been seen with a fanatical looking in his eye, igniting a whole packet of them behind unsuspecting beduin. Away in his outpost Zaid sent a truck all the way to Dubai to fetch four large packing cases of them. Quite appropriately, they are forbidden in Sharjah, as also are bicycles in the suq.

ABU DHABI:

Hamid bin Bati has now settled down in Doha, after a visit to Saudi Arabia on which, it is said, he did not fare financially as well as was generally expected. It is feasible, of course, that the Qataris rather than the Saudis are intending to use his connections[26] with Khor al Odaid to support their frontier claims.

Shaikhs Khalid, Said, Zaid and Haza all visited Dubai during the month, where some of their womenfolk were being treated at the Maktum hospital. Shaikh Khalid afterwards left by B.I. steamer for Bombay accompanied by Said bin Shakhbut and other members of the family.

Shaikh Haza has been encamped at Bida Haza[27] for most of the month.

D'ARCY EXPLORATION COMPANY:

The "Calypso" finished operating in Abu Dhabi waters on 6th April, and left for the Maldives Islands, where she is to be engaged on biological work. The Commander

25 The distinction between staff (presumably European) and employees (all others).

26 The Qubaisat tribe, of whom Sheikh Hamid bin Buti was the chief, have always considered Khor al Odaid to be their territory.

27 The place was named after Shaikh Haza as he found fresh water there at about 40 to 50 feet. Bida Haza is in western Abu Dhabi territory about 15 kilometres southeast of Bida Mutawa and about 50 kilometres south of the coast at Ruwais.

of the "Calypso" Cousteau, found little of interest in the fish of the Persian Gulf, and states that the fish in the Gulf are only migratory.[28]

Before the departure of the "Calypso", many shots[29] of Shaikh Shakhbut, Abu Dhabi, Dubai, pearl diving etc. were taken for the film which the crew of the ship are making for D'Arcy.

Asked by the Ruler as to why the "Calypso" had not worked in the Western parts of Abu Dhabi waters, the representative of D'Arcy requested permission from the Political Agent to inform the Ruler of the restrictions which had been placed on his Company's operations by H.M.G. The Political Agent was much opposed to this, and told the Representative that he would have to fob the Ruler off with technical difficulties, and this led to an exchange of views which did not leave the Representative on very good terms with the P.A.

Although D'Arcy has established an office in Dubai, and the news of the formation of a Company to take over the Dubai Sea Rights has been publicised in the press, the Representative has been embarrassed at not being able to inform the Ruler[30] of the reason for his Company's presence in Dubai. Apparently the formation of the new Company (with one third French interests) has not been as finalised as the press notices state.

COMPANY OPERATIONS:

Gravity Meter Party 1A, which is now based at Tarif, began its reconnaissance of the Bainuna/Dhaffara/Liwa sands by helicopter during the month, but the start of this operation was rather marred by the loss by fire of one of the supply carrying Rapides, at the No.1 Advance Base, (about 15 miles south-west from the Murban rig).

Drilling at Murban No.1 reached a depth of about 10,900 feet at the end of the month, and seems to be continuing satisfactorily.[31]

The R.A.F. wishes to take over part of the hospital building in Sharjah which is now on lease to the Company. It is feared that the Headquarters may instruct the local Commanding Officer to invoke the clause of the lease, which gives it the right to take back the whole building at only one month's notice. The matter is still being discussed.

Codrai
Representative.

---

28 It appears that the writer, Codrai reflecting the views of many, considered that Cousteau's work was of only limited value.

29 Photographic.

30 Ruler of Abu Dhabi Shaikh Shakhbut.

31 The well was spudded in (drilling commenced) on 18 January 1953.

TRUCIAL COAST DIARY FOR PERIOD ENDING 31 MAY 1954

GENERAL:

Ramadan began on sight of the moon, on 4th May in all the Shaikhdoms except Abu Dhabi where it was a day later.

There has been no reaction, and a surprising lack of concern, at the death of the Imam[32] of Oman. It was over two weeks before the news of his death filtered through to the Trucial Coast, prior to which rumour had it that the Imam was very ill and had appointed a successor.

Large swarms of locusts have been reported from many parts of the Trucial Coast during the month, and the gardens and plantations at Ras al Khaima, Dhaid and elsewhere are believed to have been badly ravaged.

POLITICAL AGENCY:

The accommodation of the new Agency in Dubai is already proving to be inadequate, and the Passport Office has been extended to an old caravan within the compound, whilst the old Bank House in Derra is about to be taken over as living accommodation for the A.P.A. It has also been observed that the barbed wire around the agency compound has been laid to keep people in, rather than out.[33]

TRUCIAL OMAN LEVIES:

The trial of the Adeni levies held on the charges of murder was due to begin on 24th May. It was to be a Sharia Court in which a British Legal Observer was to be present. The Qadi is a Muscati, and the Prosecuting and Defending Counsellors both Lebanese.

On the night of 16th May two British Levy N.C.O's in a Land Rover mistook the track and drove into Hamasa where they were taken prisoners by the Saudis. They were released, together with their vehicle, on the 18th May, on the orders of the Saudi government, to whom the matter had been referred by the Commander of the Hamasa garrison, Turki bin Ataishan, It was made clear to Turki, in an ultimatum handed to him by the Political Agent, that HMG would have taken whatever measures were necessary to have secured the release of these two Levies. The freed prisoners both stated that they were well treated during their confinement in Hamasa.

---

32 The Imam of Oman, Mohamed Abdullah al-Khalili, was the religious leader in the Sultanate who controlled much of the interior of the land and defied the Sultan. His authority over the interior stemmed from the 1920 Treaty of Seeb. The actual document was treated with great secrecy.

33 In those days Europeans were discouraged from going into town, and if they did they were accompanied by a guide/guard.

Trucial Coast subjects at present comprise about 85% of the total strength of the T.O.L., and it is hoped that more Adenese will be got rid of, and this percentage increased, before long. A Company of the R.A.F. regiment are still based in Sharjah, to support the T.O.L.

Wheels and other fittings were stolen off three T.O.L. Land Rovers outside the new Officers' mess in Sharjah, during the month.

RAS AL KHAIMA:

No progress was made during the month on the settlement of the Ras al Khaima/ Umm al Quwain boundary problem.

SHARJAH:

The Ruler of Sharjah[34] was entertained by the Representative to dinner in the Company guesthouse, in Sharjah, on 12th May.

On 22nd May the Royal Air Force held a ceremony in the R.A.F. Station at which the Political Agent unveiled portraits of the Ruler of Sharjah, in the presence of the Ruler. This was followed by dinner given by the Ruler in his Palace.

The Rulers uncle, Sheikh Mohammed bin Saqr, has extended his tour from Doha to Bahrain, Kuwait and Saudi Arabia. It is said that he receives the sum of Rs. 6000 annually from the Saudis. His son, who was recently forbidden by his father to work with the Company, now works as a fitter in Sharjah.

DUBAI:

Lt. Col. D.G. McCaully, the quarantine Medical Officer, left on home leave during the month and has been relieved by his new Pakistani assistant.

The labour troubles in the British Bank of Middle East have yet to be fully settled, and it seems that to do this most of the clerical staff will have to be changed.

ABU DHABI:

Shaikh Haza visited the Company camp at Tarif twice during the month, and Shaikh Zaid once. During his visit, Shaikh Zaid distributed baskets of dates among the Bedouin squatters near the camp.

About the 18th May it was reported that the Ruler of Abu Dhabi's post at Khor al Odaid was abandoned and it was feared that the garrison of 12 men had deserted. Sultan bin Shakhbut visited the post some days later and returned with the glad news that all the men were present, correct and presumably in good heart.

On the 25th May intelligence was received that a Saudi party was expected to make an incursion into Trucial Oman territory. Preparations were made by the P.A.,

34 Shaikh Saqr bin Sultan.

the R.A.F.[35] and T.O.L.[36] to locate, intercept and turn back any such party that might appear. In these arrangements the Company assisted by undertaking to provide water where necessary (and possible) and a surveyor to fix the position of any interception that might take place. Transport for the P.A. would have been provided if necessary. On the 29th R.A.F. reconnaissance reported a party encamped just south of the Qatar Peninsula and a few days later they were reported to be camped at an unnamed well at a position roughly 24° 27' N and 51° 10' E, just about on the Abu Dhabi border. Bedu reports estimated that the party consisted of 46 Americans and about 70 armed guards with many vehicles. It is likely that this is an exaggeration. Groups of two or three vehicles were observed moving in Abu Dhabi territory in the Khor al Odeid area and may have been engaged on geophysical work.

Since then (i.e. early June) the R.A.F. have dropped a warning that the party was trespassing. It is understood that the authorities are intending to land a force near Khor al Odeid so that the intruders can be intercepted and turned back. This plan was made because it was felt that the T.O.L. would experience difficulty in crossing the sand on the North shore of Khor al Dhuwein.

It was arranged that the T.O.L. would embark at the Company's port at Zubaya.[37]

BARAIMI:

On 29th May it was reported that some Naimi tribesmen attempting to enter Hamasa were fired on by the Levy post. One was killed, one died of wounds and one wounded.

D'ARCY EXPLORATION COMPANY:

The Representative of the D'Arcy Exploration Company left for England on home leave early in the month, and expects to return sometime in September, when his company hopes to resume its operations in Abu Dhabi territory with a Seismic Party.

COMPANY ACTIVITIES:

Earlier in the month the Ruler of Abu Dhabi cancelled Khan Sahib Hussein's 'license' to work in Abu Dhabi territory. This took the form of the Ruler telling the Representative of D'Arcy Exploration Company that he could no longer use Khan Sahib Hussein, and sending for the Company Representative[38] to tell him the same thing. However, Khan Sahib Hussain visited the Ruler before the Company Representative and by a stroke of good fortune, met Shaikh Zaid in Abu Dhabi,

35 Royal Air Force.

36 Trucial Oman Levies.

37 70 kilometres west of Abu Dhabi.

38 PD(TC).

who intervened on his behalf and, after Khan Sahib had paid Shakhbut Rs. 23,000/- succeeded in getting Khan Sahib's contractor's 'license' renewed.

According to the agreement between Khan Sahib and the Ruler of Abu Dhabi, 25% of the Contractor's profits have to be paid to Shaikh Shakhbut, who seems most incredulous of the small profits being made by a contractor from an Oil Company. Also, Shakhbut has refused to believe that the contractor has made only small profits on such projects as the Abu Dhabi causeway, the Company Bungalow in Abu Dhabi and the new jetty at Zubaya and, in the case of the new house in Abu Dhabi for D'Arcy Exploration Company that he has actually sustained a loss. This suspicion of Khan Sahib Hussain's balance sheet has left the Ruler with a receptive mind for overtures made to him by other merchants, who have promised him considerably larger payments provided that he will support them in their moves to exploit the Company. One of these merchants is Khalifa bin Yusif, the Ruler's former secretary, who has been given considerable encouragement by the Representative of D'Arcy to establish himself as a contractor. The other merchants who have made offers to Shakhbut (one is Fakri), are all from Dubai.

The Political Agent, C. Pirie-Gordon, O.B.E., was the guest of the Company at Tarif for two days during the month and, as well as being shown the installations and drilling operations, was given a short trip in a helicopter. His visit was concluded by a flight in a Company Dove[39] over some of the Liwa settlements, after which he was taken by R.A.F. Anson to Baraimi, to deal with the incident reported on the above.

REPRESENTATION:

S.K. Watt took over from R.A.T. Codrai, who is going on home leave, as the Company Representative on 26th May.

S.K. Watt
Representative

39 De Havilland Dove. A small aircraft seating about six people and capable of landing on quite rough air-strips. The Company used Doves quite extensively throughout the Middle East, and was still using them for several years after I arrived in 1963.

TRUCIAL COAST DIARY FOR PERIOD ENDING 30 JUNE 1954

GENERAL:

The Eid al Fitr[40] began on second June in Sharjah, Ajman and Ras al Khaima and on 3rd June in Dubai, Abu Dhabi and Umm al Quwain. A strong body of opinion in Dubai was in favour of declaring Eid on the second but Shaikh Said squashed the move until the moon was clearly seen. In Dubai tens of thousands of fire-crackers were used in the Eid celebrations.

The Representative visited all Rulers except for Fujairah during the Eid and presented and received the compliments of the season.

The Saudi/American activity in the Khor al Odaid area had come to an end by the 15th when the T.O.L. forces landed. Early in the month Locusts were again reported to be attacking the various gardens but the ripening dates did not suffer.

POLITICAL AGENCY:

On the 25th a meeting of the Trucial States Council was attended by all the Rulers. It is reported that a discussion on schools was brought to an end by the Ruler of Abu Dhabi impatiently remarking that he had no educational problems because he had no schools.[41]

The Rulers (except, we understand Abu Dhabi,) have agreed verbally to accept the P.A.'s Boundary awards. This work has been in the hands of the A.P.A.[42] and he states that much progress has been made recently and it is hoped shortly to settle the Umm al Quwain/Ras al Khaima boundary.

TRUCIAL OMAN LEVIES:

The C.O. of the T.O.L. is very pleased with the performance of his men and vehicles in the Khor al Odaid. It is well to remember that the operation met no

---

40 At the end of the fasting month of Ramadan.

41 I can imagine that maybe he was teasing them! Mohamed Morsy Abdullah wrote 'In Abu Dhabi another enlightened and very rich pearl merchant, Khalaf b. 'Utaibah founded a school and entrusted the teaching to Shaikh 'abd-Latif b. Ibrahim, a member of the Al Mubarak family, famous as scholars of the Maliki teachings in al-Hasa.' Morsy Abdullah does not give a date but judging from the context it must have been in the early part of the 1900s. At that time similar schools were opened in Hirah and Dubai. However economic decline in the 1930's seriously reduced the provision of education until the late 1940's. The al-Falahiyyah school in Abu Dhabi opened and closed in 1958. It was not until 1960-61 that 'modern schools' (Morsy Abdullah's words) were opened in Abu Dhabi and Al 'Ain. ABDULLAH, M. M. (1978). *The United Arab Emirates, a Modern History.*

42 Assistant Political Agent. Julian Walker. WALKER, J. (1999), *Tyro on the Trucial Coast.* The Memoir Club, London, 1999. Walker wrote that Abu Dhabi (town) had 3,000 inhabitants.

resistance and only a few men and vehicles were involved. Our Landing Craft 'Afri' gave close support and was the source of water. Both the T.O.L. and the R.A.F. are on the lookout for further signs of Saudi activity.

The trial of the 3 Adeni Levies accused of murder took place before a Muscati Qadi. The men demanded a trial before the Sultan and when this was refused, attempted to declare the court incompetent to try them. The trial, nevertheless proceeded and, although the Sharia court found that the evidence was insufficient for a conviction, the three men are now imprisoned in Muscat jail for an indefinite period.

R.A.F.:

The new C.O. Wing Commander Garbett, arrived during the month.

UMM AL QUWAIN:

The Ruler now spends much of the time at his Falaj and returns to the heat of Umm al Quwain only if business calls him.

An ex-gratia payment was made to the Ruler for disbursements to the heirs of the late Abdulla al Masawi, Head guard at the company compound.

RAS AL KHAIMAH:

The Representative visited the Ruler during The Eid but found nothing to report.

SHARJAH:

The Representative exchanged Eid visits with the Ruler.

Mohd. bin Saqr returned from the travels and seems to have enjoyed himself.

On the 24th June the Golden Valley's labour on Abu Musa went on strike and the Navy was called in to evacuate the manager and his family and to restore peace. Details of the disturbances are not known but after two or three days the labour went back to work and cleared a ship which had been loading at the time. The manager and his family were put up by the P.A. for a few days, after which they moved to the Fort.[43]

The P.A. and the Ruler of Sharjah have sent for Khansahib Hussain to effect a final settlement on the island. Khansahib is still in Tarif but is expected home shortly.

Earlier this month Barnett, Golden Valley's manager, approached Khansahib regarding the oxide loading contract but they did not reach an agreement. Khansahib, in view of his previous unhappy experience, did not seem very interested. Now the P.A. is said to be anxious to see Khansahib once again controlling labour on Abu Musa and may use his influence to achieve this end.

Earlier this month a K.L.M. airliner in distress landed at Sharjah and unloaded an assortment of monkeys, tigers, peacocks and other exotic birds. The Ruler was

43 The B.O.A.C., British Overseas Airways Corporation, rest house.

much interested but turned down the pilot's offer of a brace of monkeys - he was keen on acquiring a peacock which the cautious Dutchman would not give away. After two days the plane left but the smell of the animals remained. All four peacocks were carefully tallied aboard by the pilot himself.

Two engineers are surveying the creek under the auspices of the P.A. but are not very hopeful. After Sharjah they will examine Dubai Creek.

DUBAI:

During the month Shaikh Rashid visited Doha and returned much impressed especially by the reception given him by the Company. He says he will build a power house[44] in Dubai and, more practical, he will move the dried fish market out of town.

Shaikh Rashid has with characteristic generosity given up the income derived from the rents of the Maktum hospital.

ABU DHABI:

The Representative visited the Ruler on 4th June. In spite of the happy occasion the Ruler that could not avoid bringing up certain matters and found an opportunity to criticise the condition of the approach road to Abu Dhabi built by the company. Shaikh Haza and Sultan bin Shakhbut were then in Abu Dhabi.

The Ruler and Shaikh Zaid visited Dubai for the Trucial States meeting, camping at Al Mirr, south-east of Jebel Ali. The Representative spent some fruitless hours seeking his camp, but only reached the spot after the party had left. Shaikh Zaid has now returned to Baraimi.

As reported above the party of intruders in Khor al Odaid withdrew before the arrival of the T.O.L. It is understood that the Americans claim to have been pursuing a normal surveying program. The T.O.L. force embarked on the Afri from Khor Zubaya. Although they swept through the area in which the R.A.F. reported activity they found no one and withdrew after a week.

BARAIMI:

The tightening of the blockade led to protests that disease was rampant in Hamasa, and the P.A. has sent in medicine to relieve the plight of the besieged. An offer of food was turned down altogether on the grounds that it was insufficient to feed the 3000 inhabitants of Hamasa. Turki's curious arithmetic has caused surprise in many quarters. The population is at present about a tenth of that figure.

It is reported that when Turki and his followers saw the Hilal they fired a feu-de-joie which provoked a withering fire from the investors.[45] Only one woman was

44 For generating electricity.

45 The Trucial Oman Levies.

accidentally killed, but her death was loudly used as propaganda. The besiegers' ten posts are now closely arranged around Hamasa.

A Daily Telegraph correspondent visited Baraimi during the month.

COMPANY AFFAIRS:

Well No.1 Murban has reached a depth of 12,330 feet and should shortly be completed.

A disastrous fire almost destroyed the stores at Tarif - the main building being a total loss. Re-building is going ahead fast.

The helicopter/gravity survey has encountered many difficulties[46] and will shortly close down temperately to re-equip.

The question of the R.A.F. Hospital building was again discussed with the R.A.F. and, partly because of our protests, they are having second thoughts about moving in.

VISITORS:

Mr Innis who is the Foreign Minister[47] of Muscat, Sayyid Thuwaini,[48] Messrs G.W. and E.F. Henderson visited Sharjah and Dubai.

Watt
Representative.

46 The main problem was that the helicopters were not powerful enough to operate in the heat of the day.

47 Innes was Foreign Minister of the Sultanate of Oman from 1953 to 1958.

48 Thuwaini bin Shehab was an Omani government official who was frequently at Innes side, particularly when he was travelling in the Sultanate. He spoke English and had been at the American University in Beirut. Innes wrote 'I could not have wished for a pleasanter person with whom to share a tent for the three weeks of the campaign.'

TRUCIAL COAST DIARY FOR PERIOD ENDING 31 JULY 1954

GENERAL:

The main event during the month was the signing of the arbitration agreement with the Saudi government which took place on the 30th. There is general satisfaction that Turki bin Ataishan is leaving Baraimi,[49] although many people find the arrangements for arbitration rather difficult to follow. The Ruler of Abu Dhabi endorses H.M.G.'s action but nevertheless has grumbled unofficially at the withdrawl of forces from the "Disputed Zone" where there is no reciprocal withdrawal of Saudis as in Baraimi.

Arrangements for the withdrawal of Trucial Oman Levy forces from Baraimi and the "Disputed Zone" are already in hand and the Royal Air Force have discontinued their reconnaissance flights over Western Abu Dhabi. Two of these planes have already left for Amman and it is possible that the Royal Air Force station in Sharjah will be considerably scaled down and the detachment at Tarif withdrawn altogether. Final decision is awaited on this point.

Some Rulers and many others have either gone abroad or to Ras al Khaima to escape the heat.

POLITICAL AGENCY:

The hoped for progress on boundaries did not materialise during the month and settlements will probably be left over till the autumn, so that the fieldwork can be done in reasonable comfort.

The Assistant Political Agent Mr. J.F. Walker, will shortly be going to Bahrain and a relief is expected soon. After a two months absence Walker will return and concentrate his efforts on Boundary work.

TRUCIAL OMAN LEVIES:

The Commanding Officer and the Captain and Quarter Master were stuck[50] overnight on a trip from Tarif to Sharjah. The Quarter Master suffered severely from heatstroke, but quickly revived when he returned to Sharjah. Air-conditioning is to be installed in the Officers mess but the Commanding Officer is still without light or even a refrigerator.

---

49 One of the conditions was that Turki bin Ataishan should leave Hamasa.

50 Bogged down in the sabkhah – the coastal salty mud/sand/gypsum that extends from the sea inland to the sand.

FUJAIRAH:

The Ruler has gone on the Haj. He left Sharjah with two followers by Charter Gulf on 29th July. The Ruler still hopes to improve the flow of a spring by dynamiting and has again sought the Company's assistance.

RAS AL KHAIMAH:

The Ras al Khaima – Umm al Qaiwain Boundary has not yet been settled although the Political Agent keeps himself very busy mapping the last details.

UMM AL QUWAIN:

The Ruler again spent most of his time in Falaj-al-Ali.[51]

SHARJAH:

Shaikh Saqr bin Sultan left Sharjah on the 26th for an extended tour of Kuwait, Iraq, Syria and Lebanon.

Earlier this month a commission consisting of Shaikh Rahamma and Khansahib Hussain went over to Abu Moussa[52] to enquire into the dispute between Golden Valley Company and the labour there. On their arrival they discovered that the manager had arrived the day before without having warned anyone on the mainland of his intentions. The labourers had immediately seized his launch and pulled it up on the beach, mixed his fuel and his water, and made his position so difficult that a Levy Officer and some men were needed to restore order. A final settlement has been effected but operations on the island have been stopped until after the worst part of the summer is past. It is understood that the Political Agent is insisting that Khansahib take over the labour contract in Abu Moussa again, even though Khansahib is not very willing.

DUBAI:

Earlier this month Shaikh Rashid bin Said left for Miraj in India to undergo a second hernia operation at the Mission Hospital there. Shaikh Rashid admits that his first operation only failed because he did not take his convalescence seriously enough, this time he intends to take it easy. Although burdened with the duties of Ruler, Shaikh Said has found time to visit his date garden at Ras al Khaima. It is said that he is eagerly looking forward to the return of Rashid, fit to relieve him once again. The latest news of Rashid is that he successfully underwent his operation and is progressing well.

51 His inland oasis retreat in the mountain foreland.

52 The large Sharjah island in the middle of the Gulf.

Shaikh Hasher[53] paid a visit to the Batinah[54] and returned complaining of the heat and damp climate.

ABU DHABI:

The General Manager[55] paid a visit to the Ruler in Abu Dhabi on the 10th and entertained him to lunch aboard the Ghazal. In spite of the heat the Ruler enjoyed the visit and was pleased to have met the G.M. again. The General Manager left soon after lunch. On the same day the Representative entertained Sultan, Hamdan[56] and many followers who had not been able to join the luncheon aboard for lack of space.

During one of the Representative's later visits a woman fell down a well just outside the palace and was rescued, unhurt but terrified, among great hullabaloo and amusement.

Shaikhs Said bin Shakhbut and Khaled bin Sultan returned from India by British India steamer on the 27th. After spending a few days camped between Sharjah and Dubai they went to Abu Dhabi. After a very short stay Said went off to Buraimi but Khaled remained in the Palace at Abu Dhabi.

BURAIMI:

Up to the moment of the agreement incidents were reported by the investing posts around Hamasa. There were some casualties among tribesman trying to break out, but the Trucial Oman Levies did not suffer loss.

On the 8th the Assistant Political Agent[57] with an International Red Cross Representative and Ali Bustani, the Agency Interpreter, visited Turki in Hamasa. He stayed four hours to investigate Saudi complaints of starvation and disease, but found none. The Egyptian doctor promised to produce cases of malnutrition but did not do so; this doctor was able to keep and feed a pet gazelle in spite of the alleged sufferings of the inhabitants. Unfortunately a sandstorm prevented the Assistant Political Agent visiting Zayid bin Sultan and telling him what was afoot and this omission considerably annoyed the Ruler of Abu Dhabi, but relations were soon restored to a friendly basis.

---

53 Sheikh Hasher bin Rashid bin Maktum. A cousin of the Dubai Ruler's father.

54 Indian Ocean coast of Oman.

55 G. Heseldin.

56 Sheikhs Sultan bin Shakhbut and Hamdan bin Mohamed.

57 J. Walker. Walker wrote about his visit to Hamasa with the Red Cross representative. 'As we came to a halt, crowds of Hamasites gathered around the car shouting "We are starving. Go home you brutal imperialist British!" and other slogans...They had the festive air of a group of holiday makers as they chanted, they were laughing and chattering, and peering at us full of curiosity rather than resentment and anger. WALKER, J. (1999).

At the end of the month arrangements were being made to evacuate Turki[58] under the terms of the Arbitration Agreement. Turki has had hopes of a triumphal exit through Sharjah and Dubai, H.M.G. are taking pains to avoid such an occurrence. He has now (13th August) left Hamasa and, so far as is known, travelled quietly along the coast road without touching any towns.[59]

COMPANY OPERATIONS:

Drilling has been discontinued at Murban No. 1 and testing operations are in progress.

Both the Helicopter Gravity Survey and the Seismic Survey in the Subkhat Matti were temporarily stopped during the month. The first had made little progress during the first 12 days of the month because the temperature was affecting the performance of the helicopters adversely. It is understood that an attempt will be made to modify the present machines or obtain a different type because even under the best conditions they are barely able to meet the lifting and range requirements of the survey party. The Seismic Survey closed down at the end of the month to overhaul machines, give leave to staff and to avoid the worst of the summer heat. This party had been doing excellent work under trying conditions in the Sabkhat Matti.[60]

The removal of the remaining material from Jebel Ali has now begun and the L.C.T. Afri called on the 27th to pick up the first load.

Since writing the above, the Representative, Dubai, has sent in the following report[61] on Turki's movements. Turki is now believed to be back in Saudi Arabia.

Stuart Watt
Representative.

---

58 The Saudi Turki bin Ataishan.

59 There were no towns in those days. There was the PD(TC) camp at Tarif and the associated village. Then nothing of significance until the small settlements at and near Markhia and Bida Matawa.

60 The far west of Abu Dhabi where the sabkhah extends up to 100 kilometres inland from the coast.

61 This report is included in the next Diary.

TRUCIAL COAST DIARY FOR PERIOD ENDING 31 AUGUST 1954

GENERAL:

The Eid al Adha was celebrated in all Shaikhdoms except Dubai and Abu Dhabi on 9th August and the days following. The two exceptions delayed their celebrations until the 10th. The Representative visited the Rulers of Dubai, Abu Dhabi, Sharjah and Ajman and exchanged greetings with the other Rulers.

As already reported[62] Turki bin Ataishan left Buraimi on the 13th. He encountered a good deal of trouble and all his trucks were stuck[63] or broken down and, when rescued by the Trucial Oman Levies, he was exhausted.

The Police Forces of both sides have been established in Buraimi. Claim and counterclaim abound but no serious incidents have been reported. The outbreak of banditry last month has subsided. So soon as Turki was out of the way the Trucial Oman Levies established posts at Qahil,[64] Dhaid and Huwailat (as well as minor posts) and these have given the bandits pause and there have been no further incidents. Tuwairish has kept quiet in the face of this opposition.

POLITICAL AGENCY:

The Political Resident visited Dubai on the 21st and discussed the security of the area. As a result the above mentioned posts were established.

A small percussion rig is expected in a few days time and two drillers have already arrived. They will drill the water wells sited by Colonel Merilees and commence in Dubai. The cost of these sited wells will be borne by the Agency but the Rulers may drill other wells at their own expense.

TRUCIAL OMAN LEVIES:

The Trucial Oman Levies have been much engaged during the month and have done excellent work in seeing Turki off the premises and dealing with bandits.

ROYAL AIR FORCE:

The Royal Air Force have been reduced to one Anson used for communications. The strength of the establishment is to be cut in the near future. The commanding officer, whoever he maybe, will not have the rank of Wing Commander. The squadron of Royal Air Force Regiment are under orders to move on 25th of September.

---

62 See letter below.

63 Stuck in the sand and/or in the sabkhah.

64 Near Mahadhah, towards the south west.

ABU DHABI:

Early this month the Ruler alleged that Khansahib was not fulfilling the terms of their agreement in respect of Khansahib's Company contracts in Abu Dhabi. He also complained that Khansahib had not called since the crisis in May, and that a final settlement of accounts was still outstanding. Khansahib has been dilatory in this matter, and on the advice of the Representative visited the Ruler, and after some discussion made a satisfactory settlement. Accounts were agreed and Khansahib is continuing with his work in Abu Dhabi. It is felt that if Khansahib had not paid this visit his 'license' would have again been revoked. As it is the Ruler has promised to extend the present agreement which expires soon.

On the 7th Messrs Colwill and Lippett of Chandler Brothers, Colwill and How of Liverpool visited the Ruler and made an agreement whereby they would enter into business in Abu Dhabi as Civil Engineering Contractors and General Traders. The agreement involves the formation of a new Company of which the Ruler is Chairman. Lippett was previously employed by Golden Valley on the Trucial Coast and during his previous stay earned an unenviable reputation and left under a cloud. Colvill returned to the UK but Lippett remained in Abu Dhabi, where he made attempts to discredit Khansahib and spread ridiculous stories that he was about to import £80,000,000 worth of goods. Later he fell sick and on his way to Bahrain elected to strike an Arab for an imagined insult. This has resulted in his resignation and return to the UK. Colwill returned and is attempting to repair the damage done in Abu Dhabi.

The Agency were much concerned over Lippett's antics and there is general relief that he has had to leave so soon.

Shakhbut with Haza, Khaled and Zaid camped on the Dubai side of Jebel Ali for several days from the 29th and visited the Political Agent. They discussed several matters, the main interest being centred on the Arbitration Agreement and the extent of Al Abu Falah jurisdiction over Buraimi and the Disputed Zone. It is understood that the Politicals consider tribal affairs to be in the hands of Shakhbut. The visit of Al bu Falah gave rise to the usual scare in Dubai and the more excitable feared an attempt on the lives of Shaikhs Said and Rashid.

On the 2nd September it was reported that Shakhbut's mother was ill and he and his brothers went to Buraimi to visit her.

DUBAI:

Shaikh Rashid bin Said has returned from India and is looking fit and well. He is confident that this second operation will be fully successful. Shaikh Said has thankfully withdrawn from the active duties of Ruler.

Mohamed Sharif, the head of the commercial community and a great friend of Rashid, died suddenly on September 2nd.

SHARJAH:

Shaikh Saqr is still away and is reported to have arrived in Cairo. Shaikh Rahamma, the Acting Ruler, has been greatly occupied during the month assisting the Trucial Oman Levies in controlling marauders.

All is quiet in Abu Moussa and the Manager and his family have returned to the island. It is reported that the Ruler of Sharjah intends to ask for a large increase in Royalty on the export of red oxide. Apparently the Royalty has remained unchanged since before the war.[65]

AJMAN:

Shaikh Rashid has been in good form and has done what he can to help chastise bandits.

FUJAIRAH:

The Ruler has returned from the Haj. He spent the minimum possible time in Saudi Arabia but was held up three days at Dammam when a tyre burst on his plane.

BARAIMI:

The arrival of Shakhbut in Buraimi has considerably upset the Saudis who are protesting volubly. Captain Clayton[66] was making considerable progress with his Saudi vis-a-vis, Abdulla Bin Naimi, when Shakhbut arrived to strain relations. This is Shakhbut's first visit to Buraimi for two years and the Agency wish that he had not selected this particular time to make a visit.

Abdulla, the Saudi Officer was at one time connected with the British Military Mission to Saudi Arabia at Taif and knows the Commanding Officer and some of the Trucial Oman Levies Officers.

COMPANY OPERATIONS:

Testing operations at Murban No.1 were marred by a tragic accident on the 6th when Mr. J.G. Johnston a petroleum engineer, lost his life. Then, and for several days afterwards, the well was very difficult to control and conditions were dangerous because of the presence of toxic gases.

The Ruler expressed his deep regret when he heard of the death of Mr. Johnston.

On the 21st the casual employee, Saif bin Obaid, died whilst working in the Sabkhat Matti. It is understood that the cause was heat exhaustion. The Ruler has been

65 World War 1939-1945.

66 See CLAYTON, P. *Two Alpha Lima, The First Ten Years of the Trucial Oman Levies,* Janus Publishing Company, 1994, p. 57.

informed. The build up to the El Feidh[67] area for Gezira location[68] is well underway and two ships were loaded from Jebel Ali during the month. The labour working at Jebel Ali proved a little fractious. However, after the discharge of two undesirable characters and small improvements in working conditions they have worked willingly.

Watt
Representative

LETTER DATED 14 AUGUST 1954

Turki bin Ataishan left Buraimi yesterday (13th August) morning and went out by the Coast Road. The first arrangements were that he should leave on the evening of the 10th but he succeeded in delaying his departure by last minute quibbles. The arrival of the Saudi receiving party was delayed because they disdained H.M.G.'s guides and consequently got handsomely stuck in the Sabkhat Matti.

As a Parthian shaft Turki stirred up the Awamir, Al bu Shams and some Naim, and there has been an outbreak of banditry. There have been various incidents on the Muscat road and eight travellers have been killed. Two of the bandits were accounted for, and it is reported that this party have returned home to enjoy the spoils. However, a second band, led by the redoubtable Tuwairish (now nicknamed Tovarisch), is said to be travelling up through Bani Ka'ab country and can be expected to start making trouble in the next day or two. The Political Agent has got the Rulers of Sharjah, Ajman and others to call out their forces and a serious effort is being made to give Tuwairish a beating up. There will also be Trucial Oman Levy forces available to help. The Rulers seem to be co-operating madly,[69] and Shaikh Rahama (the Ruler in Sharjah during Saqr's absence) has taken the field in person whilst Rashid of Ajman is simply breathing fire.

One supposes that Turki intends to demonstrate that when he leaves, peace goes with him, a variation of "Apres moi le deluge", but he has not been very successful. Everyone has seen through the plan, and even Saudi sympathisers are annoyed that the peace of the countryside has been so wantonly destroyed. Town-dwellers, with

67 On the coast in the western part of the Sabkhah Matti about 70 Kilometres west of Jebel Dhanna. They were getting ready to drill a well about 35 kilometres south of the coast. The preparation was undertaken secretly, in so far as it was possible to keep anything secret! Secrecy was necessary because the Arbitration Agreement was still being negotiated and secrecy was maintained until the agreement was announced in Parliament in London.

68 The geologist still believed that the best prospect for finding oil in Abu Dhabi territory was in the west. The Company was also keen to support Abu Dhabi's territorial rights in the west of Abu Dhabi in land claimed by Saudi Arabia.

69 With enormous enthusiasm.

their natural antipathy towards the Bedouin, very much object to this lawlessness, and a defeat of Tuwairish will tell heavily against Turki and the Saudis.

TRUCIAL COAST DIARY FOR PERIOD ENDING 30 SEPTEMBER 1954

GENERAL:

The Muscat post at Aswad[70] has been collecting customs from all travellers including Trucial Coast subjects on their way to Fujairah, Khor Fakkan and Kalba. This has led to protests, particularly from Rulers, such as Fujairah who are likely to find their progresses impeded by the post.[71] It is understood that the Agency have raised the matter with the Government of Muscat.

The pearlers have begun to return and some good hauls are reported. Two boats from Jazeerat Za'ab[72] are reported to have sold their catches for a total Rs. 110,000.

Messrs. H.M. Thomson and K.M. Jackson[73] paid a visit to the Trucial Coast so that Mr. Thompson could meet the Rulers and Mr. Jackson say goodbye. During an energetic three days from the 19th they met all the Rulers, except for Fujairah and many notables.

POLITICAL AGENCY:

The Agency and in particular the Political Agent,[74] is very popular at present. All Rulers without exception praise the Political Agent, and the value of the Trucial Oman Levies as a peace-making force is appreciated. The water well rig has been at work but encountered trouble on the first well which was abandoned at 40 feet. Grey, moving sand was encountered and the hole filled in as fast as it was holed out until there was a danger of the collapse of the top layer of sand.

TRUCIAL OMAN LEVIES:

Lieutenant Colonel Martin, The commanding officer, is in the process of handing over the command of Trucial Oman Levies to his second in command,

---

70 The only motorable route between Dubai/Sharjah and Fujairah/Kalba over the mountains was though the Wadi Qor. This track passed from Ra's al-Khaimah into Sultanate of Oman territory and then back into Sharjah territory. The Omani police post was at Aswad in the Wadi.

71 We have seen earlier in these diaries that the route from Sharjah to Fujairah, the Wadi Ghor (Qor), passed through territory of the Sultanate of Oman, and the Ruler of Fujairah had to take that route on his way home from Sharjah.

72 Ra's al-Khaimah.

73 Both PD(TC) employees.

74 C.M. Pirie-Gordon.

Major Johnston. Colonel Martin expects to leave for the United Kingdom to rejoin his regiment about the middle of November. It is not known whether Major Johnston will be permanently appointed as Commanding Officer of the Trucial Oman Levies.

ROYAL AIR FORCE:

The Squadron of Royal Air Force regiment left for Aden on the 25th.

ABU DHABI:

The Ruler returned from Buraimi on the 15th. His mother had recovered from her illness sometime before. His visit caused a considerable stir[75] but has not led to any particular incidents. He said he enjoyed the trip.

Two directors of the Abu Dhabi Development Company (Chandler Bros., Colewill and How) visited Abu Dhabi. They waited some days for Shakhbut to return but when he did not, they came back to Dubai. On the way in they had an accident and one of the directors was injured superficially. Nothing daunted they made another visit after the Ruler's return from Buraimi. They seem to have settled matters and repaired any damage done by Lippitt, but are no longer so anxious to rush into operation. At present they are seeking a new Representative in Abu Dhabi. An article in their Agreement whereby they were required to operate the Abu Dhabi customs has been cancelled by mutual consent. The Ruler denies that such had ever been his intention; this in spite of the article written into the agreement.

Khansahib Hussain again visited Abu Dhabi and, although he has not signed a new agreement with the Ruler, is confident that he will continue to operate in Abu Dhabi.

Mr. Hillyard of D'Arcy Exploration arrived about the middle of the month and has installed himself with his family in the house in Abu Dhabi. D'Arcy have sought assistance from the Company[76] under an arrangement made in London.

Mohamed Bu Hulaiba of the Al Bu Shaar[77] visited the Representative in Dubai on the 30th. He had come from Liwa and stayed two days with Shakhbut before travelling to Dubai. He reported that all was quiet in the Liwa but said that the dates had suffered badly from the ravages of locusts.

Shaikh Said bin Shakhbut visited Tarif and stayed for ten days. Everyone in camp including the Ruler's Representative was vexed, but Shaikh Said behaved himself. It was rumoured that Said had been exiled from Abu Dhabi by his father, but this is apparently untrue. Another tale has it that Shakhbut now employs Said as an

75 Seen by some (not Sheikh Shakhbut) as an infraction of the Standstill Agreement.

76 The Company. PD(TC).

77 Manasir tribe.

"intelligence agent", but there is nothing to support this except the fact that the Ruler is certainly very interested in the well in Tarif.[78]

DUBAI:

Shaikh Said bin Maktum left for Bahrain on the 19th and stayed until the 24th. He saw Dr. Snow who examined his eyes and pronounced that an operation (presumably cataract) can be performed in six months.

Shaikh Rashid has done a good deal of travelling and it is difficult to know at any one time whether he is at home or at Ras al Khaima. Because of his operation he has been forbidden to ride in a Land Rover or any other rough riding vehicle, so he goes about in a saloon or pick up.

Shaikhs Rashid, Juma and Khalifa[79] were entertained to dinner in Dubai house on the 19th.

Dr. McCauley returned on 1st September and is very busy.

SHARJAH:

The Ruler returned from his holiday in Lebanon and Egypt on 2nd October. He was met by about 150 of his loyal subjects, most of whom kissed him once, if not twice. He was still smiling after it all and shook hands with the Representative and smiled manly.

It is reported that a party of travellers from Muscat stopped at a well (probably Tawi Sinh) and found a boy drawing water. They demanded the use of his leather bucket which he refused at once. The travellers grabbed the bucket and soundly boxed the boy's ears. He rushed off to his people, who were Bani Kitab, and in the resulting fracas one of each side was killed. Nothing much has come of the incident although the travellers appealed to Shaikh Rashid bin Said.

A Bahraini launch with 45 passengers aboard had engine trouble close to Sir Bu Nair[80] and the nakhuda put his charges ashore on the island and proceeded to Abu Dhabi under sail promising that he would either repair his launch and return or send a rescue vessel. He neglected to do either and the castaways remained marooned and in great distress until they were able to hail a passing launch. One person died. One feels that the passengers were a very gullible lot, however much they have suffered.

Khaled bin Sultan[81] has gone on a visit to Bahrain and hopes that he will never return. So do many others.

---

78 Well Murban No. 1.

79 Sheikhs Rashid and Khalifa are sons of the Ruler, Sheikh Saeed, while Sheikh Juma is a brother of the Ruler.

80 Sharjah island in middle of Gulf.

81 Brother of the Ruler.

Shaikh Ahmad bin Muhammad Ali Harthi returned by company plane from Salala.[82] He had a cold and stayed with the Acting Ruler for a few days till he was fit to travel.

AJMAN:

Shaikh Rashid is on the friendliest terms with his brother-in-law of Fujairah. Shaikh Mohammed bin Hamid as Sharqi stayed at Ajman after his return from the Hajj. Shaikh Ali bin Rashid[83] called and offered to hire his launch to the Company. It is possible Khansahib can make use of the vessel.

RAS AL KHAIMAH:

The Ruler spends a lot of time travelling around his territory and improving his influence. His eldest son Khaled has gone to Kuwait to continue his education.

FUJAIRAH:

As already stated the Ruler stayed with Shaikh Rashid of Ajman. Later they travelled together to Fujairah. After Rashid's return Shaikh Mohamed took his wife to the hospital in Muscat.

COMPANY OPERATIONS:

During the month Seismic and Gravity operations got underway again.

At Murban No. 1 abandonment operations are now in hand.

Watt
Representative

82 Dhofar, Sultanate of Oman. The Sultan's favourite retreat where he spent most of his time.

83 Eldest son of Ruler.

TRUCIAL COAST DIARY FOR PERIOD ENDING 31 OCTOBER 1954

GENERAL:

Events in Ibri and in the Wadi Jizzi have been followed with great interest on the Trucial Coast.[84] The arrival of refugees from Ibri on the 16th October spread the news, but even before then it was known that the Imam's forces were on the move. The fall of Ibri[85] and Obeid bin to Jumma's attack on the Abdulla bin Salem's post at Ra'abi shortly after caused great concern, particularly among the Al Bu Falah, but the reversal of fortunes which followed so soon after has raised them from depressed gloom to joy.[86]

The unheralded arrival of a Saudi Dodge in Hamasa spawned a wild crop of rumours. For example it was reported that two vehicles have been seen at Jebel Hafit loaded with arms, ammunition and sackfulls of money, destined for Ibri and Suleiman bin Himyar. The Saudis claimed to have brought only pay for their men in Baraimi, and they travelled as directly and as quickly as possible between Salwa[87] and Buraimi. However the vehicle did undoubtedly enter undisputed Abu Dhabi territory and it is understood that the Resident is to protest at this contravention of the Arbitration Agreement.

The General Manager companied by Mrs. and Miss Heseldin paid farewell visits to the Rulers of Sharjah, Dubai and Abu Dhabi on the 19th and 20th. On the 19th the British Community in Dubai and Sharjah was entertained to a buffet supper party.

POLITICAL AGENCY:

The Political Resident made his annual tour of the Trucial States from the 11th to the 16th October but only visited Abu Dhabi, Dubai and Sharjah and called upon the respective Rulers. It is understood that the Political Resident will shortly make another tour to include Ajman, Umm al Quwain, Ras al Khaima and Fujairah and he plans to camp at Umm al Quwain and Khor Fakhan.

The Agency's water well rig moved to a new site and has drilled ahead to 245 feet. Progress is disappointedly slow due to the unexpected presence of white clay. Colonel Merilees the water diviner, arrived during the month and is superintendenting

---

84 The Imam controlling most of the interior of Oman, Imam Mohamed Abdulla Khalili died on 3 May 1954. He was succeeded by Imam Ghalib Al Hinai. Imam Ghalib sought to extend his influence throughout Oman. The tribes in Ibri were not parties to the Sib agreement (secret treaty) which concerned the spheres of influence of the Imam and the Sultan.

85 Fall to the forces of the Imam.

86 First the defeat of Obaid bin Juma by Abdullah bin Salem. Then the quick removal of the Imam's forces from Ibri on 27th October. HENDERSON, E. (1988). p. 138ff.

87 Saudi Arabia, near the Abu Dhabi border.

operations. He is confident of success and became most excited when the bit reached a strata of water-worn gravel, but this lasted for only 3 inches and was dry.

A new assistant Political Agent, the Hon I.T.M. Lucas with his wife, is expected at the Agency. He will relieve Mr. Walker who is then to devote himself to boundary settlement problems. Since there is no other accommodation the new assistant Political Agent and his wife will stay with the Political Agent.

TRUCIAL OMAN LEVIES:

The Levies took part in operations in the Wadi Jizzi[88] and greatly contributed to their successful outcome. In the west, the squadron stationed at Tarif is endeavoring to prevent any more Saudi vehicles passing undetected, but they are very thin on the ground and would be fortunate to intercept a single vehicle travelling fast.

ROYAL AIR FORCE:

On the 16th an RAF Anson[89] on a flight from Sharjah to Bahrain force-landed near Doha due to engine trouble. A few days later an Anson taking part in night flying exercises struck an obstruction while taxying and suffered considerable damage.

ABU DHABI:

Since the 16th a state of considerable anxiety has prevailed in Abu Dhabi. It was reported to the Ruler that Diab bin Saqr bin Sultan[90] and Hamdan bin Hamdan bin Sultan[91] were preparing a Coup d'etat and that Diab had received Rs. 133,000/- from Saudi Arabia. Diab and Hamdan are the sons of previous Rulers, the uncles of Shakhbut, who were assassinated, and although they have long been in exile Shakhbut fears that they have become ambitious.

The reports are discounted in Dubai and Sharjah, both by the Rulers and the general public, but in Abu Dhabi extra-ordinary precautions have been taken. Extra men under the command of Sultan bin Shakhbut are posted at the Mugta,[92] and all who approach are halted by a sentry some four hundred yards from the Guard Tower. This man checks the approaching vehicle and runs back to Sultan to obtain permission for the travelers to proceed. Sentries have also been posted along the beaches and launches are watched. Although the Ruler apologized to the Representative for the inconvenience caused, the checks were carefully carried out both entering and leaving Abu Dhabi.

---

88 Concerning Abdullah bin Salem, above.

89 There is also an Anson aircraft in the Sharjah Mahatta museum.

90 Not 'bin Sultan'. The writer is incorrect. Should be 'bin Zayed'.

91 Not 'bin Sultan'. 'bin Zayed'.

92 The crossing to Abu Dhabi island.

The Ruler was very pleased to receive a visit from the General Manager. Mr. Heseldin with Mrs. Heseldin and his daughter called on the Ruler in his palace and were entertained to lunch. Later the Ruler and his brothers Haza and Khaled were entertained aboard the Ghazal.

On the 23rd Shaikh Haza camped near Jebel Ali and later called on the Political Agent. They discussed various matters, most particularly the situation in Oman. Haza at first expressed his grave concern, but the situation improved during the visit and he left in a much happier frame of mind.

On the 17th a Saudi Dodge travelled through Abu Dhabi territory and arrived in Buraimi the following day. At first the vehicle stopped in Hamasa but later reported to Abdullah bin Naimie the officer in charge of the Saudi detachment.[93] From investigations made by the Representative it appears that the vehicle drove along the coast road from Aglat al Nakhla to Jabal Baraka[94] (where it was seen by Company drivers) and then turned south east to Agaila and on through Argaiyib, Qume Gharab and slightly north of Bu Hasa. The vehicle apparently entered undisputed territory 7 miles south west of Mirfa, passed between the Biban and a small unnamed hill to the north and continued past Qashash, crossing the road just north of the rig at Murban.[95] The vehicle's tracks rejoined the main road east of Tarif having passed South of Barq Al Jo. Thereafter it travelled along recognised tracks to Buraimi. The vehicle returned by the same route a week later.

The Saudi guide was a certain Nasir bin Majid of the Manasir (Al bu Rahma). It is said that he lived with Turki in Hamasa for many months.

The Levies have since established posts around Tarif so that vehicles should not again be able to sneak past unobserved, but even so there are many routes to the south which cannot be covered since they are in disputed territory. Guards and personnel at the Company's locations at El Feidh, Gezira and with Seismic have been requested to report any movements which they may observe.

In Buraimi Zaid fell sick towards the end of the month. He was suffering from a boil which turned septic. Fortunately Dr. McCaully was visiting Buraimi at the time and was able to deal with the situation. Dr. McCaully stayed in Buraimi for seven days and, as well as Zaid, treated many patients.

DUBAI:

The General Manager called on Shaikh Rashid. Shaikh Rashid and Shaikh Said were ill during the month. Rashid suffered from food poisoning for a day or two but

93 In Hamasa.

94 Near where the 'secret' preparations were being made to drill a well further south.

95 Murban well No. 1.

quickly recovered. Said had an attack of malaria following a hunting trip and for one day he was very ill. However, he recovered quickly and a week later set off on another hunt.

Shaikh Mubarak bin Beshait who was a Qadi in Hamasa during Turki bin Ataishan's stay has returned to Hamasa. He had been living in Dubai since Turki's departure.

A Lebanese optician visited Dubai and brought new glasses for Shaikh Said. It appears that this optician examined Said's eyes during his visit to Bahrain in September.

SHARJAH:

The General Manager called upon Shaikh Saqr and lunched with him.

Shaikh Saqr announced the birth of a daughter in Kalba. It was at first announced that a son had been born, but this was untrue and Saqr was consequently disappointed.

After his return Saqr dismissed his uncle Rahamma who had been Representative during his absence. The cause of the trouble seems to have been domestic, Rahamma and Saqr's wife in Sharjah quarrelled and Saqr supported his wife. Although the Political Agent expressed his disapproval there has been no reconciliation and Rahamma is still in disgrace. It is expected that he will leave Sharjah.

AJMAN:

Shaikh Rashid has been in his usual robust health and towards the end of the month left Ajman for a visit to his gardens in Manama.[96]

RAS AL KHAIMA:

The Ruler has had difficulty with Ali bin Saif of the Khawatir. He wished to stop the annual payment of Rs. 11,000 and appealed to the Agency for aid. Since the agreement whereby the payment is made, is registered at the Agency, the Political Agent was bound to refuse Saqr's request for Levies to intimidate Ali Saif.

MUSCAT AND OMAN:

On the 14th Shaikh Sultan bin Said al Husini arrived by car from Muscat and stayed as a guest of the Company in Dubai. Two days later a party of the Ibri Shaikhs, Yakubis, Duru and Kalbanis, arrived as refugees from Ibri and on the following day most of these left on Company charter for Duqm.[97] Others left for the Dhahira by car and three followers remained behind. These three returned home overland after the recapture of Ibri.

96 Sheikh Rashid's inland oasis in the mountain foreland.

97 On the coast more than 350 kilometres south of Muscat. After failing to obtain access to the interior of Oman through Buraimi or the Wadi Jizzi, the Company chose Duqm as their starting point for expeditions into the interior, in particular to the Fahud structure where they wished to drill an exploration well.

A party of Wahiba and Junaibi Shaikhs including Hamad bin Yasir al Majaali and Humud bin Said bin Rashid Al Jaafi arrived in Dubai and offered their assistance. Since there was no immediate need for their presence in Duqm they stayed for some time as guests of the Company and later left for the interior. The swift capture and even more sudden re-capture of Ibri has led many people to reconsider their position and the Sultan appears to have gained much support.

On the 20th Obaid bin Juma with the strongest forces he could muster attacked Abdulla bin Salem al Kaabi in the Wadi Jizzi. Obaid himself came to witness the expected victory but, like the ancient Persian, he saw his men driven off, having lost three killed and others wounded. Abdulla followed up this success and with assistance from Shaikh Sakhr and the forces of Sohar cleared the Wadi Jizzi. Sometime later Obaid was driven from Khalwa,[98] this time with the assistance of the Trucial Oman Levies and finally took refuge in the neutral zone in Buraimi. It appears that at Khatwa the officer in charge of the Levy Force fired a few rounds of 2 inch mortar high explosive. Although this was done without the authority of the Politicals it won the day in a matter of minutes.

It is reported that Shaikh Saqr bin Sultan al Naimie did not follow his usual custom of raising the Saudi flag on Friday, but on the following day raised the Sultan's flag instead. Apparently he has decided to swim with the current.

COMPANY OPERATIONS:

The build-up of the new location (named Gezira) in the Sabkhat Matti continues. Considering the remoteness of the location progress is swift and most buildings are well advanced. The erection of the derrick has begun. Seismic operations continue some 13 miles to the south of Gezira whilst the Gravity Survey with the assistance of helicopters to the south of Tarif continues with increasing speed.

The Sharjah base was shut down early in the month and its remaining functions, such as Local Purchase and Aviation, were transferred to Dubai Office.

Watt
Representative

98 He means Khatwa, a short distance north of the western entrance to the Wadi Jizzi.

TRUCIAL COAST DIARY FOR PERIOD ENDING 30 NOVEMBER 1954

ABU DHABI:

Shaikh Zaid has recovered completely from his recent illness and visited Ibri[99] during the month where he stayed nearly a week.

Shaikh Shakhbut bin Sultan turned down verbally an offer made to him in writing during the month of a loan[100] of Rs. 500,000 on the grounds that the sum was not sufficient. The Ruler stated a loan of Rs. 2 million would be acceptable.

Tension still continues in Abu Dhabi over the possibility of a Coup D'etat. Buildings are being put up on the mainland end of the Muqta. It is believed that Diab bin Saqr[101] has offered to go away permanently to Bombay, if Shaikh Shakhbut will pay his fare and no doubt give him an allowance to live there but it would seem that the Ruler is not agreeable to doing this as Diab bin Saqr is still in Dubai.

The Political Agent presented 60 rifles to Shaikh Shakhbut. The Ruler had hoped to receive 200 rifles which might have given him the chance of building up his own fighting force similar to that of the Trucial Oman Levies.

During the visit of the Representative to Abu Dhabi on 30th November the Ruler expressed great concern at the slowness with which the Company were arranging to pay him customs duties on items imported into Abu Dhabi territory by the Company.

During the early part of the month Shaikh Shakhbut posted Diab bin Said as Assistant Head Guard to Tarif without first discussing the matter with the Representative. The Area Superintendent, Tarif, reported to the Representative towards the end of the month that Diab bin Said was causing him great concern and he requested to have him removed. On being approached the Ruler agreed to remove this man from the Company area. It is believed that Diab bin Said who was transferred from Abu Dhabi to Tarif, had been causing the Ruler a great deal of trouble, so, much for the Company's misfortune he was posted to Tarif.

Fresh rumours which were circulating on the movement of Saudi trucks in the vicinity of Muqatara proved to be false. Even so there appears little doubt that everyone is on edge and wonders what will happen next.

99 In the Sultanate of Oman. The Sultan's forces re-entered Ibri without blood-shed after the garrison surrendered on 27th October.

100 Loan from the Company PD(TC).

101 Sheikh Diab bin Saqr bin Zayed.

DUBAI:

Shaikh Said bin Maktum's daughter Mousa flew to Bahrain for medical attention.

Shaikh Rashid bin Said spent much time during the month travelling to and from his gardens in Ras al Khaima.

The Indian Bharat line is now operating to Dubai under the agency of Tulsidas. On the 17th one of their ships ran aground much to the ill-concealed delight of Messrs Gray Mackenzie, & Co.

Whilst moving towards her anchorage during the hours of darkness on 28th one of the B.I. ships m.v. Dwarka collided with a dhow which was proceeding from Bahrain to India via Muscat. All passengers who were mainly Dhofaris going back to their homes lost not only their kit but their savings. The Captain, First Officer and another officer were on the bridge at the time of the collision and stated that the Dhow had no lights whatsoever on board. The crew and all 70 passengers of the Dhow stated they had navigation lights showing.

At the end of the month the Agency water-well drillers had reached 560 feet without finding water. It is believed they will continue to drill to just over 600 feet.

RAS AL KHAIMA:

It is rumoured that on completion of the drilling of the present water-well in Dubai the rig will be moved to Ras al Khaima.

SHARJAH:

The Ruler visited the Political Resident at Kalba during the latter's stay there.

During the month arrangements were made verbally between the Political Agent and the Ruler for the handing over ceremony of the new school building which the Agency were presenting to the Ruler. Unfortunately the Ruler's official invitation to the Political Agent for the ceremony to take place on the 18th did not reach him until a few hours before the ceremony. The Political Agent regretted he was unable to be present at such short notice, and the ceremony was postponed.

Lt. Col. Martin, Commanding Officer of the Levies, accompanied by his wife and family left Sharjah on posting to his regiment. His second-in-command Major E.F. Johnston, M.B.E., M.C., took over command and it was learned later in the month that his appointment as Commanding Officer has been confirmed.

Shaikh Saif bin Abdul Rehman has taken his brother's place as the Ruler's Representative.

AJMAN:

Shaikh Rashid bin Humaid entertained the Political Resident and Mr. C. Pirie-Gordon to lunch at Manama during their visit to Ajman. The Political Resident presented Shaikh Rashid with a rifle and 2,000 rounds of ammunition.

POLITICAL AGENCY:

The Political Resident Mr. B.A. Burroughs paid a second visit to the Trucial Coast within a month and accompanied by the Political Agent visited Kalba, Fujaira, Ras al Khaima, Umm al Quwain, and Ajman.

GENERAL:

Mr. S.K. Watt left Dubai on posting to Ibri on 20th November. Mr. R.A.T. Codrai who was accompanied by his wife returned to Dubai from home leave on 5th November, left on 24th November on posting to Umm Said. Mr. R.L. Reed, accompanied by his wife, arrived Dubai on 23rd on posting as Company Representative.

The greater part of the Trucial Coast had a heavy rain storm which started on 13th and lasted for three days, during which hail-stones fell and did a certain amount of damage to every building. Sharjah airstrip was unserviceable for over a week. Owing to the unserviceability of the Sharjah airfield during that period the Managing Director[102] who was on a visit to the Persian Gulf was unable to visit Sharjah.

Hamad bin Nasir, a Shaikh of Wahibi[103] tribe accompanied by 23 followers arrived in Dubai and was accommodated in Company accommodation. Hamad bin Nasir had wished to visit Saudi Arabia but had been turned back on the grounds that his tribe has now joined the Sultan of Muscat. On his way back he visited Qatar where he received help to proceed on to Dubai. At Dubai the Company assisted him and his party to proceed to Muscat.

Great interest has been shown here over the possibilities of a general strike starting in Bahrain.

The director Mr. Thomas of the Golden Valley Co., arrived in Sharjah from London on 1st December by air on his way to visit the Company location at. Abu Musa.

Reed
Representative

102 Managing Director of IPC and associated companies.

103 From the central part of the Sultanate of Oman.

TRUCIAL COAST DIARY FOR PERIOD ENDING 31 DECEMBER 1954

During the month visits were paid by the Representative to the Rulers of Ras al Khaima, Fujairah, Umm al Quwain, Abu Dhabi, Sharjah and Dubai.

ABU DHABI:

The building of accommodation for the guards at the Muqta[104] is still going on but the work is very slow and little progress was noted between the Representative's visit in November and the one he made this month.

Khansahib Hussain reported that on a recent visit to Abu Dhabi he found on arriving at the Muqta that Shaikh Sultan bin Shakhbut who is the i/c of the post was not there and although he is a well-known personality in the Abu Dhabi territory he was not allowed to pass until Shaikh Sultan returned to the post some four hours later. The same thing happened to him again when he arrived at the Muqta on his way back to Sharjah.

It was learned during the month that Shakhbut will be paid the sum of £100,000[105] by D'Arcy Exploration during the month of March 1955. This fact may account for the independent attitude shown by the Ruler in turning down our offer of an interest free loan of Rs. 500,000 on the grounds that the sum was not large enough.

The Area Superintendent, Trucial Coast, has confirmed that Diab bin Said, the Assistant Head Guard, who was at Tarif and was causing the Company considerable trouble has now been taken away from the Company location by the Ruler.

Mr Hillyard advises that the seismic party are covering an average of 50 knots per day and on one occasion completed a survey of 65 knots [in one day].

DUBAI:

The Agency water-well drillers drilled to 640 feet without success. Drilling was then stopped and the well was closed.

Shaikh Rashid bin Said left Dubai on 28th for a hunting trip in southern Persia and it is expected he will return about 20th January 1955.

The seventy survivors from the Dhow which sank after colliding with m.s. Dwarka left Dubai on another B.I.[106] ship on 5th for Muscat.

RAS AL KHAIMA:

The Agency water-well drillers left Dubai during the middle of the month for Ras al Khaima, where they hope to have more success than they had in Dubai.

---

104 The crossing from the mainland to Abu Dhabi island.

105 1.33 Million Rupees.

106 Both British Indian Steamship Navigation Company boats.

SHARJAH:

Shaikh Saqr bin Sultan spent much time during the month out hunting and visiting his gardens at Kalba, Khor Fakkan and Dhaid.

It is believed that Shaikh Khaled bin Sultan, the Ruler's brother who has been on an extended visit to Saudi Arabia has now decided to take up residence in Dhahran. Furthermore it is stated that King Ibn Saud has publicly announced that besides the Rials 6000/- per year which the Saudi Arabian government were paying to Shaikh Khaled, a further sum of Rials 1000/- per month would now be paid to him. It can be well understood that the Ruler is extremely annoyed at his brother's decision.

It was reported during the month that trouble had arisen between the Ruler of Sharjah and the Sultan of Muscat as to who was the "Lord and Master" of a small village named Madhha'[107] situated near Kelba. Until the Political Agent gives a decision in this matter the villagers have been evacuated. No doubt in due course they will creep back again.

FUJAIRAH:

The Representative left Dubai on 16th on a two day visit to Kalba, Fujairah and Khor Fakhan. The night was spent at Fujairah.

Shaikh Mohammed bin Hamad Al Sharqi, the Ruler of Fujairah repeated his request previously made to Mr. Watt[108] for the gift of some explosives for the purpose of enlarging one of his water wells. Mr. Watt agreed at the time for this issue to be made, but the Political Agent has stated that this issue can only be made when he is satisfied that Shaikh Mohammed has found a suitable and reliable person to handle the dynamite.

The Ruler of Fujairah also mentioned that he was thinking of asking the Company for an advance on his third year's dues, but later in the month when he was in Dubai on the visit he stated that he did not wish to press this request.

POLITICAL AGENCY:

Admiral Morris, C in C, East Indies on board the flagship H.M.S. Newfoundland arrived at Dubai on the 2nd on a four day official visit. H.M.S. Newfoundland was escorted by H.M.S. Flamingo and H.M.S. Loch Insh.

On Saturday 4th the C.in C. invited all the Rulers of the Trucial States on board the ship for exercise "shop window" which lasted three hours during which the H.M.S. Newfoundland attacked and fired on H.M.S. Lock Insh and also defended herself against a 'mock' bombing attack from three R.A.F. aircraft.

---

107 This is a small Omani enclave extending inland about 15 kilometres from near the coast; south west of Khor Fakkan and surrounded by Sharjah territory.

108 PD(TC) representative prior to Reed, the current author of this diary.

When the Representative visited a number of Rulers later in the month, he learned that all were considerably impressed by the experience through which they had been. The Ruler of Abu Dhabi took three quarters of an hour in giving a glowing account of all that happened.

During the month permission was granted to the Saudi Arabian Government for a Saudi Arabian aircraft to land at the Cahill[109] for the purpose of changing the Guard at Buraimi. The Political Agent and the Commanding Officer of the Trucial Oman Levies visited Cahill especially to meet the aircraft and to ensure no liberties were taken. The aircraft did not land at Cahill but Buraimi, the American pilot stated on landing that his instructions were to land there, this caused much annoyance to those who were waiting for the arrival at Cahill and much consternation to those in Buraimi who were not expecting it.

The Political Agent visited the Political Resident on the 6th. It is believed that the main object of the visit was to discuss and plan the future water drilling program. The rig is now at Ras al Khaima and if the drillers have no success there a final effort will be made to find sweet water in Abu Dhabi.

During the month there was great excitement in the Agency, a slave dealer was caught with the goods on him – metaphorically speaking. He and his party consisting of one Arab girl and four Baluchi girls were located at the foot of the hills near Ras al Khaima by Major Smith of Trucial Oman Levies, who was accompanied by an enthusiastic Shaikh Saqr bin Sultan.[110]

The dealer was tried on 28th before Judge W.P.R. Maudsley from Bahrain, and having pleaded guilty was sentenced to four year's imprisonment.

At the Political Agent's request the Rulers of the Trucial States attended a conference at the Agency on 26th.

GENERAL:

During the early part of the month there were rumours that 300 Saudi Arabians had succeeded in reaching Hamasa, but there was no foundation in this rumour.

Considerable interest to still being taken by many people on the Trucial Coast with regard to the political situation in Bahrain.

Abdulla bin Salim, Amir of Mahadha[111] and [the] Wali of Sohar, whilst travelling through Wadi Jizzi were fired on by a party of bandits. Abdulla bin Salim's party

---

109 In territory of the Sultanate of Oman, north of Buraimi and south west of Mahadhah.

110 Sharjah ruler. Is the writer correct? Perhaps it was Sheikh Saqr bin Mohamed as it appears that the event took place in Ra's al-Khaimah territory.

111 Sheikh Abdullah bin Salim appears earlier in these diaries. He ejected Sheikh Odaid bin Juma from Mahadha in 1953. Sheikh Abdullah's allegiance to Saudi Arabia was short-lived, just briefly a convenience. KELLY, J. (1964), p. 232.

retaliated and injured two. The rest fled. Instead of continuing their journey to Batinah coast Abdulla bin Salim and Wali of Sohar decided to return the way they had come and travel via Wadi Ghor and eventually arrived at their destination.

During the latter part of the month there was a strong rumour that the Sultan of Muscat was sending troops up to the Buraimi area, but there has been no confirmation of this move and it may have originated from the fact that Sultan of Muscat dispatched extra patrols to Wadi Jizzi after the incident mentioned in the paragraph above.

Reed
Representative.

1955

TRUCIAL COAST DIARY FOR PERIOD ENDING 28 FEBRUARY 1955

ABU DHABI:

The concession payment for 1955 which was due in the middle of January was not paid until 29th January. The Ruler insisted that the payment was settled in cash, but owing to the heavy rains during the second week of that month, it was not possible for the Representative to be certain of getting through by road[1] until 29th January. Arrangements had been made for the payment to be made on 22nd but they were cancelled at the last moment owing to the condition of the road. The Trucial Oman Levies kindly supplied an escort for the journey. It was learned during the last week of February that it was the Ruler's wish that D'Arcy pay by cheque their concession payment due on 10th March of £70,000 approximately plus £30,000[2] which is the salaries due to the Rulers representatives.

During the Representative's visit on 29th January the old and outstanding problem of the village which exists very close to our daily paid lines at Tarif was discussed. Efforts have been made on numerous occasions in the past to get the Ruler's authority for the village to be moved without success. It was therefore with considerable surprise that the Representative learned on his visit to Tarif on 6th February that the Ruler had written to his representative to get the village moved to an area at least a mile away from the Company accommodation.

The death occurred in an accident on 13th January of Ali bin Mohamed (an Abu Dhabi subject).

On receiving the sad news, the Representative immediately advised the Political Agent by letter and also wrote informing the Ruler and expressing the Company's

1 The track, largely across the sabkhah between Dubai and Abu Dhabi. There was no road!

2 A total of Rs. 1.33 million.

regret. The Ruler in his reply thanked the Company for its expression of sympathy, but insisted that the driver, (a Jordanian Christian) of the vehicle concerned in the accident be tried by him. This matter was referred to the Political Agent who has confirmed that the Ruler is not entitled to try a case in which the accused is a foreigner. The Political Agent is still deciding whether he should try the case or not.

The Representative visited the Ruler on 21st February and endeavoured to pay to the relatives through the Ruler the sum of Rs. 2500/- as compensation to the relatives of Ali bin Mohd but the Ruler refused to accept it until Salim Yousef Ammary had been tried. It is difficult to know exactly why the Ruler is pressing so persistently for a court case, but the most likely reason is his hope that the court will insist on the Company paying the relatives a larger sum of money,[3] in which case the Ruler and/or his brothers will get a larger percentage for passing the money on to the relatives. There appears to be little doubt that on the last occasion that the sum of Rs. 2500/- was paid by the Company as compensation to relatives through the Ruler, the relatives received only Rs. 1200/-, the remainder was divided between the Ruler and his two brothers, Shaikh Haza and Shaikh Khalid.

LAUNCHES:

It is well known that Shaikh Shakhbut pays his launch crew as little as possible. The result of this economy is that the Company usually have considerable trouble with Abu Dhabi launches. During the latter half of January it was learned that the crews of three launches out of six owned by the Ruler had left their ships and come to Dubai for work.

During the Representative's visit on the 22nd February the Ruler eventually agreed that all future payments whether concession payments, payments for hire of launch or for guards etc could be paid by cheque and not as before in cash.

On this visit the Ruler was advised that the Company intended to start as early as possible to repair the causeway. It is estimated that this work will cost Rs. 40,000 of which the company will pay two thirds and D'Arcy has agreed to pay one third. The Ruler was delighted with the news.

Sheikh Sultan bin Shakhbut, the Ruler's second son was married at the end of February.

ABU DHABI MARINE AREAS LIMITED:

At the request of Abu Dhabi Marine Areas Ltd. Representative, Gulf Aviation have arranged a Dove schedule to call in at Abu Dhabi on the second Wednesday on its way to Sharjah and again on the Thursday on its way back to Bahrein. The Representative felt that this would encourage the local merchants to travel on the

3 We would call this tax levied by Government.

aircraft, but Abu Dhabi is still a small village and money is scarce, and it is felt that the scheme is a little premature.

It was hoped during the early part of February that the seismic party on the Sonic would complete its work (including work for the PDTC) by 28th February. Unfortunately bad weather and the very shallow water in which the Sonic had to work towards the end caused a number of hold-ups, and it is improbable that the work will be completed before the middle of March.

On 17th January Sonic called in at Abu Dhabi. The opportunity was taken to show the Ruler of Abu Dhabi over the ship, and trial runs were made whilst he and his relatives were on board.

Dr. Gaskell, one of the senior BP Geophysicists visited Abu Dhabi during the latter part of February. Arrangements were made by the Representative for him to visit Dukhan.[4]

DUBAI:

Soon after Shaikh Rashid bin Said left Dubai for Persia on his hunting trip, the guards at the watch towers at the entrance to Deira and Dubai took a more active part in the security of the towns. Shots were fired by the guards at any vehicle proceeding towards the towns which failed to stop at the towers for examination.

Rumour has it that while Shaikh Rashid was away, Shaikh Juma bin Maktum[5] felt there was a possibility of an attack on the towns from the Abu Dhabi sheikdom.

Shaikh Juma besides being very pro-Saudi is generally becoming a nuisance and causing the Politicals a head-ache.

Shaikh Rashid returned to Dubai on 4th February. The Representative called on him the same day and learned that the hunting trip although a very wet one owing to the heavy rains, was a great success and 900 lesser bustards were either shot or brought down by Falcons. The fact that Shaikh Rashid went for only 20 days and stayed over 40 is sufficient proof that a good hunting was had by all.

The Representative entertained the Ruler, Shaikh Said bin Maktum, Shaikh Rashid bin Said and numerous other relatives to a lunch on 12th February. The only important relative who was not able to attend was Shaikh Juma bin Maktum.

H.M.S. Flamingo visited Dubai with S.N.O.P.P.G.[6] on board between 13th and 15th January.

Mr. L Baker arrived in Dubai on 19th January to take over from Mr. C. Ross-Hyder as manager B.B.M.E. Mr Ross-Hyder left for Baghdad on the 8th February.

4 The IPC (QPC) base in Qatar.

5 Uncle of Sheikh Rashid and brother of Sheikh Said, the Ruler.

6 Senior Naval Officer Persian Gulf.

SHARJAH:

Shaikh Saqr bin Sultan sent Shaikh Mohammed bin Saqr[7] to Saudi Arabia during January in the hope that he could convince his brother Khaled bin Sultan who has taken up permanent residence there, how foolish he was and how much wiser he would be by returning to Sharjah. The Shaikh argued that the Saudis might give them nearly everything he wanted now, but later on Shaikh Khalid would not be so generously treated. Unfortunately Shaikh Mohammed returned without success.

It was confirmed during the early part of January that the slave trader who was captured, tried and sentenced to four years imprisonment had paid Rs. 30,000/-for his four young – and I trust at that price – attractive ladies. He has since admitted that he hoped to sell them for Rs. 50,000/-. It would seem that purchase tax is not only confined to the British Isles.

BARAMI:

On 8th February a Saudi Arabian aircraft which had had permission to land at Barami landed at Cahill[8] and did not go on to Burami. Next day the same aircraft flew in from Saudi Arabia again. This time was expected to land at Cahill, but it did not, it landed at Burami.

The Political Agent accompanied by the Assistant Political Agent and Mr. van Ollenbach, an agriculturalist from Bahrain visited Cahill during January.

POLITICAL AGENCY:

Mr. Walker, who is now working on the boundary question, spent most of the latter half of January and first half of February in the Fujaira, Kalba, Khor Fakhan area. He is now working in the Ras el Khaima area.

The Political Agent, after the first failure to find sweet water at Ras el Khaima, decided to allow the drillers to try again, which they did with great success some 6 miles inland at 47 feet. On test this well produced 2000 gallons per hour. Encouraged by this success the Political Agent authorised the drilling of a further well some 30 yards from the second one. This well has also been a success. It is now learned that on the recommendation of Mr. Ayre, a Middle East agricultural expert, who has recently visited the area, a further four wells will be drilled.

RAS EL KHAIMA:

Shaikh Saqr bin Mohammed was married to a third wife at Deira on 4th January. The third wife is a daughter[9] of Ahmed bin Gherrair who is quite a wealthy Dubai merchant.

---

7 The Ruler sent his uncle.

8 A few kilometres north of Buraimi.

9 Mother of Sheikh Saud bin Saqr, Ruler of Ra's al-Khaimah.

On 18th January Shaikh Saqr came specially from Ras el Khaima to visit his new wife at Deira, but on reaching the watch post at the entrance to Deira town he and his followers were instructed to leave their rifles behind until they returned. It appears that Shaikh Saqr was so infuriated at this demand that he immediately turned about and returned to Ras el Khaima. Shaikh Saqr made no further attempt to visit this wife until Shaikh Rashid returned from his hunting trip, when such restrictions to local Shaikhs were no longer carried out.

Shaikh Saqr bin Sultan of Sharjah had a similar experience when he and his followers wished to visit the cinema[10] but Shaikh Saqr bin Sultan is a much more determined individual than his cousin and he and his followers carried on with their rifles to the cinema.

The Representative visited Ras el Khaima on 26th February.

AJMAN:

The Representative visited Shaikh Rashid bin Humaid on 14th February.

UMM EL QUWAIN:

The Representative visited Shaikh Ahmad bin Rashid on 12th January and again on 5th February.

R.L. Reed
Representative.

10 Cinema in Deira.

TRUCIAL COAST DIARY FOR PERIOD ENDING 31 MARCH 1955

On the 1st March the General Manager Mr. P.R.A. Ensor accompanied by the Chief Local Representative Mr. H.M. Thomson, passed through Sharjah en route to Muscat from Dukhan. They lunched in Sharjah.

From the 16th to the 18th the General Manager Mr. P.R.A. Ensor, paid a visit to the Trucial States. Accompanied by Mr. J. Morgan and Sayid Ali Tajir[11] he landed at Abu Dhabi airfield on the 16th, was met by Mr. R.L. Reed and then paid a visit to Shaikh Shakhbut. Afterwards he called on Mr T.A.W. Hillyard, Representative of the Abu Dhabi Marine Areas ltd. After having lunch with Mr. and Mrs. Hillyard Mr. Ensor and party left for Dubai by car.

On the 17th the General Manager called on the Ruler of Dubai Shaikh Said bin Maktum and later left by road for Sharjah where he called on the Ruler Shaikh Saqr bin Sultan. The Political Agent Mr. Pirie- Gordon was visited on the return journey and then lunch was taken with Shaikh Rashid bin Said of Dubai. During the afternoon a visit was paid to the Dubai and Deira souks. In the evening the Company Representative gave a party for the General Manager to which all the British community were invited.

On the 18th in the morning the General Manager visited the Ruler of Ajman Shaikh Rashid bin Humaid and the Ruler of Umm al Quwain Shaikh Ahmed bin Rashid. He left in the afternoon by air for Dukhan.

Mr. J. de. R. Morgan took over the duties of Representative Dubai from Mr. R.L. Read on the 26th. Mr. and Mrs. Reed left Sharjah by air for Bahrain on the 26th.

ABU DHABI:

During the period of the 6th to the 12th the Representative of the Abu Dhabi Marine Areas Ltd. handed over to the Ruler quantities of petrol and kerosene in accordance with their agreement. The concession payment was made by cheque on the 10th. Shaikh Zaid bin Sultan of Buraimi made a rare visit to Abu Dhabi, a visit which coincided with the receipt of the concession payment.

Mr. E.F. Henderson arrived in Abu Dhabi territory on the 16th and was able to confer with Shaikh Zayed among others.

---

11 Ali Tajir was the man who collected information about the tribes, their occupations and loyalties to support the Abu Dhabi case in the border dispute with Saudi Arabia. This information gathering was overseen by Codrai and Henderson, but much of the credit should go to Ali. His cousin Mohamed Mahdi Tajir, also originally from Bahrain, came to Dubai in December 1955 to run the customs department. Years later in 1971 Mohamed Mahdi Tajir was the first UAE Ambassador in London. Ali Tajir passed away in 2006.

Mr Colwell, a partner in the firm Abu Dhabi Development Company Ltd., arrived in Abu Dhabi on the 23rd and is taking up residence there.

The Ruler was visited by Mr. Morgan and Mr. Read on the 24th.

The younger son of the Ruler, Shaikh Sultan, was married during the month to an Abu Dhabi subject.

RAS AL KHAIMA:

Shaikh Saqr bin Mohammed was visited by Mr. Reed and Mr. Morgan on the 21st.

POLITICAL AGENCY:

Mr. A.A. Ackland, the new Assistant Political Agent, arrived in Dubai on the 18th.

Morgan
Representative.

TRUCIAL COAST DIARY FOR PERIOD ENDING 30 APRIL 1955

The month of Ramadan commenced in Dubai and in all other states of the Trucial Coast on the 24th.

ABU DHABI:

A courtesy visit was paid by the undersigned to Shaikh Shakhbut on the 16th. In the early part of the month the Ruler had been absent for about a week on a hunting trip as a relaxation from the number of visitors he had been receiving.

Shaikh Zaid visited Abu Dhabi twice during the month, and the Ruler and his three brothers met together on both occasions. Later, Sheikh Zaid went on a brief visit to Muscat. Earlier he had been to Ibri in company with Salim bin Ham, and successfully arranged a truce for one year between the 'Awamir and the Duru', following a minor upset between the two tribes arising from a blood feud.

The Hon. Martin Buckmaster (formerly A.P.O., Sharjah) and Messrs. Henderson and Codrai were all engaged on duties in Abu Dhabi Territory, during part of the month, and a reconnaissance was made by Messrs. Codrai and Sheridan (a field geologist) to Liwa.

DUBAI:

Shaikh Said bin Maktum was absent in Qatar from the 3rd to the 10th for medical treatment for his eyes. On his departure he was presented with three saloon cars by Shaikh Ali bin Abdulla.[12]

SHARJAH:

Shaikh Saqr bin Sultan was absent in Saudi Arabia from the 6th to the 19th. He was visited by the undersigned on the morning of his departure.

Arrangements were made for Sheikh Mohammed bin Saqr[13] to travel by Company aircraft from Sharjah to Qatar on the 12th.

The undersigned attended the Sharjah school sports on the 22nd. The Rulers of Ras al Khaima and Ajman and also Shaikh Rashid bin Said[14] were present.

Three prizes of the total value of Rs. 116 were presented by the Company.

AJMAN:

A visit was paid by the undersigned to the palace on the 5th. Shaikh Ali bin Rashid[15] was present but Shaikh Rashid[16] was absent in Dubai.

UMM AL QUWAIN:

Shaikh Ahmed bin Rashid was visited by the undersigned on the 3rd and again on the 13th when he was given lunch.

POLITICAL AGENCY:

The Political Agent made several visits to Abu Dhabi during the month and was absent in Muscat over Easter, travelling there and back by road.

A party was given by the frigate H.M.S. Lock Insh to all members of the British community in Dubai and Sharjah on the 17th.

DUBAI OFFICE:

Mr. D. Christie, Construction Supervisor Gezira,[17] was in Dubai from the 6th to the 9th to inspect the M/R and D/R[18] mess building, a part of which had collapsed.

---

12 Ruler of Qatar.

13 The uncle of the Ruler and father of the present Ruler, Dr. Sheikh Sultan bin Mohamed.

14 Son of Dubai Ruler.

15 Ruler's eldest son.

16 Sheikh Rashid bin Humaid Ruler of Ajman.

17 The drilling location in western Abu Dhabi.

18 Monthly Rate, (clerks and artisans) and Daily Rate (workers).

Padre Jenkins[19] was in Dubai from the 12th to the 13th and gave Easter services at the R.A.F. station Sharjah and at the Agency.

Mr. H.M. Thompson arrived by car from Muscat on the 19th and left for Dukhan on the 20th.

Mr. E.F. Henderson arrived in Dubai on the 27th and was still in Dubai at the end of the month.

PETROL CONVOY – IBRI:

Arrangements were made with the Dubai contractor Ali Hajji Abdullah Awazi for a convoy of seven trucks to transport petrol from Dubai by the Ramlat Anaij route to Ibri. The convoy departed from Dubai on the evening of the 30th and travelling by night only because of Ramadan and by-passing the Burami zone they reached Ibri on the morning of 4th May. An escort was arranged with the Trucial Oman Levies who handed over the convoy to the Muscat Field Force. One truck broke down en route but all the petrol originally carried was delivered, making a total of 151 drums (each carrying 43.3 gallons). Is reported that the returning convoy was fired on at Aflaj Bani Qitab.

Morgan
Representative.

<u>POLITICAL SUMMARY APRIL 1955</u>

<u>MUSCAT AND OMAN</u>[20]

n.b. The reports in this section have been divided under the headings of Muscat and Ibri, according to where they originated.

<u>Muscat</u>

On 30th April the Sultan sailed from Muscat to Salalah[21] aboard the British tanker 'Reliance', having spent a period of two months in Muscat. He is expected to remain at Salalah until the middle of June, when he will be going on a visit to the UK, after which he is expected to return to Salalah until his next visit to Muscat in October.

The first day of Ramadhan fell on 24th April.

---

19 He was based at Umm Said in Qatar.

20 I have decided to include these reports for the months of April, May, June, July, August and September 1955 because 1). These 6 are included in the files - the reports for other months are missing. 2). The events in the Sultanate of Oman and Trucial Oman (Trucial Coast) were at that time very much bound up with one another.

21 The coastal town in the Dhofar province of the Sultanate. The Sultan's favourite retreat.

During a visit to Muscat, the Sheikhs of the Wahiba tribe nominated Mohammed bin Hamad Al Daghail to represent them in their dealings with the Muscat government. This was at the request of the Sultan. Mohammed Bin Hamad is a Shaikh, but not the Tamima of the tribe.

The suspected increase in traffic of arms into Oman from Saudi Arabia is causing some anxiety.

Sayed Saud bin Harib, the former Wali of Barka, and father of the present Wali of Ibri, has been appointed by the Sultan as Wali in Ibri.

A letter from Yahyayi to the Manadhir Sheikhs was recently intercepted by HILAL BIN SULTAN, and it is said that it made reference to the promise by the advisor of the Egyptian Consulate in Jiddah to give the Iman 12 lacs Rupees,[22] and arms, to help him to recapture the Ibri and Tanam areas.

It is reported that at the recent meeting in Nezwa the Imam[23] offered to abdicate on the grounds that he was not receiving the cooperation of the Sheikhs in the Imamate. The Sheikhs among his followers immediately reiterated their loyalty and signed documents of allegiance. Immediately afterwards, the Imam appointed Talib Bin Ali[24] and Mohamed Bin Abdulla Al Salmi as advisers, Salih Hamad al HARTHI as Wali of Rastaq[25] and Ali bin Hilal as Wali of Ja'alan.

Lt. Col. Waterfield and 50 troops of the Muscat infantry recently carried out manoeuvres in the Russ al Had[26] area lasting one week.

Of the 12 Landrovers and 11 Bedford trucks purchased from the British army, 3 Landrovers and 6 Bedfords were sent in convoy from Muscat to Ibri, by the Wadi Jizzi route, under the command of a new M.F.F.[27] Officer, and later joined by Major Maxwell at Sohar. The convoy took the wrong track, and arrived at Al AIN, Buraimi. The Saudis later complained of this incident to H.M.G., and stated that any further occurrences of this nature would be regarded as a breach of the Standstill Agreement.[28]

22 Twelve hundred thousand Rupees.

23 Ghalib bin Ali, brother of Talib bin Ali. The Imam dominated the interior of the Sultanate, where the Sultan's authority was weak. This was specified in the 1920 'Treaty of Sib'.

24 The Imam's brother.

25 On the north side of Jebel Akhdhar, one-time capital of the Sultanate of Oman. At the time of writing this diary most of the territory apart from Muscat and the coastal areas was beyond the Sultan's writ. Jebel Akhdhar is the 3,000 metre high mountain. Terraced gardens high up in the mountain produce fruit and vegetables and roses for making the famous rose water.

26 The most easterly point in the Sultanate.

27 Muscat Field Force.

28 26th October 1952 H.M.G. and the Government of Saudi Arabia announced a 'Standstill Agreement not to disturb the current situation in respect of the Bureimi oases'.

New recruits for the expanding Muscat Field force are to be trained at GOBRA, 15 miles from Muscat under the command of Major Pope, who was formerly the second in command of the Batinah Force.

Mr. J.W. Carrigan, the United States' Consul General from Dhahran, visited Muscat during the month to discuss with the Sultan the proposal to appoint an American Consul at Muscat next year.

Ibri

The Dhahira Shaikhs returned from their visit to Muscat during the first week in April. They appeared to have enjoyed the trip, and to have been much impressed by the Sultan, but they were critical of their reception and the length of time they had been kept waiting. This, unfortunately, is a common complaint from baduin shaikhs visiting Muscat.

During the visit of the Sheikhs the Sultan dealt with many problems, namely the appointment of a permanent Wali in the Dhahira. At first he appeared to favour the confirmation of Sultan bin Saif in his temporary appointment. This, it is thought, would not have been a wise decision, for Sultan bin Saif was becoming unpopular in the Dhahira, and could not be expected to command the same respect as one of the Sayeds. Instead, the Sultan appointed Sayed Saud.[29]

The Duru (Mahmudi) Shaikhs returned from Muscat early in April. One of their internal tribal dissensions seems to have been settled in Muscat, but one of the several outstanding ones seems to centre round the employment of labour at Fahud, the quarrel being as to which section of the tribe the recruits should be taken. It is hoped that the new Wali from Muscat will be of assistance in settling this disagreement.

During their visit to Muscat Sayed Ahmed seems to have promised the Duru Shaikhs all that they asked for, which encouraged, rather than quelled, quarrels within the tribe. There seems to have been no attempt to appoint a Tamima of the tribe, possibly as a deliberate policy, but this makes the Company Representative's task in Ibri exceedingly tiresome when dealing with the Shaikhs.

In accordance with the arrangements made in Muscat, HILAL BIN SULTAN (the son of SULTAN BIN SAIF, the MUSCATI WALI IN IBRI[30]) handed over Arraqi fort[31] to Hamud bin Hamad al M'amri and twenty M'amri soldiers. Afterwards, Hilal left for Muscat, having been the Government's sole representative in Ibri for nearly three months. He did very good work during his term of office, but at seventeen he could hardly hope to command the respect of an older man. Most of the Beni Hawasinah also went home, except 40 who remained behind to garrison Salaif.

29 Saud bin Harib.

30 Former temporary Wali, see above.

31 Baluch town a few kilometres north of Ibri.

The Company Representative in Ibri visited Muscat, during the month, travelling overland by the Wadi Jizzi route. It was his impression that officials in Muscat had very little knowledge of affairs in the interior, and that the liaison between the government and its outposts left much to be desired.

An incident occurred at Party 2's camp towards the end of the month in which the Camp Boss was struck a blow with a rifle. The Harassis concerned were sent to Muscat, where six of them were each sentenced to 15 days imprisonment in Jalili Fort. The Minister of the Interior, who dealt with the case, drew attention to the fact that the Company had not recruited its labour through an authorized agent, nor had it provided proper guards for Party 2 camp, and he felt that these omissions may have contributed to the incident.

H. M. Thomson
b.c.c. Representative, Dubai
Representative, Doha
Representative, Ibri
Representative, Muscat
E.F.Henderson, Esq., P.C.L., Bahrain.

TRUCIAL COAST DIARY FOR PERIOD ENDING 31 MAY 1955

The 'Id al Fitr' commenced in all Trucial States apart from Ras al Khaima on the 23rd, in Ras al Khaima it commenced on the 22nd.

ABU DHABI:

At the request of the Area Superintendent Tarif Shaikh Shakhbut was requested by letter on the 7th to consider the replacement of the head guard at Gezira,[32] Mana bin Abdulla. It was considered best during Ramadan to write concerning this matter rather than to call in person, as it was reported that Shaikh Shakhbut was not receiving any visitors on business affairs. It was later pointed out that Mana's replacement might have undesirable repercussions as he is head of the Bu Muhair[33] tribe in the Liwa

32 The drilling location in the west of Abu Dhabi. The third Abu Dhabi exploration well. Drilled from January 1955 to February 1956 to a total depth of 12,500 feet, without discovering oil. PD(TC) geologists still believed that the best prospect for discovering oil in Abu Dhabi territory was in the west.

33 Al Bu Muhair is one of the Bani Yas group of tribes, in those days found mostly in Batin in Abu Dhabi and in Dubai. The writer does not explain why he would not be welcome at Gezira, unless it is that someone from the Manasir would be more appropriate.

district. After absence for a month during Ramadan Mana returned to Gezira after the 'Id', evidently reproved but not replaced by Shaikh Shakhbut. The matter was still in abeyance at the end of the month.

Shaikh Shakhbut was visited by the undersigned on the third day of the 'Id' the 25th. Shaikh Haza and Shaikh Khalid were also present. Great interest were shown in any information that could be given regarding the recent events at Mazam.[34]

DUBAI:

The departure of Shaikh Juma with his four sons for Saudi Arabia on the 14th has already been reported to you in a memo.[35]

The undersigned called on Shaikh Rashid in the evening on the first day of the 'Id' the 23rd. He also attended a dinner party given by Shaikh Rashid for the new Political Agent and his wife, Mr. and Mrs. J.F. Tripp, on the 28th.

The general reaction in Dubai to the events at Mazam was as only to be expected, unfavourable.

SHARJAH:

Shaikh Saqr bin Sultan was visited by the undersigned on the morning of the second day of the Ede the 24th. Present also were Shaikh Rashid of Ajman and his sons Ali and Humaid; and Shaikh Mohammed bin Saqr uncle of the Ruler.

UMM AL QUWAIN:

A visit was paid by the undersigned on the 25th to the Ruler's house. Shaikh Ahmed was absent in his gardens at Falaj al Ali and his son Shaikh Ali presided in his place.

---

34 Mazam is an important Baluch village about half way between Ibri and Dhank. The writer does not tell us about the events. Thesiger wrote that Al Mazim was the settled Baluchi's tribal capital. Others say that the main centre of the Bani Baluch was 'Araqi, a short distance north of Ibri. At the time of this diary the new Imam Ghalib was adopting a more aggressive stance, in contravention of the Treaty of Seeb. He had occupied and the been driven out of Ibri and 'Araqi in late 1954 by the Sultan. Rentz wrote that in 1951 the sheikh at Mazam had declared in favour of Saudi Arabia. See THESIGER, W., 1950. And RENTZ, G. Ed. RAGHID EL-SOL 1997. However the Mazam affair is reported in detail in the May 1955 Political Report, included below.

35 Memo missing. The sons of Juma, were Obaid, Maktum, Hamad and Ahmed. However there is a note on the files recording that apparently Sheikh Rashid had been warned that there was a plot among Juma and his followers to kill him during the Eid. The help of the Agency was enlisted in serving Juma his notice to leave, and the T.O.L. were brought in to guard the Agency until his departure for Saudi Arabia. We see later that Sheikh Saeed, the Dubai ruler was not altogether happy with his son being deported. Perhaps he did not believe the reports.

RAS AL KHAIMA

Shaikjh Saqr bin Mohd was also visited on the 29th and was informed that arrangements have been made as requested for his concession payments to be paid monthly instead of quarterly.

POLITICAL AGENCY:

Mr. C.M. Pirie-Gordon handed over to Mr. J.P. Tripp and departed on the 16th. A party was given at the Agency on the 14th to introduce the British Community to Mr. and Mrs. J.P. Tripp. On his departure on the 16th from Sharjah airfield, Mr Pirie-Gordon was seen off by the Rulers of Sharjah and Ras al Khaima; a guard of honour was provided by the Trucial Oman Levies. A guest night was given by the R.A.F. Station Sharjah in honour of Mr. Pirie-Gordon on the 10th.

DUBAI OFFICE:

Mr. Midgley of the Times[36] and his wife spent the day in Dubai on the 3rd. Padre Jenkins and Mr. K.G. Cleverton, camp boss party 5, arrived in Dubai on the 10th and departed on the 11th.

Mr. E.F. Henderson left Dubai on the 7th and returned for one night on the 17th.

Morgan
Representative

POLITICAL SUMMARY

MUSCAT AND OMAN

n.b. The reports in this section have been divided under the headings of Muscat and Ibri, according to where they originated.

Muscat

On 23rd May Major F.C.L. Chauncy left Muscat for Salala,[37] via Bahrain, to visit the Sultan. It is understood that Mr. Robin Dunn Q.C. met him at Salala, and

---

36 Correspondent of the London Times newspaper.

37 Salala is the Sultan's coastal summer retreat in the Dhofar province of the Sultanate of Oman and about 1,000 kilometres south of Muscat.

together they explained to the Sultan the case which H.M.G. has prepared for the boundary arbitration.[38]

At the beginning of the month, members of the Jawasim[39] partially demolished the boundary wall at MAJAZAH, a village near Aswad in the mouth[40] of the Wadi Qor, stating that the wall was theirs and that they were opening up a new camel route. After their departure the Wali of Shinas[41] visited MAJAZAH and instructed the villagers to rebuild the wall.

Later in the month, the Wali of Sohar and his father, the new Wali of Ibri,[42] were stopped by members of the Jawasim at MAJAZAH. Fighting broke out and the two Walis retreated to Sohar and enlisted the support of the Batinah Force. Leading fifteen troopers, Major Maxwell quickly had the situation under control, and the Jawasim retreated from the scene. There were no casualties. A Batinah Force patrol has been left in the area, and the Muscat government has protested about this incident to the Political Resident.

Recruits for expanding the Muscat Field Force are slow in coming forward, but the authorities hope to have the first batch of 200 men ready for field service by January 1956, and the second batch of 200 by June 1956.

Whilst on a visit to Muscat, on 19th May, H.M.S. Loch Killisport received instructions to proceed immediately to a point near the Quoins in the Straits of Hormuz, where two tankers were in difficulty after a collision in heavy fog. The damaged tankers were escorted to Bahrain.

Lt. Col. Waterfield, Commandant of the Muscat Infantry, left Muscat on 18th May for two months leave.

Major Barren, who is situated at Ibri, has resigned from the M.O.F.F.[43]

<u>Ibri</u>

The petrol convoy from Dubai was met at Mahadha[44] by a detachment of M.O.F.F., under the command of Lieutenant Colonel Waterfield, which took over

---

38 The boundary with Saudi Arabia. The Saudi Arabian military force present in the Buraimi group of oases was in Hamasa, one of the Sultanate of Oman villages and not an Abu Dhabi village. Access to Hamasa from Saudi Arabia was through Abu Dhabi territory.

39 Jawasim, Al Qasimi are a Sharjah and Ra's al-Khaimah tribe/family. The people involved here probably would have been from Ra's al-Khaimah.

40 Facing the Indian Ocean. Aswad is in the territory of the Sultanate of Oman and about 10 kilometres from the sea.

41 Shinas is on the coast about 50 kilometres north of Sohar and about 20 kilometres from Aswad. Shinas to Fujairah town is also about 50 kilometres.

42 Saud bin Harib.

43 Muscat and Oman Field Force.

44 North of Buraimi.

the escort duties from the T.O.L.[45] Lacking guides familiar with the area, the escort and convoy took the old tracks to Ibri, instead of DARB ZAID, which had been used in recent months to avoid clashes with the Bani Kitab and Baluch. The convoy was fired on at Aflaj Bani Kitab and again near MAZAM. The Company Representative accompanied the convoy on its return, but had to take the same AFLAJ/MAZAM route to collect a vehicle broken down at AZIZI, and the convoy was again fired on at BAKHABEH.

The Muscat government was asked to take punitive action against the offenders, and despite a warning that the Sultan's Forces would be discredited if this was not done, it declined to take action.

Shortly afterwards, the newly appointed Wali on his way from Muscat to Ibri was fired on by the Baluch of Al Mazam. Three of his party were wounded (including a corporal of the M.O.F.F. returning from leave).

When the Wali arrived at Ibri on 14th May it was decided to send a squadron of the M.O.F.F. to Mazam to bring back the leaders of the trouble-makers. The demand for the delivery of these people having been rejected, the M.O.F.F. opened fire on Mazam, but only two of twelve mortar bombs fired, and the operation was abandoned.

On 18th May an enlarged M.O.F.F. detachment was again sent to Mazam, this time with some mortar experts. All appeals for the surrender of the leaders, and finally for the evacuation of women and children, before the expiration of an ultimatum, failed, and the force opened fire. A pause was made in the bombardment, to allow surrender, but this was ignored, and the operation was continued until the village was entered, and finally surrendered. Baluch casualties were eight killed and three wounded. There were no M.O.F.F. casualties.

After the occupation, the fort was burnt down, and the M.O.F.F. withdrew. Later, Rashid Bin Said, the Tamima of the Baluch, and representatives of the three villages of MAZAM, SUBAIKHA and HARAT BALUCH, arrived in Ibri and expressed their allegiance to the Sultan, at the same time declaring AHMED BIN BATTI (the chief trouble-maker at Mazam, who escaped during the operation to Saudi Arabia) an outlaw.

Immediately Mazam surrendered, messengers were sent to the Bani Kitab of MAMUR summoning them before the Wali. They duly arrived and agreed to sign their allegiance to the Sultan, and the Wali allowed them 15 days in which to inform their people of this intention, so as to avoid any impression of coercion.

These actions revealed some of the weakness in the organisation of the M.O.F.F. and its transport and equipment. The question of concentrating more of the forces on Ibri has still to be dealt with, and it is interesting to note that only 100 troops could

45 Trucial Oman Levies.

be got into the field for the second Mazam operation. The remainder of the force was engaged on garrison duties at Ibri, Fahud, Awaif, and Party two's camp.[46]

The incident at Mazam was watched with great interest by the people of Dhank,[47] as elsewhere, and there is every reason to suppose that it has done much to make the small tribes in this area reconsider their positions with a view to accepting the sovereignty of the Sultan. It is reported that Mattar bin Salim of Dhank is on the verge of a visit to Muscat, and further news from this quarter is eagerly awaited.

Early in the month a Company engineer, accompanied by Sultan bin Saif[48] and an escort of Baluch Force Levies, began the survey of the proposed road from Khaburah[49] to Ibri, via the wadis Hawasinah and Al Kabir. It would appear that Muscat had given no thought to political arrangements for this survey, and the party was obstructed at many places in the hills by the villagers demanding payments before they would allow the party to pass, particularly at Miskin and Najaid. Villagers of the latter places have since visited Ibri, and have been informed that the road building project now awaits the Sultan's consideration: should it be decided to build a road, they will be approached before work begins. All the negotiations of the right-of-way of the survey party were carried out by the Company's Representative from Ibri, the Sultan's Representatives finding this task a little beyond them. The actual survey has been made the subject of a separate report.

H.M. Thomson.
b.c.c. Representative, Dubai
Representative, Doha
Representative, Ibri
Representative, Muscat
E.F. Henderson, Esq., P.C.L., Bahrain.

46 Geophysical Party 2.

47 Loyal to the Imam.

48 The Sultan's former temporary Wali in Ibri.

49 Khaburah is on the Indian Ocean coast. Some 120 kilometres over the mountains and northeast of Ibri.

TRUCIAL COAST DIARY FOR PERIOD ENDING 30 JUNE 1955

ABU DHABI:

Shaikh Shakhbut visited Dubai on the 2nd to make his official call on the Political Agent; as usual he was only present in Dubai for as short a time as possible and returned quickly to Abu Dhabi territory. However he was absent from Abu Dhabi town itself for approximately five days, spending two or three nights in the desert on the journey to and from Dubai.

The undersigned visited Abu Dhabi to call on Shaikh Shakhbut on the 5th and again on the 27th and 28th, on the latter occasion spending the night at the house of Mr. T.A.D.W. Hillyard.[50] On the morning of the 28th our visit coincided with the return of Shaikh Zaid from his visit to Muscat and Ibri.

Four Abu Dhabi Shaikhs[51] – Mana bin Mohamed, Mohammed bin Khadim Bu Halaibah, Rashid bin Said and Said bin Saif – arrived to stay in Company quarters on the 6th and remained until the 15th. A special dinner party was given by the Company for them on the 7th.

Shaikh Zaid[52] with Shaikh Mohammed bin Salamin[53] of the Al Bu Shamis arrived in Sharjah with many of their followers on the 8th. Shaikh Zaid stayed at the I.A.L.[54] Fort;[55] Shaikh Mohamed Salamin and other Shaikhs from the Baraimi area who arrived at the same time were accommodated by the T.O.L.

A special dinner party for Shaikh Zaid and Shaikh Mohammed bin Salamin was given by the Company on the 10th; Shaikh Rashid of Dubai, Shaikh Saqr of Sharjah and Mr. Acland and Mr. Walker of the Agency were also present. The undersigned attended a dinner given the following night for Shaikh Zaid and Shaikh Mohammed bin Salamin by Shaikh Rashid of Dubai.

Shaikh Zaid and Shaikh Mohamed Salamin together with other Buraimi Shaikhs departed from Sharjah by special air charter for Muscat on the 13th.[56]

---

50 Abu Dhabi Marine Areas/BP representative.

51 Manasir tribe from Liwa and western region.

52 Shaikh Zayed bin Sultan, brother of Ruler Sheikh Shakhbut bin Sultan.

53 From Qabil and Sunainah in the Sultanate of Oman. Sheikh Zayed married his daughter, later divorced.

54 I.A.L., International Aeradio, a communications company set up by B.O.A.C., British Overseas Airways Corporation, to manage airport communications. They also provided the first telephone service in Abu Dhabi.

55 The BOAC Fort at the airport, the rest house for overnight stays and hotel.

56 Wilkinson wrote 'Muhammad bin Salimin, Shaikh of the Al Bu Shamis, along with some lesser Na'im shaikhs, accompanied Shaikh Zayid of Buraimi to Muscat where they signed

It is reported that a Kuwaiti merchant Ahmad Katani has withdrawn his financial support from the Abu Dhabi Development Company, an event which has caused them to reconsider the scope of their immediate activities. To date the Company has sold three or four Land Rovers in Abu Dhabi, has established a garage looked after by a competent Assyrian fitter and is making preparations to construct an underground concrete water tank for the storage and sale of fresh water. A special ship has been procured to transport this water from Bander Abbas in Persia.

The Representative of Abu Dhabi Marine Areas[57] is trying to arrange with Shaikh Shakhbut for the establishment of an emergency refuelling depot at Abu Dhabi aerodrome.

It will be recalled that up to a few years ago, drinking water was shipped to Abu Dhabi from Sha'am, in Ras al Khaimah territory, and sold at prices varying from Rs. 8/. to Rs. 15/. per drum.

At the request of the Political Resident, the Company has agreed to loan its bungalow in Abu Dhabi for the use of the Political Officer who is arriving shortly.

Two water-well digging parties, sent out under the auspices of the Company, have already dug several wells in Bainunah/Dhafara areas.

DUBAI:

An operation was successfully carried out on Shaikh Said's eye by a Lebanese specialist in the early part of the month. He was visited in the hospital by the undersigned on the 13th.

The Political Resident was in Dubai from the 15th to the 18th. On the 16th the undersigned attended a lunch party given by Shaikh Saqr of Sharjah in the P.R.'s honour; and in the evening a drinks party and then a dinner party given by the Agency in Dubai, also a luncheon party given by Shaikh Rashid of Dubai on the 17th.

Mr. J.F. Walker of the Agency left by air from Bahrain for London on completion of his tour of duty[58] on the 13th.

U.S.S. Valcour paid a visit to Dubai from the 21st to the 23rd. Parties were given at the Agency and on board for the officers and British community in Dubai and Sharjah.

The inspection of well drilling equipment acquired by the Agency[59] for Shaikh Zaid was carried out by the fitter loaned from Q.P.C. who arrived on the 23rd.

---

documents of allegiance to the Sultan.' WILKINSON, J., *The Imamate Tradition of Oman,* Cambridge University Press, 1987, ISBN 0 521 32713 X, p. 314.

57 Previously D'Arcy. The concession was held 66⅔% D'Arcy and 33⅓% Total. D'Arcy (BP) were the operator.

58 His chief responsibility was investigating, and where possible, determining the boundaries between the Sheikhdoms.

59 British Political Agency.

Another convoy consisting of twelve trucks carrying petrol, kerosene and lubricants left Dubai for Ibri on the 25th. One truck broke down en route and had to return to Dubai with its load; the others reached Ibri and returned to Dubai without incident.

Shaikh Sultan bin Saif al Husseini[60] visited Dubai to buy a Land Rover and visited the Political Agent on the 25th and 26th; he also visited the undersigned.

SHARJAH:

Shaikh Saqr is continuing work on the construction of a concrete jetty at Layyah. It is hoped that when his jetty is complete a deep enough anchorage will be provided for boats as a substitute for Sharjah Creek, which has silted up too much to be serviceable any longer. However the local manager of Gray Mackenzies, who is the local expert on such matters, is sceptical about the success of this new jetty.

Doubts are generally entertained as to how Shaikh Saqr will finance his European holiday on which he is going to embark in July. He is being accompanied by the wealthy pearl merchant Sultan bin Ali bin Awais who has already made a free present of 1500 bags of cement for the jetty at Leyyah.

Mr. Platt of the Desert Locust Survey has been posted to Aden and has been replaced by a Mr. L.A. Tillen.

Shaikh Zaid, accompanied by Mohd. Salimeen, and many of the Al Bu Shamis and Naim from the Buraimi area, arrived in Sharjah on 6th June, en route to Muscat.

UMM AL QUWAIN:

Shaikh Ahmed bin Rashid was visited on the 21st.

RAS AL KHAIMA:

It is reported that Shaikh Saqr bin Mohamed has been forcibly recruiting men for the T.O.L. and as a result quite a few of his younger subjects have escaped into Dubai and Sharjah to avoid conscription.

BURAIMI:

It was reported by one of Shaikh Zaid's followers that Shaikh Mohammed bin Salamin occupied the village of Bu Buqra at the end of the month; the village had until then been occupied by Ahmad as Saif[61] of the Naim.

60 Innes writes 'Al Hasni' for one of the Hawasinah tribe. The writer has referred to Wadi Hawasinah on many occasions.

61 The writer means Ahmed al Salf, or Ahmed as Salf.

DUBAI OFFICE:

The following Company and non-Company personnel paid duty visits as shown to Dubai and were accommodated in the mess.

		Arrived	Departed
Mr. M.C. Watterson	Personnel Office Tarif	1	2
Mr. T.A.D.W. Hillyard	A.D.M.A.	3	4
Mr. E.F. Henderson	Bahrain	4	11
		30	*
Mr. Ali Tajir	Bahrain	4	13
		22	29
Mr. Dodd	Director Abu Dhabi Development Company	7	8
Mr. J.F. Drake	D.A.P.G	11	12
Mr. E.A. Thorpe	Assistant D.A.P.G	11	12
Mr. R.A.T. Codrai	Dukhan	13	15
Mr. P.R. Johnson	Tarif	15	16
Mr. D.J.R. Sheridon	Geologist	18	22
Padre K.T. Jenkins	Umm Said	29	*
Mr. G. Fennemore	Maintenance Engineer	30	*

Morgan
Representative.

POLITICAL SUMMARY JUNE 1955

MUSCAT AND OMAN

n.b. The reports in this section have been divided under the headings of Muscat and Ibri, according to where they originated.

Muscat

During the month the authorities have been actively engaged in trying to prevent the smuggling of arms and ammunition into the Imamate, and have had several successes. Early in the month information was received that a consignment of arms and ammunition had been off-loaded from a Saudi launch at Sib[62] and conveyed to Khodh, from whence they were distributed to Rostaq,[63] Nizwa and Sharkiya.[64] A few days later news was received that a further consignment was expected to arrive, and the Muscat Infantry laid an ambush at Sib, but the gun-runners were not encountered. The coast from Shamaileeya[65] to Swaik[66] is still being patrolled, and the detachments of the Muscat infantry engaged on this operation are in radio contact with Muscat.

A search of Sib and its environs was later carried out, and nine sacks of .303 ammunition of 1914-18 vintage were seized, and Shaikh Saif bin Said of the Yal Hadid, a section of the Bani Hinai tribe, has been imprisoned in Jalali Fort,[67] together with six of his followers, and their property at Sib has been confiscated and sold by public auction. Also seized with the ammunition was a somewhat antiquated machine for filling cartridge cases.

On 23rd June Sayed Tariq[68] and Major Maxwell were fired on whilst carrying out a reconnaissance of the Khodh area, but no casualties were inflicted and the fire was not returned.

The Minister of the Interior, Sayed Ahmed bin Ibrahim, protested to Shaikh Mubarak Bin Omair of the Bani Hinai against the part played by the Khodh Shaikhs in the foregoing incidents, and requested that the smuggled arms and ammunition should be handed over to the Government. This request was refused, and it is understood that Shaikh Hilal bin Ali of the Bani Ruwahah is acting as intermediary between the two parties.

Talib, the brother of the Imam, and Ahmed bin Abdullah, the Wali of Samail,[69] are both reported to be at Khodh.

The Batinah Force has been no less active than the Muscat Infantry, in its operations against the gun-runners. At Sib a patrol seized 600 rounds of .303 ammunition, whilst at Khaburah they arrested a Muscati in possession of ammunition and lead suitable for making bullets, all of which he is stated to have bought in Dammam.

---

62 Sib, the site of the modern international airport, is on the coast some 50 kilometres west of Muscat.

63 Rostaq is 160 kilometres from Muscat on the south west side and at the foot of the Jebel Akhdhar. (Green Mountain).

64 The Sharkiya, the eastern region of the Sultanate.

65 The name indicates the northern region.

66 On the coast 140 kilometres west of Muscat.

67 The fort on the rocky island in Muscat bay.

68 Tariq bin Taimur, brother of the Sultan Saeed bin Taimur.

69 Samail is about 100 kilometres south of Muscat on a main route between Jebel Akhdhar on the west side and the Sharkiya on the east side.

A letter being carried by one Khaluf, a servant of Talib, from Abdullah Majid Al Ghanaim of Dubai, to his master, was intercepted by Major Maxwell. The letter stated that the sum of Rupees 20,000 had been credited to Talib. Further investigations are being carried out to discover the significance of the exchange.

During the month the Batinah Force established a check- post at Sahaila, in the Wadi Jizzi which is used in communicating with M.O.F.F. at Ibri.

Only 35 men have so far been recruited under the scheme to expand the M.O.F.F by 400 troopers.

Ten 107 inch base Landrovers, ordered through the Company on behalf of the Muscat Government, have been distributed as follows:- seven to M.O.F.F., two to Batinah Force, one awaiting repairs. M.O.F.F. vehicles were sent in convoy by the Wadi Jizzi route, under the command of the Minister for Foreign Affairs, who returned by camel to see the proposed Wadi Hawasinah route.

During the month the Muscat porters went on strike for three days, claiming an increase in carrier rates from 4 Annas to 8 Annas a load. Sayed Ahmed intervened, granted an increase of two Annas a load, and then put the two leaders of the strike in Jalali Fort.

A Saudi subject was recently arrested at Hazam[70] when travelling by car to Rostaq. He claimed that the object of his visit was to collect a debt of 5000 Riyals from Talib, but it is suspected that he was going to become an instructor in the Imam's army.

Ibri

In the Dhahira, the period under review was possibly the most favourable to the Sultan's cause since the capture of Ibri last autumn. This was almost entirely due to the strong action taken with the Baluch tribe at Mazam during the preceding month. Whereas previously a certain disregard for the law and for bona fide travellers had caused many tribesmen to oppose the passage of vehicles and discharge their rifles at will, the M.O.F.F. action at Mazam had suddenly shown them that they could not always act as they wished with impunity. A certain awe of the Sultan and his forces immediately became apparent, and visitors to Ibri, coming to pay their respects to the Wali, increased considerably.

International reactions to Mazam prevented the fullest advantage being taken of the opportunities presented, and Dhank, a key point in the central Dhahira, remained an unfulfilled objective. By the end of the period, some of the most favourable chances for gaining the allegiance of the more lukewarm tribes and villages had passed, and it was reported that Saudi influence and penetration, which had earlier received a severe check, was once more on the increase.

70 Between Rostaq and the coast.

In Ibri itself, the new Wali, Sayyed Saud bin Harib, a member of the Sultan's family, has already made a very considerable impression on all and sundry with his courtesy, resolution and common sense. He has received many visits from the chiefs of the surrounding tribes, and, despite his age, has himself visited the majority of the nearby villages. His latest expedition, accompanied by the M.O.F.F, was to all the Baluch and Beni Kitab villages, where the Sultan's flag now flies atop the forts.

The Sultan left Salalah for England by boat in the middle of the month (June), arriving there at the beginning of July. He is not expected to return before September. Ibri, had many visitors, including Brigadier Baird and Group Captain Coates from Bahrain; Mr. Innes Minister of Foreign Affairs in Muscat; Major Somerville of the War Office, London; Major Barnes; C.L.R. Dukhan; Messrs Houlder, Richardson, Donaldson and Baden, all P.D. (O);[71] and Shaikhs Zaid and Haza bin Sultan from Buraimi and Abu Dhabi with some of the Al Bu Shams and Naím chiefs.

Mr. G. Khimji, the Muscat merchant, also visited Ibri to discuss contracts with the M.O.F.F., and investigate the possibilities of opening a shop.

The Eid was celebrated with much feasting and noise of firearms between the 23rd and 27th of May. During this period, there was little movement of tribesmen, or news of developments, with the exception of a scare in Nizwa area. It was reported that the Imam's forces were massing to attack the loyal Ahmed Mohamed Al Harthi at Qabil. RAF reconnaissance, over Nizwa, however, showed little sign of any major move.

There has been much disturbance among the chiefs of the Duru tribe during this period, and considerable difficulty in getting and keeping labour at Fahud. Mayuf bin Khalifain and Musellim bin Hamad wished to confine recruitment of labour to their own sections; whilst Ali bin Hilal and Mohamed Bin Said wanted to send their men to work. Finally, towards the end of May, coolies were sent from all the areas, resulting four days later in a general strike. This was partly due to a mistake, which had been made in the monthly payments as well as the general feeling of indulging in a spending spree once payment had been made. But in addition three or four trouble-makers, almost certainly encouraged by Mayuf, presented impossible demands for higher wages, more food and water and less work. It was decided not to accede to these demands and to send all coolies back to their homes. After four days, instructions were sent to the Duru' Shaikhs by Sayed Ahmed ordering them to co-operate with the Company and arrange for coolies to return to Fahud at once. The Wali of Ibri preferred to deal with Shaikh Ali bin Hilal only, and the latter shortly afterwards despatched sixty workmen to Fahud. This undoubtedly caused yet more friction between Mayuf and Musellim on the one hand and Ali and Mohamed on the other.

71 The IPC associated company Petroleum Development (Oman).

Towards the end of June, the Wali called a meeting of all the Duru' Shaikhs in Ibri to try to resolve their differences, but he met with only partial success. Shaikh Zaid bin Sultan, on his visit from Buraimi, also tried to mend these differences, but could not entirely succeed despite his great influence and standing with the tribe.

By the end of the month, an uneasy peace seemed to prevail among the Duru' leaders, but it will not last indefinitely.

With the increasing heat, all coolies again refused work at the end of June. Half of them were returned to their homes, but the others were prevailed upon to stay by Shaikh Ali.

Sheikh Huwaishil bin Ali arrived in Ibri at the end of June, offering his services to the Government or the Company in any capacity required. On instructions from Muscat, he was informed that until he went to Muscat and signed his allegiance to the Sultan, he was not considered sufficiently reliable to entrust with any specific project. Huwaishil withdrew without commenting on this, but it is considered possible that he has once again been approached by the Saudis, and that his reason for coming to Ibri was to gauge the Government's attitude to himself first.

A reconnaissance has been made to Ashaish, a well in the Wadi Adam, south of Jebel Salakh, with one Army and one Air Force Officer from Bahrain to choose a possible air field site. An admirable stretch of hard gravel was found about 6 miles west of Ashaish. This well itself was located, but no tribesmen have been there this year, and the well had not been dug out.

Company transport at Ibri suffered minor reverses during the period, but there was always one Landrover on the road. The need for a new vehicle, however, is rapidly becoming apparent.

The M/T Officer of the M.O.F.F., accompanied by the Representative, Ibri, as far as the Wadi Jizzi, visited Muscat towards the end of June, returning with seven or eight new long wheelbase Landrovers, and a considerable amount of spares.

Shaikh Hamad bin Sultan Al Janabi from 'Izz (inside Jebel Salakh) visited Tanaam and Ibri. He has many connections with the Duru' tribe by marriage, and a visit seemed to be mainly social, but with an invitation to the Duru' chiefs to visit their villages inside Jabal Salakh in the near future. The intention thereby seemed to be to influence the neighbouring tribes in the direction of Nizwa.[72] Shaikh Said bin Sultan El Janabi from Ras Duqm[73] also visited Ibri to see the local 'leech' and get bled. He returned to Duqm in what seemed a very frail condition about 15 days later. His visit was in no way political.

72 Where the Imam resided.

73 Duqm is on the coast some 500 kilometres south of Muscat. The Company established a base there for operations at Fahud more than 300 kilometres to the north-west.

Shaikh Hamad bin Saif el Kilbani, who lives in Ibri, and who has a tribal section living in one quarter of Dhank, visited the latter place for a week in mid-June. He returned with the news that Mattar Bin Salim el Azzizi and Abdulla Bin Hamad Al Kilbani would hand the town over to the Sultan, provided the M.O.F.F. lent their support. Abdulla visited Ibri, but the more faint hearted Mattar sent a messenger to report the Government's reaction to the proposal. Despite much pressure from all Ibri chiefs, the Wali and Shaikhs Zaid and Haza bin Sultan (at that time in Ibri), the Government refused to consent to the proposal. The importance of this large town at the mouth of one of the most important wadis of Dhahira cannot be over emphasized, and its occupation would probably gain for the Sultan the allegiance of all the remaining tribes of the area.

Due largely to the action at Mazam and the influence of Sheikh Zaid bin Sultan, the Bedu Al Bu Shams under Shaikh Mohamed Salimeen agreed to sign their allegiance to the Sultan. Sheikh Mohamed (with some minor Naím chiefs) visited Dubai, and then flew to Muscat accompanied by Shaikh Zaid, where they met Sayyed Ahmed Ibrahim. The party then travelled by road to Ibri with the new MOFF vehicles, accompanied by the Minister of Foreign Affairs, Mr. Innes. In the meantime Shaikh Haza bin Sultan drove from Buraimi to Ibri with other vehicles to meet the party there and escort them home.

Shaikh Mohamed Salimeen succeeded in getting permission to establish a post of MOFF at the bedu palm grove of Suneina, some 10 or 12 miles[74] out from the hills west of Dhank. On the 23rd of June, a patrol left for Suneina to establish the post, the mission being successfully accomplished. Subsequently, it was learnt that the people of Dhank thought that the expedition was aimed at them, and many of the pro-Saudi element fled the town only to return later when it was discovered that the force was going to Suneina. Shaikh Mohammed Salimeen now wishes to move the post on to Qabil or Hafit,[75] which are more strategically placed.

Wadi Kebir – Wadi Hawasina. On June 27, Mr. Innes left Ibri to return to Muscat by car and camel via the shortest route. A night was spent at Miskin, where once again unruly inhabitants (Beni Kilban) let loose a fusillade of a rifle fire in the direction of the Wazir and the Wali of Ibri,[76] who also accompanied the party. Mr. Innes ordered the entire village population to be assembled and informed them that such conduct would not be tolerated in the future, and action would be taken against them, if the passage of travellers was impeded again.

Nizwa area. Several tribal leaders of the Saidi tribe from near Nizwa (the Sultan's own tribe) arrived in Ibri at the end of June. They brought news of gun running and

74 More than 20 miles.

75 Almost on the border with Abu Dhabi.

76 Innes and Saud bin Harib.

increased supplies of money from the Saudis into the Imam's capital. They also asserted that apart from the Imam and the powerful tribal heads, most of the people were very much pro-Sultan and tired of the Imam's unsuccessful pretentions.

Thomson.

b.c.c. Representative, Dubai
Representative, Doha
Representative, Ibri
Representative, Muscat
E.F. Henderson, Esq., P.C.L., Bahrain.

TRUCIAL COAST DIARY FOR PERIOD ENDING 31 JULY 1955

ABU DHABI:

The Representative travelled to Tarif by car on the 11th and on the 12th accompanied by Mr. K.M. Maude and Mr. R. Hayes. The Representative visited Shaikh Shakhbut in Abu Dhabi to introduce Mr. R. Hayes on his taking over the duties of Area Superintendent Trucial Coast from Mr. Maude. Another visit was paid by the undersigned to Shaikh Shakhbut on the 26th on which occasion he was given lunch.

The sum of Rs. 2500 was paid into the account of Shaikh Shakhbut with the British Bank of the Middle East Dubai on the 17th as compensation for the accidental death on 13th January 1955 of WSP1461 Ali Mohammad.

At least 50 huts were destroyed by fire in Hamasa in the Baraimi Zone in the early part of the month. Clothes, barrasti matting and rice were dispatched to Hamasa by the Trucial Oman Scouts but the Shaikh of Hamasa, Rashid bin Hamad apparently made difficulties about the proper distribution of this aid.[77]

Mr. Henshaw of B.P. Limited Tripoli, Libya, was present with Mr. Hillyard of Abu Dhabi Marine Areas Ltd. during the month to gain experience of the post in case a relief should be required.

The activities of Abu Dhabi Development Corporation have almost come to a stand-still. The fitter in charge of their garage has left for Iraq as a result of sickness, and there are no prospects of the return in the near future of Mr. Colwill from England.

77 The material was refused and returned to Dubai.

DUBAI:

Shaikh Said departed from Dubai for Ras al Khaima on the 13th and remained there for the remainder of the month.

The undersigned attended a lunch party given by Shaikh Rashid for Mr. Hammond of the British Bank of the Middle East, Bahrain on the 1st.

Accompanied by Mr. Hayes, an Eid call was made on Shaikh Rashid on the 30th.

During the month an order was made that with immediate effect all customs payments due to the Ruler must be paid through the British Bank of the Middle East Dubai and not as previously to the Customs Superintendent Rashid bin Ahmed. It has been estimated that a large amount of revenue has been lost to the Ruler over the past three or four years due to the procedure of customs payment that was in force. However although Rashid bin Ahmed has become rather inexplicably a wealthy man, he still maintains his position of Customs Superintendent, but without the financial control.

General concern is being felt over the possible silting up of Dubai Creek within the next few years to such an extent that sea-going launches will not be able to pass over the harbour bar even at high tide. An estimate has been made by the British firm of Sir William Halcro and Partners of the cost and measures required to remedy this problem. They stipulate that the building of break-waters near the harbour mouth would be necessary and the total cost would be Rs. 5,000,000. Guided by the Agency,[78] Shaikh Rashid now realises that all other schemes such as electricity plants will have to be shelved until the creek problem is solved. Apparently the British Bank of the Middle East are prepared to put forward a certain sum as a loan for this project. It is possible that this Company[79] may be approached too. The Political Agent mentioned this matter to Mr. Hayes, the Area Superintendent, during the latter's visit to Dubai over the Eid.

Zayani[80] from Bahrain is in the process of establishing a Land Rover Agency in Deira. Mr. Waghorn, the Rover agent, was in the area in the early part of the month; the future shop has yet to be built and temporary premises are occupied at the moment at the east end of Deira suq.

It has apparently been decided that due to the volume of work, a second Administrative Officer is required at the Political Agency. Extra office buildings are at present being built and an extension wing is also being added to the Political Agent's house to provide more Guest accommodation.

H.M.S. Flamingo visited Dubai from the 21st to the 23rd. There were the usual parties on shore and on board.

---

78 British Political Agency.

79 PD(TC).

80 The Bahraini merchant Zayani.

AJMAN:

Ajman was visited on the 21st by the Representative and again with Mr. Hayes during the Eid on the 31st. Shaikh Rashid bin Humaid spent most of the month at his gardens at Manama, but was present in Ajman over the Eid. He informed the Representative that he knew two places where he was certain there was oil in his territory and wanted to know when the Company proposed to come to drill for it.

Shaikh Ali, the Ruler's eldest son, recently returned from a visit to Bombay.

SHARJAH:

Shaikh Saqr left Sharjah by air on 9th July for the Levant, Egypt and, perhaps Europe, accompanied by the pearl merchant Sultan bin Ali bin Awais.

UMM AL QUWAIN:

A visit was paid to Umm al Quwain on the 20th. Shaikh Ahmed was absent in his gardens in Falaj al Ali where he remained most of the month. Shaikh Rashid, his son deputised for him.

FUJAIRAH:

Shaikh Mohammed bin Hamad al Sharqi visited Dubai from the 15th to 17th July. He called on the Political Agent and then on the Representative at this office to collect a box of dynamite and detonators which he had previously been promised to enable him to enlarge a certain well in Fujairah. No progress on this project has yet been reported; apparently the expert, who had been produced from Abu Mousa,[81] discovered he had no previous experience of the type of dynamite supplied.

Before coming to Dubai, Shaikh Mohammed had apparently returned recently from a visit to Kuwait and Saudi Arabia, where he had visited Medina.

DUBAI OFFICE:

The following Company and non-Company personnel paid duty visits as shown to Dubai and were accompanied in the mess.

81 The Golden Valley Red Oxide Company.

		Arrive	Depart
Mr. E.F. Henderson	Bahrain	*	4
Padre K.T. Jenkins	Umm Said	*	1
Mr. G. Fenimore	Maintenance Engineer	*	2
Mr. T.A.D.W. Hillyard	A.D.M.A.	6	9
Mr. Hayes	Area Superintendent Trucial Coast	30	*
Dr. K.F. Thompson	Medical Officer, Trucial Coast and Oman	30	*

A private drinks and buffet supper party was given in the Representative's flat for the British community in Dubai and Sharjah on the 14th.

Morgan
Representative.

POLITICAL SUMMARY JULY 1955

MUSCAT AND OMAN

n.b. The reports in this section have been divided under the headings of Muscat and Ibri, according to where they originated.

Muscat

During the early part of the month the Muscat Infantry, under the command of Major Maxwell, Commandant of the Batinah Force, encamped at Sib in readiness to attack Khodh, should Shaikh Mubarak bin Ameer have failed to hand over the 500 rifles recently smuggled into the village, via Sib. Numerous excuses were made in the initial stages, and ultimately the arms were handed over to the Infantry and despatched to Muscat. The rifles were said to have all been of the 1914-18 type.

Rumour has it that 2000 rifles were ordered through the Saudi Embassy in Egypt at £18 each, some three months ago, when Talib paid a visit to Egypt. It is strongly suspected that many more than 500 rifles have been smuggled into the Imamate via the sea route. Sayed Ahmed[82] received information that arms and ammunition had already been landed at Khrais, a village near Gobra, and the further consignment was expected to be off-loaded at Khor Fakhan.

82 Ahmed Ibrahim, the Minister of the Interior.

Talib returned to Rostaq[83] after the Khodh incident, and it is rumoured, the Imam himself paid a quick visit to the village. Life in Khodh is back to normal, but a section of the Muscat infantry, under a local officer, was standing by at Sib for a few more days.

Upon information being received that a Saudi launch was expected to arrive within the next few days carrying a consignment of arms, ammunition and Saudi agents, the Minister of Foreign Affairs[84] left Muscat on 21st July in one of the Sultan's armed launches, to patrol the coast[85] between Sib and Sohar. The Minister returned on the 26th with no untoward incident to report.

Suleiman bin Himyar, together with his son Sultan and 40 followers, arrived in Muscat on 18th July. Prior to departing two days later for Jebel Akhdar, he was presented with Rs. 10,000 by the Government, and, a radio set by Her Britannic Majesty's Consul General.

The discussions between Sayed Ahmed and Suleiman bin Hamyar centred around (a) co-operation between H.H. The Sultan and the Imam (b) the unrestricted travel of motor transport between Muscat territory and Rostaq. (c) Cessation of arms smuggling into the Imamate. The discussions were friendly, but inconclusive.

Shaikh Saif bin Said of the Yal Hadid, referred to last month as having been arrested, has been released from Jalali Fort together with his six tribesmen, and all confiscated property has been returned to them.

Towards the latter end of the month Talib, commanding 80 armed tribesmen, set up camp at Qarn El Shubaika, in the mountain range between Rostaq and Hazam,[86] from where Hazam and the coast receive their water supply. As a precautionary measure a detachment of the Batinah Force has been moved from Sohar to Hazam.

The Government recently passed a censorship law and instructed the Batinah Force to censor, seize and confiscate any doubtful correspondence.

Brigadier Baird and Captain Laird visited Muscat for two days during the month.

Group Captain Coates of the R.A.F. Bahrain, visited Muscat from the 24th to 28th July. The object of the visit was to inspect the present airstrip and also to endeavour to find alternative sites. Needless to relate he did not succeed in the latter.

Ali bin Mudhaffer has been appointed Wali of Sib.

A Company Dove landed at Muscat on 18th July, with Colonel Cheeseman. The latter remained at Muscat for four days and returned to Ibri by road.

A fire at Mutrah destroyed 24 "barastis", fortunately without any loss of life. The fire was caused by a primus stove catching fire in one of the houses.

---

83 Rostaq is in the mountain foreland on the north side of the Jebel Akhdhar. At one time capital of the Sultanate.

84 Foreign Minister, Innes.

85 Known as the Batinah coast.

86 Hazam, a large oasis with a fine fort, is about halfway between Rosatq and Khabura on the coast.

The Eid Al Adha was celebrated on 31st July in Muscat and the Batinah. The Representative conveyed the company's felicitations to senior government officials.

Ibri

After the more spectacular events of May and June, the month of July was something of a disappointment in the Dhahira.[87] Many of the advantages which had seemed to accrue to the Sultan's cause were counteracted by a rather passive attitude adopted by both the Foreign Office[88] and the Muscat Government to what was earlier so favourable a situation. There were many reasons for this: among them, the Sultan's absence in Europe, the Muscat Government's preoccupation with gun-running and political events on the coast, and the Foreign Office's fear of prejudicing the future of Buraimi. In addition, the M.O.F.F. at Ibri and Nafun had troubles of their own, both administrative and mechanical, whilst the heat, at its greatest during the month, was not conducive to the successful outcome of complicated ventures.

Domestic issues, such as the pacification of tribes liked the Bani Kitab and Bani Kilban, were, however, well to the fore, and Shaikh Sultan bin Saif El Howasani was sent to Ibri by Sayed Ahmed as his special emissary to achieve these and other objects.

At Fahud, the month was fairly quiet. Work continued, but rather at half pressure, the heat and the date harvest together ensuring that most of the Duru' labour would keep away from this somewhat inhospitable spot.

The Duru'

Most of the Duru' tribesmen seemed to retire to the Hamrat or the villages behind Jabal Salakh and around Ibri during this month of heat. Labour was difficult to obtain at Fahud,[89] and despite the efforts of the leading Shaikhs no new labour could be found to come in until after the Eid Al Kabir. As a result the work at Fahud was somewhat held up. There seemed to be little improvement in relations between the Chiefs, although Shaikh Sultan bin Saif may have done something to lessen their differences during his visit from Muscat. But even a strong personality such as his is entirely unable to rub out the jealousies in a tribe which stretches from Ibri in the north to Adam in the south.

Dhank

Shaikh Abdulla Bin Hamad Al Kilbani paid his usual monthly visit to Ibri on the 27th. He reported little movement in his town, where an uneasy peace seems to reign. Shaikh Saqr bin Sultan from Buraimi earlier visited his property there, and in

87 The area between Nizwa and Buraimi, the mountains and the Abu Dhabi desert.

88 Foreign Office in London.

89 The Company was drilling a well at Fahud.

fact stayed there over the Eid. There seems little doubt that his prolonged stay was intended to hearten his own people, and the lesser tribes nearby. This success was shown by the fact that several leading personalities from the Yahyai, Na'im and Beni Ali flew to Riyadh from Buraimi, ostensibly as pilgrims.

Shaikh Rashid Bin Ali of Dut (in Wadi Dhank) visited Ibri. He is the first important chief from the wadi to "come in" and express his allegiance of loyalty to the Government. He demanded a 'markaz' at Dut with M.O.F.F. soldiers, but this the Muscat authorities refused to consider. Although his is only a small tribe, Shaikh Rashid is reported to be an independent chief, and not, as Muscat imagines, a subordinate of Shaikh Saif bin Amer Al Alawi of Yunkul.[90] Shaikh Rashid spend three days in Ibri from the 11th to 14th.

Al Bu Shamis

On the night of the 14th some Beni Ali tribesmen raided Seneina (where the M.O.F.F. have a post) and shot dead one Al bu Shamsi. Sheikh Mohammed Salimeen with the soldiers gave chase next morning and succeeded in overtaking the three Beni Ali men. One man was shot by the soldiers and the others escaped. It was discovered that the incident was in no way political, a blood feud having existed between these two tribes for years. The Wali of Ibri has been instructed to call representatives of the tribes to Ibri to arrange a truce.

Sheikh Mohammed Salimeen still clamours for a "markaz"[91] at Qabil at the southern end of Jabal Hafit. On the 18th a visit was paid to Qabil, which is a considerable settlement of far greater size than Suneina and more strategically placed,[92] and the matter was discussed with Shaikh Mohammed. A report has now been referred to Muscat.

M.O.F.F.

The Force carried out a mobile patrol from Ibri in the area north and west of Dhank, and fairly close to the hills, in the middle of the month. The object was to intercept any lorries or camel trains, search for illegal goods and generally obtain information. It had been suspected that guns were possibly being run into Dhank, but on this particular occasion none were found. Numbers of Baluch and Bani Kitab tribesmen were encountered, however, going to and from Buraimi. Patrols such as this are undoubtedly very effective by the mere fact of movement in the area, and with luck might well encounter important news.

90 In the mountains north of Dhank.

91 Military or police centre or post.

92 Very near the border with Abu Dhabi.

The Force met with some internal difficulties of their own during the month concerning pay and discipline. Colonel Cheeseman flew to Muscat for urgent discussions, and later returned by land through the Wadi Jizzi, a small convoy of three vehicles having been sent from Ibri under Captain Ayliffe-Jones.

Shaikh Sultan bin Saif

Sheikh Sultan arrived in Ibri towards the end of the month as a special emissary of Sayed Ahmed from Muscat. He had several missions to carry out: the necessity for bringing in the Ayyal Rubaia section of the Beni Kitab and obtaining their allegiance: the posting of Ghafiri askars to Maazam from Dariz: the willingness of the Beni Kilban to see through the Wadi Hawasinah - Wadi Al Kabir road project, and gain the subjugation of the people of Miskin; the labour problems at Fahud, etc. The solving of all these problems is essential to the strengthening of the Sultan's position around Ibri, and the Wali has been unable to devote enough of his time to see that this is done. With his usual energy, Shaikh Sultan sped round the area on his errands, and seems to have been remarkably successful, although at the same time not entirely placating all the personalities involved. Tact is not his strong suit.

Bani Kitab

On the 27th the Ayyal Rubaya section of the Beni Kitab tribe arrived in Ibri under the Shaikh Dhiban bin Ali and signed their allegiance to the Sultan. The other chief of the section, Ali Bin Mohamed, flew to Riyadh. Hamood, the son of Shaikh Dhiban, had previously set off for Muscat to visit Sayed Ahmed on behalf of his father.

Beni Kilban

Sheikh Saeed bin Saif Al Kilbani, brother of Hamad bin Saif, came to Ibri from Mikonyat on a visit. He appears to have little influence, and it is improbable that his visit was in any way political.

Ibri water

The leading townspeople of Ibri raised what might have been an awkward subject: the supplying of Fahud with water from Ibri, and the Company's intentions in the future. Fortunately, at the same time, the well team in Wadi Amairi near Fahud at last encountered what appears to be a constant supply of good water at Abaili, and no Nubians[93] have been to Ibri for water since.

93 Large lorries used for transporting water.

Eid Al Kabir

The last day of the month heard the first fusillades of shots welcoming in the three day period of the Eid Al Kabir. The usual visits were made.

Thomson.

b.c.c. Representative, Dubai.
Representative, Doha
Representative, Ibri
Representative, Muscat
E.F. Henderson, Esq., P.C.L. Bahrain.

TRUCIAL COAST DIARY FOR PERIOD ENDING 31 AUGUST 1955

A Trucial States Council meeting was held at the Agency on the 23rd August. This meeting was attended by all the Rulers of the Trucial States and the Agency were very gratified at the friendly and cordial atmosphere that prevailed throughout the conference itself and the lunches given by the Agency, Shaikh Rashid and by Shaikh Shakhbut at his camp near Jebel Ali in the desert.

It is understood that among matters discussed at the Council meeting itself was a proposal by the Agency for the registration of all fire-arms, the main object being to assist the prevention of the smuggling of arms into the Buraimi zone. However, although the Abu Dhabi Shaikhs agreed to try to enforce this proposal, Shaikh Rashid of Dubai said it was too extensive a scheme to be undertaken in Dubai territory. Apparently the proposal was not pressed.

Another question discussed was the prohibition or discouragement of traffic in 'araq, opium and hashish throughout the States. A lecture was also given on the advantages of education and the teachings of the Prophet by a visiting member of the British Council.

On the 24th the Rulers all attended a meeting to discuss the affairs and recent progress of the government hospital run by Dr. D.G. McCaully.

Without doubt the most notable and gratifying feature of these meetings was the good relationship that existed between Shaikh Shakhbut and the other Rulers, notably Shaikh Said of Dubai. Shaikh Shakhbut was in excellent spirits the whole time, and very cordial and friendly towards everybody. His camp in the desert between Jebel Ali and Dubai was much nearer Dubai than usual, and on the evening of the 24th he gave a dinner party at this camp which was attended by all of the Rulers except Sharjah and Fujairah. The undersigned was also invited to this particular dinner party.

The Agency consider that one of the reasons for the improvement of relations between Shaikh Shakhbut and Shaikhs Said and Rashid of Dubai is the absence from the scene of Shaikh Juma[94] who they believe to have been a bad influence in this respect.

ABU DHABI:

The undersigned visited Shaikh Shakhbut in Abu Dhabi on the morning of the 16th before the arrival of Messrs. Zylstra and Franklin by air from Umm Said to inspect launches for possible employment for the Marine Seismic Survey. Shaikh Zaid had apparently arrived in Abu Dhabi from Buraimi three days before on the 13th and he remained in Abu Dhabi to accompany Shaikh Shakhbut, Haza and Khalid to Dubai for the Council meeting on the 23rd. Shaikhs Zaid and Haza remained in the area of Dubai and Sharjah until they finally departed by special air charter from Sharjah for Bahrain and Geneva on the 30th. Their departure and destination was kept very secret and this office was not aware of same until after they had left. They both called on the undersigned at the office on the 23rd; Shaikh Haza had not previously seen the Dubai Company office building and apparently wished to do so; he seemed suitably impressed.

DUBAI:

Mr. I. Cuthbert has been posted to Dubai to be an assistant to Mr. T.A.D.W. Hillyard and to look after the Dubai office of the Dubai Marine Area Limited.

Muhammad bin Khadim Bu Halaibah of the Manasir was accommodated by the Company from the 23rd to the 31st, when he departed for Bahrain to be medically inspected by Mr. R.D. Wilkins.

The Political Agent Mr. J.P. Trip was absent in Bahrain from the 29th to the 31st.

Shaikh Hilal bin Sultan Al Hussaini[95] stayed in Company quarters from the 27th to the 31st, when he was flown to Salalah.

DUBAI OFFICE:

The following Company and non-Company personnel paid duty visits and were accommodated in the Company mess:

94 The Ruler's brother currently in exile in Saudi Arabia.

95 Al Hasni (Innes spelling). The Hawasinah tribe.

		Arrival	Departure
Mr. R Hayes	Area Superintendent, Trucial Coast	*	1st
Dr. Thomson	Medical Officer Trucial Coast and Oman	*	1st
Mr. B.B. Howard	Secony Vaccuum New York	2nd	3rd
Padre Jenkins	Umm Said	7th	8th
Mr. J.V. Collier	Geophysicist Party 1A	23rd	24th
Mr. R.R. Hayes	Area Superintendent, Trucial Coast	31st	*
Mr. H.R. Chantler	Geologist	31st	*

Morgan
Representative.

POLITICAL SUMMARY AUGUST 1955

MUSCAT AND OMAN

n.b. The reports in this section have been divided under the headings of Muscat and Ibri, according to where they originated.

Muscat

His highness the Sultan returned to Salalah via Baghdad and Bahrain on about 9 August, having paid a short visit to the United Kingdom.

The authorities appear to have had some success in preventing the further smuggling of arms and ammunition into the Sultanate and military patrols have now been considerably curtailed. The armed launch continues to patrol as far as Sohar once every fortnight, and is in radio contact with Muscat and Sohar.

A messenger camel post from Ibri to Khaburah and thence to Muscat by taxi, and conversely, has been opened by the Minister of Foreign Affairs.

The authorities are desirous of increasing animal and vegetable production in order to cope with Company and Military requirements, and the possibility of recruiting an Agricultural Advisor is being investigated. Unless something is done quickly, there appears to be a serious risk of local inflation and of depreciation of flocks of sheep and goats.

H.H. The Sultan has appointed Hilal bin Sultan as I/C Askars[96] to City Services[97] at Dhufar.[98]

96 Soldiers, guards.

97 The USA oil company.

98 The west province of the Sultanate.

Major T.J.M. Scott, late of the M.O.F.F. has been appointed Commandant of the Gobra training school. There are 35 recruits to date but training has been impeded owing to a shortage of water at the proposed site. He has been allocated a sum of Rs. 15,000 for the construction of the training school at Gobra.

On the 22nd of the month Sultan bin Saif returned from Tanam and Miskin, claiming to have accomplished the object of his mission. He presented Sayed Ahmed bin Ibrahim a document signed by all the Duru Shaikhs to the effect that their tribal differences had been settled, and that they would co-operate to the best of their ability with the Government and the Company. A further document signed by the Beni Kalban, Beni Umr and Hawasana Shaikhs acknowledges that the Company vehicles may traverse their territories without hindrance, but they request permission to visit the Sultan prior to the commencement of the proposed road construction from Khaburah to Ibri.

Talib, referred to last month as having encamped at Qarn El Shubaika with 80 armed tribesmen, has now returned to the hinterland. It is generally believed that the object of the move to Qarn El Shubaika was to facilitate the smuggling of arms and ammunition from the coast to the interior. The counter move of posting of a detachment of the Batinah Force to Hazam appears to have deterred Talib from the scheme.

It is reported that the Imam is holding a conference at Nezwa with all minor shaikhs present, including an Egyptian emissary Mohamed Ishaq Itfeesh, who is said to have presented the Iman with three lakhs of rupees.

Once again rumour has it that the Imam is desirous of massing his supporters with the objective of invading the Dhahira and capturing Ibri, Tanam, and Dhank. This is countered by other reports that quite a number of shaikhs together with a high percentage of tribesmen are gradually losing patience with the Imam and his prevarications. Government circles reiterate the opinion that the Imam has missed his opportunity, if ever there was one, insofar as his untrained tribesmen could never stand up against the M.O.F.F. with modern weapons, transport and trained personnel.

Two Saudi army instructors and an Egyptian school teacher are reported to have arrived at Nezwa, the object being to train and teach the Iman's forces. Talib is now reported to be at Rostaq, awaiting the Egyptian emissary, Mohammed Ishaq Itfeesh.

The Imam has passed a censorship order, and is prepared to pay 6 Dollars to anyone intercepting subversive correspondence or literature.

Lt. Col. Waterfield returned from home leave on the 5th of August and took over the duties of Minister of Foreign Affairs from Mr. Innes, who proceeded on home leave on 9th August.

Ibri

The main events of the month were focused largely on Ibri. There was little to report from the central Dhahira or the Jabal Hafit area. In the south, the only rumours emanated from Nizwa, and these could never be adequately checked. Most of the local movement centred around the colourful figure of Shaikh Sultan bin Saif, who proved himself energetic, if at times unpredictable. At one time he would be in Ibri or Silaif, then out in the Duru' country, and later in the mountains visiting the Beni Kilban. There was no doubt about his efforts and his self-importance: considerable doubt about the extent and scope of his achievement. In the middle of the month, his list of missions apparently completed, he left for Muscat.

Much time was taken up recruiting labour and organising work at Fahud. A force of between 60 and 70 coolies was signed on largely from the Ibri area and the country inside Jabal Salakh. In the course of the recruiting, Mamur, one of the so called 'forbidden' villages to the north of Salakh was visited, whither many of the Duru' had migrated during July, and where Shaikh Huwaishil bin Ali has a house. Due to the efforts of Shaikh Ali bin Hilal and Mayuf bin Khulaifin labour was not difficult to come by, and in fact many of Mayuf's men had to be turned away. It was agreed to appoint a junior shaikh from the tribe each month to act as representative in Fahud and oversee the coolies. Shaikh Salim bin Saif from Tanaam was the first, and he rapidly proved that he had the respect of the coolies and was capable of seeing that work continued satisfactorily. Indeed, there was probably less trouble and more work in Fahud during August than at any time since the Duru' started providing labour.

Unfortunately, internal dissension in the tribe, although apparently smoothed over by Shaikh Sultan bin Saif, keeps on breaking out, and there is no doubt that a watchful eye must be kept on the Shaikhs, as each is constantly endeavouring to score off the other with resulting ill effects on the tribe as a whole and the labour at Fahud. Sayed Ahmed approved a scheme for labour recruitment put up by the Representative, Ibri, and some days later achieved a volte-face by approving a totally different scheme put up by Shaikh Sultan bin Saif. He later reapproved the first scheme. Shaikh Sultan's scheme had neither been referred to the Wali nor to the Representative, Ibri.

Mr. F. T. Halan, a male nurse loaned to the M.O.F.F by the Company in the absence of the Force Medical Officer, has rapidly established a reputation for efficiency and hard work. He constantly visited Ibri Town and the surrounding villages and has won great esteem from the local populace for his successful work. Many have asked for his retention, but with the return of Dr. Quraishi of the M.O.F.F. from leave this will probably not be possible.

On the return of the Sultan to Salalah, it was at last possible to get a decision on the question of monthly payments to the Duru' sheikhs. The Sultan refused to consider the matter until next year, as he has already made considerable payments to the Duru' during their visit to Muscat in April. This will undoubtedly cause some coldness between the Sultan and this tribe, and could result in minor intrigue with the Saudis.

The Party 2 camp was moved from Mankab south to a point near the Wadi Amairi in anticipation of the arrival of the new geophysical party during the early part of September.

Except for a short outing to Bat, no patrols were carried out during the month, beyond the normal relieving of the garrison at Seneina every week to 10 days. This was disappointing, as it was rumoured that there was some considerable movement by the Saudis in the Al Bu Shams territory. But vehicle breakdowns and administrative work in Ibri kept the Force somewhat tied down.

There was one incident during the month when what was probably a shooting star over Silaif was thought to be a red Very light[99] by the camp sentry on duty. This, from Silaif, means danger. A force admittedly turned out from Ibri and sped to Silaif to find a quiet sleeping town. As an exercise, however, the evening was a success, and the force turned out remarkably quickly and enthusiastically.

News from Dhank was sinister and unreliable. Saqr bin Sultan was still reported there – building a house (fort?). Saif bin Amer el Alawi was said to have visited from Yunkul, and a vague rumour circulated that Talib, the Imam's brother, was on his way there from Nizwa. The whole situation seems most unsatisfactory.

Sheikh Sultan bin Saif accompanied by Representative, Ibri, and Colonel Cheeseman met the Beni Kilban sheikhs from Njaid and Mikonyat (Ali bin Humaid and Ghusn bin Nasir) at Bat[100] on the 12th. The purpose of the meeting was to discuss the proposed Ibri-Khaburah road, get the support of the local tribesmen and induce the chiefs to visit Muscat. No representatives of the village of Miskin appeared and the talks were conducted without them. Later, the sons of the two chiefs visited Ibri. Different impressions of the meeting were widespread, ranging from 'complete success and agreement' on Shaikh Sultan's part to 'tentative plans' for the future on the part of Shaikh Ghusn. The latter is an old man but definitely a personality and appears to have far more prestige and weight with his somewhat lawless tribesmen than anyone else. The nonentity, Shaikh Hamad bin Saif, as at Ibri, did not attend the meeting.

Shaikh Mohammed Salimeen visited the Wali at Ibri to arrange about the 'Sulh'[101] between his tribe and the Beni Ali. The latter tribe also sent a representative, and the Wali reported that peace between the tribes had been successfully achieved. Shaikh Mohammed also saw Colonel Cheeseman and Representative, Ibri, and continued to press for the Qabil post. If, as it is rumoured, he has been offered Rs. 30,000 by the Saudis to break his allegiance to the Sultan, with a further monthly payment in perpetuity, it would obviously be a good thing if Qabil were occupied.

---

99 Military warning light, shot from a pistol as a signal.

100 Villages on the west side of Jebel Akhdhar.

101 Reconciliation.

H.M. Thomson.

b.c.c. Representative, Dubai
Representative, Doha
Representative, Ibri
Representative, Muscat
E.F. Henderson, Esq., P.C.L., Bahrain.

TRUCIAL COAST DIARY FOR PERIOD ENDING 30 SEPTEMBER 1955

It is reported that the pearling season this year for crews from the Trucial States has been a very good one. In particular one owner of two Dubai launches which were operating brought back pearls weighing one thousand Mithgal[102] valued at approximately one lakh.[103]

A pneumatic well drilling equipment demonstrator from Dukhan[104] was in Dubai from the 22nd to the end of the month and it was arranged by the Agency that he gave demonstrations at Falaj al Ali and Manama to followers of the Rulers of Umm al Quwain and Ajman respectively. Mr. R. Huntington, who has recently been appointed by the Residency as the government Agricultural Advisor to Ras al Khaima, assisted with these demonstrations. The original purpose of this scheme, which was to instruct followers of Shaikh Zaid to be able to use this equipment in the Buraimi area, was thwarted by the non-arrival of these followers in spite of repeated prior notifications from the Agency. It is intended now that the equipment will in course of time be sent to Buraimi after both Ajman and Umm al Quwain have benefited from it for a while. Although the equipment is of no use for enlarging existing underground falaj, it can be used effectively to some purpose to dig new channels in hard rock and stone. Apparently both the Rulers of Ajman and Umm al Quwain are very glad to have the use of it.

ABU DHABI:

The undersigned visited Abu Dhabi for the day to see Shaikh Shakhbut on the 19th and again on the 26th. On the first occasion the Ruler enquired again about the Company's intention concerning the payment of Customs duty. After consultations with the Agency, who said they could see no objection to the proposal, an official letter

102 One thousand mithgals is about 3.6 Kilograms.

103 100,000 Rupees.

104 The Company base in Qatar.

was written to the Ruler declaring the Company's intention as a concession to pay a 2½% duty on all food imported by the Company into Abu Dhabi since 1949 and in the future. This letter was delivered by the hand of Mr Leon-Hart[105] to the Ruler after the end of the month and until the time of writing there has been no reaction.

The Ruler was visited by Mr. Hayes on the morning of the 29th when the latter was en route to Dubai from Tarif. Shaikh Shakhbut was apparently in a very affable mood showing a great interest in all the operations at Gazira[106] among other things. From the experience of the undersigned, this particular interest has previously to all outward appearance has been rather lacking – taking the form of a 'could not care less' attitude.

The Agency are at the moment displeased with the Abu Dhabi Ruling family as detailed arrangements were made in Sharjah, Bahrain and Cairo for Khalifa, the son of Zaid, to proceed to Alexandria at the end of the month to attend a school as previously arranged. However Khalifa, instead of coming to Sharjah to catch the aircraft to Bahrain, went to Abu Dhabi instead and all the arrangements as made were disorganised.

The Hon. Martin Buckmaster arrived in Dubai from Bahrain and the U.K. at the middle of the month and after approximately a week proceeded to Abu Dhabi to establish the post there of Political Officer.

The regrading by the Company machine of the road between Gazira and Dubai has greatly improved the speed and comfort of the journey by car to Abu Dhabi from Dubai.

The work carried out by Khansahib Hussain under instruction from the Area Superintendent Trucial Coast to ensure an all-weather route over the Sabkha at Abu Dhabi is nearly completed; so also is the renovation of the causeway between the mainland and Abu Dhabi island.

Mr. Hillyard of the Abu Dhabi Marine Areas returned to Dubai from his visit to the U.K. on the 17th and in due course made arrangements with the assistance of the Area Superintendent Tarif for the recruitment of labour from the Liwa area to carry out the construction of jetties and other work on Das Island. Mohd. bin Khadim bu Halaibah, a Shaikh of the Manasir was enlisted by Hon. Buckmaster as a rather unwilling assistant to recruit this labour; we understand Mohd. thought the task was rather beneath him.

105 Was this Peter Lienhardt? He was a social anthropologist who first went to Kuwait in 1953. He was employed by Sheikh Shakhbut for a few months in early 1963 on the recommendation of HMG. There is no indication as to why he delivered this letter. He was in Kuwait in the 1950's LIENHARDT, PETER, EDITED AHMED AL-SHAHI, *Disorientations, A Society in Flux Kuwait in the 1950's*, Ithica Press, 1993, ISBN 0 86372 166 4.

106 The location of the drilling rig.

We understand that sufficient Liwa labour has also been recruited now by Area Superintendent Trucial Coast to commence work on the construction of the jetty at Baraka.[107]

The well-digging parties sent out by the Company to the Dhafara area, some three months ago, report the completion of over twenty wells.

OMAN:

A P.O.L. convoy of seven vehicles left Dubai for Ibri on the 5th; apparently the journey there and back was without incident. The number of vehicles was restricted to seven at the request of the Commanding Officer of the Levies, who stated that any larger number made the convoy very difficult to control – especially when crossing over the Ramlat Anej.

DUBAI:

Shaikh Said was absent in Bahrain from the 10th to the end of the month. He requested the Political Resident that he should be allowed to bring back Shaikh Jumma and his family with him to Dubai from Saudi Arabia; the request was refused.

The undersigned was absent from Dubai on a visit to Dukhan, Bahrain, Gazira and Tarif from the 7th to the 14th and again in Dukhan from the 21st to the 23rd.

A fire occurred in Dubai town on the morning of the 25th and approximately one hundred barasti houses in the Bastaqi quarter were destroyed. Damage was done to roofs and doors of mudbrick houses as well. There was only one fatal casualty. Various estimates of the cost of the damages have been made; the committee of Dubai merchants who have organised a relief fund put it as high as five or six lakhs,[108] which is probably excessive. Twenty five new labourers' tents were brought in from Tarif on the same day the fire occurred and have since been presented to Shaikh Rashid to be kept and used for similar emergencies in the future. Rs. 5000 in cash was also presented to the relief fund committee by the Company. The Agency are supplying all the barrasti matting valued at Rs. 22,000 which was refused in July by the Shaikh of Hamasa on the occasion of that fire. Shaikh Rashid and the British Bank of the Middle East have each contributed Rs. 10,000 to the relief fund and various merchants Rs. 4,000 each.

Work has commenced on the construction of a new palace for Shaikh Rashid between two or three miles to the south of Dubai town at a location where there are palm trees and fresh water.

107 A short distance west of Jebel Dhanna.

108 500,000 to 600,000 Rupees.

AGENCY:

The Administration Officer of the Agency Mr. R.F. Coleman left Dubai for the U.K. on completion of his tour of service on the 5th. He has been replaced by Mr. R. Featonby.

For the last 10 days of the month the Political Agent Mr. J.P. Tripp has been sick and is only recovering at the time of writing.

DUBAI OFFICE:

The following Company and non-Company personnel paid duty visits as shown to Dubai and were accommodated in the mess.

		Arrival	Departure
Mr. H.R. Hayes	Area Superintendent Trucial Coast	*	2
Mr. H.R. Chantler	Geologist	*	2
Padre K.T. Jenkins	Umm Said	13	14
Sayed Ali Tajir	Bahrain	26	*

Morgan
Representative.

<u>POLITICAL SUMMARY SEPTEMBER 1955</u>

MUSCAT AND OMAN

n.b. The reports in this section have been divided under the headings of Muscat and Ibri, according to where they originated.

<u>Muscat</u>

According to rumour, the smuggling of arms and ammunition into the Nezwa area via the coast has stopped, but recommenced via Buraimi.

The proposed site for the Gobra training school has been abandoned owing to lack of water. A second site has been chosen at Ghali, approximately 5 miles west of Gobra, and 50 recruits under Major Scott and Captain Hoggarth have pitched camp there. Apparently the local inhabitants are protesting strongly against the presence of troops in the vicinity, and the authorities are wondering what illegitimate business the tribesmen are engaged in, and strongly suspect that smuggling is being carried on there.

During the month 10 Pilgrims returning to Samail from Mecca, via Dammam and Bahrain, were refused permission to disembark from a B.I. steamer at Muscat, and were over carried to Gwadar, and returned to Dubai by the next ship. They were in possession of travel documents issued by the Imam which, of course, the Muscat authorities refused to recognise.

A proposal by the Minister of Foreign Affairs to make regular monthly remittances to the Duru Shaikhs has not met with the approval of H.H. the Sultan.

The Indian Consul has been approached by the Muscat Government to make preliminary arrangements with an Indian contracting company to lay a 3 inch water line from Belad to the village of Sur, a distance of approximately 4 miles. The consul, Maqbul Hussain Khan Bahadur of the Muscat Government, recently visited Sur to discuss the proposed project on the spot.

Government proposes to build a track suitable for motor vehicles from Ras al Hadd to Sur, and thence on to Al Kahil. Initially the track is intended for military transport only, and will not be used by public or private vehicles. At the moment there are no vehicles, military or private, at Sur.

It is reported that the Imam recently granted permission to his followers to own and use radio sets.

H.M.S. "Loch Lomond" visited Muscat from the 11th to 13th September, and the usual courtesy calls were made between ship and shore personnel.

Ibri

September saw a renewed outbreak of political activity in the Nezwa area, where the Saudis and the Egyptians are determined to strengthen the Imam to the detriment of the Sultan of Muscat. An Egyptian emissary loaded with money was reported to have arrived at Nezwa to organise a fighting force of 2000 men, subvert the neighbouring tribes and generally distribute largesse. The usual route through Hamasa was used; then the Wadi Dhank route to Yunkul, the Beni Kilban country and Nezwa. News of these movements usually reached Ibri too late for the M.O.F.F. to do anything about them, but the Egyptian and Talib, the Imam's brother, narrowly escaped meeting an M.O.F.F. patrol near Wadi Dhank at the beginning of the month, which was going to Mahadha to meet the incoming POL convoy from Dubai. Were the M.O.F.F. capable of sending out mobile patrols every week to scour the countryside, this would have a considerable deterrent effect on the movement of Saudi and Imamate supporters; but so far there have been too many transport and administrative difficulties to do this, with the result that the enemies of the Sultan can do as they please, almost with impunity.

Dr. Quraishi, the M.O.F.F. medical officer, returned from leave in India at the end of the month.

The Duru', as usual, occupied much of the Representative's time during the month. The experiment of having a junior shaikh in charge of the coolies at Fahud has worked reasonably well to date. On the whole there are less complaints about work, and a small nucleus of men prepared to become permanent workers.

Many rumours circulated round the tribe concerning the activities in the Nezwa area. Most of the leading sheikhs admitted to having received messengers from Suleiman bin Hamyar, or the Imam himself, inviting them to visit Nezwa; all said that these advances had been refused. Shaikh Mohamed Bin Saeed (Taina), however, visited Mamur (towards Nezwa) with his son Ali, and Mayuf bin Khulaifin also said that he had been there, consulting Shaikh Huwaishil Bin Ali. The fact that the Sultan refused to consider the Duru' sheikhs' request for monthly payment in lieu of an annual remuneration must undoubtedly have given rise to some coldness between the sheikhs and Sayed Said bin Taimur. The temptation for them to go to Nezwa and get their share of the latest 'comforts' must be considerable.

There are reports of renewed contact between the Duru of the outlying parts of Wadi al 'Ain and the Saudis in Buraimi. Rashid Bin Hamad of Hamasa was said to be in touch with a certain Dur'i named Humaid bin Ali near the old Party 2 site.

Representative, Ibri, accompanied a M.O.F.F. patrol to Hafit and Mahadha at the beginning of the month to meet the POL convoy from Dubai, and escort it to Ibri. The patrol was a strong one consisting of six vehicles, three of which were returning to Sohar.

Between Wadi Dhank and Hafit two Landrovers belonging to Shaikh Saqr bin Sultan Al Naimi of Buraimi where encountered. After six weeks stay in Dhank, Shaikh Saqr was returning home. The two cars were stopped by units of the patrol (which had dispersed and was proceeding independently) no less than three times, and Shaikh Saqr was considerably upset and frightened by this. Little wonder, when it is remembered that two days earlier the Egyptian emissary and Talib, the Imam's brother, were transported in the same vehicles from Yunkul to Buraimi on route to Riyadh and Cairo by air. Finally, Shaikh Saqr stopped in the sand country, near Hafit, and waited till nightfall before proceeding cautiously on to Buraimi by a circuitous route. The M.O.F.F. patrol spent the night near Hafit doing night exercises and forming a roadblock.

The POL convoy was met the following day at Mahadha and safely escorted to Ibri.

Shaikh Hamad[109] Bin Rashid an Naimi of Hafit met the patrol near his village and requested the establishment of a post there. The matter has been referred to Muscat.

During the patrol Shaikh Abdulla Bin Salim Al Kaabi was met at Mahadha.

Shaikh Amer bin Saif of Fida in the Wadi Dhank visited Ibri in the middle of the month and stayed two days. He is chief of a small section, but there is no doubt that, given some encouragement by Muscat, he and other minor chiefs of the area could be excellent sources of information from the Wadi. A considerable traffic seems to pass through the Wadi at present.

109 Humaid bin Rashid. Al Khuraiban section.

Abdulla Bin Hamid el Kilbani paid his monthly visit to Ibri and confirmed the movements of Shaikh Saqr bin Sultan and the Imam's party from Nizwa.

Shaikh Mattar bin Salim al Azzizi was reported as having visited Dariz, near Ibri, at the end of September. Dariz is the village of Shaikh Ali bin Said Al Ghafiri. Far from continuing his journey to Ibri, however, he apparently met there Shaikh Nasir bin Isa el Harthi, brother of Salih bin Isa, and escorted him back to Dhank en route for Baraimi. Shaikh Ali's attitude to all this, in view of his supposed great loyalty to the Sultan, is a little suspicious, to say the least.

Members of the Bani Kilban and Maqabil tribes were also said to have visited Nezwa. Certainly there seems to be no grounds for satisfaction concerning the loyalty of the mountain Sheikhs to the Sultan at the present time.

After the long hot summer at Ibri, the following maximum and minimum temperatures statistics may be of interest. The thermometer was hung in the coolest place available – a barasti hut.

Month	Average Max.	Average Min.
May	103°	74°
June	112°	83½°
July	113½°	85½°
August	111°	85°
September	106°	80°

(All readings Farenheit).

The hottest night of the summer was July 3rd with a minimum of 93°, and hottest days July 20th and 21st with maxima of 119°.

H.M. Thomson.

b.c.c. Representative, Dubai
Representative, Doha
Representative, Ibri
Representative, Muscat
E.F. Henderson, Esq., P.C.L., Bahrain.

TRUCIAL COAST DIARY FOR PERIOD ENDING 30 OCTOBER 1955

BURAIMI:

The main event which of course overshadowed any others during the month was the occupation of the Baraimi area on behalf of the Sultan of Muscat and Ruler of Abu Dhabi. The occupation began in the early hours of the 26th. The Saudi police detachment was taken completely by surprise and having surrendered were flown out of the area the same morning. The only incident in this connection was when Abdulla bin Nami[110] attempted to hold Major Smith of the T.O.L. Levies by the waist in order to enable another Saudi to try to escape with a box containing Rs. 147,000 in cash. Major Smith warned Nami that he would shoot unless he released him and eventually Nami received a very minor flesh wound in the thigh. Nami was treated for this wound in Dubai hospital and then with the remainder of the Saudi detachment was embarked on a British naval frigate.

Quite stiff resistance was encountered by the force occupying Hamasa. A detachment of the Levies reached Turki's house in Hamasa and were besieged there most of the 26th. It is thought that this resistance was inspired mainly by Obeid bin Juma'.[111]

However negotiations with Saqr bin Sultan, Rashid bin Hamid,[112] and Obaid bin Juma' were carried out during the 26th, and eventually their forces surrendered just before zero hour for an attack which was going to be launched against them. Apparently their resolution began to waiver immediately the news came through of Abdulla bin Nami's capture and evacuation.

Although Sultan bin Saqr[113] was allowed temporarily to stay on in his village, both Rashid bin Hamid and Obaid bin Juma' were evacuated immediately to Sharjah where they were kept in custody. All three have since with their families been evacuated to Saudi Arabia.

Reaction in Dubai and Sharjah to these events has been lukewarm.

Mohamed bin Salamin as Shamsi stayed in Company accommodation in Dubai from the 12th to the 17th, when he left by Company transport with Ali Tajir for Muscat. He returned to Dubai on the 30th to wait for an air passage by a R.A.F. aircraft to Salala.

ABU DHABI:

The undersigned visited Abu Dhabi for the day to see the Ruler on the 11th and again on the 29th. The questions of Customs payment and employment by the Company of non-Abu Dhabi launches were discussed.

---

110 The Saudi.

111 The Ka'abi Sheikh.

112 Sheikh Saqr bin Sultan Nai'mi, Buraimi Sheikh and Sheikh Rashid bin Hamid al Shamsi, Hamasa Sheikh.

113 The writer means Sheikh Saqr bin Sultan.

Shaikhs Hazza and Zaid returned to Abu Dhabi after their visit to Europe on the 21st. They were both present in the Baraimi area from the 26th onwards.

DUBAI:

Shaikh Said bin Maktum returned to Dubai on the 17th from his visit to Bahrain and Ras al Khaima.

The General Manager and Chief Local Representative paid a visit to Dubai on the 18th to meet the Political Agent Mr. J.P. Tripp. A call was also made on Shaikh Rashid.

A Mr. G. Chapman[114] has taken over the Dubai office of Messrs. Gray MacKenzie from Mr. K. Cook who has gone on leave.

SHARJAH:

Shaikh Saqr returned from his visit to Egypt, Iraq and Lebanon on the 15th. He has brought back with him two Egyptian school masters to teach at Sharjah school. One of his first actions on his return was to query with the Political Agent the drilling obligation date stipulated in the Company concession agreement with him. He was informed that it was September 1957 and not September 1956 as he had thought. The undersigned called on the acting Ruler on the 9th and on the Ruler himself on the 23rd.

AJMAN AND UMM AL QUWAIN:

Visit was paid by the undersigned to the Rulers of Ajman and Umm al Quwain on the 10th.

DUBAI OFFICE:

The following Company personnel paid duty visits as shown to Dubai and were accommodated in the mess:

		Arr.	Dep.
Mr. H.R. Hayes	Area Superintendent, Tarif	+	2nd
Mr. E.F. Henderson	Admin. Assistant PDTC & PDO	24th	+
Padre K.T. Jenkins	Umm Said	29th	31st

Morgan
Representative.

114 Chapman lives in retirement in Dubai today in 2020.

TRUCIAL COAST DIARY FOR PERIOD ENDING 30 NOVEMBER 1955

The Political Agent held a Trucial Coast Council meeting on the 8th which was attended by all the Rulers of the Trucial States. Among the matters discussed were:

1. The future development plans of the Agricultural advisor for finding and protecting water in the States.
2. Education, building of schools and provision of teachers.
3. Improvement of medical services.
4. Possibility of certain road or track repairs.
5. Police.
6. Law Courts.
7. Narcotics.

ABU DHABI:

Visits were paid to Abu Dhabi by the undersigned on the 6th and on the 15th. On the former occasion an invitation was received to attend a lunch given by Shaikh Khaled for Shaikh Zaid, who had returned temporarily from Buraimi.

A.D.M.A.:

Abu Dhabi Marine Areas are continuing with their work on Das Island constructing jetties etc., and have been prospecting for an area in which to build an airstrip.

DUBAI:

During a large part of the month, both Shaikhs Said and Rashid (especially the latter) have been absent from Dubai on hunting trips. They both attended a luncheon given for them in the Company office building on the 23rd.

The new Commercial Counsellor Mr. Gale paid a visit to Dubai from Bahrain from the 19th to the 23rd. Mr. and Mrs. Gale and Mr. and Mrs. Tripp came to dinner at the representative's flat on the 21st.

The General Manager Mr. P.R.A. Ensor and Mrs. Ensor and the Chief Local Representative Mr. H.M. Thompson and Mrs. Thomson paid a visit to Dubai from the 26th to the 27th. A buffet supper party for the British community in Dubai and Sharjah was given on the evening of the 26th. A visit was also paid to Shaikhs Rashid and Said on the 26th.

AJMAN, UMM AL QUWAIN AND SHARJAH:

The undersigned called on the Rulers of Ajman and Umm al Quwain on the 13th and on the Ruler of Sharjah on the 28th. The latter has been absent from Sharjah most of the month in Kalba or on hunting expeditions.

DUBAI OFFICE:

The following company and noncompany personnel paid duty visits as shown to Dubai and were accommodated in the mess.

		Arrival	Departure
Mr. R.L. Moore	Acting Drilling Superintendent	1	2
Mr. E. Foxall	Assistant Petroleum Engineer	1	2
Mr. D. Christie	Construction Supervisor	2	4
		22	23
Mr P Johnson	Assistant Air-conditioning Engineer	2	4
		22	23
		30	*
Mr. W.F. Miller	Electrical Foreman	2	4
Dr. K.F. Thompson	Medical Officer PDTC and Oman	10	12
Mr. R. Hayes	Area Superintendent Trucial Coast	11	12
Mr. E.F. Henderson	Administrative Assistant PDTC and PDQ	21	25
Mr. M.O. Watterson	Personnel Officer T.C.	23	25
Mr. Y.G. Keep	i/c Commissariat Trucial Coast	23	25
Mr. E.J. Nott	Acting Stores Officer Trucial Coast	28	*
Mr. & Mrs. T.A.D.W. Hillyard	A.D.M.A. Abu Dhabi	30	*

Morgan
Representative.

TRUCIAL COAST DIARY FOR PERIOD ENDING 31 DECEMBER 1955

ABU DHABI:

Shaikh Shakhbut caused general surprise by travelling to Dubai on the 5th especially to attend a luncheon party given by the B.B.M.E. on the occasion of the visit of their Chairman and General Manager.

The undersigned visited Abu Dhabi on the 19th and was given lunch by Shaikh Shakhbut, who was in a very benevolent mood.

Shaikh Shakhbut travelled to Buraimi at the end of the month, where he met the Political Agent Trucial States[115] and the Sultan of Muscat.[116]

DUBAI:

The establishment of law courts in Dubai presided over by a Bahraini Mohamed Abdul Khalik has been a further source of friction between Shaikh Said and Shaikh Rashid. They have been established at the instigation of the Political Agent and Shaikh Rashid and have proved very popular generally in Dubai. However Shaikh Said maintained that the people would still prefer and should have their cases tried by the Ruler and not by a court presided over by a foreigner. He therefore withdrew his guards from the courtroom and tried to prevent it from functioning any more. However Shaikh Rashid produced some guards of his own and ordered that the court was to continue its work.

A new Director of Customs for Dubai – a Bahraini called Mahdi Tajir[117] and a cousin of Ali Tajir[118] – has been appointed to replace Rashid bin Ahmed, who has been somewhat discredited. Mahdi Tajir is reported to be carrying out some much needed re-organisation of the department. Apparently at the present time of year when the entrepot trade is at its highest the Ruler receives approximately two lakhs[119] of Rupees per month customs dues.

Shaikh Rashid left Dubai on the 28th for Bandar Abbas on a hunting expedition.

---

115 J. P. Tripp the Political Agent in Dubai.

116 This historic meeting with Sultan Saeed bin Taimur, the Sultan of Oman, took place a few days after Shaikh Shakhbut had called on Hillyard at home on Christmas day. Shaikh Zayed was present at the Buraimi meeting. Although Sheikh Zayed had met the Sultan, Saeed bin Taimur, on a number of occasions there is no record that Sheikh Shakhbut had ever met him on any other occasion. HILLYARD, SUSAN, *Before the Oil*, Ashridge Press, 2002. ISBN 1 901214 02 8. OWEN, RODERIC, *The Golden Bubble*, Collins. 1957.

117 Later the first UAE Ambassador (To the Court of St. James) in London.

118 Ali Tajir was well known in Abu Dhabi and had worked for IPC/PD(TC) for many years. He lived in retirement in Dubai and died in 2006.

119 Rupees 200,000.

A call was made on the Ruler of Sharjah on the 17th.

The undersigned was absent from Dubai on a visit to Iraq from the 22nd to 27th inclusive.

DUBAI OFFICE:

		Arrival	Departure
Mr. and Mrs. T.A.D.W. Hillyard	A.D.M.A. Abu Dhabi	*	1
Mr. E.J. Nott	Assistant Stores Officer	*	2
Mr. P.J. Bullen	Assistant Driller Gezira	15	17
Mr. E.F. Henderson	Administrative Assistant	23	27

Morgan
Representative.

1956

TRUCIAL COAST DIARY FOR PERIOD ENDING 31 JANUARY 1956

ABU DHABI:

Shaikh Shakhbut was absent from Abu Dhabi on a hunting expedition in the area of and to the south of Buraimi during the greater part of the month. He returned to Abu Dhabi on the 24th.

The Managing Director,[1] accompanied by Messrs de. Grouchy, P.R.A. Ensor and R. E.R. Bird, paid a visit to Abu Dhabi on the 31st, called on the Ruler and was given lunch. Points discussed at this meeting have been covered in a memo.

A.D.M.A. Ltd have stationed a European (Mr. P. Townsend) permanently on Das Island. They have contracted with Messrs. Wimpy to carry out core drilling in their marine areas.

The activities of the Abu Dhabi Development Corporation are very limited, and their affairs are still being supervised locally by a Cypriot Mr Leslie; no member of the U.K. staff has come out this winter.

The undersigned paid a visit to Gezira and Tarif on the 24th and 25th.

DUBAI:

Shaikh Rashid has been absent from Dubai for the whole month on a hunting trip in Persia.

Plans for the preservation of Dubai creek are proceeding. The loan raised locally of 4½ lacks will be used to finance core drilling by Messrs Wimpy in mid-April to test the seabed in the place where it is proposed subsequently to dredge the mouth of the creek and in the places where a mole and two training walls will be constructed. It is estimated that the dredging and the construction of the mole and walls will cost in

---

1 IPC and PD(TC). H.S. Gibson.

the region of £388,000,[2] depending on the findings of the core drilling; a loan of this amount has apparently been promised by the Rulers of Bahrain and Qatar.

In conjunction with Sir William Lindsay, visits were paid to Ras al Khaima on the 11th, Ajman and Umm al Quwain on the 12th, Sharjah on the 16th and Kalba, Fujairah, Khor Fakkan and Dibbah between the 13th and 15th. In order to see the Ruler of Fujairah who was in Dibbah, it was necessary to hire a launch and travel by sea from Khor Fakkan. The special Company diaries were presented at the time to the Rulers of all the States mentioned above, except Shaikh Rashid of Ajman, who was absent on the 12th and had to be visited again on the 29th.

A visit was paid to Ras al Khaima to the experimental vegetable and crop farm supervised by the Agricultural Adviser Mr. R. Huntingdon. Experiments are being carried out quite successfully with various crops and a variety of types of vegetable.

DUBAI OFFICE:

The following Company and non-Company personnel paid duty visits as shown to Dubai and were accommodated in the mess:

		Arrived	Departed
Mr. E.F. Henderson	Administration Assistant PDTC and PDQ	4	5
		16	17
		22	26
Mr. H.R. Hayes	Area Superintendent Tarif	6	9
The Rev. K.T. Jenkins	Umm Said	6	9
Sir William Lindsay	Dukhan	10	18
Mr. C.W. Woolley	Dukhan	16	18
Mr. W. Neil	Party 1	16	18
Mr. D. Christie	Civil Engineer, Gezira	31	*
Mr. P.R. Johnson	Air conditioning Engineer	31	*

Morgan
Representative.

2 About Rs. 4,000,000.

TRUCIAL COAST DIARY FOR PERIOD ENDING 28 FEBRUARY 1956

ABU DHABI:

A visit was paid to Abu Dhabi on the 9th when an invitation was received to attend a large luncheon given by Shaikh Haza for Shaikh Zaid who was on a visit from Baraimi.

Another visit was paid on the 16th, when the annual concession payment was made in cash. On this occasion Shaikh Shakhbut raised the question once again of the future of Gezira and the site and date of a new location. He also complained that the Company had not finished yet the approach road over the sabkha to the causeway or the causeway itself; did not seem to occur to him to spend some of his own money on these projects.

On the 18th Shaikh Shakhbut departed on a hunting expedition to the Bainuna and was absent from Abu Dhabi town until the end of the month.

On the 20th the undersigned proceeded with Mr E. F. Henderson to Baraimi and stayed there until the 24th. Shaikh Zaid was not present in Baraimi at the time and had deputised Mr Henderson to act on his behalf in the falaj dispute between the Abu Dhabi and the Muscat villages.

This dispute concerned the falaj for the Jimi and Qattarah (Abu Dhabi) villages which run under the Baraimi and Hamasa (Muscat) villages. Baraimi and Hamasa, although they have got their own separate falaj, have dug wells into the Jimi and Qattarah falaj and use these falaj for drinking and washing purposes. As a result Jimi and Qattarah villages maintain that they cannot drink from their falaj due to pollution. The Abu Dhabi supporters state that when this complaint was first brought before the Wali representing the Muscat government, he agreed that all the wells dug by the Baraimi and Hamasa villages in the Jimi and Qattarah falaj should be closed up; whereupon the necessary work was begun. However it is maintained that the Wali later changed his mind and gave his instructions that those wells which had been closed should be opened up again.

This situation led to friction between the villages and Mr Innes, Muscat Minister for Foreign Affairs, arrived in Buraimi to meet with the head Muscat Qadhi in an attempt to reach a solution. After further discussion between the Wali, the Qadhi and Messrs. Innes and Henderson, a compromise was reached allowing certain wells to be closed and others to remain open. However when this agreement was written down in Arabic for the Wali's signature, he apparently refused to do so. At the time of writing, it is not known whether any agreement on this matter has been reached or not.

Mr Henderson also accused the Wali of attempting to increase taxation and customs duty in the Baraimi area.[3]

3 For more on this see INNES. N. (1987), p. 182ff.

DUBAI:

Shaikh Rashid returned from his hunting trip to Persia on the 5th. He stated that he had accounted for 1035 hibara, but had suffered from heavy rain and the cold.

Mr. A. A. Acland, Assistant Political Agent Trucial States, left Dubai on transfer to Kuwait on the 10th. His place has been taken by Mr. J. M. Edes.

DUBAI OFFICE:

The following company personnel paid duty visits as shown to Dubai and were accommodated in the mess.

Mr. F. R. Johnson	Air Conditioning and refrig. engineer
Mr. D. Christie	Civil Engineer
Mr. E. F. Henderson	Admin. Assist. PDTC and PDO
Mr. H. R. Hayes	Area Superintendent Trucial Coast.

Morgan
Representative.

TRUCIAL COAST DIARY FOR PERIOD ENDING 31 MARCH 1956

A Trucial Coast Council meeting was held at the Agency in Dubai on the 26th. The meeting was attended by all the Rulers, and Shaikhs Zaid and Hazza accompanied Shaikh Shakhbut from Abu Dhabi. The Political Resident had arrived the same morning from Bahrain on a visit that had been frequently postponed due to the troubles in Bahrain et cetera. He was therefore able to attend the meeting too and, according to rumours circulating in Dubai, created a stir by announcing that he considered that no oil would be found on the Trucial Coast and that the Rulers should divert their attention and energies to the encouragement of crop cultivation etc. in their territories and to similar methods of economic support.

As on previous similar occasions, the ruling families of Dubai and Abu Dhabi seem to be on very friendly terms. Apparently Shaikh Zaid of Abu Dhabi has stated that he would like to marry the daughter of Shaikh Rashid of Dubai. This proposal is being encouraged by Shaikh Rashid's wife who originally came from the Abu Dhabi ruling family herself.[4] However apparently Shaikh Rashid has not yet decided that the relations between the two states are sufficiently friendly to allow the marriage.

---

4 Latifa, the daughter of Sheikh Hamdan bin Zayed bin Khalifa, a cousin of Sheikh Shakhbut.

On the 14th a luncheon party was held in Dubai House for Shaikh Saqr of Sharjah and Shaikh Rashid bin Humaid of Ajman.

A visit was paid to Abu Dhabi on the 19th.

On the 22nd a visit was paid to the Ruler of Umm al Quwain and to an exhibition of paintings and artistic work held at Sharjah school.

DUBAI OFFICE:

The following Company personnel paid duty visit to Dubai and were accommodated in the mess.

		Arrival	Departure
Mr. E.F. Henderson	Administration Assistant PDTC, PDQ	*	1
Mr. H.R. Hayes	Area Superintendent Trucial Coast Tarif.	4	6
Mr. M.O. Watterson	Personnel Officer Trucial Coast, Tarif	5	6
Rev. K.T. Jenkins	Umm Said	11	13

Morgan
Representative.

TRUCIAL COAST DIARY FOR PERIOD ENDING 30 APRIL 1956

The month of Ramadan commenced in all the Trucial States on the 12th.

ABU DHABI:

Shaikh Haza and Shaikh Zaid travelled to Muscat in the early part of the month. While in Muscat Shaikh Haza saw the American missionary doctor who diagnosed a malignant growth in the intestines; Shaikh Haza has now gone on to India with Shaikh Zaid to have an operation. Apparently the possible seriousness of Shaikh Haza's illness has not been passed on to Shaikh Shakhbut.

A visit was paid to Shaikh Shakhbut on the 21st, when, as mentioned elsewhere he raised the question of the new location in his territory and of contractors employed by the company.

DUBAI:

Lord and Lady Louis Mountbatten spend the night of the 23rd in Dubai on their way back to the U.K. from India.

The P.R.[5] and Lady Burroughs were in Dubai from the 23rd to the 25th.

DUBAI OFFICE:

The following company personnel paid duty visits to Dubai and were accommodated in the mess.

		Arrival	Departure
Mr. J.E. Sager	Firemaster and safety officer	1	2
Mr. R.G. Boardley	Acting stores officer	1	2
		30	*
Mr. E.D. King	Driller	15	16
		20	23
Rev. K.T. Jenkins	Umm Said	8	9
Mr. P.R. Johnson	Air conditioning engineer	16	19
		28	*
Mr. J. McCreath	Electrical Foreman	16	19
		28	*
Mr. Rose	Tarif	21	23
Mr. H.R. Hayes	Area Supt. Trucial Coast Tarif	24	27

5 The Political Resident and his wife.

Mr. E.J. Nott Acting stores officer 30 *

Morgan
Representative.

TRUCIAL COAST DIARY FOR PERIOD ENDING 30 MAY 1956

Mr. G. Littledale arrived in Dubai on the 3rd to take over the duties of Representative Trucial Coast from Mr. J. Morgan during the latter's absence on short U.K. leave.

Mr. Morgan left Sharjah by air on the 17th.

On the 23rd the General Manager Mr. P.R.A. Ensor accompanied by the Assistant Chief Representative Mr. W.A. Livingston visited Sharjah and Dubai, after lunch with the Representative Trucial Coast in Dubai they proceeded by air to Tarif, where they spent the night and returned to Qatar the next day.

Courtesy "Eid al Fitr" calls were made on all the appropriate Muslim notables on the 12th and 13th of May.

During the month visits were paid by the undersigned to the Rulers of Abu Dhabi, Ras al Khaima, Umm al Quwain, Sharjah and Dubai.

ABU DHABI:

On the 9th a visit was paid to Shaikh Shakhbut, who appeared to be in rather poor health, which perhaps accounted for the fact that he made no fresh demands or requests from the Company.

Apart from dwelling briefly on the question of his mysterious "Rights" to extort a cut from the profits of Company contractors working in his sand rich domain, no questions of business raised by him.

On the 15th the son of Shaikh Shakhbut, Shaikh Said bin Shakhbut left Sharjah airport for India via Bahrain.

It is stated that he is going to India for medical treatment, … .

On the 31st Shaikh Khalid bin Sultan, brother of Shaikh Shakhbut left Abu Dhabi for medical treatment in India, he was accompanied by his son and three retainers.

DUBAI:

Visits with paid to Shaikh Said and Shaikh Rashid by the undersigned on the 12th and the 21st.

Under the tolerant and reasonable Rule of Shaikh Rashid, Dubai and Deira continue to develop fast.

Jashanmal the well-known Indian merchants in Bahrain and Kuwait, have completed a fairly large building in Deira and intend to open a branch there in the very near future.

Messrs. Wimpey have started core drilling in Dubai Creek as a prelude to its dredging.

Shaikh Rashid has started recruiting a Dubai Police Force, mainly for use in Dubai and Deira towns.

This Police Force will prove a blessing to the inhabitants, as with the growth of Dubai as a port there is a large transitory population, certain elements of which are rather unruly and light fingered.

On the 26th Shaikh Rashid left Sharjah for Kuwait by a special Dakota plane which was sent for him by the Shaikh of Kuwait.

It is reported from a hitherto reliable source that the object of Shaikh Rashid's visit to Kuwait was to seek financial assistance to enable him to carry out improvements in his state.

It was originally thought that he would try to obtain the loan or gift of Rs. 5,000,000 from the Shaikh of Kuwait, to enable him to pay for the dredging of the creek, but it is now believed that H.M.G. are prepared to back him in his project and his demands in Kuwait were to enable him to start electricity and educational projects in Dubai.

Shaikh Rashid returned to Dubai on the 31st having, it is reported, been successful in his request for financial assistance in Kuwait.

During the last week of May two stabbing incidents occurred among the Indian community.

Some 40 Indians, a lot of whom did not possess proper travelling documents were involved and all of them were arrested and locked up in the Dubai jail for two days while the stabbings were investigated, later two of them were deported back to India.

This is the first incident of its kind to take place among foreigners in Dubai and it is believed that strict action will be taken against Indians who try to enter Dubai in future if they are not in possession of valid travelling documents.

The recent order by the Sultan of Muscat prohibiting the centuries old trade between his Sultanate and the Trucial States has had a very adverse effect on the Trucial States, especially in Dubai.

The merchants of Dubai are very critical of what they consider to be a senseless and useless example of the Sultan's despotism as they used to have a comparatively thriving trade with Oman and Muscat.

SHARJAH:

The Ruler of Sharjah, Shaikh Saqr bin Sultan was visited on the 12th, 27th and 28th.

On the 13th the Ruler visited the Company offices in Dubai and discussed a certain radio broadcast (the undersigned confidential memo 16th of May 1956 refers) [missing]

On the 14th the undersigned, at the Rulers invitation, attended a school play given by Sharjah boys' school.

After arrival it was learned that the object of the play was to raise funds for enlarging the school.

The theme of the play was generosity and lists of donation from unfortunate victims were read out at the end of the play.

On the 27th and 28th the undersigned accompanied Messers. Van der Plaats, Woolley, Cooper, Badcock and Welsh on a recce trip in the Dhaid and Falaj Ali areas.

The bedouin tribes in the Dhaid area who apparently owe allegiance to Sharjah, seem to be rather dissatisfied as the Ruler was not paying them any money.

On the 28th the undersigned dined with the Ruler in his Palace in Sharjah.

UMM AL QUWAIN:

The Ruler of Umm al Quwain was visited on the 26th, he had no problems with the Company to discuss and his agricultural projects in Falaj Ali were discussed.

Umm al Quwain was visited again, by the undersigned on the 28th in company with Mr. Van der Plaats and his party when the marine landing base and Company compound were inspected.

RAS AL KHAIMA:

The undersigned visited the Ruler of Ras al Khaima on the 26th.

The Ruler raised the question of a request made by him for a loan of Rs. 100,000 from the Company last year, the undersigned stated he had recently taken over and had not heard of the request but would enquire into the matter.

Agricultural projects in Ras al Khaima under the supervision of Mr. Huntingdon (member of the H.B.M. Political Agency Staff) seem to be progressing well.

POLITICAL AGENCY:

Mr. Julian Walker returned to Dubai from Bahrain on the 15th to resume his boundary fixation and the delimitation work in the Trucial States.

He has started on the disputed areas of Sharjah State, these disputed areas involve Dubai, Ajman and Umm al Quwain.

Whether the respective Rulers will observe the frontiers laid down, despite their promises to do so, remains to be seen.

RUMOURS AND GOSSIPS:

There appears to be a strong undercurrent of feeling among the Rulers and notables of the Trucial States that the Company is acting in the Trucial States under the orders of H.M.G. and they have been instructed by H.M.G. not to discover oil yet, so that the Protectorate can be turned into Mandate or Trusteeship.[6]

Considerable feeling against the British Bank of the Middle East in Dubai has been aroused by a rumour that when the Ruler approached them for a loan, to dredge the creek, they stated that a condition of the loan would be a 15 year extension of their present 25 year monopoly in Dubai and adjoining states.

The majority of local merchants would like to see other banks come in, perhaps to enable them to start new overdrafts.

In the last week of May an Arab soldier of the Trucial Oman Scouts was Court-martialled and sentenced for ... on a truck whilst in transit between Sharjah and Buraimi.

DUBAI OFFICE:

The following personnel paid duty visits to Dubai and were accommodated in the mess.

		Arrived	Departed
Mr. E.J. Nott	Store keeper Tarif	*	4
Mr. R.G. Boardley	Store keeper Tarif	*	4
Mr. P.R. McDonald	Rig Maintenance Engineer Tarif	1	5
Mr. J.B. Latham	Transport Engineer Tarif	11	14
Mr. J.M. Kennedy	Foreman Mechanic Tarif	11	14
Mr. J. McCreath	Electrical Foreman Tarif	18	20
Mr. S. Wantling	Electrical Foreman Tarif	18	20
Mr. H.R. Hayes	Area Superintendent Trucial Coast Tarif	24	26
Mr. R.L. Stevenson	Photographer Dukhan	24	31
Mr. H.J. van der Platt	Senior Geophysicist Dukhan	26	29
Mr. C.W. Woolley	Assistant to Senior Geophysicist Dukhan	26	29
Mr. D. Cooper	Area Superintendent Tarif	26	30
Mr. I. Badcock	Camp Boss Party 5	26	30
Mr. K.L.N. Welsh	Seismic Party	26	30

Littledale
Representative.

6 Some muddled thinking here.

No Diaries June to November 1956.

TRUCIAL COAST DIARY FOR PERIOD ENDING 31 DECEMBER 1956

ABU DHABI:

The Chief Representative accompanied by Messrs. Livingston, Littledale, Ali Tajir and myself visited Shaikh Shakhbut on 2nd December during which visit three main points were discussed; firstly the invitation to El Hamra[7] on 17th December, secondly the withdrawal by the Ruler of his claim against the Company for custom's dues and thirdly increasing of the concession payment. Shaikh Shakhbut became so incensed at the second of these points that he refused to either discuss or consider the third and intimated that he proposed to refuse to accept anything further from the Company.

This interview, however, had no detrimental effect on the visit of the Ruler to El Hamra on 17th December which passed off in a happy atmosphere. H.B.M.'s Political Officer at Abu Dhabi[8] accompanied the Ruler to El Hamra. In accordance with the wishes of the Political Officer advantage was taken of this occasion to get the Ruler to go hunting thus allowing himself to be seen by some of his subjects[9] who live in an area which he only rarely visits. The Ruler took considerable interest in the Company's operations and had the opportunity of meeting many of his subjects employed by the Company.

Abu Dhabi was also visited on 10th and 30th December by me[10] but on both occasions no business of any sort was discussed.

Mohamed Al Rahma[11] came to Abu Dhabi from Muscat during the month and left afterwards for Buraimi. He was accompanied from Muscat by two of his sons who remained in Dubai until he left for Buraimi when they followed their father.

Shaikh Khalid, a brother of the Ruler left for India during this month for medical treatment. He travelled by air via Sharjah.

El Hamra was visited on 15th December and a number of administrative points were discussed.

---

7 Al Hamra was the base for the drilling operations further south at Gezira and Shuweihat. The Ruler visited the drilling rig at the new location at Shuwaihat, where drilling started early in November.

8 M. Buckmaster. He lived in Dubai as a Political Officer and was preparing to take up residence in Abu Dhabi.

9 Mostly Manasir, and some Murra in this area.

10 I.S. Kirkbride.

11 Mohamed bin Salimeen Al Shamsi from Sunainah, Sultanate of Oman.

AJMAN:

The Ruler of Ajman was visited on the 11th December when Mr Littledale introduced me and took his leave. The Ruler was concerned about the date on which the Company intended to start operations in his territory.

The Ruler of Fujairah stayed here during the period he was receiving medical treatment from Dubai hospital.

DUBAI:

Trade continues to flourish in Dubai although strong winds during the latter part of the month made passage of the creek a hazardous affair.

There have been several occasions on which pro-Nasser slogans were shouted at British subjects seen in Deira.[12]

On Friday 7th December during the midday prayers both Shaikh Rashid and Shaikh Abdul Rahman Al Dajani the Chief Justice, were denounced as traitors for allowing themselves to sit with foreigners. Shaikh Rashid was present in the Mosque at the time, the Chief Justice was not. The latter, a Syrian national who had many years' service in Palestine before the termination of the Mandate, immediately submitted his resignation. It took the Political Agent some considerable time and much work to get the matter patched up.

The Chief Justice is reported to be thoroughly unpopular with other members of the bench due to his avowed intention to remain un-corruptible and bring the Law Court to the same standard. This has already resulted in one of the Mullas leaving.

The British Foreign Office films on Port Said have been shown to selected audiences. Public showing is not apparently possible since the proprietor of the cinema firstly does not believe that the films were taken at the time of the Anglo-French occupation and secondly fears that his cinema will be wrecked by the pro-Egyptian elements in Deira.

Shaikh Rashid left for Iran on a hunting expedition during the third week in December.

A number of notables and merchants called at the house on the occasion of Christmas Day.

A case of smallpox was discovered earlier in the month in Dubai and the Government hospital undertook mass vaccinations. The number of such vaccinations given in Dubai, Deira and Sharjah totaled about 70,000.

---

12 This was after the Anglo-French-Israeli military operation, in August 1966, to occupy the Suez Canal Zone after President Nasser of Egypt had nationalised the Suez Canal. There was a wave of Anti-British protest throughout the Arab world.

FUJAIRAH:

Mr. Littledale and myself were unable to visit Fujairah before the former's departure, due to lack of time.

However on 7th December the Ruler called at the office. Sometime ago he had suffered from a stroke which left half of his face immobilised and was currently receiving treatment at the Government hospital. He proposed to visit either India or Iraq to obtain further treatment.

It was explained to him that due to the closing of the Suez Canal, arrival of the two Land Rovers which the Company had agreed to present to him would be delayed. Delivery to him was promised at the earliest opportunity after arrival in Dubai.

RAS AL KHAIMA:

During the tour of introduction at the beginning of the month Ras al Khaima was visited on 5th December, the previous night being spent at the Agricultural Experimental station some twelve miles away.[13]

Mr. Huntingdon reported that his friends in the town had been warned that it would be unwise with him to visit the suq area as a number of persons were feeling very strongly anti-British. Later the need for this caution disappeared and by the end of the month things were reported to be back to normal.

When we called on the Ruler, he was not present having gone to Dubai earlier that very day. He was visited on 7th December in Dubai. He was concerned about his application for an advance from the Company and was later advised that this could not be granted.

The Manager of the British Bank of the Middle East has concluded an agreement with the Ruler, the basic clauses of which included:

(a) Validity of 20 years from 1956.
(b) Opening of a branch in Ras al Khaima at the latest within six months of the Oil Company (whether land or sea) confirming in writing to the Ruler that they have started commercial exploitation of oil discovered in his territory.
(c) For four years dating from the opening of a full-time branch, the Ruler undertakes to allow no other bank to open a branch or operate in his territory.
(d) The payment for the concession will be annually in advance.
(e) A specific sum was paid at the time of signing the agreement.

SHARJAH:

Like many of his colleagues the Ruler of Sharjah spent a considerable part of the month away from the affairs of state, hunting.

13 At Digdaga, south of Ra's al-Khaimah town.

There were some reports by personnel of Party 5 of pro-Nasser[14] slogans being shouted out when they appeared in the town.

Earlier in the month two incidents occurred; the first was an attempt to burn down the garage belonging to Lieutenant Colonel E. Johnson the Commanding Officer of the Trucial Oman Scouts[15] and the second was the cutting of one of the two water lines supplying the R.A.F. station and airfield, of all things, by a hacksaw during one night. The culprit of the last incident was traced as a result of identification of his footprints and was flogged.

Shortly after these incidents, the Ruler held a meeting of Sharjah intellectuals at which he exhorted his subjects to refrain from anti-British activities and asked them if they were unable to cooperate with the British at least to keep quiet.

On being advised that the Company was not prepared to grant him the advance asked for sometime ago, the Ruler became angry and threatened to sever connections with the Company except through the Political Agent, to advise the Political Agent that he could no longer be responsible for Company equipment, and to refuse payments of any sort. None of these threats were carried out. It is believed that the Political Agent talked privately to the Ruler. A few days later the Ruler was again discussing the advance.

For some time the Manager of the British Bank of the Middle East had been pressing the Ruler to repay his overdraft and the latter had tried to obtain relief from this by promising that there would be no difficulty over obtaining an advance from the Company. The loan was finally obtained from local merchants.

It is rumoured that the Ruler is trying to raise money by various means connected with the levying of custom's dues.

Difficulty was experienced over the supply of water to Party 5 from the wells at Dhaid immediately prior to the Company's refusal to grant the advance mentioned above. Blame for this state of affairs appears to fall on both sides and an amicable agreement was reached shortly after the Party returned from its Christmas leave period.

During the lunch party given by him on 7th December, the Ruler showed considerable interest in the proposed date of the start of the new location.[16] No information was available to give him.

The Ruler appointed his brother Abdullah, to be his representative on matters concerning Party 5. This arrangement has proved reasonably successful in spite of obvious language difficulties.

---

14 Egyptian President Nasser.

15 The Trucial Oman Levies were renamed Trucial Oman Scouts, effective 1 March 1966. In Al Ain they occupied Jahili Fort from November 1955 having used Murabah Zayed from the time of their first arrival in the area in September 1952.

16 New drilling location. The Company drilled a well at Juweiza in 1957/1958 to a depth of 12,916 feet but did not find oil.

Several cases of scarlet fever were reported in the outlying districts during the early part of the month, and some Trucial Oman Scout's personnel are reported to have contracted the disease.

UMM AL QUWAIN:

The Ruler of Umm al Quwain was visited on 6th December during the introductory tour of the states. No business was discussed and the only point relevant to oil raised was the question of why, when oil production is on the increase around the world, does the price of its products continue to rise!

In the middle of the month the company craft "Jumana" landed the equipment to be used for the drilling of water wells in the Sharjah concession area.

Party 5 operators, spent some four days in this territory during the month. Due to the short period they stayed in the area, the Ruler agreed to allow the Sharjah subjects to continue to work without hindrance.

AGENCY:

Mr Julian Walker is again operating on boundary delineation between the states of Sharjah and Ras al Khaima at the base of the Oman mountains[17] which run from south to north on the eastern side of the Trucial States territory.

Kirkbride
Representative.

17 The Hajar mountain range.

1957

TRUCIAL COAST DIARY FOR JANUARY 1957

ABU DHABI:

Abu Dhabi was visited on 3rd, 19th and 29th January on the last occasion with Ali Tajir of P. C. L. Bahrain.

On 3rd January the night was spent with the Political Officer, and the Ruler was visited on 4th January. No business was discussed with the Ruler on this occasion. He showed considerable interest in the Shell rig disaster off Qatar and rumours which were subsequently said to be incorrect, gave the figure of Abu Dhabi subjects missing as anything from 100 to 250.

In discussion the Political Officer said that an attempt was being made to get Messrs. African and Eastern Limited interested in the development of Abu Dhabi with the idea, presumably, to take over from the Abu Dhabi Development Company which went bankrupt last year.

Dr. McCaully also called on the Ruler on 4th January and the latter did not appear particularly pleased when he learnt that Dr. D'Sousa was in Buraimi at the time without his knowledge.

The purpose for the visit of 19th January was to introduce Mr. G. D. Entwistle to the Ruler. The party from El Hamra consisted of Messrs. Cooper, Entwistle, Chandler and Smith.[1] The last two did not call on the Ruler. No business was discussed with Shaikh Shakhbut.

Messrs. Buckmaster and Hillyard were also visited. Both were concerned about a report that there had recently been another incident at Gezira between the Shaikh's guards there and a hunting party from Qatar. Subsequently this proved to be a reiteration of the November incident.

1 All IPC.

Hillyard mentioned that Shaikh Shakhbut was considering employing British officers for his 'Police' force.

Hillyard was having some trouble with the Ruler over a traffic accident involving a Britisher and an Abu Dhabi subject. The Ruler insists that the case is taken to court and the whole legal procedure followed in spite of both A. D. M. A.'s[2] and the victim's willingness to settle the matter out of court. The Ruler is apparently trying to establish a precedent to be followed on all future occasions.

It was understood that the radio telephone link between the Political Officer[3] and the Agency[4] will be opened early in February. This will relieve A. D. M. A. of their responsibilities for keeping the two parties in radio touch with each other.

Shaikh Abdulla bin Isa al Khalifa, uncle of the Ruler of Bahrain arrived in Abu Dhabi during the afternoon of 19th January, remained there until the 22nd when with a party of Abu Dhabi Shaikhs led by Shaikh Zaid proceeded to Bainuna[5] on a hunting expedition. This party spent the night of the 22nd at Mirfa, where, not having warned the Trucial Oman Scouts of their intended arrival, they were held up until their identity was established.

El Hamra was visited from 21st to 23rd January. Whilst there a long discussion was held between Messrs. Cooper, Entwistle[6] and myself on the question of the Ruler's guards and ways and means of trying to stop petty pilfering. The Area Superintendent was informed of our very weak position over the guards in Abu Dhabi territory since the Company had ceased all payments there for. It was admitted that under these conditions it would not help matters to continue complaining about the inefficiency of the guards. As soon as the position is restored, it is the Area Superintendent's intention to continue with these complaints for he feels that there is some benefit to be gained by such a policy in spite of the fact that the present situation is a direct result of it. It was agreed that it is almost impossible to move the small village which has grown up outside the camp area. Again our views on the desirability of the village being there, were directly opposed.

Very heavy rain fell over almost all the Abu Dhabi territory on 21st and 22nd of January and the roads became almost impassable during the first day.

---

2 Abu Dhabi Marine Areas. The offshore oil company operated by BP and owned ⅔ BP and ⅓ Total.

3 Buckmaster was the Political officer in Abu Dhabi, reporting to the Political Agent in Dubai.

4 Tripp was the Political Agent in Dubai reporting to the Political Resident in Bahrain.

5 Central in Abu Dhabi territory.

6 From the Office in London. Ten years later I took him, when he was again visiting Abu Dhabi, to the drilling rig at Shah to the south of Liwa.

On 29th January the annual payment was taken to Shaikh Shakhbut and was refused in accordance with the Shaikh's statement to the Chief Representative on 2nd December 1956.

Shaikh Khalid who was reported in December's edition of this diary as having gone to India on medical grounds, returned to Abu Dhabi on 29th January having undergone an operation whilst in India. He is reported to be much better after this treatment.

According to Mr. Hillyard, Shaikh Shakhbut invited Shaikh Abdulla bin Issa to visit Abu Dhabi in order to ask him for the hire of the Government water drilling outfit used in Bahrain. Another version of the reason of the visit was that Shaikh Abdulla tried to go to Saudi Arabia for hunting as is his usual practice but was either told that he was not welcome or he was made to feel unwelcome.

AJMAN:

Ajman was not visited this month.

DUBAI:

Throughout the month Shaikh Rashid was in Iran on the hunting trip mentioned last month.

The main cause for concern this month in Dubai has been the weather. On 12th January during a period of very high winds, 2 fishing boats were washed ashore and wrecked. Several fishermen were found to be seriously ill, and 2 died as a result of exposure. Later in the month on 22nd, 23rd and 24th January the heavy rains brought transport to a standstill and caused considerable damage to shops and storehouses in the town. Some merchants are said to have lost goods worth quite large sums of money.

Mr. Lewis from the distribution side of B.P. in Bagdad arrived in Dubai on 13th January and has been travelling round the Trucial States with a view to starting sales. At the present moment he is awaiting arrival of the first shipment from Abadan. There are still rumours that Shell are also going to set up some sort of sales organization in the Trucial States which will be run from Dubai although there are no signs of any activity as yet.

Shaikh Abdulla bin Isa[7] arrived from Bahrain by B.I.[8] boat on 18th January.

The Senior Naval Officer, Persian Gulf visited Dubai on 18th January and his arrival by air was followed shortly afterwards by the arrival of H. M. S. Loch Killesport[9] one of the frigates stationed in the Persian Gulf. H. M. S. Loch Killesport left Dubai on 21st January for Abu Dhabi and thereafter for shooting practice somewhere off Sir Bani Yas island.

---

7 Uncle of Bahrain Ruler.

8 British India Steamship Navigation Company.

9 Her (or His) Majesty's ship Loch Killesport. A British Royal Navy vessel.

It was rumoured in Dubai that the Shah of Persia was sending an aircraft to Bandar Abbas to take Shaikh Rashid to Teheran for a meeting. Later this was changed to the Shah sending Shaikh Rashid a present.

Nothing more was heard of either the smallpox or scarlet fever scare mentioned in last month's diary.

FUJAIRAH:

As far as can be ascertained in Dubai the Ruler of Fujairah has not yet returned from abroad.

RAS AL KHAIMA:

The wave of anti-British feeling in Ras al Khaimah has passed, according to reports.

At the instigation of the Political Agency, a British geologist visited the agricultural station in Ras al Khaima during the early part of the month to try and help solve the problems Mr. Huntington has been experiencing over the supplies of water from the wells there.

Another visitor was Mr. Ollenbach the Manager of the Bahrain Government Experimental farm.

Ras al Khaima was not visited this month.

SHARJAH:

The difficulties regarding the supply of water from Dhaid which were mentioned in last month's diary, were overcome after discussions with Shaikh Saqr on 2nd January.

In the morning of 7th January Shaikh Saqr had a car accident. His car was stationary at the time of impact and only a few of the occupants of the other car involved were superficially injured.

The Manager of the British Bank of the Middle East called on 12th January and discussed Shaikh Saqr's position. As a result of the latter's failure to obtain an advance from the Company, Mr. Baker has been restricting his credit.

He also asked whether the rumours that the Company were about to start drilling in Sharjah territory were true and also the position of the location.

During a visit which took place on 15th January, the Ruler asked when the Seismic Party was proposing to complete its work in the area. He showed concern over the large proportion of Arab labourers recently discharged from the Party as opposed to the number of other nationalities. He asked us to try and arrange the discharge of all labourers of other nationalities.

Also on 15th January, Mr. Taylor the "Times" correspondent from Kuwait visited Party 5 and took lunch there. The purpose of his visit to the Trucial States was not directly connected with oil. He had come to see what was being done with regard to the "Trucial States Development Scheme".

During the middle of the month it was necessary to visit the proposed site for a water well at Tawi Hussain near Dhaid as there was some doubt to start with, as to whether this was located in Sharjah or Umm al Quwain territory (see also Umm al Quwain).

Shaikh Abdulla bin Issa spent the night of 18th in Sharjah the Ruler having managed to complete his new majlis just in time for this visit.

On 24th January while visiting the Political Agent, the latter said that the Ruler had asked him to use his influence in helping him obtain an advance from the Company. The Political Agent seemed satisfied with the Company's policy on this matter and later it became apparent that he had intimated to Shaikh Saqr that he supported this view.

Shaikh Ali the son of Abdulla bin Issa arrived in Sharjah on 30th January and stayed with Shaikh Saqr until his father returned from Abu Dhabi during the first days of February. He called at the office on 31st January, and was given assistance in communicating with his father.

Whilst on their hunting trip, the Ruler and Shaikh Ali called on Party 5 on 31st January.

UMM AL QUWAIN:

Umm al Quwain was visited on 8th and 17th January. With the possibility of its importance increasing as a result of it being used as a beach head for landing equipment for the second location,[10] visits to Umm al Quwain are being increased.

During the second visit at which lunch was taken, the Ruler showed considerable interest in the site of the new water well drilling about which he had heard. He appeared convinced that it was not in his territory although it took some discussion before he came round.

He had had a visit from Mr. Lewis (see Dubai above) and again raised the possibility of this newcomer to the market, reducing the price of petrol in spite of the fact that he admitted that he bought the cheapest available which is smuggled from Iran. After lunch he suddenly appeared to be quite sick due presumably to his affliction of diabetes.

Acting on behalf of the Ruler, Mr. Tripp[11] approached the Company for permission to allow the British Bank of the Middle East to conclude an agreement with Umm al Quwain.

---

10 Second drilling location on the Trucial Coast, excluding Abu Dhabi. The well was in Sharjah territory.

11 Political Agent Dubai.

AGENCY:

Throughout the month Mr. Walker[12] continued with his investigations into the correct positions of the borders between the states of Ras al Khaimah and Sharjah.

On his way back to Bahrain from Muscat, the Political Resident[13] stayed 3 days in Dubai arriving on 11th January and leaving on 14th. It is understood that he had a serious talk to Shaikh Saqr with regard to the latter's financial position.

Kirkbride
Representative.

TRUCIAL COAST DIARY FOR FEBRUARY 1957

ABU DHABI:

In spite of the Ruler's refusal to accept the annual payment from the Company, relations continue to be friendly. The Political Agent[14] was informed of the position of this payment on 5th February in the presence of Mr. E. F. Henderson[15] of the Political Residency, Bahrain. Although they were both somewhat surprised at Shaikh Shakhbut's refusal, the Political Agent later appeared to be rather disinterested. During the latter part of the month it became apparent that the Political Officer[16] in Abu Dhabi had been informed of the position, and in addition to which Mr. Hillyard of A.D.M.A. had found out about the matter.

The radio telephone between the Political Agency in Dubai and the Political Officer in Abu Dhabi was installed and put into operation during the month.

The annual consignment of free petrol supplied by B. P. to the Ruler of Abu Dhabi arrived on 5th February.

During the visit to Abu Dhabi on 19th February, Shaikh Shakhbut was presented with the photographs taken on the occasion of his visit to El Hamra on 17th November 1956, and showed great pleasure in the gift, going through the album many times.

Among other matters discussed at this meeting, was the camel racing which had taken place at Beda al Mughani[17] on 17th February. The Ruler was keen to ensure that the populace of Dubai were told that a camel of his tribe had won the race from a camel of Shaikh Rashid.

---

12 Mr. Julian Walker.

13 Sir Bernard A.B. Burrows.

14 J. P. Tripp.

15 Previously with the Company PD(TC).

16 The Hon. M. Buckmaster.

17 Bida Al Mughani is in Abu Dhabi territory about 40 Kilometres north-north-west of Al 'Ain.

Mr. Buckmaster was, on this occasion, in an extremely critical mood and this is the first time that I have ever heard him criticize the Ruler. The subject was the proposal of H.M.G. to open a dispensary in Abu Dhabi, to which the Ruler's attitude was that excellent proposal that it was, he himself was not prepared to assist if it meant putting himself out in the slightest. This meant, apparently that he was not even prepared to provide accommodation or the supply of water to the orderly.

Shaikh Zaid from Buraimi was in Abu Dhabi during the visit of the Political Resident[18] (see below under "Agency") and remained there for a few days afterwards.

AJMAN:

Ajman was not visited during the month.

DUBAI:

Shaikh Abdulla bin Issa[19] returned from his hunting trip[20] in Abu Dhabi territory on 2nd February staying from that date until his departure on 4th February at a tented camp in Umm Isqaim.[21] He was joined there by his son.

On 8th February Shaikh Rashid returned to Dubai from his hunting trip in Iran. During the whole time he was away his party killed some 800 bustard only which compared to previous years is rather poor.[22]

Whilst in Iran Shaikh Rashid was invited to visit the Shah in Teheran, but declined. The Shah sent him a present of a sporting rifle and a considerable quantity of literature on the Bagdad Pact[23] and anti-communism activities.

There has been an increase in the amount of activity from the sales organizations of the major oil companies wishing to market products in the Trucial States. B.P. received their first consignment from Abadan in 4 gallon tins and by the end of the month according to their own statement, were very satisfied with the sales being made. Shell have had a representative travelling around. The Ruler is understood to have told this man that it would be quite useless his firm trying to sell products at a price which will exceed the price of smuggled products from Iran. Presumably to keep abreast with this activity, three members of the BAPCO[24] sales organisation also visited Dubai during the latter part of the month. At the present moment BAPCO's

---

18 Sir Bernard Burrows.

19 From Bahrain.

20 In those days bustard were found in the Abu Dhabi desert in season.

21 Today a Dubai suburb.

22 The reported numbers of birds killed are surely an exaggeration.

23 A British inspired group of nations, Iraq, Iran, Turkey, Pakistan and the UK came together from 1955 to 1979.

24 Bahrain Petroleum Company.

products are the cheapest, provided the drums in which they come are returned. The market for empty 4 gallon tins has popularised the BP products, whether or not this will be the case when this market has absorbed all the cans it can, is open to question.[25] The relative prices and quality of the products is a matter of continual discussion here.

Plans for the new Municipality in Dubai appear to be nearing completion. The Iraqi expert is to go to Bagdad in the near future to complete the greater part of the initial statistical work. Naturally, there has been some opposition to some of the ideas put forward, but generally speaking a large proportion of the more important people have reached agreement. Sensibly it is intended to start slowly and with not too rigid a plan so that amendments can be made when this is found necessary.

Shaikh Abdul Rahman, the Syrian Qadhi of Dubai has decided not to stay after the completion of his contract with the Ruler. It would appear that he feels that he cannot continue to operate justly while there is interference from interested persons.

On 14th February a lunch party was given for Shaikh Rashid and his father. The latter, however, was unable to attend.

Mr. Allcard, a Director of Gray Mackenzie & Co. Ltd., visited Dubai on 27th February.

FUJAIRAH:

It has now been discovered that the Ruler of Fujairah did not in fact visit either Iraq or India for medical treatment.

During the visit of the Political Resident to the Trucial States (see under "Agency" below) the Ruler was in Ajman.

RAS AL KHAIMA:

A visit was made to Ras al Khaimah on 12th February. Although he did not mention this at the time it is understood that the Ruler is far from satisfied about the new borders which have been delimited by Mr. Walker of the Political Agency.

Mr. Huntingdon's Agricultural Experimental Station has been producing a considerable variety of fine vegetables. Attempts to emulate this example by local growers has not been such a success as there is a tendency to try and get Mr. Huntingdon to do all the work.

The Ruler was very friendly during the visit to his capital, but was rather concerned over the fact that there appeared to be no prospect of the Company starting work in his area.

25 The BP cans were very popular for many purposes ranging from seats for a cinema to building blocks (when filled with sand or cement).

SHARJAH:

During the early part of the month, the Political Agent showed considerable interest in our handling of the advance requested by the Ruler. From the fact that after supporting the Company's attitude vide last month's report, he appeared pleased when payment of the first half-yearly instalment was made before it was due, the Political Agent appears to find Saqr's financial difficulties rather embarrassing.

Mr. Moore of the British Council in Kuwait visited the Sharjah school at the beginning of the month. He appeared to be quite impressed with what was being done.

The Ruler continued to show interest in the start of operations connected with the second location[26] this subject being brought up at every interview.

Shaikh Saqr expressed the hope that if such a method of transportation is to be used, the Company would use Sharjah for landing stores from ships during the build-up of the second location.

Shaikh Saqr attended the camel racing mentioned in the "Abu Dhabi" paragraph above, but because of misunderstanding over the date on which the big race was to take place would not let his camels race for the first two days.

B. P. started building a storage depot for their products in Sharjah.

Mr. J. A. Court, the Manager of the Eastern Bank in Bahrain visited Sharjah early in the month with a view to ascertaining the value of his bank opening a branch there. He found the Ruler co-operative.

On 28th February, Shaikh Saqr left Sharjah for Kuwait with his son who has been taken seriously ill with an appendicitis. This considerably upset the local medical authorities who had prepared for the operation to take place in the hospital in Dubai. Unfortunately it is most probable that this sudden change of heart on the part of the Ruler is due to the general unpopularity of Dr. McCaully.

Party 5[27] personnel working just to the east of their camp site experienced some difficulties this month when the inhabitants of the village through which they had to pass refused to allow them to enter. The Ruler, being away at the time, his deputy, Shaikh Saif, was called in to settle the matter, which he did with commendable speed.

The Ruler gave a dinner party on the night of 8th February to which four members of Party 5 were invited.

UMM AL QUWAIN:

The Ruler of Umm al Quwain was advised on 18th February of the initial aspects of our operations in his area. He was very pleased to hear that we were about to start operations and proved most co-operative.

He appeared to be in better health than has previously been the case.

26 The second drilling location on the Trucial Coast excluding Abu Dhabi.

27 Seismic survey Party 5.

The Political Agent was advised towards the end of the month that the Company had considered his letter on behalf of Shaikh Ahmed as fulfilling the latter's obligations regarding the proposal to allow the British Bank of the Middle East to negotiate the opening of a branch in Umm al Quwain territory.

AGENCY:

The most important happening under this heading during the month was undoubtedly the official visit to the Trucial States of the Political Resident from Bahrain. This year he based himself in Ras al Khaima and all the Rulers except those of Abu Dhabi and Fujairah paid their official respects and were entertained to dinner there. He then visited the Rulers in turn, including the Ruler of Fujairah who had travelled to Ajman especially for this purpose. Abu Dhabi, in view of its geographical location was visited later. The Political Resident also visited El Hamra, Party 5 and Das Island.

Mr. Walker continued his mapping of the boundaries in the north eastern part of the Trucial States.

The new General Officer Commanding in Aden visited Sharjah on 8th February.

H. M. S.[28] Newcastle carrying the Commander-in-Chief of the East Indies station arrived in Dubai on 23rd February and sailed on 25th.

Dr. Mackenzie of the Foreign Office paid an extended visit to the Trucial States and Muscat during the month, inspecting medical facilities.

On 28th February the Political Agent was advised that the Company did not consider the monopolistic trend of the agreements between the British Bank of the Middle East and the Rulers of Umm al Quwain and Ras al Khaimah to be in the interest of the latter. The Political Agent advised that he intended to look into the matter.

Captain Binns of thc Trucial Oman Scouts who acts as the Company's medical officer in this area, returned from leave on 18th February.

Kirkbride.

---

28 Her (or His) Majesty's Ship.

TRUCIAL COAST DIARY FOR MARCH 1957

ABU DHABI:

Relations with the Ruler continued to be friendly, even when certain business subjects were discussed.

Visits were paid on 3rd, 10th and 31st March.

Although almost a month before the beginning of Ramadhan the Ruler was already fasting during the first of these visits for having been obliged to forgo the full fasting period some years ago he still fasts for a few days before the beginning of each month of Ramadhan to make up for his failure on the previous occasion.

During the second visit, which took place at a well named Umm al Muraikha[29] some 20 miles from Abu Dhabi the Ruler was informed of our intention to move Seismic Party 5 back into his territory in the Tarif area. He promised his co-operation.

This was duly brought into effect during the third and last visit when a request for guards for the party was made. The guards were subsequently provided.

The last visit was somewhat protracted, lasting including lunch for about four hours. Many subjects were discussed in the most friendly atmosphere. The Ruler showed considerable interest in oil, going into quite technical reasons as to how different types of oil from world wide sources manage to produce approximately the same standard of products.

Mr Buckmaster, the Political Officer, spent about half the month visiting Buraimi and was somewhat disappointed to find Shaikh Zaid absent.

In spite of the Ruler's lack of co-operation which was mentioned in last month's diary in the 6th paragraph under this heading, H. M. G. are reported to have decided to go ahead with their plan to build and operate a dispensary in Abu Dhabi.

El Hamra was visited on 10th and 11th March and the recently discovered thefts were discussed together with the problem of forbidding the entry of bedouin into the camp area.

Abu Dhabi was visited by the Manager of the British Bank of the Middle East together with his relief (see "Dubai") on 13th March. This party also visited the Ruler at Umm al Muraikha.

Mr. Hillyard, the Chief Local Representative of Abu Dhabi Marine Areas Ltd. has been experiencing some trouble over questions of medical compensation for workers on Das Island. There have been cases where workers have refused to accept medical treatment and have then claimed compensation. The Ruler, apparently, has been supporting the workers, in this particular matter.

29 Inland and northwards in the direction of Dubai.

Mr. Hillyard in the early part of the month gave up the agency for Gulf Aviation[30] who awarded this to one Khalifa bin Yousef[31] an Abu Dhabi subject. Mr. Hillyard then endeavoured to arrange for this man to become our agent in Abu Dhabi to deal with such matters as collection of the shift labour who take leave every week in that town. Unknown to Mr. Hillyard this man has previously worked as a contractor for the Company and since according to one source, his service was not entirely satisfactory, Mr. Hillyard's efforts have been resisted.

On 28th March in the mouth of the Dubai creek one of the Ruler's launches sank.[32] According to the Ruler's son this was the fault of Gray Mackenzie's barge which rammed the launch, although Gray Mackenzie contend that the launch was both aground and holed at the time of being rammed. Latest news indicates that the Ruler intends to file a suit for damages against Gray Mackenzies with the Political Agent.

AJMAN:

Ajman was visited on 27th March.

DUBAI:

Activity in the field of sales of petroleum products was somewhat less this month except in the case of B. P. who sent a British salesman here on 15th March to supervise their sales side. Latest rumours state that ARAMCO[33] is about to enter the market, although there were no signs of any action being taken in this respect by the end of the month.

Prices of the various makes now available in Dubai are as follows:-

BAPCO[34]	Rs. 80/- per drum
BP ex Abadan	Rs. 8/10 per 4 gallon tin[35]
	Rs. 7/8 per 4 gallon without tin
Smuggled ex Bahrain	Rs. 72/75 per drum[36]
Ex Abadan	Rs. 7/- per 4 gallon
Ex Qatar	Rs. 54/55 per drum

30 The forerunner of Gulf Air.

31 In due course the agency for Gulf Aviation/ Gulf Air, British Overseas Airways Corporation (BOAC) and other airlines was held by the brothers Khalifa and Omeir bin Yousef.

32 Sheikh Shakhbut's launch.

33 Arabian American Oil Company in Saudi Arabia.

34 Bahrain Petroleum Company.

35 Rs. 8 to 10.

36 Rs. 72 to 75 per drum. A drum is 55 US gallons or 46 imperial gallons. In this case Imperial gallons were used at that time both in Abadan and BAPCO.

The new Municipality was brought into being during the month. Ali Bustani, the Arab Assistant in the Political Agency was appointed Assistant President of the Council on 6th March with executive powers, and by the end of the month its work had started. Immediately noticeable were the cleaning of the streets, the widening of the streets in Deira, the filling of the worst depressions in the streets, and the 10% tax on intoxicating liquor.

The Syrian Qadhi left for Bahrain on 9th March. He is expecting to be offered a post in Bahrain by the Political Resident.

Visitors to Dubai included Miss Munroe of the Economist, Mr. Ritchie of the Foreign Office for whom the Political Agent gave a dinner party to which all the Rulers were invited, Mr. Clark of B.P. sales in London into whose sphere of responsibility this territory falls and Mr. Ursell of B.P. who accompanied Mr. Clark.

Mr. Baker Manager of the British Bank of the Middle East left Dubai on 27th March for Kuwait having handed over to Mr. King. Before leaving he toured all the states except Fujairah accompanied by Mr. King.

On 10th March whilst drunk a Lebanese building contractor shot and killed a Pakistani laundryman. This killing caused much comment in the town where the normal way of dealing with such matters is to kill the killer in cold blood. Since both these persons were foreigners the Political Agent had to try the case and to everyone's surprise awarded a punishment of 9 months imprisonment and deportation from the Trucial States.

Ali Tajir, a cousin of Mahdi Tajir the Director of Customs here, who until recently was employed by P.C.L. Bahrain[37] has come to Dubai where he intends to start a business importing and selling foods of every description except frozen foods.

The school in Deira held its annual celebrations and it is alleged that a number of anti-British speeches were made.

Shaikh Ali bin Thani, the Ruler of Qatar, took lunch with Shaikh Rashid on 29th March before continuing his journey by B.I. boat from India to Umm Said.[38] The guests included the Ruler of Sharjah, the Ruler of Ajman, the Political Agent and his assistant and myself.[39]

On 2nd March in Deira, as a result of an argument between a weight lifter who was putting on an exhibition and some of the audience, two persons were arrested and put in prison. This infuriated the prisoners' friends to such an extent that they attacked the prison and released them. Next morning the President of the Court again arranged

37 Ali Tajir's employment with the Company went back to pre-war (1939-1945) days. He was also extremely helpful in collecting information to assist in supporting the Abu Dhabi case in the border dispute with Saudi Arabia.

38 The Company's oil export terminal on the south east coast of Qatar.

39 Kirkbride.

for the arrest of the two miscreants, but on the pleas of some of the elders of the town, the Ruler agreed to release them.

FUJAIRAH:

The Ruler of Fujairah called at the office on 18th March. There was a general discussion on Fujairah of which the only interesting item brought to light was that at the present moment Fujairah obtains its supplies of petrol, etc. from Dubai but application had been made to the Political Agent to allow direct shipments to be made. So far, for some reason unknown to the Ruler, permission to do this had been withheld.

The Ruler asked about the delivery of two Land Rovers promised as a gift to him by the Company.

He intends to go to Iraq for medical treatment after having completed a pilgrimage to Mecca this year. He stated that the Political Agent had advised him that the doctors in Iraq were among the best in the vicinity.

The Ruler stayed in Dubai and Ajman for the greater part of the month.

RAS AL KHAIMA:

Ras al Khaimah was only visited in company of the Chief Representative (see Chief Representative's tour below).

SHARJAH:

The Ruler returned from Kuwait (see last month's diary 8th paragraph under this heading) on 20th March with his son whose operation for appendicitis was successful.

During the month there was an exchange of visits between school boys from Sharjah and Kuwait and Qatar.

Party 5 completed its operations on 19th March except for a small field party. The main camp had moved out of Sharjah territory by 22nd March.

The Ruler continued to show great interest in the Company's progress towards the new drilling location to become operative in his territory and asked about this as soon as he returned from Kuwait.

The annual sports of the Sharjah school were held on 29th March. All the Rulers of the Trucial States were present with the exception of Shaikh Shakhbut from Abu Dhabi.

For those that were present at last year's sports the omission of Arab national flags from the ground came as something of a surprise. It was not long before the story as to how this occurred came out. Remembering last year, the Political Agent suggested that if flags other than Sharjah were to be flown it would be a pleasant gesture to include the Union Jack. The Principal pleaded that this was impossible as there was no such flag available in the school. This was countered by the Political Agent lending them a flag, with the result that the organizers decided to fly no flags.

However, the point was brought out in the speech of the Principal of the school, the Governments of Kuwait and Egypt were thanked for their co-operation in sending teachers, whereas reference to H.M.G. who provided the building was omitted.

The organizers did a good job and very nearly had the disappointment of not being able to complete the programme due, through no fault of theirs, to the ceremonies starting almost an hour and a half late.

A scouts troop from Dubai also took part.

See below for details of the visit of the Chief Representative to Sharjah.

The house for the teachers which is being built at the expense of the Kuwait Government is progressing well.

UMM AL QUWAIN:

The arrival of M.V. Jessoura and the posting of a Civil Engineer to Umm al Quwain heralded the opening of operations for turning the stores yard into a receiving depot for stores for the second drilling location.

It was arranged that the Ruler would visit the Jesoura the day after arrival, 14th March, but due to the extremely inclement weather this had to be delayed until the following day and almost did not take place at all. The Ruler took tea with the crew and technical personnel on board before inspecting the vessel and watching unloading operations. He was presented with some cases of fresh fruit later in the evening.

By the end of the month progress had been made and with the exception of some trouble with the guards who appeared to dislike taking orders from the engineer in charge of operations, there were no political teething troubles.

Umm al Quwain was visited on 5th, 14th, 15th and with the Chief Representative.

On the first occasion the work to be carried out in the territory was explained in greater detail to the Ruler. This was followed on 14th by introducing Mr. Christie, the Engineer in charge of operations to the Ruler at a lunch party given by the latter. Just before the end of the month the Northern Area[40] artisans paid their respects to the Ruler.

AGENCY:

Having completed his work with the frontiers Mr. Walker returned to the United Kingdom in the early part of the month.[41]

---

40 Arabs from Iraq, Palestine etc. The Company had difficulty in finding and attracting to the Trucial Coast enough Arab artisans, clerks, mechanics, carpenters etc. As the scale of the operations grew they had, increasingly, to look to India and Pakistan to fill posts.

41 Julian Walker's work met with considerable criticism from all the Shaikhdoms. However with relatively minor modification it formed the basis for boundaries which became, in general, accepted. After the establishment of the UAE in 1971 some areas were still in dispute and there were requests that Walker should return and help resolve problems.

As a result of the departure of the Syrian Qadhi to Bahrain, the Political Agent is considering obtaining the services of an Iraqi Kurd to replace him.

TRUCIAL OMAN SCOUTS:

During the month new outposts were set up at Rams[42] and Ain Khatt[43] in the Ras al Khaima area which must have done little to allay the fears of the Ruler that the Agency was about to force on him, what he considered, an unfavourable decision regarding the frontiers between Ras al Khaima and Fujairah.

The Lt. Colonel who will eventually replace Lt. Colonel Johnson arrived during the month but had not taken up his duties by the end thereof.

CHIEF REPRESENTATIVE'S TOUR:

The Chief Representative accompanied by the Assistant Chief Representative arrived in Sharjah on 15th March, on a visit the purpose of which was to call on all the Rulers except that of Fujairah, through lack of time, and of Abu Dhabi who had been visited earlier.

On 25th March the Rulers of Sharjah and Dubai were visited. Conversation was kept on general subjects including the Company's operations in their various territories.

On 26th Umm al Quwain and Ras al Khaima were visited. During the visit to Ras al Khaimah, the Ruler complained about the decision of the Political Agency regarding his frontiers with Fujairah. Mr. Huntingdon[44] was also visited. Dinner that evening was taken in Dhaid at the invitation of Shaikh Saqr the Ruler of Sharjah.

On the following day, the last day of the visit, a call was made on the Ruler of Ajman.

The visitors left Sharjah for Umm Said[45] after lunch on 27th March.

Kirkbride
Representative.

H.M.G. however stood firm in their belief that any outstanding disputes should be resolved within the UAE and the services of Walker were not required. Walker did return on a number of occasions many years later but by then almost all differences had been resolved.

42 A short distance north of Ra's al-Khaimah town, where the Ruler had to assert his authority earlier. See the diary for March 1952.

43 South east of Ra's al-Khaimah town. Near the foothills and very near the border with Fujairah. Hab Hab is the Fujairah settlement a few kilometres south of Khatt. Khatt is known for its hot springs.

44 At the Digdaga experimental farm.

45 The Qatar Petroleum Company Oil Export Terminal.

TRUCIAL COAST DIARY FOR PERIOD ENDING 30 APRIL 1957

ABU DHABI:

Abu Dhabi was visited on 14th April only due to the fact that April coincided with the month of Ramadhan.

This visit was considered necessary as there had been a large theft of electrical materials from El Hamra.[46] The Ruler was charming throughout the interview and granted the concession we sought which was the inspection of the Farij[47] in El Hamra after such thefts. In fact he went further without our prompting, by stopping all leave for guards for a period of six months and, if the materials were not recovered, the guards will not be paid for three months.

By the end of the month no progress on recovery has been made.

Whilst in Abu Dhabi visits were paid to Mr. Hillyard[48] and Mr. Buckmaster.[49]

Mr. Hillyard was apparently apprehensive that the Ruler might refuse to accept payment of the annual concession payment which fell due in the middle of the month, as a result of which he allowed payment in a case of medical compensation which he had previously been fighting. The annual payment was not refused but by the end of the month it is understood that the Ruler complained that he felt that Abu Dhabi Marine Areas Ltd. had lost confidence in him.

Mr. Buckmaster appeared somewhat annoyed that the Company would not let Mr. Nott make a written statement on the Gezira incident on last November[50] and rather worried over the Ruler's refusal to accept our annual payment.

Mr. Hillyard expressed a wish to interview Ali Tajir whom he had heard had left our service, with a view to employing him with ADMA.

---

46 This was the base for drilling the wells Gezira (abandoned 9 March 1956) and Shuwaihat. The drilling rig, active at Shuwaihat from November 1956 to November 1957 reached a depth of 12,360 feet. At that time the geologists still believed that the best prospects for finding oil were in the west of Abu Dhabi territory. This was nearer to the Qatar and Saudi Arabian oilfields with known oil bearing rock formations. These same rocks were found in Abu Dhabi territory, but much deeper down and without oil.

47 Village. It was inevitable that wherever the Company established a camp, a small settlement (Farij) would be set up nearby by the local employees so that they could have their families with them.

48 Abu Dhabi Marine Areas. BP and Total.

49 Political Officer at Abu Dhabi.

50 Nott was at Gezira to complete clearing of the location. When his team arrived they were met by a party of Arabs in seven cars. The Ruler's guards said that they had fired on them to prevent them from going further to Gezira.

On 13th April Shaikh Haza and Shaikh Khalid accompanied by Shaikh Zaid[51] left Abu Dhabi for the United States where they will undergo medical treatment.

As a result of Mr. Hillyard's efforts to come to an agreement with the Ruler over matters of workers' compensation, the Agency requested the Residency in Bahrain to send their labour official to consolidate everyone's ideas on this matter.

The question arising from the sinking of the Ruler's launch in Dubai have yet to be settled.

It is rumoured in Abu Dhabi that there is a possibility of Gulf Aviation[52] ceasing to land there due to lack of traffic.

Mr. Hillyard who is building a jetty outside the ADMA offices suggested that P.D.T.C. might consider contributing towards the cost since, in his opinion, a good jetty in Abu Dhabi would naturally result in our getting our supplies through that town instead of Dubai. He stated that the contractor providing food for Das was doing so at a cheaper price than the Dubai contractor previously used by them.

It would appear to be the policy of ADMA to deal with Dubai as little as possible. In the early part of the month their British Representative, Mr. Townsend was transferred to Bahrain and the running of the office handed over to the representative of BP Trading as a part time job. ADMA is not expected to replace Mr. Townsend.

El Hamra was not visited during the month.

Party 5 (Seismic) started operations from their new camp at Zenab[53] during the first week of the month.

Dr. Kelly[54] of Chatham House[55] visited Buraimi in the first week of the month accompanied by Mr. Hillyard.

It is rumoured that during Mr. Hillyard's forthcoming leave, Mr. R.A.T. Codrai of IPC will be acting for him during the summer.

AJMAN:

Ajman was visited on 16th, 21st and 24th April in connection with the guards employed on the road camp.

The Ruler,[56] as usual, showed considerable interest in what was going on and several times visited the road camp privately. He also showed considerable interest

51 The three brothers of the Ruler, Sheikh Shakhbut bin Sultan.

52 The old name for Gulf Air.

53 Zenab in Abu Dhabi territory.

54 Dr. J.B. Kelly was visiting in connection with his research which resulted in his publishing a book entitled 'Eastern Arabian Frontiers'.

55 Chatham House in London. An internationally recognised political research centre.

56 Shaikh Rashid bin Humaid. Ruler 1928-1981.

in the affairs of his fellow Rulers and as always was disarmingly straight forward in his questioning.[57]

DUBAI:

There was no change in the sales of Petroleum products during the month. Something was heard of the promised introduction of Shell's sales service but nothing materialized.

The Ruler[58] was visited on 28th April when the rents due for the offices and other buildings were paid.

By the end of the month the Ruler decided that the launch belonging to the Ruler of Abu Dhabi which was sunk at the entrance of the creek last month, should be removed as it is partially blocking the creek, and, more important, causing a sand bank to build up behind it.

Nothing further has been heard of how this case is to be settled.

The Municipality was again active about the town, filling in ditches in the roads, cleaning the streets and where possible widening the roads. The first attempts at raising money from the populace were made during the month and some progress reportedly although generally speaking, since no coercion was used to try and obtain payment, everyone is watching the reaction of his neighbours.

The Municipality are very short of funds.

The market of Dubai was closed for 24 hours starting from noon on 27th April on the occasion of the death of the father of the Ruler of Qatar.

FUJAIRA:

The Ruler of Fujairah is reported to have spent the whole of Ramadhan in Fujairah.

RAS AL KHAIMAH:

During the early part of the month the Ruler[59] left for Bahrain to discuss the question of the frontier with Fujairah with the Political Resident. He was still absent at the end of the month.

The town of Ras al Khaimah suffered badly in the storms during the early part of the month when a tidal wave broke over the sands.

57 Extract from Political Report. 'He particularly wanted to know how the Ruler of Ras al Khaimah was progressing with his complaint about the frontiers with Fujairah. In view of the fact that he has land in that area this is not surprising.' The land is his inland oasis at Manama which lies north of Dhaid.

58 Shaikh Saeed bin Maktoum. Ruler 1912-1958.

59 Sheikh Saqr bin Mohamed. Ruler 1948-2010.

The Political Agent recommended that relief to the amount of £1,000 be granted. This was cut down to £500 by the Treasury,[60] the final figure being a compromise at Rs. 10,000. As usual it was not possible to keep these negotiations secret and the final figure was known to the inhabitants of the town. This had the unfortunate result of their refusing to accept any aid at all, for the first two lorry loads of clothes etc. to arrive were considered to be the total amount forthcoming which the inhabitants thought to be rather little for such expenditure.

SHARJAH:

The Ruler of Sharjah was called on, on 29th April, when he was advised that the Company had started operations in the area of the new rig site.[61] Arrangements were made for the supply of labour and guards.

During the month the Ruler proclaimed that a customs fee of one Anna per Tola (worth about 70 Rupees) would be charged on all gold passing through Sharjah. This resulted in a complete suspension of importation for a short time while the gold merchants visited Shaikh Shakhbut with a view to importing gold through Abu Dhabi. It is reported that Shaikh Shakhbut demanded 4 Annas per Tola. Trade commenced again towards the end of the month with every importer complying with the Ruler's order.

The Ruler visited Doha on 28th April to offer his condolences to the Ruler of Qatar on the death of the latter's father.

The suq was closed on this account.

The well drilled by the Company at Tawi Hussain[62] was reported to have been blocked up. It is believed that this was done by persons trying to obtain water therefrom.

The Field Party left behind by Party 5 completed its work by the end of the month.

AGENCY:

Mr. Edes left the Trucial Coast on transfer at the beginning of the month and is replaced by Mr. Melhuish.[63]

Group Captain Coates together with his relief visited the Trucial States in the first week of the month.

Another visitor was Mr. Given the relief of Mr. Brookes-Richards in Bahrain, and his wife.

Kirkbride
Representative.

---

60 In London.

61 At Juwaiza.

62 A water well, not a deep oil exploration well. About 10 Kilometres west of Dhaid.

63 Political Officers.

TRUCIAL COAST DIARY FOR MAY 1957

ABU DHABI:

Abu Dhabi was visited on 2nd, 18th and with Mr. Livingstone on 27th May.

Generally relations have continued to be friendly although the Ruler showed signs of losing control once during the last visit when an approach was made on business matters which touched on what he considered to be his unfulfilled rights.

An interesting feature of the last meeting was that after some discussion with the Ruler, in which he refused to listen to our attempts to explain certain misconceptions in his mind, Mr. Buckmaster arrived and the Ruler immediately tried to start a three way discussion. Mr. Buckmaster, however, stated that he never became involved in Company matters. The Ruler did not appear pleased at this statement, particularly as we had been going to some length to explain that it was H.M.G. that decided frontiers and not our Company.

Mr. Hillyard has spent a considerable part of this month travelling between Abu Dhabi, Das Island and Bahrain. This increased activity is no doubt due to the approach of his company taking over from George Wimpey & Co. whose task of completing the camp on Das Island has almost finished.

Towards the end of the month a special copy of "The Golden Bubble" autographed by the author[64] was presented to the Ruler by Mr. Hillyard.

During the last two weeks of this month the Agency in conjunction with the T.O.S, R.A.F and R.N.[65] were undertaking search in order to find and prevent the entry into Abu Dhabi territory of alleged gun smugglers. It is believed that they met with no success.

AJMAN:

Ajman was not visited during the month except on the occasion of paying off of guards from that territory on 25th May. The Company is no longer employing people from this area.

DUBAI:

The news that caused the most comment this month came from Dubai.

Taking advantage of their presence in Sharjah, the band of the Cameronians[66] visited both Sharjah and Dubai and "Beat the retreat' for entertainment of the populace. After such a parade in Deira on 5th May, some students of the local school

64 The author was Roderick Owen, who was visiting Abu Dhabi at the time of Sheikh Shakhbut's meeting with Sultan Saeed bin Taimur at Buraimi/Al Ain in December 1955.

65 Trucial Oman Scouts, Royal Air Force and Royal Navy.

66 A Scottish regiment.

tried to remove the Union Jack[67] from the Political Agent's car and to stone both him and his family who were shopping in Jashanmal's store. This resulted in the Political Agent obtaining from the Ruler an order for the Jordanian school teacher's removal and return to Kuwait.

The following day all the school children came out on strike. On 7th May the school children held a demonstration carrying anti-Imperialism and Colonialism banners. This was broken up by the Ruler's men who were told to show no mercy, however small the child. The school master involved left Sharjah by air on 8th May and the situation settled down to normal again.

The Ruler visited Doha on 2nd and 3rd May to convey his condolences to the Ruler of Qatar on the occasion of his father's death in April and to offer his felicitations on the occasion of the Eid al Fitr.

The new Indian currency arrived Dubai during the month but was not issued for use by the public.

Apart from a visit by the Shell sales representative, Mr Read, no progress has been made by this company towards starting up. The B.P. representative stated that he expected a drop in the price of petroleum products in the near future. Kerosene, according to his statement, will be particularly effected.

It is understood that Shell have obtained permission to use the B.O.A.C. jetty, the attached buildings and an adjacent area for storage of their products. The use of the jetty by other concerns is to be retained.

On 25th May, Mr. Lorrimer arrived from Bahrain on a visit prior to his being appointed to the Dubai police force. He is expected to return to Dubai to take up his appointment in July. He is at present a member of the Bahrain police force.

Trade this month has declined. This is due to the fact that in the first place Iran has apparently come by extra supplies of foreign currency and that one of the bigger Pakistani smugglers has been caught by the Pakistani authorities.

FUJAIRA:

With the imminent arrival in Dubai of two motor vehicles to be presented to him by the Company, the Ruler spent the greater part of the month in this city. The vehicles were handed over to his representative on 27th May.

The Ruler called at the office twice during the month.

It appears that the vehicles given to him by the Company are the only two serviceable ones he now owns, and that until they arrived he was unable to return to his home territory.

He advises that he intends to go on a pilgrimage to Mecca and Medina shortly after returning to Fujairah. Having been before he was full of complaints about how the Saudi Arabian authorities extract money from pilgrims from foreign lands.

67 British flag.

Due to the extreme coldness of the weather this year the date crop in Fujairah and along the Batinah coast has been a failure.

RAS AL KHAIMA:

The Ruler of Ras al Khaimah returned to his home during the earlier part of the month without receiving any satisfaction over the question of frontiers from the Political Resident in Bahrain.

It is understood that he would like to raise some sort of trouble over the failure of the Political authorities to recognise his rights in the matter, but it is reported that so few people are interested in the question he could not expect to get much support.

SHARJAH:

Owing to the beginning of our operations in Sharjah territory there was much liaison work done in this month, dealing with such matters as recruitment, guards, approach roads, supply of transport and supply of food. After a few difficulties at the start various procedures were evolved which, by the end of the month, appeared to be working satisfactorily.

The realignment of the road to the rig site from Umm al Quwain proved harder than was first visualised due to the soft nature of the sand and some trips by loaded vehicles were only accomplished after extreme difficulty had been experienced.

The Ruler, during one of the many interviews which took place during the month, asked the Company to consider raising the wages of the guards, but after making enquiries from other concerns likely to be affected by such a change, it was considered that there was no real case to do so.

Towards the end of the month the main sphere of influence of the Company's operations was moved from Umm al Quwain to Juweiza[68] location. This resulted in a lightening of visits to Umm al Quwain of representatives of the Ruler of Sharjah which was becoming so frequent as to cause us some embarrassment.

During the last three days of the month, the Manager of the Eastern Bank in Bahrain paid a visit to Sharjah. He was taken on a visit to Dhaid by the Ruler on 28th May and reported that his bank intended to open up a branch in Sharjah in the near future. As far as can be gathered the agreement to be signed between the Ruler and the Bank includes clauses which forbid the opening of a third bank for a period of five years, and provision of living and office accommodation by the Ruler on a repayment basis.

There were two fires in Sharjah this month the first being of considerable proportions and resulting in the destruction of 30 houses. Assistance in dealing with

68 The Sharjah drilling location.

the fires was given by R.A.F. and T.O.S.[69] Financial assistance was given to Company employees who suffered hardships.

It was rumoured that as a result of the incidents in Dubai (see above) the Political Agent advised the three Jordanian school teachers of Sharjah that no re-entry visas would be granted to them and they would not be allowed to return from their summer leave.

It is reported that the Ruler has received a gift of six lakhs of Rupees[70] to be used towards the building of the jetty in Sharjah. The Ruler has approached us requesting an inspection and advice on this project by one of our engineers.

UMM AL QUWAIN:

Some difficulties arose over the supply of fish from the local market this month. The Company relies on Khansahib Hussain for its fish supplies and he found that it was not possible to supply at the Company's price for this commodity due to the fact that all fish had to be bought through the third son of the Ruler, who has put up the price to the Company buyer to almost three times the normal amount. The Company stood firm and at the end of the month Khansahib Hussain was said to be losing some Rs. 20/- per day. He had made an attempt to obtain fish from other villages but found it uneconomical to do so.

Along with many vehicles from Sharjah, three lorries were hired from the Ruler for the transport of Company equipment to the rig site. These amounted to the Ruler's complete fleet.

An agreement was signed with the Ruler for the constant surveying of the positions of the Company's buoys in the channel leading into the Khor.

The launch now plying between Baraka[71] and Umm al Quwain carrying Company supplies is from Umm al Quwain and is yet another way in which the Ruler and people of that town are obtaining benefit from the Company's presence there.

AGENCY:

Mr. Marshall, the First Secretary (Labour) at the Political Residency in Bahrain, visited Dubai at the beginning of the month to ascertain the views of the various British firms regarding a medical disability compensation scheme. This has become necessary as a result of attempts by Abu Dhabi Marine Areas to come to some agreement with the Ruler there on this question. These attempts have been crowned

69 Royal Air Force and Trucial Oman Scouts.

70 The amount received was £50,000, or about Rs. 667,000, or 6⅔ Lakhs. The donor was the Ruler of Qatar.

71 For the base at Al Hamra west of Jebel Dhanna.

with some success but are apparently by no means complete. By the end of the month, the results of Mr. Marshall's visit had not appeared.

Mr. E.F. Henderson visited Dubai on 6th and 7th May. It is rumoured that he will be relieving Mr. Tripp as Political Agent when the latter goes on leave this summer.

Mr. Tripp visited Bahrain on 9th and 10th May.

A visit by H.M.S. Loch Alvie was paid to Dubai on 15th and 16th May.

For the house to be built for the new head of police force, the Political is to adopt a system similar to that used by us in building the new Company house.

Mr. R. Malhuish was replaced by Mr. J. Adams as Assistant Political Agent on 29th May.

Kirkbride
Representative.

TRUCIAL COAST DIARY FOR JUNE 1957

ABU DHABI:

Abu Dhabi was visited on 11th, 22nd, 26th and 28th June. Mr. Ensor, Mr. Livingstone and Sayed Ibrahim Arrayedh visited Abu Dhabi on 22nd and 26th June.

The visit of the Chief Representative resulted, after much discussion of both relevant and irrelevant subjects, in the acceptance of an increased annual payment by the Ruler. Shaikh Zaid was present almost the whole time that these discussions were taking place. Shaikh Hazza also had comments to make on one occasion. The Ruler on accepting the payments made it clear that it would be necessary for the Company to seriously consider other outstanding problems and a promise was made that the question of Customs payments would be taken up in the middle of July.

Shaikhs Hazza, Zaid and Khalid returned to Abu Dhabi from their trip to America on 20th June. Shaikh Khalid had received some benefit from the treatment he had received, but the outcome of treatment of Shaikh Hazza appears to have been to confirm that his health is not likely to improve.

The recording made by Shaikh Zaid during the short period he spent in England was broadcast from London and was heard in Dubai on 14th June. Shaikh Shakhbut had not been informed of the proposed broadcast and as a result did not hear his brother speaking.

Shaikhs Hazza, Zaid, Khalid and the elder[72] of Shaikh Shakhbut's sons travelled to Buraimi on 29th June where they intended to spend the summer.

72 Sheikh Said bin Shakhbut.

There were strong rumours in Abu Dhabi at the beginning of the month that considerable quantities of oil had been found in Shuwaihat No, 1. Since a visit was made to El Hamra shortly after these rumours reached this office, it was possible to contradict them with some authenticity. It is regrettable that far from waiting to discover the truth of the matter, the British community in Abu Dhabi managed to convince themselves that these rumours were quite authentic.

Further news of the sunk launch of Shaikh Shakhbut will be found under "Dubai".

El Hamra was visited on 16th June and Party 5 on 18th June.

There were accusations and counter accusations between Abu Dhabi and Sharjah subjects in the Party 5 camp in the middle of the month and the beating of a Sharjah subject by one of the Abu Dhabi guards resulted in all the Sharjah subjects returning to Sharjah. Unfortunately they arrived just as Shaikh Saqr was leaving for Abu Dhabi and as a result it was two days before they could be persuaded to go back to work. The matter was settled between the two Rulers concerned but not before the Ruler of Sharjah had involved the Political Agent.

Mr. Hammond, the Manager of the British Bank of the Middle East in Bahrain and who has charge of the general policies of all branches of this bank in the Persian Gulf, arrived in Abu Dhabi on 6th June and later came to Dubai.

AJMAN:

Ajman was not visited this month.

The Ruler left for Manama[73] in the middle of the month and apart from occasional visits to Ajman intends to spend the summer there.

DUBAI:

There is no further activity to report regarding the sale of Petroleum products.

Trade generally is still at a low level.

The sunk launch belonging to Shaikh Shakhbut was moved from the entrance to Dubai creek during the month and placed where it can do no harm. Gray, Mackenzie & Co. Ltd., as expected, disclaim all responsibility for the sinking so this problem remains a thorn in the side of the Political Agent who will have to settle the case as best he can. It is understood that Shaikh Shakhbut is claiming Rs. 70,000/-.

The Municipality continue to keep up their high standard of workmanship, the latest improvement being the repair of the steps for landing the small ferrying craft in the creek.[74] New taxes introduced this month include taxes on these ferry boats, and motor vehicles.

---

73 His inland oasis in the mountain foreland and north of Dhaid.

74 Those were the days before the tunnel and bridges. The presence of the Abras (meaning across) saved people valuable time and money as it was a long journey round the inner end

The Company gave Rs. 1000/- to the Municipality as a gift to encourage their work.

It was rumoured in Dubai at the time when the resignation of Sir Stephen Gibson[75] became known that he was to be replaced by the Hon. M. Bridgman of British Petroleum. It being stated that such a statement was made by the B.B.C. in one of its news broadcasts.

It was learnt on 30th June that 4 Dubai subjects had been deported for smuggling arms into the Trucial States.

FUJAIRA:

There was no contact with Fujaira this month, but it is understood that the Ruler has left for Mecca.

RAS AL KHAIMA:

There has been no outstanding news from Ras al Khaima.

It would appear to be the policy of H.M.G. to let the Ruler try and forget his grievance over the boundary settlement by leaving him alone.

It is understood that the Ruler's son, Khalid, who is a boy of approximately 16 years of age, is to visit England where he will stay with Mr. Huntingdon and later be shown round under the auspices of the British Council.

SHARJAH:

The newness of our methods of operating continued to cause a considerable amount of extra work in this office, but towards the end of the month matters appeared to be settling down well.

The Ruler in continuation of his policy to use the arrival of the Company in his territory to try and obtain benefits for all, approached the Company with a view to increasing the amount of rations granted to employees and to putting them on the same wage scale as oil workers in other Arab states: Qatar, Kuwait and Saudi Arabia being specifically mentioned in this connection.

At one time it was rumoured that he had given instructions to the Head Guard at the location[76] to advise the labour not to accept the present ration scale which might be acceptable to Abu Dhabi subjects but not to the population of Sharjah.

The only trouble in the location to date was entirely due to the Head Guard thrashing, apparently without sufficient justification, one of the kitchen staff in public.

---

of the creek.

75 Sir Stephen Gibson was the IPC/PD(TC) etc Managing Director. He resigned on 30th June 1957. He was succeeded by G. H. Herridge. At the time the Chairman was Admiral Sir John Cunningham.

76 Meaning the drilling location.

It is interesting to note that it was exactly this treatment by the Head Guard of Party 5 that the Ruler of Sharjah took such strong objection.

In an attempt to help the Company over the transport difficulties it is facing, the Ruler lent one of his guides to the Area Superintendent on 3rd June. Who in company with the MT[77] Engineer, and the Civil Engineer sought a different and more favourable route from Umm al Quwain to the location. Unfortunately the attempt failed.

The Ruler's attempts to collect customs duty on gold imported through Sharjah airfield continued to cause anxiety to the merchants. The Manager of International Aeradio has been keeping records of all gold entering by air, but when asked to pay the duty, the merchants from Dubai, supported by the Ruler of Dubai, refused to do so. At one time during the month it was reported the British Bank of the Middle East had undertaken collection of the money, but this report proved to be false. This looked like being another sticky problem which the Political Agency would be left to straighten out when the Ruler of Sharjah stated that he would not allow gold arriving by air to be released until the duty had been paid. This resulted in the merchants agreeing to pay, under protest. Whether or not large quantities of gold will continue to be imported by air, is now the question.

Kelba was visited by the Ruler several times during the month.

The Ruler advised that during the middle of July he intends to leave on a trip abroad, probably to Iran and Iraq, which will get him away from the heat of the Trucial Coast which he states he finds too oppressive.

UMM AL QUWAIN:

The Company is continuing its policy of trying to give as much benefit from its operations in the area as possible to the people of Umm al Quwain. It was found necessary to discharge the launch used for carrying stores from Baraka as the Nakhuda was obviously being very un-conscientious.

The Ruler was visited on 5th and 29th June.

The Ruler has moved his family to Falaj al Ali where he intends to spend most of the summer months.

At the beginning of the month the Ruler advised that some damage had been done to the reed houses in the town by transport on hire to the Company, and arrangements were made to forbid the entry of large vehicles into the town.

AGENCY:

Mr. C.A. Gault accompanied by his wife visited Dubai from 1st to 3rd June.

Mr. E.F. Henderson visited Dubai on 5th to 12th June.

---

77 MT. Motor transport.

The Political Agent[78] paid a visit to Abu Dhabi on 27th and 28th June to welcome the Ruler's brothers on their return from the U.S.A.

BANKING:

It is rumoured that the recent improvement in the relations of the British Bank of the Middle East with the merchants throughout the Trucial States, is the direct result of the intention of the Eastern Bank to open branches. It is understood that one of the improvements is a lowering of the rate of interest on loans.

The agreement between the Ruler of Sharjah and the Eastern Bank is now complete and the signing is expected in the near future. With regard to this bank opening a branch in Abu Dhabi, it is rumoured that the Ruler is to receive 25% of the profits.

Kirkbride
Representative.

TRUCIAL COAST DIARY FOR JULY 1957

ABU DHABI:

Abu Dhabi was visited by Mr. Ensor,[79] Mr. Hahn[80] and Sayed Ibrahim Arraydh[81] on 17 July 1957. During the meeting with the Ruler the problem of the Custom's payments was discussed at length. It was hoped that Shaikh Zaid was to be present but his arrival was delayed due to the visit to Buraimi of the Acting Political Resident concerning events in the Oman.[82]

Apart from this, Abu Dhabi was visited on the following occasions, 5th, 9th on the occasion of the Eid al Adha and 13th.

78 Based in Bahrain.

79 The General Manager Qatar and the Trucial Coast.

80 IPC.

81 Bahraini who later became prominent in Bahrain as a poet and leader of the literary movement. The Bahrain House of poetry was named after him. At the time of this diary and for many years he was employed by the Company PD(TC) and Abu Dhabi Petroleum Company.

82 Rebellion had broken out in Oman on 16th July after the exiled Talib bin Ali had returned and routed the Sultan's forces at Balad Sait near Nizwa. The Political Resident ordered the TOS to go to the assistance of the Sultan of Oman.

Mr. Stockwell[83] of the Abu Dhabi Marine Areas Ltd. spent some time at the beginning of the month in Abu Dhabi discussing the Custom's problem with which they are faced. It appears that these discussions incurred the Ruler's ill favour.

The Ruler did not show any extraordinary interest over the events in Oman and neither asked for nor gave any news.

Mr. Buckmaster visited Buraimi in the early part of the month and later the Liwa. These visits were in the nature of farewell visits before he proceeds on leave early in August. During his trip to the Liwa he called at Al Hamra to pick up a guide and also at the Party 5 location.

On 15th July news was received in Dubai that Rashid bin Hamad ash Shamsi ex Ruler of Buraimi[84] and the man who is said to have arranged for a Saudi representative to go to Buraimi, had died.

By the end of the month British troops had taken over Trucial Oman Scouts posts at Baraka[85] and Buraimi.

During the early part of the month Colin Lawson a correspondent of the Daily Express[86] visited Abu Dhabi where he interviewed the Ruler. Later he managed to get a lift to Buraimi, albeit unofficially, in an RAF aircraft. It is understood that the pilot of this machine was reprimanded for this lapse in security. Originally Lawson had come to the Trucial States to write an article on the development of the area and had arrived before the events in Oman changed his objective.

It is believed that over half the population of Abu Dhabi were smitten by the "Asiatic flu" but no deaths were recorded.

---

83 He negotiated the ADMA concession agreement with Sheikh Shakhbut in 1952/53. In the late 1970's and early 1980's he was appointed Managing Director of the Abu Dhabi Petroleum Company. It was in those latter years that I accompanied him on many courtesy calls on Sheikh Shakhbut.

84 Not correct. He was the Sheikh of Hamasa the next village to Buraimi, also in the territory of the Sultanate of Oman. He did accompany the Saudi Arabian Representative, Turki bin Ataishan when he first arrived in Hamasa on 31st August 1952. He was expelled to Saudi Arabia after the Saudi delegation left on 27th October 1955. The Sheikh at Buraimi was Shaikh Saqr bin Sultan, Al Nu'aimi.

85 In the west of Abu Dhabi territory, about 40 kilometres west of Jebel Dhanna. The T.O.S. post was placed there to watch for possible intrusions into Abu Dhabi territory from the west. British troops were replacing soldiers of the TOS who were engaged in operations in the Sultanate of Oman.

86 Colin Lawson wrote on 17 July 1957 under the headline 'Oil Sheik snaps an order – Britain told: start drilling or else.' Lawson, after being hosted generously on the Trucial Coast wrote an article for his paper which being far from the truth, infuriated the Company IPC. To this day that newspaper still favours the sensational rather than accuracy. The Sheikh referred to was the Ruler of Sharjah, Sheikh Saqr bin Sultan. The Company had already been preparing the drilling site for several months.

AJMAN:

Ajman was not visited during this month due to the absence of the Ruler.

DUBAI:

The main topic in the local news this month was the announcement of the forthcoming marriage between one of the Ruler's daughters to Shaikh Ahmed the son of the Ruler of Qatar. The marriage is expected to take place during the autumn immediately the hot weather has abated.

Some concern was shown by the Iranian merchants at the length of time it was taking for the Sultan's forces to overcome the rebels in Oman. It was considered that every day's delay in dealing successfully with the situation increased the possibility of encouraging other likely dissidents in the Trucial States to cause trouble.

Trade remained at a low level, events in the Oman doing nothing to increase the people's confidence.

Mr. Lorrimer arrived from Bahrain in the early part of the month to take charge of the Dubai police force. His first allotted task has been to check up on outlets allowing the sale of alcohol without permits. By the end of the month little success had crowned his efforts. Other restrictions resulting from the arrival of this officer are likely to include, the checking of passports and movements of persons to and from Dubai whether by road or sea.

A courtesy call was paid on the Ruler on the occasion of the Aid al Adha.

On 29th July the Ruler accompanied by his father, and numerous officials left for Iran by boat. It is said that the Ruler will fulfil his promise to go to Teheran in accordance with the invitation extended to him by H.M. the Shah last winter (please refer to February edition of this diary).

FUJAIRA:

Again there has been no contact with the Ruler of Fujaira this month as he is believed to be away in Saudi Arabia on the annual pilgrimage.

RAS AL KHAIMA:

As occurred in the territory of Abu Dhabi, the Trucial Oman Scouts post in Ras al Khaima territory was replaced by British troops. The Ruler is said to have shown signs of forgetting his grievance over the boundary dispute previously mentioned.

Ras al Khaima was not visited.

SHARJAH:

Owing to the presence of the airport adjacent to the town, Sharjah more than any other town was effected by events in Oman.

It is understood that the Ruler showed no hesitation in allowing R.A.F. attacks on the rebels to be launched from this airport, but is said to have stated in Qatar that the rebels had shot down a small number of R.A.F. machines.

An article in the Egyptian periodical "Akhr Sa'a" stated that the British were placing the whole of the blame for events in the Oman on Shaikh Saqr's shoulders.

The number of newspaper reporters who invaded Sharjah as a result of the Oman events caused considerable embarrassment not only from the accommodation angle but also from the stories that they were sending home. The authorities came in for a considerable amount of criticism in their handling of this invasion. However one cannot lay all the blame at the authorities' door since the articles which were being written and the behaviour of the correspondents would make the most cooperative of authorities shudder.

The marriage of the son of Qatar Shaikh Mohamed bin Ali to the daughter of one of the Ruler's uncles, Shaikh Mohamed, was celebrated on 10th July.

The Ruler left Sharjah for Kuwait on 19th July on his annual summer holiday in Arab countries. Although invited to do so by H.M. the Shah he does not intend to visit Iran this year as he felt that such a visit would not be welcomed immediately after the disastrous earthquake which occurred in Northern Iran.

The opening of a branch by the Eastern Bank in Sharjah towards the end of this year is now confirmed from all sides. Probably as a result of this the British Bank of the Middle East have decided to open their branch in the town every day instead of twice a week.

The Company's operations[87] in Juweiza continued more smoothly than last month although a visit by Shaikh Abdulla the Ruler's brother, towards the end of the month caused some upset.

It is said that thc duty on gold being imported through Sharjah airport is now being paid by merchants dealing in this commodity.

It was reported that the Trucial Oman Scouts were seriously infected with the "Asian Flu", about 150 men contracting the disease.

On 12th July the flag of Sharjah was seen to be flying at half mast on the Ruler's palace. This was in memory of the Ruler's brother-in-law Shaikh Saqr bin Sultan bin Salim the … ,[88] who was reported to have died in Saudi Arabia.

Kelba was visited by the Ruler several times during the month.

A courtesy call on the occasion of Aid al Adha was made on the Ruler.

---

87 Preparing to drill an exploration well. In those days the tower of the drilling rig was built piece by piece. It was another 5 years before rigs were introduced to the country where the tower was raised, lowered and transported in one piece.

88 Sheikh Saqr laid claim to Kalba after the death of the last Ruler, Sheikh Hamad bin Said.

UMM AL QUWAIN:

Umm al Quwain was visited on 2nd and 8th July.

The Company's operations continue to run smoothly in the territory although during this month the number of persons employed on permanent jobs here were reduced considerably.

The Ruler spent much of the month in Falaj Al Ali, leaving his second son, Sultan, in charge of state affairs.

AGENCY:

This summer Messrs. Tripp and Buckmaster will be away on leave in the United Kingdom. Mr. Tripp should have left Dubai in the early part of this month but was asked to remain until the end of the Oman affair. Neither are being replaced for the duration of their respective leaves which means that the Agency will be run by Mr. W.J. Adams and the Political Office in Abu Dhabi will close.

Kirkbride
Representative.

TRUCIAL COAST DIARY FOR AUGUST 1957

ABU DHABI:

Abu Dhabi was visited on 9th to 10th, 17th and 25th August. On all these occasions the Ruler was well except for the last when he was suffering from the after effects of a cold.

Relations continued to be good although he did not accept the Company's view of the articles on which customs duty was due.

It is believed that Abu Dhabi Marine Areas have made no progress towards settling their customs problem. Mr. Hillyard's relationship with the Ruler appears to have improved since last month. The Ruler has visited the ADMA cinema shows.

During the month some minor repairs were effected to the Company house in Abu Dhabi.[89] Khalifa bin Yousef, an Abu Dhabi contractor, was used to carry out this work. The Ruler is pleased that this house is again in use by the Company's representative.

Mr. Wainwright who, it is understood, will be in charge of the Abu Dhabi Marine Area project, arrived in Das about 19th August.

89 In the far north east of Abu Dhabi island.

Shaikh Zaid, who at the beginning of the month was in Ibri[90] at the instigation of the Political Agency, returned to Buraimi on or about 14th August.[91] He did not visit Abu Dhabi.

At the end of the month, the British troops[92] were still replacing those of the Trucial Oman Scouts for which see 7th paragraph under "Abu Dhabi" in last month's diary.

Mr. Orde of Gray Mackenzie's Bahrain branch accompanied by Mr. Brown of the Dubai branch and an interpreter called on the Ruler on 25th August to discuss the question of compensation for the sinking of the Ruler's launch in the Dubai creek (see page 2 of June Diary under "Dubai" 3rd paragraph for main details). It is understood that Mr. Orde offered to settle for the sum of Rs. 2,000; an offer which was rejected by the Ruler.

Al Hamra was visited on 26th August.

AJMAN:

Ajman was visited on 22nd August. The Ruler was in Manama and his second son was acting on his behalf.

Considerable interest was shown in the Oman situation and the young shaikh appeared to be fairly well informed even as regards the outcome of the complaint to the United Nations.[93]

On oil matters he was not so well informed and asked if the Company was already preparing to build a pipeline in view of his having seen some pipes of considerable diameter being transported from Umm al Quwain to Juweiza.

DUBAI:

The Ruler remained absent throughout the month.

On 2nd August a large area of "barasti" dwellings, was devastated by fire. In all some 400 houses were said to have been completely destroyed. Fortunately the number of deaths, even by the most pessimistic estimators, did not exceed 3 persons. Considering that the Ruler was absent, a fair amount of relief work was done by the end of the month and a considerable sum of money had been collected. This appears

90 In the Sultanate of Oman. 150 kilometres south of Buraimi/Al 'Ain. In 1954 Ibri was taken by Talib and the forces of his brother, the Imam Ghalib. It was regained by the Sultan's forces after a very short time in October 1954.

91 By the middle of August the Sultan's forces, with the help of the Trucial Oman Scouts (100 men) and the Cameronians, had regained control of Nizwa, Tanuf and other important centres, excluding the formidable Jebel Akhdhar. See INNES, (1987).

92 The Cameronian regiment from Scotland.

93 Many Arab countries, including Egypt and Saudi Arabia, sided with the Imam Ghalib bin Ali.

to have been by far the worst fire in living memory due to the rapid spreading of the flames by a very dry and very strong easterly wind which blew throughout the day.

The police continued to be active and are said to have dumped a large quantity of useless and useful arms in the sea. A number of arms dealers were warned that there would be some tightening up of controls. Four persons are said to have been convicted of arms smuggling and given prison sentences.[94]

The end of the Oman affair[95] resulted in a slight improvement in trade, although the police activities were probably the cause of making this of a limited nature.

FUJAIRA:

The Ruler of Fujaira returned from his pilgrimage on the 19th August and is believed to have left for Fujaira towards the end of the month.

He did not visit the office.

RAS AL KHAIMA:

Ras al Khaima was not visited during this month.

SHARJAH:

Sharjah, with the lessening of air sorties over the Oman, was considerably quieter this month. However, slogans appeared on the walls of the houses now being built for the school teachers which either praised Ghalib,[96] or condemned the Sultan of Muscat and Oman. One even returned to the 'Long live Jamal Abdul Nasser' theme. There appears to have been no live demonstrations of such feelings.

The Ruler was away throughout the month.

International Aeradio, after a prolonged stay in Sharjah, were advised in the middle of the month that their contract with the Ministry of Aviation for the managing of the airport is not being renewed. As a result of this, their organisation intends to move to Dubai where it will continue to operate agencies for Cable and Wireless, and Gulf Aviation. Reaction by the Ruling family was unexpectedly marked to the extent that the Ruler is said to have gone to the British Embassy in Beirut to complain of this change. It is understood that the British Political authorities were not forewarned of the change over.

---

94 The destination for most of the smuggled arms was to the rebels in the Sultanate of Oman.

95 In the space of a couple of weeks the Imam's forces were expelled from Nizwa and all the main towns in central Oman. British troops and the T.O.S. were withdrawn from the Sultanate in the middle of the month.

96 Brothers Talib and Ghalib bin Ali. The leaders of the insurrection against the Sultan Saeed bin Taimur. Ghalib was elected Imam after the death in 1954 of the previous Imam Khalili.

Company operations continued to run smoothly and although contact with the Deputy Ruler on Company matters was frequent, there were no problems left unsolved. The Deputy Ruler has been most cooperative and has never failed to agree to reasonable requests put forward by the Company.

Kalba was visited by the Ruler's brother Abdulla, in the middle of the month.

UMM AL QUWAIN:

Umm al Quwain was visited on 4th August. The Ruler was away in Falaj Ali and his second son was acting in his stead.

The Company's operations in this territory continued smoothly.

AGENCY:

Mr. J.P. Tripp left for the United Kingdom on his annual leave on 19th August.

Kirkbride
Representative.

TRUCIAL COAST DIARY FOR SEPTEMBER 1957

ABU DHABI:

The Ruler was visited on 10th, 18th, and 29th of this month. Shaikh Zaid was present at the first of these meetings.

Relations continued to be cordial although there was some cooling off when some views of the Company concerning custom's problems, were made known to the Ruler in writing.

It is understood that the Abu Dhabi Marine Areas Ltd. have made some progress in relation to their custom's problem in that Mr. Hillyard is convinced that the Ruler now realises firstly, the Company is not prepared to move from its stand: secondly, there is nothing to be gained from taking the matter to arbitration.

The ADMA drilling platform is rumoured to have suffered from recent storms in the Atlantic Ocean and has had to put into Gibraltar for inspection and repairs.[97]

The Abu Dhabi Police Force which was started a short time ago, is now in evidence in the town and new barracks for it is in the process of being built. The commander of this force is the Ruler's second son, Shaikh Sultan.

97 The drilling platform (jack-up) was manufactured in Hamburg and towed to Abu Dhabi. It was reported to have broken loose from the towing barge in the Bay of Biscay in the storms. This was the first of its kind in the Gulf.

Negotiations have been afoot with one of the merchants of Dubai, Shaikh Ahmed Mustafa, to set up a water distillation unit. An agreement is said to have been signed with the Ruler, but that almost immediately afterwards the agreed sale price was considered to be too high.

This merchant is also said to have been given a contract for the refacing of the palace in Abu Dhabi.

There was much rejoicing at the arrival of the Ruler's first grandson from the male side of the family. The child was born to Shaikh Said and has been named Tahnoon, by the Ruler.

AJMAN:

The Ruler was visited at Manama on 7th and at Ajman on 24th September.

The Trucial Oman Scouts are making arrangements with the Ruler to be allowed to send detachments to go to Manama to undergo training in that area.

DUBAI:

The Ruler returned from Iran on 1st September and was visited in honour of this occasion on 3rd September.

He enjoyed his trip immensely. During his stay there, he called on the Shah in Teheran and travelled extensively in the north; reaching the Caspian Sea.

On his return the Ruler was quick to start some action for the relief of the victims of the fire which occurred on 2nd August by distributing the money collected. The sums given varied, the average being about Rs. 250/-.

Trade was again disappointing although there was some improvement as a result of the cancellation of some police restrictions; which, the Oman[98] affair having ended, appeared now to be unnecessary. The Ruler considers that the fall in trade is partly due to new restrictions in Iran which are making smuggling from that country more difficult.

Contact with the Ruling family of Qatar was extensive during the latter part of the month as the date set for the marriage of one of the Ruler's daughters to the son of the Ruler of Qatar, draws near.

Just as everything appeared to be going well a surprise occurred on the last day of the month when, according to popular belief, the lady became reluctant to go through with the plans.

This is due, apparently, to her desire to marry her cousin who is head of the courts in Dubai, and the unfavourable impression created by the brother of the bridegroom, of whom, since his marriage to the daughter of Shaikh Mohamed bin Saqr, nothing has been seen or heard of the bride.

98 It was declared that the rebellion against the Sultan had been defeated. But not entirely and British troops were again called on to support the Sultan in 1959.

The Ruler, being a little short of accommodation for the marriage, has found it necessary to build a new house in Zabil.

Dr. McCauly, the Senior Medical Officer of the Trucial States, returned from England at the end of the month. A second medical officer from India arrived at the close of the month also.

FUJAIRA:

There has been no contact with the Ruler of Fujairah this month.

RAS AL KHAIMA:

Ras al Khaimah was visited at the beginning of the month and a call made on the Ruler on 8th September.

As usual, he was interested in the Company's operations although he strongly criticised the Company's failure to operate in his territory.

The damage done last winter by the excessively high seas (see this diary for April 1957) was inspected. It is considerable: a breach about 200 yards long has been made in the sand bank on which the town is built.

Mr. Huntingdon returned from leave in England at the beginning of the month and is full of new ideas and enthusiasm for the experimental station. He has acquired a further garden from the Ruler in Ain Khatt, which, unlike the other gardens when new, is a going concern. He proposes to use this garden to plant fruit trees from the Lebanon and India.

There is some talk of livestock being introduced into the station.

Mr. Huntingdon advises that considerable progress has been made towards getting local farmers to use his methods and a good crop of vegetables is expected from this source this summer, thus allowing the station to be used for experimental purposes.

There was some discussion on the supplying of vegetables to Company locations and it is hoped that a visit to Ras al Khaimah by the Area Commissariat Supervisor will be arranged later so that he may inspect the quality of the produce.

Still enthusiastic for his scheme for damming the wadi which runs from the direction of Manama to Ras al Khaimah, Mr. Huntingdon is to visit Aden where similar schemes for the conservation of water are employed.

SHARJAH:

The Ruler remained absent throughout the month.

The Eastern Bank which is to open a branch in Sharjah in December of this year, has already appointed a Manager, whose task, for the time being, is to supervise the construction of the building.

The school opened in the middle of the month, but without the Palestinian, Egyptian or Syrian teachers formerly employed there.

Several visits were paid to the Deputy Ruler and a number of minor points relating to the Company's operations in Juweiza were discussed and settled.

Company operations continue to run smoothly with complaints to the Deputy Ruler being much reduced.

British Air Services, the successors to International Aeradio as controllers of flying at Sharjah airfield, are expected to be operating by the middle of October. In the meantime arrangements for the move of International Aeradio to Dubai are in hand.

UMM AL QUWAIN:

Umm al Quwain was visited on 8th September but the Ruler was still absent, returning from Falaj al Ali much later in the month.

What Company operations remain in this town continue smoothly, although there were some cases of theft reported and the Head Guard had to be warned that any future incidents of this nature would result in action being taken against him.

AGENCY:

Mr. Fletcher of the Information Section of the Residency in Bahrain called at the office on 19th September. He intimated that all were very disappointed that the Company could not see its way to making a film on the development of the Trucial States.

It is intended to station a mobile cinema in the Trucial States in the near future.

We were offered facilities for borrowing films from the Residency's library.

Kirkbride
Representative.

TRUCIAL COAST DIARY FOR OCTOBER 1957

ABU DHABI:

The Ruler was visited on the 16th and 22nd of the month. On the first visit the Ruler's reception was cold and discussion on the main outstanding problem between him and the Company; that of Custom's dues was unpleasant. During the last visit this same problem was brought up by the Ruler but the discussion was friendly and free. No progress towards a settlement was made on either occasion.

Hon. M.S. Buckmaster the Political Officer returned from leave at the beginning of the month and almost immediately left for the Liwa. He had not returned from there by the day of the last visit from this office to Abu Dhabi.

Shaikhs Hazza and Khalid and the families returned from Buraimi towards the middle of the month. The party was accompanied by Shaikh Zayed who having delivered them safely to Abu Dhabi, himself went on a visit to Bainunah.[99]

Paragraph removed.

The ADMA drilling platform is reported, at the end of the month, to be between Suez and Aden and is expected to arrive off Das[100] in about three weeks' time. There seems to be some doubt as to whether the harbour that has been built on Das is large enough to take this vessel.

Work has begun on the refacing of the palace of Abu Dhabi and during the last visit to the Ruler he was complaining that this was not progressing fast enough for his taste.

Company operations continue to run smoothly and the Ruler has taken a considerable interest in the El Hamra well[101] since drilling has stopped.

An outing for persons of importance and those who have had some connection with the building of thc installations there, was arranged by ADMA to Das on 6th October. Two members of P.D.T.C. staff attended.

AJMAN:

Ajman was not visited during the month.

---

99 Central desert area of Abu Dhabi between the coastal sabkhah and the high sands of the Liwa oases.

100 Das island where ADMA constructed oil collecting, storage and loading facilities as well as a base for the offshore drilling and oil production operations.

101 Shuwaihat well near Al Hamra. Drilling had reached 12,360 feet deep without finding oil. The second well in the west of Abu Dhabi, the area where the Company geologists were most interested in, partly because of it being nearer to oil fields in Saudi Arabia and Qatar.

DUBAI:

After many delays and postponements, the marriage between Shaikh Ahmed[102] of Qatar and the daughter of Shaikh Rashid of Dubai took place on 19th October. Shaikh Ahmed arrived on 14th and left on 29th October, his bride remained in Dubai.

As was expected this occasion resulted in a social whirl with daily lunch and dinner parties.

It was almost impossible to get any business done with either the Rulers of Dubai or Sharjah whilst this visitor was here.

Due, it is believed, to the intervention of Shaikh Ahmed,[103] Shaikh Rashid allowed his deported cousin Maktum bin Juma[104] to return to Dubai. Later this man left for India where he is to undergo medical treatment.

Trade improved slightly this month but has not yet got back to its previous level.

FUJAIRAH:

Shaikh Mohamed visited the office on 19th October during a short visit he was paying to Dubai and Ajman.

He was presented with the Arabic portable type-writer bought for him by the Company, for which he was very grateful.

According to his statement Fujairah is flourishing and much enthusiasm has been raised by the proposal now being put forward by the Agency to make a road through the mountains to allow at least Land Rovers to proceed from Fujairah to the other Trucial States without going through Muscat territory, as at present.

Shaikh Mohamed was most co-operative over the proposal to carry out a geological survey in his territory and promised to remain in the area of the survey until the work is completed.

As usual Shaikh Mohamed is short of money.

RAS AL KHAIMA:

No visits were paid to Ras al Khaima this month.

The Ruler has been causing the Agency some anxiety over his continued refusal to recognise the frontier as demarcated by them between Ras al Khaima territory and Fujairah.

The Trucial Oman Scouts are carrying out route reconnaissances in the disputed area between Ain Katt and Diba and this is being used to show the Ruler that he is the only one who is being uncooperative. It is believed that the Agency with the approval

---

102 Son of Ruler Shaikh Ali bin Abdullah al Thani. Shaikh Ahmed was Ruler of Qatar from 24th October 1960 to 22nd February 1972.

103 The writer probably means Shaikh Ahmed bin Ali of Qatar, Shaikh Rashid's new son-in-law.

104 The second son.

of the Residency, is proposing to threaten the Ruler with dire consequences if he does not ... .

Shaikh Khalid the Ruler's son whose return to Ras al Khaima from his visit to England was reported in last month's diary, is now studying in Cairo.

Mr. Huntingdon visited Aden early in the month as was expected (see September's diary) and on his return he was as enthusiastic as ever for his scheme of water conservation. He has now been lent a bull dozer by the Company for a period of six weeks, to carry out this work.

The seeds for this season's crop have arrived and sowing is proceeding according to plan.

SHARJAH:

The Ruler of Sharjah returned to his home town on 10th October.

The Ruler paid an official visit to the Company's location at Juweiza on 22nd October when he was welcomed and conducted round the site by the General Manager.[105] Senior members of the Company's staff from Qatar were present. After taking lunch the Ruler went hunting, regrettably without success.

Shaikh Saqr seemed rather worried about the situation on the Turko-Syrian border and was inclined to believe that as a result of this and America's foreign policy, a third world war was probably unavoidable.

Shaikh Mohamed of Qatar accompanied his brother to Dubai and then lived in Sharjah. Shaikh Mohamed married the daughter of one of the Ruler's uncles (see Diary for July).

Shaikh Mohamed is said to believe firmly the Cairo broadcast that British troops are still heavily involved in fighting in the Oman.[106]

International Acradio closed at the end of the month, at the same time removing the Cable and Wireless office from Sharjah. This transfer seemed to most people to be quite unnecessary since it was the only means of communication for private firms between Dubai and Sharjah.

UMM AL QUWAIN:

The Ruler was visited on 1st October.

105 The General Manager in Qatar was P. Ensor. Operations on the Trucial Coast still came under Qatar Petroleum Company management.

106 In those days Radio Cairo (Arabic) was listened to throughout the Middle East and the Gulf. The Anti British rhetoric appealed to many Arabs, particularly the younger generation. Unfortunately Cairo used the radio to spread propaganda which often was exaggerated and sometimes quite untrue. The Soviet Union was also voicing Anti British propaganda, while the USA was not always silent in this matter.

There was considerable discussion on the different Arabic broadcasts received in this town, much interest being shown in a station which has only recently been received which calls itself "Saut al Haq"[107] It is Anti-Nasser[108] in inclination. The closing of the Cyprus broadcasting station was considered to be a pity.[109]

The Ruler and his sons visited Sharjah on 24th to attend a dinner by Shaikh Saqr in honour of Shaikh Ahmed of Qatar.

AGENCY:

The Political Agent and his family returned to Dubai from leave in England on 17th October.

When approached about the proposed geological survey in the territory between Ras al Khaimah and Fujairah which is under dispute, the Political Agent was at first concerned about the party crossing the border but after consulting the Residency agreed to provide an escort to allow the survey to be carried out as planned. It is certain that the Agency hope to use this survey as further chance to impress on the two Shaikhs that the border is settled and recognised.

Mr. Marshall the First Secretary Labour in the Residency, held a meeting in the Agency on 17th October to discuss and get agreement to the Residency implementing some sort of legislation in regard to Worker's Compensation for injuries. This agreement was obtained although several firms opposed the idea. The matter is now to be brought before the forthcoming meeting of the Trucial Council where the agreement in principle of the Rulers is to be sought. Since this is not expected to be an easy task, those who opposed legislation may well win the day. (For background see Diary for May).

VISITORS:

Capt. Beaching and another member of Kanoos[110] of Bahrain visited the Trucial Coast during the month and included the states of Dubai, Sharjah and Abu Dhabi in their itinerary. Kanoos apparently are considering setting up business in this area as building contractors and shippers although there seems to be little work for new competitors in either field. It is believed that it is bound to depend on oil being found at either Juweiza or by ADMA in their offshore drilling.

107 "Voice of truth".

108 Egyptian President Gamal Abdel Nasser. 1956-1970.

109 The BBC relay station.

110 Haji Yousef bin Ahmed Kanoo, the founder of the Bahrain family business was a frequent and welcome visitor to all the Trucial States in the years between the two World Wars (1918-1939). He died in 1945.

Mr. Pike, Sales Manager of Aden Airways, visited Dubai and Sharjah to try and increase the number of bookings on the recently opened service between Sharjah and Aden and to ascertain whether or not it would be possible to import vegetables into the Trucial States from Asmara in Kenya.[111]

Mr. Newton, the BOAC[112] Sales Representative in Bahrain also paid a visit to the Trucial States during the month.

Kirkbride
Representative.

TRUCIAL COAST DIARY FOR NOVEMBER 1957

ABU DHABI:

The deterioration of the health of Shaikh Hazza has overshadowed everything in Abu Dhabi, this month. The turn for the worse came in the middle of the month and both ancient and modern methods of medical treatment were tried in order to relieve the sufferer of as much pain as possible. Although there are occasions when Shaikh Hazza shows signs of reviving, it is generally felt that he is unlikely to get over this attack. There is an air of gloom and depression throughout the palace which is very hard to dispel. As is usual with the medical profession the views of the various doctors as to how long Shaikh Hazza is likely to continue to live vary from 6 weeks to 6 years.

The Political Agent visited Abu Dhabi with Mrs. Tripp on 12th November to pay their respects on their return from leave. They were accompanied by E.F. Henderson.

The two portraits painted by Michael Scott of Shaikhs Hazza and Zaid were delivered to the palace on 13th November. Unfortunately this was mistaken by some as being a presentation ceremony which, of course, had taken place in London some months ago.

The ADMA drilling platform arrived towards the end of the month after a delay in the Sohar[113] area where the tug broke down.

Work on the re-facing of the palace at Abu Dhabi continues but there appears to be little likelihood of the distillation plant becoming operative.

Company operations ran without trouble throughout the month with some minor thefts in Tarif being reported.

---

111 Asmara is the capital city of Eritrea. The writer, Kirkbride, may have meant to write 'Asmara and/or Kenya.

112 British Overseas Airways Corporation. Now British Airways.

113 Sohar is on the coast of the Sultanate of Oman.

The search for the assassins of Faris bin Ghanim was called off after the failure to find any trace of the culprits inspite of Shaikh Zaid joining the search.

AJMAN:

Ajman was not visited during the month.

The Cameronian[114] detachment stationed at Sharjah have been carrying out exercises in the hills to the east of Manama using live ammunition.

DUBAI:

The event of most importance this month in Dubai was the storm which occurred during the night of 22nd November although reports reaching the outside world and later broadcast by various radio networks seem to have been exaggerated.

It has been established that 13 persons lost their lives with the possibility of one or two more succumbing to injuries. Although some 2,000 reed[115] houses are estimated to have collapsed the material damage to persons in this sort of dwelling does not appear to have reached that occasioned by the fire which took place on 2nd August. Some three boats were damaged beyond repair while a larger number were turned over and later recovered.

Persons who suffered most in the storm, apart from the injured, were those who live in stone dwellings on which the rooves proved insecure.

The roof of the Political Agency was damaged by hail stones which attained some considerable size in certain areas and to add to the confusion a filing cabinet disintegrated allowing the contents to be drawn out through a hole caused by the hail.

It is alleged that BP in the shape of ADMA in a burst of enthusiasm sent a cable to their principals asking permission to utilise the services of a cine cameraman who happened to be on board their rig platform, to take pictures of the devastation. However the populace of Dubai speedily rebuilt their houses and as a result, the cameraman, when he did arrive, was forced to make full use of the cinema's licence for fantasy. This he did by photographing buildings which have been in the course of demolition for the last six months.

The news that a Dubai driver had been captured by the rebels in the Oman was the occasion of much talk in the town, and the father, at first, refused to believe the Company's assertions that the man was fit and well.

---

114 Scottish regiment. They were sent to the Trucial Coast to take over some of the duties normally performed by the Trucial Oman Scouts who had been deployed to help the Sultan in Oman.

115 Reed houses. Dubai has many stone (often coral) houses. However there were many houses constructed of palm fronds (areesh or khaimah). The reeds that the writer refers to would have been imported from Basra and they were formed into what was known as Basra board. This was a more solid construction than the areesh.

The visit to Dubai of H.M.S. Gambia[116] flagship of the C-in-C[117] East Indies station, which was scheduled to take place on 26th and 27th of November was cancelled as a result of the storm mentioned above.

Mohamed bin Rahma[118] spent two weeks in Dubai as a 'guest' of the Company. He had come to complain about the fact that the Sultan of Muscat under whose jurisdiction he falls in Buraimi, was not paying him any money.[119] He had hoped to get the Political Agent to agree to his being kept by H.M.G. He also hinted that the Company should consider offering him some sort of salary on the grounds of loyalty.[120]

Rivalry in the oil business showed some signs of revival with the appearance of a number of Shell posters advertising the advantages of this type of motor oil over all others. There are, as yet, no signs of the arrival of any petroleum products to be marketed by this organisation.

FUJAIRAH:

Although the Ruler attended the meeting of the Trucial States Council, he did not call at the office.

He arranged to give us the assistance of guides from his territory for the use of the geologists who carried out a survey extending into his territory. These two persons earned their master a rebuke from the Political Agent by their attempt to prevent camels from Ras al Khaima tribes from entering the territory of the Ruler of Fujairah.

After the meeting the Ruler spent some time in Ajman before returning to his capital.

RAS AL KHAIMA:

As a result of the Geological Department's intention to carry out a survey stretching from Ras al Khaima territory across the disputed border into Fujairah, the Ruler was visited three times in an attempt to settle the matter without resorting to the use of the Political Agency for support. All this was of no avail since the Ruler

116 An 8,000 ton cruiser.

117 Commander-in-Chief.

118 This is Shaikh Mohamed bin Salimeen bin Rahma al bu Shamis from Hafit, Qabil and Sunaineh. He had an agreement with the Company signed by himself and Bird on 21st April 1948. Bird was the Company representative at that time in Jahili (Al Ain) and the agreement was for three years with a possible extension for two more years. The Company could explore in his lands which extended south in the Sultanate of Oman to just north of Dhank. The agreement was repudiated by the Sultan in Muscat, but Shaikh Mohamed did receive his first year's rent. Clearly he felt he was due more. He enjoyed a good relationship with Shaikh Zayed bin Sultan.

119 Records indicate that 10 years earlier he was receiving a small amount from the Sultan.

120 His claim of loyalty to the Company was correct, but perhaps more applicable a few years earlier.

refused to have anything to do with a party which contained anyone from Fujairah. The survey was therefore accomplished with the aid of the Trucial Oman Scouts. The Ruler made no attempt to prevent the use of camels from his area although such action would have been in keeping with his mood.

During a visit early in the month the Ruler showed considerable concern at the way in which his son Shaikh Khalid had gone to Egypt and the young man's mother was particularly upset over the matter. Later in the month when letters started arriving their concern abated a little, but the mother remained convinced that it would have benefitted her child more to have gone to England.

The Ruler was disappointed that the Company was unable to lend him the use of the bulldozer which had been lent to Mr. Huntingdon.

An extension of Mr. Huntingdon's activities outside the area of Ras al Khaima will be found below under "Agriculture".

SHARJAH:

The Ruler of Sharjah continues to pay unofficial calls at the drilling location. He apparently causes little trouble to the inmates although he often has complaints to bring back with him. These visits often coincide with his hunting trips, which as a result of the recent rains are likely to increase.

Although he has spent some considerable time hunting his efforts have not been crowned with success.

Sharjah was not greatly affected by the storm which caused the damage to Dubai although the airfield was out of action for three days as a result of flooding.

A great stir was caused by the rescinding of the decision to close International Aeradio Ltd. at Sharjah. It appears that the firm to whom the contract for controlling the airfield was awarded, found it impossible to find sufficient staff to undertake their commitments and rather than allowing this to result in the closing of Bahrain[121] airfield, the Minister[122] himself, according to reports from here, intervened and reversed the decision. Other reports say that the reversal of the decision was the result of intervention on the part of the Ruler.

UMM AL QUWAIN:

Umm al Quwain was not visited this month but it is understood that this town did not suffer from the storm which overtook Dubai.

Company operations in this township continue to run smoothly.

121 The writer must mean Sharjah airport.

122 In London.

TRUCIAL STATES COUNCIL:

The meeting of the Trucial States Council was held on 5th November and the programme included visits to the hospital in Dubai and the Trucial Oman Scouts lines where lunch had been prepared.

The highlight of the meeting was the departure of the Ruler of Ras al Khaima who was refused permission to again raise his frontier problem in front of the meeting although reference was made to it during the reading of the minutes of the previous meeting.

Shaikh Shakhbut who was very worried over the condition of Shaikh Hazza, excused himself from attending the visits to the hospital and Trucial Oman Scouts.

It was agreed at the meeting that in future an announcement would be issued by the Council so that the populace have some idea of what items of interest to them, were discussed.

The first of these was published after this meeting and included the following information:

(a) Agriculture: The Rulers had agreed to the establishment of gardens in their territories under the guidance of Mr. Huntington to encourage the produce of vegetables and other crops. A school taking boys between the ages of 12 and 18 from all parts of the Trucial States is to be opened in Ras al Khaimah to teach modern cultivation practices.

(b) Water: A drilling rig has been purchased by H.M.G. and will be used to drill wells for water throughout the States.

(c) Education: It is intended to build 4 new schools in the coming year from funds from H.M.G. A technical training school is to be opened in Sharjah this winter to teach carpentry, mechanics, building construction and maintenance of cars, and electrical engineering. There are seven teachers being trained in Bahrain at the expense of H.M.G.

(d) General health: Five male nurses who have completed training in the Dubai hospital are now employed in out stations. Four clinics have been completed this winter and a new Pakistani doctor has been engaged to travel between these clinics giving treatment. Four more clinics are to be built in the next year and applicants for the job of running them are solicited.

AGRICULTURE:

It is good news indeed to learn that Mr. Huntington now has authority to establish gardens in all the Trucial States, but for how much longer he is going to run these without some other assistance is debateable. At present he has, in addition to the three original gardens in the Kharan, one in Khatt, one in Adhn and one in Manama, one in Falaj al Mu'alla, one in Fujairah and just recently acquired one in Buraimi.

AGENCY:

It is understood that the majority of Rulers at the Trucial Council meeting agreed that it would be an advantage to have a law covering workmen's compensation and Mr. Marshall of the Residency is to produce a draft. Wisely enough, no details as to how this is to be implemented were discussed.

Kirkbride
Representative.

TRUCIAL COAST DIARY FOR DECEMBER 1957

ABU DHABI:

The health of Shaikh Hazza continued to cause concern to those near him although there was some slight improvement in his general condition towards the end of the month. During the time of the visit of the Political Resident (see below under "Agency") Shaikh Hazza's condition was so bad that the former's visit to Abu Dhabi was postponed and the proposed visit to Buraimi cancelled.

Abu Dhabi was visited only on 2nd December when the Ruler was found to be very depressed over Shaikh Hazza.[123]

All attempts to open the distillation unit in Abu Dhabi appear to have been unrewarding.

Shaikh Sultan, the second son of the Ruler and Commandant of the Abu Dhabi Defence Force, spent a considerable part of the month in the Bainuna[124] area. He visited El Hamra[125] on a number of occasions, and was rescued by Company personnel when he had the misfortune to overturn his car near Baraka[126] after the rain storms which occurred late in November. Luckily neither he nor his companions were seriously injured.

It was learnt on 12th December, that the Political Agency and the Trucial Oman Scouts were concerned over an unexpected and large concentration of camels and tents in Liwa. An air reconnaissance having failed to identify these people, at attempt was made to contact them from the ground. This, however, proved impossible.

The Ruler inspected the drilling platform at Das Island on 26th December.

---

123 Sheikh Hazza bin Sultan died on 21 January 1958.

124 Central Abu Dhabi between the coastal sabkhah and the high dunes of the Liwa oases in the south.

125 About a kilometre east of the drilling location Shuwaihat which is itself about 25 kilometres west of Jebel Dhanna, along the coast.

126 A short distance to the west of Shuweihat drilling location.

With the return of Company operations to the Tarif area,[127] the Ruler's Representative is showing some concern over the possibility of renewed frequent visits by members of the Ruler's family.

El Hamra was visited on 10th December.

AJMAN:

Ajman was not visited this month.

The Trucial Oman Scouts have been carrying out training exercises in the hills around Manama.[128]

DUBAI:

The Municipality has been active during the month and have instituted a number of new taxes as well as improvements in various fields.

New taxes are being levied on factories making ice and cement blocks as well as leather tanneries, workshops and garages. The following trades are also included in the new taxes: Bakers, hoteliers, masons, tailors, sellers of goods from barrows or movable stores and barbers.

Other innovations include a speed limit in the town area, a rule against obstructing the streets with either movable or immovable objects, a rule allowing the police to fine shop keepers who leave their shops unlocked during the night, the examination of gold and certain ornaments to ascertain their correct value, a rule allowing the Municipality to repair at cost plus 10% any drains found open and leaking and a proposal to establish an electric company. Until this latter proposal takes effect it is proposed to levy a tax on all generators.

The Commandant of the Police has come in for severe criticism over the arresting of a member of a well known Sharjah family. Apparently this man and some of his friends were found drinking in the desert between Dubai and Sharjah and were thrown into the Dubai jail until Shaikh Saqr of Sharjah obtained their release. The criticism was due to the fact that these persons were outside the limits of Dubai town; although in Dubai territory; thereby causing no one any harm, and that the Commandant is seen at parties drinking with persons who he knows are forbidden to do so.

The hunting season now being in full swing there is much competition between the various Rulers and other hunters as to who can obtain the largest bag. In one day alone Shaikh Rashid bin Said brought back 29 bustard. Shaikh Said, his father, spends almost all of his time out of town in this manner.

---

127 Preparations had started for the return to Tarif and Murban (Bab) to drill a second well on the structure.

128 The Ruler of Ajman's oasis in the mountain foreland 20 kilometres north east of Dhaid.

FUJAIRAH:

There has been no contact between the Company and the Ruler of Fujairah this month, although he attended the lunch party given by the Political Agent[129] in Dubai in honour of the Political Resident and Lady Burrows.

RAS AL KHAIMA:

The Ruler of Ras al Khaimah was visited on 30th December in connection with the forthcoming geological survey in his territory. Since there is no question of using any person from Fujairah, he gladly consented to give every possible assistance.

He had not had any communication from his son Shaikh Khalid who is in Egypt at school, since 16th November and this absence of news is causing both himself and the boy's mother some anxiety.

Although there had been some rain early in November the fact that none has fallen for over a month had adversely affected the crop of barley and wheat which he had sown following the first rains.

Although the Ruler threatened to boycott all functions connected with the visit of the Political Resident after having been forced to submit to the Company's geological survey which took place in November against his will, he did, in fact, attend the lunch party given by the Political Agent in this connection.

SHARJAH:

The Ruler visited Kelba twice during the month and was also away hunting whenever the opportunity arose.

He also visited the location at Juweiza[130] unofficially. One of which visits happened to coincide with the incident when four rig labourers refused to work This was fortunate as he was able to stop any growth of the trouble. His considerable faith in the Company's fairness in dealing with his subjects is shown up on such occasions as this; since on the one hand he told the labourers that they were never to take any action as drastic as refusing to work without consulting him, whilst on the other hand he neither queried or interfered when the Company settled the question by refusing to allow the incident to alter the official attitude on the points raised.

On one thing he is absolutely adamant and that is that his subjects are not to be treated less favourably than those of other oil companies with particular reference to Q.P.C., K.O.C. and ARAMCO.[131]

---

129 J. P. Tripp.

130 The well was drilled to 12,916 feet and was abandoned without finding oil in September 1958.

131 Qatar Petroleum Company, Kuwait Oil Company and Arabian American Company (Saudi Arabia).

The Ruler was invited to attend the Islamic Conference held in Pakistan in December, but declined the invitation.

UMM AL QUWAIN:

Umm al Quwain was visited on 5th December.

AGENCY:

The Political Resident paid his annual official visit to the Trucial States from 4th to 6th December. He visited all the states except Abu Dhabi. His original programme included a visit to Buraimi instead of Abu Dhabi town but it was felt that it would be unkind to ask the Ruler to leave his capital whilst his brother was so ill. A tour of Abu Dhabi territory, including Buraimi is expected to take place sometime in January 1958. Shaikh Shakhbut, unexpectedly, attended the lunch party given by the Political Agent in honour of Sir Bernard Burrows. The Political Resident was accompanied by Lady Burrows.

VISITORS:

Mrs Thayer of the Washington Post visited the Trucial States under Company sponsorship; including in her programme Dubai, Sharjah, Umm al Quwain, Ajman and Abu Dhabi. During her stay in the latter place she had the fortune of accompanying the Ruler on his inspection of the ADMA drilling platform.

(No signature)

Photographs

1. Sheikh Shakhbut bin Sultan, 1957. Ruler of Abu Dhabi 1928-1966.

2. A Liwa oasis on the edge of the Empty Quarter, 1950's.

3. Family at a Liwa water well, 1969.

4. Family in transit from Liwa to Abu Dhabi, 1950's.

5. Mountain fort in Sharjah territory, 2005.

6. *Ra's al-Khaimah in 1950's.*

7. Khan Saheb Hussain Ahmed, 1950's. Residency Agent 1935. AIOC agent. Contractor and merchant.

8. Rapide aircraft used by the Company throughout the Middle East, 1950's.

9. Site for first Company (PD(TC)) house on Abu Dhabi island, 1950.

10. PD(TC) house, north-east corner Abu Dhabi island. Now in the harbour, circa 1962.

11. Survey party in south of Abu Dhabi. Note the theodolite on the left, 1961.

12. Sheikh Saqr bin Sultan, Ruler of Sharjah (driving) with Ensor (PD(TC)), 1957.

13. Old drilling rig, built and later dismantled piece by piece, 1950's.

14. Sheikh Shakhbut bin Sultan with Jackson (PD(TC)) on floor of the drilling rig, 1950.

15. Camels passing in front of an old drilling rig. Water is waste from drilling, 1960.

16. PD(TC) Medical Centre, 1950's.

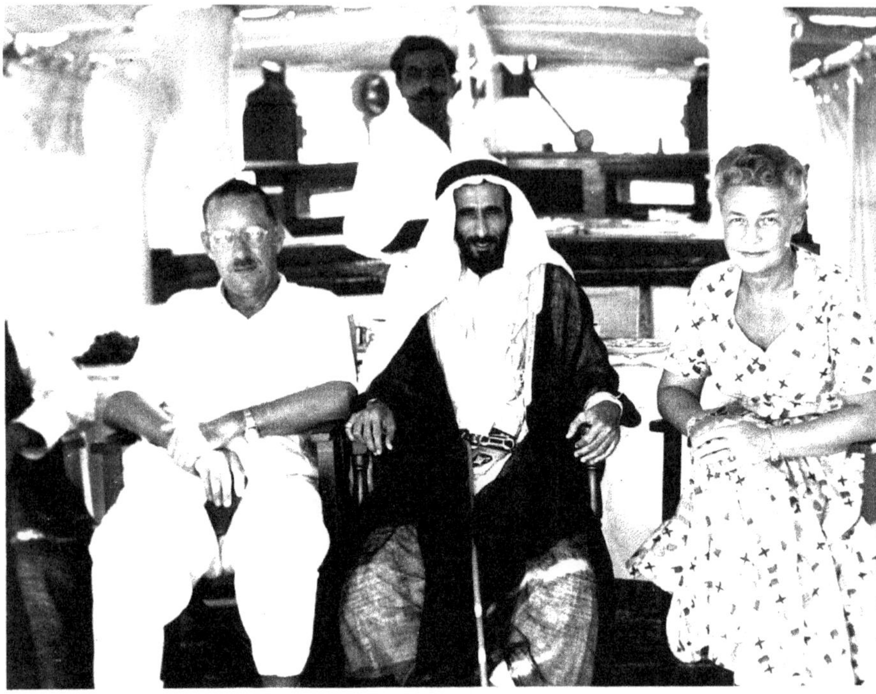

17. Sheikh Shakhbut bin Sultan in a boat with the Heseldins (PD(TC)), 1954.

صاحب العظمة الشيخ زايد بن سلطان آل نهيان

18. Sheikh Zayed bin Sultan, early 1960's. Ruler's representative Muwaiji/Al 'Ain 1946-1966. Ruler of Abu Dhabi 1966-2004. President United Arab Emirates 1971-2004.

19. Thani bin Murshid al Romaithi, 1950's. Ruler's representative Tarif.

20. Codrai in a Land Rover, 1954.

21. Mohamed bin Haufan with a Falcon, 1950's.

22. Hamdun, Grandson of Ghannam bin Ali. Head Guard at Dubai, early 1950's.

23. Sheikh Shakhbut bin Sultan with Ibrahim Arrayadh (PD(TC)), 1950's.

24. Sheikh Saqr bin Sultan, Sharjah Ruler, with PD(TC) Ensor, Kirkbride (on left) and Mohamed Abdulrahman, 1957.

25. *Sheikhs Hazza and Zayed bin Sultan in London, June 1957.*

Bibliography

The following books have been referred to or quoted from in this volume.

ABDULLAH, MOHAMED MORSY, *The United Arab Emirates, A Modern History*, Hurtwood Press, London, 1994, ISBN 0 903696 37 1.

AL-GURG, Sir EASA SALEH, *The Wells of Memory*, John Murray, London. 1998, ISBN 0 7099 1915 8.

AL TAKRITI, WALID YASIN, *Archaeology of the Falaj*, Department of Historic Environment, Abu Dhabi, 2011, ISBN 978 9948 01 949 7.

BIBBY, GEOFFREY, *Looking for Dilmun*, Collins, London, 1970.

BOSCH, DR. DONALD AND LOUISE, *The Doctor and the Teacher*, Apex Publishing, Muscat, 2000.

CLARK, Sir T., *Underground to Overseas, The Story of Petroleum Development Oman*, Stacey International, ISBN 978 1 905299 46 1.

CLAYTON, PETER, *Two Alpha Lima, The First Ten Years of the Trucial Oman Levies*, Janus Publishing Company, 1994, ISBN 1 85756 196 1.

FENELON, KEVIN, *The United Arab Emirates*, Longman Group Ltd., London, 1973, ISBN 0 582 78041 1.

HAWLEY, SIR DONALD, *The Trucial States*, George Allen and Unwin, 1970, ISBN 0 04 953005 4.

HEARD, DAVID, *Oil Men, Territorial Ambitions, and Political Agents*, Gerlach Press, Berlin, 2019, ISBN 978 3 95994 064 1.

HEARD-BEY, FRAUKE, *From Trucial States to United Arab Emirates*, Longman, 1982, ISBN 0 582 778032 2.

HENDERSON, EDWARD, *Arabian Destiny*, Motivate Publishing, Dubai, 1999, 2002, ISBN 1 86063 029-4.

HILLYARD, SUSAN, *Before the Oil*, Ashridge Press, 2002, ISBN 1 901214 02 8.

INNES, N. M., *Minister in Oman, A Personal Narrative*, The Oleander Press, 1987, ISBN 0 900891 89 0.

KELLY, J. B., *Eastern Arabian Frontiers*, Faber & Faber, London, 1964.

KELLY, J.B., Edited by S.B. Kelly, *Desert dispute*, Gerlach Press, Berlin, 2018, p. 317. ISBN 978 3 95994 024 5.

LIENHARDT, PETER, Edited by AHMED AL-SHAHI, *Disorientations, A Society in Flux Kuwait in the 1950's*, Ithica Press, 1993, ISBN 0 86372 166 4.

OWEN, RODERIC, *The Golden Bubble*, Collins, 1957.

STANLEY-PRICE, NICHOLAS, *Imperial Outpost in the Gulf,* Book Guild Publishing, 2012, ISBN 978 1 84624 684 5.

THESIGER, SIR WILFRED, *Arabian Sands,* Longmans, 1959, Collins, Motivate, 1990.

THOMAS, BERTRAM, *Arabia Felix: Across the Empty Quarter of Arabia*, Jonathon Cape, 1938.

TOWNSEND, JOHN, *Oman, The Making of the Modern State*, Croom Helm, London, 1977, ISBN 0 85664 446 3.

WALKER, JULIAN, *Tyro on the Trucial Coast*, The Memoir Club, London, 1999, ISBN 1 84104 005 3.

WILKINSON, JOHN, *The Imamate Tradition of Oman,* Cambridge University Press, 1987, ISBN 0 521 32713 X.

About the Editor

David Heard CBE studied physics and geology before joining the London based Abu Dhabi Petroleum Company in Abu Dhabi in August 1963. Working for more than a decade as a Petroleum Engineer he participated in the discovery of oil in the Abu Dhabi desert. Thereafter he was for more than two decades the Representative of the same company in Abu Dhabi. He married in 1967 the historian Dr. Frauke Heard-Bey who then joined him in Abu Dhabi, where they both still live in retirement. They have a son and two daughters. David and Frauke were fortunate to meet both Sheikh Shakhbut bin Sultan and Sheikh Zayed bin Sultan on many occasions. David is a member of Chatham House, The Royal Society for Asian Affairs, the Travellers Club, and is a Fellow of the Energy Institute, all based in London. He published 'From Pearls to Oil, How the Oil Industry came to the United Arab Emirates' in 2011 (Motivate, Dubai) and 'Oil Men, Territorial Ambitions and Political Agents, From Pearls to Oil in the Trucial States of the Gulf' in 2019 (Gerlach Press, Berlin).

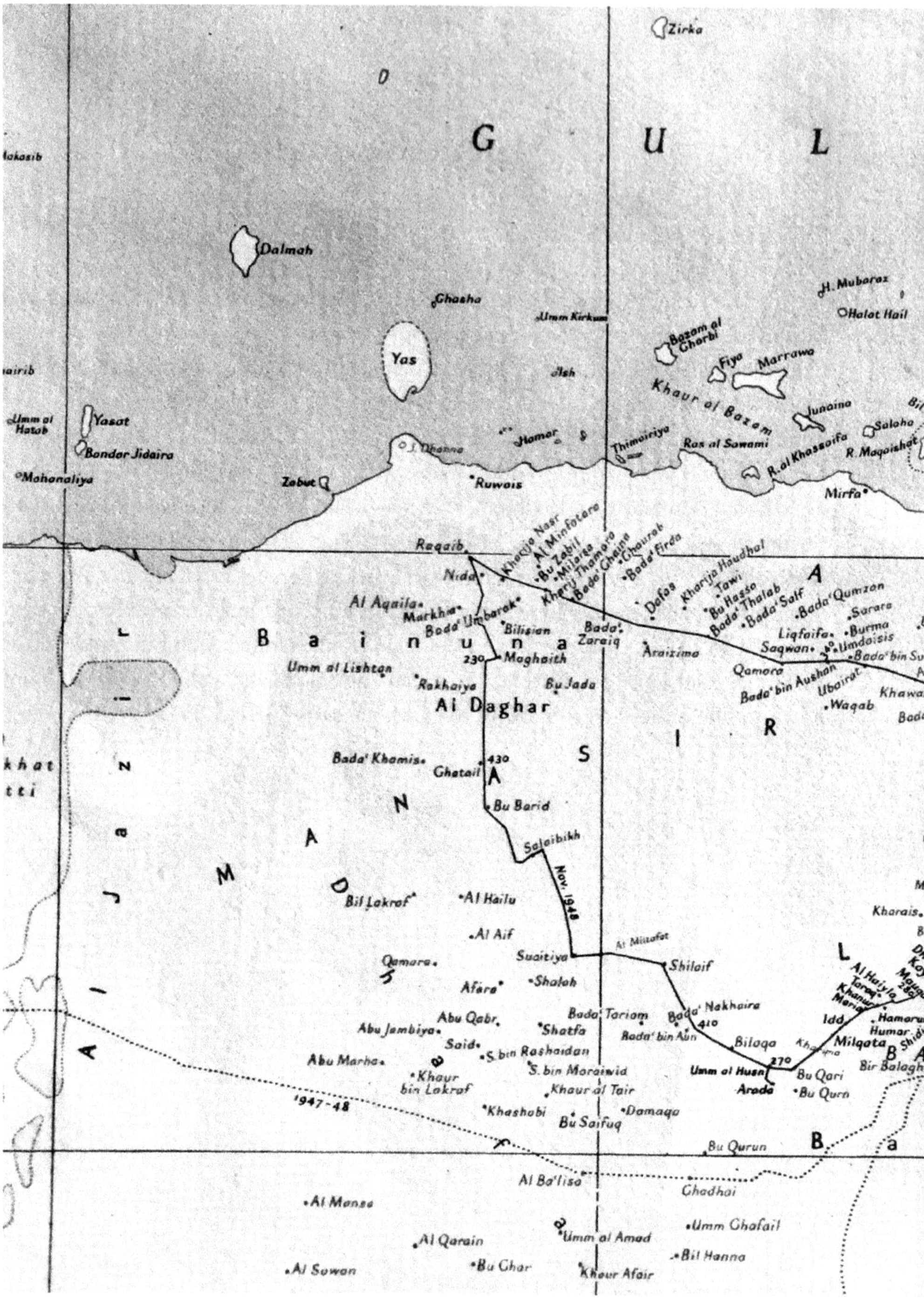
Zirka
G U L
Dalmah
Ghasha
Umm Kirkum
Yas
Bazam al Gharbi
Fiya
Marrawa
Khaur al Bazam
Junaina
H. Mubaraz
Halat Hail
Saloha
Yasat
Umm al Hatab
Bandar Jidaira
Mohonaliya
Hamar
Thimairiya
Ras al Sanami
R. al Khassaifa
R. Maqaishat
Zabut
Ruwais
Mirfa
Raqaib
Nida
Al Aqaila
Markhia
Bada' Umbarak
Bilisian
B a i n u n a
Bada' Zaraiq
Dafas
Araizima
Kharija Haudhal
Tawi
Bu Hasso
Bada' Thalab
Bada' Salf
Bada' Qumzan
Sarara
Burma
Umdaisis
Bada' bin Sul
Liqfaifa
Saqwan
Qamara
Bada' bin Aushan
Ubairat
Waqab
Khawai
Bada
230
Maghaith
Umm al Lishtan
Rakhaiya
Bu Jada
Al Daghar
Bada' Khamis
430
Ghatail
Bu Barid
S I R
A
Salaibikh
Nov. 1948
Bil Lakraf
Al Hailu
Al Aif
Al Mitzafat
Suaitiya
Shilaif
Qamara
Shaloh
Afara
Bada' Tariam
Bada' Nakhaira
410
Bada' bin Aun
Biloqa
Abu Qabr
Abu Jambiya
Shatfa
Said
S. bin Rashaidan
S. bin Maraiwid
Abu Marha
Khaur bin Lakraf
Khaur al Tair
Umm al Husn
270
Arada
Bu Qari
Bu Qurn
Milqata
Idd
Bir Balagh
Kharais
1947-48
Khashabi
Damaqa
Bu Saifuq
Bu Qurun
B a
Al Ba'lisa
Ghadhai
Al Manse
Umm Ghafail
Al Qarain
Umm al Amad
Bil Hanna
Al Sawan
Bu Ghar
Khaur Afair
A I J A N A
M A N A S I R
D h a f r a
L
kha t
t t i
Makasib
airib

Thesiger's map.